Violence Prevention

Totally Awesome™ Teaching Strategies for Safe and Drug-Free Schools

Linda Meeks · Philip Heit · Randy Page

The Ohio State University   The Ohio State University   University of Idaho

Preface by David Sleet, San Diego State University

Meeks Heit Publishing Company

Editorial, Sales, and Customer Service Office
P.O. Box 121
Blacklick, OH   43004
(614) 759-7780

Project Editor: Julie R. DeVillers
Production: Meeks Heit Publications
Production Editors: Julie R. DeVillers, Ann G. Turpie
Director of Art and Design: Jim Brower
Illustrators: Jim Brower, Jennifer King
Director of Marketing: David Willcox

Printed in the United States of America

1 2 3 4 5 6 7 8 9 1099 98 97 96 95 94

Library of Congress Catalog Number: 94-76121

ISBN: 0-9630009-4-2

REVIEWERS

Sergeant Joyce Baker
Peace Officers Standards and Training Instructor
State of Georgia Police
Resource Officer/Staff Instructor
Drug Education Program
Savannah-Chatham County Board of Education
Savannah, Georgia

Donna Breitenstein, Ed.D.
Coordinator and Professor of Health Education
College of Education
Appalachian State University
Boone, North Carolina

Betsy Gallun, M.Ed.
Supervisor of Drug Programs
Prince George's County Public Schools
Upper Marlboro, Maryland

Sheryl Gotts, M.S.
Curriculum Specialist
Office of Health and Physical Education
Milwaukee Public Schools
Milwaukee, Wisconsin

Nancy Green, M.Ed.
Supervisor of Physical Education, Health, and Girls'
Athletics
Jefferson County Public Schools
Birmingham, Alabama

Major William Greer
Millen Police Department
Millen, Georgia

Janet Henke, B.S.
Middle School Team Leader
Old Court Middle School
Baltimore County Public Schools
Baltimore, Maryland

Peggy Holstedt, M.S.
Health Promotion Specialist
Oregon Department of Education
Salem, Oregon

Joseph M. Leake, B.S., C.H.E.S.
Health Education Curriculum Specialist
Baltimore City Public Schools
Baltimore, Maryland

Mary Moren, M.A.
Coordinator
North Carolina School Health Training Center
Apalachian State University
Boone, North Carolina

Billette D. Owens-Ashford
Program Assistant
Drug-Free Schools and Communities
Atlanta Public Schools
Atlanta, Georgia

Linda Peveler
Master Teacher
Columbiana Middle School
Shelby County Public Schools
Birmingham, Alabama 35244

Michael Schaffer, M.A.
Supervisor of Health Education, K-12
Prince George's County Public Schools
Upper Marlboro, Maryland

Barbara Sullivan, M.S.
Wellness Team Leader
Sudbrook Magnet Middle School
Baltimore County Public Schools
Baltimore, Maryland

TABLE OF CONTENTS

Section 3
Totally Awesome™ Teaching Strategies

Chapter 3
USING THE *TOTALLY AWESOME*™ TEACHING STRATEGIES

Section 4
Violence Prevention Literature

Chapter 4
USING THE VIOLENCE PREVENTION
LITERATURE

Section 5
Family, Teacher, and Student Masters

Chapter 5
USING THE FAMILY, TEACHER, AND STUDENT MASTERS   577

Section 6
Violence Prevention Resources

Chapter 6
USING THE VIOLENCE
PREVENTION RESOURCES

Preface

Violence Prevention: An Awesome Responsibility

When you turn the page, you will read the news as reported in a fictitious newspaper, *Violent Times*. However, each of the articles in *Violent Times* contains factual information. References for these and other facts appear immediately after the newspaper to help you find more information. This Preface is written in a newspaper-style to give these facts added impact. Some of the articles keep you abreast of the threat of violence in young people. Two of the articles are about young people who were victims of horrific crimes. Information for these articles was provided by family members. Other articles focus on ways schools and communities can work together to promote safe schools. Also included are articles containing information on grants and other monies available to help schools with violence prevention programs. Finally, of special interest is an article that describes a program involving young people that is aimed at stopping violence.

Violence prevention is an awesome responsibility for each of us. As an educator, you have an important role in protecting the health and safety of the youth of this nation. This book, *Violence Prevention: Totally Awesome™ Teaching Strategies for Safe and Drug-Free Schools,* contains a violence prevention curriculum; facts about violence prevention; *Totally Awesome™* Teaching Strategies; violence prevention literature; family, teacher, and student reproducible masters; and violence prevention resources. It is a valuable resource for educators.

David Sleet, Ph.D.
Professor
San Diego State University

the Violent Times

STORMY
High 70/Low 42

VIOLENCE THREATENS NATION'S YOUTH

Recent polls indicate that America's youth are vitally concerned about crime and violence. According to state and national survey data, their worries are justified. A violent crime occurs near a school every six seconds, and nearly 40 percent of school administrators report an increase in violence within their school districts in the last five years.

Nearly 8 percent of all students in grades 9-12 say they have been in at least one physical fight that resulted in a treatable injury in the past 30 days. Nearly three million thefts and incidents of violent crime occur on or near school campuses each year.

Among eighth and tenth graders, almost 7 percent of boys and 2 percent of girls carry knives to school nearly every day. More than half of students in grades 6-12 say they are able to get a handgun if they want one. Nearly one of 5 students in grades 9-12 say that they have carried a weapon at least once during the past 30 days. One in 20 students carried a gun. Among young people ages 15 to 24, homicide is the second most common cause of death, surpassed only by unintentional injuries. Homicide is the most common cause of death for both African-American females and males ages 15-34. Eighty two percent of homicides among teenagers 15-19 years of age are associated with a firearm, 91 and 77 percent among black and white males respectively.

For every homicide victim, there are at least 90 people over age 12 who are injured in an interpersonal violent event. From 1987 to 1991,

juvenile arrests for violent crimes have increased by 50 percent; juvenile arrests for murder have risen an alarming 85 percent; and 3 of 10 juvenile murder arrests involved a victim under the age of 18.

More than 15 percent of youth ages 12 to 17 say that gangs exist in their schools. Gang members are 10 times more likely to have carried a weapon in the last year; they are 10 times more likely to have been in gang fights; they are 4 times more likely to have used drugs or alcohol, and 5 times more likely to steal or buy drugs.

Violence in school-age youth is costly. In 1987, violence to people age 12 and older resulting from rape, robbery, assault, murder, and arson caused about ten billion dollars in potential health-related costs. A single crime-related injury costs an average of $41,000 for medical and psychological care.

School-age youth are disproportionately represented among the perpetrators and victims of violence. The average age of both perpetrators and victims of violence has been growing younger and younger.

Students Still Mourn Shooting Death Of Classmate

Students at Margaret Leary Elementary School in Butte, Montana still mourn the shooting death of their classmate, Jeremy Bullock. Jeremy died April 12, 1994, of a head wound he suffered when a fellow student fired a gun at a line of students on the school playground. The 10-year-old boy who shot Jeremy was angered by a pair of arguments he had had, one on the playground and another after school near his home. The arguments appear to have led the boy to bring a gun to the school, intending to shoot one of the boys with whom he had argued. However, the boy apparently was not

Jeremy Bullock, shooting victim

familiar with the gun. When he began firing the gun, there were first, fourth, and fifth grade students lined up at the door of the school. One of the bullets struck Jeremy. One struck a book bag lying on the ground, and the other traveled through a student's coat without striking the student.

Ironically, Jeremy had previously sensed that the boy was having difficulties in his relationships. He had invited him to have lunch at school. The day before the shooting, they had had lunch. Students at Margaret Leary admired his helping attitude.

Jeremy was involved in many school activities. He was an avid reader and good student. Jeremy was a member of Boy Scout Troop #8. Students described him as being skilled at many sports, including soccer, basketball, karate, hockey, skiing, and swimming. Jeremy and

Shooting from 1

his identical twin brother, Joshua, shared interests in the outdoors. They enjoyed rafting, fishing, and camping.

Students still mourn the tragic death of Jeremy. They worry about the violence in our country. They want young people with problems to be helped in order to prevent other tragedies.

Jack Copps, Jeremy's grandfather and Deputy State Superintendent of The Office of Public Instruction, shares the concerns of these students. He said the family is comforted to know that the students at Margaret Leary Elementary School want an end to violence at school.

Safe Schools Act Implemented

Signed into law on March 23, 1994 as part of the Goals 2000 legislation, the Safe Schools Act authorizes competitive grants to local education agencies to enable them to carry out projects of up to two years designed to achieve Goal 7 (formerly Goal 6) of the National Education Goals by helping to ensure that all schools are safe and free of violence. This goal recognizes that violence prevention is a key to the success of educational reform.

Grants are used to support a variety of activities, that includes identifying school violence, addressing discipline problems, conducting school safety audits, planning comprehensive violence prevention programs, training school personnel, acquiring metal detectors, hiring security guards, and other prevention/protection measures. The Safe Schools Act also authorizes the Secretary of Education to conduct a variety of national activities, that includes research, program development and evaluation, data collection, and training and technical assistance to school districts and local education agencies. Congress appropriated twenty million dollars for the program in 1994.

Unsolved Murder Plagues Family

The afternoon of September 21, 1982, eight year old Kelly Prosser left Indianola Informal Elementary School in Columbus, Ohio, to walk to her grandmother's house. Kelly never

Kelly Prosser, homicide victim

arrived. Four days later she was found, the victim of a brutal rape and murder.

A number of years have passed since Kelly's tragic death. Kelly's family members, like other homicide survivors, have many unanswered questions. What happened on that crisp, clear, autumn day? Who was the perpetrator of this crime? Why did Kelly have to be the victim of such a horrific crime? Did Kelly know her murderer? Will her murderer ever be apprehended and convicted? Family members relive the event when police call to review the details as they attempt to link recent homicides to Kelly's death. They also are concerned that police will no longer give priority to the investigation of this homicide because of the recent increase in violence and other homicides in the community. The pain continues. Family, friends, and others in the community know that one less child completed school, attended the high school prom, went off to college, and embarked on adulthood.

One of a dozen billboards promoting SWELP

SWELP THWARTS JUVENILE DELINQUENCY

SWELP, the Summer Work Experience Leadership Program, is one of many programs sponsored by the Columbia Urban League of Columbia, South Carolina, aimed at stopping violence. According to James McLawhorn, President and CEO of the Columbia Urban League, the program was initiated ten years ago as a result of research findings from a longitudinal study done by George E. Vaillant while at Harvard Medical School. The study followed the lives of 456 teenage boys from inner-city Boston, many who were reared in impoverished and/or broken homes. Vaillant and his team of researchers compared the men's mental health scores to boyhood activity scores. The boyhood activity scores were determined by a compilation of points awarded for part-time jobs, household chores, extracurricular activities or sports, school grades relative to I.Q. (a measure of effort in school), and ability to cope with problems.

When follow-up interviews were conducted as these young men reached ages 25, 31, and 47 years

Cynthia Hardy, Urban League staff conducting orientation for SWELP participants and parents.

old, one finding was clear: those who had worked as boys, even at simple household chores, were happier and more productive than those who had not worked. Those highest on the boyhood activity scale were twice as likely to have warm relations with a wide variety of people, five times as likely to be well paid and 16 times less likely to have been significantly unemployed. On the other hand, the group who had worked least in childhood were far more likely to have been arrested, ten times more likely to have been mentally ill, and six times as many of them had died. When researchers examined the activities that made up the boyhood scale, they found that I.Q., amount of school, and family and socioeconomic class made no significant difference. The key activity influencing the futures of these young men was whether they had part-time jobs and/or household chores.

McLawhorn recognized that many programs aimed at helping young people to be successful and avoid the pitfalls of juvenile delinquency are expensive. SWELP was initiated as a cost-effective program to prevent juvenile delinquency. And, SWELP has been well-received by the young people and their sponsors in Columbia, South Carolina. This past summer more than 400 young people participated in SWELP. To be eligible, participants must be between the ages of 12 and 16, sign up for an internship for a minimum of two weeks (most sign up for four weeks), and agree to work for twenty hours per week. During the internship, participants are paired with a mentor. They shadow this mentor in a career-oriented job. They are paid a stipend of three dollars an hour for this work. When they complete the program, they are awarded a framed certificate.

"The response from the community is very positive," said McLawhorn. "Businesses as well as private citizens donate money to sponsor the young people who participate.

They recognize that young people under age 16 have had little opportunity to gain job-related experience and they want to help. Many of the mentors in the program continue to work with their interns after the summer program ends." McLawhorn is hopeful that cities across the nation will adopt programs similar to SWELP. SWELP is cost-effective and helps prevent juvenile delinquency.

Private Foundations Provide Monies For Violence Prevention

Private foundations are increasingly interested in funding violence prevention programs. From 1988 to 1992, 17 foundations gave more than one million dollars each for violence prevention. Among them are the largest philanthropists such as Robert Wood Johnson Foundation, W. K. Kellogg Foundation, Ford Foundation, the Henry J. Kaiser Foundation, the Harry Frank Guggenheim Foundation, and the Carnegie Foundation. Only about 2 percent of the total grants in 1990 were awarded for projects directly related to preventing school violence.

State Agencies Offer Assistance

State Maternal and Child Health (MCH) agencies (defined as the offices that receive federal Title V Bloc Grant monies), state health departments, state education agencies, and the office of the state Attorney General frequently provide grants to schools and school-based health centers to support violence prevention programs. MCH may provide grants to schools and school-based health centers to support violence prevention programs such as positive parenting, violence reduction education, and mentoring programs. Health departments may assist schools to develop a violence reporting system or aid in victim counseling and health services. State education agencies, through federal funding, may fund state and local violence prevention curricula and teacher training. The Attorney General's office and state law enforcement agencies may assist in legal issues, help review school policy regarding disciplinary procedures, and support alternative programs for violent offenders as well as recreational and after-school programs, parent training, and violence reduction education.

Federal Agencies Support Violence Prevention Activities

The National Center for Injury Prevention and Control (the lead agency for violence prevention) and the National Center for Chronic Disease Prevention and Health Promotion, Division of Adolescent and School Health (the lead agency for school health) (both at the Federal Centers for Disease Control and Prevention, Atlanta, Georgia) provide technical assistance and funding through state and local health departments for violence prevention activities. CDC conducts the Youth Risk Behavior Surveillance System and other data collection efforts that help track risks for

violence among youth and has published many helpful resource guides. Schools are a major focus for the implementation and evaluation of strategies such as conflict resolution, and are an integral part of funding larger, community-based programs.

Office of Justice Programs, the National Institute of Justice, the Bureau of Justice Assistance, and Office of Juvenile Justice and Deliquency Prevention (all at the United States Department of Justice) provide funding for demonstration programs to schools; provide technical assistance to schools in developing school safety plans (through the National School Safety Center); operate state grant programs; conduct research and evaluation on violence and violence prevention; collect and report data on violence, crime, and victimization in schools; and operate state juvenile justice programs.

The Department of Education, through the Office of Educational Research and Improvement, helps track changes in school violence trends over time and provides assistance to schools, school districts, and state and local education agencies to conduct and evaluate violence and drug education programs in the schools. They have been instrumental in cosponsoring a number of conferences and publications related to safeguarding our youth from violence.

The Center for Substance Abuse and Prevention at the Substance Abuse and Mental Health Services Administration conducts and sponsors research and demonstration programs involving the prevention of drug and alcohol use and violence, much of which is focused on school-aged youth. Community groups and schools are frequent recipients of these broad-based programs.

Schools And Communities Work Together For Safe Schools

Many school districts and state education agencies are collaborating with other community resources to forge comprehensive plans for violence prevention in schools. Although the solutions to school violence differ from one school or district to another, some guiding principles for school-based programs, derived from planning exercises and coalition development in various states, point to some general guidelines:

In the community

- Publicly support violence prevention as a long-term, high priority program in the community where the school is located.
- Intervene early with very young children and with youth at high risk of violence and aggression.
- Support community development activities intended to reduce community violence, such as restricting access to firearms.
- Consider programs that keep schools open before and after the normal school day.
- Encourage wide participation of students, teachers, administrators, parents, and community groups in developing and implementing a violence prevention program.
- Provide neighborhood outreach programs to serve the needs of disruptive youth.

- Expand access for at-risk students to programs known to improve school success, such as Head Start and Chapter 1.
- Provide young people with positive adult role models or mentors for nonviolence.
- Develop means to restrict access to weapons in the community.
- Develop violence prevention plans in partnership with local governments, businesses, and parents as well as medical and law-enforcement, and community-based organizations.

In the school

- Publicly support violence prevention as a long-term, high priority program for the school.
- Develop strong and consistent discipline policies, widely communicated, fairly administered, and consistently enforced.
- Assess school safety problems through school safety audits, environmental analysis, and reviewing discipline and violence-related school data.
- Assess and measure program outcomes, such as reductions in violent behavior, school incidents, or changes in student/teacher/parent behaviors and risks.
- Install emergency communications systems or classroom telephones throughout the school to facilitate

rapid response.
- Implement developmentally appropriate, culturally sensitive, and culturally relevant violence prevention programs in all grades.
- Endorse district policies that enable schools and administrators to know the school-violence history of disruptive or aggressive students.
- Provide inservice education in violence prevention and control for teachers, administrators, school-service personnel, staff, teachers aids, groundskeepers, and school bus drivers.
- Require student photo identification.
- Prevent weapon-carrying and weapon-storage at school.

These and other strategies should be tailored to local needs and policies and developed with the broadest input from school and community groups. While it is true that some schools are seriously affected by violence problems, most schools remain safe places for teachers and students. But as violence invades the community, it surely will find its way into the schools unless schools take action to prevent it.

NEWSPAPER BIBLIOGRAPHY

Earls, F., Cairns, R.B., & Mercy, J.A. (1993) The control of violence and the promotion of nonviolence in adolescents. In S.G. Millstein, A.C. Petersen, & E.O. Nightingale (Eds.), *Promoting the Health of Adolescents* (pp. 285-304). New York: Oxford University Press.

Fingerhut, L. (1993) Firearm mortality among children, youth,and young adults 1-34 years of age, trends and current status: United States 1985-1990. *Advance Data from Vital and Health Statistics 231.* Hyattsville, MD: National Center for Health Statistics, March 23.

Fingerhut, L., & Kleinman, J.C. (1990) International and interstate comparisons of homicide among young males. *Journal of American Medical Association*, 263:3292-3295.

Hammett, M. et al. (1992) Homicide surveillance, 1979-1988. In Centers for Disease Control and Prevention Surveillance Summaries, 29 May 1992, *Morbidity and Mortality Weekly Report*, 41(SS-3):1-33.

Heymann, P. (1994) Opening speech. *Proceedings of Forum on Safeguarding Our Youth: Violence Prevention for Our Nation's Children.* Washington, DC: U.S. Department of Education.

Holinger, P.C., Offer, D., Barter, J.T., & Bell, C.C. (1994) *Suicide and Homicide Among Adolescents.* New York: Guilford Press.

Keister, E., & Keister, S. (1986) How to raise a happy child. *Reader's Digest*, January.

Lazaroff, S. (1992) Youth gangs: Not new but more violent. *Family Life Educator*, 11(1):13-15.

Lowry, R., Sleet, D., Duncan, C., Powell, K., & Kolbe, L. (in press) Adolescents at risk for violence. Special Issue of *Educational Psychology Review.*

Mercy, J., & O'Carroll, P.W. (1988) New directions in violence prediction: The public health arena. *Violence and Victims*, 3(4):285-301.

Mercy, J., Rosenberg, M., Powell, K., Broome, C., & Roper, W. (1993) Public health policy for preventing violence. *Health Affairs*, 12(4):7-29.

Metzger, D.E., & Strand, V.C. (1993) *Grantmaking in the Field of Violence Prevention.* Tarrytown, NY: Center for Training andResearch in Child Abuse and Family Violence. (As quoted in Metzger, D.E., & Strand, V.E. (1993) Violence prevention: Trends in foundation funding. *Health Affairs*, 12(4):209-220, Winter 1993.)

Miller, T.R, Cohen, M.A., & Rossman, S.B. (1993) Victim costs of violent crime and resulting injuries. *Health Affairs*, 112(4):186-197, Winter.

National Center for Injury Prevention and Control. (1993) *The Prevention of Youth Violence: A Framework for Community Action.* Atlanta, GA: Centers for Disease Control and Prevention.

National Research Council. (1993) *Understanding and Preventing Violence.* Washington, DC: National Academy Press.

National School Boards Association. (1993) *Violence in the Schools: How America's School Boards Are Safeguarding Our Children.* Alexandria, VA: National School Boards Association.

O'Carroll, P.W., Harel, Y., & Waxweiler, R.J. (1993) Measuring adolescent behaviors related to intentional injuries. *Public Health Reports*, 108(Supplement 1):15-19.

Roper, W.L. (1991) The prevention of minority youth violence must begin despite risks and imperfect understanding. *Public Health Reports*, 106(3):229-231.

Rosenberg, M.L., and Mercy, J.A. (1991) Introduction. In M.L. Rosenberg and M.A. Fenley (Eds.), *Violence in America: A Public Health Problem.* New York: Oxford University Press. Satcher, D. (1994) Speech to Phoebe Putney Memorial Hospital, Albany, GA, September 2.

Sleet, D.A. (1994) Injury prevention. In P. Cortese & K. Middleton (Eds.), The Comprehensive School Health Challenge: Promoting Health Through Education (pp. 443-489). Santa Cruz,CA: ETR Associates.

Strauss, M.A. (1986) Violence and homicide antecedents. *Bulletin of New York Academy of Medicine*, 62:446-62.

United States Department of Education. (1994) *Proceedings of Forum on Safeguarding Our Youth: Violence Prevention for Our Nation's Children.* Washington, DC: U.S Department of Education.

-----. (1993) *Reaching the Goals: Goal 6: Safe, Disciplined, and Drug-Free Schools.* Document #ED/OERI 92-46, Washington, DC: U.S. Government Printing Office.

Virginia Association of School Superintendents. (1992) *Violence in Schools: Recommendations for Action by the Education Summit.* Charlottesville, VA: Virginia Association of School Superintendents.

SECTION

1

The Violence Prevention Curriculum

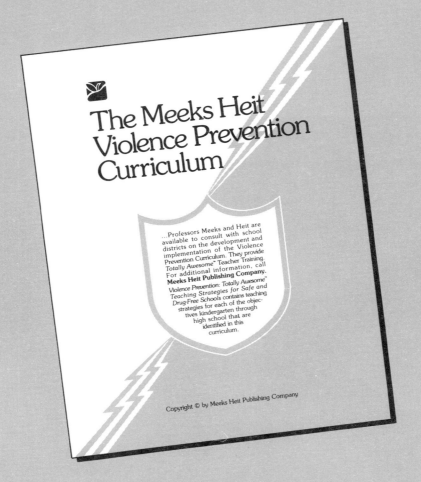

The Meeks Heit
Violence Prevention
Curriculum

...Professors Meeks and Heit are
available to consult with school
districts on the development and
implementation of the Violence
Prevention Curriculum. They provide
Totally Awesome™ Teacher Training.
For additional information, call
Meeks Heit Publishing Company.

Violence Prevention: Totally Awesome™
*Teaching Strategies for Safe and
Drug-Free Schools* contains teaching
strategies for each of the objectives kindergarten through
high school that are
identified in this
curriculum.

USING THE VIOLENCE PREVENTION CURRICULUM

CHAPTER

1

The material in this book is organized and presented within a framework the authors believe provides the best sequence in which educators might learn how to educate about violence prevention. In this sequence, educators first examine the desired outcomes for an effective violence prevention curriculum. Then they examine the facts about violence their students need to know. Next, educators review *Totally Awesome*™ Teaching Strategies and violence prevention literature that can be used to motivate students to learn and practice life skills for violence prevention. There are family, teacher, and student masters to accompany many of the *Totally Awesome*™ Teaching Strategies. Also included is a list of violence prevention resources.

Accordingly, this book is organized into six sections:
Section 1: The Violence Prevention Curriculum
Section 2: Facts About Violence Prevention
Section 3: *Totally Awesome*™ Teaching Strategies
Section 4: Violence Prevention Literature
Section 5: Family, Teacher, And Student Masters
Section 6: Violence Prevention Resources

The following discussion introduces the material included in Section 1. The Violence Prevention Curriculum. The discussion focuses upon developing a violence prevention curriculum and using *The Meeks Heit Violence Prevention Curriculum*.

DEVELOPING A VIOLENCE PREVENTION CURRICULUM

The beginning step in initiating violence prevention education is to develop a violence prevention curriculum. A **violence prevention curriculum** is an organized plan for the effective implementation and

evaluation of violence education. Educators need to consider the following when developing the curriculum:
• What is the rationale or philosophy for educating about violence prevention?
• How might students be taught to make responsible decisions that prevent violence or keep it from escalating?
• How might students learn to resist pressures to be violent?
• What does research say about risk factors for and protective factors that prevent violence?
• What are age-appropriate objectives and life skills that can be carefully interwoven into a scope and sequence or spiral of learning?
• What teaching strategies might be used to reach each of the objectives in the scope and sequence and help students develop appropriate life skills?
• How might literature be used to enhance the learning experiences of students?
• Into what curriculum areas might the teaching strategies on violence prevention be infused?
• How might critical thinking skills and character education be infused into the violence prevention teaching strategies?
• How will the students and the curriculum be evaluated to learn if the desired outcomes have been reached?

USING *THE MEEKS HEIT VIOLENCE PREVENTION CURRICULUM*

It is by no means easy to develop, implement, and evaluate an effective violence prevention curriculum. To facilitate this task, the authors have included *The Meeks Heit Violence Prevention Curriculum*. Much time was devoted to the development of the curriculum. *The Meeks Heit Violence Prevention Curriculum* is based on 20 risk factors and 20 protective factors. And, it was reviewed by your colleagues who know the history and background of this program and have expertise in violence prevention and education. Your school district might decide to use *The Meeks Heit Violence Prevention Curriculum* rather than spend valuable time and resources writing one. Of course, your school district may want to make some modifications based upon the specific needs of your school and community. Should your school district or you choose to use this curriculum, the authors ask you to keep the copyright statement on each of the pages.

The Meeks Heit Violence Prevention Curriculum includes:

1. A carefully formulated statement of goals and philosophy;
2. A Responsible Decision-Making Model that students can study and use to help them make decisions that are healthful, safe, legal, respectful of self and others, consistent with guidelines of responsible adults such as their parents, and/or guardians, and are indicative of character;
3. A Model For Using Resistance Skills that students can study and use to enable them to resist negative peer pressure;
4. An explanation and listing of the risk factors and protective factors that were used to develop the objectives and life skills for *The Meeks Heit Violence Prevention Curriculum*;
5. A Scope and Sequence Chart including objectives, life skills, and protective factors for grades K–2, grades 3–5, grades 6–8, and grades 9–12 that

serves as a blueprint for planning, implementing, and evaluating instruction;

6. An explanation of the design of the *Totally Awesome*™ Teaching Strategies that can be used to involve students in learning about violence and practicing life skills to prevent violence;
7. A rationale for including violence prevention literature to afford students the opportunity to explore the types of behavior and feelings experienced by themselves and others;
8. Identification of curriculum areas into which violence prevention might be infused;
9. A rationale for infusing critical thinking skills into the *Totally Awesome*™ Teaching Strategies;
10. A rational for infusing character education into the *Totally Awesome*™ Teaching Strategies;
11. A discussion of inclusion of students with special needs in the regular classroom for violence prevention education;
12. Suggestions for implementing the violence prevention curriculum with family, school, community, and professional involvement;
13. Suggestions for evaluating the objectives and life skills, identified for different grade levels, in the Scope and Sequence Chart.

Carefully review *The Meeks Heit Violence Prevention Curriculum*. Focus on the desired outcomes for students at grades K–2, grades 3–5, grades 6–8, and grades 9–12. The remaining sections of this book contain all of the teaching strategies, violence prevention literature, and family, student, and teacher masters needed to reach these desired outcomes.

The Meeks Heit Violence Prevention Curriculum

...Professors Meeks and Heit are available to consult with school districts on the development and implementation of the Violence Prevention Curriculum. They provide *Totally Awesome*™ Teacher Training. For additional information, call **Meeks Heit Publishing Company.**

Violence Prevention: Totally Awesome™ *Teaching Strategies for Safe and Drug-Free Schools* contains teaching strategies for each of the objectives kindergarten through high school that are identified in this curriculum.

Goals and Philosophy...

Wellness is the quality of life that includes physical, mental-emotional, family-social, and environmental health. The **Wellness Scale** depicts the ranges constituting the quality of life—from optimal well-being to high level wellness, average wellness, minor illness or injury, and premature death. At least six factors influence health and wellness:

1. the behavior a person chooses;
2. the situations in which a person participates;
3. the relationships in which a person engages;
4. the decisions that a person makes;
5. the resistance skills that a person uses;
6. the level of self-esteem that a person develops.

Health status is the sum total of the positive and negative influences of behaviors, situations, relationships, decisions, use of resistance skills, and self-esteem on a person's health and wellness. Each influence that is positive is viewed as a plus (+) while each influence that is negative is viewed as a minus (-). A person's health status fluctuates on the Wellness Scale, depending on these influences.

The goal of violence prevention education is to promote wellness in students. The philosophy of **The Meeks Heit Violence Prevention Curriculum** focuses on helping students develop life skills for violence prevention. **Life skills** are actions that keep young people safe and that are learned and practiced for a lifetime. **Life skills for violence prevention** help young people resist behaving in violent ways, protect themselves from the violent actions of others, and develop resiliency. **Resiliency** is the ability to prevent or to recover, bounce back, and learn from misfortune, change, or pressure. When young people are resilient, they bounce back when unexpected and difficult events occur in their lives. They learn from their experiences and use what they have learned wisely.

A Responsible Decision-Making Model...........

The Meeks Heit Violence Prevention Curriculum helps students learn to make responsible decisions. A decision-making model is applied consistently at every grade level with emphasis placed on making responsible decisions. The steps in the model are as follows:

- Clearly describe the situation.
- List possible actions that can be taken.
- Share the list of possible actions with a responsible

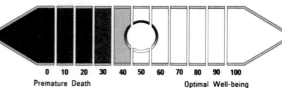

Wellness Scale
Factors That Influence Health and Well-Being

Risk behaviors	Wellness behaviors
Risk situations	Healthful situations
Destructive relationships	Healthful relationships
Irresponsible decision making	Responsible decision making
Lack of resistance skills	Use of resistance skills
Negative self-esteem	Positive self-esteem

0 10 20 30 40 50 60 70 80 90 100
Premature Death   Optimal Well-being

Health status is the sum total of the positive and negative influences of behaviors, situations, relationships, decisions, use of resistance skills, and self-esteem.

adult such as someone who protects community laws and demonstrates character.

- Carefully evaluate each possible action using six criteria. A responsible action is one that is:
  1. healthful,
  2. safe,
  3. legal,
  4. respectful of self and others,
  5. consistent with guidelines of responsible adults such as parents and guardians,
  6. indicative of character.
- Decide which action is responsible and most appropriate.
- Act in a responsible way and evaluate the results.

Model for Using Resistance Skills.........

The Meeks Heit Violence Prevention Curriculum helps students learn to resist harmful peer pressure. A model for using resistance skills or "say NO" skills is applied consistently at every grade level. Students practice the model as they:

- use assertive behavior,
- avoid saying "NO, thank you" to people who pressure them to behave in violent ways or use drugs (there is no need for them to thank people who want them to behave this way),
- use nonverbal behavior that matches verbal behavior,
- influence others to choose responsible behavior,
- avoid being in situations in which there will be pressure to make harmful decisions,
- resist pressure to engage in illegal behavior.

Risk Factors and Protective Factors...................

The Meeks Heit Violence Prevention Curriculum is based on what we know about risk factors and protective factors. **Risk factors** are ways that people might behave and characteristics of the environment in which they live that increase the likelihood that something negative will happen to their health, safety, and/or well-being. Some risk factors that promote violence are listed in Figure 1. Risk factors refer only to the statistical probability that something negative will happen. When young people have risk factors in their lives, it does not mean that they will actually behave in violent ways or be harmed by others. Young people have varying degrees of control over the different risk factors. For example, young people can control whether they use drugs or belong to gangs. However, they do not have control over the family in which they were reared and whether their families are rich or poor. **Protective factors** are ways that people might behave and characteristics of the environment in which they live that promote their health, safety, and/or well-being. Some protective factors that prevent violence are listed in Figure 2. Protective factors refer only to the statistical probability that a person's health, safety, and/or well-being will be protected. There is a chance that something beyond a person's control will affect health, safety, and/or well-being in negative ways. For example, a young person might be a victim of random violence such as a drive-by shooting. However, the more protective factors that apply to a young person, the more likely (s)he is to be protected from violence. **The Meeks Heit Violence Prevention Curriculum** encourages students to shield themselves from violence by avoiding risk factors and practicing life skills that focus on protective factors to prevent violence.

Figure 1
Risk Factors
That Promote Violence

Risk Factors are ways that you might behave and characteristics of the environment in which you live that increase the likelihood of having something negative happen to your health, safety, and/or well-being.

1. Failing to recognize violent behavior.
2. Having negative self-esteem.
3. Being reared in a dysfunctional family.
4. Living in an adverse environment.
5. Lacking social skills.
6. Being unable to manage anger.
7. Being unable to manage stress.
8. Not participating in physical and recreational activities.
9. Having suicidal tendencies.
10. Resolving conflict in harmful ways.
11. Practicing discriminatory behavior.
12. Lacking responsible decision-making skills.
13. Being unable to resist negative peer pressure.
14. Using alcohol and other drugs.
15. Carrying a weapon.
16. Belonging to a gang.
17. Challenging authority and breaking laws.
18. Being in risk situations.
19. Avoiding recovery if a victim.
20. Repeating violence if a juvenile offender.

Figure 2
Protective Factors
That Prevent Violence

Protective Factors are ways that you might behave and characteristics of the environment in which you live that promote your health, safety, and/or well-being.

1. Recognizing violent behavior.
2. Having positive self-esteem.
3. Being reared in a healthful family.
4. Living in a nurturing environment.
5. Using social skills.
6. Practicing anger management skills.
7. Practicing stress management skills.
8. Participating in physical and recreational activities.
9. Practicing suicide prevention strategies.
10. Practicing conflict resolution and peer mediation skills.
11. Avoiding discriminatory behavior.
12. Making responsible decisions.
13. Practicing resistance skills.
14. Avoiding alcohol and other drugs.
15. Practicing responsible behavior around weapons.
16. Resisting gang membership.
17. Respecting authority and abiding by laws.
18. Practicing self-protection strategies.
19. Participating in recovery if a victim.
20. Changing behavior if a juvenile offender.

Scope and Sequence: Objectives, Life Skills, and Protective Factors Grades K Through 12............

The Meeks Heit Violence Prevention Curriculum is organized into a sequential spiral of learning. The objectives are grouped as follows: grades K–2, grades 3–5, grades 6–8, and grades 9–12. For each objective, specific life skills that are age appropriate are identified. The life skills are stated "I will…" as they are actions students will learn and practice for the rest of their lives. The life skills are based on the 20 protective factors that shield students from violence. Below each life skill is the protective factor that is being reinforced by practicing the stated action. For each objective in **The Meeks Heit Violence Prevention Curriculum,** there is a specific *Totally Awesome™* teaching strategy in *Violence Prevention Skills: Totally Awesome™ Teaching Strategies for Safe and Drug-Free Schools.* There also are short stories, poems, puppet shows, and reader's theatre scripts for many of the objectives.

. . . .

OBJECTIVES, LIFE SKILLS, and PROTECTIVE FACTORS: Grades K–2

Students will:

1. **Name types of violence.**
   I will not act in ways that harm others.
   (PF1) *Recognizing Violent Behavior*
   I will not say hurtful words or act in harmful ways toward others who are different.
   (PF11) *Avoiding Discriminatory Behavior*
   I will change the way I act if I act in harmful ways toward others.
   (PF20) *Changing Behavior If A Juvenile Offender*

2. **Tell ways to say "NO" when other children want them to act in ways that would harm others.**
   I will develop positive self-esteem.
   (PF2) *Having Positive Self-Esteem*
   I will make wise choices.
   (PF12) *Making Responsible Decisions*
   I will say NO when others want me to act in harmful ways.
   (PF13) *Practicing Resistance Skills*
   I will stay away from gangs.
   (PF16) *Resisting Gang Membership*

3. **Tell ways to handle disagreements without fighting.**
   I will use manners and treat others fairly.
   (PF5) *Using Social Skills*
   I will try to work out disagreements without fighting.
   (PF10) *Practicing Conflict Resolution And Peer Mediation Skills*

4. **Tell healthful ways to express anger.**
   I will express my anger in healthful ways.
   (PF6) *Practicing Anger Management Skills*

5. **Tell healthful ways to handle stress.**
   I will choose healthful ways to handle stress.
   (PF7) *Practicing Stress Management Skills*
   I will participate in physical activity.
   (PF8) *Participating In Physical And Recreational Activities*

6. **Tell ways to stay safe from people who might harm them.**
   I will follow rules to stay safe from persons who might harm me.
   (PF18) *Practicing Self-Protection Strategies*

7. **Explain that drugs may change the way a person acts.**
   I will not try alcohol or other drugs.
   (PF14) *Avoiding Alcohol And Other Drugs*
   I will stay away from persons who use harmful drugs.
   (PF14) *Avoiding Alcohol And Other Drugs*

8. **Explain the difference between safe and unsafe touch.**
   I will expect family members to treat me in kind ways.
   (PF3) *Being Reared In A Healthful Family*
   I will tell someone if family members treat me in harmful ways.
   (PF3) *Being Reared In A Healthful Family*
   I will say NO if someone tries to touch me in an unsafe way.
   (PF18) *Practicing Self-Protection Strategies*
   I will get help if I have been touched in an unsafe way.
   (PF19) *Participating In Recovery If A Victim*

9. **Tell what to do when they are around weapons such as guns and knives.**
   I will follow the SAFE rule: Stop, Avoid getting closer, Find an adult, Explain what I saw.
   (PF15) *Practicing Responsible Behavior Around Weapons*

10. **Name persons who can help them stay safe.**
I will try to be in places where I can stay safe.
    (PF4) *Living In A Nurturing Environment*
I will listen to wise adults and follow rules and laws.
    (PF17) *Respecting Authority And Abiding By Laws*
I will act in ways to keep myself safe.
    (PF18) *Practicing Self-Protection Strategies*

. . . .

OBJECTIVES, LIFE SKILLS, and PROTECTIVE FACTORS: Grades 3–5

Students will:

1. **Name kinds of violence and ways to protect against violence.**
I will recognize that violent behavior is wrong.
    (PF1) *Recognizing Violent Behavior*
I will practice suicide prevention strategies.
    (PF9) *Practicing Suicide Prevention Strategies*
I will avoid discrimination.
    (PF11) *Avoiding Discriminatory Behavior*
I will practice self-protection strategies.
    (PF18) *Practicing Self-Protection Strategies*

2. **Identify resistance skills that can be used when pressured to engage in violent behavior.**
I will develop positive self-esteem.
    (PF2) *Having Positive Self-Esteem*
I will make responsible decisions.
    (PF12) *Making Responsible Decisions*
I will practice resistance skills.
    (PF13) *Practicing Resistance Skills*

3. **Describe ways to resolve conflicts without fighting.**
I will develop social skills.
    (PF5) *Using Social Skills*
I will practice conflict resolution and peer mediation skills.
    (PF10) *Practicing Conflict Resolution And Peer Mediation Skills*

4. **Identify healthful ways to express anger and disappointment.**
I will respond to my environment in an empowering way.
    (PF4) *Living In A Nurturing Environment*

I will practice anger management skills.
    (PF6) *Practicing Anger Management Skills*

5. **Outline ways to manage stress.**
I will practice stress management skills.
    (PF7) *Practicing Stress Management Skills*
I will participate in physical activity.
    (PF8) *Participating In Physical And Recreational Activities*

6. **Differentiate between people and groups who choose responsible behavior and people/gangs who are violent.**
I will resist gang membership.
    (PF16) *Resisting Gang Membership*

7. **Explain why drug use increases the risk of violence.**
I will avoid alcohol and other drugs.
    (PF14) *Avoiding Alcohol And Other Drugs*

8. **Identify and describe types of abuse: emotional, sexual, physical, and neglect.**
I will strive for healthful family relationships.
    (PF3) *Being Reared In A Healthful Family*
I will develop resiliency to "bounce back" if I was reared in a dysfunctional family.
    (PF3) *Being Reared In A Healthful Family*
I will practice self-protection strategies.
    (PF18) *Practicing Self-Protection Strategies*
I will participate in recovery if a victim.
    (PF19) *Participating In Recovery If A Victim*

9. **Describe procedures to follow for safety around guns.**
I will practice responsible behavior around weapons.
    (PF15) *Practicing Responsible Behavior Around Weapons*

10. **Identify the advantages of cooperating with law enforcement officers and other people with authority.**
I will respect authority and abide by laws.
    (PF17) *Respecting Authority And Abiding By Laws*
I will change behavior if a juvenile offender.
    (PF20) *Changing Behavior If A Juvenile Offender*

OBJECTIVES, LIFE SKILLS, and PROTECTIVE FACTORS: Grades 6–8

Students will:

1. **Identify types of crime and violence.**
   I will recognize that violent behavior is wrong.
   (PF1) *Recognizing Violent Behavior*
   I will avoid discrimination
   (PF11) *Avoiding Discriminatory Behavior*

2. **Identify protective factors and risk factors for violence.**
   I will develop positive self-esteem.
   (PF2) *Having Positive Self-Esteem*
   I will strive for healthful family relationships.
   (PF3) *Being Reared In A Healthful Family*
   I will develop resiliency to "bounce back" if I was reared in a dysfunctional family.
   (PF3) *Being Reared In A Healthful Family*
   I will develop social skills.
   (PF5) *Using Social Skills*

3. **Examine the importance of resiliency in dealing with life crises.**
   I will respond to my environment in an empowering way.
   (PF4) *Living In A Nurturing Environment*
   I will develop resiliency to "bounce back" if I live in an adverse environment.
   (PF4) *Living In A Nurturing Environment*
   I will practice suicide prevention strategies.
   (PF9) *Practicing Suicide Prevention Strategies*

4. **Identify resistance skills that can be used when pressured to engage in violent behavior.**
   I will make responsible decisions.
   (PF12) *Making Responsible Decisions*
   I will practice resistance skills.
   (PF13) *Practicing Resistance Skills*

5. **Describe sources of hidden anger and healthful ways to express it.**
   I will practice anger management skills.
   (PF6) *Practicing Anger Management Skills.*
   I will practice stress management skills.
   (PF7) *Practicing Stress Management Skills*
   I will participate in physical activity.
   (PF8) *Participating In Physical And Recreational Activities*

6. **Identify effective approaches to conflict resolution that exclude fighting.**
   I will participate in physical activity.
   (PF8) *Participating In Physical And Recreational Activities*
   I will practice conflict resolution and peer mediation skills.
   (PF10) *Practicing Conflict Resolution And Peer Mediation Skills*

7. **Discuss rape, acquaintance rape, rape prevention, and guideline to follow if raped.**
   I will practice self-protection strategies.
   (PF18) *Practicing Self-Protection Strategies*
   I will participate in recovery efforts if a victim.
   (PF19) *Participating In Recovery If A Victim*

8. **Discuss sexual harassment and guidelines to follow with regard to sexual harassment.**
   I will practice self-protection strategies.
   (PF18) *Practicing Self-Protection Strategies*

9. **Discuss ways to prevent assault and homicide.**
   I will practice self-protection strategies.
   (PF18) *Practicing Self-Protection Strategies*

10. **Discuss ways to prevent suicide.**
    I will practice suicide prevention strategies.
    (PF9) *Practicing Suicide Prevention Strategies*

11. **Outline procedure to follow to be safe around weapons.**
    I will practice responsible behavior around weapons.
    (PF15) *Practicing Responsible Behavior Around Weapons*

12. **Discuss ways to resist pressure to belong to gangs and to participate in group acts of violence.**
    I will resist gang membership.
    (PF16) *Resisting Gang Membership*

13. **Examine the role that drug use and drug trafficking play in increasing the risk of violence.**
    I will avoid alcohol and other drugs.
    (PF14) *Avoiding Alcohol And Other Drugs*

14. **Identify ways to reduce violence by following laws and cooperating with law enforcement authorities.**
    I will respect authority and abide by laws.
    (PF17) *Respecting Authority And Abiding By Laws*
    I will change behavior if a juvenile offender.
    (PF20) *Changing Behavior If A Juvenile Offender*

15. **Identify support systems available for people who have been victims of violence.**
    I will participate in recovery if a victim.
    (PF19) *Participating In Recovery If A Victim*

OBJECTIVES, LIFE SKILLS, and PROTECTIVE FACTORS: Grades 9–12

The student will:

1. **Identify types of violence.**
   I will recognize that violent behavior is wrong.
   (PF1) *Recognizing Violent Behavior*

2. **Identify protective factors and risk factors associated with violent behavior.**
   I will develop positive self-esteem.
   (PF2) *Having Positive Self-Esteem*
   I will strive for healthful family relationships.
   (PF3) *Being Reared In A Healthful Family*
   I will develop resiliency to "bounce back" if I was reared in a dysfunction family.
   (PF3) *Being Reared In A Healthful Family*
   I will respond to my environment in an empowering way.
   (PF4) *Living In A Nurturing Environment*
   I will develop social skills.
   (PF5) *Using Social Skills*

3. **Discuss the role of resiliency in dealing with hopelessness, poverty, discrimination, life crises.**
   I will avoid discrimination.
   (PF11) *Avoiding Discriminatory Behavior*
   I will respect authority and abide by laws.
   (PF17) *Respecting Authority And Abiding By Laws*

4. **Demonstrate resistance skills that are effective in resisting pressure to engage in violent behavior and/or belong to gangs.**
   I will make responsible decisions.
   (PF12) *Making Responsible Decisions*
   I will practice resistance skills.
   (PF13) *Practicing Resistance Skills*
   I will resist gang membership.
   (PF16) *Resisting Gang Membership*

5. **Examine ways in which unexpressed anger contributes to violence.**
   I will practice anger management skills.
   (PF6) *Practicing Anger Management Skills*
   I will participate in physical activity.
   (PF8) *Participating In Physical And Recreational Activities*

6. **Describe effective means of conflict resolution and peer mediation to avoid fighting.**
   I will practice stress management skills.
   (PF7) *Practicing Stress Management Skills*
   I will practice conflict resolution and peer mediation skills.
   (PF10) *Practicing Conflict Resolution And Peer Mediation Skills*

7. **Describe guidelines to follow when sexual harassment occurs.**
   I will practice self-protection strategies.
   (PF18) *Practicing Self-Protection Strategies*

8. **Describe ways to prevent rape and guidelines to follow when rape occurs.**
   I will practice self-protection strategies.
   (PF18) *Practicing Self-Protection Strategies*
   I will participate in recovery if a victim.
   (PF19) *Participating In Recovery If A Victim*

9. **Describe guidelines to follow when there are weapons in the environment.**
   I will practice responsible behavior around weapons.
   (PF15) *Practicing Responsible Behavior Around Weapons*

10. **Describe strategies to prevent assault and homicide.**
    I will practice self-protection strategies.
    (PF18) *Practicing Self-Protection Strategies*

11. **Describe suicide prevention strategies.**
    I will practice suicide prevention strategies.
    (PF9) *Practicing Suicide Prevention Strategies*

12. **Evaluate the consequences of belonging to a gang.**
    I will resist gang membership.
    (PF16) *Resisting Gang Membership*

13. **Evaluate the consequences of using drugs and being involved in drug sales and trafficking.**
    I will avoid alcohol and other drugs.
    (PF14) *Avoiding Alcohol And Other Drugs*

14. **Describe the importance of respecting laws and law enforcement authorities.**
    I will respect authority and abide by laws.
    (PF17) *Respecting Authority And Abiding By Laws*
    I will change behavior if a juvenile offender.
    (PF20) *Changing Behavior If A Juvenile Offender*

15. **Describe ways that people who have been victims of violence may be helped toward recovery.**
    I will participate in recovery when a victim.
    (PF19) *Participating In Recovery If A Victim*

Totally Awesome™ Teaching Strategies.........

Totally Awesome™ teaching strategies are creative ways to involve students in learning about violence and practicing life skills to prevent violence. For each of the objectives identified in the violence prevention curriculum K through 12, there is a *Totally Awesome™* teaching strategy providing in *Violence Prevention: Totally Awesome™ Teaching Strategies for Safe and Drug-Free Schools.*

The design of the *Totally Awesome™* teaching strategies:

- *Clever Title.* A clever title is set in boldfaced type in the center of the page.
- *Designated Grade Level.* The designated grade level for which the teaching strategy is appropriate appears in the upper left-hand corner.
- *Designated Curriculum Objective.* The designated curriculum objective that will be met by using the teaching strategy is identified directly beneath the designated grade level that appears in the upper left-hand corner.
- *Designated Protective Factors.* The designated protective factors that are discussed when using the teaching strategy are identified directly beneath the curriculum objective that appears in the upper left-hand corner.
- *Infusion into Curriculum Areas.* The teaching strategies are designed to be infused into several curriculum areas other than health education: art studies, foreign language, home economics, language arts, physical education, math studies, music studies, science studies, social studies, and visual and performing arts.
- *Critical Thinking.* Several of the teaching strategies help students develop critical thinking skills. A symbol to the right of the title of the teaching strategy is used to designate critical thinking.
- *Character Education.* Several of the teaching strategies focus on helping students develop character. A symbol to the right of the title of the teaching strategy is used to designate character education.
- *Objective.* The objective for the teaching strategy is listed under this boldfaced subheading. The objective helps the professional focus on what is to be learned and how to measure the learning that has taken place.
- *Life Skills.* The life skills that are reinforced by using the teaching strategy are listed under this boldfaced subheading. Life skills are actions that help keep young people healthy and safe and they are learned and practiced for a lifetime. Next to each life skill a reference is made to the number of the protective factor that is being reinforced by practicing this action.
- *Materials.* The materials are items that the professional must gather to do the teaching strategy. They are listed under this boldfaced heading.
- *Motivation.* The motivation is the step-by-step directions the professional follows when using the teaching strategy. The directions are listed under this boldfaced subheading.
- *Evaluation.* The evaluation is the means of measuring the student's mastery of the objective and life skills. The evaluation is described under this boldfaced subheading.
- *Inclusion.* Suggestions for adapting the teaching strategy to assist students with special learning challenges are included under this boldfaced subheading.

Violence Prevention Literature...................

Violence prevention literature affords students the opportunity to explore the types of behavior and feelings experienced by themselves and others. For each of the grade level groupings (grades K–2, grades 3–5, grades 6–8, and grades 9–12) in **The Meeks Heit Violence Prevention Curriculum,** there are short stories, poems, puppet shows, and/or reader's theatre in *Violence Prevention: Totally Awesome™ Teaching Strategies for Safe and Drug-Free Schools.* Each of the literature selections is accompanied by a *Totally Awesome™* teaching strategy.

Curriculum Infusion of Violence Prevention

The objectives, life skills, and protective factors identified for each grade level are appropriately taught within the health education curriculum. *The Totally Awesome™ Teaching Strategies for Safe and Drug-Free Schools* are designed to be taught within the health education curriculum. However, today the trend in education is to infuse learning into many curriculum areas. Thus, the *Totally Awesome™* teaching strategies are designed so that they might be infused or integrated into the following curriculum areas other than health education: art studies, foreign language, home economics, language arts, physical education, math studies, music studies, science studies, social studies, and visual and performing arts.

Critical Thinking..........

The Meeks Heit Violence Prevention Curriculum is designed to help students develop critical thinking skills. Some of the *Totally Awesome™* teaching strategies provide an opportunity for students to examine responsible decision-making and to learn to evaluate the consequences of actions.

Character Education.......

The Meeks Heit Violence Prevention Curriculum is designed to help students build character and develop sound moral values. Some of the *Totally Awesome™* teaching strategies provide an opportunity to examine laws and community responsibility. They help students recognize that being responsible and respectful involves choosing actions which are best for the self, others, the environment, and the community. Character education promotes citizenship.

Inclusion of Students with Special Needs.......

A current trend in education is to include students with special needs in the regular classroom. Inclusion is believed to promote learning as well as social development. In order for inclusion to be effective, teachers may need to make adaptations to teaching strategies. These adaptations facilitate learning and bolster self-esteem in students with special needs.

Implementation: Parental, School, Community, and Professional Involvement..

An advisory team including parents, administrators, teachers, community leaders, and allied health professionals might be formed to review the *Violence Prevention Curriculum* prior to implementation. A current trend is to schedule a parent meeting in which the goals and objectives for *The Violence Prevention Curriculum* are discussed and several *Totally Awesome™* teaching strategies from *Violence Prevention: Totally Awesome™ Teaching Strategies* for *Safe and Drug-Free Schools* are presented. The policies regarding violence and regarding drugs should be presented. Parents are encouraged to discuss these policies with their children. Professionals from various community agencies and from the allied health professions might describe the services they provide.

Evaluation. . . . .

The Meeks Heit Violence Prevention Curriculum might be evaluated in a number of ways. The objectives identified for each of the grade levels might be used to evaluate student mastery of information, attitudes, and skills confidence regarding violence prevention. Surveys might be conducted to evaluate student mastery of life skills and to evaluate the incidence of violence in the school and community. Teachers may observe students to determine attitudes and behavior regarding violence prevention. Role play might be used to help risk situations appear lifelike to students and help them practice behavior they may choose. Health behavior contracts might be used to evaluate change in student behavior. Portfolio assessment might be used to document student knowledge and track student progress.

Facts About Violence Prevention

GRADES K-2

Violence prevention

Special Me
and Violence-Free

ISBN: 0-9630009-9-3

GRADES 3-5

Violence prevention

Super Cool
and Violence-Free

ISBN: 0-9630009-8-5

GRADES 6-8

Violence prevention

Awesome Me
and Violence-Free

ISBN: 0-9630009-7-7

GRADES 9-12

Violence prevention

How To Be Hip, Cool
and Violence-Free

ISBN: 0-9630009-6-9

Using The Violence Prevention Student Books

To be effective, violence prevention education must include facts about risk factors and protective factors. **Risk factors** are ways that people might behave and characteristics of the environment in which they live that increase the likelihood that something negative will happen to their health, safety, and/or well-being. *The Meeks Heit Violence Prevention Curriculum* identifies 20 risk factors for violence. These risk factors refer only to the statistical probability that something negative will happen. When young people have risk factors in their lives, it does not mean that they will actually behave in violent ways or be harmed by others. Young people have varying degrees of control over the different risk factors.

Protective factors are ways that people might behave and characteristics of the environment in which they live that promote health, safety, and/or well-being. *The Meeks Heit Violence Prevention Curriculum* identifies 20 protective factors to prevent violence. Protective factors refer only to the statistical probability that a person's health, safety, and/or well-being will be protected. There is always a chance that something beyond a person's control will affect health, safety, and/or well-being in negative ways.

Four student books accompany *The Meeks Heit Violence Prevention Curriculum*. The student books include information on risk factors and protective factors that is age-appropriate for grades K–2, grades 3–5, grades 6–8, and grades 9–12. The *Totally Awesome*™ Teaching Strategies and Violence Prevention Literature with the accompanying teaching strategies in this book can be used with these valuable student books. The following discussion includes information about each of the following student books:

- *Violence Prevention: How To Be Hip, Cool, And Violence-Free*
  Grades 9–12
  ISBN: 0-9630009-6-9

- *Violence Prevention: Awesome Me And Violence-Free*
  Grades 6–8
  ISBN: 0-9630009-7-7

- *Violence Prevention: Super Cool And Violence-Free*
  Grades 3–5
  ISBN: 0-9630009-8-5

- *Violence Prevention: Special Me And Violence-Free*
  Grades K–2
  ISBN: 0-9630009-9-3

VIOLENCE PREVENTION: HOW TO BE HIP, COOL, AND VIOLENCE-FREE (Grades 9–12)

Violence Prevention: How To Be Hip, Cool, And Violence-Free, is designed to be used with students in grades 9–12. The content in this book is correlated to the objectives and life skills in *The Meeks Heit Violence Prevention Curriculum*. Unique in design, this student book is divided into the 20 protective factors that help prevent violence. As each of the 20 protective factors is discussed, facts pertaining to the correlating risk factor are included. At the end of each protective factor, there is a violence-free pledge. Each violence-free pledge lists the life skills students can practice to be hip, cool, and violence-free.

The entire copy of the student book, *Violence Prevention: How To Be Hip, Cool, And Violence-Free*, is included in Section 2 of this book. The authors want you to have the latest facts pertaining to risk factors and protective factors. In addition, rather than learning these facts while reading material written for teachers, the authors think it is valuable for you to read this information in the format of the student book to promote rapport with students and to facilitate discussions. The actual student book, *Violence Prevention: How To Be Hip, Cool, And Violence-Free*, is available as a hardbound textbook and can be purchased for classroom use and for libraries.

VIOLENCE PREVENTION: AWESOME ME AND VIOLENCE-FREE (Grades 6–8)

Violence Prevention: Awesome Me And Violence-Free is designed to be used with students in grades 6–8. The information is correlated to the objectives and life skills in *The Meeks Heit Violence Prevention Curriculum*. This student book is similar in design to *Violence Prevention: How To Be Hip, Cool, And Violence-Free*; however, it contains age-appropriate information and the readability is carefully controlled for its audience. It also is divided into the 20 protective factors that prevent violence. As each of the 20 protective factors is discussed, facts pertaining to the correlating risk factor are included. At the end of each protective factor, there is a violence-free pledge. Each violence-free pledge lists the life skills students can practice to be awesome and violence-free. One of the unique features of this student book is the inclusion of violence prevention literature for each of the protective factors.

VIOLENCE PREVENTION: SUPER COOL AND VIOLENCE-FREE (Grades 3–5)

Violence Prevention: Super Cool And Violence-Free is designed to be used with students in grades 3–5. The information in this book focuses on factual information and life skills relevant to this age group. It is correlated to the objectives and life skills in *The Meeks Heit Violence Prevention Curriculum*. Students learn to recognize violence and take the position that violence is wrong. They learn: why it is important to treat others with respect, how to make responsible decisions, how to use resistance skills, ways to resolve conflicts without fighting, ways to express anger, how to manage stress, ways to avoid gangs, why it is important to avoid drugs and stay away from others who use drugs, what to do if they are abused, ways to stay safe around weapons, and how to cooperate with law enforcement officers and other people with authority. There is an emphasis on practicing self-protection strategies. Throughout this book, there are violence-free pledges. Each violence-free pledge lists the life skills students can practice to be super cool and violence-free.

VIOLENCE PREVENTION: SPECIAL ME AND VIOLENCE-FREE (Grades K–2)

Violence Prevention: Special Me And Violence-Free is designed for the primary grades. Teachers can help their students read this book. Each concept is presented in a manner that is easily understood. The illustrations involve students in learning. The information and illustrations in this book are correlated to the objectives and life skills in *The Meeks Heit Violence Prevention Curriculum*. Students learn why it is important to stay safe, help others stay safe, speak kindly to others, feel good about themselves, make wise choices, say NO when asked to do something that is wrong, stay away from gangs, use manners, work out disagreements without fighting, express anger in healthful ways, talk with parents about stress, choose physical activity, follow rules, stay away from people who use drugs, tell a grownup if they are treated badly or touched in an unsafe way, tell a grownup if they find a weapon or see someone with a weapon, and name people who keep them safe. Adult family members may want to read this book with their children after it has been read at school. This provides added learning opportunities.

Notes

Notes

Notes

Notes

Meeks Heit
Publishing Company

pViolence Prevention

how to be
hip, cool,
and
violence-free

Meeks Heit Publishing Company

Editorial, Sales, and Customer Service Office
P.O. Box 121
Blacklick, OH   43004
(614) 759-7780

Project Editor: Julie R. DeVillers
Production: Meeks Heit Publications
Production Editors: Julie R. DeVillers, Ann G. Turpie
Director of Art and Design: Jim Brower
Illustrators: Jim Brower, Jennifer King
Director of Marketing: David Willcox

Printed in the United States of America

1 2 3 4 5 6 7 8 9 10   99 98 97 96 95 94

Library of Congress Catalog Number: 94-79481

ISBN: 0-9630009-6-9

advisory board

reviewers

Sergeant Joyce Baker
Peace Officers Standards and Training Instructor
State of Georgia Police
Resource Officer/Staff Instructor
Drug Education Program
Savannah-Chatham County Board of Education
Savannah, Georgia

Donna Breitenstein, Ed.D.
Coordinator and Professor of Health Education
College of Education
Appalachian State University
Boone, North Carolina

Joanne Fraser, Ed.D.
Education Associate
South Carolina Department of Education
Columbia, South Carolina

Betsy Gallun, M.Ed.
Supervisor of Drug Programs
Prince George's County Public Schools
Upper Marlboro, Maryland

Sheryl Gotts, M.S.
Curriculum Specialist
Office of Health and Physical Education
Milwaukee Public Schools
Milwaukee, Wisconsin

Nancy Green, M.Ed.
Supervisor of Physical Education, Health, and Girls' Athletics
Jefferson County Public Schools
Birmingham, Alabama

Major William Greer
Millen Police Department
Millen, Georgia

Janet Henke, B.S.
Middle School Team Leader
Old Court Middle School
Baltimore County Public Schools
Baltimore, Maryland

Peggy Holstedt, M.S.
Health Promotion Specialist
Oregon Department of Education
Salem, Oregon

Linda Johnson, M.Ed.
Health Coordinator
Department of Public Instruction
Bismarck, North Dakota

Joseph M. Leake, B.S., C.H.E.S.
Health Education Curriculum Specialist
Baltimore City Public Schools
Baltimore, Maryland

Mary Moren, M.A.
Coordinator
North Carolina School Health Training Center
Appalachian State University
Boone, North Carolina

Billette D. Owens-Ashford
Program Assistant
Drug-Free Schools and Communities
Atlanta Public Schools
Atlanta, Georgia

Linda Peveler
Master Teacher
Columbiana Middle School
Shelby County Public Schools
Birmingham, Alabama

Michael Schaffer, M.A.
Supervisor of Health Education, K-12
Prince George's County Public Schools
Upper Marlboro, Maryland

Barbara Sullivan, M.S.
Wellness Team Leader
Sudbrook Magnet Middle School
Baltimore County Public Schools
Baltimore, Maryland

table of contents

table of contents

preface

You are very special. The way you think, feel, and act is important because you have an awesome task ahead of you. You and other young women and men your age will provide the leadership for this nation in the 21st Century. Take a moment to imagine a nation in which all people are treated with dignity and respect. There is no discrimination against people who are different. Imagine living in a nation in which all people are safe. There is no crime or violence. Imagine living in a nation in which illegal drugs are not used or sold. Recognize that you and other young people can create a nation in which all people have dignity and respect, all people are nonviolent and safe, and all people are drug-free. At this very moment, you and other young people are shaping the future. Everything that you do counts. This book, **Violence Prevention: How To Be Hip, Cool, And Violence-Free,** will give you the information that you need to act and think in ways that keep you and others healthy, safe, and drug-free. You will learn how to treat others with respect. You will learn how to be nonviolent and to protect yourself from harm. Then it is up to you to use this information. Remember, your future and the future of this nation are influenced by your actions.

how to be
hip, cool,
and
violence-free

You can be hip, cool, and violence-free in a world that is heated and unsettled. You can be hip, cool, and violence-free when others are not. But to do this, you need to develop and practice life skills for violence prevention. **Life skills** are actions that keep you and others healthy and safe and that are learned and practiced for a lifetime. Life skills for violence prevention help you resist behaving in violent ways, protect yourself from the violent actions of others, and develop resiliency. Life skills for violence prevention are based on what we know about risk factors and protective factors.

Risk Factors

Risk factors are ways that you might behave and characteristics of the environment in which you live that increase the likelihood of having something negative happen to your health, safety, and/or well-being. Some risk factors that promote violence are listed in Figure 1. As you read through this list, you may find some risk factors that describe your behavior or the characteristics of the environment in which you live. If so, then you have some risk factors for violence. You

may be more at risk for behaving in violent ways. You may be more at risk for being harmed. Risk factors refer only to the statistical probability that something negative will happen. This does not mean that you will actually behave in violent ways or be harmed by others. You have varying degrees of control over the different risk factors. For example, you do have control over whether or not you carry a weapon to school. However, you do not have control over the family in which you were reared. You also had little control over whether you were born rich or poor. Knowing about risk factors is an important step in being hip, cool, and violence-free in a heated and unsettled world. Knowing about protective factors will help you stay healthy and safe and protect your well-being.

Protective Factors

Protective factors are ways that you might behave and characteristics of the environment in which you live that promote your health, safety, and/or well-being. Some protective factors that prevent violence are listed in Figure 2. As you read through this list, you may find some protective factors that describe your behavior or characteristics of the environment in which you live. If so, then you have some protection from violence. You are more likely to behave in non-violent ways. You are less likely to be harmed by others. Protective factors refer only to the statistical probability that your health, safety, and well-being will be protected. There is a chance that something beyond your control will affect your health, safety, and/or well-being in negative ways. For example, you might be a victim of random violence such as a drive-by shooting. However, the more protective factors that apply to you, the more likely you are to be protected from violence. Having protective factors in your life also promotes resiliency. **Resiliency** is the ability to prevent or to recover, bounce back, and learn from misfortune, change, or pressure. When you are

resilient, you bounce back when unexpected and difficult events occur in your life. You learn from your experiences and use what you have learned wisely. You do not act out in violent ways.

How can you be hip, cool, and violence-free in a heated and unsettled world? How can you be hip, cool, and violence-free when others are not? You can learn all about risk factors and avoid the risk factors over which you have control. You can learn all about protective factors that prevent violence. You can pledge to be violence-free. This book will give you information you need to act and think in ways that keep you and others healthy and safe. This book is divided into 20 Protective Factors that help prevent violence. At the end of each Protective Factor, there is a Violence-Free Pledge. Each Violence-Free Pledge includes life skills you can practice to be hip, cool, and violence-free.

Figure 1
Risk Factors
That Promote Violence

Risk Factors are ways that you might behave and characteristics of the environment in which you live that increase the likelihood of having something negative happen to your health, safety, and/or well-being.

1. Failing to recognize violent behavior.
2. Having negative self-esteem.
3. Being reared in a dysfunctional family.
4. Living in an adverse environment.
5. Lacking social skills.
6. Being unable to manage anger.
7. Being unable to manage stress.
8. Not participating in physical and recreational activities.
9. Having suicidal tendencies.
10. Resolving conflict in harmful ways.
11. Practicing discriminatory behavior.
12. Lacking responsible decision-making skills.
13. Being unable to resist negative peer pressure.
14. Using alcohol and other drugs.
15. Carrying a weapon.
16. Belonging to a gang.
17. Challenging authority and breaking laws.
18. Being in risk situations.
19. Avoiding recovery if a victim.
20. Repeating violence if a juvenile offender.

Figure 2
Protective Factors
That Prevent Violence

Protective Factors are ways that you might behave and characteristics of the environment in which you live that promote your health, safety, and/or well-being.

1. Recognizing violent behavior.
2. Having positive self-esteem.
3. Being reared in a healthful family.
4. Living in a nurturing environment.
5. Using social skills.
6. Practicing anger management skills.
7. Practicing stress management skills.
8. Participating in physical and recreational activities.
9. Practicing suicide prevention strategies.
10. Practicing conflict resolution and peer mediation skills.
11. Avoiding discriminatory behavior.
12. Making responsible decisions.
13. Practicing resistance skills.
14. Avoiding alcohol and other drugs.
15. Practicing responsible behavior around weapons.
16. Resisting gang membership.
17. Respecting authority and abiding by laws.
18. Practicing self-protection strategies.
19. Participating in recovery if a victim.
20. Changing behavior if a juvenile offender.

types of violence

We live in a society in which violence occurs every day. We see violence on television and videotapes. When we listen to certain types of music, we hear lyrics that describe violent behavior. Unfortunately, being exposed to violence again and again may result in getting used to it. It may lead to being unable to recognize what is violent and what is nonviolent. In fact, it might lead to being unable to tell the difference between what is right and wrong. STOP! It is dangerous not to know what is violent and what is not violent. You need to know that it is wrong to harm yourself or others. You need to know that it is wrong for others to harm you. This is the first step in being hip, cool, and violence-free in a heated and unsettled world. The following discussion will help you learn about different kinds of violence. You will learn why you are at risk if you do not recognize violent behavior. You will learn why the kind of behavior that you choose affects your likelihood of being involved in violence. When you behave in appropriate ways, you help protect yourself from violence.

Facts: Violence

Violence is the threatened or actual use of physical force to injure, damage, or destroy yourself, others, or property. **Nonviolence** is the avoidance of the threatened or actual use of physical force to injure, damage, or destroy yourself, others, or property. A

perpetrator is a person who commits a violent act. A **victim** is a person who is harmed by violence.

Figure 3 defines different kinds of violence: bullying, fighting, assault, homicide, suicide, sexual harassment, rape, child abuse, and domestic violence. You will need to learn about each of these kinds of violence.

Bullying is an attempt by a person to hurt or frighten people who are perceived to be smaller or weaker. A **bully** is a person who hurts or frightens people who are perceived to be smaller or weaker. There are different ways that a bully might act. A bully might place a hand in the face of someone in order to threaten that person. You might have heard someone say, "Get outta my face" because a bully had done this to him/her. Most young people have been bullied at one time or another. In fact, 75 percent of students in middle school and high school say they have been bullied. More than 10 percent of students in high school say they have been bullied in an extreme way (CDC, 1993). Being bullied is harmful. Bullying someone else is violent behavior and is wrong.

Fighting is taking part in a physical struggle. The first experience young people have with fighting is often a fistfight. About 40 percent of high school students say they have been involved in at least one fight per year. Eight percent of high school students say they have been in a fight in the last 30 days in which someone needed medical treatment for an injury. Males are more likely to get into fights than are females. Fighting is risky behavior. Many young people are injured. In most cases where a young person was murdered by another young person, it began with a fight.

Assault is a physical attack or threat of attack. Young people may assault others or be assaulted for different reasons. In some cases, assault occurs because a person wants to harm another person. In other cases, assault occurs as a result of another type of crime. For example, one young person might push another person down in order to take something such as a jacket. In this case, the physical attack or assault was part of a robbery. More than two million people are victims of assault each year. More than one-half million of these victims require emergency medical care. There are more assault injuries to people in your age group than there are to people of any other age group. Later in this book, you will learn ways to protect yourself from assault.

Homicide is the accidental or purposeful killing of another person. **Murder** is a homicide that is purposeful. Homicide or murder is death from injuries that resulted when one person harmed another. Most homicides follow arguments and fights between people who know each other. A gun is used as the weapon in more than 60 percent of homicides (CDC, 1993). Homicide is a serious problem in the United States. Homicide is the tenth leading cause of death. It is the second leading cause of death in people ages 15 to 34. Males, young adults, and minority group members, particularly African-Americans and Hispanics, are the most common homicide victims (Mercy et al., 1994). Knowing these statistics should help convince you that it is important to resolve problems without fighting.

Suicide is the intentional taking of one's own life. Unfortunately, suicide is a deadly and final solution to temporary problems. People who commit suicide have experienced depression, anger, hopelessness, alcohol and other drug use, family problems, and relationship problems for which they could have received help. In the United States, more people commit suicide than are murdered. Suicide is the eighth leading cause of death. It is the third leading cause of death among young people. Females in your age group are three times more likely to commit suicide than males. The suicide rate is highest for white Americans and American Indians. Later in this book, you will learn what to do if you or someone you know shows signs of suicide. Keeping yourself and others alive should be a priority.

Sexual harassment is unwanted sexual behavior that ranges from making unwanted sexual comments to forcing another person into unwanted sex acts. Sexual harassment sometimes occurs in schools. Sexual harassment also may occur in the workplace. There are laws to protect you and others from sexual harassment. Title IX, a federal law, makes it clear that sexual harassment should never occur in your school.

Figure 3
Types of Violence

Bullying	An attempt by a person to hurt or frighten people who are perceived to be smaller or weaker
Fighting	Taking part in a physical struggle
Assault	A physical attack or threat of attack
Homicide	The accidental or purposeful killing of another person
Suicide	The intentional taking of one's own life
Sexual Harassment	Unwanted sexual behavior that ranges from making unwanted sexual comments to forcing another person into unwanted sex acts
Rape	The threatened or actual use of physical force to get someone to have sex without giving consent
Child Abuse	Harmful treatment of a person under 18 and includes physical abuse, emotional abuse, sexual abuse, and neglect
Domestic Violence	Violence that occurs within the family or within other relationships in which people live together

9

Unfortunately, one study reported that sexual harassment often occurs in schools. More than 85 percent of the high school females and more than 75 percent of the high school male students reported that they had been sexually harassed (UUAWF, 1993). Later in this book, you will learn what to do if sexual harassment occurs.

Rape is the threatened or actual use of physical force to get someone to have sex without giving consent. An important part of this definition is "without giving consent." There are laws to interpret what this means. The first interpretation is obvious. If a person does not willingly agree to sex, there is no consent and sex is considered rape. The second interpretation is one designed to protect people who are under a certain age and people who may not have the ability to know what they are deciding. The law states that people under a certain age and people who do not have certain mental abilities are considered people who are not able to give consent. Even if these people willingly agree to have sex, the law considers them unable to give consent. A person who has sex with someone who is described as not able to give consent is guilty of committing rape.

There are many facts to know about rape. Rape is a violent act. It is estimated that more than one million people in your age group are raped each year. Females are raped far more often than males, but males are rape victims too. Experts agree that many rapes are not reported. You should know that nearly eight of ten rape victims knew the person who raped them. Some studies have reported that half of all rapes occur while the people involved are on a date. You always need to trust your feeling when you are around others. Later in this book, you will learn more about rape, ways to protect yourself, and what victims of rape should do.

Child abuse is the harmful treatment of a person under the age of 18 and includes physical abuse, emotional abuse, sexual abuse, and neglect. The most common type of child abuse is neglect. This is followed by physical abuse and emotional abuse. Abuse is another serious type of violence in the United States. More than 2.5 million young people under the age of 18 are abused or neglected each year. More than 160,000 of these young people are seriously injured because of abuse. And, 1,100 young people die from abuse each year. A family member is the person who is the abuser 85 to 90 percent of the time.

In most cases, the family member who harms a young person was abused as a child. Young people who are abused often are abusive when they are older and become parents. And, over 80 percent of people in prison report they were abused during their childhood. The cycle of abuse will be discussed in more detail later in this book. You have a right to be protected and kept safe by the important adults in your life. No one has the right to abuse you.

Domestic violence is violence that occurs within the family or within other relationships in which people live together. You have already learned about one type of domestic violence, child abuse. There are other types of domestic violence. Sometimes there is abuse in a marriage. One marriage partner abuses or harms the other. This person may physically beat a partner. This person might emotionally harm a partner by repeatedly making cruel and critical comments. This person also might force a partner to have sex without consent. These are all types of domestic violence. Domestic violence also includes ways other family members interact. Brothers and sisters also might behave in these ways. Stepbrothers and stepsisters also might behave in these ways.

Sometimes children are guilty of abusing their parents. This is a type of domestic violence known as parent abuse. **Parent abuse** is the physical and emotional assault of parents by their children. Recently, domestic violence has been a topic in the media. People are being made aware that domestic violence is much more common than they might have believed. It is estimated that one-half of all families experience some type of domestic violence. Half of all married couples say that violence has occurred at least once during their marriage. In one survey, one-eighth of the husbands said they had beaten their wives. Females are more likely to be killed by their husband or partner or by their former husband or partner than by anyone else. It is frightening to know that people who love one another or at one time loved one another might harm one another. Domestic violence must be stopped.

You have just learned about types of violent behavior. Remember, each of these types of behavior is wrong. You do not want to get used to seeing, hearing, or reading about these types of behavior and begin to think they are all right. A risk factor for becoming a perpetrator or victim of violence is failure to recognize violent behavior.

Risk Factor #1

Failing To Recognize Violent Behavior

A number of years ago a serial killer named Jeffrey Dahmer was arrested by the police and later found guilty of murder. Dahmer would meet young males, invite them back to his home, murder them, cut up their bodies, and store some of their body parts in his refrigerator. The news reports of his behavior shocked everyone. Why would Dahmer behave this way? What was his childhood like? Were there any signs of strange behavior? The media gathered as much information as they could find about Dahmer. What they found was not too surprising. Friends and neighbors said Dahmer had no close friends and described him as a "loner." His classmates said he acted out in a bizarre manner to gain attention. There were reports that he enjoyed skinning animals and was fascinated with dead animals. At the time, the people who observed Dahmer's behavior did indeed question if his behavior was normal (*Vanity Fair*, 1991).

What is normal behavior? When does behavior indicate that a person might be violent and dangerous? It is important to learn the difference between nonviolent behavior and violent behavior at an early age. Yet, there seems to be at least two reasons some young people might have difficulty doing this.

The first reason that young people may have difficulty recognizing violence is that they have gotten used to it. Today, newspaper headlines often mention a recent murder or robbery. Television shows and videotapes show acts of violence. Young people can view one shooting after another. And, music often is filled with lyrics about violence and about drugs. When young people see, hear, and read about violence again and again, they can become desensitized.

Desensitization is a process of lessening a person's response to certain things by overexposing that person to those same things. Desensitization to violence involves the lessening of a person's response to violence by overexposing that person to acts of violence. This is very risky. Young people may begin to respond to acts of violence in a casual way. Then they are less likely to recognize when their own behavior is violent.

A second reason some young people cannot recognize violence is that they grew up with it. Being exposed to violence in the community or in the home can desensitize young people. Young people with this experience might begin to believe that this is the way everyone acts or that it is acceptable to act this way. In fact, young people who experienced violence at home often begin to show the same violent behavior when they are with others.

Young people who were abused often become very aggressive. They are often depressed and withdraw from others. They may harm themselves. Young people who were abused during childhood are more at risk for attempting suicide than are other young people (Division of Injury Control, 1992).

Protective Factor #1

Recognizing Violent Behavior

You need to be able to recognize violent behavior. Then you will know when you are behaving in violent ways. You will know when it is best for you to change your behavior. You will know when others are behaving in violent ways and you need to protect yourself.

Figure 4 includes information about passive behavior, aggressive behavior, and assertive behavior. You can learn to recognize these types of behavior in yourself and others. You can learn ways that passive behavior and aggressive behavior are linked to violence. You can learn how to behave in an assertive way and why this will help protect you.

Passive behavior is the holding back of ideas, opinions, and feelings. People who have passive behavior have difficulty expressing their concerns. They often make unnecessary apologies and excuses for what they have said or done. They might look away or laugh when they are trying to express serious feelings. People who have passive behavior usually do not show disrespect for others. They do not call others names or provoke fights. They usually keep angry feelings inside rather than expressing them. Suppose they continue to keep angry feelings inside and they become more angry. At some point, the anger will be

11

expressed. They may explode because it has been kept inside so long.

You may have read about someone who was described as being very nice and pleasant who acted in a very violent way. People who have passive behavior may become perpetrators of violence because their anger has been kept inside so long that they act out. People who have passive behavior also are at risk for being victims. They often are chosen as victims because they are not as likely to resist the violent behavior of others. They also are less likely to tell others if they are harmed.

Aggressive behavior is the use of words and/or actions that show disrespect toward others. People who have aggressive behavior might call other people names and make loud and sarcastic remarks. They interrupt others and monopolize conversations. They may glare at others, use threatening hand gestures, and sit with very rigid posture. They are domineering and threaten and intimidate others.

People who have aggressive behavior may become perpetrators of violence. They may try to force others to do what they want by using violent behavior. People who have aggressive behavior also are more likely to become victims of violence. Because they threaten others, people around them may become angry and defend themselves. In other words, they may cause a fight and end up being harmed themselves.

Assertive behavior is the honest expression of thoughts and feelings without experiencing anxiety or threatening others. Assertive behavior is healthier than passive or aggressive behavior. People who have assertive behavior are more likely to have good interpersonal relationships. They are able to clearly communicate with others. They have a confident body posture. Their hand gestures are nonthreatening. They listen to what is said and have comfortable eye contact with others. People with assertive behavior are least likely to become victims of the violent actions of others.

Figure 5 contains a self-test that you can complete to check your behavior. You will learn how you behave in different situations. You can check to see if your response is passive, aggressive, or assertive. Then you can think about other situations and decide what behavior is most typical of you. It is important to regularly examine your behavior. Check your likelihood of becoming a perpetrator or victim of violence. Change your behavior when needed.

To reduce the likelihood of being a perpetrator, recognize situations when you act in passive ways. Know when you are holding angry feelings inside you and these angry feelings are increasing. Do something to

---

Figure 4
How Behavior Influences the Likelihood of Being a Perpetrator or Victim of Violence

People with Passive Behavior:

- Hold back ideas, opinions, and feelings;
- Have difficulty expressing concerns;
- Rarely start arguments with others.

They may be **perpetrators** because they hold back feelings for so long that they may become angry and act out in unexpected ways.

They may be **victims** because they have difficulty resisting abusive and harmful actions of others, which invites further harm.

People with Aggressive Behavior:

- Use words and actions that show disrespect for others.

They may be **perpetrators** because they often bully, threaten, and fight others.

They may be **victims** because they may provoke others, causing them to retaliate.

People with Assertive Behavior:

- Express thoughts and feelings honestly without experiencing anxiety or threatening others.

They are less likely to be **perpetrators** because they resolve conflict by sharing thoughts and feelings and listening to others.

They are less likely to be **victims** because they resist abuse from others.

Figure 5
Patterns of Behavior Self-Test

Directions: Read each of the following scenarios. Determine how you might respond. Think about your response. Are you behaving in ways that might provoke others? Are you behaving in ways that might invite others to abuse you? Are you behaving in ways in which anger and resentment is building inside you? Do you have any patterns of behavior that may lead to violence? If so, how might these behavior patterns be changed?

1. You are playing softball on the playground after school. It is your turn to bat. One of the other players grabs the bat out of your hand and runs up to the plate. You respond by:
   a. pushing him/her off the plate and calling him/her names
   b. not saying anything, after all, your turn will come
   c. calling to him/her and asking if he realized that it was your turn to bat

2. You have taken your friend to a restaurant for his/her birthday. You made reservations but the host tells you that you must wait for a table. After waiting for a long time, you notice that customers who arrived later than you are being seated. You respond by:
   a. complaining loudly so that all the customers can hear about your situation
   b. remaining quiet to avoid spoiling the birthday celebration
   c. asking the host about your order in line and explaining that you are having a special celebration

3. You are working on a paper in class and are trying to concentrate. The student behind you keeps kicking your chair. It is driving you crazy. You respond by:
   a. turning around and kicking his/her desk so that his/her books fly off the desk
   b. ignoring it as best as you can
   c. telling him/her that (s)he might not realize that (s)he is kicking your desk, but it is making it hard for you to concentrate, and to please stop

4. You have invited your friend to sleep at your home. Your friend begins to snore so loudly you can't fall asleep. You respond by:
   a. knocking your friend off the bed and saying if you can't sleep, neither can (s)he
   b. putting your pillow over your head and trying to ignore it
   c. nudging your friend carefully until (s)he changes positions and quiets down

5. A new teammate on your basketball team is not playing very well. (S)he keeps missing the basket, never looks where (s)he is going, and keeps bumping into you. You respond by:
   a. bumping him/her back and yelling that (s)he stinks at the game
   b. ignoring him/her, hoping that it won't happen again
   c. taking him/her aside and asking if (s)he wants to stay later to practice with you so that you two can figure how to play together best.

If most of your responses are a:
You are choosing **aggressive** responses to situations. If you demonstrate aggressive behavior, you are at risk of being a perpetrator or victim of violence. When you demonstrate aggressive behavior, you use words and/or actions that tend to communicate disrespect toward others. People who demonstrate aggressive behavior are likely to be violent. Because aggressive behavior tends to provoke others, people who demonstrate aggressive behavior also are at risk for being victims of violent actions of others.

If most of your responses are b:
You are choosing **passive** responses to situations. If you demonstrate passive behavior, you are at risk for being a victim or a perpetrator of violence. When you demonstrate passive behavior you tend to hold back ideas, opinions, and feelings. People who demonstrate passive behavior often hold angry feelings inside and may become perpetrators. When angry feelings that are held back begin to build up inside, the result may be an explosion of violence. People who demonstrate passive behavior also are more often selected to be victims of violence because they are less likely to resist and less likely to tell someone else when they are harmed.

If most of your responses are c:
You are choosing **assertive** responses to situations. Assertive behavior is healthier than passive or aggressive behavior. People who demonstrate assertive behavior clearly communicate with others. Assertive behavior promotes high-quality relationships. People who demonstrate assertive behavior are least likely to be perpetrators and/or victims of violence.

change your behavior. You will learn ways to express anger later in this book. Also, recognize situations when you act in aggressive ways. Know when you are domineering or forceful. Know when you are being disrespectful of others. Do something to change your behavior. Later in this book, you will learn how to work out disagreements without being aggressive.

To reduce the likelihood of being a victim, recognize situations in which you are passive and other people are taking advantage of you. Later in this book, you will learn about resistance skills you can use. You also need to change aggressive behavior so you will not provoke hostility in others. Again, later in this book you will learn how to work out disagreements with others without being hostile. And finally, to reduce the likelihood of being a perpetrator or a victim, you can get training in assertiveness skills.

Violence-Free Pledge

I will recognize that the following are acts of violence and are wrong: bullying, fighting, assault, homicide, suicide, sexual harassment, rape, child abuse, and domestic violence.

I will tell a trusted adult if someone around me behaves in violent ways.

I will choose television programs, videotapes, and movies carefully to avoid watching acts of violence.

I will choose music carefully to avoid listening to violent lyrics.

I will behave in an assertive way to avoid being a perpetrator or victim of violence.

Self-esteem

To be hip, cool, and violence-free, you need to like yourself. Having good feelings about yourself motivates you to protect yourself. You are likely to recognize that others are worthy too. You are less likely to act in ways that harm others. **Self-esteem** is what you think or believe about yourself. You have positive self-esteem when you believe you are worthy and lovable. You have negative self-esteem when you believe you are unworthy and unlovable. The following discussion focuses on self-esteem. You will learn why having negative self-esteem is a risk factor for violence. You will learn ways to develop positive self-esteem.

Facts: Self-Esteem

How do you feel about yourself? Do you believe that you are worthwhile? Your feelings about yourself were most likely formed by the age of four or five (Black, 1991). The people who most influenced your beliefs about yourself were the members of your family. The people who had the greatest influence were your parents or other significant adults in your life.

You received messages about your worthiness from these people. These messages often influence what you believe about yourself. For example, if you were comforted and your needs were met, you began to believe that you were worthy of attention and care. If your parents or other significant adults spent time with you, you began to believe that being with you

was valuable. If your parents taught you how to do things and then praised you for doing them, you gained confidence in yourself. If your parents treated you with respect, you learned that you deserve respect. When you believe you are capable and deserve the attention, care, and respect of others, you begin to develop positive self-esteem.

Now imagine that you were treated differently. Suppose you were neglected. You may have begun to believe you were not worthy of attention and care. If no one had time for you, you would have begun to doubt your value. If your parents harmed you in any way, you may have begun to believe that you were not worthy of respect. These early messages may have caused you to develop negative self-esteem. People who have negative self-esteem, do not feel good about themselves. They do not believe that they are capable and worthy of attention, care, and respect from others.

Messages about worthiness that you received at a young age from your parents or significant adults are very lasting. They carry into other situations. As you grew up, these messages may have influenced your feelings about yourself in other situations. Suppose these messages were positive. Because you felt good about yourself, you may have walked into school the first day with confidence. You probably held your head high and spoke in a friendly manner to students you were meeting for the first time. Suppose these messages were negative. You may replay these messages and think poorly of yourself. You would have felt differently on the first day of school. You might have felt self-conscious and thought that others did not like or respect you. You might have been reluctant to introduce yourself to students you did not know.

Although your family greatly influenced your self-esteem, there is another important influence. Being able to do things well also influences self-esteem in positive ways. To improve self-esteem, you can set goals and work toward reaching them. At a younger age, this included tasks such as learning to ride a bicycle. Do you remember the positive feelings you had about yourself when you were able to ride and keep your balance? A positive feeling accompanies achievement. It is important for you to continue to develop new skills. Always set realistic goals for yourself. Your goals should not be too difficult or too easy for your abilities.

Throughout life, you will want to get feedback from people you respect. People you respect can offer suggestions on how to do things better. They can reward and praise your work when it is well done. Getting clear feedback about your performance is more helpful than getting false praise. It is more important to be praised for tasks that are challenging than tasks that require little effort. Praise for poor work, or insincere

praise communicates to you that a person lacks faith in your abilities. False praise can lessen your self-esteem.

It also is wise to get feedback on your behavior. Having high standards for your behavior is important. This means being honest, fair, loyal, trustworthy, and self-disciplined. Being praised for having high standards for behavior is important. When your behavior does not meet high standards, you need to know why. If not, you may keep behaving in inappropriate ways.

Now that you know more about self-esteem, let's learn why having negative self-esteem is a risk factor. Then we will look at ways you can develop positive self-esteem.

Risk Factor #2

Having Negative Self-Esteem

There are many reasons why having negative self-esteem is a risk factor for violence. People with negative self-esteem are more likely to be self-centered and self-destructive. **Self-centered behavior** is behavior in which you act in ways that fulfill your needs and wishes with little regard for the needs and wishes of others. In other words, self-centered people "want what they want when they want it." Why might this increase the likelihood that these people will be violent? If people have so little regard for the belongings of others, they might become involved in shoplifting or burglary. They might disregard the safety of others and carry a weapon to school. They might feel that it is all right to injure others in a fight. Being self-centered is very risky.

Self-destructive behavior is behavior in which you harm yourself. Remember, people with negative self-esteem do not feel they are worthy. These people may be self-destructive. They might have so little regard for themselves that they participate in criminal behavior. Later, they will be punished. They might harm themselves in another way. The rate of suicide and suicide attempts is much higher in people with self-destructive behavior.

People with negative self-esteem are likely to experience difficulty in social situations. It is more difficult for

---

Figure 6
Ways to Develop Positive Self-Esteem

1. Set goals and make plans to reach them.
2. Develop a special skill or talent.
3. Make a list of things you do well.
4. Work to do your best in school.
5. Be involved in school clubs and community activities.
6. Develop a trusting relationship with at least one adult.
7. Choose friends who encourage you to do your best.
8. Spend time with friends and adults who give you support.
9. Volunteer to help another person.
10. Keep a neat appearance.

---

these people to get close to others. They might choose to be around others who also have difficulty in social situations. Unfortunately, these people are more likely to be involved in violent behavior.

Young people who belong to a delinquent peer group are very likely to engage in violent behavior. Behaving in violent ways may be a way of gaining acceptance from peers. They behave this way because they feel unworthy and unlovable. They feel better when they are accepted by the delinquent peer group. They believe any relationship is better than none.

People with negative self-esteem are less likely to try hard in school. As a result, they may do poorly in school. When young people do poorly in school, they are more likely to use alcohol and other drugs. They are more likely to drop out of school. Young people who drop out of school are much more likely to become involved in crime (Wodarski and Hedrick, 1987).

There is no doubt that a person's self-esteem influences the likelihood of violence. If you have positive feelings about yourself, you will want to continue these feelings. If you have negative self-esteem, you will want to improve your self-esteem so you are not at risk. That is why you will want to learn ways to develop positive self-esteem.

Protective Factor #2

Having Positive Self-Esteem

Having positive self-esteem has many benefits. Having positive self-esteem helps you feel confident. When you feel good about yourself, you can handle problems. You are less likely to choose harmful ways of coping such as using drugs, overeating, or becoming sexually active.

When you have positive self-esteem, you feel valuable. Because you believe yourself to be of value, you engage in self-loving behavior. **Self-loving behavior** is healthful and responsible behavior that indicates you believe you are worthwhile and lovable. An example of self-loving behavior might include locking your doors to protect yourself from harm. Another example might be saying NO if someone wants you to do something that is wrong. Also, you would say NO if someone tries to abuse you. You know that you do not deserve to be abused. You expect others to treat you with respect.

You will want to have self-loving behavior. You will want to have positive self-esteem. You can actively do something to improve and maintain positive self-esteem. Ways you can develop positive self-esteem are listed in Figure 6. The following discussion focuses on these ways to develop positive self-esteem.

Set Goals And Make Plans To Reach Them. Doing things well improves self-esteem. For this reason, it is important for you to work to achieve goals. You need to set goals and make plans to reach them. It is important to set realistic goals and recognize the skills that will help you achieve the goals that have been set.

Develop A Special Skill Or Talent. An important way to improve self-esteem can be to identify a special skill or a talent upon which you can work. By practicing a skill or talent, you can experience personal progress. Forward progress is essential to having positive self-esteem.

Make A List Of Things You Do Well. It is helpful to keep a list of things you do well. This list will help you focus on your strengths and will motivate you when you are struggling with a new skill. You can refer to this list to boost your self-confidence. This helps you remember how hard you worked to accomplish each task that is now well done. Then you will learn not to give up when things are difficult. This is a key to being successful.

Work To Do Your Best In School. Doing well in school improves self-esteem. If you do well in school, you are at less risk for many violence-related problems. To do well in school, you should attend school regularly, keep track of all your assignments, study each day, hand in all homework assignments, and participate in class discussions. If you are having difficulty with school work, get outside help.

Be Involved In School Clubs And Community Activities. Besides doing well in school, you need to feel a sense of belonging at school. Feeling like you are part of what is happening at school gives you good feelings. Examine the various activities and clubs your school offers and participate in at least one. Sports and recreation activities are of particular value. Participating in these activities helps you cope with stress. Besides being involved in school activities, you might get involved in community activities.

Develop A Trusting Relationship With At Least One Adult. Regardless of the number of friendships you have, contact with adults who are trustworthy and positive role models is important. You need to have a trusting relationship with at least one adult. This person can be a role model for you. (S)he can help you examine standards for your achievement and behavior. This adult can give you feedback. The feedback you receive from this adult can help you recognize and take pride in your achievements.

Choose Friends Who Encourage You To Do Your Best. Select your friends carefully. Spend time with friends who encourage responsible behavior. Your friends who have high standards will encourage you to have high standards.

Spend Time With Friends And Adults Who Give You Support. Sometimes you might fall short of the standards you set for yourself. When you do, it is helpful to spend time with friends and adults who give you support. Friends and adults who support your best efforts rather than expecting perfection from you help you with self-esteem. They help you remember these important messages, "I won't give up just because things are difficult" and "I am worthwhile even if I have not accomplished this task at this point in my life."

Volunteer To Help Another Person. Another important way to develop positive self-esteem is to volunteer to help others. You might complete chores for your family or volunteer to do community work. Helping others provides the sense that "I make a difference to someone else, therefore I am valuable."

Keep A Neat Appearance. A neat appearance is important for at least two reasons. A neat appearance helps you feel good about the way you look. It influences how others see you, which in turn influences your self-image.

Violence-Free Pledge

I will act in ways to improve self-esteem.

I will avoid self-centered behavior.

I will avoid self-destructive behavior.

family relationships

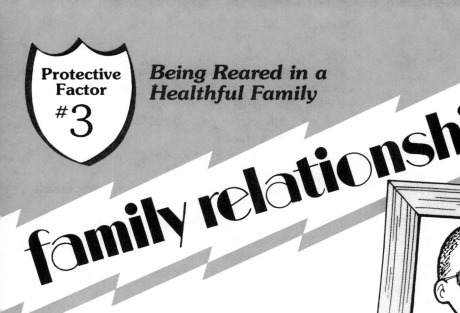

Being close to your family is a powerful protective factor in preventing violent behavior. Having a supportive relationship with a parent or parents is especially important. Parental trust, warmth, and involvement are necessary for you to feel secure. Having a strong attachment to parents motivates you to behave in responsible ways. It increases the likelihood that you will choose friends who are responsible. In addition to parents, you might choose to have supportive relationships with other responsible adults such as teachers, relatives, and community leaders. These adults also can show you how to be responsible and nonviolent. The following discussion focuses on family relationships. You will learn why being reared in a dysfunctional family is a risk factor for violence. You will learn why having healthful relationships with family members and other adults helps to prevent violence.

Facts: Family Relationships

Relationships are the connections that you have with other people. **Family relationships** are the connections that you have with family members, including extended family members. **Extended family members** are family members in addition to parents, brothers, and sisters. Extended family members might include stepparents, stepbrothers, stepsisters, grandparents, aunts, uncles, and foster brothers and sisters. Some families consider significant people who live in the home and who have significant influence on family interactions as family members. For example, an adult who is not related to your family might live with you and be considered an extended family member.

The Family Continuum is a scale marked in units ranging from zero to 100 that shows the quality of relationships within families (Figure 7). The dysfunctional family is at the zero end of the Family Continuum. The quality of the relationships within the dysfunctional family is low. The healthful family is at the 100 end of the Family Continuum. Notice that a family does not have to be at one end or the other of the continuum. A family might be somewhere in between. For example, some of the items listed under the dysfunctional family and some of the items listed under the healthful family might describe a family. If more items describe the healthful family, then this family would be closer to the right end of the continuum. Now suppose more of the items describe the dysfunctional family. Then this family would be closer to the left end of the continuum. Being reared in a dysfunctional family is a risk factor for violence.

Being Reared in a Dysfunctional Family

Being reared in a dysfunctional family is rated as the greatest risk factor for behaving in violent ways or becoming a victim of violence. To understand why this is so, you will need to learn more about the dysfunc-tional family. **A dysfunctional family** is a family in which feelings are not expressed openly and honestly, coping skills are lacking, and family members do not trust each other. In a dysfunctional family, one or more of the family members:

1. do not show respect for each other;
2. do not trust each other;
3. are confused about guidelines for responsible behavior;
4. are not punished or are punished severely for wrong behavior;
5. do not spend time with each other;
6. do not share feelings or do not share feelings in healthful ways;
7. do not have effective coping skills;
8. resolve conflicts with violence;
9. abuse alcohol and other drugs;
10. abuse each other with words and actions.

Violent behavior is usually learned early in life by observing the ways parents and other adults act. Children who have observed violence begin to show aggressive behavior at an early age. When children are treated in harmful ways, they are more likely to become juvenile delinquents. A **juvenile delinquent** is a young person who has antisocial behavior or refus-es to follow the law. The most important factor lead-ing to juvenile delinquency seems to be the kind of par-enting a person received. Parents of juvenile delin-quents often lacked skills in how to raise children. They may have become parents when they were teenagers. Parents who lack parenting skills often are unable to set guidelines for their children's behavior. They may not know how to get their children to do what they are supposed to do. They may attempt to get their chil-dren to do what they expect them to do by using force. Their children learn this way of dealing with others. When children watch their parents behave in violent ways, they are more likely to be violent when they are frustrated. Often, parents who have violent behavior allow their children to treat other children in harmful ways. They allow their children to push, kick, fight, and call other children names.

Cycles Of Family Violence. Violence in the family tends to be repeated. People reared in families in which there was violence are likely as adults to have violence in their families. Young people who have a family member who is a criminal are more likely to become juvenile delinquents (Developmental Research and Programs, 1993). In other words, there seems to be a cycle of family violence that is repeated.

Figure 7
The Family Continuum

The Family Continuum depicts the degree to which a family promotes skills needed for lov-ing and responsible relationships.

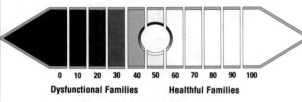

0 10 20 30 40 50 60 70 80 90 100
Dysfunctional Families   **Healthful Families**

Dysfunctional Families
1. do not show respect for each other;
2. do not trust each other;
3. are confused about guidelines for responsible behavior;
4. are not punished or are punished severely for wrong behavior;
5. do not spend time with each other;
6. do not share feelings or do not share feelings in healthful ways;
7. do not have effective coping skills
8. resolve conflicts with violence;
9. abuse alcohol and other drugs;
10. abuse each other with words and actions.

Healthful Families
1. show respect for each other;
2. trust each other;
3. follow guidelines for responsible behavior;
4. experience consequences when they do not follow guidelines;
5. spend time with each other;
6. share feelings in healthful ways;
7. practice effective coping skills;
8. resolve conflict in nonviolent ways;
9. avoid alcohol and other drugs;
10. use kind words and actions.

20

Children with violent behavior often disobey their parents. When parents make reasonable requests, these children do not do what has been asked. Parents may become frustrated and resort to harsh physical punishment. Their children copy the harsh ways they are treated. They begin to believe using harsh treatment is an appropriate way to get others to do what they want them to do. They begin to behave in the same way with their friends and at school.

Characteristics Of Families With Violent Children. It is important to know that violent behavior is learned. This learned behavior accounts for the cycles of abuse that are repeated over and over again. Young people are abused in their families, they become abusive when they form families as adults, they abuse their children, and their children become abusive.

It is important for you to examine characteristics of violent families. Studying these characteristics may help you examine your own family background. Remembering these characteristics will help you if you decide to be a parent when you are an adult. Some characteristics of families in which children behave in violent ways are (Hawkins et al., 1990):
• parents allow their children to behave in violent ways;
• parents excuse their children when they break laws or harm others;
• parents have little skill in setting limits;
• parents are involved in criminal activities;
• parents are aggressive and punish their children in harsh ways;
• parents abuse their children;
• family members watch television too often;
• family conflicts occur often;
• older children behave in violent ways;
• parents are inconsistent when they discipline their children;
• parents allow their children to do whatever they want;
• children do not bond or become close to the family;
• children are not involved with their mother;
• there are very few expectations for achievement in school;
• a pattern exists in which one parent is overly involved with the children while the other is uninvolved;
• there is harmful family communication including criticism, blaming, and shaming;
• parents set unrealistic goals for children;
• parents do not supervise their children;
• parents do not have time for their children;
• parents do not protect their children from harm;
• parents do not encourage their children;
• parents have marriage problems.

There has been much interest in how family breakdown influences the likelihood of violence. Young people whose parents are divorced have somewhat higher rates of delinquency. However, the divorce may not have caused the juvenile delinquency. It may be that the way that the family dealt with feelings and conflict led to divorce. And, the way the family dealt with feelings and conflict also may have led to the delinquency. Children reared in families in which there is frequent conflict are more likely to behave violently. Conflict between parents, even in unbroken families, is associated with antisocial behavior in children (Hawkins, Catalano, and Miller, 1992).

Characteristics Of Dysfunctional Families. It is difficult for children being reared in dysfunctional families to know how to behave in responsible ways. Usually, one or both parents behave in irresponsible ways. They may behave in violent ways. Soon other family members behave in harmful, irresponsible, and violent ways. Some contributing causes to family dysfunction are: chemical dependency, violence, workaholism, neglect, emotional abuse, physical abuse, sexual abuse, abandonment, mental disorders, eating disorders, and extreme pressure to succeed.

Members of dysfunctional families often are self-destructive. **Self-destructive behavior** is behavior in which you harm yourself. In most dysfunctional families, the significant adults behave in self-destructive ways. They may drink too much alcohol or use other harmful drugs. They may harm one another by being physically abusive, emotionally abusive, or sexually abusive. Young people reared in these families often begin to copy this behavior. They begin to behave in self-destructive ways.

Adults in dysfunctional families often have difficulty with love. They may choose inappropriate sexual behavior. For example, they often have difficulty accepting their sexuality and forming close relationships. As a result, they are unable to teach their children how to form close relationships. When their children reach puberty and need to understand how to cope with sexual feelings, they are unable to do so. These young people may make unwise choices as they try to cope with sexual feelings. They may confuse sexual feelings with the need for power and control. This

21

confusion is often the basis for sex crimes such as sexual harassment and rape. In these crimes, people use sexuality to control and harm others.

+In healthful families, parents assist their children in understanding what they are feeling, why they feel the way they do, and how to show what they are feeling in healthful ways. As a result, children learn to trust their feelings. They know what feels appropriate or right and what feels wrong. However, in a dysfunctional family, denial and dishonesty replace the expression of feelings and truthful explanations. **Denial** is a condition in which a person refuses to recognize what (s)he is feeling because it is extremely painful. Denial can take many forms including: minimizing problems, blaming the cause of problems on other people, making excuses for problems, pretending that a problem does not exist when it really does, changing the subject to avoid threatening topics, and avoiding issues.

Young people who use denial hide or control their feelings. The feelings they work hardest to control are those considered to be immature, dangerous, uncomfortable, or simply bad: anger, fear, sadness, rage, embarrassment, bitterness, and loneliness. Unfortunately, it is impossible to put a lid on such feelings without also stopping the expression of other feelings, such as happiness. In healthful families, parents tend to cope with life pressure by working out problems through openly communicating, exploring options, and not being afraid to seek outside help if they need it.

Young people reared in dysfunctional families are not able to communicate openly or cope adequately with stress. A mental disorder called codependence results. **Codependence** is a mental disorder in which a person loses personal identity, has frozen feelings, and copes ineffectively. Young people who develop codependence have certain feelings and behavior in common. Although healthy people demonstrate many of these feelings and behavior, young people with codependence demonstrate these more often. People who have codependence are sometimes called codependent.

The messages people with codependence have learned from their families include:
1. I should not talk to others about family problems.
2. I should get others to believe that everything in my family is fine.
3. I would be better off continuing to behave the

way that I am than attempting to deal with the dysfunction in my family.
4. I am safer if I keep my feelings to myself.
5. I do not deserve to be treated with respect.
6. I am better off being dishonest because if I told others the truth they might not like me.
7. I am more comfortable being serious than playful and having fun.
8. I cannot trust others.

These messages destroy the ability to form healthful relationships with those outside the family. Unfortunately, these messages also contribute to attempts at coping by means of risk-taking behavior. Violence, alcohol and other drug use, and sexual experimentation are much more common in young people who have difficult family relationships. Acting in violent ways may be an attempt to express the anger and hurt that is felt. The alcohol and drug use may be an attempt to numb the painful feelings these young people experience. Sexual experimentation is often an attempt to make up for affection that is lacking at home. Sexual violence may be an attempt to control others because one has felt powerless. Young people often choose risky behavior to receive temporary relief from pain rather than deal with the difficult and painful issues that face them. Recovery from codependence always involves dealing with painful issues and learning to express feelings and get needs met in healthful ways.

Homeless Youth. Homeless youth consist of young people who:
• along with their families, lack shelter;
• leave home without parental consent (runaways);
• are thrown out of their homes (throwaways).

Approximately 1.5 million young people between the ages of 11 and 18 are homeless. Homeless youth are at risk for violence. They have little protection from the harmful actions of others. They may engage in violent behavior in order to gain the resources to live.

Protective Factor #3

Being Reared in a Healthful Family

Being reared in a healthful family is a powerful protective factor to prevent violence. The **healthful family** is a family in which feelings are expressed openly and honestly, coping skills are adequate, and family members trust each other. Nonviolent young people are likely to have been reared in healthful families. In a healthful family, family members:

1. show respect for each other;
2. trust each other;
3. follow guidelines for responsible behavior;
4. experience consequences when they do not follow guidelines;
5. spend time with each other;
6. share feelings in healthful ways;
7. practice effective coping skills;
8. resolve conflict in nonviolent ways;
9. avoid alcohol and other drugs;
10. use kind words and actions.

Let's examine the characteristics of members of healthful families more closely.

Show Respect For Each Other. Respect is having esteem for someone's admirable characteristics and responsible and caring actions. When parents and other responsible adults show respect for children, children learn to respect themselves. Self-respect is very important. It helps you want to protect yourself and stand up for yourself so that you are not a victim of violence. When you respect yourself, you are more likely to respect others. Much of fighting and conflict occurs when people do not show others respect. Learning to respect people who are different is important.

Trust Each Other. Trust is needed to feel secure. If you trust someone, you feel safe and comfortable with them. Feeling safe is important. When you feel safe, you are able to express yourself more honestly. You are able to share difficult situations with family members and know that they will help you. You do not feel that you will be harmed by family members.

Follow Guidelines For Responsible Behavior. When parents and other responsible adults guide and discipline children, the children become responsible. Children who have been given guidelines and know the consequences for not following them are less likely to engage in delinquent behavior than children whose parents allow them to do whatever they want to do. When faced with a decision, the children have guidelines to follow to know whether what they are doing is right or wrong. They have observed their parents struggling with decision-making and know that it can be difficult. But, they learn that people are responsible for what they do.

Experience Consequences When They Do Not Follow Guidelines. Parents and other significant adults who care about their children punish them in appropriate ways when they break rules. They are consistent. They explain right and wrong and discuss the consequences of choosing what is wrong. When children do something wrong, they pay the price. This teaches children that there are always consequences for actions. It helps them to think about the consequences of their actions before deciding what to do.

Spend Time With Each Other. Setting aside time to spend with family members is an important protective factor. Young people who are successful at school tend to eat dinner with parents and exchange ideas. Young people value time with parents. Quality and quantity of family time spent together is very important

Share Feelings In Healthful Ways. Children reared in healthful families learn ways to share feelings. Their parents help them by encouraging them to express their feelings. They help their children examine what they are feeling, why they feel a certain way, and how they can express their feelings in healthful ways. They do not try to shut out feelings, including feelings of anger, sadness, or depression. They allow their children to have these feelings and work through them. As a result, children learn to trust their feelings. This sharing serves as an important protective factor. When children feel they are in danger around someone, they learn to trust this feeling and share it with adults. When these feelings are shared with parents, the parents pay close attention rather than overlook what has been said.

In the healthful family, parents demonstrate through their behavior healthful ways to express anger. They teach their children that it is all right to be angry, but

23

that angry feelings cannot be expressed in ways that harm self or others. They recognize that holding anger inside can interfere with relationships. They allow children to practice expressing anger within the family setting. The family setting is a safe place for practicing anger.

Practice Effective Coping Skills. Parents and other significant adults in a healthful family teach children coping skills and the need to delay gratification when necessary. **Delayed gratification** is allowing oneself to sacrifice in the present so that a benefit will be achieved in the future. Most people will experience a series of difficult life crises throughout life. Adults in healthful families prepare their children for these difficult life crises by teaching them how to cope. They help their children by allowing them to cope under their guidance rather than fixing the problems for them.

Children who learn to cope are much more likely to delay gratification. For example, young people may be asked to complete homework before watching television or to earn a certain amount of money before receiving a reward. By doing difficult tasks before receiving a reward, delayed gratification is learned. Being able to delay gratification is an important protective factor. Consider actions such as shoplifting or stealing from someone's locker at school. The motivation for such actions might be to have something desirable at that moment. Criminal actions might be taken because a person is unable to wait for something.

Resolving Conflict In Nonviolent Ways. Conflict occurs within all relationships. A conflict is a disagreement between two or more people or between two or more choices. Conflicts within families might arise over events such as who gets to use the bathroom first or who gets to drive the car. Conflicts might arise over how to spend money and what purchases to make. Other conflicts might arise when someone's feelings are hurt or when someone becomes very angry. Parents and other responsible adults within the healthful family practice conflict resolution skills. Conflict resolution skills are skills a person can use to resolve a disagreement in a healthful, safe, legal, respectful, and nonviolent way (These skills are described in detail in Protective Factor #10).

It is important for young people to observe adults practicing conflict resolution skills. This is the single best way to learn these skills. There are many other messages that are learned from watching parents and other adults resolve conflict. These include:

- People who care about each other can be in conflict.
- Conflict does not have to be avoided.
- There does not have to be a winner and a loser when a conflict occurs.
- It may take time to resolve a conflict.
- When conflict occurs, it is important to show respect for the other person.
- A relationship often becomes stronger when people have worked through a conflict.

Avoid Abusing Alcohol And Other Drugs. Parents and other significant adults in healthful families avoid the abuse of alcohol and other drugs. They know that these drugs harm health. They are aware that alcohol and other drugs change the way that people think and behave. Because they do not abuse these drugs, they are in control of their behavior and do not act out and harm themselves and others. They are good role models for children.

Use Kind Words And Actions. **Abuse** is the harmful treatment of a person. Abuse includes the following behavior: neglect, sexual abuse, physical abuse, and emotional abuse. Parents and significant adults in healthful families are not abusive. Children do not learn this type of behavior from them. Further, children learn that abusive behavior is wrong. Their parents protect them from abuse from others.

In summary, young people reared in healthful families gain the skills they need to be nonviolent and to stay safe. Their parents and other significant adults serve as valuable role models.

All young people need and want supportive adults present in their lives. Unfortunately, many young people are not reared in healthful families. Many young people, especially those growing up in high-crime, drug-infested neighborhoods, do not have stable, loving adults in their lives. These young people may be uninvolved in school activities and youth groups, and may not have jobs where they might interact with adults. If young people do not have responsible adult role models, they are at risk for joining gangs or spending time with friends who get into trouble. Having a relationship with an adult mentor can help a young person to be nonviolent and stay safe. **Mentors** are persons who guide and help younger persons.

Mentors may include youth leaders, teachers, coaches, and clergy. A mentor may serve as a role model, friend, and confidant. If you do not have an adult mentor, you may wish to explore opportunities to find one. You may wish to find an adult mentor by enrolling in an organized mentoring program. You may contact an organized mentor program and express your interest in finding an adult mentor. Organized mentoring programs include the Big Brothers and Big Sisters programs that are found in many communities. In these programs, adult mentors ("Bigs") are matched with young people ("Littles") with whom they spend time. Another example of a formal mentoring program is Baltimore's Choice program. In this program, recent college graduates work with troubled youth in the city's most difficult neighborhoods. Typically, Choice workers see the young people to whom they are assigned three to five times a day, *every* day of the year. The purpose of the program is to provide guidance and discipline for young people who are in need of attention.

If there is no organized mentoring program in your community or school, you may find a mentor on your own. There may be a responsible adult in your community or school you admire and who you feel would be a positive role model. You might ask this person to be an adult mentor for you, or you may write him/her a letter explaining that you are interested in establishing a mentor relationship. Or, you might join a group such as a youth fellowship group or an athletic team that is led by a responsible adult. Often, young people who establish a relationship with a mentor discover a special bond that may last a lifetime.

Violence-Free Pledge

I will treat family members with respect.

I will share feelings with family members.

I will resolve conflict with family members in nonviolent ways.

I will tell a trusted adult if a family member abuses me.

I will establish a relationship with a mentor if I am not close with adults in my family.

The **environment** is everything that is around you in the place in which you live. A **nurturing environment** is a set of conditions and surroundings in which a person lives that promotes growth, development, and success. An **adverse environment** is a set of conditions and surroundings in which a person lives that interferes with growth, development, and success. To some extent the saying, "Life is not fair" is true when we examine the environment in which people live. The environment in which you live can and does limit the choices available to you.

You may live in a nurturing environment that provides the chance for you to grow, develop, and succeed. In this type of environment, you are more likely to remain safe from violence. The choice is up to you to act in nonviolent ways and to protect yourself from the violent actions of others. On the other hand, you may live in an adverse environment in which you feel the odds are stacked against you. You may be exposed to dangerous situations. You may have witnessed violence in your home and learned violent ways to handle disagreements. However, if you live in an adverse environment, life is not hopeless. Although you are at greater risk for being a perpetrator or victim of violence, the choice to make responsible decisions is still yours.

The following discussion focuses on environment. You will learn why living in an adverse environment is a risk factor. Finally, you will learn what to do if you live in an adverse environment.

Facts: Nurturing Environment

A nurturing environment provides the best opportunity for you to be at your best. Living in this kind of environment decreases the likelihood that you will be violent. It increases the likelihood that you will be safe.

If you live in a nurturing environment, your parent(s) and other significant adults who helped raise you:
- are loving, affectionate, and supportive;
- earn enough money to provide food, clothing, and shelter;
- are actively involved in your schooling;
- supervise your free time;
- advise you to spend time with friends who choose healthful behavior;
- discipline you in a fair and consistent way;
- teach you clear values;
- expect you to be responsible;
- get along well with others and teach you social skills;
- are trustworthy and honest;
- teach you how to resolve conflict without violence;
- teach you to express anger in appropriate ways;
- help you set goals and look forward to your future.

Besides your parent(s) and other significant adults, family members help provide a nurturing environment. Extended family members such as grandparents, cousins, aunts, and uncles can help you grow, develop, and succeed. The ways in which family members interact is important, too.

If you live in a nurturing environment, you have the opportunity to get a quality education. Adequate medical care and social services are available if you need them. Your neighborhood and school are safe. There is little crime where you live.

Living in a nurturing environment gives you hope. **Hope** is the feeling that what is desired is possible and that events in life may turn out for the best. Hope is necessary to motivate you and keep you positive. Without hope, you may lack goals and wishes. Having hope increases your overall ability to cope with stress and reach your potential. Certain things happen when you are filled with hope:

1. you develop relationships in which there is caring, sharing, trust, and a feeling of belonging and being needed;
2. you develop a positive attitude about your future;
3. you abandon the attitude that you must have everything you want to be happy;
4. you have patience and trust as you wait for things you desire in your future;
5. you set goals and make plans to reach them;
6. you have a plan to cope with stress;
7. you have a sense of purpose for living;
8. you do not feel trapped;
9. you have a positive outlook about your past, present, and future;
10. you participate in mental and physical activities to feel that you are growing.

If you live in a nurturing environment, you have much for which to be grateful. Appreciate what you have and take advantage of all opportunities. Remember, you will not be successful without personal effort. And, you will not be safe from violence unless you pay attention to other protective factors.

Risk Factor #4

Living in an Adverse Environment

Living in an adverse environment is a risk factor for violence. Before examining why this is so, you should learn what it is like to live in an adverse environment. If a person lives in an adverse environment, the neighborhood might be described in the following ways:

1. Many of the families living in the neighborhood are poor.
2. Many of the people are unemployed and have few job skills.
3. Families in the neighborhood do not have enough food or clothing.
4. It is difficult for people in the neighborhood to get the medical and dental care that is needed.
5. People in the neighborhood experience discriminatory behavior. **Discriminatory behavior** is to make distinctions in treatment or to show behavior in favor of or prejudiced against an individual or group of people.
6. There is overcrowding. For example, many family members may live in a small area.
7. People in the neighborhood may use or sell illegal drugs.
8. People in the neighborhood may purchase illegal guns and carry them.
9. There is crime in the community.
10. There is a high student dropout rate.
11. There are not very many families in which there is both a female and male head of household.

Unfortunately, too many people in this country live in adverse environments. Four million young people live in deeply troubled neighborhoods in which there is poverty and unemployment. This represents approximately six percent of the young people in the nation. One-half of these young people live in the six largest states--New York, California, Texas, Ohio, Illinois, and Michigan. The rural states in the deep south have some of the highest percentages of young people in troubled neighborhoods (Usdansky, 1994).

The amount of violence in these areas is very high. Homicide and other forms of violence are closely related to poverty and high rates of unemployment. Young people who are poor are the most likely to be victims and perpetrators of violence. Young people who live in inner-city areas are far more likely to be perpetrators or victims of violence than people who live in rural areas. This is particularly true when young people live in inner-city areas in which there is poverty, poor housing, crowded living, and a high unemployment rate. The feelings that often accompany these conditions, such as hopelessness about life options and anger about poverty, increase the risk of violent behavior. Being poor often means living in crime-ridden neighborhoods, growing up in a family without a father, and going to schools where most students fail and are expected to fail. There are fewer adult males in many of these communities. When there are few adult males from which to learn how to behave, there is an increase in the number of young people who join gangs. (Committee on Prevention of Mental Disorders, 1994).

Many young people being raised in adverse environments have problems as teenagers. They do poorly in school, drop out, become teenage parents, become delinquent, and use alcohol and/or other drugs (Kazdin, 1993). It is important to realize that young people at risk for violence do not have to come from adverse environments (Dougherty, 1993). Yet, when they do, they need extra skills because they must break out of the vicious cycle of school failure, juvenile delinquency, drug use, teenage pregnancy, and unemployment.

The Changing Family Environment. Today, more than one million young people have experienced divorce in their families. One out of five young people lives in a single-parent family usually with a female who is the head of the household (Webb, 1992). Four percent of children ages three to six care for themselves while their mothers work. The following changes in the family influence the environments in which young people are reared (Steinberg, 1991).

1. The majority of young people will live in a single-parent household for at least some time before the end of the teenage years.
2. More than half of young people will experience separation and/or divorce of parents.
3. Approximately one-fourth of young people will experience a parent remarrying.
4. Approximately one-eighth of young people will experience parents divorcing, remarrying, and divorcing again.
5. The majority of young people will be reared in homes in which adults responsible for their care are working. As a result, they will spend some

time in child care during infancy and early childhood.
6. A large number of young children will need supervision after school during elementary and middle school.

Just because young people live in single-parent families does not mean they live in an adverse environment. However, there are many reasons that living in a single-parent family increases this risk. Unfortunately, unless there is an extended family there is only one adult responsible for raising children. Young people miss the opportunity to watch two adults love one another. They are unable to watch two adults disagree and work out disagreements in healthful ways. In single-parent families, there is only one adult to supervise the children. Often, this means young people spend much time alone without supervision. There is more opportunity to get into trouble.

Females who are head of household make the least amount of money of all groups of people. They are more likely to be poor. This means many young people raised by single parents are often poor. Because they are poor, there are other risk factors. They are more likely to live in neighborhoods that are overcrowded. There is more crime and drug use in these neighborhoods.

Young people experiencing some of these conditions as a result of living in single-parent families can still respond in positive ways. For example, if they live with

---

Figure 8
The Nurturing Environment

I have only just a minute.
Only sixty seconds in it,
Forced upon me–
Can't refuse it
Didn't seek it,
Didn't choose it,
But, it's up to me to use it.
I must suffer if I lose it,
Give account if I abuse it.
Just a tiny little minute–
But eternity is in it.

Benjamin Eligah Mays
Former President of Morehouse College

---

their mother, they can develop a relationship with an adult male who can provide direction. Joining an athletic team or club supervised by a male is helpful.

Protective Factor #4

Living in a Nurturing Environment

Many young people are reared in a nurturing environment. As you have already learned, these young people need to be grateful. They want to take advantage of opportunities. They need to behave in nonviolent ways and protect themselves from harm. Suppose you are one of these young people. You know the choice is yours.

But, what about the young people who are reared in adverse environments? Although they have no control over the environment in which they live, they can control their responses. They can become resilient. To be **resilient** is to be able to prevent or to recover, bounce back, and learn from misfortune, change, or pressure. Many young people who are reared in adverse environments become resilient.

To do this, young people must feel empowered. **Empowerment** is the belief that you control your own destiny. Although people cannot control the environment in which they live, they can control what they do. Consider the words of the late Benjamin Eligah Mays, President of Morehouse College. Dr. Mays inspired many young people with the message in Figure 8. Suppose you live in an adverse environment. You can be empowered. You can control your own destiny. You can review the protective factors that are in this book. There are suggested actions that you can take for each of these protective factors. You can make a commitment and choose these actions.

Violence-Free Pledge

I will be grateful, take advantage of opportunities, and protect myself and others if I live in a nurturing environment.

I will behave in empowering ways and practice as many protective factors as possible if I live in an adverse environment.

Protective Factor #5 | *Using Social Skills*

social skills

Using social skills reduces the risk of violence. **Social skills** are skills that can be used to relate well with others. People who are **socially competent** use social skills effectively. They have positive relationships with peers. **Peers** are people who are similar in age or status. Young people who lack social skills often have difficulty relating with peers. They may feel rejected by their peers. Rejection by peers may lead to aggressive and violent behavior. The following discussion examines social skills. You will learn why young people who lack social skills are more at risk for violence. You will learn why young people with social skills have more protection from violence.

Facts: Social Skills

Some young people have better relationships with peers than do others. They seem to have better social skills. In many cases, they learned these skills from the parents or other adults who reared them. They felt a close bond and felt a sense of belonging. They began to feel good about themselves and about others. This, in turn, helped them to relate well with peers.

By practicing social skills in the family and then with friends, young people develop social competence.

Young people with social competence are at an advantage. Other people like them better. They have fewer disagreements with others. When they disagree, it is easier to work things out. Being accepted by peers is important. Some of the skills that encourage peer acceptance include (Henggler and Borduin, 1989):

1. being able to understand the feelings and thoughts of others;
2. being able to determine what is expected in a given situation and using this information to decide what to do;
3. being able to fit in different social situations;
4. being able to solve problems without fighting;
5. being able to set goals and overcome obstacles to reach them;
6. being able to begin and have a conversation;
7. knowing how much to say to another person;
8. being able to influence others;
9. responding in a friendly way when approached by others;
10. cooperating with others during school activities.

Young people with social competence understand how to begin relationships. They are aware that new relationships develop gradually. They take time and are patient as they get to know someone. They do not expect to be accepted by others right away. They avoid forcing themselves on others. When they experience difficulties with peers, they talk things over with parents or other trusted adults.

30 Copyright © by Meeks Heit Publishing Company.

Lacking Social Skills

Young people who lack social skills are at risk for violence. Most juvenile offenders lack social skills. A **juvenile offender** is a person below the age of 18 who breaks a criminal law. Juvenile offenders often have difficulty relating with peers. They behave in aggressive ways and usually do not think about the consequences of their actions (National Center for Environmental Health and Injury Control, 1992). Juvenile offenders usually are not close to their families, have few friends, and are not involved with school activities. Again, this is probably because they lack social skills.

Social skills are learned at a young age. Young children who have difficulty with social skills are prime candidates to become juvenile offenders. As early as kindergarten and first grade, these children show aggressive behavior. Some signs of this behavior include: acting out, being impatient, being very mean, responding in very negative ways, and bullying others. Other children who lack social skills do not act out. They withdraw from others because they cannot relate. Young males who either are very angry and negative or are very shy and withdrawn are at risk for being juvenile offenders when they are teenagers (Developmental Research and Programs, Inc., 1993).

As young people mature, they have a need to feel close to others. **Alienation** is the feeling that one is apart from others. Young people can feel this way even when they are around others. For example, they might attend a school function but not feel like they are a part of what is happening. They do not feel included even though they are present with others. This feeling is very painful.

Loneliness is an anxious, unpleasant, and painful feeling that results from having few friends or from being alienated. Most young people feel lonely some of the time. However, some young people feel lonely most of the time. Young people whose families are broken are more at risk for feeling lonely. They are more at risk for failing in school, dropping out of school, having mental health problems, and choosing negative behavior. They are more at risk for becoming juvenile offenders.

Young people who are lonely are likely to be shy and lack self-confidence. When they are unable to gain acceptance by peers, they feel more lonely. They may feel more alienated. Sometimes they become angry and aggressive. They may respond to peers who ignore them in aggressive ways. They may begin fights. Teaching these young people social skills would help to keep this from happening.

Using Social Skills

Figure 9 lists social skills that help young people become socially competent. Juvenile offenders usually lack these skills. By learning these skills, they might become socially competent. Young people who have these skills need to continue to use them. Social skills should never be taken for granted. Here are some suggestions for using these social skills.

Using Manners. Always use good manners. Saying please, thank you, excuse me, and pardon me shows others that you respect them. When you listen without interrupting, you also show respect for others. You can show others that you are thinking about them by writing notes to express thankfulness, sympathy, congratulations, or to acknowledge something important such as a birthday. Select cards and paper carefully. Use your best handwriting. Manners make a lasting impression.

Asking For Help. When you are in a difficult situation, try to describe the situation clearly. Decide if you need help. Make a list of people who might help you. Select someone. Explain to this person what you are facing. Ask for suggestions. Listen carefully. Express your thankfulness.

Giving And Following Instructions. There are guidelines to follow for giving others instructions: say what needs to be done, tell who should do it, explain how it is to be done, tell how fast it must be done, and explain why it must be done. After you give instructions, ask others if your instructions are clear. Ask if there are any questions. After others give you feedback, you may need to go over instructions again.

There are some guidelines for following instructions: listen carefully, repeat the instructions to yourself, ask questions if you are not clear, imagine yourself following the instructions before you begin, and set a time for getting things done.

Expressing Affection. Expressing affection in appropriate ways is an important social skill. First, decide if you have warm, caring feelings for a person. Then decide if this person would like to know about your warm, caring feelings. Consider the most appropriate way to express your feelings. Select an appropriate place and time to share your feelings.

Expressing And Responding To A Complaint. Sometimes it is important to express a complaint. Before expressing a complaint, spend time identifying the problem and who is responsible for it. Consider your suggestions for solving the problem. Then explain the problem to the appropriate person. Share the suggestions that you have. Listen to the response of the person. Show that you understand the person's viewpoint. Work together to solve the problem. Identify specific steps to take.

Suppose another person shares a complaint with you. You might be hurt or offended. However, it is best to be calm and objective. Listen to what the person says. Ask for suggestions for how to solve the problem. Respond to the suggestions. Share your feelings about what has happened. Work together to solve the problem. Identify specific steps to take.

Dealing With Rejection. Being rejected can be painful. Try not to blow it off and pretend you do not care. Do not attack or harm people who reject you. There are positive actions you can take:

- Determine whether you are being left out or rejected.
- Try to learn why other people are not including you.
- Brainstorm a list of ways that you might deal with the situation.
- Discuss this list with a close friend or trusted adult.
- Select a healthful way to deal with the rejection and try it.

Dealing With A Stressful Conversation Or Event. Sometimes you know you are about to experience a stressful conversation or event. You may want to have a mental rehearsal ahead of time. A **mental rehearsal** is a technique that involves imagining yourself in the stressful conversation or situation, pretending that you say and do specific things, and imagining how the other person will respond. You can have several mental rehearsals until you are comfortable with what you will say and do. You can practice until you are comfortable with the response you expect. Then you are more prepared when the conversation or event actually happens.

Dealing With Shyness. You may be shy. If you are shy, it may be helpful to know how other shy people feel. If you are not shy, know about the feelings of shy people. Most shy people do not like others to call them "shy." They also do not want others to force them to participate. They do not want others to call attention to them. They like to be gently encouraged. When shy people participate, they like to succeed. They like praise or helpful suggestions. If you are shy, you might want to know that these feelings lessen with time and more social experience. If your shy feelings do not lessen, talk to an adult. There are ways adults can help you.

Responding To The Feelings Of Others. **Empathy** is the ability to share in another person's emotions or feelings. Empathy is more than understanding another person's point of view. It involves caring. Empathy is an important part of violence prevention. When you have empathy, you are able to understand how people who are victims feel. You are involved at a caring level. When people are harmed, you care about their hurt and fear. You can show empathy for another person:

- Pay attention to the person's actions and words.
- Try to understand what the person is feeling.

- Decide whether or not it would be helpful to let the person know that you understand how (s)he feels.
- Express your thoughts and feelings in a warm and sincere way.

Dealing With Excessive Fear. You may have excessive fear. If you do, you may avoid specific objects, situations, or people. This may be helpful especially if you are in real danger. For example, you may fear being around a person you know. Suppose this person is violent. Your gut level feelings are wise--be fearful and stay away from this person. But sometimes, your fears are not appropriate. You are not in real danger. Talk to someone about these fears. If your fears do not lessen, it may be wise to ask your parents for help from someone else. Therapists help some people overcome excessive fear by using systematic desensitization. **Systematic desensitization** is a process in which a person is gradually exposed to something that arouses fear and learns to respond less to it. Another process that is used is called flooding. **Flooding** is the sudden, rather than gradual, exposure of a person to what causes the fear. This also can help a person become more comfortable with what causes the fear. Eventually, the person will not have the same response.

You may want to work on some of the social skills that were discussed in this protective factor. Being socially competent helps you have a good feeling about yourself. When you get along well with peers, you have a feeling of belonging. You are less likely to get involved with people who act in violent ways.

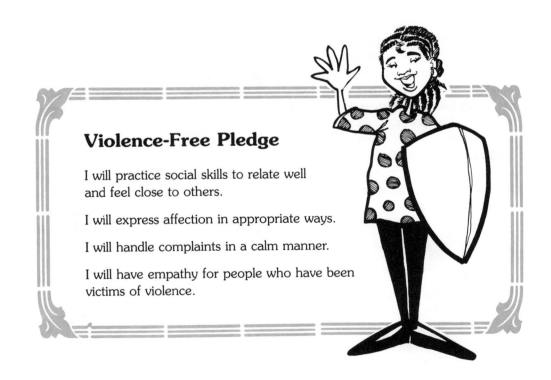

Violence-Free Pledge

I will practice social skills to relate well and feel close to others.

I will express affection in appropriate ways.

I will handle complaints in a calm manner.

I will have empathy for people who have been victims of violence.

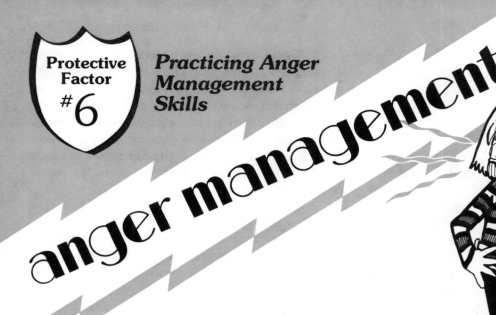

anger management

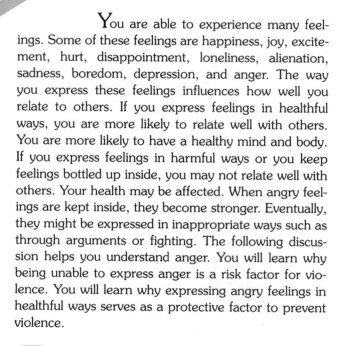

You are able to experience many feelings. Some of these feelings are happiness, joy, excitement, hurt, disappointment, loneliness, alienation, sadness, boredom, depression, and anger. The way you express these feelings influences how well you relate to others. If you express feelings in healthful ways, you are more likely to relate well with others. You are more likely to have a healthy mind and body. If you express feelings in harmful ways or you keep feelings bottled up inside, you may not relate well with others. Your health may be affected. When angry feelings are kept inside, they become stronger. Eventually, they might be expressed in inappropriate ways such as through arguments or fighting. The following discussion helps you understand anger. You will learn why being unable to express anger is a risk factor for violence. You will learn why expressing angry feelings in healthful ways serves as a protective factor to prevent violence.

Facts: Anger

Communication is the sharing of feelings, thoughts, and information with another person. One way to share your feelings in healthful ways is to use I-messages. An **I-message** is a statement that contains (1) a specific behavior or event, (2) the effect the behavior or event has on the individual, and (3) the feeling that resulted. I-messages are statements that refer to the individual, the individual's feelings, and the individual's needs (Figure 10).

When you use I-messages, you take responsibility for sharing your feelings. There are benefits to using I-messages. When I-messages are used, feelings are not bottled up inside. When I-messages are used, the communication with other persons remains open. The use of an I-message invites a response. Positive health status is maintained. The following example shows how to use an I-message:

Juan and Miguel made plans to go to a baseball game together. Juan waited patiently for Miguel, but Miguel did not pick him up. Juan was very angry with Miguel. Later, Miguel called and told Juan how much he enjoyed the game. Juan was even more angry, but he waited a moment, took a deep breath,

Figure 10
I-Messages

The three parts of an I-message are:

1.	**2.**	**3.**
The specific behavior or event… ▼ (When you…)	The effect of the behavior or event… ▼ (It affected me because…)	The feeling that resulted… ▼ (and I felt…)

and shared an I-message with Miguel, "I waited for you (the specific behavior) and missed the game (the effect of the behavior), and I am very angry (the feeling that resulted)."

In this situation, the use of an I-message allowed Miguel to respond to Juan's angry feelings. Juan did not judge Miguel. Suppose Juan used a you-message. A **you-message** is a statement that blames or shames another person instead of expressing feelings. A you-message puts down the other person. It is usually taken as a personal attack. Juan might have used the following you-message, "You are the most thoughtless and careless knucklehead in the world." Miguel would probably defend himself. He might even attack Juan in his response. These personal attacks do not help the friends communicate. They may even cause them to fight.

The best place for you to learn and practice using I-messages is at home with your family. If your parents and other significant adults use I-messages, listen and copy their way of sharing feelings. However, if I-messages are not being used by your family, you can still learn to use and practice them in school.

You also can learn to listen carefully. **Active listening** is a type of listening in which you let others know you heard and understood what was said. When you use active listening, you avoid shutting out the feelings that another person is trying to express. In the example given, Miguel might have demonstrated active listening by saying, "I can understand why you are annoyed with me." There are four ways to use active listening (Figure 11). A **clarifying response** is a response in which a person asks for more information. A restating response could be in the form of a question. Miguel might have used a clarifying response, "What might I do to show you that I am sorry?" A **restating response** is a response in which a person repeats what the speaker has said in his/her own words. This response allows the listener to confirm that the meaning is understood. Miguel might have used a restating response, "So what you're telling me is that you are angry with me because I forgot to pick you up for the game?" A **summarizing response** is a response to review the major idea or ideas expressed. Miguel might have used a summarizing response, "It seems the main problem is that you missed the game because I didn't pick you up." A **confirming response** is a response to acknowledge the feelings that the speaker expressed and to show appreciation for expressing the feelings. Miguel might have used a confirming response, "I don't blame you for feeling angry and I appreciate that you told me how you feel."

There are two important factors to remember about the healthful expression of feelings. First, the use of I-messages is a healthful way to express feelings. Second, the use of active listening helps others express their feelings and keeps communication positive.

Anger is the feeling of being irritated, annoyed, and/or furious. Anger is usually a response to being hurt or frustrated. The hurt might be emotional, psychological, social, and/or physical. **Anger triggers** are thoughts or events that cause you to become angry. Anger may be caused by physical pain. If someone hits you, you are likely to feel angry and may want to hit back. Frustration is another cause of anger. Other sources of anger include situations that insult you or cause you to feel poorly about yourself such as: being rejected by peers, failure, or being criticized. You may become angry if a group with which you identify (family, racial or ethnic group, gender, sexual orientation, or religious group) is treated unfairly or is insulted (Alschuler and Alschuler, 1984).

Anger cues are changes in the body that are signs that a person is angry. When a person is angry, the anger response begins. The anger response (fight or

---

Figure 11
Active Listening

Active listening is a type of listening in which you let others know you heard and understood what was said. Active listening includes the following types of responses:

Type of Response	The Listener...
Clarifying Response.......	Asks for more information.
Restating Response	Repeats what the speaker said in his/her own words.
Summarizing Response ..	Summarizes the main idea or ideas.
Confirming Response	Acknowledges and shows appreciation for the speaker's feelings.

flight) causes the following changes to occur in the body:

- rapid breathing;
- increase in heart rate;
- rise in blood pressure;
- increased sweating from the sweat glands in the face;
- sweaty palms;
- dryness of the mouth;
- increased muscle strength as a result of increased availability of blood sugar to the muscle;
- extra cortisol and adrenaline entering the bloodstream;
- decreased sensitivity to pain;
- increased alertness;
- tensed eyebrows;
- pursed lips;
- reddening of the face.

Anger is also one of the five stages that occurs in other life crises. When you experience different life crises, you may respond with denial, anger, bargaining, depression, and acceptance. Let's use an example. Suppose you learn that your family is going to move. At first, you may respond with denial and not discuss it. You pretend that the move will not actually occur.

Figure 12
Coping with Life Crises

Anger is one of the five stages that occur in life crises. When a person experiences a life crisis, (s)he may go through five stages. Using the example of parents getting a divorce, this is how the person might respond:

1. **Denial** .... (My parents won't really get a divorce.)
2. **Anger** .... (I hate my father for wanting a divorce.)
3. **Bargaining** ...... (If I promise to behave better, they won't get a divorce.)
4. **Depression** ...... (I can't stop crying when I think about my parents' divorce.)
5. **Acceptance** ..... (At least I will still see my father every weekend after the divorce.)

Adapted from Elisabeth Kübler-Ross (1975)

Then your family begins to make plans to move. You realize that you will not live near friends. You become angry and don't believe this is fair. You might begin to bargain. You offer to get a part-time job to earn money for your family. Then your parent(s) will not need a different job and have to move. When this doesn't work, you become sad. After all, you will miss your friends, your home, your school, and the activities in which you participate. Eventually, you work through the sadness and reach acceptance. You pitch in and help the family. You begin to think of ways to meet new friends and activities you will join at the new school.

This situation is not as difficult as some life crises that you might experience. You might experience separation or divorce of parents or stepparents. Perhaps a family member will be very sick and die. A person close to you may die of AIDS or violence. Your home may be damaged by a tornado, fire, or earthquake. Should you experience any difficult life crisis, you will need to work through your feelings. Refer to Figure 12 and remember the stages of a life crisis that most people experience. Learning to express feelings during difficult times helps you to become emotionally mature.

Risk Factor #6

Being Unable to Manage Anger

Sometimes it is difficult to express anger and to work through the feelings that you have during a life crisis. However, if you do not express feelings, you may develop hidden anger. **Hidden anger** is anger that is not recognized or is expressed in a harmful way and may result in inappropriate behavior and poor health (Figure 13). The following types of behavior may be signs of hidden anger: being negative, making cruel remarks to others, being flippant, procrastinating, blowing up easily, having very little interest in anything, being bored, sighing frequently, and being depressed. If you have hidden anger, it may affect your health. You may experience tense facial muscles, stiff or sore neck and shoulder muscles, ulcers, headaches, sleeplessness or excessive sleeping, stomachaches, high blood pressure, some types of cancer, and weight gain or weight loss. It is important to examine what is currently known about hostility and health. The **Hostility Syndrome** is the body changes that result

Figure 13
Hidden Anger

Hidden anger is anger that is not recognized or is expressed in a harmful way and may result in inappropriate behavior or poor health. The following types of behavior may be signs of hidden anger:
- Being negative
- Making cruel remarks to others
- Being flippant
- Procrastinating
- Blowing up easily
- Having very little interest in anything
- Being bored
- Sighing frequently
- Being depressed

from stronger responses of the sympathetic nervous system and weaker responses of the parasympathetic nervous system and immune system (Williams and Williams, 1994). The **sympathetic nervous system** is part of the nervous system that prepares the body for emergencies. The **parasympathetic nervous system** is part of the nervous system that maintains the body's normal state and restores balance after an emergency. The body of a person showing the Hostility Syndrome is in a constant state of emergency. Unfortunately, the body does not easily return to balance and the person's immune system does not work well. When the immune system is not working well, a person may have headaches, stomachaches, and sleeplessness. There may be an increase in certain kinds of cancers and other diseases.

People who show the Hostility Syndrome often have lowered brain serotonin. **Serotonin** is a naturally occurring chemical found in the brain, blood, and other parts of the body, that helps regulate primitive drives and emotions. The effects of lower levels of brain serotonin and the risks of showing the Hostility Syndrome are discussed further in Protective Factor #10.

Most important, hidden anger often is the underlying cause of violence. People may not express the anger they feel because they were abused, rejected, or mistreated. They may not express the anger they feel because a group to which they belong has been treated unfairly. They may be angry due to discrimination. People may have hidden anger because of a misfor-

tune or accident. When angry feelings are not recognized and expressed, they usually increase. Hidden anger builds up. Eventually, people cannot keep hidden anger inside. They often act out in inappropriate ways. They may have an outburst, temper tantrum, start a fight, say something inappropriate, harm themselves, or harm others.

The ways people express hidden anger are often inappropriate for the situation. Inappropriate expressions of anger can lead to violence. **Projection** is blaming others for actions or events for which they are not responsible. Projection can lead to violence. For example, a person who is angry about a failing grade on a test may take out anger on a classmate who received a higher grade on the test. This person might call the classmate a name that is a put-down, or destroy one of the classmate's belongings. **Displacement** is the releasing of anger on someone or something other than the cause of the anger. For example, a person who is angry about a family situation might destroy school property or harm someone. Unfortunately, some people do not know why they are behaving in inappropriate and/or violent ways. They are unaware that they have so much hidden anger inside them.

Protective
Factor
6

Practicing Anger Management Skills

Feeling angry is a normal and healthful response to many situations. It is not harmful to feel angry in certain situations. However, it is essential that you learn anger management skills in order to express anger in appropriate ways. Important anger management skills are identified in Figure 14. A discussion of each of these anger management skills follows.

Keeping An Anger Self-Inventory. You can become skilled in recognizing anger triggers and deciding how to express anger. You can examine what you do when you are angry by using the Anger Self-Inventory (Figure 15). The Anger Self-Inventory helps you examine the situations that cause you to feel angry and your responses to these situations. Once you complete the Anger Self-Inventory, you can work on your ways of responding. You might learn that you overreact in some situations. You can change this response. The Anger Self-Inventory can help you determine if a situation is worth your attention, if the anger is warranted, and how you might respond.

Using Self-Statements To Control Your Anger. Self-statements are words you can say to yourself when you experience anger triggers and cues. Some examples of self-statements you can practice and use to control your anger include: (Goldstein and Keller, 1987):

- This is going to upset me, but I know how to deal with it.
- I can manage the situation.
- Try not to take this too seriously.
- Time for a few deep breaths of relaxation. Feel comfortable and relaxed.
- Easy does it.
- As long as I keep cool, I'm in control.
- I don't need to prove myself.

- I'm not going to let it get to me.
- Getting upset won't help.
- It's just not worth it to get so angry.
- I'm not going to get pushed around, but I'm not going haywire either.
- (S)he would probably like to get me angry. Well, I'm going to disappoint him/her.
- Can I laugh about it? It's probably not too serious.
- Don't take it personally.
- I handled that one pretty well. It worked.
- I could have gotten more upset than it was worth.
- My pride can sure get me into trouble. But, when I don't take things too seriously, I'm better off.

Participating In Physical Activities. Vigorous physical activity can work to lessen the effects of anger and relieve tension by providing a physical outlet for the energy that builds up with anger. To lessen the effects of anger, choose physical activity that reduces physical tension. Fantasizing revenge toward the person with whom you are angry may increase anger rather than defuse it. Participating in activities such as dancing, jogging, swimming, martial arts, weight lifting, and team athletics can help lessen anger.

Using Physical Expression To Blow Off Steam. Another way to blow off steam involves expressing anger in a physical way. The extra energy provided by the anger response is used during this physical expression rather than in an action that might harm yourself or others. Some suggestions for lessening the effects of anger with physical expression include:

- stomping on the floor;
- striking the air;
- screaming into a pillow;
- hitting a pillow;
- throwing a fluff ball at a wall in a way that will not cause damage;
- hammering in a way as not to damage anything;
- squeezing a fluff ball or tennis ball.

Using I-Messages And Active Listening. An I-message can be used to express the anger you feel for the behavior of another person. An I-message also might be used to express the anger you feel about a specific situation. For example, the people who lost their homes and possessions as a result of the earthquake in California might express anger using I-messages. An I-message might be, "When our apartment was destroyed by the earthquake (the event), I lost some of my valuable possessions (the effect of the event), and I became angry (the feeling that resulted)." I-messages allow you to express your anger rather than keeping it bottled up inside.

Active listening, especially when coupled with clarifying responses, also is effective in anger management. When you use active listening techniques, you are able to gain control of your emotions and gather more information about the situation that is making you angry. This helps to keep you from acting out when, with more information, you may find a resolution to your present difficulty.

Keeping A Sense Of Humor. Keeping a sense of humor when you are angry is a valuable skill. When you stop and examine your angry feelings, you often realize that you are overreacting to a situation. Finding the humor in a situation and laughing at yourself in a good-spirited manner can help lessen anger. Using humor helps in situations where others are angry as well. Telling a joke or poking fun at a situation or yourself (in a good-spirited and not an attacking way) can lighten up a situation.

Expressing Yourself Through Creative Activities. Another way to lessen the effects of anger is to express yourself in a creative way. You might want to write a poem that expresses how you feel. You might want to draw a picture or take clay and mold something. You may want to paint a picture or make a craft. Many community centers offer opportunities for young people to express themselves in creative ways. Besides lessening the effects of anger, these activities give you a sense of accomplishment.

Talking With Parents And Mentors. Talk with parents and mentors when you experience anger triggers and cues. Adults can be helpful in helping you recognize what you are feeling, why you are feeling this way, and what are some healthful ways to cope with these feelings. It can be very reassuring to have trusting adults understand your angry feelings. For example, if you feel rejected as a result of being left out of a social activity, you might share your feelings of rejec-

tion and resulting anger with a parent or other trusted adult. They can help you examine ways to handle this situation.

Writing Letters To Express Your Angry Feelings. It can be helpful to write letters to express angry feelings. For example, you might be very angry about a situation that has occurred at school or within the family. You might not feel that you can approach the person(s) with whom you are angry. Writing a letter helps to lessen the anger by providing a way to express it without confronting the person. Sometimes you might feel that during the conversation you are not able to express yourself clearly. You might feel you will have an outburst of anger that is not appropriate. Writing a letter provides a safer way to talk to the person. It gives you the time that you need to clearly express what you are feeling. Sometimes just writing the letter without mailing it lessens the anger you feel. At other times, it may be important to send the letter to the appropriate person. Consider the appropriateness before sending the letter you have written. You may choose to wait until you are less angry before you send the letter. Then, you can read it again and decide if you want to send it. You may choose not to mail the letter and to throw it away.

Planning Ahead To Deal With Your Anger. As you become more experienced in recognizing when you are angry and knowing what makes you angry, you can begin to plan ahead. You can practice ahead of time what you will do. You can practice in school with peers, in another setting with friends, with your parent(s), or with a school counselor. You might even practice at home in front of a mirror so that you can watch your response. During practice, you can ask other people to play certain roles or pretend they are a specific person. You can practice different responses and see which ones work best for you. This can be very helpful. Then, when you are actually in a situation, you will be comfortable expressing your anger. You are more likely to manage your anger and to keep from doing something harmful.

Violence-Free Pledge

I will use I-messages to express angry feelings.

I will use active listening when others express their angry feelings.

I will practice anger management skills.

I will express my feelings in healthful ways if I experience a life crisis.

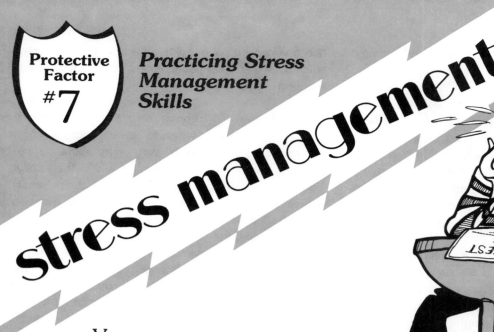

stress management

You probably have heard someone say, "I am stressed out." This person was experiencing many demands and finding it difficult to cope with them. **Stress** is the response of the body to the demands of daily living. Think about the demands on you. You may feel pressure to do well in school. Your family situation may be difficult. You may have concern about your personal safety. Peers may be pressuring you to engage in harmful behavior. No one escapes the demands of daily living. Everyone experiences stress. Yet, people respond differently to stress. The following discussion examines stress. You will learn why being unable to handle stress is a risk factor for violence. You will learn how using stress management skills serves as a protective factor to prevent violence.

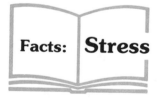

Facts: **Stress**

Stressors are the sources or causes of stress. A **stressor** is a demand that causes changes in the body. A stressor can be physical, such as running a race, being exposed to germs, using drugs, or breathing the cigarette smoke of another person. A stressor can be mental, such as trying to solve a math problem, taking a test, or having poor self-esteem. A stressor can be emotional, such as learning that a relative is very ill, being filled with hidden anger, or having new feelings of love for another person. A stressor can be social, such as meeting someone for the first time, being teased, or having an argument. A stressor might be environmental, such as living in a crowded place,

experiencing loud noise, or being poor. Each of these stressors is different, yet each causes changes in the body.

Your response to stressors can be positive or negative. **Eustress** is a healthful response to a stressor that produces positive results. For example, as a student you might be actively trying to get a college scholarship. You respond to this stressor by keeping a rigorous study schedule, keeping up to date on classroom assignments, and getting adequate sleep. You envision yourself as a very likely scholarship recipient. Your response to stress has been healthful and positive. This is eustress.

You might respond to the same stressor in a different way. **Distress** is a harmful response to a stressor that produces negative results. For example, you might be overwhelmed by how difficult it will be to earn a college scholarship. You respond by skipping meals, having difficulty sleeping, and being so anxious that you are unable to perform well on tests. Your response does not benefit you. Later in this section, you will learn how distress might cause harmful changes in the body.

Everyone experiences stress. It is impossible to avoid having demands placed on you. Your response to stress can be either healthful or harmful. In order to understand why, you need to know more about how the body responds to stress.

The Stress Response. The **general adaptation syndrome (GAS)** is a series of changes that occur in the body when stress occurs. There are three stages in the general adaptation syndrome. The **alarm stage** is the first stage of the GAS in which the body gets ready for action. During this stage, adrenaline is released into the bloodstream. **Adrenaline** is a hormone that helps your body get ready for an emergency. Your heart rate and blood pressure increase, digestion slows, muscles contract, respiration and sweating increase, and mental activity increases. Your pupils dilate so you can see sharply, and your hearing sharpens as well. In the alarm stage of the GAS, you experience a burst of quick energy. Sometimes this response is called the fight-or-flight response because the GAS gets you ready to take action or to run quickly away to protect yourself. The **resistance stage** is the second stage of the GAS in which the body attempts to regain balance and return to normal. The body is no longer in the emergency state and now the body wants to go back to normal. Adrenaline is no longer secreted. Heart rate and blood pressure decrease, digestion begins again, muscles relax, respiration returns to normal, and sweating stops.

When you experience a stressor, it is normal and healthful for your body to get ready for an emergency (alarm stage), for the body changes to help you do something positive, and finally for your body to recognize that you no longer are in a state of emergency and to return to normal (resistance stage). Unfortunately, this does not always happen. Some people worry needlessly and as a result their bodies are in the alarm stage for long periods of time. Other people do not know positive actions to take when stress occurs, so their bodies remain ready to do something for long periods of time. The body is not capable of being ready for an emergency for long periods of time. Eventually the body will become exhausted. The **exhaustion stage** is the third stage of the GAS in which there is wear and tear on the body, lowered resistance to disease, and an increased likelihood of disease or death. Fortunately, people who practice stress management skills will not experience the exhaustion stage. Later, there will be a discussion of stress management skills.

Sources Of Stress. You and your peers are exposed to many different stressors. The following list shows the results of a survey that asked high school students what they found to be stressful (Zitzow, 1992). The events causing stress are listed below in rank order; the most serious are listed first. There are parentheses with numbers inside after each life event. The number is the percent of students who said that they had experienced this event in their life.

1. Death of a brother or sister (7.9)
2. Death of a parent (13.8)
3. Being responsible for an unwanted pregnancy (16.4)
4. Being suspended from school or placed on probation (17.0)
5. Having parents who are separated or divorced (21.8)
6. Receiving a D or F on a test (78.4)
7. Being physically hurt by others while in school (24.6)
8. Giving a speech in class (82.3)
9. Feeling that much of life is worthless (56.5)
10. Being teased and made fun of (45.5)
11. Feeling guilty about things I've done in the past (92.3)
12. Pressure to get an A or B in a course (48.4)
13. Pressure from friends to use drugs or alcohol (88.4)
14. Fear of pregnancy (29.4)
15. Failure to live up to family expectations (62.4)
16. Feelings of anxiousness or general tension (78.8)
17. Pressure to have sex (83.6)
18. Feeling like I don't fit in (86.4)
19. Fear of being physically hurt by other students (72.4)
20. Past/present sexual contact with a family member (10.8)

Certainly, major life events such as these are stressful. Yet, it is now believed that young people experience most of their distress from the accumulation of daily hassles. **Daily hassles** are the day-to-day stressors of normal living. These include such things as concern about physical appearance, struggles with peers, worrying about too much to do, homework assignments and tests, misplacing or losing belongings, and being bullied or criticized. Personal safety also has become a daily hassle for many young people. They worry about their personal safety at school and in their neighborhoods. They may worry about gang activity and other violent acts.

Daily hassles can result in more than worry and frustration. When daily hassles pile up, health and well-being can be affected. For these reasons, it is important to understand stress, causes of stress, and what to do about stress.

Risk Factor #7

Being Unable to Manage Stress

Being unable to manage stress is a risk factor. When you are unable to manage stress:

1. your health may be harmed;
2. you may cope in ways that harm health;
3. you may cope poorly and become a perpetrator or victim of violence.

Stress And Your Health. Long periods of stress can keep your body in a constant state of emergency. When this happens, your body works too hard. Your blood pressure and heart beat rate stay high. You continue to breathe more often. Eventually, your mind tires from trying to be mentally alert. Your muscles tire from being tensed for long periods of time.

Something else happens to your body during periods of stress. Your immune system does not work as well as it might. The **immune system** is the body system that fights disease. It contains white blood cells that destroy germs. When you experience long periods of stress, the number of these white cells decreases. Thus, you are more likely to become ill.

Long periods of stress place too much wear and tear on your body. You begin to feel the symptoms of stress. These symptoms might include high blood pressure, headaches, stomachaches, sleeplessness, and nervousness. If you have allergies or asthma, your condition may worsen. Long periods of stress also increase the risk of heart disease and cancer.

Stress And Harmful Coping. Long periods of stress are difficult. Often, people who are unable to manage their stress in healthful ways will find the stress so overwhelming that they begin to engage in harmful behavior. Some young people turn to drugs as a means of coping. Life becomes so painful for them that they attempt to numb the pain with drugs. This only worsens their problems. Other young people choose different harmful behavior to escape their problems. Eating disorders, such as anorexia nervosa and bulimia, are believed to result from having poor self-esteem and inadequate coping skills. **Anorexia nervosa** is an emotional disorder in which there is excessive preoc-

cupation with food, starvation, and exercising to lose weight. **Bulimia** is an emotional disorder in which an intense fear of being overweight and a lack of self-esteem result in secret binge eating, followed by self-induced vomiting. Another response to too much stress might be to eat too much and gain weight. Still other young people attempt to escape from their problems by becoming sexually active. They become overly dependent and involved with someone as a way of avoiding problems. These harmful actions result from young people not being able to manage stress in healthful ways.

Stress And Violence. Being unable to manage stress is linked to violence in many ways. Young people who have long periods of stress may become depressed. If depression is not treated, then there is an increased risk of personal violence. Suicide is a leading cause of death in young people. In most cases, suicide might be prevented by knowing how to handle pressures that lead to depression and drug use.

Long periods of stress increase anxiety and tension. Young people who are anxious and tense have difficulty relating to others. When there is conflict in their relationships, they may be unable to remain calm and in control. They may say offensive things to others or start a fight. Being unable to manage stress is often the

---

Figure 16
Stress Management Skills

1. Using Responsible Decision-Making Skills
2. Using Breathing Techniques
3. Eating A Healthful Diet
4. Getting Enough Rest And Sleep
5. Participating In Physical Activities
6. Using A Time Management Plan
7. Writing In A Journal
8. Having Close Friends
9. Talking With Parents And Other Trusted Adults
10. Helping Others
11. Expressing Affection In Appropriate Ways
12. Caring For Pets
13. Changing Your Outlook
14. Keeping A Sense Of Humor

---

underlying reason that a person becomes a perpetrator or cause of crime.

These negative ways of behaving may cause others to respond with negative behavior. Other people might be offended or threatened by the behavior of a young person who is stressed. They may retaliate. They may begin an argument or a fight. In this way, being stressed increases the likelihood of becoming a victim of a crime. Juvenile delinquency is common in young people who are unable to manage stress. Certain types of behavior, such as destroying property, writing graffiti, and stealing, are often attempts to manage stress. However, these attempts at stress management produce negative results.

Protective Factor #7

Practicing Stress Management Skills

Fortunately, you can protect yourself from the risks of being unable to manage stress. You can practice stress management skills. **Stress management skills** are techniques that can be used to cope with the harmful effects produced by stress. There are two types of stress management skills. The first type of skill focuses on doing something about the cause of stress. Using responsible decision-making skills can help to solve a problem or situation that causes stress. The second type of skill focuses on keeping your body healthy and relieving anxiety. Exercising and eating a healthful diet are ways to keep your body healthy and relieve anxiety. However, this may not change the cause of stress. It is important to do something about the cause of stress as well as to do something to keep the body healthy and relieve anxiety. Stress management skills that you can use are listed in Figure 16. The following discussion focuses on these stress management skills.

Using Responsible Decision-Making Skills. The Responsible Decision-Making Model is discussed in detail in Protective Factor #12. You can use this same model for deciding how to cope with a stressful situation. The steps to follow are:
1. Identify the cause of the stress and anxiety.
2. Identify ways to cope with the situation.

3. Evaluate each way of coping:
   - Will this way of coping result in an action that will protect my health and that of others?
   - Will this way of coping result in an action that will protect my safety and that of others?
   - Will this way of coping result in an action that will protect the laws of the community?
   - Will this way of coping result in an action that shows respect for myself and others?
   - Will this way of coping result in actions that are acceptable to my parents and other responsible adults?
   - Will this way of coping show that I have good character and moral values?
4. Choose a responsible action to cope with the source of stress.
5. Keep a journal to record the way in which you solved the problem.
6. After a period of time, evaluate the action you selected.

When you apply the steps in the Responsible Decision-Making Model to a difficult situation, you feel less anxious. You feel more in control. You will have more confidence that you can handle a situation.

Using Breathing Techniques. When you feel stress, your body begins the stress response. Your body gets ready for an emergency. It can be helpful to reverse this response and calm yourself. You can breathe in deeply through your nose, keeping your mouth shut. Then, slowly blow the air out through your mouth. This breathing technique has a calming effect on the body. It also helps you take a time out from thinking about the cause of stress.

Eating A Healthful Diet. Eating a well-balanced diet is always wise, but it is especially important when you are stressed. During the alarm stage of stress, adrenaline is secreted into the bloodstream. When adrenaline is secreted, your body uses vitamins B and C. It is very important that you obtain sources of these vitamins. Vitamin B is needed for a healthy nervous system. Vitamin B is found in foods such as whole grain cereals, rice, legumes, and breads. Vitamin C helps the immune system to function. Vitamin C is found in foods such as oranges, grapefruit, tomatoes, limes, lemons, and broccoli.

Caffeine is a stimulant drug that increases the rate of bodily activities. Caffeine is found in coffee, tea, cola beverages, and chocolate. Because bodily activities are already increased during the stress response, it is helpful to avoid caffeine when you are stressed. Some people have special diet needs when they are stressed. There are some individual differences in how people respond to different foods. For example, some people find that spicy foods are not easily digested at this time.

Getting Enough Rest And Sleep. Without rest and sleep you will find it difficult to reduce your stress levels. You may feel irritable, exhausted, and anxious. When you are resting, your blood pressure lowers and heart rate slows. Your muscles relax, and your body has a chance to rest. After getting enough sleep, you feel invigorated and ready to face the day's challenges. Many people need to have at least nine hours of sleep each night to function at their best.

Participating In Physical Activities. Physical activities such as running, walking, swimming, rollerblading, and playing basketball can help reduce stress. Vigorous physical activity relieves tension by providing a physical outlet for the energy that builds up with stress. When you are physically fit, you recover from the effects of stress more quickly. You are less likely to develop diseases because of stress. Improved physical fitness levels have been linked to a decrease in the severity of the stress response, a shorter recovery time from stress, and improved resistance to disease.

Using A Time Management Plan. Your life is very busy with school, homework, sports, and family activities. You may be overwhelmed by the number of tasks you have to complete in a day. The following suggestions may help you manage your time and reduce stress.

1. Keep a daily calendar to learn how your time is spent.
2. Write down what you need to do.
3. Decide in what order to complete the tasks. Remember, it is sometimes best to tackle bigger or more difficult tasks first.
4. Decide how much time it will take to finish each task.
5. Plan to finish each task.
6. Build time into your plan for unexpected delays.
7. Check off each task as it is completed.
8. Review your plan each day and make changes if they are needed.

You may find that you procrastinate. **Procrastination** is putting off doing something until a future time. If you find yourself putting off unpleasant tasks, try to understand why. It may be helpful to plan something fun as a reward for finishing something difficult. For example, if you have a research paper to write, plan to do something you enjoy when you complete the paper.

Writing In A Journal. Writing about your stress is a healthful way to express your feelings and may help you work through your stress (Meeks and Miller, 1995). Try to find a quiet place where you can write in your journal. The easiest way to start a journal is simply to write about issues that concern you today. Writing in a journal has been shown to elevate the number of Helper-T cells in the body. **Helper-T cells** are a type of white blood cell that fights pathogens and destroys cancerous cells. Reviewing regularly what you have written can help you learn more about how you cope with stress. You may want to share what you have written with someone you trust.

Having Close Friends. Having close friends helps you cope with stress. When you are with friends, you can share your feelings and experiences without being judged. Your friends can listen and offer suggestions on ways to handle the situations that are causing stress. They may share similar experiences. Often, just having friends listen can make you feel better and reduce stress.

Talking With Parents And Other Trusted Adults. You can express thoughts, feelings, and concerns with parents and other adults. They can listen and be supportive. They can help you solve the problem that is causing stress.

Helping Others. There are many ways that you can help others. You might tutor a younger student, volunteer at a nursing home, or help an elderly person in your neighborhood. When you are stressed, helping others gives you a different outlook. You feel important because you are able to help. This results in a feeling that has been called a "helper's high." Helping people less fortunate than yourself can make stressful situations seem less important.

Expressing Affection In Appropriate Ways. Expressing affection reduces stress and provides feelings of closeness. Giving a parent a hug, sending a card to a friend, or spending time with a grandparent can bring about feelings of happiness that reduce feelings of stress.

Caring For Pets. Caring for a pet can be rewarding and can reduce stress. Nursing homes have discovered that caring for an animal raises patients' spirits. A visit with animals is often cited by patients as the highlight of their day. Caring for a pet involves physical contact. Petting an animal is comforting and relaxing. Many people report that playing ball with a dog or talking to their cat helps them reduce feelings of stress. And, spending time with a pet helps to lessen feelings of loneliness.

Changing Your Outlook. **Reframing** is changing your outlook in order to see a situation in a more pos-itive way. Changing your outlook helps to turn life's obstacles into challenges. For example, your family may move into a new school district. Instead of being stressed because you have left your friends, you feel challenged and look forward to making new friends.

Keeping A Sense Of Humor. A good laugh is a posi-tive way to manage stress. Heart rate, blood pressure rate, and muscular tension drop below normal levels after a hearty laugh. As a result, you are more relaxed. The greatest benefit of humor is its ability to alter your outlook (Meeks and Miller, 1995).

Violence-Free Pledge

I will practice stress management skills.

I will seek help if I cope with stress in harmful or violent ways.

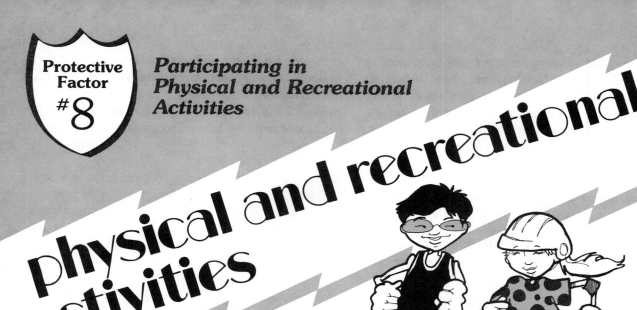

physical and recreational activities

After school, do you hang out with friends on the street? On weekends, are you a couch potato? Do you keep your eyes glued to the television screen? If you do, you are missing out on the opportunity to be active. Participating in physical and recreational activities helps prevent violence. **Physical activities** are activities that require you to use energy and to move your muscles. Examples include riding your bike, playing basketball, dancing, running, walking, lifting weights, and rollerblading. **Recreational activities** are activities that involve play, amusement, and relaxation. Examples include shuffleboard, bowling, board games such as monopoly, and attending a sporting event or a theater performance. The following discussion provides suggestions for activities you might enjoy. You will learn why you are at risk for violence when you are not active. You will learn why participating in physical and recreational activities helps prevent violence.

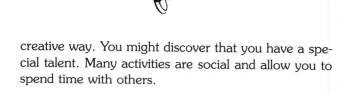

Facts: Physical and Recreational Activities

You can participate in many different physical and recreational activities. Some of these activities are physical and help you become physically fit. Some of these activities stimulate your mind and keep you mentally sharp. Other activities are educational. You learn new facts and skills when you participate in these activities. Some activities allow you to express yourself in a

creative way. You might discover that you have a special talent. Many activities are social and allow you to spend time with others.

Let's examine the many activities from which you can choose. You need equipment for some of these activities. For others, you need money to pay for the activities. You also might need lessons or training. All activities require your willingness to participate. You can have fun trying different activities. When you choose several different ones, you avoid getting into a rut.

Physical activities help you become physically fit. They help increase your level of energy. They help reduce stress. You are more likely to sleep well at night and keep a healthful weight. Participating in physical activities can improve appearance. You have better muscle tone and a healthful glow to your skin. You feel good about yourself.

Most likely, you have physical education classes at your school. These classes are very important. During physical education, you learn new skills that you can use the rest of your life. There is time in your school day for you to exercise and use energy. This relieves stress. It also helps you to think more clearly in your other classes. Be dedicated and involved in your physical education class. Always remember to bring what is needed. For example, remember your tennis shoes or comfortable clothing when needed. Participate with enthusiasm. Ask your physical education teacher about activities to enjoy after school and during weekends. Your teacher knows about physical activities available in your community. For example, there may be basketball, baseball, softball, and soccer leagues you can join. There may be a race in which you can run. If you have a disability, there are special events in which you can participate. A **disability** is a condition in the body that may require a person to do things in a different way. For example, some people are not able to move their legs. They may use wheelchairs to move about.

The following list includes physical activities that require energy and keep you fit. Some of these activities can be done alone while others can be done with family and friends. In some cases, you need to join a team. Examine this list and choose physical activities to enjoy:
• Ping pong
• Bowling
• Walking
• Running
• Rollerblading
• Dancing
• Playing basketball
• Hiking
• Playing baseball
• Playing golf
• Playing soccer
• Skiing
• Playing tennis
• Swimming
• Karate
• Martial arts

Most likely, you have heard the saying, "You lose it if you don't use it." People have made this statement to describe the importance of using muscles. When muscles are not used, you lose muscle tone. Your body may appear flabby. The mind also needs regular exercise. You can stimulate your mind, learn new things, and discover new interests. You need to keep your mind in top shape with activities that are mental and help you learn. Your school may have clubs you can join. The community center or park near you might offer activities. Examine this list and choose mental activities to enjoy:
• Chess
• Checkers
• Monopoly
• Reading books
• Working jigsaw puzzles
• Completing crossword puzzles
• Visiting museums
• Participating in science fairs
• Collecting stamps
• Debate clubs

Creative activities give you a chance to express yourself. You can do something in a way that no one else has done it. You can develop new skills and talents and share these with others. Creative expression relieves stress. It gives you a feeling of well-being. You learn new things about yourself. Other people appreciate how special you are. Others enjoy the things you make. They enjoy watching you perform.

There might be opportunities at your school. You might sing in the school choir or play in the band. You might try out for the school play. There might be classes offered where you can learn to sew or develop woodworking skills. Your school district may have a special school that provides training. This is sometimes called an alternative school. Your teachers might direct you to other places in your community. Community centers and parks often provide arts and crafts. If you have a special talent and need money, equipment, or lessons, someone at school or in your community might help you. For example, there usually is money available to help young people with musical talent purchase instruments. Do not give up on trying to get what is needed to pursue your talent. Examine the following list and choose creative activities you can enjoy:
• Drawing
• Woodworking
• Leathercraft
• Sculpting
• Making pottery
• Singing in a choir
• Ballet dancing
• Acting in theater or plays
• Playing a musical instrument (your school band)
• Needlework
• Sewing

Social activities give you a chance to be with your friends. You also can meet and enjoy new people when you participate in social activities. You can practice your social skills. Many of the activities on the previous lists also provided the chance to be with others.

Here are some additional ways that you can be with people who share your interests:
- Carnivals
- Attending concerts
- Hobby clubs
- Card games
- Attending parties
- Attending sporting events

Today, there are many activities and programs in which young people can participate. You may want to take part in one of these programs or a similar program in your area. Following are descriptions of several different programs that are popular with young people. Read what other young people are doing.

Outward Bound USA. **Outward Bound USA** is an outdoor adventure program in which young people are challenged physically and mentally in a wilderness setting. Outward Bound activities are not easy. Tasks include climbing a rock face, whitewater rafting, and spending days alone in the wilderness. Here is a description of one of the activities in this program (Buchanan, 1993):

> By negotiating a series of high-wire acts, they experience the risks of leadership and stretch the limits of their courage. Staff members supervise every step to ensure that students are properly clipped to ropes to prevent them from falling. Students climb a rope ladder, walk a cable 50 feet above the ground, and ride a harness down a zipline from a platform to the ground. In the "flying squirrel" exercise, they are hooked into a harness so that the rest of the group can haul them down toward the roof of the gym by means of a rope-and-pulley system. On the way down, they take a shot at a basketball hoop from midair. Michael Jordan never had it so good!

Young people learn from these activities. By successfully completing them, they develop self-confidence, self-awareness, and trust in others. Outward Bound offers special programs for young people who are poor, have had substance abuse problems, have disabilities, and have been in trouble with the law. If you are interested in participating in an Outward Bound Program, call the national office at 1-914-424-4000.

Midnight Basketball. Many communities offer midnight basketball. **Midnight Basketball** is a basketball program that is held late at night to keep young people from being on the streets. The purpose of these programs is to keep young people from being out late at night in areas where there is much crime and drug use. The basketball games are carefully supervised. When young people arrive to play basketball, they cannot have been drinking alcohol or have used other harmful drugs. They cannot be carrying a weapon. They must agree to follow rules. You can check with your school, recreation center, or community center to learn if Midnight Basketball is offered in your community.

El Puente. **El Puente** is a community-based youth center in Brooklyn, New York, that offers a wide range of services and activities for young people. Young people can participate in programs such as team and individual sports, dance, drama, and art. Health services and peer counseling also are available through the center (Lovell and Pope, 1993). You can check with your school counselor or look in the phone directory for information about community-based youth centers available to you.

Gang Alternative And Prevention Program. The **Gang Alternative And Prevention Program** is a program in Los Angeles, California, that refers at-risk young people in elementary and junior high school to a variety of recreational activities (Moss-Manson, 1993). These young people live in areas with high rates of crime, gang activity, and drug use. They are encouraged to participate in basketball and football leagues and weightlifting and boxing programs to keep them from becoming involved in harmful behavior. They work with program officers. If you live in an area with a high rate of crime, gang activity, and drug use, check with the local police or recreation departments to learn about similar programs.

Community Service Center Of San Gabriel Valley, California. There are many community service centers that offer programs for young people. Community Service Center of San Gabriel Valley, California, is a good example. The local police department, local schools, the Boys and Girls Club, and other community organizations work with the center to offer services and activities. The center is staffed with counselors who speak different languages. There are many volunteers as well as probation officers. College interns help supervise the many activities that are offered. Drug and gang awareness classes are offered. Young people can get free tutoring. There are many fun activities in which they can participate. You can check to learn if there is a similar community service center near you.

Cherokee Nation Youth Fitness Camp. The **Cherokee Nation Youth Fitness Camp** is a summer program in Oklahoma for young people who belong to the Cherokee Nation. The camp offers swimming, sports, and outdoor adventure. Young people participate in community service to learn ways to help others. You may belong to a specific group. There may be camps and organizations to meet the needs of the group to which you belong. Check with adults who belong to the same group as you do.

You have learned about many different physical and recreational activities. Imagine how much fun you might have participating in these. Select several and get involved.

Risk Factor #8

Not Participating in Physical and Recreational Activities

Young people who do not participate in physical and recreational activities are more likely to get into trouble. They are more likely to get into fights and to engage in crime. They are more likely to hang out in the streets where there is violence and illegal drug use. They are more likely to join gangs. There are other risks as well. Let's examine the risks of not participating in physical and recreational activities.

You Become A Couch Potato. When you are not active, you have less energy. You are not physically fit and not in the best condition you can be. As a result, you tend to take part in activities that require little physical activity. You might become a couch potato. The biggest factor contributing to low levels of physical activity is watching too much television. The average young person in America watches television for more than 22 hours per week. Typical activity for many young people is watching television or playing video games while snacking on high-fat, high-calorie snacks (Robbins, Powers, and Burgess, 1994). If you watch television much of the time, most likely you see violence again and again. Watching violence over and over again may increase the likelihood that you will act in violent ways.

You Have Too Much Time To Get Into Trouble. One of the main reasons young people get into trouble is

that they are bored. Young people who are bored also are more at risk for joining gangs, using alcohol and other drugs, and being involved in criminal activity.

You Do Not Have A Way To "Work Off" Anger. When you become angry, you have a surge of energy. Without a physical outlet for your anger, you may use your energy in another way. You may explode and harm someone else. You may harm yourself.

Your Stress Level Increases. When you do not participate in physical and recreational activities, your stress level is higher. You may find your stress level so overwhelming that you act out in harmful ways. Young people with long periods of stress often become depressed. The rate of suicide is higher in depressed youth. Young people under severe stress do not relate well with others. They are more likely to have conflicts. When they have conflicts, they are less likely to remain calm and in control of their temper. They may harm someone.

You Rob Yourself Of A Chance To Practice Social Skills. When you participate in activities with others, you have a chance to practice social skills. Having social skills help you relate well with people your age. Young people who lack social skills are often left out by peers. Peers do not want to spend time with them. Being left out has been shown to cause young people to become aggressive. Aggressive behavior leads to violence.

You Feel Left Out And Lonely. A major reason young people join gangs, give in to peer pressure, and join others to behave in violent ways is to keep from feeling left out. **Alienation** is the feeling that one is apart from others. **Loneliness** is an anxious, unpleasant, and painful feeling that results from having few friends or from being alienated. When you are not involved with others in healthful activities, you overcome your feelings of loneliness by getting involved with those people who get into trouble.

You Miss The Chance To Follow Rules And Respect Authority. When you participate in many activities, you are required to follow rules and respect people who make and enforce them. If you are not involved, you miss this opportunity. Young people who do not learn to follow rules and respect authority are more likely to break laws. They are more likely to challenge people in authority.

You Might Not Learn To Be A Good Sport.
Sportsmanship is taking losing without acting out or without bragging, and treating other players to whom you have lost or beaten in fair and courteous ways. When you do not participate in activities, it is difficult to learn to handle defeat. You miss the chance to learn to express your disappointment and anger in appropriate ways. In other situations, you might be a sore loser or bad sport. This can cause others to reject you. Rejection by peers is a risk factor for violence.

Your Self-Esteem Might Suffer. You need a "to do" list for self-esteem. As you complete this list, you feel good about yourself. When you do not participate in activities, you miss the opportunity to develop skills and talents that improve self-esteem. You miss the opportunity to improve your appearance with regular physical activity.

You Might Not Develop Self-Discipline. **Self-discipline** is the effort or energy with which you follow a plan to do something. Many activities require that you practice. You develop self-discipline by practicing. Many activities require that you have a plan. You develop self-discipline by following this plan. When you do not participate in sports and hobbies, you might not learn the commitment that is needed to be self-disciplined.

Protective Factor #8

Participating in Physical and Recreational Activities

Participating in physical and recreational activities can benefit you in many ways. Figure 17 lists some of the benefits. Participation is a protective factor because it helps prevent violence. Let's examine each of the benefits and how they prevent violence.

You Develop Physical Fitness. When you exercise for at least 25 minutes a day, three times a week for more than seven weeks, your body releases beta-endorphins. **Beta-endorphins** are substances produced in the brain that help reduce pain and create a feeling of well-being. They cause what people who run regularly describe as a "runner's high." In other words, you can

---

> Figure 17
> ## Benefits Of Physical And Recreational Activities
>
> 1. You Develop Physical Fitness.
> 2. You Use Your Time Wisely.
> 3. You Have A Physical Outlet To Work Off Anger.
> 4. You Reduce Your Stress Level.
> 5. You Practice Social Skills Such As Cooperation.
> 6. You Feel A Sense Of Belonging.
> 7. You Learn To Follow Rules And Respect Authority.
> 8. You Learn How To Accept Defeat.
> 9. You Improve Self-Esteem.
> 10. You Develop Self-Discipline.

get high naturally from regular, hard exercise. Being physically fit increases energy and improves your health. You feel better about your appearance. When you have these good feelings, you are not as likely to behave in violent ways. You do not need drugs to get high because you experience natural highs.

You Use Your Time Wisely. One reason young people become violent is that they want excitement. They are bored because they are not involved in activities. When you participate in activities, you do not have time to behave in illegal and violent ways. You are too involved. There is no time left.

You Have A Physical Outlet To Work Off Anger. When you are angry, there is physical tension in your body. If you are involved in activities such as playing a sport or playing in the band, you have a physical outlet to work off the tension that accompanies anger. You work off this tension in a healthful way rather than arguing or fighting.

You Reduce Your Stress Level. When you are involved in activities, you can take your mind off problems for a while. This can reduce your stress. Being involved in physical activities helps you to be fit. When you are fit, your body is more healthy and the effects of stress on your body are lessened. Participating in recreational activities can be fun and relaxing. Your spirits may be lifted. This changes your outlook. Then you are not as likely to be depressed. You are less likely to harm yourself and others when problems occur.

You Practice Social Skills Such As Cooperation.
When you participate in activities with others, you can practice social skills. You practice manners and cooperation. You have the opportunity to give and follow directions, to assume the role of leader, and to learn to resolve conflict. These skills help you relate well with others. Then when you are in disagreements, you know how to cooperate and get cooperation. You know how to communicate with others. These skills reduce the risk of violence.

You Feel A Sense Of Belonging. One reason youth gang members say they joined gangs is to gain a sense of belonging. There are better ways to gain a sense of belonging. Belonging to a school team or playing in a summer league are healthful ways to feel a part of a group. Being in a school play or singing in the choir also create a sense of belonging. When you belong to groups that are involved in healthful activities, you are less likely to get in trouble and to be involved in violence.

You Learn To Follow Rules And Respect Authority.
Many activities can be enjoyed only if there are rules for those who participate. When you choose these activities, you learn the importance of rules. If you break rules, there are consequences. You are penalized in some way. You know that it is wise to respect the official, captain, coach, or band leader. You recognize that these people are helping you. You recognize that it is their responsibility to discipline others and you allow them to do it. These lessons carry into other aspects of living. You recognize that there are consequences for breaking laws so you follow them. You know that parents, police officers, and school officials are trying to help you so you obey them. You know that there are ways to handle people who break the law. When someone harms you, you allow the appropriate people to handle the situation. These types of behavior help protect you from violence.

You Learn How To Accept Defeat. You have heard the saying, "It's not whether you win or lose, but how you play the game." Most people do not win all the time. Learning to accept defeat and to overcome defeat is important. These life lessons can be learned and practiced while you play sports and games. You can practice what to do and how to express feelings of disappointment or anger when you lose or have a poor performance. When someone else is the winner, you offer congratulations. Defeat does not get you down. You do not choose harmful actions when you feel defeat.

You Improve Self-Esteem. Regular physical exercise improves appearance. You feel good about your appearance. Participation in different activities increases your skills. You feel good because you master new skills. When you compete, you might have a chance to win an award or experience victory. You feel a sense of accomplishment and pride. These good feelings help you improve self-esteem. When you have positive self-esteem, you protect yourself from harm. You feel better about those around you and are less likely to harm them.

You Develop Self-Discipline. When you regularly participate in activities, you learn to discipline yourself. You set goals and make plans to reach them. For example, if you are on an athletic team, you regularly go to practice. You practice the same skills over and over again. If you are a member of the school band, you also go to practice. You play certain tunes again and again to get them just right. You work hard to perform well. You develop self-discipline. Being self-disciplined helps to prevent violence. You expect yourself to behave in nonviolent ways and you do not allow others to change your mind. When others behave in violent ways, you stick to your way of doing things.

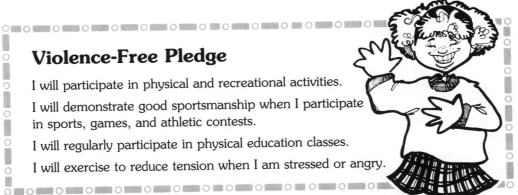

Violence-Free Pledge

I will participate in physical and recreational activities.

I will demonstrate good sportsmanship when I participate in sports, games, and athletic contests.

I will regularly participate in physical education classes.

I will exercise to reduce tension when I am stressed or angry.

Protective Factor #9

Practicing Suicide Prevention Strategies

Suicide prevention strategies

The philosopher Joseph Addison once said, "The three grand essentials to life are something to do, someone to love, and something to hope for." Think about his message for a moment. Having something to do and doing it well gives you a feeling of accomplishment. Having people to love gives you the opportunity to share your feelings, hopes, dreams, and disappointments. Having something to hope for gives you a reason to live. When you have something to hope for, you look forward to your future. Young people who do not have things to do, people to care about, and something to which they look forward, are more at risk for suicide than are other young people.

Suicide is the intentional taking of one's own life. Some young people view suicide as a way to escape problems. Other young people view suicide as a way to gain attention. Others view suicide as a way to get even with those who have rejected them. However, suicide is a final choice. Suicide cannot be undone. Suicide is a permanent solution to temporary problems. Suicide does not solve problems--it creates additional problems. There is always a better choice. The following discussion focuses on suicide. You will learn why having suicidal tendencies is a risk factor for self-inflicted violence. You will learn why practicing suicide prevention strategies serves as a protective factor to prevent violence.

Facts: Suicide

Suicide is the third-ranked cause of death among people ages 15 to 24. Each year, thousands of young people attempt suicide. To prevent suicide, you should learn the facts about suicidal thoughts, suicide attempts, suicide completions, and parasuicide.

Thoughts. It is believed that at least once in their lives, some people have the thought "I would be better off dead." For most of these people, this remains just a brief passing thought. Unfortunately, too many young people dwell on thoughts of suicide. In one survey, more than one quarter of high school students reported that they had seriously considered suicide. One in 12 reported they had made a specific plan to commit suicide (Youth Risk Behavior Survey, 1991).

Attempts. Each year, almost one-half million young people attempt suicide. The majority of people who attempt suicide do not receive medical or mental health care (Smith and Crawford, 1986). Without medical or mental health care, the person who attempts suicide often continues life in the same pat-

52   Copyright © by Meeks Heit Publishing Company.

tern as before making the attempt. Suppose this person was depressed and/or used drugs, and continued this behavior after the attempt. (S)he has an extremely high risk for attempting suicide again.

Completions. Approximately 5,000 people ages 15 to 24 commit suicide each year (National Center for Health Statistics, 1993). The number is probably even higher because many suicides go unreported. Young people who have lost a friend or family member because of suicide also need help. They are more at risk for making a suicide attempt.

Parasuicide. **Parasuicide** is a suicide attempt in which a person does not intend to die. Parasuicide is usually a cry for help. People who make an attempt but do not want to die are in pain. They want others to know this. They may hope to bring about a change in other people's behavior. They may hope to bring to the attention of their family or friends that they have problems they cannot solve. A cry for help always should be taken seriously. People who make an attempt are at high risk for making another attempt unless help is received.

Having Suicidal Tendencies

Having suicidal tendencies is the greatest risk factor for self-inflicted violence. The following discussion helps you recognize suicidal tendencies. You will learn how to identify young people who are at risk for making a suicide attempt.

Young people who are at risk for suicide may have one or more of the following characteristics:
- Aggression
- Excessive perfectionism
- Hopelessness
- Low self-esteem
- Inadequate social skills
- Mental disorders
- Depression

Many young people who attempt suicide have recently had a difficult life experience such as a breakup of a relationship, an unwanted pregnancy, or failure at school. Young people also are more likely to attempt suicide if they:
- abuse alcohol or other drugs;
- have experienced the death of a parent, parental separation, or parental divorce;
- feel alienated from family and friends;
- are teased by or rejected by peers;
- have difficulty coping with bodily changes and sexuality.

Young people who are most vulnerable to attempting suicide are those who are treated poorly at home, desire to punish their family or friends, have difficulty in school, and/or have worries about their appearance and health. Young people who attempt suicide often are very depressed. **Depression** is a feeling of hopelessness, sadness, or helplessness. It is normal to experience depression for short periods. However, long periods of depression are not normal. Signs of severe depression include loss of interest in appearance, family, friends, and school. Other signs include loss of appetite and inability to concentrate. Young people who are depressed usually withdraw from others. They may be sad and cry frequently. They also may be irritable and hostile. There are at least five main causes of depression in young people: disappointment, a sense of hopelessness, loss of self-esteem, illness, and unfair comparisons.

Disappointment. When young people expect something that does not happen, someone lets them down, or they let someone else down, they may feel disappointed and depressed. For example, if parents expect high grades, a young person may be very disappointed with a failing grade.

A Sense Of Hopelessness. There are many changes during the teenage years. A teenager is not a child anymore, yet teenagers do not have the privileges that adults have. Teenagers sometimes feel trapped. They may be uncertain about the future. They may feel they have no control over their lives. A sense of hopelessness is a risk factor for suicide.

Loss Of Self-Esteem. Some young people expect too much of themselves. They are perfectionists and set unrealistic goals for themselves. Or, they feel that other people, such as their parents, have expectations for them that are too high. Because of the pressure they put on themselves, these young people have low self-esteem and are depressed.

Illness. Young people who have a long-term illness may become depressed. They may be unable to participate in activities that they enjoy. There may be limits on social activities. Since they do not feel well physically, they may not feel emotionally healthy either.

Unfair Comparisons. Young people often compare themselves to others--to people they see on television or in the movies and to people they see in magazines. They often feel that other people are smarter, more attractive, thinner, and more successful than they are. They feel they do not measure up to others. Comparing oneself to heroes, famous athletes, and movie stars is unfair.

Signs Of Suicide. Young people who are thinking about suicide often provide warning signs. By trying to warn others, young people are often crying out for help and hoping that someone will step in to help them. Young people who are thinking about suicide might do some of the following:

- make a direct statement about killing oneself, such as, "I don't want to live anymore;"
- make an indirect statement about killing oneself, such as, "I wonder where I can get a gun;"
- have a change in personality;
- withdraw from family and other people;
- lose interest in personal appearance;
- have a preoccupation with death and dying;
- make frequent complaints about physical symptoms that are related to emotions such as stomachaches or headaches;
- use alcohol and other drugs;
- lose interest in schoolwork;
- give away possessions;
- talk about getting even with others;
- fail to recover from a disappointment or loss;
- run away from home;
- have a close friend or relative who has committed suicide.

Figure 18
Suicide Prevention Strategies

1. Know Suicide Hotline Numbers
2. Know What To Do When You Feel Down
3. Build A Network Of Support
4. Get Involved In Rewarding Activities
5. Know What To Do If Someone Shows Warning Signs

Protective Factor #9

Practicing Suicide Prevention Strategies

Practicing suicide prevention strategies is a powerful protective factor. **Suicide prevention strategies** are techniques that can be used to help prevent a person from thinking about, attempting, and completing suicide (Figure 18). Some important suicide prevention strategies are examined in the following discussion. There also are recommendations on what to do if you suspect someone is considering suicide.

Know Suicide Hotline Numbers. Write down suicide hotline numbers and other crisis hotline numbers. Keep these numbers handy so you will them when needed. One national suicide hotline service is the National Youth Suicide Hotline. The toll-free phone number is 1-800-621-4000. This 24-hour hotline is available to all young people. The phones are staffed by trained volunteers who listen to problems and offer support and help. They provide information on resources, youth programs, and support groups available in the community.

Know What To Do When You Feel Down. When you feel depressed, decide on a plan of action. Try to determine what is bothering you. Make a list of your strengths and the positive aspects in your life and review your list. Make a list of what you can do to make yourself feel better; for example, planning an activity you enjoy. If you are angry, practice the anger management skills in Protective Factor #6. If you feel stressed, practice the stress management skills discussed in Protective Factor #7. Tell others that you are feeling down.

Build A Network Of Support. Develop a support network of caring people who will listen to you, offer advice, and help you during hard times. Share your fears, feelings, and disappointments. Your support network may include friends, family members, adult mentors, school counselors, clergy, and teachers.

Get Involved In Rewarding Activities. When you are involved in rewarding activities, you are more productive. You have something for which to live. If you are involved in activities you enjoy, you will be happier, have more self-esteem, and be better able to manage your stress. Playing a sport, learning a craft, or helping others through community service are examples of activities you might find rewarding. One warning sign of suicide is a lack of interest in activities. If you find yourself losing interest in activities you once enjoyed, make an effort to discover new activities in which you can become involved.

Know What To Do If Someone Shows Warning Signs. You can use the following suggestions if you suspect someone is suicidal.

1. Look for warning signs when someone is depressed.
2. Do not ignore any signs or take them lightly.
3. Ask a responsible adult such as a school counselor or teacher for help.
4. Let the person who shows warning signs know you care. Always show sincere concern and respect for this person's feelings.
5. Listen and try not to be shocked by what this person says.
6. Ask the person directly if (s)he is considering suicide. Many people are relieved because they want help. Others will deny suicidal thoughts at first.
7. Help the person think of better ways to solve problems.
8. Identify other supportive people with whom the person can talk.
9. Get professional help. Call a suicide hotline or school officials, the person's physician, clergy, or the police.
10. Do not leave the person alone. Stay with the person, at least until professionals take over.
11. Use a contract for life. A contract for life is a written agreement in which a suicidal person promises not to hurt himself/herself for a certain period of time and/or until the receives professional help.

Violence-Free Pledge

I will practice suicide prevention strategies.

I will recognize suicidal tendencies in others and get help for them.

Conflict resolution and peer mediation

Conflicts occur in many aspects of life. Conflicts occur within relationships--in the family, in the school, and in the community. Conflicts occur between strangers. Conflicts also may occur within you and be centered on different needs and values that you have. Strong emotions often accompany conflicts. These emotions might be helpful as they might motivate you to resolve a conflict in a nonviolent and responsible manner. At other times, these emotions might cloud judgment and you might want to resolve a conflict with violence. The following discussion focuses on types of conflict and conflict response styles. You will learn why being unable to resolve conflict and mediate with peers is a risk factor for violence. You also will learn why practicing conflict resolution skills and peer mediation serves as a protective factor to prevent violence.

Facts: Conflict

A **conflict** is a disagreement between two or more people or between two or more choices. Conflict usually involves one or more of the following:
- Availability of resources
- Fulfillment of psychological needs
- Upholding of personal values
- Maintaining self-preservation

Resources are available assets and may include time, money, and material possessions. Conflicts may occur when there are not enough available resources. **Psychological needs** are things that are needed to feel important and secure and may include friendship, belonging, accomplishments, and status. Conflicts may occur when something happens that may interfere with people getting what they need. **Values** are the beliefs, goals, and standards held by people. Conflicts may occur when decisions must be made and people have different standards and beliefs. **Self-preservation** is the inner desire to keep oneself and others safe from harm and may include preserving physical, mental, and social health. Conflicts may occur when people harm or threaten to harm others.

When asked, young people identified the following as sources of conflict (McClure, Miller, and Russo, 1992):
- learning that someone had said something negative behind their back;
- having someone cut in front of them in a line while waiting to take a turn;
- being teased;
- being called a name or being sworn at;
- wanting the same item at the same time as somebody else;
- disagreeing with another person;
- being with someone who did not follow the rules;
- being blamed for something that they did not do;
- having something stolen from them;
- being ignored by someone;

- being threatened by someone;
- being bossed around by someone;
- having someone else take credit for something they did;
- being punched, kicked, or hit;
- being denied a fair chance to participate in a game or other activity.

Types of Conflict. There are four different types of conflict.

1. An **intrapersonal conflict** is a conflict that occurs within a person. For example, you may have an intrapersonal conflict involving the amount of a resource you have--time. Your conflict also might involve your needs and values. You experience this intrapersonal conflict when you hear internal voices that disagree. You may say to yourself, "I would like to be accepted and go with my friends to the movies." You also may say, "I should do my homework to meet my goal of getting good grades." You are experiencing intrapersonal conflict.

2. An **interpersonal conflict** is a conflict that occurs between two or more people. Suppose you arrive at the movie theater at nearly the same time as another person. Each of you believes you were first and wants to purchase a ticket first. You and the other person begin to argue. You and the other person are involved in an interpersonal conflict.

3. An **intragroup conflict** is a conflict that occurs between people that identify themselves as belonging to the same group. Suppose your family is planning to take a trip during vacation. Some family members want to go camping while the other family members want to go to the beach. You and other family members are involved in intragroup conflict.

4. An **intergroup conflict** is a conflict that occurs between two or more groups of people. The conflict may involve different neighborhoods, schools, gangs, racial groups, religious groups, and/or nations. For example, you may be on an athletic team. Your team is playing another school. A player who is a member of the team at your school bumps into a player who is a member of the other team. The team members at the other school believe the action of the player at your school was intended to harm their team member. Members of both teams begin to argue. Players from your school and players from the other school are involved in intergroup conflict.

Examining Conflict Response Styles. It is unlikely that you will journey through life without experiencing conflict. Since you cannot always control the sources of conflict identified, the most important focus should be on how to respond to conflict in a healthful and responsible way. A **conflict response style** is a pattern of behavior a person demonstrates when conflict arises. There are three conflict response styles. Figure 19 includes information to help you understand each of the conflict response styles.

Figure 19
Conflict Response Styles

Conflict Avoidance
A person denies that there is a conflict and/or attempts to please others at his/her expense.

Conflict Confrontation
A person attempts to settle a disagreement in a hostile, defiant, and aggressive way.

Conflict Resolution
A person uses conflict resolution skills to resolve a disagreement in a healthful, safe, legal, respectful, and nonviolent way.

Conflict avoidance is a conflict response style in which a person denies that there is a conflict and/or attempts to please others at his/her expense. A person may bury his/her head in the sand to avoid acknowledging that conflict exists. A person may allow those people with whom (s)he is in conflict to solve a conflict in a manner of their choosing.

There are several reasons why a person might choose conflict avoidance as a conflict response style. Usually conflict avoidance is learned from a person's family during childhood. A child observes the conflict response styles of the significant adults within the family. Perhaps one or more of the significant adults does not want conflict or disagreement to occur. Disagreements are avoided at any cost. The child learns the message, "It is not all right to disagree." The child does not want to admit there is a problem. The child may even deny there is a problem. Denial often occurs in homes where there is substance abuse and in which one or more adults denies the abuse.

There is another reason some people respond to conflict with conflict avoidance. Perhaps when a person was a child, there was violence in the home. When disagreements occurred, one or more of the significant adults became out of control, abusive, and threatening to the health and safety of others. As a result, the child came to the following conclusion, "If I avoid disagreements, I will be safer." Even though something might be gained by resolving the conflict, the young person avoids the conflict rather than risking the danger of explosive behavior.

Another way people learn conflict avoidance is by listening to family messages that relate to being loved and lovable. In some families, significant adults send the following message, "If you agree with me and do exactly what I tell you to do, you are lovable and I will love you." Agreement is met with verbal and, most important, nonverbal approval. However, disagreement is met with disapproval and withholding of support and love. The messages are, "If I want to be loved, have friends, and succeed in relationships, I cannot disagree," and "The way to be loved and lovable is to allow others to have their way even if they do things that I do not want them to do."

Conflict confrontation is a conflict response style in which a person attempts to settle a disagreement in a hostile, defiant, and aggressive way. If people adopt conflict confrontation as their primary conflict response style, they usually view conflict as a win-lose proposition. When conflict occurs, they will choose a position and disagree with the opposition. A confronter wants to win or be right at all costs. The conflict often increases because the confronter refuses to consider any other side to the issue.

People who use conflict confrontation as a conflict response style have usually observed this pattern of behavior from significant adults in their family. As children, they may have observed at least one significant adult approach most conflict situations with a win-lose attitude. This adult conveyed the message that (s)he was always right. Any disagreement was met with verbal and/or physical retaliation. If, as children, they observed two adults using this conflict response style, they most likely observed a great deal of hostility and fighting. They viewed relationships as being hostile and argumentative. In some families, children experienced one significant adult who was confrontational in family interactions. This adult bullied others within and outside the family. These children might have felt very

intimidated and insecure. When they become adults, these people become confrontational within other relationships to resist being dominated by others.

Conflict resolution is a conflict response style in which a person uses conflict resolution skills to resolve a disagreement in a healthful, safe, legal, respectful, and nonviolent way. **Conflict resolution skills** are skills a person can use to resolve a disagreement in a healthful, safe, legal, respectful, and nonviolent way. If you adopt conflict resolution as your conflict response style, you view conflict as a natural part of life. You are able to be rational and think clearly. You see the potential for win-win in situations and relationships in which conflict arises.

People who use conflict resolution as a conflict response style have usually observed this pattern of behavior from significant adults in their families. As children, they observed significant adults who respected the rights and needs of others and who attempted to work through disagreements in healthful and responsible ways. These adults were less concerned about winning than resolving a situation and allowing all people involved to keep their dignity and maintain integrity. These adults did not avoid conflicts but viewed conflict as necessary and important. Children reared in these situations gained self-confidence as they learned to resolve disagreements with others. They gained the sense of intimacy that is obtained from working through problems to the benefit of all people involved.

You will want to practice conflict resolution. When you are skilled at conflict resolution, you are likely to have healthful interpersonal relationships. You are less likely to be a perpetrator and victim of violence than people who use conflict avoidance or conflict confrontation. If you are not skilled in conflict resolution you might:

* keep a journal about the conflicts you are experiencing
* examine your patterns of behavior
* review how you learned these patterns of behavior
* seek help learning and practicing conflict resolution-skills.

Resolving Conflict in Harmful Ways

There are at least three serious threats that result from being unable to use conflict resolution skills and peer mediation:

- People experience threats to their physical health status.
- People are less likely to have inspiriting relationships.
- People are more likely to become victims and/or perpetrators of violence.

Threats To Physical Health Status. People who practice conflict avoidance and conflict confrontation may compromise health status. In conflict avoidance, people deny that there is conflict or please others at their own expense. In some cases, the conflict does not continue and people are glad they avoided dealing with it. However, this often is not the case, and the people who avoid conflict on the outside are in a constant state of inner conflict. As they continue to bury their feelings, they develop hidden anger. **Hidden anger** is anger that is not recognized or is expressed in a harmful way. On the outside, the person may appear as if nothing is wrong but on the inside (s)he may be very angry and hostile. **Hostility** is a feeling of ill will and antagonism.

In conflict confrontation, people attempt to settle disagreements in defiant, hostile, and aggressive ways. These people show outward signs of hostility and aggression. People who demonstrate conflict avoidance have inward hostility and are often passive-aggressive. People who are **passive-aggressive** appear cooperative and pleasant while inside they feel very angry and hostile.

It is important to examine what is currently known about hostility and health. In their national bestseller, _Anger Kills_, Redford and Virginia Williams describe the Hostility Syndrome (Williams and Williams, 1994). The **Hostility Syndrome** is a group of characteristics that result from stronger responses of the sympathetic nervous system and weaker responses of the parasympathetic nervous system and immune system. The

sympathetic nervous system is the part of the nervous system that prepares the body for emergencies. The **parasympathetic nervous system** is the part of the nervous system that maintains the body's normal state and restores balance after an emergency. The **immune system** is the body system that fights disease. The Hostility Syndrome places people at higher risk of developing severe, life-threatening illnesses.

When people demonstrate the Hostility Syndrome, their bodies are in a constant state of emergency. Unfortunately, the body does not easily return to balance. The immune system is not as able to fight disease. Often these people have lowered brain serotonin levels. **Serotonin** is a naturally occurring chemical found in the brain, blood, and other parts of the body, that helps regulate primitive drives and emotions. These primitive drives and emotions include sex, mood, appetite, sleep, arousal, pain, aggression, and suicidal tendencies. It is interesting to note that people who demonstrate the Hostility Syndrome are more likely to engage in behavior that is harmful in the first place: smoking, overeating, and increased drinking. The lowered brain serotonin levels further compromise health status. These people become more aggressive; enjoy pleasurable effects from nicotine, food, and alcohol; and may increase smoking, eating, and drinking.

Recall that people who are hostile have strong responses from the sympathetic nervous system and weak responses from the parasympathetic nervous system. The sympathetic nervous system is responsible for beginning the flight-or-fight response. It prepares the body for emergency by sending signals from the brain to the adrenal glands to increase the secretions of adrenaline and cortisol. The body responds with an increase of blood flow to the muscles and a decrease of blood flow to the internal organs such as the stomach. Heart and respiration rates increase. These changes are important during an emergency such as when a person needs to run from danger. However, people who have the Hostility Syndrome have these changes in their bodies because they feel hostile, not because of a real emergency.

People are more likely to have heart diseases and respiratory diseases. They are more likely to have headaches, stomachaches, restlessness, sleeplessness, and irritability. When the immune system does not work as it should, people are more likely to develop certain kinds of cancers.

Lack Of Inspiriting Relationships. **Inspiriting relationships** are relationships that lift the spirit and contribute to a sense of well-being. **Dispiriting relationships** are relationships that are characterized by a state of low spirits. People who practice conflict avoidance and conflict confrontation are more likely to experience dispiriting relationships. When practicing conflict avoidance, people usually are dishonest with others. They do not share their true feelings about what is happening. There are at least two reasons that this behavior prevents close relationships. First, the other people are unable to respond to the needs and feelings of people because the needs and feelings are not known. This prevents closeness from developing. Second, the people who practice conflict avoidance often harbor resentment. Although they accommodate other people through outward behavior, inside they wish their relationships were otherwise.

Relationships also are hampered when people practice conflict confrontation. People engaging in relationships with confronters lack the safety that is needed to develop closeness. It is difficult to have psychological safety when people are hostile and aggressive. Instead, the people feel uneasy and lack the comfort that intimacy might otherwise provide.

Increased Likelihood Of Becoming A Perpetrator Or Victim Of Violence. Both conflict avoidance and conflict confrontation are associated with increased risks of violence. As mentioned previously, people who demonstrate conflict avoidance often experience inner hostility and hidden anger. They are often passive-aggressive. This means that much of the time they behave in a passive and pleasing way yet they continue to be irritated, annoyed, and furious on the inside. The newspaper is full of stories of people who were believed to be very passive and pleasant and suddenly reached a boiling point and were violent.

Conflict avoiders also might become victims. Because they are pleasers and attempt to keep the peace, they may not stand up for themselves. They are the people who are described as having kept the family secrets such as rape, incest, and abuse of alcohol and other drugs. Because of this pleasing and secretive behavior, they are more likely to be victims of the harmful actions of others.

It is more obvious why people who demonstrate conflict confrontation are more likely to be perpetrators

and victims of violence. Their defiant, hostile, and aggressive behavior may cause others to be angry and respond. When their controlling, hostile, and antagonistic behavior is challenged by others, they are more likely to act out and to harm others.

There is evidence that patterns of dysfunctional conflict resolution spread from parent to child, spouse to spouse, and sibling to sibling. Parents who are perpetrators of child abuse often were abused themselves as children. Spouse abusers tend to have been reared in families with spouse-abusing parents. Families experiencing spouse abuse are likely to have occurrences of child abuse. A history of having experienced abuse/and or neglect as a child is associated with later delinquent and criminal behavior (Morton and Ewald, 1987).

Young people lacking conflict resolution and peer mediation skills often rely upon coercion in managing interpersonal relationships. **Coercion** is the use of force to influence another person. People who have been treated in a forceful manner have a strong tendency to treat others in the same way. This process for dealing with problems has been linked with delinquency, violence, and other problems (Patterson, 1982).

Protective Factor #10

Practicing Conflict Resolution and Peer Mediation Skills

Fortunately, people can change their way of responding to conflict and learn conflict resolution and peer mediation skills. To repeat the definition, **conflict resolution skills** are skills people can use to resolve disagreements in healthful, safe, legal, respectful, and nonviolent ways (Figure 20). A guiding principle of conflict resolution is the concept of win-win. It is important to appreciate that many conflicts can be settled with those involved feeling they have won (win-win). Rather than spending time and energy bickering and fighting over positions, participants in a conflict can focus instead on finding creative ways to resolve their problems (Roderick, 1987, 1988). It is important to recognize that there does not have to be a loser in every conflict.

1. Remain Calm. Whenever a conflict arises, regardless of whether it is within a person or between a person and others, it is important to remain calm. Ralph Waldo Emerson, a nineteenth-century American philosopher, once said, "We boil at different degrees." Make a personal assessment of your boiling point. Try to increase your patience. For some people, counting to ten is helpful. For others, a few deep breaths may help. Still others need a timeout before trying to resolve a conflict. An important rule to follow is: Do not begin to resolve a conflict if your temperature is boiling. Calm down first.

2. Set The Tone. When conflict arises between you and another person, each of you will naturally want to meet your own needs. It may be difficult for you to convince the other person that you want to play fair and find a mutually acceptable solution if good communication skills are not practiced. The following tips help to set the tone for positive communication: avoid blaming, avoid interrupting, affirm others, be sincere, avoid putdowns, reserve judgment, avoid threats, separate the person from the problem, help others save face, use positive nonverbal messages.

3. Define The Conflict. After calming down and setting the tone, the first step in resolving conflict is to define the conflict. You might define the conflict by describing it in writing. The best way is to use as few sentences as possible. The description should be short and to the point. If the conflict is between you and another person(s), each of you should describe the conflict clearly and briefly. In describing the conflict, it is important to continue following the rules for setting the tone. The focus should be on the conflict and not on the people involved. For example, suppose you and another person arrive at nearly the same time to purchase tickets for a rock concert and each of you believes you were first. You may describe the conflict as, "I think I arrived first and should be able to buy my tickets first," rather than "You cut in line." The second message blames the other person and also is a putdown. The first message helps the other person save face.

4. Take Responsibility For Personal Actions. It is always important for a person to take account of personal actions that may have led to the conflict. For example, in the situation described, if you shoved the other person out of line, you should take responsibility for this action. Even if you believed you were first, this behavior is not appropriate. Harming another person is not appropriate behavior unless this behavior occurs as a result of defending yourself or others from personal harm and injury. Even in this case, good judgment must be used. It is important to take responsibility for personal actions, to recognize what one has done, and to apologize when you are wrong.

Figure 20
Conflict Resolution Skills

Conflict resolution skills are skills a person can use to resolve a disagreement in a healthful, safe, legal, respectful, and nonviolent way.

1. Remain Calm.
2. Set The Tone.
   - Avoid blaming.
   - Avoid interrupting.
   - Affirm others.
   - Be sincere.
   - Avoid putdowns.
   - Reserve judgment.
   - Avoid threats.
   - Separate the person from the problem.
   - Help others save face.
   - Use positive nonverbal messages.
3. Define The Conflict.
4. Take Responsibility For Personal Actions.
5. Use I-Messages To Express Needs And Feelings.
6. Listen To The Needs And Feelings Of Others.
7. List And Discuss Possible Solutions.
   - Will the solution result in actions that are healthful?
   - Will the solution result in actions that are safe?
   - Will the solution result in actions that are legal?
   - Will the solutions result in actions that are respectful of all involved people?
   - Will the solution result in actions that are nonviolent?
8. Agree On A Solution.
9. Keep Your Word And Follow The Agreement.
10. Ask For The Assistance Of A Trusted Adult Or Obtain Peer Mediation If The Conflict Cannot Be Resolved.

61

5. Use I-Messages To Express Needs And Feelings.
The needs and feelings of the people involved in a conflict are important in finding a successful resolution. An **I-message** is a statement that contains (1) a specific behavior or event, (2) the effect that the behavior or event has on the individual, and (3) the feeling that resulted. An I-message is a statement that refers to the individual, the individual's feelings, and the individual's needs. A win-win solution usually recognizes the feelings and needs of people involved. For example, if a person calls you a derogatory name, most likely you will be angry and hurt. It is important for you to express the anger and hurt you experience, "When you called me...(behavior), I felt put down (effect,) and I am very angry (feeling)." When you express feelings rather than calling the person a name, it is easier to work out the problem.

6. Listen To The Needs And Feelings Of Others.
To resolve a conflict in a peaceful manner, it is important to listen. This means taking the time to allow other people to share their needs and feelings. Again, certain principles need to be followed: no interrupting or judging. Listening to people shows that you sincerely want to resolve a conflict in a manner that will be win-win if possible. Usually when people feel that they have the opportunity to clearly express themselves and are being taken seriously, they are more open to different ways to solve a conflict.

7. List And Evaluate Possible Solutions.
This step involves brainstorming as many solutions as possible for the conflict. Identify all possible solutions before discussing each. When discussing each solution, predict the outcome. How will each solution affect you and the other people involved? Will the solution be viewed as win-win by both? Will the solution result in actions that are healthful, safe, legal, show respect for all involved, and be nonviolent?

8. Agree On A Solution.
After each solution is evaluated, the people involved should agree on the solution. To avoid future conflicts, restate or summarize what each of you will do to honor the agreement reached. Sometimes it is helpful to put the agreement in writing so that the agreement might be reviewed at a later time.

9. Keep Your Word And Follow The Agreement.
You should always intend to do what you say you will do. Sometimes, people need help keeping their word and following the agreement that has been reached. If this is the case, people need to share the difficulty that they will have and examine ways they can be helped. Good faith is very important in conflict resolution.

10. Ask For The Assistance Of A Trusted Adult Or Obtain Peer Mediation If The Conflict Cannot Be Resolved.
When you cannot resolve interpersonal conflict, you might talk with a trusted adult or seek professional help. When conflict between you and other people cannot be resolved, it is wise to ask for the assistance of a trusted adult or to obtain peer mediation. A discussion of peer mediation is included.

Young people gain many benefits from learning and practicing conflict resolution skills. These benefits include:

- developing greater awareness and tolerance for people who are different;
- developing empathy for the feelings of others;
- respecting the rights of others as well as personal rights;
- developing a sense of responsibility for personal actions;
- taking positive action to resolve conflicts;
- stating complaints in ways that leave open the possibility of a peaceful settlement;
- protecting the dignity of those involved in a conflict;
- focusing on conflicts to be resolved rather than on people.

When people are unable to resolve disputes using conflict resolution skills, peer mediation can be helpful. A **peer** is a person who is similar in age or status. To **mediate** is to bring people who are in conflict together. **Peer mediation** is a process used to resolve conflicts, in which a person helps peers resolve disagreements in healthful, safe, legal, respectful, and nonviolent ways. A **peer mediator** is a person who assists the people who have a conflict in reaching a solution. There may be more than one mediator involved in peer mediation. Your school may have a peer mediation program in which you might get involved. Or, you may be involved in a peer mediation program in the future. The process of peer mediation involves several steps (Figure 21). Each of these steps is examined in the following discussion.

1. The Peer Mediator Introduces Himself/Herself And Explains That (S)he Will Maintain A Neutral Position.
The role of the peer mediator is to bring the people in conflict together. This means arranging a meeting place that is agreeable and neutral. The peer

Figure 21
The Process of Peer Mediation

Peer mediation is a process used to resolve conflicts, in which a person helps peers resolve disagreements in healthful, safe, legal, respectful, and nonviolent ways. A peer mediator assists the people having a conflict in reaching a resolution.

1. The peer mediator introduces himself/herself and explains that (s)he will maintain a neutral position.
2. The peer mediator establishes ground rules and the peers in conflict agree to follow them.
   - Tell the truth.
   - Commit to resolving the conflict.
   - Avoid blaming.
   - Avoid putdowns.
   - Avoid threats.
   - Avoid sneering, pushing, and hitting.
   - Reserve judgment.
   - Listen without interrupting.
3. Each of the people in disagreement clearly defines the conflict.
4. Each of the people in conflict expresses his/her needs and feelings about the conflict.
5. Each of the people in conflict identifies possible ways to resolve the conflict.
6. The peer mediator offers additional ways to resolve the conflict.
7. Each of the suggested solutions is evaluated.
   - Will the solution result in actions that are healthful?
   - Will the solution result in actions that are safe?
   - Will the solution result in actions that are legal?
   - Will the solution result in actions that are respectful of all people involved?
   - Will the solution result in actions that are nonviolent?
8. The people in conflict attempt to resolve the conflict by agreeing to a solution. If this is not possible, the peer mediator negotiates an agreement.
9. An agreement is written and signed by all people.
10. A follow-up meeting is set to discuss the results of following the agreement.

mediator needs to explain that it is the responsibility of the people involved to resolve their disagreement. The mediator has no authority over the people involved.

2. The Peer Mediator Establishes Ground Rules And The Peers In Conflict Agree To Follow Them. This is perhaps one of the most important aspects of peer mediation. Often, the people in disagreement express hostility and suspicion for each another. The use of humor by the peer mediator may help to relieve tension. When those involved follow ground rules, they are more likely to focus on the conflict than upon their feelings toward one another. Appropriate ground rules include: tell the truth, commit to resolve the conflict, avoid blaming, avoid putdowns, avoid threats, avoid sneering, avoid pushing, avoid hitting, reserve judgment, and listen without interruption.

3. Each Of The People In Disagreement Clearly Defines The Conflict. The people involved need to begin by identifying and describing the conflict. This needs to take place before solutions can be identified. The peer mediator uses his/her skills to focus the discussion on the conflict. (S)he might use clarifying questions or summarize what has been said to be certain that the conflict is clearly defined and that people involved are focusing on the same issue.

4. Each Of The People In Conflict Expresses His/Her Needs And Feelings About The Conflict. The people involved need to share what they believe led to the conflict. They need to share their current feelings using I-messages and avoiding blaming, putdowns, and threats. Constructing an I-message is described in Figure 10. They need to express how their needs might be met.

5. Each Of The People In Conflict Identifies Possible Ways To Resolve The Conflict. The peer mediator assists with brainstorming. It is helpful to make a list in writing of the possible solutions. At this stage, it is best to avoid evaluating each possible solution. The purpose of the brainstorming is to identify as many solutions as possible, and evaluation may cut off some of the solutions that people might mention.

6. The Peer Mediator Offers Additional Ways To Resolve The Conflict. The peer mediator may identify solutions that the people involved have not identified. These solutions can be added to the list. Again, at this point, the solutions should not be evaluated.

7. Each Of The Suggested Solutions Is Evaluated.
When evaluating each solution, it is important to use the same criteria. The peer mediator assists by identifying the criteria to be used:
- Will the solution result in actions that are healthful?
- Will the solution result in actions that are safe?
- Will the solution result in actions that are legal?
- Will the solutions result in actions that are respectful of all people involved?
- Will the solution result in actions that are nonviolent?

If criteria are not established, the people involved might view a solution as acceptable when it is not. For example, two opposing gangs might decide that participating in gang warfare is an appropriate way to solve a disagreement over who should occupy specific turf. When the criteria identified are used to evaluate this option, it is clear that this option leads to actions that are not appropriate.

8. The People In Conflict Attempt To Resolve The Conflict By Agreeing To A Solution. If This Is Not Possible, The Peer Mediator Negotiates An Agreement. At this stage, the peer mediator may meet separately with the people involved and brainstorm further ideas. During these meetings, the peer mediator may suggest making tradeoffs in order for all people involved to experience a compromise that is viewed as win-win. Sometimes the peer mediator recommends a combination of meetings. In some, all people meet together; and in others, only one side meets with the peer mediator at a time. This step of peer mediation may take time and it is particularly important for the peer mediator to remind the people involved about their commitments to the mediation process.

9. An Agreement Is Written And Signed By All People. The people involved should enter into the agreement in an entirely voluntary manner. After they agree to do so, a written agreement should be designed. This agreement specifically states what those involved will do. Time should be allotted for those involved to review the written document and to ask questions. The people involved and the peer mediator should then sign and date the document. The people involved and the peer mediator should keep a personal copy of the agreement. The agreement can be used as a reference point should questions or further conflicts arise.

10. A Follow-up Meeting Is Set To Discuss The Results Of Following The Agreement. The peer mediator will encourage the people involved to set a date for a follow-up meeting. The people involved might mutually decide upon the desired length of time that might pass before this meeting. They might even determine an agenda for this meeting. The purpose might be to review how well the agreement is working. If the agreement is not working, the process of peer mediation might begin again.

One example of a model peer mediation program is the Conflict Manager Program developed and implemented by the Community Board of San Francisco. Selected students serve as "conflict managers" by helping fellow students resolve disputes. Selected students work in teams of two as facilitators, listening to each side of a conflict and helping those who disagree listen to each other and work toward a resolution. Conflict managers receive intensive training in communication, conciliation, critical thinking, and leadership skills.

Schools instituting peer mediation programs similar to the Conflict Manager Program report fewer fights, reduced tensions, and less need for adult involvement in disciplinary matters. Students who serve as peer mediators develop leadership skills, increase their self-esteem, and learn new ways to resolve conflict nonviolently.

Violence-Free Pledge

I will take a time-out if I am in a conflict where tempers are rising.

I will change my behavior if I practice conflict avoidance as my usual conflict response style.

I will change my behavior if I practice conflict confrontation as my usual conflict response style.

I will practice conflict resolution skills.

I will practice peer mediation when I am unable to resolve conflict.

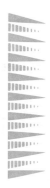

Protective Factor #11

Avoiding Discriminatory Behavior

We live in a society in which there are many different people. People differ in age, gender, racial and ethnic heritage, socioeconomic class, and sexual orientation. Yet all people are alike in some ways. All people want the respect of others. All people want to be treated fairly. Unfortunately, some people single out certain people or groups of people and treat these people in unfair and disrespectful ways. They may tell jokes about them. They may make up lies about them. They may stereotype them in unfair ways or harass them. They may single them out and harm them. These ways of treating others are considered discriminatory behavior.

Discriminatory behavior is making distinctions in treatment or showing behavior in favor of or prejudiced against an individual or group of people. **Prejudice** is suspicion, intolerance, or irrational hatred directed at an individual or group of people. Discriminatory behavior and prejudice divide people. Those who are the targets of discriminatory behavior and prejudice are angry because they are treated unfairly. Discriminatory behavior and prejudice often result in violence. The following discussion examines discrimination. You will learn why engaging in discriminatory behavior is a risk factor for violence. You also will learn why avoiding discriminatory behavior is a protective factor to prevent violence.

Facts: Discriminatory Behavior

Behavior that discriminates against others is learned. People are not born prejudiced; they learn to be prejudiced. Training in how to treat and respect other people begins early in life. Very young children observe how the adults in their lives treat people who are different. Suppose a young person witnesses a father treating the mother with disrespect. The message that is learned may be: females do not deserve to be treated with respect. Suppose a young person hears significant adults tell jokes or make snide remarks about a specific racial group. The message that is learned may be: this racial group is inferior, and joking about this group is funny. Suppose a young person hears significant adults in the family make unkind remarks about people of a different sexual orientation. The message that is learned may be: my parents won't care if I harm people of a different sexual orientation. Unfortunately, young people who have these experiences may not recognize that these ways of thinking and behaving are wrong. They may begin to think this way. They may copy this behavior.

Copyright © by Meeks Heit Publishing Company.

65

To avoid discriminatory behavior, it is helpful to examine "isms." An **ism** refers to beliefs, attitudes, assumptions, and actions that subject individuals or people in a particular group to discriminatory behavior. Common "isms" include ageism, sexism, racism, and heterosexism. **Ageism** refers to behavior that discriminates against people in a specific age group. **Sexism** refers to behavior that discriminates against people of the opposite sex. **Racism** refers to behavior that discriminates against members of certain racial or ethnic groups. **Heterosexism** refers to behavior that discriminates against people who are gay, lesbian, or bisexual.

Anything that sets one group apart from another can cause people to discriminate against others and to be prejudiced. People of color, women, people with disabilities, people who are overweight, people who are Jewish, people with HIV/AIDS, and people who are homosexual have experienced discrimination. People of different racial and ethnic groups such as those who are Iranian, Hispanic, Cambodian, Korean, African-American, Vietnamese, Asian-American, and Native American have experienced discrimination. Because some people practice this behavior, laws have been passed to guarantee all people the same rights, regardless of their differences. However, laws are not enough. Individuals must willingly treat others fairly and with respect.

Risk Factor #11

Practicing Discriminatory Behavior

Ageism, sexism, racism, heterosexism and other forms of discrimination harm relationships between people. When these types of behavior are practiced, individuals or groups of individuals act in ways that show they believe they are superior to others. As a result, those who are the target of discriminatory behavior recognize that others believe them to be inferior. Being continually abused, patronized, or left out harms self-esteem. People who are continually treated in these ways may begin to believe they are inferior. This is very damaging. Having negative self-esteem and feeling unworthy is one of the risk factors for violence. People who have negative self-esteem are more likely

to be victims because they may begin to believe they do not deserve the respect of others.

People who are prejudiced and who practice discriminatory behavior are at risk for being both perpetrators and victims of violence. They may be perpetrators and commit hate crimes. **Hate crimes** are crimes motivated by religious, racial, ethnic, sexual orientation, or other bias. Hate crimes are sometimes called bias crimes. Hate crimes have included violent attacks, intimidation, arson, and other property damage. It is difficult to count the number of hate crimes because it is not always possible to determine what caused a perpetrator to commit a crime. However, it is known that the number of hate crimes rose throughout the 1980s. At least 30 states responded by passing laws that add extra penalties for crimes committed out of racial or other prejudice.

One example of a hate crime is gay-bashing. **Gay-bashing** is a physical assault on people who are homosexual that is motivated by prejudice. The National Gay and Lesbian Task Force reported an increase in gay-bashing in recent years. Some of the factors that appear to have contributed to the rise in gay-bashing are (Cotton, 1992):

- failure of the courts and society to give a clear message that this type of violence is wrong and will not be tolerated;
- lack of official condemnation by the media, churches, schools, and courts;
- belief of perpetrators that this behavior reinforces their masculinity;
- peer pressure to behave in this way, especially when the pressure involves a group of young males;
- people of homosexual orientation gathering in an area that is known, making it easier for perpetrators to act as a group and assault them;

Gay bashing is discriminatory behavior that is hurtful to young people who are homosexual.

A survey was taken of young people ages 14 to 21 who are homosexual and who sought services from a community-based agency. More than 40 percent stated they had been physically attacked because of their sexual orientation. After being victims of these attacks, they had lower self-esteem. They were more likely to be truant from school and to have thought about making a suicide attempt (Hunter, 1992).

People who experience discrimination and prejudice are likely to become angry. At first, they may experience hidden anger. **Hidden anger** is anger that is not recognized or is expressed in a harmful way and may result in inappropriate behavior and poor health. But, eventually their anger will not be contained. This anger may be directed at self. The suicide rate is higher in people who have experienced discrimination. The anger may be directed at others. An individual or group may decide to fight back or demonstrate to others what it is like to be harmed. In this situation, people who have experienced discrimination become perpetrators. Unfortunately, the confrontations that occur often result in serious injury and death to those involved.

Protective Factor #11

Avoiding Discriminatory Behavior

It is important to show respect for all people. When you show respect for others, you increase the likelihood that others will be at their best and contribute to society. You increase the likelihood that all people will be able to live together, will be productive, and will behave in nonviolent ways. To avoid discriminatory

---

Figure 22
Ways To Avoid Discriminatory Behavior

In his famous speech, Martin Luther King said, "I have a dream...my four little children will one day live in a nation where they will not be judged by the color of their skin but by the content of their character." Unfortunately, our society is still not living this dream. Change begins with the individual. Your efforts are very important in stopping discriminatory behavior. You can:

1. Challenge Stereotypes
2. Create Synergy Through Diversity
3. Show Empathy For All People
4. Avoid Discriminatory Comments
5. Ask Others To Stop Discriminatory Behavior
6. Learn About People Who Are Different

---

behavior, you must recognize this behavior and challenge others who choose to behave in these ways (Figure 22).

Challenge Stereotypes. A **stereotype** is a prejudiced attitude that assigns a specific quality or characteristic to all people who belong to a particular group. Stereotypes imply that an individual is the same as every other member in the group with which (s)he is identified. It is unfair to make generalizations about people based upon stereotypes. People who belong to a specific racial, religious, ethnic, or gender group do share something in common. They have their race, religion, ethnicity, or gender in common. However, they are different in other ways. Suppose you have had an unfortunate experience with an individual who belongs to a specific racial, religious, ethnic, or gender group. You must avoid believing that other people belonging to the same group are exactly the same. Then you will not treat anyone unfairly. Fair treatment of others promotes nonviolence.

Create Synergy Through Diversity. Suppose you were making chocolate chip cookies. You would mix together several ingredients before baking the cookies. Some of the individual ingredients, such as the chocolate chips, would be tasty by themselves. But, blending the ingredients would be even better. You might look at society in the same way. Most likely, you enjoy, appreciate, and respect others who are like you. But, when you enjoy, appreciate, and respect all people in your environment, you experience synergy. **Synergy** is a positive outcome that occurs when different people cooperate and respect one another and, as a result, more energy is created for all. **Diversity** is the quality of being different or varied. When there is synergy, people with different backgrounds, talents, and skills work together to produce better solutions than would be possible if everyone were exactly alike. When there is synergy, others are valued and respected, and both the strengths and weaknesses of individuals are accepted (Newell, 1992). Synergy promotes nonviolence.

Show Empathy For All People. **Empathy** is the ability to share in another's emotions or feelings. When you have empathy for another individual, you not only understand what this individual is feeling but also you express your understanding when possible. You might express this understanding with words or actions. For example, you learned that some people live in an adverse environment. Their lives may be difficult because of overcrowding or poverty. Their lives may be difficult because they have been abused. Having empathy for these people includes caring about the conditions in which they live. You might help them to better their lives when possible. You might help those who have been abused to get help toward recovery. Empathy for people who have been victims of violence is particularly important. Recognizing the hurt and pain that result from violence helps you to know that it is best to behave in nonviolent ways.

Avoid Discriminatory Comments. You have probably heard the saying, "Sticks and stones will break my bones, but words can never hurt me." There is little truth to this statement. Although sticks and stones may break bones, words may break the heart and spirit. Words often cause emotional wounds that are more difficult to heal than physical wounds. For this reason, always think before you speak. Avoid making jokes or snide remarks about other people. Avoid laughing or affirming others when they make jokes or snide remarks about other people. There is a saying, "Much truth is said in jest." Remember, the more often you say something negative about others, the more likely you are to believe what you have said. If you make a commitment to say kind and respectful comments about others or nothing at all, you promote nonviolence.

Ask Others To Stop Discriminatory Behavior. One way to support discriminatory behavior is to say or do nothing when people around you behave in a discriminatory way. When you allow others to behave in this way, they have your passive approval. Remember, it is best for you to be an active participant in creating synergy. You can and should share with others your feelings about discriminatory behavior. When someone makes a snide remark or tells a joke about an individual belonging to a specific group, share your disapproval. Do not laugh or go along with the behavior. You can make your feelings known without sounding self-righteous. You might tell the individual making the remarks or telling the joke that you know (s)he meant no harm, but that this behavior is hurtful to people belonging to that specific group. In this way, you are educating others. You will help them to behave in ways that promote nonviolence and respect for others.

Learn About People Who Are Different. As you learn more about others, you appreciate the talents they have to offer. You are more likely to develop empathy for the pain they may feel. You are better able to see how people who are different might live and work together. There are many ways in which you can learn about people who are different. You might study a foreign language in school. You might read about other races or cultures in the library. Get to know a student in your school or community who is different from you. This will help you see others as valuable. You will want others who are valued to be protected and safe.

Violence-Free Pledge

I will avoid discriminatory behavior.

I will ask others to stop discriminatory behavior.

I will show empathy for all people.

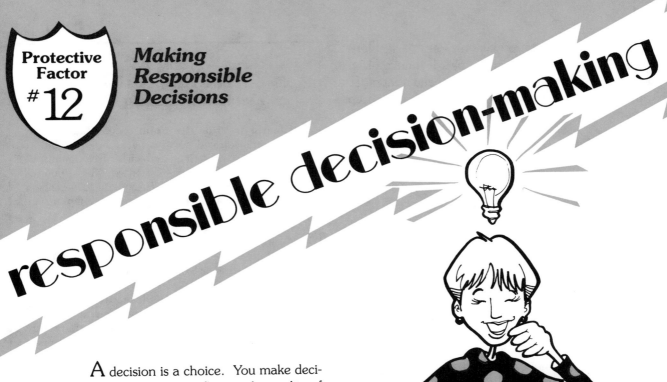

responsible decision-making

A decision is a choice. You make decisions every day. Your decisions influence the quality of your life as well as the lives of others. It is critical for you to learn that you can decide to be nonviolent and to behave in ways that protect you from the violent actions of others. The following discussion examines decision-making. You will learn why lacking decision-making skills is a risk factor for violence. You also will learn how using the Responsible Decision-Making Model is a protective factor to prevent violence.

Facts: Decision-Making

Most people have one or a combination of three decision-making styles. An **inactive decision-making style** is a decision-making style in which you fail to make choices, and this failure determines what will occur. A person who has an inactive decision-making style usually procrastinates. **Procrastination** is putting off something until a future time. Most of us have known people who have an inactive decision-making style. They often put off making decisions when they are faced with something difficult. Often they put off making a decision because they do not know what they want to do. They may never make a decision and one option merely plays itself out. Unfortunately, people who have this style have little control over the direction their lives take. It is difficult for them to develop the self-confidence that might be gained from feeling that they control their own destiny.

A **reactive decision-making style** is a decision-making style in which you allow others to make decisions for you. Most of us also have known people who have this style. They are easily influenced by what others think, do, or suggest. They are easily pressured by peer pressure, lack self-confidence, and have a need to be liked by others. Unfortunately, people who adopt this style have difficulty owning their behavior. They are not in control of their own destiny. Instead, they give this control to others.

A **proactive decision-making style** is a decision-making style in which you examine the decision to be made, identify and evaluate actions that can be taken, select an action, and assume responsibility for the consequences. Most of us have known people who have this style. Rather than being driven by circumstances and conditions or being influenced by others, they take responsibility. They are principle-centered. People who are **principle-centered** have guidelines that direct their decisions. These include fairness, integrity, honesty, human dignity, service, quality or excellence, potential, growth, patience, nurturance, and encouragement. These principles guide their behavior.

People with a proactive decision-making style are empowered. **Being empowered** is the feeling of being inspired because you believe that you control your own destiny. People who are empowered believe they have the capacity to make responsible decisions, change habits, develop and uphold morals, keep promises and trusts, exercise courage, and treat others with kindness and respect. They are willing to accept responsibility.

Risk Factor #12

Lacking Responsible Decision-Making Skills

Young people who lack responsible decision-making skills are more likely to harm others and to be harmed. Delinquent and aggressive teenagers consider fewer consequences of their actions than nondelinquent teenagers (Hollin, 1993). When young people do not stop and think about consequences, they often see only immediate benefits. A decision made in the moment may have consequences that last a lifetime. There is no way to change the following: death, injury, disability, disfigurement, imprisonment, and loss of educational opportunity.

Young people who lack responsible decision-making skills are more easily pressured by peers to believe, "It must be all right to do this because everyone else is." Young people with responsible decision-making skills know that wrong is wrong regardless of how many peers are doing something. Young people who lack responsible decision-making skills are not as self-confident as those who have these skills. Young people feel good about themselves when they know they are doing the right thing or what is responsible.

Protective Factor #12

Making Responsible Decisions

For obvious reasons, it is important to master responsible decision-making. You can learn and practice decision-making skills using the Responsible Decision-Making Model. The **Responsible Decision-Making Model** (Figure 23) is a series of steps to follow to assure the decisions you make lead to actions that:

1. protect health;

Table 23
The Responsible Decision-Making Model

1. **Clearly describe the situation you face.**
   If no immediate decision is necessary, describe the situation in writing. If an immediate decision must be made, describe the situation out loud or to yourself in a few short sentences. Being able to describe a situation in your own words is the first step in clarifying the question.

2. **List possible actions that can be taken.**
   Again, if no immediate decision is necessary, make a list of possible actions. If an immediate decision must be made, state possible actions out loud or to yourself.

3. **Share your list of possible actions with a responsible adult such as someone who protects community laws and demonstrates character.**
   When no immediate action is necessary, sharing possible actions with a responsible adult is helpful. This person can examine your list to see if it is inclusive. Responsible adults have a wide range of experiences that can allow them to see situations maturely. They may add possibilities to the list of actions. In some situations, it is possible to delay decision making until there is an opportunity to seek counsel with a responsible adult. If an immediate decision must be made, explore possibilities. Perhaps a telephone call can be made. Whenever possible, avoid skipping this step.

4. **Carefully evaluate each possible action using six criteria.**
   Ask each of the six questions to learn which decision is best.
   a. Will this decision result in an action that will protect my health and the health of others?
   b. Will this decision result in an action that will protect my safety and the safety of others?
   c. Will this decision result in an action that will protect the laws of the community?
   d. Will this decision result in an action that shows respect for myself and others?
   e. Will this decision result in an action that follows guidelines set by responsible adults such as my parents or guardian?
   f. Will this decision result in an action that will demonstrate that I have good character and moral values?

5. **Decide which action is responsible and most appropriate.**
   After applying the six criteria, compare the results. Which decision best meets the six criteria?

6. **Act in a responsible way and evaluate the results.**
   Follow through with this decision with confidence. The confidence comes from paying attention to the six criteria.

2. protect safety;
3. protect laws;
4. show respect for self and others;
5. follow guidelines set by responsible adults such as parents and guardians;
6. demonstrate good character and moral values.

Using the Responsible Decision-Making Model has many benefits. Because there are guidelines for what is responsible behavior, you always know how to evaluate a situation. You identify the possible actions to be taken and then ask the following questions.

1. Will this decision result in an action that will protect my health and that of others?
2. Will this decision result in an action that will protect my safety and that of others?
3. Will this decision result in an action that will protect the laws of the community?
4. Will this decision result in an action that shows respect for myself and others?
5. Will this decision result in an action that follows guidelines set by responsible adults such as my parents and guardians?
6. Will this decision result in an action that will demonstrate good character and moral values?

Having carefully established guidelines helps you approach decision-making in a rational manner. You will not be tempted to choose what seems best for the moment. Instead, you will think about your future.

The criteria or guidelines used to evaluate actions are helpful when you want to tell peers that you will not do something. You can use the criteria to state why you are saying NO. For example, if peers want you to join a gang, you can say, "NO, I want to remain safe." If peers want you to steal something from someone's locker at school, you can say, "NO, stealing is illegal and I need to follow laws." If your peers want you to carry a knife or gun in a backpack, you can say, "NO, it is not safe to carry a weapon." If peers continue to pressure you, you can continue to repeat the reason over and over again.

Violence-Free Pledge

I will make responsible decisions.

I will use a proactive decision-making style if I have a reactive decision-making style.

I will change my decision-making style if I have an inactive decision-making style.

practicing resistance skills

A **peer** is a person who is similar in age or status. **Peer pressure** is pressure that people of similar age or status place on others to encourage them to make certain decisions or behave in certain ways. Peer pressure can be positive or negative. For example, if peers pressure you to stay away from gangs, this is positive peer pressure. However, if peers pressure you to join a gang, this is negative peer pressure. You need to resist negative peer pressure. You can use resistance skills. **Resistance skills** are skills that are used when a person wants to say NO to an action and/or leave a situation. This discussion will focus on the importance of using resistance skills when needed. You will learn why lacking resistance skills is a risk factor for violence. You will learn why using resistance skills is a protective factor to prevent violence.

Facts: Resistance Skills

Think about the following for a moment. You have learned responsible decision-making skills. You have criteria to help you know what is right and what is wrong. You know that it is right to do something healthful, safe, legal, respectful, and nonviolent. You know that it is wrong to do something that is harmful, unsafe, illegal, disrespectful, or violent. There are three reasons why you might do something wrong. The first reason is: you do not know the difference between right and wrong. But, now you will know the difference because you have decision-making skills. The sec-

ond reason is: you are not motivated to do what is right. The third reason is: you give in to peer pressure to do what is wrong.

Let's look at whether or not you are motivated to do what is right. Young people who choose to do the right thing most of the time know that they will benefit. If you are motivated to do what is right, you might be described as follows:

1. You have positive self-esteem because you say NO to wrong behavior.
2. You are close to your family and want your family to be proud of your behavior.
3. You have goals and plans to reach them and do not want harmful actions to interfere.
4. You have friends who are responsible and you do not want to lose their friendship.
5. You are involved in school and community activities and want to keep the privilege of being able to participate.
6. You value your education and do not want anything to get in the way of graduating from high school.
7. You regularly spend time with responsible adults who would not approve of wrong behavior.
8. You do not use alcohol or other drugs, so you think clearly when pressured.
9. You avoid dangerous situations because you want to be safe.
10. You select entertainment that promotes responsible actions because you do not want to be influenced in negative ways.

Perhaps you choose wrong behavior. If you do, take a moment to understand why. Do any of the following statements describe you:

1. You have negative self-esteem and do not feel good enough to take care of yourself.
2. You are being reared in a dysfunctional family and have watched adults choose risky behavior.
3. You lack goals and plans to reach them and you do not view risky behavior as blocking goals.
4. Your friends choose risky behavior and you join with them.
5. You are not involved in school and community activities so you have more free time to get into trouble.
6. You do not value your education.
7. You are not close to adults who help you decide when and how to say NO to risky behavior.
8. You might use drugs that interfere with your ability to think clearly and say NO.
9. You are bored and spend time looking for excitement.
10. You select entertainment that shows risky behavior and then behave in the same ways.

If you choose behavior that is harmful, illegal, unsafe, disrespectful, or violent, you need to change. An important first step is to be honest with yourself. You can review the list of reasons why you might choose wrong behavior again. Are you bored? Do you spend time with friends who encourage wrong behavior? Are you using drugs that interfere with your thinking? Once you know what you need to change, make a plan. Ask trusted adults to help you. Remember the many benefits of being responsible.

The third reason why you might choose wrong behavior is being unable to resist the negative pressure of peers. Later, you will learn how to use resistance skills. Then you will be able to say NO when peers pressure you to do anything harmful, illegal, unsafe, disrespectful, or violent. You will be able to stick to your decision to say NO.

Figure 24
Model for Using Resistance Skills

1. **Use assertive behavior.**
   There is a saying, "You get treated the way you 'train' others to treat you." Assertive behavior is the honest expression of thoughts and feelings without experiencing anxiety or threatening others. When you use assertive behavior, you show that you are in control of yourself and the situation. You say NO clearly and firmly. As you speak, you look directly at the person(s) pressuring you. Aggressive behavior is the use of words and/or actions that tend to communicate disrespect. This behavior only antagonizes others. Passive behavior is the holding back of ideas, opinions, and feelings. Holding back may result in harm to you, others, or the environment.

2. **Avoid saying, "NO, thank you."**
   There is never a need to thank a person who pressures you into doing something that might be harmful, unsafe, illegal, or disrespectful or which may result in disobeying parents or displaying a lack of character and moral values.

3. **Use nonverbal behavior that matches verbal behavior.**
   Nonverbal behavior is the use of body language or actions rather than words to express feelings, ideas, and opinions. Your verbal NO should not be confused by misleading actions. For example,
   if you say NO to cigarette smoking, do not pretend to take a puff of a cigarette in order to resist pressure.

4. **Influence others to choose responsible behavior.**
   When a situation poses immediate danger, remove yourself. If no immediate danger is present, try to turn the situation into a positive one. Suggest alternative, responsible ways to behave. Being a positive role model helps you feel good about yourself and helps gain the respect of others.

5. **Avoid being in situations in which there will be pressure to make harmful decisions.**
   There is no reason to put yourself into situations in which you will be pressured or tempted to make unwise decisions. Think ahead.

6. **Avoid being with persons who choose harmful actions.**
   Your reputation is the impression that others have of you, your decisions, and your actions. Associate with persons known for their good qualities and character in order to avoid being misjudged.

7. **Resist pressure to engage in illegal behavior.**
   You have a responsibility to protect others and to protect the laws of your community. Demonstrate good character and moral values.

Risk Factor #13

Being Unable To Resist Negative Peer Pressure

Being unable to resist negative peer pressure is a risk factor for violence. Some young people are unable to resist negative peer pressure even when they want to resist it. Their need to belong is so great that they will do anything to be accepted by peers. They may feel unloved or rejected at home. They may have difficulty making friends. Peers who choose negative behavior are often very accepting. They will allow anyone to be a part of their group if the person follows along. This means they will accept those young people who are not accepted elsewhere.

Young people who join gangs often are motivated to do so by the need for acceptance. The gang offers security, belonging, and identity. Young people may accept dares and do things that are wrong in order to have the security the gang provides.

Sometimes young people are unable to resist negative peer pressure because they are unable to use resistance skills. They may be in situations in which they want to say NO, and find themselves going along with peers. They lack self-confidence. When negative peer pressure increases, they cave in. Much of violence occurs in this way. Young people might become caught up in the emotion of the moment and join others in harmful behavior. For example, a group might decide to damage school property. A young person might know this is wrong. But, when the group begins to spray paint the school and the young person is given the can of spray paint, (s)he caves in. Later,

there may be serious consequences for having joined in. The young person regrets not standing up for himself/herself and saying NO.

Although you might get away with wrong behavior some of the time, eventually you will be caught and punished. You will pay the price for not resisting negative peer pressure. The cost can be very high. You might harm someone. You might damage property. You may be harmed. Your injury might be permanent, such as loss of an arm or an eye. You might not finish high school. You might spend time in jail. Knowing when and how to say NO when there is negative peer pressure is essential.

Protective Factor #13

Practicing Resistance Skills

Being comfortable using resistance skills will help you to be safe. **Resistance skills** are skills that are used when a person wants to say NO to an action and/or leave a situation. **The Model For Using Resistance Skills** (Figure 24) contains a list of suggested ways for effectively resisting pressure to engage in actions that:
1. threaten health;
2. threaten safety;
3. break laws;
4. result in lack of respect for self and others;
5. disobey guidelines set by responsible adults;
6. detract from character and moral values.

You need to practice using resistance skills in non-threatening, lifelike situations. This practice provides carryover value--when you are actually in real life situations and are pressured, you will know what to do.

Violence-Free Pledge

I will practice resistance skills.

I will say NO when I am pressured to by peers to behave in ways that I know are wrong.

I will change my behavior if I am not motivated to resist behaving in ways that I know are wrong.

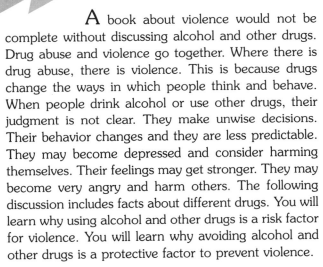

Protective Factor #14

Avoiding Alcohol and Other Drugs

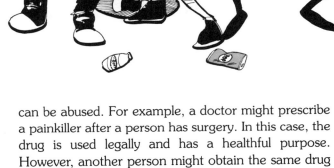

A book about violence would not be complete without discussing alcohol and other drugs. Drug abuse and violence go together. Where there is drug abuse, there is violence. This is because drugs change the ways in which people think and behave. When people drink alcohol or use other drugs, their judgment is not clear. They make unwise decisions. Their behavior changes and they are less predictable. They may become depressed and consider harming themselves. Their feelings may get stronger. They may become very angry and harm others. The following discussion includes facts about different drugs. You will learn why using alcohol and other drugs is a risk factor for violence. You will learn why avoiding alcohol and other drugs is a protective factor to prevent violence.

Facts: Alcohol and Other Drugs

Drugs are substances that change the way the body and/or mind work. **Drug use** is the legal or illegal way in which people use drugs. There are laws to help people know when they are involved in drug abuse. **Drug abuse** is the use of drugs that lessens the user's ability to function normally or that is harmful to the user or others. For example, young people who drink alcohol are involved in drug abuse. Not only is it illegal for young people to drink alcohol, young people do not function normally when drinking alcohol. And young people are at special risk for harming themselves and others when they have been drinking. Sometimes a drug may be used in a healthful way or the same drug

can be abused. For example, a doctor might prescribe a painkiller after a person has surgery. In this case, the drug is used legally and has a healthful purpose. However, another person might obtain the same drug in an illegal way. This person might use the drug for a harmful purpose.

You need to know facts about drugs to make responsible decisions. Figure 25 lists different drugs and gives their effects. The following discussion provides even more facts about these drugs.

Alcohol. **Alcohol** is a drug that depresses the nervous system and often changes behavior. Alcohol is the most widely used and abused drug. Drinking alcohol may lead to changes in health. It may harm the liver, stomach, and heart. There is an increased risk of some kinds of cancer. Alcohol is known to interfere with clear thinking. People who have been drinking have more accidents. They are more likely to drown, fall, or be burned. Drinking alcohol and driving is very dangerous. The number one cause of death in teenagers is traffic accidents in which someone was drinking and driving. When people use alcohol, they are more violent. This is because alcohol makes feelings stronger. People who are angry or aggressive get stronger feelings. They may act on their feelings and harm themselves or others. Many young people who attempt or commit suicide have been drinking. Many people who harm young people have been drinking. Many cases of

75

Figure 25
Different Types Of Drugs

Alcohol. A drug that depresses the nervous system and often changes behavior.

Sedative-Hypnotics. Drugs that depress the central nervous system and are "downers."

PCP. A drug that changes the way people see things.

Cocaine. A drug that stimulates the central nervous system and frequently results in dependence.

Crack. A drug that is pure cocaine, which produces rapid ups and downs.

Amphetamines. Drugs that "speed up" the central nervous system.

Heroin. A drug that slows body functions such as heart rate and breathing and produces drowsiness and mood swings.

Anabolic Steroids. Drugs made from male hormones, that produce muscle growth and can change health and behavior.

Marijuana. A drug containing THC that impairs short term memory and changes mood.

---

domestic violence and abuse occur after drinking. Murder is often the result of a fight that occurred when someone was drinking.

Sedative-Hypnotics. **Sedative-hypnotic drugs** are drugs that depress the central nervous system and are "downers." Barbiturates and tranquilizers are examples. These drugs are sometimes prescribed by a physician. Some people need them to relax. But, often they are bought in the drug world. They are used illegally. They are second to alcohol in contributing to violent behavior. Because these drugs dull the way people think, people who use them are not as likely to think about what will happen if they do certain things. People using these drugs often start senseless fights with others.

PCP. **PCP**, or angel dust, is a drug that changes the way people see things. It is also known as angel dust. People who use this drug may have memory and speech problems. They may have hallucinations. They may become very depressed. PCP can cause very vio-

lent behavior. People who use this drug become more and more angry over time. They are more likely to commit murder or suicide. Use of PCP also can cause death due to changes in health.

Cocaine. **Cocaine** is a drug that stimulates the central nervous system whose use frequently results in dependence. **Dependence** occurs when people have to have a drug or they experience withdrawal. Cocaine is snorted through the nose, smoked, or injected into a vein. The effects occur quickly. Heart rate and blood pressure increase. The heart may work so hard that the heartbeat becomes irregular. People who use this drug can have a heart attack. Cocaine use can change personality. People can change in different ways. Some become very hostile toward others. Others get very depressed. Cocaine use might result in harming others or suicide. There are other deadly risks. People who share needles to inject cocaine into their veins are at risk for HIV infection. They may develop AIDS and die. People also have been known to die after using cocaine only once.

Crack. **Crack** is a drug that is pure cocaine which produces rapid ups and downs. People who use this drug get a very quick "high" that is followed by a rapid drop to "low." Crack is usually smoked. People who smoke crack can become dependent right away. Then they will have a real urge to get more. They may steal to get money for crack. They may harm others. Using crack only once can lead to death. And, of course, the rapid changes in behavior can cause violence.

Amphetamines. **Amphetamines** are drugs that "speed up" the central nervous system. This is why they are called "speed." They are widely abused by high school students. They are very dangerous. Young people who use them become overactive. They get impulsive and out of control. They may provoke fights. When young people stop using them, severe depression follows. It becomes difficult to be motivated. Young people who use these drugs also are at risk for suicide.

Heroin. **Heroin** is a drug that slows body functions such as heart rate and breathing, and produces drowsiness and mood swings. Because heroin is injected into the vein, users who share needles are at risk for HIV infection. People who use heroin can become dependent on the drug. Withdrawal symptoms are strong. Heroin use increases violent behavior.

Anabolic steroids. **Anabolic steroids** are drugs made from male hormones, that produce muscle growth and can change health and behavior. Steroids can be taken as pills or injected into a vein. Some athletes use them to develop more muscle without realizing how risky their use is. They produce acne, changes in breath, sexual problems, high blood pressure, cancer, and liver damage. People who use them can experience "roid rages." These are outbursts of very angry behavior. During roid rages, users may harm others. After using these powerful drugs for some time, depression may occur. Users are at risk for suicide.

Marijuana. **Marijuana** is a drug containing THC that impairs short term memory and changes mood. In the past, marijuana usually had about one to five percent THC in it. Today, it may have as much as eight to fifteen percent THC in it. This is why use of marijuana has become more dangerous. It increases heartbeat rate and damages the lung. Use of this drug blocks short-term memory and causes restlessness and mood swings. People who use this drug may have hallucinations. They may become extremely worried and feel threatened.

Risk Factor #14

Using Alcohol and Other Drugs

Using and/or selling alcohol and other drugs is a risk factor for violence. Using alcohol and other drugs impairs the way people think and behave. As a result, people behave in aggressive and violent ways. They are less likely to respect the rights of others. When people use alcohol and other drugs, they drop their guard and do not protect themselves. They are more likely to become victims of violence. You will learn more about the use of alcohol and other drugs in the following discussion. You also will learn why people involved in drug trafficking are at extremely high risk of violence.

In order to choose responsible behavior, you need to be in control. You need to be able to think clearly and to respond quickly to different situations. You need to be able to think about the consequences of your behavior. And, you need to be caring, compassionate, and

respectful of others. Because alcohol and other drugs change the way you think and feel, use of these substances is risky. Consider the following evidence.

Fighting And Assaults. People who use alcohol and other drugs often are not rational. They are unable to manage their anger when they experience stressful situations. They are unable to identify peaceful ways to resolve conflict. Instead they may explode and begin a fight. Many, if not most, instances of assault follow drug use. This leads to many injuries. Some of these injuries are permanent. Young people who spend time with people who use drugs increase their risk of being assaulted.

School Expulsion. Using alcohol and other drugs places young people at risk for not finishing their education. There are a number of reasons. When drugs are used, it is difficult to think clearly and focus on learning. Young people may drop out of school. Some get expelled when they use drugs. Most school drug policies have a provision for the school to expel students who use drugs. Drug use increases the likelihood of fighting. Fighting has become another reason for expelling young people.

Sexual Assault And Acquaintance Rape. Using alcohol and other drugs is a risk factor for sexual assault and rape. **Rape** is the threatened or actual use of physical force to get someone to have sex without giving consent. When young people use alcohol and other drugs, their thinking is impaired. Their inhibitions are reduced. They are less likely to recognize the feelings of others. Let's examine how this might increase sexual assault and rape. Suppose a female has been drinking alcohol or smoking marijuana. She is not thinking clearly. As a result, she gets in a risk situation in which she normally would not be. For example, she might leave a party with a male she hardly knows. She might go to a male's home when no adults are home and listen to music in his bedroom. She is now in a risk situation. It will be harder for her to defend herself from unwanted rape.

Let's take another example. Suppose a male has a strong sexual desire for a female he is dating. The female tries to make her limits for expressing affection clear. However, the male has been drinking or using other drugs. He is unable to think clearly and to respond in an appropriate way to others. He does not respect his female companion's NO response. He forces her to have sex with him. In these two situations, unwanted sexual intercourse or rape occurred because drugs impaired judgment.

There is another way in which alcohol and other drugs contribute to rape. Rape is an act of violence. Rapists often have a strong need to control others. Using alcohol and other drugs may intensify feelings and the need for control. These rapists are more likely to act out after using drugs. Indeed, many rapes are reported to occur after the rapist has been drinking alcohol.

Theft. Use of alcohol and other drugs can be very expensive. When people who use drugs run out of money, they may become desperate. To obtain money to purchase more drugs, they might steal money or property from family members of friends. They might break into homes of unknown people or rob stores.

Domestic Violence. **Domestic violence** is violence that occurs within the family or within other relationships in which people live together. Most acts of domestic violence occur after a family member has been drinking or using other drugs. This is because alcohol and other drugs increase angry, hostile, and aggressive feelings. In addition, drugs cause unclear thinking. People are not rational and they may act in wrong ways. Disagreements are handled in a violent way. In some cases, domestic violence occurs for no reason at all. People who are violent become so angry that they harm other family members. Each year, 675,000 children are seriously abused by a caretaker who uses alcohol or other drugs. The use of alcohol and other drugs has become one of the main reasons that many children are taken from their homes.

Suicide. Alcohol and many other drugs are depressants. People who are depressed and use these drugs become even more sad, angry, and confused. They are unable to think clearly and may believe that suicide is a solution to their problems. More than half of the cases of teenage suicide follow drug use. Alcohol and other drugs are often the cause of suicide.

Homicide. **Homicide** is the accidental or purposeful killing of another person. The use of alcohol and other drugs is considered a factor in more than half of homicides. Blood alcohol tests and drug tests are commonly used on homicide victims to determine the levels of these substances in their bodies. In one survey of New York City homicides, drugs or alcohol were judged to be a factor in 53 percent of homicides. Most of the drug-related homicides were associated with drug traf-

ficking. Cocaine was involved in 84 percent of the drug-related homicides.

Protective Factor #14

Avoiding Alcohol and Other Drugs

A **drug-free lifestyle** is a lifestyle in which people do not use harmful and illegal drugs. When you choose a drug-free lifestyle, you help protect yourself and others from violence. When you avoid the use of alcohol and other drugs, you are making a responsible choice. If you are drug-free, you are more likely to:

- be in control of your behavior;
- make responsible decisions;
- desire to resolve conflicts in nonviolent ways;
- relate well to others;
- express emotions in healthful ways;
- be skillful in managing stress;
- have a positive self-concept;
- abide by laws.

In order to stay healthy and safe, it is important for you to choose a drug-free lifestyle. Here are some suggestions for you to follow.

Choose Drug-Free Activities. Drug-free activities can help relieve boredom so that you will not be tempted to get high on drugs. These activities also may provide an opportunity to spend time with friends. Many schools offer alcohol-free and drug-free activities such as proms, graduation parties, and other celebrations. Volunteer to be on the planning committees for these events. When they are offered, show your support by attending them and encouraging your friends to go too. Suggest other drug-free activities that might be offered by your school and in your community. Consider the following:

- After-school and weekend activities
- Dances
- Rap contests
- Drama events
- Carnivals
- Talent shows
- Multicultural events
- Food fairs
- Fashion shows

Be Involved In Peer Programs. **Peer programs** are programs in which young people serve as role models, facilitators, helpers, and leaders. You may want to get this special training and become involved in helping others. Or, you may want to join a peer program to receive help from other young people.

Support Drug-Free Zones. A **drug-free zone** is a defined area around a school for the purpose of sheltering young people from the sale of drugs. Increased penalties for using and selling drugs have been set for drug-free zones. School officials and law enforcement officers pay particular attention to the drug-free zones. They want to stop drug trafficking. They want to reduce the risk of violence. They need your help and support. Encourage your friends to support the drug-free zone at your school.

Know And Follow School Policies Regarding Drugs. You need to know the policies that your school has for the possession, use, and sale of drugs. These school policies have been made for your protection. You will want to support these policies. You will want to know your school's policies regarding intervention and treatment for those people who have used drugs. If you are using drugs, you will want to ask for help. If you know someone who is using drugs, you can suggest to this person that help is available.

Violence-Free Pledge

I will not use alcohol or other harmful drugs.

I will not buy or sell alcohol or other harmful drugs.

I will stay away from people who use, buy, or sell harmful and illegal drugs.

I will ask for help if I abuse alcohol or other drugs.

I will talk to a trusted adult if there is drug abuse in my family.

I will know and follow school policies regarding drugs.

I will attend only drug-free activities.

Protective Factor #15

Practicing Responsible Behavior Around Weapons

weapons

WEAPON FREE ZONE

SCHOOL

Weapons are widely available in the United States. According to several surveys, one in five high school students has carried a gun, knife, or club to school or someplace else (Miller, 1993). Today, young people are more likely to use weapons to solve disagreements than they were in the past. In many cases, fighting with fists has been replaced by fighting with guns or other weapons. You already know that weapons can be very dangerous. The following discussion will help you examine facts about weapons. You will learn why carrying a weapon is a risk factor for violence. You also will learn why practicing responsible behavior around weapons serves as a protective factor to prevent violence. It may save your life.

Facts: Weapons

A **weapon** is an instrument or device used for fighting. A variety of instruments and devices might be considered weapons. The types of weapons most commonly used by young people are guns and knives. Other weapons include razor blades, pipe bombs, brass knuckles, clubs, and stun guns. Most likely, you would identify each of these objects as weapons. A frying pan or a broomstick also might be considered a weapon. A weapon might be an object that is not designed specifically to harm another person. However, when used to harm another person, the object is classified as a weapon. Be cautious when you think someone might use an object as a weapon. Be very cautious around guns. Guns are the weapons that are most likely to be used to harm young people.

Because a gun can cause a serious or deadly injury, most states have laws regarding their possession and use. These laws forbid the sale of handguns to people under the age of 21, and rifles to people under the age of 18. Many states also have strict regulations regarding the sale of ammunition. The law forbids people of any age from carrying a concealed weapon without a permit. A **concealed weapon** is a weapon that is hidden partially or fully from view. There also are laws that regulate the way guns may be transported in cars. Most states have laws forbidding the sale of guns to anyone under the age of 18. They also have passed laws that prohibit carrying weapons to school.

These laws are designed to protect young people. Unfortunately, many young people disobey the law and carry weapons. Today, many young people are killed with guns. Among young people ages 15 to 24, one in four deaths is caused by a gun. The leading cause of death in teenage males in this country is gunshot wounds (Koop and Lundberg, 1992). More than three-quarters of all homicide victims ages 15 to 19 were killed with a gun.

Today, guns are readily available. Many people have them illegally, do not know how to use them, misuse them and have accidents, or intend to use them to harm others. It is estimated that over 66 million handguns and 200 million other kinds of guns are in circulation in this country (Larson, 1994). In about one-half of all households, someone owns a gun. In one-quarter of all households, someone owns a handgun. It is possible for young people to obtain a gun from their homes without their parents or guardians knowing.

Unfortunately, young people can buy guns on the street, from drug dealers, and from pawnshops. In fact, more than half of students in grades six through 12 said they could "get a handgun if they wanted one" (Newsweek, 1993). Guns can be purchased for as little as ten dollars. Young people also may be able to borrow guns from questionable sources.

One in 20 high school students has reported carrying a gun. When asked why they carried a gun, different reasons were given. Some said carrying a gun safeguarded them from being jumped or assaulted by others (Price, Desmond, and Smith, 1991). Others said it gave them status and recognition. Still others said that a gun was their only protection against older or larger youth and gangs who bullied them.

Many schools have taken security measures to prevent students from carrying guns to school in bookbags or lockers. They want to stop students who hide guns. They may require students to carry see-through backpacks to school. Students may have to pass through metal detectors as they enter the school. There may be unannounced locker searches. Extra police may be hired for extra security on school grounds. These security measures are costly. Walk-through metal detectors often cost $10,000. X-ray equipment may cost as much as $17,000. The hiring of extra security also is expensive. Yet, many schools are willing to pay for these measures. It is a top priority to keep you and others safe. But, you play a vital role as well. Remember, it is against the law for you to purchase a weapon or carry a weapon to school. In the next discussion, you will learn why this is so risky.

Risk Factor #15

Carrying a Weapon

Many young people disobey the law and carry a weapon. Carrying a weapon, particularly a gun, increases the risk that a person will be seriously injured or murdered. It increases the risk that a person will seriously injure or murder another person. Young peo-ple who carry guns are more likely to be involved in gangs, drug trafficking, and crime (Webster, Gainer, and Champion, 1993).

Every day, a young person dies or is seriously injured in a gun accident. In most cases, the victims were "fooling around with the gun." The victim may not have known how to handle the gun. The victim may have been showing off the gun to impress others or gain status. The victim may have been wondering what it would be like to pull the trigger, thinking the gun was not loaded. The victim may have been handling a gun that was bought in an illegal manner. Or, the victim may have been around a person who was handling a gun for one of the above reasons. The person handling the gun or someone else nearby became the victim.

Other young people die or are seriously injured because they are carrying a weapon and get into a fight with someone. If they had not had the weapon, they might have settled their disagreement in a different way. But, when emotions are strong and someone has a weapon, it is easy to use that weapon. Once the weapon has been used, there is no way to take back any injury that has been inflicted. When a person has a weapon, there also is the possibility that the other person will wrestle the weapon away. Then, the other person might use the weapon to get even with the owner.

There is another reason that it is risky to have a weapon. Sometimes young people experience hard times. They may feel depressed. They may be taking harmful drugs. They may be confused and unable to identify ways to deal with their difficulties. These situations can lead to thoughts of suicide. In most cases, thoughts of suicide pass. However, if a weapon is available, a person might use it. This action cannot be taken back. The person may be seriously injured or die. In many of these cases, outside help would have been available to help this person.

Carrying a gun for the purpose of a crime is very risky. People who have a gun with them may not intend to use it. They may intend to use the gun only to frighten their victim. But, they may use the gun if the victim puts up a fight. A person who carried a gun and planned only to rob a store has been known to use it to kill during the robbery. Once a bullet is fired and it injures or kills someone, there is no way to undo what happened.

Protective Factor #15

Practicing Responsible Behavior Around Weapons

To protect yourself, you can practice responsible behavior around weapons. Figure 26 lists some guidelines for you to follow. Each of these guideline is explained.

1. Do Not Purchase A Weapon Illegally. Remember, most states have laws forbidding the sale of guns to people under the age of 18. Suppose you want to purchase a weapon for hunting or another purpose. Ask your parents or guardian for permission. Learn how to use the weapon properly. Keep it in a safe place. Never carry it with you at inappropriate times.

2. Do Not Carry A Concealed Weapon. Remember, carrying a concealed weapon without a permit is against the law for a person of any age. Always follow

---

Figure 26
Safety Around Weapons

1. Do not purchase a weapon illegally.
2. Do not carry a concealed weapon.
3. Do not carry a weapon to school.
4. Encourage others to avoid buying, carrying, and/or concealing a weapon.
5. Do not pretend you are going to use a weapon.
6. Avoid being around people who buy, carry, conceal, or use weapons.
7. Do not argue with someone who has a weapon.
8. Avoid being in situations in which there will be weapons.
9. If you find a weapon, leave it where you found it.
10. Tell a responsible adult when you find a weapon.

---

laws because they are made to protect you. If someone should ask you to conceal a weapon, say NO. You risk your safety when you have a weapon with you. You also threaten the safety of others.

3. Do Not Carry A Weapon To School. Remember, you are forbidden to carry a weapon to school. You need to graduate from high school and do not want to be suspended. You want your school to be a safe place for yourself and others.

4. Encourage Others To Avoid Buying, Carrying, And/Or Concealing A Weapon. You can have a positive influence on others. You might encourage others to help keep your school and community safe. The fewer weapons there are in your community, the less the likelihood that there will be accidents and crimes in which people are injured or killed.

5. Do Not Pretend You Are Going To Use A Weapon. Do not joke about weapons. This behavior may threaten others into violence. For example, do not joke around by pointing your finger in your pocket to pretend you have a gun. Should you find a gun, do not point it at yourself or anyone else, even if you think it is not loaded. Because weapon use is so dangerous, people should always take others seriously when they talk about weapons. Pretending may be misinterpreted.

6. Avoid Being Around People Who Buy, Carry, Conceal, Or Use Weapons. You want to stay safe, and you cannot be certain what will happen if another person has a weapon. If you are around people who sell weapons to young people, you are around people who are involved in criminal activity. These people might be involved in drug trafficking, theft, or other illegal activity. Stay away.

7. Do Not Argue With Someone Who Has A Weapon. When you see someone with a weapon, keep your distance. Try not to provoke or argue with this person. Remember, weapons are often used to inflict injury when someone becomes emotional. Remain calm.

8. Avoid Being In Situations In Which There Will Be Weapons. You may know that other students are going to carry weapons to a specific event. If so, it is best to stay away from the event. Choose something to do where there will be no weapons and you will be safe.

9. If You Find A Weapon, Leave It Where You Found It. The weapon you find may have been used in a crime. If so, it may have fingerprints on it that would help solve the crime. The exact location of the weapon also may be important. It is always best not to touch a weapon.

10. Tell A Responsible Adult When You Find A Weapon. You already know that you should not touch a weapon should you find one. However, someone needs to know the location of the weapon. A responsible adult such as a parent, teacher, or law enforcement officer can make arrangements, remove the weapon, and put it in a safe place.

Violence-Free Pledge

I will practice responsible behavior around weapons.

I will not purchase a gun.

I will not carry a weapon.

I will stay away from people who buy, carry, conceal, or use weapons.

Protective Factor #16

Resisting Gang Membership

gang membership

Youth gangs are groups of young people who band together and participate in violent, unlawful, or criminal behavior. Young people who are attracted to gangs believe gangs will provide protection and a feeling of belonging. You may have seen examples of gang violence in the media. You may be aware of gang activity in your community or school. You may be a member of a gang or desire to be one. Gangs are an increasing problem in our country. Research shows that gang membership and the number of gangs have increased rapidly in recent years. The following discussion focuses on facts about youth gangs. You will learn why belonging to a gang is a risk factor for violence. You will learn why resisting gang membership serves as a protective factor to prevent violence.

Facts: Youth Gangs

There is much information available to help you understand more about youth gangs. Gangs usually have names and an area they believe to belong to them. They often use graffiti to mark their territory. Gang members hang out only with each other. They often commit crimes against other youth gangs or against the general population. Gang members often wear certain colors and dress in ways to be easily recognized. Youth gangs are usually made up of members from the same backgrounds—white Americans, African-Americans, Hispanic-Americans, or Asian-American members. Gang members often refer to the groups to which they belong as "crews" or "posses."

The following characteristics describe many youth gangs:

1. Gangs are often made up of a core of leaders, a group of regular or full-time members, and a few others. The others are referred to as "hangers-on."
2. Young people who want to get into gangs may have to prove their courage and loyalty.
3. Most gang members are between the ages of 10 and 21, with an average age of 19.
4. Gang members are mostly males; however more females are becoming gang members.
5. Gang members tend to meet and stay within their territory.
6. Gangs refer to their territory as their "turf". They may draw graffiti on buildings to let others know what they consider to be their turf.
7. Gangs usually have a name and symbols.
8. Gangs give their members support and protection from other gangs.
9. Gang members follow strict codes of conduct.
10. Individual gang members are concerned about proving themselves and having a reputation.

There appear to be different types of youth gangs (Huff, 1989):

1. **Hedonistic gangs** are groups of young people who band together to get high on drugs. Gang members usually do not get involved in violent crimes.
2. **Instrumental gangs** are groups of young people who band together and commit property crimes to

get money. Most of the members use alcohol and other drugs. Some may be involved in drug trafficking. However, drug selling is not an organized gang activity.

3. **Predatory gangs** are groups of young people who band together to commit crimes and violence. They commit robberies, street muggings, group rapes, and murder. Group members often are involved in illegal drug use and drug trafficking. They want money to buy weapons.

A large city does not have to have gangs. There is much concern over violent gang members moving from large cities, such as Los Angeles and Chicago, to smaller cities.

In the past, youth gangs were primarily made up of males. Females who hung around with gangs were usually the girlfriends of gang members. Today, more females are joining gangs (Taylor, 1993). It is estimated that females now make up about 5 percent of gang members (Stephens, 1993). Females who are involved in gangs either join male gangs, form female offshoots of male gangs, or join exclusively female gangs (Campbell, 1990). Few female gangs are totally separate from male gangs. Most females who belong to gangs take their orders from males (Stikes, 1994).

Gangs have clear structures with leaders. They have specific rules. They are organized city- or country-wide with a leader and hard-core members, regular members, "wanna-be's," and "could-be's" (National Youth Gang Information Center, 1993). **Hard-core gang members** are the senior gang members with the most influence. They have an average age of early to mid-20s and they make up 5 to 10 percent of the gang. **Regular gang members** are the gang members who already belong to the gang and who back up the hard-core members. Their average age is 10 to 13. **Wanna-be's** are young people who are not yet gang members, usually dress in gang colors, and engage in dangerous behavior to prove themselves to regular and hard-core gang members. They have an average age of 10 to 13. Wanna-be's also are called claimers or associates. **Could-be's** are young people who are interested in belonging to the gang, perhaps because of a friend or family member. They also are called potentials and are usually nine to 11 years old.

To prove themselves worthy of belonging to the gang, young people often must undergo harsh initiation rites. They undergo tests of courage and loyalty. They

may be subject to any gang member's demand at any time. "Wanna-be's" often are considered the most dangerous gang members because they commit violent crimes as they try to prove themselves. Gang members often demand that "wanna-be's" commit the most serious acts of violence and illegal activity. This keeps the other gang members from being caught. Often, older gang members take advantage of younger teens who want to belong. They know that the penalties may be less severe for younger people. Initiation demands may include drug dealing or drug running, illegal weapon activity, getting tattoos, carving a gang insignia into the skin, participating in Russian Roulette, robbery, beating up other people, and beating up or killing members of rival gangs. Young people trying to get into a gang often are subject to severe emotional, physical, and sexual abuse. Because of the secrecy associated with gang initiations, many young people are unaware of what they must do to join a gang.

Females who want to belong to gangs also may undergo severe initiation rituals. Many are beaten or sexually abused by male gang members. Some gangs require that females be "tricked in." This means they are forced to have sex with several male gang members in order to become a gang member. In order to get into a gang in San Antonio, Texas, five females were dared to have sex with a male gang member who said he was infected with the human immunodeficiency virus (HIV). This is the virus that causes AIDS. The five females had sex with him and then went to a Planned Parenthood Office to be tested for HIV. The news media became aware of this. They spread the story. They wanted people to know what some young people will do to belong to a gang.

There is another way females join gangs. It involves "jumping-in." **Jumping-in** is a test for toughness in which a young person fights with two gang members at once for an established period of time (Sikes, 1994). Jumping-in is supposed to show gang members that one has courage. Jumping-in also is supposed to keep females from belonging to the gang for the wrong reasons—to gain access to boys, to act as spies for a rival group, or to use the gang to gain protection for a private dispute (Campbell, 1990).

Once young people are full-fledged gang members, it is difficult to break away. Gang members who want to leave the gang may be set up to be caught in illegal activity. They may be tortured or murdered. Their family members may receive death threats. Gang members who do manage to separate from the gang usually must leave the city or state.

Young people join gangs for different reasons. Some join because they want to feel like they belong. Others join because they live in an unsafe place. They want the protection of other gang members. Young people who are experiencing difficulties seem to be attracted to gangs. They may live in poor areas, struggle in school, and have few job skills. Still other young people join gangs for money and status. They see no other way to get these without getting involved in crime and drug trafficking.

Young people from families that have money also join gangs. They may join because they are bored or lonely. They may want to rebel against their family. They may want a sense of excitement. Other reasons young people join gangs are the excitement of gang activity, peer pressure, and family tradition. Many young people who join gangs have no idea how dangerous this will be.

Figure 27 shows characteristics of a typical gang member. Gang members are usually males who are ages 13 to 23. They usually were raised in poor families and have few social skills. They are streetwise. They usually have dropped out of school or rarely attend school. The following signs may indicate that a young person is a gang member or wants to be a member (National Youth Gang Services, 1993):

1. Wardrobes
- wearing mostly one-color outfits such as all dark clothes;
- having a scarf or item of one particular color, with every outfit;
- wearing a dark jacket or sweater with every outfit;
- regularly wearing oversized pants;
- wearing colored shoelaces in tennis shoes.

2. Tattoos
- having a tattoo of a rose, tear drops, or graffiti-like markings around the hand area, neck, forearm, shoulder, or leg.

3. Makeup
- heavy eye makeup;
- heavy rouge;
- dark lipstick.

4. Hair
- wearing hair cut in the "feathered look" at the top, and left loose in the back or pulled to the back with a pencil or Afro comb;
- wearing hair nets;
- two-tone hair coloring;
- wearing rollers and braids in hair.

5. Language
- excessive swearing;
- using code names or unusual descriptions of ordinary objects, places, or people.

6. School
- cutting classes;
- getting into fights with teachers or other students;
- acting difficult in class;
- not taking books home and/or completing homework;

Figure 27
Typical Gang Member

Characteristics Of A Typical Gang Member Include:

Wardrobes
- wearing mostly one-color outfits such as all dark clothes;
- having a scarf or one particular color with every outfit;
- wearing a dark jacket or sweater with every outfit;
- regularly wearing oversized pants;
- wearing colored shoelaces in tennis shoes.

Tattoos
- having a tattoo of a rose, tear drops, or graffiti-like markings around the hand area, neck, forearm, shoulder, or leg.

Makeup
- heavy eye makeup;
- heavy rouge;
- dark lipstick.

Hair
- wearing hair cut in the "feathered look" at the top, and left loose in the back or pulled to the back with a pencil or Afro comb;
- wearing hair nets;
- two-tone hair coloring;
- wearing rollers and braids in hair.

- no interest in subject or any kind of school activities;
- frequent truancy;
- drawing gang insignias and graffiti on book covers and notebooks.

7. Social Behavior
- lacking hobbies or something to do in leisure time;
- having friends who are gang members;
- expressing racism or hatred of people who belong to a specific religious group or who have a particular sexual preference;
- buying gifts and items with newly acquired and unexplained money.

8. Participation In Family Activities
- unwilling to attend family gatherings;
- not spending time with the family;
- not taking an interest in family situation.

Of course, this list does not describe all young people who belong to gangs. Some young people are involved with gangs and do not dress in gang attire. They may behave in different ways.

Risk Factor #16

Belonging to a Gang

Belonging to a gang can be very risky for a number of reasons. Gang members are more likely to be around illegal drugs and weapons. They get into fights more often. They are more likely to get arrested and spend time in jail. Family members of active gang members are at risk as well. They may be harmed. Their property may be stolen or damaged.

Gang activities are very risky. The two most common crimes gang members commit are robbery and assault. When compared to young people who do not belong to gangs, gang members are 10 times more likely to have carried a weapon in the past year. They are 10 times more likely to have been involved in gang fights. They are four times more likely to have used drugs or alcohol. And they are five times more likely to have stolen or bought drugs (Subcommittee on Education, Arts, and Humanities, 1993).

There are other gang activities that are risky. In one six-week period in 1991, there were 162 drive-by shootings and 26 gang-related murders in Los Angeles (Cotton, 1992). Drive-by shootings are often the result of gang warfare and drug dealing.

Belonging to a gang often means being with young people who have enemies. Rivalry exists among gangs. Gang rivalry and hatred results in fighting and other acts of violence. Gang members are injured and some are murdered. Gang members often get criminal records. Then it is difficult to get jobs.

Gangs affect young people who do not wish to join them. More than 15 percent of people ages 12 to 17 reported that gangs exist in their schools (School Crime Supplement of the National Crime Victimization Survey, 1992). African-American young people (20 percent) and Hispanic-American young people (32 percent) reported gangs at school more often than white young people (14 percent). Young people who reported gangs were at their schools reported that they were afraid. They said they avoided certain restrooms and hallways to keep from being harmed.

Gang activity in school increases violence. Gangs often stake out an area of the school as their turf. When rival gang members or other students enter this area, fighting begins. Often young people are harmed in these turf battles. In some schools, gang members have forced students to pay them money to stay safe. Students may not be able to walk in a certain place without paying a fee. Students who refuse to pay are harmed. Gang activity also may involve selling drugs to students at school. Drug-related debts or arguments can result in violence (Stephens, 1994).

The following checklist can help you determine the degree to which gangs are involved at your school (Stephens, 1994):
- There is gang graffiti or crossed-out graffiti on or near the school;
- Students wear gang clothing;
- Drugs are used and sold at or near your school;
- There is much physical fighting;
- Weapons are sold or carried to school;
- Students use beepers, pagers, and cellular phones;
- There are racial incidents;
- There has been a history of gang activity in your community;
- There are social groups who have unusual names.

Protective Factor #16

Resisting Gang Membership

You know that it is risky to belong to a gang. You can resist gang membership by making the following decisions (Jankowski, 1991):

1. Avoid being around gang members.
2. Avoid being in locations that are gang turf or where gang activity takes place.
3. Avoid wearing any color or clothing that is gang-related.
4. Avoid taking part in graffiti writing or being around graffiti-marked walls.
5. Avoid alcohol and other drugs.
6. Avoid having tattoos with gang symbols.
7. Avoid staying out late at night.
8. Attend school and school activities regularly.
9. Be involved in family activities.
10. Set goals and make plans to reach them.

If you are approached by gang members who want you to join a gang, say NO. Follow the steps in the Model for Using Resistance Skills (Figure 24) to stick to your decision. Practice using the resistance skills described in Protective Factor #13: Practicing Resistance Skills in advance. Then you will be prepared to use them if you are pressured to join a gang.

Violence-Free Pledge

I will resist gang membership.

I will avoid being around gang members.

I will avoid being in locations that are gang territories or where gang activity takes place.

Protective Factor #17

Respecting Authority and Abiding by Laws

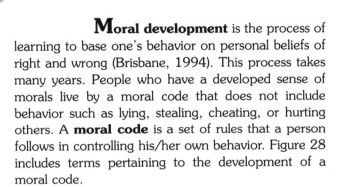

authority and laws

Moral development is the process of learning to base one's behavior on personal beliefs of right and wrong (Brisbane, 1994). This process takes many years. People who have a developed sense of morals live by a moral code that does not include behavior such as lying, stealing, cheating, or hurting others. A **moral code** is a set of rules that a person follows in controlling his/her own behavior. Figure 28 includes terms pertaining to the development of a moral code.

The development of a moral code and sound values is the foundation for learning respect for authority and laws. **Values** are the beliefs, goals, and standards held by a person. Because you must learn to live within the rules and laws of society, the development of sound values and moral behavior is essential to live safely. The following discussion examines facts about authority and laws. You will learn why challenging authority and breaking laws is a risk factor for violence. You will learn why respecting authority and abiding by laws serve as a protective factor to prevent violence.

Facts: Authority and Laws

All societies are governed by a set of rules called laws, and these laws are regulated by people in authority. A **law** is a rule of conduct or action recognized to be binding and is enforced by a controlling authority. **Authority** is the power and right to govern and to apply laws. In our country, we enjoy many freedoms

Figure 28
Terms: Authority and Laws

Moral development is the process of learning to base one's behavior on personal beliefs of right and wrong.

A **moral code** is a set of rules that a person follows in controlling his/her own behavior.

Values are the beliefs, goals, and standards held by a person.

A **law** is a rule of conduct or action recognized to be binding and is enforced by a controlling authority.

Authority is the power and right to govern and to apply laws.

Respect is having esteem for someone's admirable characteristics and responsible and caring actions.

Responsibility is being reliable and dependable.

Trustworthiness is acting in a right, responsible, and effective way.

Caring is being interested and concerned.

A **conscience** is an inner sense of right and wrong that prompts responsible behavior and causes feelings of guilt following wrong behavior.

Social reciprocity is the act of people treating others as they themselves wish to be treated.

A **commitment** is a pledge to do something.

because we have laws that protect our rights. Laws usually represent the beliefs of a majority of people in a community, state, or nation. Every citizen has the responsibility to know and obey existing laws. Those who abide by laws realize that the laws have been passed for the good of all the people. In the United States, if a person does not believe that a law is fair, there are democratic processes that can be followed to correct or change such a law.

Because laws represent what the majority of people in a community, state, or nation believe and they are designed to protect rights, you would think that all people would want to obey laws. But, this is not the case. Remember, people also operate with their own moral code. Those people who have a moral code that includes such values as respect, responsibility, trustworthiness, and caring are more likely to obey laws. **Respect** is having esteem for someone's admirable characteristics and responsible and caring actions (Eyre and Eyre, 1993). **Responsibility** is being reliable and dependable. **Trustworthiness** is acting in a right, responsible, and effective way. **Caring** is being interested and concerned. Values such as these are important not only to the individual but also to the entire society. They confirm the dignity of a human being, and promote and protect a person's rights. These values are essential to the preservation of a nation because they determine the extent of responsibility that a person is willing to assume. Basic values and moral behavior are necessary for healthy character development, caring interpersonal relationships, a humane and democratic society, and a just and peaceful world (Lickona, 1991). Young people need to think about moral issues and principles in order to be able to answer the question, "What is the right thing to do?" (Ryan, 1993; Wynne and Ryan, 1993).

Lawrence Kohlberg developed a theory that will help you understand how a person develops a moral code. This theory identifies three levels that occur over a long period of time. The first level in developing a moral code is the premoral level. The **premoral level** is a level of moral development whereby a child determines which behavior is right and which is wrong based upon which behavior is likely to be punished and which will be rewarded. The guiding factor is "Will I get into trouble?" The child has little understanding about the reasons behind the rules that parents and other caregivers use to punish or reward. In other words, a child is not born with an understanding of the differences between right and wrong. What is understood at this level is that certain actions make parents and other caregivers unhappy and may result in punishment; other actions make caregivers happy and may be rewarded.

The beginning of a conscience emerges in most children between the ages of five and seven. A **conscience** is an inner sense of right and wrong that prompts responsible behavior and causes feelings of guilt following wrong behavior (Brisbane, 1994). The moral code that children learn early in life forms the basis of the conscience. A person's conscience makes him/her feel obligated to do what is right or good and helps control behavior (Hildebrand, 1994). As a conscience develops, a child begins to know the difference between a truth and a falsehood.

Most children reach the next level of moral development, which has been called role conformity, between the ages of 10 and 13. **Role conformity** is a level of moral development whereby moral decisions are determined by answering "What will people think of me if I behave this way?" Between the ages of 10 and 13, young people are most concerned with behaving in ways that are expected by people with whom they feel close. At this age, young people now understand what behavior is expected, which behavior is right, and which behavior is wrong.

The third level of moral development is the principled level. The **principled level** is a level of moral development in which a person has a conscience, operates with a set of principles, and understands that certain actions would violate the rights of others. This level of moral development can be reached during adolescence or adulthood (Lickona, 1991; Mawhinney and Peterson, 1986).

Unfortunately, not everyone reaches the third level of moral development. There are young people your age who do not have a conscience that prompts responsible behavior and causes feelings of guilt when they are not responsible. There are young people who do not operate with a set of principles. There are young people who do not understand that certain actions violate the rights of others. Now you can understand the relationship between behaving according to a moral code and respecting authority and laws. Because of this, it is important for you to understand the risks involved for a person who challenges authority and breaks laws.

Risk Factor #17

Challenging Authority and Breaking Laws

Juvenile offenders usually have not developed the principled level of a moral code. As a result, they are unable to make responsible and moral judgments. This is illustrated in an account of a vicious attack by a pack of 13- to 16-year-old males on a young woman who was jogging in New York's Central Park. The brutality of the attack shocked the nation. The young woman was hit with rocks, brutally beaten with a metal pipe, stabbed in the head five times, and repeatedly raped. The arrested youths showed little remorse or sense of guilt for the attack. In fact, their thinking was so distorted that they blamed the young woman for being foolish enough to jog in Central Park at night. They said they were in the park that evening just "wilding" or having fun (Gibbs, 1993).

Distorted thinking and not assuming personal responsibility for personal actions is widespread among juvenile offenders (Gibbs, 1993). In cases of shoplifting, many juvenile offenders have blamed shopkeepers saying they should have been alert enough to catch a potential shoplifter. Other juvenile offenders who were arrested for stealing cars thought that car owners were at fault because they had left the keys in their cars and deserved to get "ripped off."

Young people who break laws are often experts at shifting the blame to other people or blaming circumstances for their behavior. They often blame parents, friends, teachers, or even authorities. They sometimes say that being poor or living in a certain place caused them to do something. Their immediate reaction when they are held accountable is to deny that they had any responsibility for breaking the law.

It is important for you to realize that you can promote your health and the health of others, protect your safety and the safety of others, and reach your goals and help others to reach their goals by respecting authority and by abiding by the laws of your community, state, and nation.

Protective Factor #17

Respecting Authority and Abiding by Laws

Not only developing sound values and a moral code but also learning respect for the rights of other people are necessary factors in developing a respect for authority and laws. Young people who develop respect for others have a good chance of being successful members of society and of staying out of trouble. An important principle to understand about respect is that in relationships, respect is not automatically received. It often is not received from a person until it is given. Respect should be extended first to the other person, and then expected from that person.

Having respect for the rights of others is a necessary quality that helps prevent violence. You can understand, then, how important it is for children to receive respect at home so that they learn how to extend respect to others. It is necessary to develop the ability to understand how others feel when treated in certain ways and to care about other people. This is called social reciprocity. **Social reciprocity** is the act of people treating others as they themselves wish to be treated. Fortunately, many people in our society live by a moral code that says, "I will treat others as I want to be treated."

A **commitment** is a pledge to do something. When young people are committed to respecting authority and following the laws of the community, they are making a pledge to help keep the community safe. They are pledging to support actions that are good for everyone in the community, including themselves. An important way to do this is to cooperate with those people who are involved in enforcing community laws. For example, neighborhood patrols and other related efforts send a very clear message that residents in crime-ridden neighborhood want to make things better in their community. They are willing to volunteer their efforts and time to help make law enforcement tasks more effective.

Violence-Free Pledge

I will respect authority and abide by laws.

I will be accountable for my actions and not blame others or circumstances for what I do.

Self-protection

In a recent poll by The New York Times, young people were asked, "How much of the time do you worry about being a victim of a crime?" More than one-half of the African-American young people and more than one-third of the white young people who responded said that they worried "a lot or some of the time" (The New York Times, 1994). A major source of worry is the unknown. Perhaps information about ways to protect yourself is unknown to you. You may wonder, "What situations are dangerous and put me at risk for becoming a victim of violence?" "How should I respond in the event that I am in a situation in which I might be harmed?" Having the answers to these questions will give you self-confidence. You will worry less if you know and practice self-protection strategies. **Self-protection strategies** are strategies that can be practiced to protect oneself and to decrease the risk of becoming a victim. The following discussion will examine facts about self-protection. You will learn why not using self-protection strategies is a risk factor for violence. You will learn why using self-protection strategies is a protective factor to prevent violence.

Facts: Self-Protection

You may believe that you will be a victim of violence only if you are in the wrong place at the wrong time. You may believe that you have no control over whether a perpetrator will choose to be a victim. However, in many cases you have a great deal of control. You can protect yourself. There are three keys to self-protection. First, always trust your feelings about people and situations. If you have a gut level feeling that a person is dangerous, trust yourself. Be on guard when this person is around. Avoid this person if possible. This is true for groups of people, too. When you sense that a situation might be dangerous, trust your feelings. Get out of the situation as soon as possible. Avoid the situation if you can. Second, always be on the alert. Pay close attention to people who are near you. Know how close others are. Know what others are doing. Third, gather information about how to protect yourself in different situations. Learn specific ways that you might behave to keep yourself safe. Behave in safe ways at all times. Do not let down your guard or take your safety for granted. Later in this discussion, you will be given guidelines for staying safe in different situations. Always follow these guidelines.

Risk Factor #18

Being in Risk Situations

Risk situations are circumstances that increase the likelihood that something negative will happen to your health, safety, and/or well-being. Risk situations for violence increase the likelihood that you will be a victim. When you are in a risk situation, you have dropped your guard. You do not protect yourself as well as you might. Let's look at some examples of risk situations. Suppose you hang out at night in a neighborhood in which there is much violent crime. Perhaps

Figure 29
Self-Protection When At Home

1. Keep windows and doors locked at all times, even when you are home.
2. Make sure your home has extra-security deadbolts on all entry doors.
3. Be aware that chain locks are easily ripped off a door.
4. Consider having a home security alarm system installed.
5. Consider getting a dog and placing "Beware of Dog" signs on your property.
6. Do not give out your house key to anyone other than a trusted friend.
7. Do not hide your extra keys outside your home.
8. Consider having a one-way viewer or peephole in your door.
9. At night, leave one or more lights on.
10. Have your mail, newspaper delivery, and other services discontinued when you leave for an extended period of time.
11. Ask a trusted neighbor to check your home and vary the position of the drapes.
12. Always have your keys ready before going to your door.
13. If there are signs that someone has entered your home, do not go inside. Go to a safe place and call the police.
14. Never let a stranger into your home unless you are sure it is safe to do so.
15. When speaking on the phone or answering the door, always give the impression someone else is in the home with you.
16. Ask to see identification before allowing a repair person to enter your home.
17. Do not open the door when someone asks to come in and make an emergency phone call. You can always make the call yourself if you want to do so.
18. Report any stranger who does not have identification to the police.
19. Be cautious about giving out information on where you live to people in person, on the phone, or by mail.
20. If you receive a crank phone call, do not talk to the person. Hang up immediately.
21. Report continuous, obscene, or bothersome phone calls to the telephone company and police.
22. Keep a list of emergency phone numbers such as the number for the police and fire departments by the phone.

there are muggings and assaults. Then you are in a risk situation. You are in situations where you might be harmed. Suppose you meet someone at a mall. You have never met this person before. This person offers you a ride home. You get into this person's car. You are in another risk situation. You are vulnerable because you know nothing about this person's behavior.

People your age often feel they cannot be harmed. People your age do need to take risks in order to grow. You need to test your limits. However, taking risks to grow is not the same as taking risks when it comes to personal safety. People your age are harmed by violence. Believe this. Read the newspaper and watch the news if you believe you cannot be harmed. You are at risk for being a victim of murder, assault, rape, and sexual harassment. You are at risk for having someone steal something from you. You are at risk when you are careless. You are at risk when you drop your guard. You are at risk when you become cocky and think, "Violence could never happen to me." Although you cannot prevent all acts of violence, practicing self-protection strategies will increase your chances of staying protected.

Protective Factor #18

Practicing Self-Protection Strategies

Think about your lifestyle. How do you spend time? With whom do you spend time? Where do you spend time? Most likely, you spend much time at home. And, of course, you spend time going to and from school. You also might have a part-time job. Perhaps you work at a store or care for someone's children. You may spend time walking, playing softball, or rollerblading. Perhaps you have a driver's license and enjoy driving a car. Maybe a friend drives you where you need to go. You may go to parties and socialize with people you are meeting for the first time. There are other places you might go—to the mall, movie theater, or library. Thinking about your lifestyle—what you do, where you go, how you get where you go, and with whom you spend time—helps you make a plan to protect yourself. The following discussion includes self-protection strategies you can use.

Self-Protection When At Home. Every 10 seconds there is a burglary. A **burglary** is an unlawful entry of a structure to commit a theft (FBI, 1991). Perpetrators may enter your home, intending to do more than take valuables. They may plan to commit an assault, kidnapping, rape, or murder. Consider the kidnapping of Polly Klaas. Polly was having a slumber party in her home when a man entered, kidnapped her, and later murdered her. You need a plan to protect yourself when you are at home. You need a plan to protect the contents of your home. Figure 29 provides a list of self-protection strategies to follow at home.

Self-Protection When Caring For Children. You may care for someone's children or for younger brothers and sisters. You need to protect yourself and these children. Figure 30 provides a list of self-protection strategies to follow when caring for children.

Self-Protection While Driving And In Cars. You need to protect yourself while driving your car or riding in a car with others. Some people pose as Good Samaritans and assault people who have car trouble. Others hitchhike and rob or assault people who stop and give them a ride. In recent years, there has been a concern about carjackings. A **carjacking** is a car theft that occurs while the driver and/or passengers are in or near the vehicle. Thousands of carjacking victims have been injured, kidnapped, raped, or killed. Consider what happened to Pamela Basu. She was driving her car with her baby daughter when she became the victim of a carjacking. Two males tried to force her from the car. She became entangled in her safety belt. As they drove away, she was dragged for more than a mile. She died of injuries. Figure 31 provides a list of self-protection strategies to follow while driving and riding in cars.

Self-Protection When In Public Places. You come from and go to many different places. You walk through the streets in your community. When you finish part-time work, you may walk to your car. You may stop at an automatic money machine to get some money from the bank. Whenever you are in public, others might harm you. If you follow a plan, you are less likely to be a target. Figure 32 provides a list of self-protection strategies to follow when you are in public places.

Self-Protection When Exercising Outdoors. You may enjoy jogging or walking for exercise. You may enjoy other activities such as rollerblading. Unfortunately, many people have been harmed participating in enjoyable outdoor activities such as these. Consider what happened in Central Park in New York City. Several years ago a woman was enjoying a run. She was brutally attacked by several young males. What began as an enjoyable run through the park ended in much harm and pain. You need a plan to protect yourself while you exercise outdoors. Figure 33 provides a list of self-protection strategies to follow when you exercise outdoors.

Self-Protection When In Social Situations. You are in many social situations. Sometimes you meet new people. At other times, you socialize with friends and other people you already know. When you socialize, you do not expect to be harmed especially when you

---

Figure 30
Self-Protection When Caring for Children

1. Ask the child's caretakers to show you around the home before they leave. Be aware of exits and entryways.
2. Ask the caretakers what to do if an emergency occurs.
3. Keep outside doors and windows locked.
4. Keep lights on in various rooms so it looks like others are at home.
5. Never open the door to strangers.
6. Do not allow anyone to enter the house unless the caretakers have told you in advance to expect someone. Ask the caretaker what the person looks like.
7. Never tell anyone who calls on the phone that you are alone with the children.
8. If you hear a suspicious noise or think that someone is trying to break in, call the police.
9. If the caretakers come home drunk, do not allow them to drive you home. Call your parents.
10. If the caretakers do anything that makes you feel uncomfortable, call your parents.
11. If the caretakers do not return home when they are supposed to, call your parents and tell them you will be late.
12. Do not let other people know you will be alone.
13. Never leave a young child unattended outside the home for even a brief period of time.

socialize with people you know. Unfortunately, a perpetrator might be an acquaintance, such as someone you know from school, or a neighbor. A perpetrator might be someone with whom you have had a few dates. One type of violence that occurs far too often is acquaintance rape. **Acquaintance rape** is rape that is committed by someone known to the victim. Figure 34 provides a list of self-protection strategies to follow when you are socializing.

Self-Protection When Sexually Harassed. You are learning about sexuality. You want to be comfortable with your maleness or femaleness. You may flirt with others. Others may flirt with you. You may tease some-

---

Figure 31
Self-Protection While Driving and Riding In Cars

1. Always park in a safe and well-lighted area where there are other people and other cars.
2. Take special note of exactly where you are parked in a large parking lot.
3. Lock your car at all times and keep your keys with you.
4. Have someone walk with you to your car whenever possible.
5. Check the front and back seats to make sure that no one is hiding inside before getting in your car.
6. Never leave infants or small children in an unattended car even if you are leaving only for a brief time.
7. Never leave the keys in the ignition or the engine running.
8. Always take your keys with you when leaving your car.
9. Keep wallets, purses, unattached stereos, and other valuables out of sight.
10. Do not allow yourself to run out of gas.
11. Plan ahead and fuel your car only during daylight hours.
12. Keep your car in good condition to prevent breakdowns.
13. Try to drive in safe, well-lighted areas, especially at night.
14. Install a car phone to use in case of emergency.
15. Keep a sign in your car that says "Send Help" to display if your car breaks down.
16. Keep a flashlight and road flares in your trunk.
17. Stay in your car, keep your doors locked and windows rolled up, keep a lookout for passing police cars, and honk your horn if you see a police car when your car breaks down.
18. Do not get out of the car if someone other than a police officer stops and offers help. Roll the window down only a crack and ask the person to call the police.
19. Drive to a nearby phone and call 911 if you see someone in need of help.
20. Never pick up a hitchhiker.
21. Do not drive home if you think you are being followed. Go to a store, police station, or well-lighted area where there are other people. Call the police and report that you were being followed.
22. Be cautious of anyone approaching your car when it is stopped.
23. Keep your car doors locked and windows rolled up at all times to prevent carjacking. If you need ventilation, roll the windows down only a crack. Keep your sunroof closed. Avoid driving in a convertible with the top down.
24. Keep your car in gear when at a stoplight or stop sign. Allow enough distance between your car and the car ahead to drive away.
25. If a person armed with a weapon demands your car or your keys, do not resist.
26. Do not give out your keys to other people.
27. Consider getting an inside latch for your trunk. If you are ever forced into the trunk, you could escape.
28. Do not rent cars that are marked as rental cars.
29. Be a courteous driver on the street. If another driver makes you angry, ignore this person. Never begin a fight.

one or they may tease you. Still, you want to maintain self-respect and you need to show respect for others. With regard to sexuality, there is a type of crime in which the perpetrator crosses the line and no longer shows respect for the sexuality of another person. This type of crime is called sexual harassment. **Sexual harassment** is unwanted sexual behavior that ranges from making sexual comments to forcing another person into unwanted sex acts. Sometimes sexual harassment occurs in the workplace. It may occur when someone with whom you work says sexual things to you that are not appropriate. It may occur if someone tries to force you to kiss him/her. A person might touch you in ways you do not want to be touched.

Sexual harassment also might occur at school. According to one survey, four out of five students said they were sexually harassed (AAUEF, 1993). The most common types of sexual harassment were sexual comments and sexual jokes; inappropriate gestures; staring up and down; and touching, grabbing, and pinching in sexual ways. One in ten students said they had been forced to do something sexual other than kissing. Males as well as females said they had been sexually harassed. Students who have been sexually harassed often do not want to attend school. They find it difficult to attend classes. They stay home or cut classes to avoid further harassment (AAUEF, 1993). Figure 35 provides a list of self-protection strategies to follow when you are sexually harassed.

Self-Protection When Being Stalked. **Stalking** is harassing someone with the intent to threaten or harm that person. Approximately 200,000 cases of stalking

---

Figure 32
Self-Protection When In Public Places

1. Avoid walking alone at night or in high-risk areas.
2. Stay on well-lighted streets and avoid deserted areas, alleys, and staircases when walking alone.
3. Keep your distance if someone in a car stops to ask you for directions. Ignore the person or call out the directions to them.
4. Never accept a ride from a stranger or someone you do not trust.
5. Never hitchhike.
6. Wear comfortable shoes that allow you to run from trouble.
7. Do not talk to strangers who approach you.
8. Seek help in a nearby store or building with other people. Walk briskly with your head up, and move in a confident manner if you think you are being followed.
9. Carry a loud siren, whistle, or buzzer to get attention if you need it.
10. Avoid using bank money machines whenever possible. If you use a money machine, do so during the day.
11. Stay away from areas where there are gangs.
12. Carry a chemical spray such as tear gas to use in case you are attacked.
13. Carry a flashlight at night and use it to light up potentially dangerous areas. It also can be used as a weapon in an emergency.
14. Carry your purse tucked under your elbow and hold it firmly with one hand. (Instead of carrying a purse, consider wearing a waist pack and carrying only what you need.)
15. Avoid using alcohol or other drugs so that you think clearly and make wise decisions about what you should do.
16. Wait only in safe and well-lighted areas for public transportation. After boarding, stay with a group of people or sit near the driver if possible.
17. Do not go into places that are deserted.
18. Yell, scream, or shout loudly for help if someone is bothering you in a public place.
19. Be sure to vary your walking route if you routinely walk to and from school or work.
20. Speed up, cross the street, turn around, run, or do whatever you feel is necessary if you feel a person may be following you.
21. Do not turn your back toward a street or a lobby when you are using a public telephone; turn your back toward the telephone.
22. Use pay telephones only when they are in well-lighted places where there are many other people.

occur each year. Most of the people who stalk others are male. Most of the people being stalked are female (Friedman, 1994). Typically, people who stalk others are trying to form a relationship with the person they stalk. They may feel that by stalking, they are able to get the other person's attention. The stalker may fantasize a relationship with a person and decide to take action. This situation occurred when a woman stalked television talk show host David Letterman. She entered his home and claimed to be his wife. In some cases, a stalker takes further action and stalking leads to injury or murder. Consider what happened to actress Rebecca Schaeffer. She was shot and killed at her home by a man who had been stalking her. Stalking also may begin when a relationship has just ended. The stalker is upset and wants to scare the victim into continuing the relationship. Figure 36 provides a list of self-protection strategies to follow when being stalked.

Figure 33
Self-Protection When Exercising Outdoors

1. Avoid exercising alone, at night, and at places where there are few other people.
2. Pay attention to your feelings and avoid areas that do not seem safe.
3. Vary routes and routines (change route, time of day, etc.) because people may stalk their victims and plan their attacks.
4. Avoid paths where a person could be hiding in bushes or trees and quickly grab you.
5. Run or walk quickly in the opposite direction and run to a place where there are other people if you are harassed by someone in a car.
6. Carry a personal siren, personal protection alarm, or whistle.
7. Consider taking a large dog with you when you exercise.
8. Do not use personal stereos with headphones because you will be less likely to hear someone approach you.
9. Keep your distance from strangers.
10. Carry identification and change to make a telephone call.
11. Always let someone you trust know the exact route that you will follow. Tell this person what time you expect to return.

Self-Protection Through Self-Defense. **Self-defense techniques** are techniques that can be used when someone is threatening to harm you or is in the process of harming you. You can enroll in a course to learn self-defense techniques. To find more information about courses in self-defense, check with your

---

Figure 34
Self-Protection When In Social Situations

1. Stay away from places where you will be alone when you are with a person you do not know well or whom you do not trust.
2. Do not go anywhere with a stranger even if you are supposed to meet other people.
3. Trust your gut feelings about other people.
4. Choose to be with other people when you socialize with someone the first few times.
5. Do not use alcohol or other drugs.
6. Set limits for expressing affection and communicate these limits to others.
7. Do not pressure another person to drink alcohol or to express affection beyond limits. Know that a person who has been drinking is accountable for sexual behavior.
8. Avoid behavior that might be interpreted as sexually teasing or seductive.
9. Respect the limits other people have set for expressing affection. Never pressure someone beyond limits.
10. Ask the other person to tell you clear limits when you are confused or feel you are getting mixed messages.
11. Do not assume you and another person want to express affection in the same ways or have the same limits.
12. Use physical force if someone continues sexual behavior after you have set limits.
13. Attend workshops, seminars, or classes to be clear on issues regarding acquaintance rape.
14. Pay attention to warning signs that indicate a person might harm you: disrespectful attitude toward you, dominating attitude, extreme jealousy, unnecessary physical roughness, and/or a history of violent and/or abusive behavior.

---

school counselor, local community center, karate or martial arts center, police station, or local college. Courses in self-defense help you learn what works and does not work in dangerous situations. These classes help you learn to protect yourself in threatening situations rather than being paralyzed by fear. You will learn ways to:

1. Get the attention of others. You may practice yelling, screaming, blowing a whistle, or using a personal siren to let others know that you are in danger.

2. Stop the person who is harming you. Your instructor will explain when to put up a fight and when it is best not to put up a fight. Your instructor may teach you what to do when you decide to put up a fight. You will learn the places on a person's body to strike such as the eyes, the base of the nose, the groin, and the kneecap. You will learn about products that are legal to purchase and use in dangerous situations. For example, there are chemical defense sprays that you can carry with you. If someone tries to harm you, you direct the spray at this person's eyes. The chemicals will cause the person's eyes to burn. This will block vision. The person will have to stop harming you for a moment and you may be able to get away.

3. Get away if possible. Your instructor will tell you the fastest and safest ways to get away. You might discuss where you would run if you were in a place where there were other people. You also might discuss what to do if you were in an isolated place and did not know exactly where to go.

The most valuable outcome of courses in self-defense is helping you overcome fear and panic. When you find yourself in dangerous situations, you cannot afford to panic. Remember, you must stay calm and act in ways to protect yourself from harm.

Figure 36
Self-Protection
When Being Stalked

1. Check the laws of your state regarding stalking. Thirty-seven states currently have antistalking laws. Know your rights and the best way to protect your rights. Know the limits of your protection as well.

2. Contact the police department to report the stalking. Consider pressing charges against the person who is stalking you. This may be enough to frighten and stop the person.

3. Keep a record of each case of stalking. Write down the date, time, what was said, and what happened. Save any evidence, including notes and letters that may have been written to you and answering machine tapes with messages left on them.

4. Try to obtain a restraining order. A restraining order is an order by a court that forbids a person from doing a particular act.

5. Tell your parents and school officials what is happening. They should be told everything so they can do what they can to help protect you.

6. Seek appropriate counseling or join a support group for victims of stalking.

Figure 35
Self-Protection
When Sexually Harassed

1. Ask the person who is harassing you to stop. Be direct about what behavior is bothering you. Describe the situation and behavior that made you uncomfortable.

2. Keep a record of what happened. Write down the date and time, describe the situation and behavior, and explain how you handled the situation. Save any notes, letters, or pictures.

3. Check to see if there are guidelines to follow for the specific situation. For example, if the harassment was at school, check school guidelines; if at work, check work guidelines.

4. Report the harassment to the appropriate person in charge. This may be a boss, teacher, or school counselor.

5. Determine if you want to take legal action.

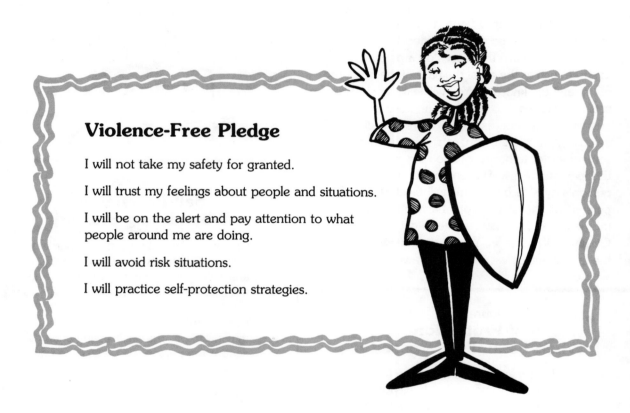

Violence-Free Pledge

I will not take my safety for granted.

I will trust my feelings about people and situations.

I will be on the alert and pay attention to what people around me are doing.

I will avoid risk situations.

I will practice self-protection strategies.

victim recovery

One out of five Americans will be a victim of a violent crime at some time (Roberts, 1990). Victims of violence may suffer physical injuries. They may lose money or property. And, victims of violence may be hurt emotionally. The emotional hurt that follows violence often is deeper and lasts longer than the physical injuries. While the physical injuries may heal, the emotional hurt may last a lifetime. The following discussion examines victim recovery. You will learn why avoiding recovery if a victim is a risk factor for violence. You will learn why participating in recovery is a protective factor to prevent violence.

Facts: Victim Recovery

Victim recovery is a person's return to physical and emotional health after being harmed by violence. Victims often need the following to fully recover:

- treatment for physical injuries;
- treatment for emotional pain;
- support from family and friends;
- repayment for money or property losses;
- skills to stop the cycle of violence.

The recovery process usually takes place over a period of time. In the time period soon after being harmed, victims may:

- be highly emotional;
- feel depressed;
- cry often;
- not want to talk with others about what happened;
- feel very angry;
- neglect every day tasks;
- have difficulty paying attention;
- feel afraid;
- sleep often or have difficulty sleeping;
- have nightmares;
- have flashbacks about what happened;
- use alcohol and other drugs;
- choose to stay away from others;
- feel ashamed;
- behave in violent ways.

Victims do not respond in the same ways. Their response may be influenced by the way they usually act. It may be influenced by the kind of violence they experienced. For example, people who have been victims of burglary may be afraid when home alone. People who have been victims of spouse abuse may have difficulties relating to other people of the opposite sex. People who have experienced the murder of a relative may fear the loss of other loved ones.

Some victims are able to recover from physical injuries and emotional hurt without help. However, most do not recover quickly or easily. Often people experience pain for many years. **Post traumatic stress disorder (PTSD)** is a condition in which a person relives a stressful experience again and again. PTSD is common in people who have experienced violence. The signs of PTSD include difficulty falling asleep or staying asleep, being irritable, and having trouble concentrating. When something reminds these people of what happened, they respond with much emotion.

Victims often experience additional pain or problems after the violence. **Secondary victimizations** are unfair treatments experienced by victims after they experienced violence. Many victims must attend the trial of the person who harmed them. The trial may be delayed several times. In order to attend the trial, they may need to miss school or their work. When they testify, they may be asked painful questions. This may cause them to relive what happened again.

Being a victim may cause other difficulties. Family and friends often have problems accepting what has happened. They may ask the victim painful questions. They may try to find fault with the victim's behavior so they can think the victim was to blame for what happened. If they can find fault, they convince themselves that this type of violence will never happen to them because they did not do what the victim did. Secondary victimizations are usually not intentional. Family members and friends do not want the victim to suffer further. But, because violence causes much emotion, people act in these ways.

Risk Factor #19

Avoiding Recovery if a Victim

There are many reasons why most victims need help to fully recover. Victims who do not fully recover are at risk for behaving in violent ways. This is especially true when violence occurred in the family. Victims who were abused by parents, may grow up and become parents some day. They have learned how to parent from their parents. Without outside help, they may parent in the same ways and abuse their children. Victims of child abuse are six times more likely to abuse their own children.

Victims of violence often have negative self-esteem. They may have been abused for so long that they actually began to believe they deserved this treatment. They began to have negative thoughts about themselves. Negative self-esteem is a risk factor for violence. Victims who have negative self-esteem are likely to allow others to abuse them. After all, they do not

believe they deserve respect. Without counseling, these feelings may continue for years.

Some victims need to practice self-protection strategies to prevent further violence. If they do not learn ways to protect themselves, they continue to be at risk. For example, a teenage female who drank alcohol may have left a party with someone she did not know well. He may have raped her. Now suppose she continues to go to parties and to drink alcohol. Drinking alcohol interferes with making wise choices. She may repeat what she did before. If she does, she may have the misfortune of leaving the party with another male who might harm her. Suppose a person belongs to a gang that fights with a rival gang. This person is stabbed by a member of a rival gang. If this victim continues to belong to a gang, another fight might occur. The result might be another injury.

Unfortunately, many victims who need treatment for injuries or counseling do not get help. Only one of six victims asks for professional help within the first year (Brown, 1991). There are different reasons for this. Victims may not want to spend money for professional services. They may not want to spend time in counseling. They may find that the effort needed to fully recover is tiring. As a result, they decide to let time pass believing they will recover without effort over time. The saying, "Time alone will not heal wounds," is true. Usually, the pain does not go away by itself. Victims often continue to suffer for years.

Protective Factor #19

Participating in Recovery if a Victim

Victims of violent crimes often experience feelings of anger, fear, shock, confusion, and depression. In many instances, they blame themselves for what happened. The world that they may have felt was safe and predictable is suddenly unsafe and unpredictable. The victim may ask, "Why me?"

The purpose of recovery programs is to help victims survive the pain, heal, and move forward with self-confidence. This may be difficult for victims. There are several steps victims can take to recover fully. Some suggestions for victim recovery are listed in Figure 37. Victims might do the following.

Talk About What Happened. It is important to share feelings, thoughts, and experiences. Victims need a support network of family members and trusted friends who can help them through the recovery process.

Get A Complete Medical Examination. Victims of violence need to get a complete medical examination if they have experienced physical injuries. They may need blood tests to determine if they have become infected with any sexually transmitted diseases. They need to learn about HIV infection.

Seek Counseling. Victims may need counseling and support services for emotional trauma. School counselors and physicians can tell them about the counseling and support services offered in the community.

Join A Support Group. There are many support groups for victims. For example, there are special support groups for survivors of rape, family members of murder victims, and survivors of domestic abuse. Victims might ask school counselors or look in the local phone directory or newspaper to find support groups for people who have had similar experiences.

Learn And Practice Self-Protection Strategies. Victims can gain confidence that they can protect themselves from further harm. They can learn about risk situations and avoid them. **Risk situations** are circumstances that increase the likelihood that something negative will happen to health, safety, and/or well-being. They can learn and practice self-protection strategies.

These suggestions help victims of any kind of violence. There also are suggestions for victims who have experienced specific types of violence.

Recovery Efforts For Rape Victims. Rape may cause physical injuries and emotional harm. Many survivors of rape experience rape trauma syndrome. **Rape trauma syndrome** is a condition in which a person who has been raped experiences emotional responses and physical symptoms over a period of time. The first phase lasts from a few hours to several weeks. During this phase, victims often feel ashamed, angry, afraid, guilty, and powerless (Mumen et al., 1991). Physical symptoms include nausea, headaches, and sleepless-

---

Figure 37
Victim Recovery

1. Talk About What Happened
2. Get A Complete Medical Examination
3. Seek Counseling
4. Join A Support Group
5. Learn And Practice Self-Protection Strategies

---

ness. The second phase lasts from several weeks to several years. During this phase, victims often change their living habits by changing their telephone numbers, moving, or moving in with others. The victim may experience problems being close with the opposite sex. Many victims fear retaliation from the rapist.

To recover and to avoid the lasting effects of rape trauma syndrome, victims need treatment for both physical injuries and the emotional hurt. Rape victims generally undergo a physical exam after the rape to determine their health status. Evidence also may be collected. They should not take a shower or bath, until after the medical examination. Rape victims may be examined by a sexual assault nurse examiner (SANE). SANEs are nurses who are trained in the examination and treatment of rape victims. **SANEs** are trained to deal with the emotional hurt caused by rape as well as the physical injuries (Allison and Wrightman, 1993). Although it is necessary, the medical examination can be a difficult experience for the rape victim.

The physical effects of rape may include more than bruises or surface injuries. Females who have been raped may have become pregnant. Both females and males who have been raped may have become infected with sexually transmitted diseases and/or HIV. **Sexually transmitted diseases (STDs)** are diseases that are transmitted from an infected person to an uninfected person during intimate sexual contact. There are more than 20 STDs. Some STDs are chlamydia, genital herpes, genital warts, gonorrhea, and syphilis. Medical treatment can be obtained for many of these STDs. However, victims who are infected with genital herpes will be infected for a lifetime. HIV is the virus that causes AIDS. Victims will need to be tested and retested at a later date for HIV. The waiting period is very stressful for victims. Currently, there is no cure for HIV. Eventually, a person who is HIV positive will develop AIDS. AIDS is fatal. Today, the

103

act of rape in which HIV is transmitted to a victim is viewed in many states as murder.

Rape victims should participate in special recovery efforts to heal from the pain they have experienced. After the rape, they may have been in shock, or felt frightened or guilty. They may have felt responsible for the rape. This is especially true of males who have been raped. Males often do not want to report a rape or seek recovery. Male rape victims may be ashamed that they were raped. They may feel that their masculinity has been threatened. They may wonder why they were chosen to be the rapist's victim. They may not want other people to know what happened to them. Both males and females who have been raped must work through personal issues.

Friends, family members, and the spouses or partners of the people who were raped also are victims. This is because the crime has affected their lives, too. Males whose female partners have been raped may feel angry, inadequate, and guilty. They may worry that their partners are pregnant, or infected with an STD or HIV. Family members may have similar worries and fears. The reactions of family members and friends can influence the recovery of the rape victim. The best ways for these people to provide support for a rape victim is to (Rape Education and Prevention Program, 1991):

• Avoid blaming the victim for the rape.
• Give the victim time to feel comfortable in discussing the rape.
• Encourage the victim to share feelings and thoughts when the victim feels ready.
• Believe what the victim says about the experience and the feelings that are shared.
• Try to be supportive but not overly protective.
• Be aware that focusing only on the sexual aspects of the rape may be traumatic. Remember that a rape is an act of violence—not a sexual act.
• Understand that it may take weeks, months, or years for the victim to begin and work through the recovery process.
• Get help from a rape crisis center, a counselor, or mental health professional.
• Encourage the victim to take courses in self-defense.

Many resources are available to help rape victims recover. Rape crisis centers are available in many communities. They are staffed with medical people and volunteers. Hospitals and women's centers offer counseling and support groups. Rape victims can call the Rape Crisis Hotline at 1-800-433-7273 for information on local support groups and resources. Some rape victims volunteer to help answer calls to the Hotline. They share their experiences with other rape victims as part of their recovery process.

Recovery Efforts For Victims Of Partner/Domestic Abuse. Every 15 seconds a female is beaten by her partner. Many victims of domestic violence feel helpless. They may even feel deserving of the beating. Victims often accept their partners' reasons for abusing them. Partners may claim they have personal problems, job problems, or money problems. They say they are stressed. Some time after the abuse, they usually say they are sorry. But, then the same thing happens again. The first step in recovery is getting the victim to believe (s)he deserves respect. This can be difficult. Victims may even protect their partners. Females often say, "He didn't mean to hurt me." Victims also must not accept blame. They must recognize that they did not cause the abuse. This is important because victims need to know abuse will continue unless something changes. Victims are powerless in changing the abuser. The abuser must decide to do this and get help.

When an abusive partner refuses to get help, a victim must decide about leaving. Many victims have few job skills, no money, and no place to go. They feel stuck in the situation. They may be concerned that no one will believe their story. They may have concerns about how they will care for their children. They may have concerns about the abuser. If they leave, they may fear the abuser will find them and harm them or kill them.

There are shelters for victims of domestic abuse. The shelters offer more than a safe place to live. Often, help is provided in training for job skills. Victims can use these resources to better themselves. Victims can build a support system. They may join support groups for survivors of domestic abuse. Victims can call the National Domestic Violence Hotline at 1-800-333-SAFE to learn about local support groups.

Young people who have lived in homes in which there was domestic abuse also need help. They are at risk for copying the behavior they have seen. They may allow others to abuse them. They may abuse others. This cycle of violence must be broken.

Recovery Efforts For Victims Of Child Abuse. Child abuse is a serious problem. Every year more than six million young people are severely assaulted (Brinegar,

1992). Others are abused in other ways. It is not easy to know which young people are being abused. They often keep what is happening a secret. They may act as model students so others will believe nothing is wrong. No one suspects they are being abused. They may try to hide abuse but their actions give clues. For example, they may abuse others.

Young people who are being sexually abused are the most secretive. Often the people abusing them will threaten them. The people abusing them make them promise not to tell. Young people who have been sexually abused often feel guilty and ashamed. They wonder what others will think of them. They may want to protect the person abusing them. They are often confused because they trusted the person who then abused them.

To begin recovery, young people being abused must tell someone they trust. If the first person they tell does not believe them, they need to tell someone else. Recovery also involves overcoming feelings of shame and guilt. Sharing these feelings with trusted adults or within a recovery group might be helpful. Victims also have angry feelings. They are angry with the person who abused them. They often are angry at someone they believed betrayed them. For example, someone in the family may have known about the abuse and did not protect them.

When sexual abuse has occurred, victims need a complete examination. A pregnancy might have resulted. There may be infection with STDs and/or HIV. Tests for these will be done. There may be treatment for STDs. Young people who get medical treatment and work through their feelings can recover from abuse.

People who suspect that a young person is being abused can call the local child protection agency. The call will be kept private and no one will know who the caller was. Someone at the agency will ask questions. Then they will investigate and make a report. If a young person is in danger, action will be taken. People can call the National Child Abuse Hotline at 1-800-4-A-Child to obtain more information on what to do.

Recovery Efforts For Homicide Survivors. A **homicide survivor** is a person who suffers because a friend, family member, or partner has been murdered. When people learn that someone about whom they care has been murdered, they often are in a state of shock. They experience disbelief. At the same time that they are struggling to accept the murder, they may have tasks to do. They may have to arrange for a funeral. They may have to notify others of the murder. The police and the news media may ask them many questions. If the person who was murdered earned money for the family, they may have worries about money. And, if the murder goes unsolved, they may worry about personal safety. They may fear people who are around them.

Homicide survivors need help too. The first six months to two years seems to be most difficult. The anniversary of the death is always painful. Holidays can be very sad times. Young people who are homicide survivors may have periods of depression. It may be difficult for them to concentrate in school. Joining a survivor group may be helpful.

Violence-Free Pledge

I will participate in recovery if I have a been a victim.

I will report violence to the police or appropriate authorities if I am a victim.

I will express empathy and show support for people who have been victims of violence.

juvenile offenders

Juvenile offenders are people below the age of 18 who break a criminal law. Juvenile offenders are involved in delinquent behavior. **Delinquent behavior** is an illegal action committed by a juvenile. Delinquent behavior includes serious crimes such as homicide, rape, drug trafficking, prostitution, robbery, assault, burglary, auto theft, and arson. Delinquent behavior also includes status offenses. **Status offenses** are types of behavior for which an adult would not be arrested, such as truancy, alcohol use, running away, defying parents, and staying out too late. Young people can be placed on probation, or placed in custody of their parents, or sent to a juvenile correctional facility for committing a status offense (Eisenman, 1994). The following discussion examines facts about juvenile offenders. You will learn why repeating delinquent behavior if a juvenile offender is a risk factor for violence. You will learn why changing behavior if a juvenile offender serves as a protective factor to prevent violence.

Facts: Juvenile Offenders

Juveniles are responsible for a large portion of violent crimes. They commit one-third of all burglaries. They commit one in seven of all rapes, and one in seven of all homicides. Consider the increase in juvenile crime between 1965 and 1989 (Barr, 1992):

- arrest rates for murder almost tripled;
- the number of aggravated assaults tripled;
- violations for carrying weapons increased two and one-half times.

Most juvenile offenders who are arrested stop committing crimes and do not go on to become repeat offenders. They fear being arrested, put on probation, or sentenced to serve time in a correctional facility. Other juvenile offenders mature and change their behavior. Another group of juvenile offenders responds favorably to programs designed to rehabilitate them. **Rehabilitation** is the process of helping juvenile delinquents change negative behavior to positive behavior.

Unfortunately, there are too many juvenile offenders who do not want to stop committing crimes. They are not stopped by the threat of punishment. They often report that the crime that was committed was "worth it because I will only be here a few years." Because of this attitude, many states have lowered the age at which juveniles charged with violent crimes can be tried as adults (Glazer, 1994).

In most cases, juvenile courts attempt to rehabilitate juvenile offenders rather than punish them. Juvenile offenders are rarely sentenced to long prison terms. They often receive special treatment such as not having their names released to the public. The following discussion describes what might happen if a young person becomes a juvenile offender.

Being Placed On Probation. **Probation** is a sentence in which an offender remains in the community under the supervision of a probation officer for a specific period of time. Probation is the most common sentence that judges use for juvenile offenders. More than two-thirds of the juveniles judged delinquent by the juvenile justice system are sentenced to probation. During probation, judges set restrictions and conditions for juvenile offenders. For example, juvenile offenders may be ordered to obey laws, obey parents, attend school, avoid contact with delinquent peers, and make some form of repayment to the victim. Repayment is a way to make up for what has been taken, damaged, or hurt. It might involve making a payment, returning stolen property, or performing community service.

Spending Time In A Juvenile Correctional Facility. When juvenile offenders engage in illegal behavior or violate the terms of their probation, they may be sent to a correctional facility. There are thousands of public and private juvenile correctional facilities in the United States. These include detention centers, training schools, ranches, forestry camps, farms, halfway houses, and group homes. Juvenile detention is the temporary physical restriction of juveniles in special facilities until the outcome of their legal case is decided. Detention centers are secure custody facilities where juvenile offenders are kept. Detention centers also are known as juvenile halls. Juvenile offenders are usually held in detention centers for a period of a several hours to 90 days. They are held in detention centers while they wait for their court hearings because they may be a threat to others, their home environment is unacceptable, or they are in need of physical or mental health treatment.

Spending Time In A Prison. A **prison** is a building, usually with cells, where convicted criminals stay. Some people feel that the best way to deal with juvenile offenders is to treat them as adults and keep them in prison. These people are concerned about juvenile offenders who repeat serious crimes. Nineteen states have recently changed their laws so that teenagers as young as the age of 14 can be tried as adults for any crime (Silverstein, 1994).

People who are against trying juvenile offenders as adults feel that the results would be negative. They are afraid juvenile offenders will spend time in prison without changing behavior. They are against placing juvenile offenders in prison without making serious efforts to help them. They believe society must do something about the factors that contribute to juvenile crime such as poverty, child abuse, unemployment, and drug abuse. In addition, they are concerned about the influence adult criminals might have on juveniles. Spending time with adult criminals may increase a juvenile's knowledge of the criminal world and may result in more criminal behavior after they are released. And, juvenile offenders may be sexually and physically abused by adult criminals while they are in prison.

Experiencing A Diversion Approach. **Diversion** is an approach to rehabilitation that involves sending juvenile offenders somewhere other than a correctional facility to learn how to obey laws. The following places offer diversion approaches: social agencies, child welfare departments, and mental health agencies; substance abuse clinics, shoplifters' programs, and crisis intervention programs; runaway shelters; alternative programs; and Youth Service Bureaus that work with troubled young people outside the formal process of the juvenile court. Youth Service Bureaus offer services such as drop-in centers, school outreach programs, crisis intervention hotlines, and programs for pregnant teens.

Adults who support diversion approaches believe this approach makes more sense than having young people go to prison. They feel young people who are labeled as delinquent will believe this is true about themselves and will continue to behave in delinquent ways (Henggler, 1989). Adults who oppose the diversion approach believe it allows juvenile offenders to get off too easy. They also believe it is very risky because juvenile offenders who are dangerous may be back on the streets (Silverstein, 1994).

Participating In A Program Such As Scared Straight. **Scared Straight** is a program in which adults who are serving prison time tell juveniles about the dangers of prison life. They tell of the physical abuse, sexual abuse, and emotional abuse. They describe what it is like to be free. The purpose of the program is to scare young people into staying out of trouble with the law by showing them what could happen if they repeat their criminal behavior (Lundman, 1993). Research has shown that these programs do not deter juvenile offenders from repeating criminal behavior. Most prisons no longer participate in these programs.

Going To A Boot Camp. A recent approach to changing juvenile offenders is to send them to a boot camp. **Boot camps** are camps that use rigorous drills, hard physical training, and structure in an effort to teach discipline and obedience to juvenile offenders. At boot camps, juvenile offenders live under very strict rules.

They may have to wake up at 5 a.m. and go to bed at 9 p.m. They may not be allowed to watch television, listen to the radio, or swear. Most boot camps include education and therapy efforts. Juvenile offenders often end up in boot camp in exchange for reduced sentences. To date, there is little evidence that spending time in boot camps discourages them from repeating crime (Glazer, 1994; Silverstein, 1994).

Being Paroled And Being Involved In Aftercare. **Parole** is a conditional release from a sentence in a correctional facility. **Aftercare** is the support and supervised services that juvenile offenders receive when they are released and must live and interact in the community. Once out on parole, juvenile offenders are assigned an aftercare officer who makes certain they follow the conditions of parole and stay out of trouble. The juvenile offender must obey parents, honor a curfew, avoid delinquent friends, agree to avoid the use of alcohol and other drugs, and make repayment of some form to the victim or victim's family. Juvenile offenders who do not follow the conditions of their parole are returned to correctional facilities.

Risk Factor #20

Repeating Violence if a Juvenile Offender

Juvenile offenders who repeat delinquent behavior are at a high risk for violence. For example, juvenile offenders arrested for being involved in gang fights and who continue to be involved in gangs are at risk of being perpetrators once again. Those people who shoplift and who are not punished may commit a robbery. Approximately 60 percent of juvenile offenders who commit crimes do not break the law again. A small proportion of juvenile offenders are sentenced to harsher penalties than probation. An even smaller proportion become serious repeat offenders. There is serious concern about juvenile offenders who repeat violent behavior. Those who are arrested three times usually continue criminal behavior for the rest of their lives (Barr, 1992).

Often, young people who become juvenile offenders have shown pre-delinquent behavior. **Pre-delinquent behavior** is behavior that leads to breaking the law. It includes disobedience, lack of respect for authority, stealing, lying, excessive aggression, inattention at school, truancy, and fighting. There is no single cause of delinquent behavior among young people. However, certain risk factors place young people at risk for being repeat juvenile offenders. These risk factors are described in the following discussion.

Living In An Adverse Environment. An **adverse environment** is a set of conditions and surroundings in which a person lives that interferes with growth, development, and success. Poor home conditions are often present in the lives of many juvenile offenders (Eisenman, 1994). Many come from homes in which parents take little responsibility for their children. One or both parents may be absent from the home. Juvenile offenders often have parents who have alcoholism, are addicted to other drugs, or have been in trouble with the law. They usually do not receive much supervision from adults. As a result, they spend their free time on the streets. This increases the likelihood they will be involved in violence. Juvenile offenders who commit violent crimes often have family histories that include neglect, physical abuse, and emotional abuse (Henggler, 1989). Poor neighborhood conditions also contribute to delinquent behavior. Communities where people who are poor live often have higher rates of crime than other communities. Young people reared in poverty and overcrowded conditions may experience a sense of hopelessness or frustration. They may see crime as the only way to overcome poverty.

Having Family Members With Criminal Records. Criminal behavior is often repeated within families. Parents, significant adults in the family, and older brothers and sisters serve as role models for young family members. Parents, brothers, or sisters choosing criminal behavior set this example for younger members of the family to follow. Younger family members learn that it is acceptable to be involved in criminal activity.

Failing In School. Young people who fail at school or who drop out are at risk for becoming juvenile offenders. When they fail, they are likely to have negative self-esteem. This is an important risk factor for violence. When young people drop out of school, they have too much free time. They are more likely to get into trouble. Without an education, they are more likely to be unemployed. This also increases the likelihood of being involved in delinquent behavior.

108

Lacking Empathy. Juvenile offenders, and in particular violent offenders, often lack empathy. **Empathy** is the ability to share in another's emotions or feelings. Juvenile offenders often lack the ability to see a situation the way another person sees it. For example, a juvenile offender may not understand how much suffering a victim experienced.

Using Alcohol And Other Drugs. Using alcohol and other drugs increases crime. Young people who are under the influence of drugs do things that they would not normally do. This is because they are not able to think clearly.

Being Involved In Delinquent Behavior At A Younger Age. The younger the age at which young people begin delinquent behavior, the more likely they are to commit more serious offenses in later years.

Being Aggressive. Aggressive behavior is a risk factor for violence. When young people are unable to manage their feelings of anger or resolve conflicts without harming self or others, they are likely to continue behaving in violent ways.

Spending Time With Delinquent Peers. Being with others who are involved in delinquent behavior increases the likelihood that young people will be involved. There may be peer pressure to choose delinquent behavior. They may gain a sense of belonging by being with other delinquent peers.

Having A Negative Self-Esteem. People have **negative self-esteem** when they believe they are unworthy and unlovable. Negative self-esteem is associated with self-centered behavior, self-destructive behavior, and violent behavior.

Protective Factor #20

Changing Behavior if a Juvenile Offender

As previously discussed, young people who commit one criminal offense usually do not continue criminal behavior. Juvenile offenders who change their behavior are selecting an important protective factor. For example, young people may be arrested for shoplifting and may be placed on probation in the custody of parents. They may recognize that shoplifting is illegal and wrong. They may return the items to the store. They may be punished by their parents. They may never commit another crime again.

For other juvenile offenders, the process of changing behavior is much more difficult. They must be taught what is right and what is wrong because they have not learned this at home. Some juvenile offenders may be encouraged by peer pressure to repeat criminal behavior and may need to learn resistance skills. Others need to learn social skills or stop abusing alcohol and other drugs in order to change their delinquent behavior. There are programs designed to teach social skills. There are 12-step programs, such as Alcoholics Anonymous, in which members give and receive help. Other groups have used Alcoholics Anonymous as a model for self-help programs. These include self-help programs for people who abuse other drugs, people who are survivors of child abuse, and people who were reared in dysfunctional families (Meeks, Heit, and Page, 1995).

Programs that seem to help juvenile offenders the most are those designed to help teach specific skills or change behavior. These programs help train juvenile offenders in study skills, job skills, social skills, and skills that help them deal with anger and conflict. One program that has been successful is EQUIP. **EQUIP** is a rehabilitation program for juvenile offenders in which they receive several kinds of help: social skills training, anger management, moral education, and support sessions with peers. EQUIP stands for Equipping Youth to Help One Another. Only 15 percent of young people jailed in a correctional facility who participated in EQUIP returned after one year of release. By comparison, 40 percent of juvenile offenders who did not participate in EQUIP returned within a year. EQUIP is believed to be successful because it helps juvenile offenders develop skills they were lacking when they became criminals.

Juvenile offenders who were sent to juvenile correctional facilities gave the following reasons for wanting to change behavior:
• "I don't want to go back to another correctional facility. We have to ask permission to do anything in here–eat, go outside, even use the bathroom. I want my freedom back."
• "I want to be able to see my family again. I have only

been allowed to see my family once since I was placed here."

• "If I commit another crime I might be sent to prison. I know prison will be much worse than being in here."

Juvenile offenders need help changing behavior. Figure 38 lists helpful suggestions.

```
Figure 38
Ways To Change Behavior
if a Juvenile Offender

1.  Improve Family Relationships
2.  Spend Time With Other Trusted Adults
3.  Ask Trusted Adults For Feedback
4.  Work To Improve Self-Esteem
5.  Choose Friends Who Obey Laws
6.  Make Repayment For Wrong Actions
7.  Become Involved in School Activities
8.  Develop Job-Related Skills
9.  Volunteer In The Community
10. Join A Support Group
```

Improve Family Relationships. In most cases, juvenile offenders have difficult family relationships. Their behavior may have caused problems. Family members may no longer trust them. In other cases, they were never close to family members. They may live in families in which there is abuse, alcoholism, or other problems. When young people are juvenile offenders, usually the entire family benefits from getting help. Family members can examine how they relate. A counselor can help them improve their relationships.

Spend Time With Other Trusted Adults. Trusted adults other than family members can be helpful. These adults should be responsible, be drug-free, and follow laws. Youth leaders, teachers, coaches, and clergy are trusted adults who may be helpful. They can teach juvenile offenders what is responsible. Offenders can learn by watching how these adults behave. They benefit from having close relationships with adults outside the family.

Ask Trusted Adults For Feedback. **Feedback** is information that helps someone know how well they are doing. Trusted adults can examine the ways in which juvenile offenders behave. They can tell them if

their behavior is responsible. They can make suggestions. They can offer praise and encouragement. When trying to change, it is always helpful to have feedback.

Work To Improve Self-Esteem. **Self-esteem** is what you think or believe about yourself. Juvenile offenders often have negative self-esteem. Figure 6 lists ways to develop self-esteem. As self-esteem improves, there is less chance of behaving in harmful ways.

Choose Friends Who Obey Laws. When juvenile offenders want to change behavior, they may need to change friends. They need friends who support responsible behavior. Friends should obey laws. They need to stay away from young people who do not obey laws. This helps prevent the temptation to do things that get them in trouble again.

Make Repayment For Wrong Actions. Repayment is a way to make up for what has been taken, damaged, or hurt. Repayment might involve paying back money that was stolen. Returning stolen property to the rightful owner is another kind of repayment. Damage to property might be repaired. Replacing property is another kind of repayment. For some wrong actions, it is difficult to make repayment. For example, when a person is injured, the injury may last a lifetime. Juveniles can tell victims that they regret their actions. They may perform a useful service for persons or families that were harmed.

Become Involved In School Activities. As part of recovery, juvenile delinquents can become involved in school activities. Then they will be with other young people with whom they share an interest. They will spend time with peers in positive ways. There will be less time to get into trouble. These peers are less likely to pressure them to behave in wrong ways. School activities are important for another reason. Becoming involved in them helps develop a sense of school pride.

Develop Job-Related Skills. It is important for young people to prepare themselves for the future by developing job-related skills. This increases the chance of obtaining and keeping a good job after finishing school. Young people can develop these skills by having after-school or weekend jobs. They can develop job-related skills through volunteer work in the community. They also may develop job-related skills by enrolling in classes such as computer courses, technical training, or courses at a local college.

Volunteer In The Community. Volunteering in the community may include helping to clean up a neighborhood or helping at a homeless shelter. Volunteering to help others is an important way to develop positive self-esteem. By helping others, juvenile offenders can be of value to others. This is a new way of behaving.

Join A Support Group. Many correctional facilities, hospitals, and social service agencies offer support groups for juvenile offenders. These support groups offer the opportunity to discuss how difficult it will be to change behavior. Members can discuss ways to help each other maintain a violence-free lifestyle. There are many kinds of support groups. Young people who have abused alcohol or other drugs may call Alcoholics Anonymous at 1-212-647-1680. Young people whose family members abuse alcohol and other drugs may call Al-Anon at 1-800-344-2466 for information on local support groups. Young people who have been victims of domestic violence may call the National Domestic Violence Hotline 1-800-333-SAFE. Telephone numbers for other support groups are listed under "support groups" in the phone directory.

Violence-Free Pledge

I will change my behavior if I have been a juvenile offender.

I will have remorse for pain and suffering I have caused others if I have been a juvenile offender.

bibliography

Ackerman, G.L. (1993) A Congressional view of youth suicide. *American Psychologist,* 48:183-184.

A.C. Nielsen Company. (1990) *Nielson Report on Television, 1990.* Northbrook, IL: Nielsen Media Research.

American Association of University Women Educational Foundation. (1993) *Hostile Hallways: The AAUW Survey on Sexual Harassment in America's Schools.* Annapolis, MD: American Association of University Women.

Andrews, A.B. (1990) Crisis recovery services for family violence survivors. In A.R. Roberts (Ed.), *Helping Crime Victims: Research, Policy, and Practice* (pp. 206-232). Newbury Park, CA: Sage.

Anspaugh, D.J., & Ezell, G. (1994) *Teaching Today's Health in Middle and Secondary Schools.* New York: Macmillan.

Asher, S.R. (1983) Social competence and peer status: Recent advances and future directions. *Child Development,* 54:1427-1434.

Barr, W. (1992) Violent youths should be punished as adults. In M. Biskup (Ed.), *Youth Violence* (pp. 212-221). San Diego, CA: Greenhaven Press.

Bart, P.B., & O'Brien, P.H. (1985) *Stopping Rape.* New York: Pergamon Press.

Bauwens, J., & Hourcade, J.J. (1992) School-based sources of stress among elementary and secondary at-risk students. *The School Counselor,* 40:97-102.

Bear, T., Schenck, S., & Buckner, L. (1992/1993) Supporting victims of child abuse. *Educational Leadership,* December/January, 42-47.

Beaver, B.L., Moore, V.L., Peclet, M., Haller, J.A., Smialek, J., & Hill, J.L. (1990) Characteristics of pediatric firearm fatalities. *Journal of Pediatric Surgery,* 25:97-100.

Bell, C. (1991) Traumatic stress and children in danger. *Journal of Health Care for the Poor and Underserved,* 2:175-188.

Berger, G. (1989) *Violence in the Media.* New York: Franklin Watts.

Biden, J.R. (1993) Violence against women: The Congressional response. *American Psychologist,* 48:1059-1061.

Blumenthal, S. (1990) Youth suicide: Risk factors, assessment, and treatment of adolescent and young adult suicidal patients. *Psychiatric Clinics of North America,* 13:511-556.

Boudreau, F.A. (1993) Elder abuse. In R.L. Hampton, T.P. Gullotta, G.A. Adams, E.H. Potter, & R.P. Weissberg (Eds.), *Family Violence: Prevention and Treatment* (pp. 142-158). Newbury Park, CA: Sage.

Brent, D.A., Perper, J.A., Allman, C.J., Moritz, G.M., Wartella, M.E., & Zelenak, J.P. (1991) The presence and accessibility of firearms in the homes of adolescent suicides: A case-control study. *Journal of the American Medical Association,* 266:2989-2995.

Brisbane, H.E. (1994) *The Developing Child: Understanding Children and Parenting.* New York: Glencoe.

Bromley, M.L., & Territo, L. (1989) *College Crime Prevention and Personal Safety Awareness.* Springfield, IL: Charles C. Thomas.

Brown, S.L. (1991) *Counseling Victims of Violence.* Alexandria, VA: American Association for Counseling and Development.

Browne, A. (1993) Violence against women by male partners: Prevalence, outcomes, and policy implications. *American Psychologist,* 48:1077-1087.

Bryant, A.L. (1993) Hostile hallways: The AAUW survey on sexual harassment in America's schools. *Journal of School Health,* 63:355-357.

Buchanan, D. (1992/1993) Outward Bound goes to the inner city. *Educational Leadership,* December/January, 38-41.

Buchsbaum, H. (1994) Guns r us. *Scholastic Update,* February 11, 18-19.

Bullock, J.R. (1993) Children's loneliness and their peer relationships with family and peers. *Family Relations,* January, 46-49.

——, (1993) Lonely children. *Young Children,* September, 53-57.

Callahan, C.M., & Rivara, F.P. (1992) Urban high school youth and handguns: A school-based survey. *Journal of the American Medical Association,* 267:3038-3042.

Cantor, P.C. (1989) Intervention strategies: Environmental risk reduction for youth suicide. *Report of the Secretary's Task Force on Youth Suicide: Volume 4*. DHHS Publication No. (ADM)89-1623. Washington, DC: U.S. Government Printing Office.

Cassidy, J., & Asher, S.R. (1992) Loneliness and peer relations in young children. *Child Development,* 63:350-365.

Center for the Prevention of Handgun Violence. (1990) *Kids and Handguns*. Washington, DC: Center for the Prevention of Handgun Violence.

Centers for Disease Control. (1991) Attempted suicide among high school students — United States, 1990. *Morbidity and Mortality Weekly Report,* 40:633-635.

———. (1991) Weapon-carrying among high school students — United States, 1990. *Morbidity and Mortality Weekly Report,* 40:681-684.

———. (1992) Suicide Surveillance Summary Report 1980-1990. Atlanta, GA: Centers for Disease Control and Prevention.

———. (1993) *Fact Sheet: Firearm Injuries and Fatalities*. Atlanta, GA: Centers for Disease Control and Prevention, 1991.

———. (1993) *Suicide Fact Sheet*. Division of Violence Prevention. Atlanta, GA: Centers for Disease Control and Prevention.

———. (1993) Violence-related attitudes and behaviors of high school students — New York City, 1992. *Morbidity and Mortality Weekly Report,* 42:773-777.

———. (1994) Deaths resulting from firearm-and motor-vehicle-related injuries — United States, 1968-1991. *Morbidity and Mortality Weekly Report,* 43:37-42.

Centerwall, B.S. (1992) Television and violence: The scale of the problem and where to go from here. *Journal of the American Medical Association,* 267:3059-3063.

Cermak, T.L. (1986) *Diagnosing and Treating Co-Dependence*. Minneapolis, MN: Johnson Institute Books.

Charney, D.A., & Russell, R.C. (1994) An overview of sexual harassment. *American Journal of Psychiatry,* 151:10-17.

Cohen, S., & Cohen, D. (1984) *Teenage Stress*. New York: M. Evans and Company.

Cole, J. (1993/1994) Moynihan is right: We must draw the line. *American Educator,* Winter, 16-17.

Colorado Department of Education. (1988) *The School's Role in Prevention/Intervention of Child Abuse and Neglect*. Denver, CO: Colorado Department of Education.

Committee on Prevention of Mental Disorders, Institute of Medicine. (1994) *Reducing Risks for Mental Disorders: Frontiers for Preventive Intervention Research*. Washington, DC: National Academy Press.

Cotton, P. (1992) Gun-associated violence increasingly viewed as public health challenge. *Journal of the American Medical Association,* 267:1171-1173.

Council on Scientific Affairs, American Medical Association. (1992) Violence against women. *Journal of the American Medical Association,* 267:3184-3189.

Covey, S.R. (1992) *Principle-Centered Leadership*. New York: Fireside.

Crooks, R., & Baur, K. (1993) *Our Sexuality*. Redwood City, CA: Benjamin Cummings.

Developmental Research and Programs, Inc. (1993) *Communities That Care: Risk-Focused Prevention Using the Social Development Strategy*. Seattle, WA: Developmental Research and Programs, Inc.

Devlin, K., & Reynolds, E. (1994) Child abuse: How to recognize it, how to intervene. *American Journal of Nursing,* March, 26-31.

Deykin, E.Y., & Buka, S.L. (1994) Suicidal ideation and attempts among chemically dependent adolescents. *American Journal of Public Health,* 84:634-639.

Division of Injury Control, Centers for Disease Control. (1992) *Position Papers from the Third National Conference: Setting the National Agenda for Injury Control in the 1990s*. Washington, DC: U.S. Government Printing Office.

Dougherty, D. (1993) Adolescent health: Reflections on a report to the U.S. Congress. *American Psychologist,* 48:193-201.

Drevitch, G. (1994) River of blood, river of tears. *Scholastic Update,* February 11, 4-5.

Dryfoos, J. (1991) Preventing high-risk behavior. *American Journal of Public Health,* 81:157-158.

DuRant, R.H., Cadenhead, C., Pendergrast, R.A., Slavens, G., & Linder, C.W. (1994) Factors associated with the use of violence among urban black adolescents. *American Journal of Public Health,* 84:612-617.

Edelman, M.W. (1993) Testimony Prepared for the Joint Senate-House Hearing on Keeping Every Child Safe: Curbing the Epidemic of Violence. 103rd Congress, 1st session, March 10.

Edmonds, P., & Price, R. (1994) Case focuses attention on spouse abuse. *USA Today,* June 21, 1A and 2A.

Eisenman, R. (1994) Society confronts the hard-core youthful offender. *USA Today Magazine,* January, 27-28.

Eyre, R., & Eyre, L. (1993) *Teaching Your Children Values.* New York: Fireside.

Fein, J. (1993) *Exploding the Myth of Self-Defense: A Survival Guide for Every Woman.* Sebastopol, CA: Torrance.

Fingerhut, L.A., Ingram, D.D., & Feldman, J.J. (1992) Firearm and nonfirearm homicide among persons 15 through 19 years of age: Differences by level of urbanization, United States 1979 through 1989. *Journal of the American Medical Association,* 267:3048-3053.

Fingerhut, L.A., Jones, C., & Makuc, D.M. (1994) Firearm and motor vehicle injury mortality — Variations by state, race, and ethnicity: United States, 1990-1991. *Advance Data from Vital and Health Statistics* (no. 242). Hyattsville, MD: National Center for Health Statistics.

Fingerhut, L.A., & Kleinman, J.C. (1990) International and interstate comparisons of homicide among young males. *Journal of the American Medical Association,* 263:3292-3295.

Fitzpatrick, K.M. (1993) Exposure to violence and presence of depression among low-income, African-American youth. *Journal of Consulting and Clinical Psychology,* 61:528-531.

Flavell, J.H. (1986) The development of children's knowledge about the appearance-reality distinction. *American Psychologist,* 41:418-425.

Flowers, R.B. (1990) *The Adolescent Criminal: An Examination of Today's Juvenile Offender.* Jefferson, NC: McFarland & Company.

Forward, S. (1989) *Toxic Parents.* New York: Bantam Books.

Friedlander, B.Z. (1993) We can fight violence in the schools. *Education Digest,* May, 11-14.

Friedman, L. (1994) What to do if you are being stalked. *Young Miss,* xxx.

Friedman, S.B., & Williams, G. (1993) Children coping with stress. *Good Housekeeping,* September, 162, 204.

Friends in Recovery. (1989) *The 12 Steps for Adult Children.* San Diego: Recovery Publications, Inc. Gallup Organization. (1991) Teenage Suicide Study: Executive Summary. Princeton, NJ: Gallup Organization.

Garbarino, J., Kostelny, K., & Dubrow, N. (1991) *No Place to Be a Child: Growing Up in a War Zone.* Lexington, MA: Lexington Books.

Garfinkel, B.D. (1989) School-based prevention programs. *Report of the Secretary's Task Force on Youth Suicide: Volume 4.* DHHS Publication No. (ADM)89-1623. Washington, DC: U.S. Government Printing Office.

Garland, A.F., & Zigler, E. (1993) Adolescent suicide prevention: Current research and social policy implications. *American Psychologist,* 48:169-182.

Garrison, C., Jackson, K., Addy, C., McKeown, R., & Walter, J. (1991) Suicidal behaviors in young adolescents. *American Journal of Epidemiology,* 133:1005-1014.

Gelles, R., & Straus, M. (1988) *Intimate Violence.* New York: Simon and Schuster.

Gelman, D. (1994) The mystery of suicide. *Newsweek,* April 18, 44-49.

Gibbs, J.C. (1993) Moral-cognitive interventions. In A.P. Goldstein & C.R. Huff (Eds.), *The Gang Intervention Handbook* (pp. 159-185). Champaign, IL: Research Press.

Gibbs, N. (1993) Hell on wheels. *Time,* August 16, 44-46.

Glazer, S. (1992) Violence in schools. *CQ Researcher,* September 11, 787-803.

——. (1994) Juvenile justice. *CQ Researcher,* 4:169-192.

Goldstein, A.P. (1986) Psychological skill training and the aggressive adolescent. In S.J. Apter & A.P Goldstein (Eds.), *Youth Violence: Program and Prospects* (pp. 89-119). Elmsford, NY: Pergamon Press.

Goldstein, A.P., & Huff, C.R. (1993) *The Gang Intervention Handbook.* Champaign, IL: Research Press.

Goldstein, A.P., & Keller, H.R. (1987) *Aggressive Behavior: Assessment and Intervention.* Elmsford, NY: Pergamon Press.

Gordon, J. (1990) *Stress Management.* New York: Chelsea House Publishers.

Green, L.W., & Ottoson, J.M. (1994) *Community Health.* St. Louis, MO: Mosby.

Greenberg, M.S., & Ruback, R.B. (1992) *After the Crime: Victim Decision Making.* New York: Plenum.

Greene, J.H., & Thompson, D. (1990) Outward Bound USA. In J.C. Miles & S. Priest (Eds.), *Adventure Education* (pp. 5-9). State College, PA: Venture Publishing Company.

Greenwood, P.W., & Zimring, F.E. (1985) One More

Chance: *The Pursuit of Promising Intervention Strategies for Chronic Juvenile Offenders.* Santa Monica, CA: The Rand Corporation.

Grossman, D.C., Milligan, B.C., & Deyo, R.A. (1991) Risk factors for suicide attempts among Navajo adolescents. *American Journal of Public Health,* 81:870-874.

Hales, D. (1994) *An Invitation to Health.* Redwood City, CA: Benjamin Cummings.

Hammond, W.R., & Yung, B. (1993) Psychology's role in the public health reponse to assaultive violence among young African-American men. *American Psychologist,* 48:142-154.

Harrington-Lueker, D. (1992) Blown away by school violence. *American School Board Journal,* 179:20-26.

Hartley, W.H., & Vincent, W.S. (1992) *American Civics.* Austin, TX: Holt, Rinehart and Winston, Inc.

Hawkins, J.D., Catalano, R.F., & Miller, J.Y. (1992) Risk and protective factors for alcohol and other drug problems in adolescence and early adulthood: Implications for substance use prevention. *Psychological Bulletin,* 112:64-105.

Hawkins, J.D., Von Cleve, E., & Catalano, R.F. (1991) Reducing early childhood aggression: Results of a primary prevention program. *Journal of the American Academy of Child and Adolescent Psychiatry,* 30:208-217.

Hazler, R.J., Hoover, J.H., & Oliver, R. (1993) What do kids say about bullying? *The Education Digest,* March, 16-20.

Heacock, D.R. (1990) Suicidal behavior in black and Hispanic youth. *Psychiatric Annals,* 20:134-142.

Henggler, S.W. (1989) *Delinquency in Adolescence.* Newbury Park, CA: Sage.

Henggler, S.W., & Borduin, C.M. (1989) *Family Therapy and Beyond: A Multisystematic Approach to Treating the Behavior Problems of Children and Adolescents.* Pacific Grove, CA: Brooks/Cole.

Hollin, C.R. (1990) *Cognitive-Behavioral Interventions with Young Offenders.* Elmsford, NY: Pergamon Press.

——. (1993) Cognitive-behavioral interventions. In A. P. Goldstein & C.R. Huff (Eds.), *The Gang Intervention Handbook* (pp. 55-85). Champaign, IL: Research Press.

Hollinger, P. (1990) The causes, impact and preventability of childhood injuries in the United States: Childhood suicide in the United States. *American Journal of Diseases of Children,* 144:670-676.

Hoover, J.H., Oliver, R., & Hazler, R.J. (1992) Bullying: Perceptions of adolescent victims in midwestern USA. *School Psychology International,* 13:5-16.

Hull, J.D. (1993) A boy and a gun: Even in a town like Omaha, Nebraska, the young are packing weapons in a deadly battle against fear and boredom. *Time,* August 2, 21-27.

——. (1993) The knife in the book bag. *Time,* February 8, 37.

Husain, S.A. (1990) Current perspective on the role of psychosocial factors in adolescent suicide. *Psychiatric Annals,* 20:122-127.

Johnson, K. (1992) Turning Yourself Around. California: *Hunter House Publications.*

Jourard, S. (1970) *Transparent Self.* New York: D. Van Nostrand.

Kazdin, A.E. (1993) Adolescent mental health: Prevention and treatment programs. *American Psychologist,* 48:127-141.

Kellerman, A.L. (1994) Annotation: Firearm-related violence — What we don't know is killing us. *American Journal of Public Health,* 84:541-542.

Kellerman, A.L., & Reay, D.T. (1986) Protection or peril: An analysis of firearm related deaths in the home. *New England Journal of Medicine,* 314:1557-1560.

Kilpatrick, W. (1993) The moral power of good stories. *American Educator,* Summer, 24-35.

Kinzie, J.D., Sack, W.H., Angell, R.H., Manson, S., & Rath, B. (1986) The psychiatric effects of massive trauma on Cambodian children. *Journal of the American Academy of Child Psychiatry,* 25:370-376.

Kissell, K.P. (1993) Guns on rise in rural schools. *The Morning Call,* March 21.

Koop, C.E., & Lundberg, G.D. (1992) Violence in America: Public health emergency, Time to bite the bullet back. *Journal of the American Medical Association,* 267:3075-3076.

Koss, M.P. (1993) Rape: Scope, impact, interventions, and public policy. *American Psychologist,* 48:1062-1069.

Koss, M.P., & Harvey, M. (1991) *The Rape Victim: Clinical and Community Approaches to Treatment.* Beverly Hills, CA: Sage. Kotulak, R. (1994) Society's ills may be changing our brains. Columbus Dispatch, January 9, G1-G5.

Kramer, Rita. (1992) The juvenile justice system is too lenient. In M. Biskup (Ed.), *Youth Violence* (pp. 212-216). San Diego, CA: Greenhaven Press.

115

Kraus, R. (1994) Tomorrow's leisure: Meeting the challenges. *Journal of Physical Education, Recreation and Dance,* April, 42-46.

Kressly, J.C. (1994) Targeting potential violence before tragedy strikes. *Schools in the Middle,* February, 27-30.

Kubler-Ross, E. (1975) Death: The Final Stage of Growth. Englewood Cliffs, NJ: Prentice Hall.

Larson, E. (1994) *Lethal Passage: How the Travels of a Single Handgun Expose the Roots of America's Gun Crisis.* New York: Crown Publishers.

Laub, J.H. (1990) Patterns of criminal victimization. In A.J. Lurigio, W.G. Skogan, & R.C. Davis (Eds.), *Victims of Crime: Problems, Policies, and Programs* (pp. 23-49). Newbury Park, CA: Sage.

Laurence, M., & Stuart, T. (1990) The use of adventure in reducing and preventing socially deviant youth behavior. In J.C. Miles & S. Priest (Eds.), *Adventure Education* (pp. 379-383). State College, PA: Venture Publishing Company.

Lewis, C.S. (1947) *The Abolition of Man.* New York: Macmillan.

Lickona, T. (1991) *Educating for Character: How Our Schools Can Teach Respect and Responsibility.* New York: Bantam.

———. (1993) The return of character education. *Educational Leadership,* November, 6-11.

Lipsitz, J. (1991) Public policy and young adolescents: A 1990s context for researchers. *Journal of Early Adolescence,* 11:20-37.

Lloyd, S.A. (1991) The dark side of courtship: Violence and sexual exploitation. *Family Relations,* 40:14-20.

Lovell, R., & Pope, C.E. (1993) Recreational interventions. In A.P. Goldstein & C.R. Huff (Eds.), *The Gang Intervention Handbook* (pp. 319-332). Champaign, IL: Research Press.

Low, B.P., & Andrews, S.F. (1990) Adolescent suicide. Medical Clinics of North America, 74:1251-1264.

Lundman, R.J. (1993) *Prevention and Control of Juvenile Delinquency.* New York: Oxford University Press.

Lurigio, A.J., & Resick, P.A. (1990) Healing the psychological wounds of criminal victimization: Predicting postcrime distress and recovery. In A.J. Lurigio, W.G. Skogan, & R.C. Davis (Eds.), *Victims of Crime: Problems, Policies, and Programs* (pp. 50-68). Newbury Park, CA: Sage.

Macallair, D. (1993) Reaffirming rehabilitation in juvenile justice. *Youth & Society,* 25:104-125.

Marecek, M. (1993) *Breaking Free from Partner Abuse.* Buena Park, CA: Morning Glory Press.

Martinez, M.G. (1993) Testimony and prepared statement. In Subcommittee on Human Resources of the Committee on Education and Labor. *Congressional Oversight Hearing on Local Gang Diversion Programs* (Serial No., 103-19).

Marwick, C. (1992) Guns, drugs threaten to raise public health problem of violence to epidemic. *Journal of the American Medical Association,* 267:2993.

Mason, J., & Proctor, R. (1992) Reducing youth violence: The physician's role. *Journal of the American Medical Association,* 267:3003.

Masters, Brian (1991) Inferno. *Vanity Fair,* November, 184-267.

Mawhinney, V.T., & Petersen, C.J. (1986) *Child Development: Parenting and Teaching.* Cincinnati, OH: Southwestern Publishing Company.

McBeath, W.H. (1991) Health for all: A public health vision. *American Journal of Public Health,* 81:1560-1565.

Meddis, S.M. (1993) In a dark alley, most feared face is a teen's. *USA Today,* October 29, 6A.

Meehan, P.J., Lamb, J.A., Saltzman, L.E., & O'Carroll, P.W. (1992) Attempted suicide among young adults: Progress toward a meaningful estimate of prevalence. American Journal of Psychiatry, 149:41-44.

Meeks, L., Heit, P., & Page, R. (1994) *Drugs, Alcohol, and Tobacco: Totally Awesome Teaching Strategies.* Columbus, OH: Meeks Heit Publishing Company.

Meeks, L., & Miller, D. (1995) Women's Health: *The Totally Awesome and Empowered Woman's Journey.* Columbus, OH: Meeks Heit Publishing Company.

Mize, J., Ladd, G.W., & Price, J.M. (1985) Promoting positive peer relations with young children: Rationales and strategies. *Child Care Quarterly,* 14:221-237.

Mizell, L.R. (1993) *Street Sense for Women: How to Stay Safe in a Violent World.* New York: Berkeley Books.

Morganthau, T. (1992) It's not just New York...Big cities, small towns: More and more guns in younger and younger hands. *Newsweek,* March 9, 25-29.

Moss-Manson, S. (1993) Testimony and prepared statement. In Subcommittee on Human Resources of the Committee on Education and Labor. *Congressional Oversight Hearing on Local Gang Diversion Programs* (Serial No. 103-19).

Murray, J. (1990) Managing stress and living longer. *USA Today Magazine,* May, 57-58.

Natale, J.A. (1994) Roots of violence. *American School Board Journal,* March, 33-40.

National Association for the Education of Young Children. (1993) NAEYC position statement on violence in the lives of children. *Young Children,* September, 80-84.

National Center for Environmental Health and Injury Control, Centers for Disease Control. (1992) Position Papers from the Third National Injury Control Conference. Atlanta, GA: *Centers for Disease Control.*

National Center for Health Statistics. (1993) Annual summary of births, marriages, divorces, and deaths: United States, 1992. *Monthly Vital Statistics Report* 41(13). Hyattsville, MD: U.S. Public Health Service.

National Center on Child Abuse and Neglect. (1991) *Family Violence: An Overview.* Washington, DC: National Clearinghouse on Child Abuse and Neglect and Family Violence Information.

National Committee for Injury Prevention and Control. (1989) *Injury Prevention: Meeting the Challenge.* New York: Oxford University Press.

National Victims Center. (1992, April) *Rape in America: A Report to the Nation.* Arlington, VA: National Victims Center.

Nelson, J. (1994) *Teaching Self-Defense: Steps to Success.* Champaign, IL: Human Kinetics.

Nelson, R.E., & Crawford, B. (1990) Suicide among elementary school-aged children. *Elementary School Guidance and Counseling,* 25:123-128.

New York Academy of Medicine. (1994) Firearm violence and public health: Limiting the availability of guns. *Journal of the American Medical Association,* 271:1281-1283.

Nordland, R. (1992) Deadly lessons. Newsweek, March 9, 22-24.

Novello, A.C., Rosenberg, M., Saltzman, L., & Shosky, J. (1992) A medical response to domestic violence. *Journal of the American Medical Association,* 267:3102.

Omizo, M.M., & Omizo, S.A. (1990) Children and stress: Using a phenomenological approach. *Elementary School Guidance and Counseling,* 25:30-36.

Page, R.M. (1991) The educationalization of adolescent suicide: The need for more evaluation of suicide awareness programs. *Wellness Perspectives: Research, Theory, and Practice,* 8:46-57.

——. (1993) Perceived physical attractiveness and frequency of substance use among male and female adolescents. *Journal of Alcohol and Drug Education,* 38:81-91.

Page, R.M., Kitchin-Becker, S., Solovan, D., Golec, T., & Hebert, D.L. (1991) Interpersonal violence: A priority issue for health education. *Journal of Health Education,* 23:286-292.

Panel on High-Risk Youth of the National Research Council. (1993) *Losing Adolescents: Adolescents in High-Risk Settings.* Washington, DC: National Academy Press.

Parry, A. (1993) Children surviving in a violent world—"choosing non-violence." *Young Children,* September, 13-15.

Peach, L., & Reddick, T.L. (1991) Counselors can make a difference in preventing adolescent suicide. *The School Counselor,* 39:107-110.

Perkins, L.K., & Giese, M.L. (1994) Cherokee Nation Youth Fitness Camp: Health promotion and disease prevention for Native American youth. *Journal of Physical Education, Recreation and Dance,* February, 60-62.

Perry, D.G., Kusel, S.J., & Perry, L.C. (1988) Victims of peer aggression. *Developmental Psychology,* 24:807-814.

Petersen, K.S. (1992) Child abuse deaths up 10 percent in '91. *USA Today,* April 3, 1(D).

Powell, E. (1991) *Talking Back to Sexual Pressure: What to Say, To Resist Pressure, To Avoid Disease, To Stop Harassment, To Avoid Acquaintance Rape.* Minneapolis, MN: CompCare Publishers.

Price, J.H., Desmond, S.M., & Smith, D. (1991) Inner city adolescents' perceptions of guns — a preliminary investigation. *Journal of School Health,* 61:255-259.

Prothrow-Stith, D., and Weissman, M. (1991) *Deadly Consequences.* New York: Harper Collins.

Proudman, S. (1990) Urban adventure. In J.C. Miles & S. Priest (Eds.), *Adventure Education* (pp. 335-343). State College, PA: Venture Publishing Company.

Quarles, C.L. (1989) *School Violence: A Survival Guide for School Staff.* Washington, DC: National Education Association.

Rape Education and Prevention Program. (1991) *If She Is Raped.* Columbus, OH: The Ohio State University.

Reducing number of repeat offenders. (1994) *USA Today Magazine,* April, 6.

Reiss, A.J., & Roth, J.A. (1993) *Understanding and Preventing Violence: Panel on the Understand-*

ing and Control of Violent Behavior. Washington, DC: National Academy of Sciences.

Resick, P.A. (1990) Victims of sexual assault. In A.J. Lurigio, W.G. Skogan, & R.C. Davis (Eds.), *Victims of Crime: Problems, Policies, and Programs* (pp. 69-86). Newbury Park, CA: Sage.

Roberts, A.R. (1990) *Helping Crime Victims: Research, Policy, and Practice.* Newbury Park, CA: Sage.

Ropp, L., Visintainer, P., Uman, J., & Trelor, D. (1992) Death in the city: An American tragedy. *Journal of the American Medical Association,* 267:2905-2910.

Rosenberg, M., Rodriguez, J., & Chorba, T. (1990) Childhood injuries: Where we are. *Pediatrics,* 86:1084.

Rosenberg, M.L., & Mercy, J.A. (1991) Introduction. In M.L. Rosenberg & M.A Fenley, (Eds.), *Violence in America: A Public Health Approach* (pp. 3-13). New York: Oxford University Press.

Roth, J.A. (1994) Firearms and violence. *National Institute of Justice: Research in Brief,* February, 1-7.

Ryan, K. (1993) Mining the values in the curriculum. *Educational Leadership,* November, 16-18.

Saltzman, L.E., Mercy, J.A., O'Carroll, P.W., Rosenberg, M.L., & Rhodes, P.H. (1992) Weapon involvement and injury outcomes in family and intimate assaults. *Journal of the American Medical Association,* 267:3043-3047.

Searles, P., & Berger, R.J. (1987) The current status of rape reform legislation: An examination of state statutes. *Women's Rights Law Reporter,* 9:25-43.

Seiger, L.H., & Hesson, J. (1994) *Walking for Fitness.* Dubuque, IA: Brown & Benchmark.

Shaffer, D., Philips, I., Garland, A., & Bacon, K. (1990) Prevention issues in youth suicide. In D. Shaffer, I. Philips, & N.B. Enzer (Eds.), *Prevention of Mental Disorders, Alcohol, and Other Drug Use in Children and Adolescents* (pp. 373-412). Office for Substance Abuse Prevention Monograph-2. DHHS Publication No. (ADM)90-1646. Washington, DC: U.S. Government Printing Office.

Sheley, J.F., McGee, Z.T., & Wright, J.D. (1992) Gun-related violence in and around inner-city schools. *American Journal of Diseases in Children,* 146:677-682.

Siegal, M. (1983) Crime and violence in America: The victims. *American Psychologist,* 38:1267-1273.

Silverstein, K. (1994) Laying down the law. *Scholastic Update,* February 11, 14-15.

Simons, R.L., Chyi-in, W., Conger, R.D., & Lorenz, F.O. (1994) Two routes to delinquency: Differences between early and late starters in the impact of parenting and deviant peers. *Criminology,* 32:247-276.

Skogan, W.G, Lurigio, A.J., & Davis, A.J. (1990) In A.J. Lurigio, W.G. Skogan, & R.C. Davis (Eds.), *Victims of Crime: Problems, Policies, and Programs* (pp. 7-22). Newbury Park, CA: Sage.

Sloan, J.H., Kellerman, A.L., Reay, D.T., Ferris, J.A., Koepsell, T., & Rivara, F.P. (1988) Handgun regulations, crime, assaults and homicides: A tale of two cities. *New England Journal of Medicine,* 319:1256-1262.

Sloan, J.H., Rivara, F.P., Reay, D.T., Ferris, J.A., & Kellerman, A.L. (1990) Firearm regulation rates of suicide: A comparison of two metropolitan areas. *New England Journal of Medicine,* 322:369-373.

Smith, K., & Crawford, S. (1986) Suicidal behavior among "normal" high school students. *Suicide and Life-Threatening Behavior,* 16:313-325.

Smolowe, J. (1993) Danger in the safety zone: As violence spreads into small towns, many Americans barricade themselves. *Time,* August 23, 29-32.

Spirito, A., Plummer, B., Gispert, M., Levy S., Kurkjian, J., Lewander, W., Hagberg, S., & Devost, L. (1992) Adolescent suicide attempts: Outcomes at followup. *American Journal of Orthopsychiatry,* 62:464-468.

Stein, N. (1993) Stop sexual harassment in schools. *USA Today,* May 18, 11A.

Steinberg, L. (1991) Adolescent transitions and alcohol and other drug prevention. In E.N. Goperlund (Ed.), *Preventing Adolescent Drug Use: From Theory to Practice* (pp. 13-52). Office for Substance Abuse Prevention Monograph-8. DHHS Publication No. (ADM)91-1725. Rockville, MD: Office for Substance Abuse Prevention.

Stephens, R.D. (1991) Bullies and victims: Protecting our schoolchildren. *USA Today,* September, 72-73.

Strauss, M.A., & Gelles, R.J. (1990) Physical Violence in *American Families: Risk Factors and Adaptation to Violence in 8,145 Families.* New Brunswick, NJ: Transaction.

Thompson, J.W., & Walker, R.D. (1990) Adolescent suicide among American Indians and Alaska Natives. *Psychiatric Annals,* 20:128-133.

Thornberry, T.P., Lizotte, A.J., Krohn, M.D., Farnworth, M., & Jang S.J. (1994) Delinquent peers, beliefs, and delinquent behavior: A longitudinal test of interactional theory. *Criminology,* 32:47-83.

Toby, J. (1993/1994) Everyday school violence: How disorder fuels it. *American Educator,* Winter, 4-9,44.

United States Department of Health and Human Services. (1991) *Healthy People 2000: National Health Promotion and Disease Prevention Objectives.* Publication No. (PHS)91-50213. Washington, DC: U.S. Government Printing Office.

United States Department of Justice. (1991) *Criminal Victimization, 1990* (Special Report No. NCJ-122743). Washington, DC: U.S. Government Printing Office.

Usdansky, M.L. (1994) 4 million kids on wrong side of track. *USA Today,* April 25, 2A.

VanWie, E.K. (1987) *Teenage Stress: How to Cope in a Complex World.* New York: Julian Messner.

Vorrath, H.H., & Brendtro, L.K. (1985) *Positive Peer Culture.* New York: Aldine.

Warshaw, R. (1988) *I Never Called It Rape.* New York: Harper and Row.

Webb, W. (1992) Empowering at-risk children. *Elementary School Guidance and Counseling,* 27:96-103.

Webster, D.W., Gainer, P.S., & Champion, H.R. (1993) Weapon carrying among inner-city junior high school students: Defensive behavior vs. aggressive delinquency. *American Journal of Public Health,* 83:1604-1608.

Weil, D.S. & Hemingway, D. (1992) Loaded guns in the home: Analysis of a national random survey of gun owners. *Journal of the American Medical Association,* 267:3033-3037.

Werner, E.E., & Smith, R.S. (1992) *Overcoming the Odds: High Risk Children from Birth to Adulthood.* Ithaca, NY: Cornell University Press.

Williams, M.M. (1993) Actions speak louder than words: What students think. *Educational Leadership,* November, 22-23.

Wilson, L.L. (1990) Alcohol and date rape: Dangerous liaisons. *Listen,* April, 11-14.

Wilson, M.H., Baker, S.P., Teret, S.T., Shock, S., & Garbarino, J. (1991) *Saving Children: A Guide to Injury Prevention.* New York: Oxford University Press.

Wintemute, G.J., Teret, S.P., Kraus, J.F., & Wright, M.A. (1987) When children shoot children: 88 unintentional deaths in California. *Journal of the American Medical Association,* 257:3107-3109.

Wodarski, J.S., & Hedrick, M. (1987) Violent children: A practice paradigm. *Social Work in Education,* Fall, 28-42.

Wynne, E.A., & Ryan, K. (1993) Curriculum as a moral educator. *American Educator,* Spring, 20-24, 44.

Zitzow, D. (1992) Assessing student stress: School adjustment rating by self-report. *The School Counselor,* 40:20-23.

Zoucha-Jensen, J.M., & Coyne, A. (1993) The effects of resistance strategies on rape. *American Journal of Public Health,* 83:1633-1634.

glossary

A

abuse: the harmful treatment of a person.

active listening: a type of listening in which you let others know you heard and understood what was said.

acquaintance rape: rape that is committed by someone known to the victim.

adrenaline: a hormone that helps the body get ready for an emergency.

adverse environment: a set of conditions and surroundings in which a person lives that interferes with growth, development, and success.

aftercare: the support and supervised services that juvenile offenders receive when they are released and must live and interact in the community.

ageism: behavior that discriminates against people in a specific age group.

aggressive behavior: the use of words and/or actions that show disrespect toward others.

alarm stage: the first stage of the GAS in which the body gets ready for action.

alcohol: a psychoactive drug that depresses the nervous system.

alienation: the feeling that one is apart from others.

amphetamines: drugs that "speed up" the central nervous system.

anabolic steroids: drugs made from male hormones, that produce muscle growth and can change health and behavior.

angel dust: see PCP.

anger: the feeling of being irritated, annoyed, and/or furious.

anger cues: changes in the body or signs that a person is angry.

anger triggers: thoughts or events that cause a person to become angry.

anorexia nervosa: an emotional disorder in which there is excessive preoccupation with food, starvation, or exercising to lose weight.

assault: a physical attack or threat of attack.

assertive behavior: the honest expression of thoughts and feelings without experiencing anxiety or threatening others.

authority: the power and right to govern and apply laws.

autogenic training: a relaxation technique that involves a series of exercises to increase muscle relaxation.

B

battered spouse: a person in a committed relationship that is physically, emotionally, or sexually abused by a partner.

being empowered: a feeling of being inspired because you believe you control your own destiny.

beta-endorphins: substances produced in the brain that help reduce pain and create a feeling of well-being.

biofeedback: a technique for getting information about involuntary processes in the body at a particular time so that an involuntary physical function can be controlled.

boot camp: camp which uses rigorous military-style drills, hard physical training, and structure in an effort to instill discipline and shock in juvenile offenders.

bulimia: an emotional disorder in which an intense fear of being overweight and a lack of self-esteem result in secret binge eating, followed by self-induced vomiting.

bully: a person who hurts or frightens people who are perceived to be smaller or weaker.

bullying: an attempt by people to hurt or frighten those who are perceived to be smaller or weaker.

burglary: an unlawful entry of a structure to commit a theft.

C

caffeine: a stimulant drug that increases the rate of bodily activities.

caring: being interested and concerned.

carjacking: car theft that occurs by force or threat of force while the driver and/or passengers are in or near the vehicle.

Cherokee Nation Youth Fitness Camp: a program in Oklahoma for young people who belong to the Cherokee Nation.

child abuse: the harmful treatment of a person under the age of 18 and includes physical abuse, verbal abuse, emotional abuse, sexual abuse, and neglect.

child neglect: maltreatment that involves failure to provide proper care and guidance.

clarifying response: a response in which a person asks for more information.

cocaine: a drug that stimulates the central nervous system and frequently results in dependence.

codependence: a mental disorder in which a person loses personal identity, has frozen feelings, and copes ineffectively.

coercion: use of force to influence another person.

commitment: a pledge to do something.

communication: the sharing of feelings, thoughts, and information with another person.

concealed weapon: a weapon that is hidden partially or fully from view.

confirming response: a response to acknowledge the feelings that the speaker expressed and to show appreciation for expressing the feelings.

conflict: a disagreement between two or more persons or between two or more choices.

conflict avoidance: a conflict response style in which a person denies that there is a conflict and/or attempts to please others at his/her expense.

conflict confrontation: a conflict response style in which a person attempts to settle a disagreement in a hostile, defiant, and aggressive way.

conflict resolution: a conflict response style in which a person uses conflict resolution skills to resolve a disagreement in a healthful and responsible way.

conflict resolution skills: skills a person can use to resolve a disagreement in a healthful, safe, legal, respectful, and nonviolent way.

conflict response style: a pattern of behavior a person demonstrates when conflict arises.

conscience: an inner sense of right and wrong that prompts good behavior and causes feelings of guilt following bad behavior.

contract for life: a written agreement in which a suicidal person promises not to hurt himself/herself for a certain period of time and/or until (s)he receives professional help.

could-be's: young persons who are interested in belonging to the gang, perhaps because of a friend or family member.

crack: a drug that is pure cocaine that produces rapid ups and downs.

D

daily hassles: the day-to-day stressors of normal living.

decision: a choice.

delayed gratification: allowing oneself to sacrifice in the present so that a benefit will be achieved in the future.

delinquent behavior: an illegal action committed by a juvenile.

denial: a condition in which a person refuses to recognize what (s)he is feeling because it is extremely painful.

dependence: when a person has to have a drug or they experience withdrawal.

depression: a feeling of hopelessness, sadness, or helplessness.

desensitization: the process of lessening a person's response to certain things by overexposing that person to these same things.

detention centers: secure custody facilities that detain juveniles on a temporary basis.

disability: a condition in the body that may require a person to do things in a different way.

discriminatory behavior: making distinctions in treatment or showing behavior in favor of or prejudiced against an individual or group of people.

dispiriting relationships: relationships that are characterized by a state of low spirits.

displacement: the releasing of anger on someone or something other than the cause of the anger.

distress: a harmful response to a stressor that produces negative results.

diversion: an approach to dealing with juvenile offenders that offers services that are designed to provide alternatives to juvenile correctional facilities.

diversity: the quality of being different or varied.

domestic violence: violence that occurs within the family or within other relationships in which people live together.

drug: a substance that changes the way the body and/or mind work.

drug abuse: the use of drugs that lessens the user's ability to function normally or that is harmful to the user or others.

drug-free lifestyle: a lifestyle in which people do not use harmful and illegal drugs.

drug-free zone: a defined area around a school for the purpose of sheltering young persons from the sale of drugs.

drug use: the legal or illegal way in which people use drugs.

dysfunctional family: a family in which feelings are not expressed openly and honestly, coping skills are lacking, and members do not trust each other.

E

elder abuse: maltreatment involving the elderly.

El Puente: a community-based youth center in Brooklyn, New York that offers a wide range of services and activities for young people.

emotional abuse: maltreatment that involves assault in a nonphysical way.

empathy: the ability to share in another's emotions or feelings.

empowerment: the belief that a person controls his/her own destiny.

environment: everything that is around a person in the place in which (s)he lives.

EQUIP: a unique rehabilitation program for juvenile offenders which combines several different approaches: social skills training, anger management, moral education, and support sessions with peers.

eustress: a healthful response to a stressor that produces positive results.

exhaustion stage: the third stage of the GAS in which there is wear and tear on the body, lowered resistance, and an increased likelihood of disease or death.

extended family members: family members in addition to parents and siblings.

F

family continuum: a scale marked in units ranging from zero to 100 to show the quality of relationships within family members.

family relationships: the connections that you have with family members, including extended family members.

fighting: taking part in a physical struggle.

flooding: the sudden, rather than gradual, exposure of a person to what causes the fear.

G

gang: see youth gang.

Gang Alternative and Prevention Program: a program in Los Angeles, California that refers at-risk young people in elementary and middle school to a variety of recreational activities.

gay-bashing: a physical assault on people who are homosexual, that is motivated by prejudice.

general adaptation syndrome (GAS): a series of changes that occur in the body when stress occurs.

H

hallucinogenic drugs: substances that have the major effect of producing distortions in perception.

handgun: a small hand-held weapon that discharges one bullet for each pull of the trigger.

hard-core gang members: the senior gang members with the most influence.

hate crimes: crimes motivated by religious, racial, ethnic, sexual orientation, or other bias.

healthful family: a family in which feelings are expressed openly and honestly, coping skills are adequate, and family members trust each other.

hedonistic gang: groups of young people whose band together to get high on drugs.

helper-T cell: a type of white blood cell that fights pathogens and destroys cancerous cells.

heroin: a drug that slows body functions such as heart rate and breathing, and produces drowsiness and mood swings.

heterosexism: behavior that discriminates against people who are gay, lesbian, and/or bisexual.

hidden anger: anger that is not dealt with in a healthful way and may result in inappropriate behavior and poor health.

HIV: see human immunodeficiency virus.

homeless youth: young people who along with their families, lack shelter; leave home without parental consent; or are thrown out of their homes.

homicide: the accidental or purposeful killing of another person.

homicide survivor: a person who suffers because a friend, family member, or partner has been murdered.

hope: the feeling that what is desired is possible and that events in life may turn out for the best.

hostility: a feeling of ill will and antagonism.

hostility syndrome: the body changes that result from stronger responses of the sympathetic nervous system and weaker responses of the parasympathetic nervous system and immune system.

human immunodeficiency virus (HIV): the pathogen that causes AIDS.

I

I-message: statement that contains 1) a specific behavior or event, 2) the effect the behavior or event has on the individual, and 3) the feeling that resulted.

immune system: the body system that fights disease.

inactive decision-making style: a decision-making style in which a person fails to make choices, and this failure determines what will occur.

inspiriting relationship: a relationship that lifts the spirit and contribute to a sense of well-being.

instrumental gang: groups of young people who band together and commit property crimes to get money.

intergroup conflict: conflict that occurs between two or more groups of persons.

interpersonal conflict: conflict that occurs between two or more persons.

intragroup conflict: conflict that occurs between persons that identify themselves as belonging to the same group.

intrapersonal conflict: conflict that occurs within a person.

ism: beliefs, attitudes, assumptions, and actions that subject individuals or persons in a particular group to discriminatory behavior.

J

jumping-in: a test for toughness in which a young person fights with two gang members at once for an established period of time.

juvenile delinquent: a young person who has anti-social behavior or refuses to follow the law.

juvenile detention: the temporary care of juveniles in physically restricting facilities while their legal case is pending.

juvenile offender: a person below the age of 18 who breaks a criminal law.

L

life skill: an action that keeps people healthy and safe and that are learned and practiced for a lifetime.

loneliness: an anxious, unpleasant, and painful feeling that results from having few friends or from being alienated.

M

marijuana: a drug containing THC that impairs short term memory and changes mood.

mediate: to bring persons who conflict together.

mental rehearsal: a technique that involves imagining oneself in a stressful conversation or situation, pretending to say and do specific things, and imagining how the other person will respond.

mentor: a person who guides and helps younger people.

midnight basketball: a basketball program that is held late at night to keep young people from being on the streets.

moral code: set of rules that a person follows in controlling his/her own behavior.

moral development: the process of gradually learning to base one's behavior or personal beliefs of right and wrong.

murder: a homicide that is purposeful.

N

negative self-esteem: the belief that a person is unworthy and unlovable.

nonviolence: the avoidance of the threatened or actual of physical force to injure, damage, or destroy yourself, others, or property.

nurturing environment: a set of conditions and surroundings in which a person lives that promotes growth, development, and success.

O

Outward Bound USA: an outdoor adventure program in which young people are challenged physically and mentally in a wilderness setting.

P

parasuicide: a suicide attempt in which a person does not intend to die.

parasympathetic nervous system: part of the nervous system that maintains the body's normal state and restores balance after an emergency.

parent abuse: physical and emotional assault of parents by their children.

parole: a conditional release from a sentence in a correctional institution.

parricide: the murder of one's parents.

partner abuse: a range of abusive actions including verbal, sexual, and physical abuse by an adult intimate partner.

passive aggressive: appears cooperative and pleasant while inside feels very angry and hostile.

passive behavior: the holding back of ideas, opinions, and feelings.

PCP: a drug that changes the way a person sees things.

peer: a person who is similar in age or status.

peer mediation: a process used to resolve conflicts, in which a person helps his/her peers resolve disagreements in healthful, safe, legal, respectful, and nonviolent ways.

peer mediator: a person who assists the people who have a conflict in reaching a solution.

peer pressure: pressure that people of similar age or status exert on others to encourage them to make certain decisions or behave in certain ways.

peer programs: programs in which young people serve as role models, facilitators, helpers, and leaders.

perpetrator: a person who commits a violent act.

physical abuse: maltreatment that harms the body.

physical activity: activity that requires a person to use energy and to move his/her muscles.

positive self-esteem: the belief that a person is worthwhile and lovable.

post traumatic stress disorder (PTSD): a condition in which a person relives a stressful experience again and again.

predatory gang: groups of young people who band together to commit crimes and violence.

pre-delinquent behavior: behavior that often lends to breaking the law and includes disobedience, lack of respect for authority, stealing, lying, excessive aggression, inattention at school, truancy, and fighting.

prejudice: suspicion, intolerance, or irrational hatred directed at an individual or group of people.

premoral level: a level of moral development whereby a child determines which behavior is right and which is wrong based on which behavior is likely to be punished and which behavior is rewarded.

principle-centered: having guidelines that direct decisions.

principled level: a level of moral development in which a person has a conscience, operates with a set of principles, and understands that certain actions would violate the rights of others.

prison: a building, usually with cells, where convicted criminals stay.

proactive decision-making style: a decision-making style in which people examine the decision to be made, identify and evaluate actions that can be taken, select an action, and assume responsibility for the consequences.

probation: a sentence in which an offender remains in the community under the supervision of a probation officer for a specific period of time.

procrastination: putting off doing something until a future time.

progressive relaxation: a relaxation technique that involves relaxing the mind by first relaxing the body.

projection: blaming others for actions or events for which they are not responsible.

protective factor: a way that a person might behave and characteristics of the environment in which (s)he lives that promote health, safety, and/or well-being.

psychological needs: things that are needed to feel important and secure and may include friendship, belonging, accomplishments, and status.

R

racism: behavior that discriminates against people who are members of a certain racial or ethnic groups.

rape: the threatened or actual use of physical force to get someone to have sex without giving consent.

rape trauma syndrome: a condition in which a person who has been raped experiences emotional responses and physical symptoms over a period of time.

reactive decision-making style: a decision-making style in which a person allows others to make decisions for them.

recovery efforts: programs a victim may undergo, support a victim may receive, and skills a victim may gain in order to manage the emotional effects of being a victim of violence.

recreational activities: activities that involve play, amusement, and relaxation.

reframing: changing a person's outlook in order to see a situation in a more positive way.

regular gang members: gang members who already

belong to the gang and who back up the hard-core gang members.

rehabilitation: the process of restoring to a normal state of constructive activity through medical or professional treatment.

relationships: the connections that a person has with other people.

resiliency: the ability to prevent or to recover, bounce back, and learn from misfortune, change, or pressure.

resistance skills: skills that are used when a person wants to say NO to an action and/or leave a situation.

resistance stage: the second stage of the GAS in which the body attempts to regain balance and return to normal.

resources: available assets and may include time, money, and material possessions.

respect: having esteem for someone's admirable characteristics and responsible and caring actions.

responsibility: reliability and dependability.

Responsible Decision-Making Model: a series of steps to follow to assure that the decisions a person makes lead to actions that protect health, protect safety, protect laws, follow guidelines set by responsible adults such as parents and guardians, and demonstrate good character and moral values.

restating response: response in which a person repeats what the speaker has said in his/her own words.

restitution: a means of compensating the victim.

risk factor: a way that a person might behave and characteristics of the environment in which a person lives that increase the likelihood of having something negative happen to a person's health, safety, and/or well-being.

risk situations: circumstances that increase the likelihood that something negative will happen to a person's health, safety, and/or well-being.

role conformity: a level of moral development whereby moral decisions are determined by answering, "What will people think of me?"

S

SANE: a nurse who has training in the examination and treatment of rape victims.

Scared Straight: a program in which adults who are serving prison time tell juveniles about the dangers of prison life.

secondary victimizations: unfair treatments experienced by victims after they experience violence.

sedative-hypnotic drugs: drugs that depress the central nervous system and are "downers."

self-centered behavior: behavior in which a person acts in ways that fulfill his/her needs and wishes with little regard for the needs and wishes of others.

self-defense techniques: techniques that can be used when someone is harming or threatening to harm a person.

self-destructive behavior: behavior in which a person harms himself/herself.

self-discipline: the effort or energy with which a person follows a plan to do something.

self-esteem: what a person thinks or believes about himself/herself.

self-loving behavior: healthful and responsible behavior that indicates a person believes (s)he is worthwhile.

self-preservation: the inner desire to keep oneself and others safe from harm, and may include preserving physical, mental, and social health.

self-protection strategies: strategies that can be practiced to protect oneself and decrease the risk of becoming a victim.

serotonin: a naturally occurring chemical found in the brain, blood, and other parts of the body, that helps regulate primitive drives and emotions.

sexism: behavior that discriminates against people of the opposite sex.

sexual abuse: maltreatment that involves inappropriate sexual behavior between an adult and a child.

sexual harassment: unwanted sexual behavior that ranges from making sexual comments to forcing another person into unwanted sex acts.

sexually transmitted diseases (STDs): diseases that are transmitted from an infected person to an uninfected person during intimate sexual contact.

sibling abuse: physical and emotional assaults directed toward a sibling.

socially competent: uses social skills effectively.

social reciprocity: the act of people treating others as they themselves wish to be treated.

social skills: skills that can be used to relate well with others.

sportsmanship: losing without acting out or winning without bragging, and treating other players in fair and courteous ways.

stalking: harassing someone with the intent to threaten or harm that person.

status offense: type of behavior for which an adult would not be arrested, such as truancy, alcohol use, running away, defying parents, and staying out too late.

stereotype: a prejudiced attitude that assigns a specific quality or characteristic to all people who belong to a particular group.

stress: the response of the body to the demands of daily living.

stress management skills: techniques that can be used to cope with the harmful effects produced by stress.

stressor: a demand that causes changes in the body.

suicide: the intentional taking of one's own life.

suicide prevention strategies: techniques that can be used to help prevent a person from thinking about attempting, and completing suicide.

summarizing response: a response to review the major idea or ideas expressed.

sympathetic nervous system: part of the nervous system that prepares the body for emergencies.

synergy: a positive outcome that occurs when different people cooperate and respect one another and as a result, more energy is created for all.

systematic desensitization: a process in which a person is gradually exposed to something that arouses fear and learns to respond less to it.

T

trustworthiness: acting in a right, responsible, and effective way.

V

values: the beliefs, goals, and standards held by a person.

victim: a person who is harmed by violence.

victim recovery: a person's return to physical and emotional health after being harmed by violence.

violence: the threatened or actual use of physical force to injure, damage, or destroy yourself, others, or property.

W

wanna-be's: young persons who are not gang members, usually dress in gang colors, and engage in dangerous behavior to prove themselves to regular and hard-core gang members.

weapon: an instrument or device used for fighting.

Y

you-message: a statement that blames or shames another person instead of expressing feelings.

youth gang: group of young people who band together and participate in violent, unlawful, or criminal behavior.

index

Totally Awesome Teaching Strategies

USING THE *TOTALLY AWESOME*™ TEACHING STRATEGIES

Totally Awesome™ **Teaching Strategies** are creative ways to involve students in learning about violence and practicing life skills to prevent violence. For each of the objectives identified in the violence prevention curriculum K through 12, there is a *Totally Awesome*™ Teaching Strategy. The following discussion focuses on the design of the *Totally Awesome*™ Teaching Strategies.

THE DESIGN OF THE *TOTALLY AWESOME*™ TEACHING STRATEGIES

The *Totally Awesome*™ Teaching Strategies include:
- <u>Clever Title</u>. A clever title is set in boldfaced type in the center of the page.
- <u>Designated Grade Level</u>. The grade level for which the teaching strategy is appropriate appears in the upper left-hand corner.
- <u>Designated Curriculum Objective</u>. The curriculum objective that will be met by using the teaching strategy is identified directly beneath the grade level designated in the upper left-hand corner.
- <u>Designated Protective Factors</u>. The protective factors that are discussed when using the teaching strategy are designated directly beneath the curriculum objective that appears in the upper left-hand corner.
- <u>Infusion into Curriculum Areas</u>. The teaching strategies are designed to be infused into several curriculum areas other than health education: art studies, foreign language, home economics, language arts, physical education, math studies, music studies, science studies, social studies, and visual and performing arts.

- <u>Critical Thinking</u>. A number of the teaching strategies help students develop critical thinking skills. A symbol to the right of the title of the teaching strategy is used to designate critical thinking.

- <u>Character Education</u>. Several of the teaching strategies focus on helping students develop character. A symbol to the right of the title of the teaching strategy is used to designate character education.

- <u>Objective</u>. The objective for the teaching strategy is listed under this boldfaced subheading. The objective helps the professional to focus on what is to be learned and how to measure the learning that has taken place.
- <u>Life Skills</u>. The life skills that are reinforced by using the teaching strategy are listed under this boldfaced subheading. Life skills are actions that help keep young people healthy and safe, and they are learned and practiced for a lifetime. Next to each life skill a reference is made to the numbered protective factor that is being reinforced by practicing this action.
- <u>Materials</u>. The materials are readily available and inexpensive items that the professional must gather to do the teaching strategy. They are listed under this boldfaced subheading.
- <u>Motivation</u>. The motivation is the step-by-step directions the professional follows when using the teaching strategy. The directions are listed under this boldfaced subheading.
- <u>Evaluation</u>. The evaluation is the means of measuring the students' mastery of the objective and life skills. The evaluation is described under this boldfaced subheading.
- <u>Inclusion</u>. Suggestions for adapting the teaching strategy to assist students with special learning challenges are included under this boldfaced subheading.

I Love You ??

Objective:

Students will name types of violence.

Life Skills:

I will not act in ways that harm others. (PF1)
I will not say hurtful words or act in harmful ways toward others who are different. (PF11)
I will change the way I act if I act in harmful ways toward others. (PF20)

Materials:

I Love My Kitten student master (page 137), a copy for each student, crayons, stickers

Motivation:

1 Introduce the term violence. **Violence** is hurting yourself or somebody else on purpose. Violent actions are unloving acts. Unloving actions are actions that harm another person. Ask students for examples of unloving actions. Students might suggest calling a person a name, biting, tripping, telling a lie about a person, hitting, fighting, stealing something, or being unkind. Have students suggest as many examples as possible.

2 Explain that sometimes a person chooses violent actions and harms another person. Sometimes a person is a victim of violence. A **victim** is a person who gets harmed. Stress that violent actions are wrong. Explain that it is wrong to harm another person. Remind students that sometimes people they know can harm them. Sometimes they can be harmed by people they do not know. These people might cause harm by stealing something; by hitting, biting, or injuring a

person in some way; or by not feeding or caring for another person.

3 Introduce the term loving actions and ask the students what they think this term means. Explain that loving actions are the ways people show how they care about others. Loving actions are different from violent actions. For example, a student remembers to thank someone who gives him/her a gift. A student remembers to put his/her toys away because (s)he loves his/her parents and they have asked him/her to do that. If a student has a pet, (s)he shows love for the pet by playing with it, feeding it on time, and taking good care of it every day.

4 Explain that you can have loving feelings about a person or pet but not show loving actions toward that person or pet. For example, a girl may love her kitten, but she may not treat the kitten in a loving way. Perhaps she kicks the kitten when she feels angry about something. Perhaps she forgets to feed the kitten. Perhaps she forgets to play with the kitten or to pet the kitten. Remind students that it is important for them to change the way they act if they have treated another person or a pet in a harmful way. They can tell the other person that they are sorry. They can decide not to act in harmful ways.

5 Remind students that where they live there are people who are different. Some people have dark skin; some have light skin; some speak a different language. Explain to students that it is important to respect others. To respect another person means not to do or say anything that would be harmful to that person. Remind students that if they have said or done anything harmful to a person who is different, they can change. They can tell the person they are sorry and not do that again.

6 Emphasize that actions such as punching and kicking are violent actions that can harm another person. Explain to students that if anyone treats them in a violent way, they should tell an adult. Review with the class who responsible adults are in their school and community (family members, a teacher, a school nurse, and so on). Explain to students that if they do not get help from the first adult they ask, they should ask another adult.

7 Explain to students that anyone who treats them in a violent way needs help so they won't do it again. This is another reason that it is important for students to tell an adult if anyone treats them in a violent way.

8 Distribute copies of the *I Love My Kitten* student master for the students to color. Explain that even though they do not have a kitten for a pet, they are to think of ways they would show loving actions toward a kitten. Have each student print his/her name on the line provided.

Evaluation:

Have students tell ways some people might harm others and why this is wrong. Have students name at least one adult in their community who would help if someone tried to harm them. Give each student a sticker that (s)he is to give to an adult who helps keep him/her safe. Ask students if they would like to share with the class to whom they are going to give a sticker.

I Love My Kitten

_____

SAY NO MITTENS

Objective:

Students will tell ways to say NO when other children want them to act in ways that would harm others.

Life Skills:

I will develop positive self-esteem. (PF2)
I will make wise choices. (PF12)
I will say NO when others want me to act in harmful ways. (PF13)
I will stay away from gangs. (PF16)

Materials:

Red construction paper, tape, scissors

Motivation:

1 Explain to students that if they are asked to do something that is not healthful or safe, they must respond in a way that makes it clear that they mean NO when they say NO. They need to show that they mean their decisions. Ask students to tell when they have said NO to something they did not want to do. Perhaps they were asked to tell a lie about someone. Perhaps they were asked to take something that belonged to another student. Explain that these are examples of actions that would harm another person. Stress that a person who would do either of these requests would not be making a wise decision.

2 Explain what a decision is. A **decision** is a choice. A wise decision is one that is right. A wise decision is one that shows you care about yourself and others. A wise decision follow the rules set by responsible adults.

3 Explain that people will make wise decisions if they have positive self-esteem or, in other words, if they like themselves. Having positive self-esteem makes people feel good about making wise decisions. They don't want to harm themselves or others. Explain that one way for a student to develop positive self-esteem is to work to do his/her best in school. Explain that a person who has positive self-esteem does not want to be around people who destroy property or harm others.

4 Instruct students to make a NO mitten (see illustration) using red construction paper. Explain that they are going to use their mittens to show when they would say NO to some situations like the ones you are going to tell them about.

5 Explain that you are going to describe different situations in which a student is being pressured to do something. After hearing each situation, each student is to decide if the situation is something that would be harmful to others. If it would be harmful, the student is to raise his/her NO mitten and to repeat what you say about the situation.

6 The following are examples of situations to use. 1) Several students are calling another student a name that is not nice. They want you to join them. (Students will raise their mittens. You will say "NO, I will not call a student by a name that is not nice because I would not want to be called a name." The students will repeat what you say.) 2) A student wants you to help steal something that belongs to someone else. (Students will raise their mittens. You will say "NO, I will not steal something that belongs to someone else because it is wrong." The students will repeat what you say.) 3) A student wants you to help him by getting into a fight with another student. (Students will raise their mittens. You will say "NO, I will not get into a fight with another student because (s)he might get hurt." Students will repeat what you say.) 4) You see some classmates after school throwing rocks at another student and they want you to join them. (Students will raise their mittens. You will say "NO, I will not throw rocks at another student because (s)he might get hurt." Students will repeat what you say.) You may want to add other situations of your own.

7 Review the answers with students and have them share the reasons for their choices.

Have students identify other situations in which they would say NO.

Evaluation:

Give students the following three scenarios that involve things their friends might ask them to do. Ask which one(s) they should say NO to. 1) A friend asks you to go home with her so that she doesn't have to be alone until her mother comes home from work. 2) A friend wants you tell another student that (s)he is not nice. 3) A friend wants you to eat lunch with him.

BULL'S EYE

Objective:

Students will tell ways to handle disagreements without fighting.

Life Skills:

I will use manners and treat others fairly. (PF5)
I will try to work out disagreements without fighting. (PF10)

Materials:

Poster paper (one sheet per student plus three extra sheets), magic marker, string, hole puncher, crayons

Motivation:

1 To prepare for this strategy, use a magic marker to make a target on one of the extra sheets of poster paper. The target should be several concentric circles with a bull's eye in the center. Use the hole puncher to punch a hole at two corners of the target and attach string so that the bull's eye can be worn around the neck. Then using the two other extra sheets of poster paper, cut out at least five arrows.

2 Explain to students that you are going to talk about conflicts. A **conflict** is a disagreement between two or more persons or between two or more choices. Explain that it is important to learn how to handle disagreements without getting into a fight. Explain that some people are bullies. A **bully** is a person who hurts or frightens other people. A bully enjoys annoying other people.

3 Explain that there does not have to be a loser in every conflict. By learning to deal with a conflict in positive ways, both sides in the conflict can "win." Getting into a fight is not a healthful way to resolve a conflict. It is better to find a healthful way to resolve a conflict rather than to get into a fight in which someone might be hurt.

4 Select one student to wear the target around his/her neck. This student will stand in front of the class. Give the five arrows to five other students. These students are going to be the bullies. They are going to try to get into a disagreement with the student who is wearing the target.

5 Have one of the students who has an arrow go to up to the student who is wearing the target and say, "I'm first." Then the bully is to touch the tip of his/her arrow to the bull's eye on the target. Suggest to the class that these two students were waiting to go down the slide. The student wearing the target was first in line, and the student with the arrow wanted to go first. Explain that the bully may have pushed the other student because bullies often push and shove to get their way. Ask students how the student who was being bullied probably felt. They may mention that the student was angry, felt like pushing or hitting the bully, or perhaps let the bully go first.

6 Now have the other students who have arrows stand next to the student wearing the target. Ask the class to tell you about times when they have been bullied or when another person tried to get them into a fight. Each time an example is given, have one of the students who has an arrow touch the bull's eye.

7 Explain that the student wearing the target allowed the arrows of the bullies to touch him/her. To stop this, the student needs some skills so that (s)he can handle a conflict without starting a fight. Explain that it is easier for a person to handle disagreements without fighting when (s)he has learned to treat others fairly and with respect. (S)he has confidence in his/her abilities to relate to others in a positive and friendly way.

8 Discuss ways that conflicts might be solved. Explain that staying calm, trying to understand the other person's actions, and looking for a solution with which both people will be happy are healthful and responsible ways to resolve conflicts. Suggest also that the person being bullied can ask for help.

9 Give each student a sheet of poster paper and instruct him/her to draw a target in the middle of the poster paper similar to the one you drew. Have them color the bull's eye. Explain that if they held the target in front of them, a bully could see that they are a target. But they do not have to be a target if they feel good about themselves. When they feel good about themselves, they will feel stronger to talk about any disagreements they have. Have students use crayons to draw pictures of ways to feel good about themselves and how to handle disagreements without fighting.

Evaluation:

Have students tell you what a bully is and how they might handle a disagreement with a bully without getting into a fight.

IT MAKES ME ANGRY

Objective:

Students will tell healthful ways to express anger.

Life Skill:

I will express my anger in healthful ways. (PF6)

Materials:

The Angry Bear student master (page 144), a copy for each student, crayons, cardboard, enough for one cardboard circle for each student, scissors, paste

Motivation:

1 To prepare for this strategy, cut circles from cardboard, one for each student. The circles should be large enough for the students to paste *The Angry Bear* (see the student master).

2 Ask students if they have ever been angry. Explain what anger is. **Anger** is the feeling of being mad. Ask students to share examples of what caused them to feel anger. Explain that it is all right to be angry but that angry feelings should not be expressed in ways that harm yourself or others. For example, if a child's younger brother broke the child's favorite toy, it would be understandable that the child would be angry. However, breaking the brother's favorite toy in return or hitting the brother would not be a healthful response.

3 Distribute copies of *The Angry Bear* master and give each student a cardboard circle. Students are to color and cut out the picture of

the Angry Bear. Using paste, they are to paste their Angry Bear to the cardboard circle.

4 Explain that it is important for students to know when they are angry and to tell someone that they are angry. Tell the students that you are going to describe different situations to them. If the situation you describe would make them angry, they are to hold up their Angry Bear circles. As they hold up their Angry Bears, you tell about the situation, and the children will then repeat it.

5 Examples of situations are as follows: 1) You are on the playground, and it is your turn next to be on the slide. Somebody cuts in front of you. (Students will hold up their Angry Bears because that is an action that would make them angry.) You will say "I was waiting for a turn on the slide and you cut in front of me and I feel angry." (The students will then repeat what you have said.) Ask students if pushing the person would be a healthful way to show their anger. Students will answer "no." 2) Your friend takes the ball you are playing with and says that she doesn't want to give it back. (Students will hold up their Angry Bears because that is an action that would make them angry.) You will say "I was playing with the ball when you took it away from me and won't give it back and that makes me angry." (The students will then repeat what you have said.) Explain that they have repeated statements that are healthful ways to express angry feelings.

6 Using the following situations, continue in the same pattern. 3) You are working on a puzzle and you have almost finished when someone comes up and pushes the puzzle pieces on to the floor. 4) You are walking to school with a friend and someone comes along and calls you a name that you do not like. 5) The person who sits behind you in school keeps pinching you. (You may wish to add other situations.)

Evaluation:

Describe the following scenarios to the students and ask them what they could say to the person who made them angry.

- Someone on the bus steals your lunch.
- Your sister takes all the cookies off your plate and eats them.
- Someone takes your pencil off your desk and breaks it.
- Someone pushes you on the playground and you fall down.

The Angry Bear

UPS AND DOWNS

Objective:

Students will tell healthful ways to handle stress.

Life Skills:

I will choose healthful ways to handle stress. (PF7)
I will participate in physical activity. (PF8)

Materials:

Ups And Downs student master (page 147), a copy for each student, crayons

Motivation:

1 Explain that everyone has times when they feel upset or "down." People feel down for different reasons. Explain that there are many reasons people may feel down. Ask students to identify circumstances that may have caused them to feel upset or down. They may say: when they had to move away from their friends, when their parents divorced, when their pet died, when they had an argument with a friend, when someone broke a favorite toy, when someone called them a name, or when they fell on the playground.

2 Introduce the term stress and explain what it means. **Stress** is the change inside a person's body caused by something they may see, hear, or feel. For example, explain that losing a pet would cause stress. Discuss what changes in his/her body might occur if a student had a pet and the pet was lost. Ask students how they would feel if their pet was lost. Students may answer that they would cry; they would be worried that something had happened to the pet; they wouldn't want to eat until the pet was found; or they couldn't get to sleep because they were upset. Explain that these are examples of stress and that everyone has stress at some time.

3 Explain that it is not healthful to let the effects of stress keep a person down or upset. It is important to bounce back. Distribute copies of the *Ups And Downs* student master and have the students color the monkey on the pogo stick.

4 When they have finished coloring, discuss how they can bounce back just like a monkey on a pogo stick when they are feeling stress. Use specific examples and ask students what they would do to bounce back. For example, what would they do if they had an argument with their best friend and they were unhappy about that. Answers might be: talk to the friend and try to settle their differences; talk to a parent or teacher and share what happened and ask for help; or get enough sleep.

5 Explain to students that it is important that they take care of their bodies when they are feeling stress. They should get enough sleep and eat healthful foods that contain vitamins. They should exercise by riding a bike, playing ball, or playing at the playground. Ask students to think of other ways they might bounce back from the effects of stress.

Evaluation:

One at a time, have each student show how (s)he colored his/her *Ups And Downs*. Have each student give an example of stress that (s)he has felt and tell how (s)he could bounce back from the effects of that stress.

Inclusion:

Students with special learning challenges can share positive ways that people have helped them when they have felt stress when they had to learn something new.

Ups And Downs

STEP UP TO SAFETY

Objective:

Students will tell ways to stay safe from people who might harm them.

Life Skill:

I will follow rules to stay safe from persons who might harm me. (PF18)

Materials:

Small risers or footstools on which students can safely step up (It is not necessary to have one for each student.)

Motivation:

1 To prepare for this strategy, collect as many risers or footstools as possible. If you do not have a riser or footstool for each student, students can take turns using the ones you have.

2 Talk about safety. Explain that there are rules or guidelines they can follow that will help them stay safe. These rules are important so that children will not be injured or harmed. Explain that there are safety rules that apply at different times and in different places. For example, there are safety rules to follow at home, school, or at play. Stress that each person must follow rules to keep himself/herself safe.

3 Discuss strangers. Explain that a stranger is someone you do not know and that most strangers are nice. However, some strangers may harm boys and girls. Explain that strangers may not look any different from other people and that most strangers do not harm children. However, each student needs to follow rules to keep safe around all people.

4 Explain to students that you are going to talk about some safety rules. Explain that as you give them a rule, they are to step up onto the riser or footstool if the rule is one they should follow. As they step up onto the riser or footstool, they should say "Step up to safety." If the rule you give them is not one they should follow, they should not step up. Those students who do not have a riser or footstool can stand by their desks and pretend to step up.

5 You may choose to add safety rules to follow in your community. If you want to mix in a few unsafe rules, turn the safe rule around. For example, you might say "I take candy if a stranger offers it to me." Following are suggested rules:

- I will not give my name and address to a stranger if I answer the telephone.
- I will not talk to strangers.
- I will not even go near a car driven by a stranger.
- I will not go near a person whom I know is using drugs.
- I will stay away from guns and knives.
- I will not go anywhere without my parent's permission.
- I will tell an adult if someone tries to touch me in an unsafe way.
- I will tell an adult if a stranger tries to give me candy.
- I will not take any pill or anything from a stranger.
- I will not cross the street except at a traffic light or crosswalk.
- I will stay with my parent when I am at the mall.

- I will know where the "Safe Home" is in my neighborhood.

Evaluation:

Review the safety rules and have students share the reasons that they should practice each one.

Inclusion:

Children with a physical handicap can call out "Step up to safety" without stepping up onto the riser or footstool.

HARMFUL CHANGES

Objective:

Students will explain that drugs may change the way a person acts.

Life Skills:

I will not try alcohol or other drugs. (PF14)
I will stay away from persons who use harmful drugs. (PF14)

Materials:

Several paper cups, water

Motivation:

1 Explain to students that alcohol is a drug. A **drug** is something other than food that changes the way a person thinks and feels. When people drink alcohol or take other drugs, their feelings become too strong and they "overflow." Explain that you are going to use paper cups and water to illustrate what happens when a person reaches this overflow point.

2 Fill cup #1 about half full of water and select a student to hold this cup over a sink or other suitable container that will hold some overflow water. Put small amounts of water in other cups. Students will be adding water to cup #1 from cups #2, 3, 4 (or as many cups as you choose to use) until cup #1 overflows.

3 Ask students to suppose that one family member might be angry with another family member and that the angry family member has been drinking alcohol. Cups #2, 3, 4 represent additional drinks of alcohol that the angry family member drinks. Select students to pour the water from these cups into cup #1 one at a time. Point out that cup #1 gets fuller with the addition of water from the other cups and then it overflows. In the same way, the angry family member will get more and more angry with each drink of alcohol and then his/her feelings will overflow. (S)he will not be able to act as (s)he usually does.

4 Explain that a person is more likely to harm another person when his/her emotions are out of control. This person will behave in ways (s)he would not behave ordinarily. Although this person normally would be able to control his/her feelings, the alcohol (or drug use) stops this from happening.

5 Ask students if they have ever felt angry. Discuss what might cause a person to feel angry. Remind them that it is important to handle their angry feelings so that they do not let those feelings overflow and do something that might harm another person or themselves. If they were to use alcohol or another drug, they would lose that control.

6 Tell students that it is very important for them to stay away from anyone who is using alcohol or other drugs. Remind them that just as the cup of water overflowed, people who are using alcohol or other drugs might reach a point at which they lose control of their emotions and try to harm other people. Remind students that they may see a person in their neighborhood, or even in their family, who is using alcohol or other drugs. They need to stay away from that person because his/her feelings may be out of control. That person may harm someone without really meaning to do so.

Evaluation:

Have students share ways they can protect themselves from a person who they know is using alcohol or other drugs.

PRIVATE BODY PARTS

Objective:

Students will explain the difference between safe and unsafe touch.

Life Skills:

I will expect family members to treat me in kind ways. (PF3)

I will tell someone if family members treat me in harmful ways. (PF3)

I will say NO if someone tries to touch me in an unsafe way. (PF18)

I will get help if I have been touched in an unsafe way. (PF19)

Materials:

My Private Body student master (page 154), a copy for each student, crayons

Motivation:

1 Explain to students that it is important for them to protect their bodies. Ask students what they think the word private means. Private means something that belongs to a particular person. Explain that every person has areas of his/her life and body that are private.

2 Explain that a person's body is special and that each person is responsible for keeping his/her body safe. Certain parts of each person's body are private. Private body parts are the parts of the body that a bathing suit protects and covers. Identify the following body parts as private: the behind; a boy's penis (the part between a boys legs); a girl's vagina (the part between a girl's legs); and breasts.

3 Explain that it is important for a person to respect himself/herself. Self-respect is feeling good about yourself. Self-respect helps you protect yourself and stand up for yourself. Children can expect family members to respect them and to treat them in loving and kind ways. Tell students that it is important for them to tell a trusted adult if a family member harms them.

4 Explain that everyone has a right to be safe. This means that *everyone* has a right to be treated in a safe manner and a right to be safe from anyone who might not treat him/her in an unsafe way. Remind students that since they were babies, they have been cared for. They have been fed, clothed, and bathed by their parents or guardians. They have been hugged and kissed. These are examples of being treated in a safe manner. They are safe touches. A safe touch is a touch that feels right and that makes a person feel special and loved. Safe touches are usually from a trusted adult such as a parent or guardian or nurse or doctor. Safe touches make a person feel respected, protected, and good.

5 Explain that it is possible to be touched in a way that does not feel right or good. This is an unsafe touch. An unsafe touch is a touch that does not feel good and usually involves private body parts. A person usually does not like an unsafe touch. A person who touches in an unsafe way might be someone the student knows. The person might be a stranger. The person might be someone in the family.

6 Instruct students how to protect themselves if they experience an unsafe touch. First, they should tell the person to stop touching them. They should get away and stay away from the person. In addition to getting away from the person, it is very important to tell a trusted adult about the unsafe touch. If the first adult is not helpful, a student should go to another trusted adult until (s)he gets help. Explain that it is important to feel safe again after experiences such as unsafe touches. Talking about the experience and sharing feelings with a trusted adult will help.

7 Distribute copies of *My Private Body* student master for the students to color. Explain that they will share their papers with their families.

Evaluation:

Have students use their pictures with their parents or guardians to tell them about safe touches and unsafe touches and what has been learned in the lesson.

My Private Body

SAFETY DETECTIVE

Objective:

Students will tell what to do when they are around weapons such as guns and knives.

Life Skill:

I will follow the SAFE rule: Stop, Avoid getting closer, Find an adult, Explain what I saw. (PF15)

Materials:

Where The Weapons Are student master (page 157), a copy for each student, *NO-NO Circles* student master (page 158), a copy for each student, crayons

Motivation:

1 Explain to students what a weapon is. A **weapon** is an object such as a gun which might harm a person. There are many different kinds of weapons. When most people think about weapons, they probably think about guns and knives because they are used so often to harm other persons. However, any object that is used to harm a person can be a weapon.

2 Explain that students need to protect themselves. If they see a gun or a knife, or if they see anyone carrying a gun or a knife, they need to stop and get away from that area or that person. They need to tell you if they saw a gun or knife at school. If they are not at school, they still need to protect themselves. They need to tell a parent or another trusted adult.

3 Explain that there are rules about having weapons such as guns or knives in school. Rules help keep all the students in the school

safe. Explain that a gun with bullets in it is dangerous. You cannot tell if a gun has bullets in it just by looking at it. It is better not to risk becoming injured. Explain that a person who carries a gun may not intend to harm anyone, but that the gun might shoot accidentally.

4 Distribute a copy of the *Where The Weapons Are* student master to each student. Discuss each picture with the students. Discuss the picture in the upper left corner. The open drawer shows a gun sticking out from beneath some clothing in the drawer. Explain that it is possible for someone to own a gun and make every effort to hide it. Ask students why someone might choose to hide a gun. Instruct students to get away from any gun they see and to never touch a gun, no matter where they see one. They should find a responsible adult and tell him/her about the gun.

5 Discuss the picture in the lower right corner. The student sitting by the open window hears a gunshot. Explain that if the student is close enough to hear the gunshot, the student is in danger. Ask students what they would do if they were that student. Instruct them that if they find themselves in a situation like that, they should get away from the window and go to a safer place in the house. They should find a responsible adult and stay with that person so that they will be safe.

6 Discuss the picture in the lower left corner. Someone has tried to get rid of a dangerous knife by throwing it in the trash can. Ask students what they would do if they saw a knife in a trash can. Discuss the importance of not touching the knife and letting a responsible adult know about the knife so that it can be removed safely and not be left in the trash can to possibly injure another person.

7 Discuss the picture in the upper right corner. A student is carrying a knife in his/her bookbag to school. The handle of the knife is sticking out of the bookbag. Instruct students that if they see a knife in another student's bookbag, they should not speak to that student about the knife. They should find a responsible adult as soon as possible to get help. They should think not only of protecting themselves but also of protecting other students.

8 Distribute a copy of the *NO-NO Circles* student master to each student. Have the students color the circles red to show danger. Students are to cut out the circles and paste them over the pictures on the *Where The Weapons Are* master. By pasting the circles on the pictures, they are indicating that they should not touch the gun in the drawer, for example. As they paste a circle over a picture, stress again that whenever they find evidence of a weapon, they should tell a trusted adult.

Evaluation:

Explain that a detective is someone who finds things. Students are to be safety detectives so that if they see a weapon, such as a gun or a knife, they will not touch the weapon and they will tell an adult if they find a weapon. Ask students to identify an adult they will tell if they find a weapon.

Where The Weapons Are

NO-NO Circles

SAFETY SHIELD

Objective:

Students will name persons who can help them stay safe.

Life Skills:

I will try to be in places where I can stay safe. (PF4)

I will listen to wise adults and follow rules and laws. (PF17)

I will act in ways to keep myself safe. (PF18)

Materials:

My Safety Shield student master (page 161), a copy for each student, paper, pencils, crayons

Motivation:

1 Explain that there are many people in a home, school, and community who protect children and keep them safe. Tell students that they are going to name some of those people and tell what they can do to keep children safe.

2 Distribute a sheet of paper to each student and have each student print his/her name in the center of the paper. Tell students that they are going to make a safety shield that will remind them that there are adults who will protect them and help keep them safe. Distribute copies of *My Safety Shield* student master. Point out that there are four sections on the shield. Students will print a name on each section and then color and cut out the shield.

3 On the chalkboard, print the word PARENT and have the students print that word in one part of the shield. Ask students how a parent helps keep them safe. They may say that a parent gives a safe home; tucks them into bed at night; teaches them how to cross a street safely; hugs them when they are afraid, and so on.

4 Print the word TEACHER on the chalkboard and have students print that word in a second part of the shield. Ask students how a teacher helps keep them safe. In school, students learn how to play safely on the playground; how to be safe on a school bus; how to follow school safety rules, and so on.

5 Print the word POLICE on the chalkboard and have students print that word in the third part of the shield. Discuss how police help keep children safe. Police are often nearby to answer questions or to help a person; they are always watching for dangerous situations; they help people when they have accidents, and so on.

6 Print the term SCHOOL NURSE on the chalkboard and have students print that term in the fourth part of the shield. Discuss how the school nurse helps keep children safe. The school nurse calls a parent when a student is ill or is hurt; the school nurse takes care of students when they fall or get hurt on the playground; the school nurse may give students medicines to keep them well, and so on.

7 Students will color and then cut out their shields. Instruct students to place their shields over their names that they printed on a sheet of paper. Stress that the people who are identified on each shield are always ready to protect students and to help keep them safe. Point out also that students can help protect themselves. They can choose to spend time with people who help them to do their best. They can make a promise or pledge to obey school rules that are made to protect all students. They can stay away from anyone who tries to harm them.

8 Stress to students that it is important that they feel safe at all times. Discuss what they might do if they are in a place in which they do not feel safe. They can go to one of the people on their shield for help.

Evaluation:

Have students take their name papers and shields home to share with their parents. Ask students to talk with their parents about other people in their families and neighborhoods who would help keep them safe.

My Safety Shield

DON'T HARM OTHERS

Objective:

Students will name types of violence.

Life Skills:

I will not act in ways that harm others. (PF1)
I will not say hurtful words or act in harmful ways toward others who are different. (PF11)
I will change the way I act if I act in harmful ways toward others. (PF20)

Materials:

Don't Harm Others student master (page 164), a copy for each student, pencils

Motivation:

1 Explain to students that there are ways that people show others that they are loved. There also are ways that people harm others. Introduce the term loving actions. Loving actions are ways people show how they care about others. Ask students for examples of ways they show others they care about them. Students might suggest giving a parent a hug, sharing toys with a friend, helping others with a chore, or telling someone that you like him/her. Have students give as many examples as possible.

2 Introduce the term violence. **Violence** is harming oneself or another person. Anything a person does to harm another person is a violent action. Explain that there are many types of violence. The following are examples:

- **Bullying** is when a person tries to hurt or scare another person.
- **Fighting** is being involved in a physical fight.

- **Homicide** is the killing of another person.
- **Child abuse** is the harmful treatment of a child. The abuse can be hitting someone, calling someone names, or not paying attention to or caring for a child.

3 Distribute copies of the *Don't Harm Others* student master. Discuss each picture on the master with the students and ask them to place an X over the pictures that show harmful actions. Ask students to explain why they placed an X over a picture. Introduce the term victim. A **victim** is a person who is harmed by violence. Ask students to explain how they might feel if they were the victim of the harmful action as shown in the picture. Explain that when a person is the victim of a harmful action, (s)he might be harmed in different ways. The person might be harmed by being beaten. (S)he might need a bandage over a cut, or might even have a broken bone as the result of a harmful action. The person might also be harmed emotionally. (S)he might be frightened and not be able to sleep. (S)he might have his/her feelings hurt by name-calling and not want to come back to school again. Point out that it is important for students to think of others and not do anything that might harm another person. This is especially true of a person who is different. This person's skin may be a different color; this person may speak a different language. No matter what the difference might be, it is wrong to do anything that might harm such a person.

4 Explain that once people get in the habit of acting in ways that are not harmful to others, they feel better about themselves. They know that they are doing the right thing when they treat others with respect. Stress that it is never too late to change. A person who has been choosing harmful actions can change. There are adults who are trained to help people who want to change their behavior.

Evaluation:

Have the students sit in a circle. One by one, they are to tell a way that a person can harm another person. After each student identifies a harmful action, the other students are to say out loud: "I will not act in ways that harm others." Then the students will identify what the opposite loving action would be.

Don't Harm Others

RED LIGHT, GREEN LIGHT

Objective:

Students will tell ways to say NO when other children want them to act in ways that would harm others.

Life Skills:

I will develop positive self-esteem. (PF2)
I will make wise choices. (PF12)
I will say NO when others want me to act in harmful ways. (PF13)
I will stay away from gangs. (PF16)

Materials:

Red construction paper, a sheet for each student, green construction paper, a sheet for each student, scissors, red crayon, one for each student, green crayon, one for each student, paper

Motivation:

1 Explain to students that sometimes other people may pressure them to make certain decisions or behave in certain ways. Students might be asked to help another person. They might be asked to push another person. Explain that these are examples of situations about which they would have to make a decision. Explain that a **decision** is a choice. If students were asked to help another person, they would make a choice. Would they make a wise decision and say yes? If so, ask students why they would say yes. Explain that there are situations about which they should be prepared to say NO. They should make a wise decision and say NO to anything that would be harmful to themselves or to another person.

2 Emphasize to students that if they are asked to do something that would harm another person, they should say NO in a firm way. They need to let others know that they mean what they say and that they are in charge of their decisions. In this way, they will convince others that they do not want to be involved in any activity that would be harmful to another person.

3 Introduce the term self-esteem. **Self-esteem** is what a person thinks or believes about himself/herself. Students with positive self-esteem like themselves. They work to do their best in school. They help others. They have friends who encourage them to do their best. People with positive self-esteem make wise decisions because they do not want to harm themselves or others. Explain that if students have negative self-esteem, they do not like themselves. They might not be positive enough to make wise decisions.

4 Explain that if there are gangs in a student's neighborhood, (s)he should stay away from any gang members. Gangs are often engaged in violence that results in people getting hurt or killed. Encourage students to say NO to any activity related to a gang.

5 Distribute a sheet of red construction paper and a sheet of green construction paper to each student. They are each to make and cut out a red traffic light and a green traffic light. Explain that you are going to read a list of activities to them. For each activity, they are to make a decision. Might this activity harm another person? If they think that an activity might be harmful to another person, they are to hold up their red traffic light. If they think that an activity would not be harmful to another person, they are to hold up their green traffic light.

6 Following is a list of activities to use for this strategy. Explain that these are examples of activities students might be asked to do by another person. You may choose to add examples of your own.
- Call someone a name
- Include a new student in a game on the playground
- Push a student in order to get to the front of the line
- Trip a student to make others laugh
- Help a person who may be ill
- Break a window
- Play in an empty house
- Help a person who has fallen
- Pick up a gun
- Scare an elderly person
- Break a window
- Throw litter into a neighbor's yard
- Kick someone
- Choose a book from the library
- Write words on the school building
- Cross a street at a crosswalk
- Laugh at a student who made a mistake
- Use bad language
- Share lunch with a student who has none
- Take another student's toy

would not be harmful, the student would use the green crayon. When you tell them the first activity, students are to write the number 1 with the correct color of crayon. For the second activity, they are to write the number 2 with the red or the green crayon, and so on. Follow this procedure for the balance of the activities.

Evaluation:

Distribute a sheet of paper, a red crayon, and a green crayon to each student. Think of five more helpful and harmful activities in which students might be involved. Explain to students that you are going to tell them five more activities that might be either harmful or not harmful. Explain that if a student thinks an activity would be harmful, (s)he would use the red crayon. If the activity

TIPS FOR CHIPS

Objective:

Students will tell ways to handle disagreements without fighting.

Life Skills:

I will use manners and treat others fairly. (PF5)
I will try to work out disagreements without fighting. (PF10)

Materials:

Low-fat, salt-free potato or corn chips, or nonfat, sugar-free chocolate chip cookies, fluff ball, wastebasket

Motivation:

1 Introduce the term conflict. A **conflict** is a disagreement between two or more persons or between two or more choices. Explain that everyone has disagreements with others at times. Some disagreements are easy to solve. For example, you may disagree with a friend about which game to play after school. You decide to play both games, the one you wanted to play and the one your friend wanted to play. Other disagreements are not as easy to handle.

2 Explain that it is important to learn skills to handle disagreements without fighting or harming others. Explain that you are going to suggest ten skills for handling disagreements without fighting. Explain that later you will give them examples of disagreements and that they will choose one of the skills they would use to handle each disagreement.

• **Stay calm.** Speak quietly. Don't try to reach an agreement too quickly. Remind yourself that you want to settle the disagreement without getting into a fight.

• **Share your feelings.** When you have a disagreement, it is a good idea to let the other person know how you feel. Be polite. Be fair. Give reasons for the way you feel about the situation.

• **Listen to the other person.** The other person may have good reasons for disagreeing with you. Listen and try to understand his/her feelings so that the disagreement can be resolved.

• **Pretend you are the other person.** Take the time to imagine that you are the other person. If you were that other person, can you understand the reasons (s)he feels the way (s)he does? Perhaps the other person's situation is different from yours and there are good reasons why (s)he is disagreeing with you.

• **Tell the other person you are sorry when you are wrong.** When you realize that you are wrong, you can resolve the disagreement by admitting that you are wrong. The other person will be glad to end the disagreement.

• **Don't use put-downs.** Put-downs are remarks that criticize another person. They make the other person feel that (s)he doesn't matter or that (s)he is not important. These kinds of remarks do not help to settle disagreements.

• **Take time to cool off.** Sometimes when you disagree with another person, the situation may make you feel angry. When you are angry, it is difficult to be calm or to listen to the other person. Walk away or ask the other person to wait for a few minutes before you discuss the disagreement. By waiting, you will be better able to settle the disagreement.

• **Do not threaten the other person.** When you threaten another person, you are saying that you intend to do something that might harm that person. Do not use terms such as "if you don't change your mind, I will...."

- **Ask an adult to help you.** Sometimes a disagreement is difficult to handle. Ask for help from a parent, a teacher, the school nurse, or a police officer if you can't get the other person to talk with you about the disagreement.
- **Run away if someone threatens you or wants to fight.** In certain situations, you need to understand that you may be harmed if you try to handle the disagreement. If you feel threatened by the other person, run away.

3 Explain that you are going to give several examples of disagreements that children the age of your students might have. When you have given an example, you will call on a student to choose one of the ten tips for handling a disagreement. The student is to tell the reason (s)he chose the particular tip. For each tip given, give the student a chip (low-fat, salt-free potato or corn chip or a nonfat sugar-free chocolate chip cookie).

Evaluation:

One at a time, students will stand five feet away from a wastebasket and try to toss a fluff ball into the wastebasket. If the fluff ball goes in, the student is to provide a tip for handling a disagreement without fighting. If the fluff ball does not go into the wastebasket, the student is to tell a harmful result that might occur from fighting.

THE ANGER HANGER

Objective:

Students will tell healthful ways to express anger.

Life Skill:

I will express my anger in healthful ways. (PF6)

Materials:

Circles cut from poster paper, one for each student, coat hanger, primary colors of yarn, hole punch, markers

Motivation:

1 To prepare for this strategy, cut circles from poster paper. The circles should be large enough for students to draw a picture on them. (See step 6.) Punch a hole in the top of each circle with the hole punch. Thread a piece of yarn (long enough to tie on the coat hanger) through the hole in the circle.

2 Introduce the term anger. **Anger** is a feeling of being irritated, annoyed, and/or furious. Explain that everyone experiences anger at times and that it is all right to feel angry. Discuss situations that might cause a person to become angry. Examples might be students taking turns on the slide, but one student pushes ahead of the other students. Or, a student wants to play with a toy, but another student won't share the toy. Perhaps a student calls another student names. Discuss other situations that might cause a student to experience anger.

3 Explain that what is important is how people deal with their angry feelings. They may deal with anger in ways that are harmful to themselves and to other people. Or they may learn to deal with anger in ways that are healthful. A healthful way of dealing with anger solves the cause of the anger and does not harm self or others.

4 Introduce the term I-messages. I-messages are statements that refer to the individual, the individual's feelings, and the individual's needs. I-messages are a healthful way to express angry feelings. An I-message can be used to express anger about another person's behavior. Use an example from step 2. One student pushes ahead of a second student who was waiting for a turn on the slide. If the second student used an I-message, (s)he might say, "I was waiting for my turn on the slide and you pushed ahead of me and I feel very angry about what you did." In this way, the student expressed his/her anger by sharing his/her feelings about the situation. Practice using I-messages using other examples of situations that might cause a student to experience anger.

5 Discuss how important it is to resolve a situation that has caused a person to become angry. Suggest some of the following healthful ways to express angry feelings:
- Talking with a trusted adult can help resolve a situation that caused anger.
- Drawing a picture of the person or situation that caused the angry feelings can help you feel better.
- Taking a few deep breaths, and thinking about fun times can help you calm down when you are angry.
- Sharing feelings with the person who caused your anger can help that person understand why you are angry.
- Riding a bike or doing some other kind of physical activity can help get rid of the extra energy you have when you are angry.

Ask students for other suggestions that are healthful ways of dealing with anger.

6 Explain that when students feel angry they should try to "hang up" their angry feelings. Explain that the class is going to make an anger hanger. An anger hanger is a mobile that will illustrate healthful ways of dealing with anger. Distribute one circle to each student. Have students draw a picture depicting a healthful way to express anger. Ask for volunteers to discuss their pictures with the class. As the example is discussed, hang the circle on the anger hanger.

Evaluation:

Have students each draw a picture to show a situation in which they experienced anger. Have them take their pictures home to share with their parents or another adult in the family. Have them talk about ways to deal with angry feelings.

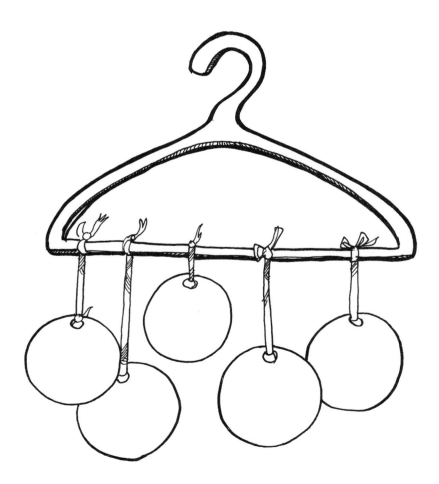

STRESS BUSTER

Objective:

Students will tell healthful ways to handle stress.

Life Skills:

I will choose healthful ways to handle stress. (PF7)
I will participate in physical activity. (PF8)

Materials:

Two posters on each of which is printed "STRESS BUSTER," a bowl, strips of paper on which examples of stressors are written, balloons, tape, pin

Motivation:

1 Introduce the term stress. **Stress** is the response of a person's body to situations. Feelings of stress may caused by many different kinds of events or situations that are called stressors. A **stressor** is a demand that causes changes in a person's body. Explain that a stressor may be a happy occasion, such as having a baby in the family, taking a test in school, or going on a vacation. A stressor also may be an unhappy occasion, such as when a grandparent dies.

2 Explain that stress may cause a person to stop eating, or to cry a lot. The person may feel sad and unhappy. The person may become physically ill. On the other hand, stress may cause a person to be very excited and impatient so that (s)he cannot sleep or eat. Explain that it is important to learn how to handle stress in healthful ways. How stress is handled may depend on the cause of the stress. For example, if a student has an argu-

ment with a friend, (s)he can speak to the friend to settle the argument. (S)he can speak to a parent or other trusted adult and ask for help.

3 Review the following healthful ways to deal with feelings of stress. 1) talk to an adult; 2) exercise; 3) spend time with good friends; 4) get extra sleep; 5) remind yourself of things you do well; 6) eat healthful foods; 7) spend time with family members; 8) draw a picture to show how you feel; 9) share your feelings. Emphasize the importance of exercise in handling stress. Exercise, such as riding a bike or playing on the playground, uses up extra energy that a person has when (s)he is feeling the effects of stress. Also point out that another healthful way to deal with stress is to do something creative, such as taking lessons in painting or taking part in a community program. These kinds of activities give people the opportunity to learn new skills, to make new friends, and to feel good about themselves.

4 Ask students for examples of stressors that affect them. As examples are identified, print them on strips of paper and put the strips of paper in a bowl. Stressors may include having a baby at home; the death of a grandparent; a friend who is moving away; an argument with a friend; parents leaving each other; an ill grandparent who comes to live with the family; a bully on the playground; a school assignment; needing surgery or dental work, and so on.

5 Have two students stand next to each other in front of the class, each holding a STRESS BUSTER poster. Have the other students form a line in front of these two students. The first student in line is to take a strip of paper from the bowl and hand the strip of paper to the teacher. The teacher reads the example of a stressor that is printed on the strip of paper. The student then names a healthful way to handle the stress and the rest of the students say "STRESS BUSTER." The two students who are holding the posters move apart and the student who named a healthful way of dealing with stress moves past them. If the student does not name a healthful way to deal with stress, (s)he goes to the end of the line. Continue in this pattern until all stressors in the bowl are named and healthful ways to deal with them are identified.

Evaluation:

Using an inflated balloon and a pin, give an example of a stressor. Stick the balloon with the pin. The balloon will pop. Use a second balloon and place a piece of tape on it. Again, name a stressor, and stick the pin into the tape on the balloon. The balloon will not pop. Explain to students that they will not "pop" or "explode" if they learn to manage stress. Give three scenarios that include a stressor and have students name a healthful way to deal with each stressor. With each answer, stick the tape with a pin each time to reinforce that stress can be handled if a person uses healthful ways to manage it.

I'M HERE TO TAKE YOU HOME

Objective:

Students will tell ways to stay safe from people who might harm them.

Life Skill:

I will follow rules to stay safe from persons who might harm me. (PF18)

Materials:

Paper, pencils

Motivation:

1 Explain to students that strangers are people they do not know. Strangers can be male or female. They can be any age. Strangers do not usually look different from other people. Explain further that most strangers do not harm children. However, it is important for students to know that there may be occasions when someone, probably a stranger, might try to harm them.

2 Discuss some rules that apply to being safe around strangers.
- Do not go near a stranger in his/her car.
- Do not go anywhere with a stranger.
- Learn to notice if a stranger is hanging around your neighborhood.
- Tell your parents or your teacher if a stranger bothers you.

3 Explain that everyone has a responsibility to protect himself/herself from people or situations that might cause him/her harm. Discuss an example, such as accepting a ride home from school. Ask how many students have been picked up after school by a parent or a relative to go to a dental appointment or to a special occasion. Usually, at such a

time, their parents have arranged for the ride and have instructed the students about the plan.

4 Ask students what they would do if they were offered a ride home with a stranger. How would they decide what to do? Should they take a ride with someone they do not know? Emphasize that it is very dangerous to accept a ride from a stranger.

5 Ask how students might know when it is safe to be picked up from school by any person other than the person they expected. Have their parents given them guidelines about accepting a ride? Students may answer that their parents have given them a code word. Explain that some parents arrange a secret code word that only the student and his/her parents know. If the parent gives someone permission to pick up the student from school, that person must provide the student with the code word. When the student hears the code word, (s)he will know that it is safe to leave the school with that person.

6 Have students take part in an activity using a code word. Ask for two volunteers. Tell a code word to the first student and instruct him/her to pretend that (s)he is leaving school. The second student is to pretend (s)he is an adult who approaches the first student as (s)he is leaving school and offers a ride home. The first student should say "no, thank you." Explain that if this were a real scenario, the student might feel threatened by the adult who offered the ride. Ask the class what this student should do if (s)he feels threatened. If the student feels threatened, this student should go back into the school building and tell a teacher what has happened.

7 Ask for two more volunteers. Repeat the steps in step 5, but this time give the code word to the second student also so that (s)he can use it when (s)he offers the ride to the first student. Have the class observe what happens under these circumstances. Review with students when it is safe to accept a ride home from school.

Evaluation:

Have each student ask an adult at home for the name(s) of a person who is allowed to take him/her home from school. Then have each student draw a picture of that person.

(Code Word)

THE DRUG MASK

Objective

Students will explain that drugs may change the way a person acts.

Life Skills:

I will not try alcohol or other drugs. (PF14)
I will stay away from persons who use harmful drugs. (PF14)

Materials:

Three large paper grocery bags, yarn, markers, scissors, construction paper, chalk, paper donkey tail

Motivation:

1 To prepare for this strategy, prepare the three paper grocery bags. On Bag 1 draw a face; the eyes are cut out and the mouth is smiling. On Bag 2 draw a face; the eyes are not cut out and the mouth shows an angry expression. On Bag 3 draw a face; the eyes are not cut out and the mouth is confused. Also, cut out a donkey tail from construction paper. On the donkey tail print the words "drug free." Draw a donkey on the chalkboard.

2 Introduce the term drugs. A **drug** is something other than food that changes the way the body and/or mind work. Explain that foods change the way the body works, but they are not drugs. The body needs food in order to live. Drugs, on the other hand, can affect the body in harmful ways. Explain that alcohol is a drug. When a person uses alcohol, (s)he is not able to control his/her feelings and behavior. For this reason, the use of alcohol often is related to violent behavior. For their own safety, encourage stu-

dents to stay away from anyone who has been drinking alcohol. In this way, they will reduce their risk of becoming victims of violence.

3 Ask for three volunteers to go to the chalkboard one at a time and indicate where the tail belongs on the donkey. All three students should do it correctly. Explain that these three students represent drug-free individuals. They are in control of their behavior.

4 Now place one of the grocery bags over each of the three volunteers. The student who has Bag 1 on his/her head will put the tail on the donkey correctly because (s)he can see. (S)he is drug free.

5 The student who has Bag 2 on his/her head will not see where to pin the tail on the donkey because no eyes were cut out. (S)he will be angry. Explain that Bag 2 represents a person who uses drugs. Using drugs affects a person's sight and can cause a person to feel angry.

6 The student who has Bag 3 on his/her head will be entirely confused. This person won't be able to decide what to do. (S)he cannot tell right from wrong. Emphasize the importance of being around people who see things clearly because they are drug free.

Evaluation:

Using construction paper, have each child draw and cut out a face. They are to draw eyes that are open and a happy face. Have the children repeat the following statements: "I will not try alcohol or other drugs," and "I will stay away from people who use harmful drugs."

UNSAFE TOUCH

Objective:

Students will explain the difference between safe and unsafe touch.

Life Skills:

I will expect family members to treat me in kind ways. (PF3)

I will tell someone if family members treat me in harmful ways. (PF3)

I will say NO if someone tries to touch me in an unsafe way. (PF18)

I will get help if I have been touched in an unsafe way. (PF19)

Materials:

Safe And Unsafe Touch student master (page 178), a copy for each student, red construction paper, roll of paper, scissors, red crayons, green crayons

Motivation:

1 To prepare for this strategy, trace and cut out an outline of a boy and an outline of a girl from the roll of paper. Tape these outlines to the chalkboard. Cut several circles, one inch in diameter, out of red construction paper.

2 Introduce the topics of safe and unsafe touches. A safe touch is a touch that feels right. A parent holding a child's hand when crossing the street is an example of a safe touch. Explain that children expect safe touches from their family members. When parents love their children, they take care of them in loving and kind ways. They provide shelter, clothing, and food for their families. Instruct students that if a family member treats them in a harmful way, they should tell a trusted adult.

3 Introduce the term unsafe touch. An unsafe touch is a touch that does not feel right. Introduce the term private body parts. Private body parts are the parts of the body that a bathing suit protects and covers. The buttocks, a boy's penis, and a girl's vagina and breasts are private body parts. Stress that a student should say NO if someone tries to touch him/her in an unsafe way.

4 Share the following examples of both safe and unsafe touches (or use some of your own suggestions). After you mention each example, ask students to tell you if it is an example of a safe touch or an example of an unsafe touch. As you mention each example, point to the area on the appropriate body outline that you have taped on the chalkboard. If the example is an unsafe touch, tape a red circle to the body outline. Explain to students that if they are unsure if a touch is a safe touch or an unsafe touch, they should ask a trusted adult.

• A stranger touches a girl on her breast.
• A teacher touches a boy between the legs.
• A parent gives a child a hug.
• A stranger hugs a girl and won't let her go.
• An older boy pulls a younger boy, who resists.
• A doctor examines a child.
• A grandparent holds a grandchild and reads a story.
• A stranger lifts a child over a puddle.
• A father holds his son on his shoulder to watch a parade.
• A nurse holds a child's arm before giving a shot.

5 Explain that it is very important for a student to get help if (s)he has been touched in an unsafe way. It doesn't matter who touched him/her. The person might be a stranger. The person might even be a family member. First of all, the student should tell the person who is touching him/her to stop. Then, it is essential to get away from the person and to stay away. Finally, the student should tell a trusted adult who will help protect the student from any further unsafe touches.

Evaluation:

Distribute a copy of the *Safe And Unsafe Touch* master to each student. Explain that you are going to give five examples of touches (one for each finger). Start with the thumb. If you give an example of an unsafe touch, students are to color the thumb red. If you give an example of a safe touch, they are to color the thumb green. Proceed in a similar way for each of the other four fingers. Use the following examples or use your own examples.

• An uncle always wants to touch your behind.
• A parent kisses you goodnight.
• A playmate gives you a hug.
• A stranger picks you up and won't let you go.
• An adult tickles you and you do not like it.

Safe And Unsafe Touch

Grade 1
- Objective 9
- Protective Factor 15

S-A-F-E T-O-U-C-H

Objective:

Students will tell what to do when they are around weapons such as guns and knives.

Life Skill:

I will stop, stay away from, and tell an adult if I see a gun or a knife. (PF15)

Materials:

S-A-F-E student masters (pages 181, 182, 183, 184), a copy of each of the four masters for each student, paper, crayons, stapler

Motivation:

1 Talk about relationships with students. **Relationships** are the way people feel close with other people. There are many kinds of relationships. However, the earliest and most important relationships occur within a family. Because of the natural bonds in a family, family relationships are very meaningful to a person.

2 Explain that it is important to learn how to get along well with others and to show respect. These are called relationship skills. The family is the first way of learning relationship skills. Explain that parents are the most important persons in a family because they are the role models from whom children learn relationship skills.

3 In families that get along well, feelings are expressed or communicated openly and honestly and family members respect each other. Explain what communication means. **Communication** is the sharing of feelings, thoughts, and information with another person. Explain that in all relationships, people disagree, and that it is important to be able to talk about differences in ways that do not harm others.

4 Introduce the topic of violence. **Violence** is hurting yourself or somebody else on purpose. People who do not communicate well can become violent. Violence often involves weapons such as guns and knives. Explain that a **weapon** is an object used for fighting. Explain that in many cases, people who use violence as a means of settling arguments or differences carry guns and/or knives with them.

5 Stress to students that anytime they see a person carrying a gun or a knife, or anytime they find a gun or knife, they should get away from that person or from that area as fast as possible. They should immediately tell an adult what they saw. Explain that there is no way to tell if a gun has bullets and there is the possibility that a gun could be shot.

6 Explain that there are school rules concerning guns and knives and that these rules are in force to protect all the students in the school. If a student breaks the rules and carries a gun or knife to school, (s)he places everyone in danger. This is one reason why it is so important to stay away from anyone carrying a gun or a knife and to tell an adult.

7 Distribute a copy of each of the four *S-A-F-E* student masters to each student. Each student also will need crayons and a blank sheet of paper. Explain that students are to make a booklet. They are to use the blank sheet of paper as a cover for the booklet. Students are to color the pictures on each of the masters. The four masters and the cover

179

should be stapled together. Students should share their booklets with their families.

Evaluation:

Mount a copy of each of the four *S-A-F-E* masters on cardboard backing. Tape these on the chalkboard, not in the correct order. Students are to take turns placing one at a time in the correct order and explaining the reason for the placement.

S-A-F-E

S — STOP

S-A-F-E

A — AVOID

S-A-F-E

F — FIND

S-A-F-E

E — EXPLAIN

SAFE HELPERS

Objective:

Students will name persons who can help them stay safe.

Life Skills:

I will try to be in places where I can stay safe. (PF4)

I will listen to wise adults and follow rules and laws. (PF17)

I will act in ways to keep myself safe. (PF18)

Materials:

Safe Helpers student master (page 187), a copy for each student, sheets of paper, crayons

Motivation:

1 Introduce the term safe. To be safe means to be away from danger. Parents want their children to be safe not only when they are with them but also when they are playing with friends or when they are in school. Ask students to give you examples of feeling safe. They may use some of the following examples. They feel safe when:
- their parents fasten a safety belt around them when they are riding in a car;
- a police officer stops to say hello when they are playing with friends;
- a crossing guard helps them cross the street;
- a grandparent reads to them;
- they obey their parents' rules;
- a nurse or doctor helps them when they are sick;
- a teacher welcomes them at school every day;
- they follow school rules.

2 Ask students to give you examples of times when they have not felt safe. They may give some of the following examples. They have not felt safe when:
- a stranger wanted them to get into a car;
- a stranger wanted to give them candy;
- they found a gun or knife on the sidewalk;
- there was no one to help them cross the street;
- someone stole something that belonged to them;
- there was no adult at home when they came home after school.

3 Discuss the importance of letting someone know when they do not feel safe. Discuss people they can trust to help keep them safe. For example, remind them that:
- a school principal makes sure that only certain people are allowed in the school building;
- a teacher keeps his/her students safe by taking care of them during the school day;
- a school nurse gives medicines to students and cleans scrapes and cuts when students fall on the playground;
- a police officer patrols a neighborhood to make sure that people who live there are safe;
- a neighbor may have a "SAFE HOME" sign in the window to let children know they can come there for help if they do not feel safe.

4 Explain how important it is to cooperate with adults who help children stay safe. Even if children do not understand why these adults have certain rules, they need to obey those rules if they are to be safe. Obeying rules is an important way for students to keep themselves safe. Encourage students as much as possible to stay around people with whom they feel safe.

5 Distribute a copy of the *Safe Helpers* student master to each student. Assist students in filling in the correct letters in each of the pictures on the master. Discuss each picture. Have students share their papers with their families and explain what each picture means.

Evaluation:

Have students each create a "Safe Helper" badge that can be given to an adult who helps keep him/her safe.

Safe Helpers

NO HARM PLEDGE

Objective:

Students will name types of violence.

Life Skills:

I will not act in ways that harm others. (PF1)
I will not say hurtful words or act in harmful ways toward others who are different. (PF11)
I will change the way I act if I act in harmful ways toward others. (PF20)

Materials:

I Will Not Harm Others student master (page 190), a copy for each student, pencils

Motivation:

1 Remind students about the meaning of the word violence. **Violence** is harming yourself, others, or property. Ask students for examples of ways that some people are violent and harm others. Students may mention hitting, fighting, or tripping. These are all examples of behavior that intends to harm another person.

2 Ask students if they know what a bully is. A **bully** is a person who tries to hurt or scare another person. A bully often will pick on one person as a victim. Bullying is a type of violence.

3 Point out that some students like to "pick" a fight. **Fighting** is taking part in a physical struggle. Someone is apt to get injured in a fight. Fighting is a type of violence.

4 Explain what homicide is. A **homicide** is the killing of another person. Point out that

homicide is an extreme type of violence because a death occurred.

5 Mention child abuse. **Child abuse** is the harmful treatment of a person under the age of 18. The most common type of child abuse is neglect. Neglect means not taking care of a child. Explain that some parents do not provide for their child. They may not provide a safe place to live, or food, or clothing. This type of treatment is harmful to a child. Child abuse is a type of violence.

6 A **victim** is a person who is harmed by violence. Explain that a person who commits a violent act is a **perpetrator**. Explain that it is always wrong to do anything to harm others. Point out that everyone wants to be treated fairly. Unfortunately, some people who are different often are the victims of hurtful words or harmful actions. These people may have a different skin color; they may dress differently; they may eat different kinds of food. It is always wrong to do anything to harm such a person.

7 Introduce the term pledge. A pledge is a promise or agreement to do a certain action. Explain to students that they are going to have the opportunity to make a pledge. Ask students if they have ever made a pledge. Perhaps they have made a pledge to a parent about not talking to strangers or always crossing a street at a crosswalk. Ask students to think about the ways they have been treating other people. If they have been acting in harmful ways, tell them that it is not too late to change their ways. They can make a pledge to change their behavior.

8 Distribute a copy of the *I Will Not Harm Others* student master to each student. Explain that the symbol of the *eye* in each illustration on the master represents the pronoun "I." Remind students that the illustrations represent only some of the ways that people harm others. Discuss each illustration and how each person in the illustration is being harmed. Explain that a person who is kicked, pushed, or punched may be physically harmed. Discuss the fourth illustration in particular. Ask students how a person is harmed when someone steals something from him/her.

9 Direct students' attention to the sentence at the top of the master that reads "I,_____, will not harm others." Instruct each student to print his/her name on the line provided in the sentence. By printing their names in this way, they are making a pledge.

Evaluation:

Compose a Dear Family letter that each student will take home. In the letter, explain to the parents that their children are studying violence prevention skills. Ask parents to watch a TV program with their child. Suggest that together they should identify any examples of violence in the program they watch together. With the letter, send the child's pledge that (s)he made on the student master. Encourage students to keep their pledges where they will be reminded not to do anything to harm another person.

I Will Not Harm Others

I, _____, will not harm others.

STAND UP FOR YOURSELF

Objective:

Students will tell ways to say NO when other children want them to act in ways that would harm others.

Life Skills:

I will develop positive self-esteem. (PF2)
I will make wise choices. (PF12)
I will say NO when others want me to act in harmful ways. (PF13)
I will stay away from gangs. (PF16)

Materials:

Sheets of paper, camera and film (optional)

Motivation:

1 Ask students if they have ever been asked to do something that they thought might harm another person. Have students share how they handled such a situation. Explain that every day everyone makes decisions about what (s)he should or should not do. Explain that a **decision** is a choice. Discuss how important it is to make wise choices. Wise choices not only protect oneself but also do not harm others.

2 Explain that it is more likely that a person can make wise choices if (s)he has positive self-esteem. People with positive self-esteem like themselves. They avoid situations and activities that might cause harm because they respect themselves and others. There are ways to gain positive self-esteem. For example, a student who does his/her best in school will gain self-esteem. A student who helps others also will gain self-esteem.

3 Explain that it is difficult to say NO when someone is telling a person to do something that (s)he is not sure about or something that (s)he thinks might be dangerous. Emphasize that it is important for students to learn to say NO and to say NO in a way that makes it clear that they mean what they say. They need to show that they are in charge of their decisions. If they do this, they will send a message to others that they do not want to take part in activities that might result in harming themselves or another person.

4 Take this opportunity to talk about youth gangs. Some students may have gangs in their neighborhoods. Explain that gangs can be violent and break the law. If students see anyone writing on a building, or carrying a weapon, they should make a wise decision to be safe and stay away from that person.

5 Tell students you are going to make several statements about a variety of activities. They will respond to each statement. If the activity is one that could harm another person, the students are to stand. If the activity is one that would not harm another person, the students are to remain seated. Explain that by standing up, they are making a decision not to take part in any activity that might be harmful. Use the following statements and add other statements that would be appropriate for your community.

- A friend wants you to ride your bike with him.
- Another student asks you to pick up a gun that is on the sidewalk.
- An older child wants you to steal a piece of candy from the store.
- A friend wants to show you a new game she got for her birthday.

- A classmate wants you to trip another student when he walks past your desk.
- A friend invites you to go swimming.
- A friend invites you to a birthday party and tells you that she is not inviting another classmate who is a friend of yours.

Evaluation:

Give each student a sheet of paper. If possible, take an individual picture of each student. Students should tape the picture on the sheet of paper. If this is not possible, ask students to draw pictures of themselves. Each student should print his/her name under his/her picture or drawing. Place the pictures or drawings on the bulletin board or tape them to the chalkboard. Each student will approach his/her picture and point to it and complete the following statement: "I stand up for myself when...."

PEACEFUL FLAKES

Objective:

Students will tell ways to handle disagreements without fighting.

Life Skills:

I will use manners and treat others fairly. (PF5)
I will try to work out disagreements without fighting. (PF10)

Materials:

Handling Disagreements transparency (page 195), transparency projector, empty cereal box, one for each student, crayons, construction paper

Motivation:

1 To prepare for this strategy, have students bring an empty cereal box from home. (An empty shoe box also could be used.)

2 Introduce the term conflict. A **conflict** is a disagreement between two or more persons or between two or more choices. Explain that it is impossible to live without having occasional disagreements. The important thing is to learn how to respond to disagreements in healthful and responsible ways. A person can learn skills to resolve disagreements without getting mad and getting into a fight.

3 Explain that you are going to suggest some skills for handling disagreements without getting into a fight. Use the *Handling Disagreements* transparency to discuss these skills with students:
- **Stay calm.** Speak softly. Do not get excited.
- **Be polite.** Show others that you want to treat them respectfully.

- **Take time to cool down.** If you are feeling angry, take time to get over the anger before you do anything.
- **Share your feelings.** Tell the other person why you feel the way you do about the disagreement.
- **Don't use putdowns.** A putdown is a remark about another person that is not nice.
- **Listen to the other person.** Listen and try to understand why the other person disagrees with you.
- **Pretend you are the other person.** Imagine that you are the other person. This often helps to understand that person's feelings.
- **Ask an adult to help.** Adults, such as a parent or a teacher, are available to help settle a disagreement.
- **Let others know when you are wrong.** If you take time to stay calm or to cool down, you may realize that you have made a mistake. When you admit that you are wrong, the disagreement will be ended.
- **Run away if someone threatens you or insists on fighting.** Realize that you might be harmed if you continue the disagreement. Protect yourself.

4 Explain to students that they are going to design a box for a new kind of cereal. The name of the cereal is "Peaceful Flakes." Explain that the "Peaceful Flakes" are going to represent ways of handling disagreements without fighting. Give a sheet of construction paper to each student. Students are to design a cover for the new cereal, including the name and the kinds of "flakes", which are skills to handle disagreements without fighting. After they have finished their designs, they will paste the new "cover" on one side of their empty cereal box. Students may add additional "flakes." Ask for volunteers to share their new cereal boxes with the class.

Evaluation:

Share examples of disagreements, such as two students who want the same book from the school library. As you state each example, call on students to choose a "flake" that would be a way to handle the disagreement without fighting.

Handling Disagreements

1. Stay calm.

2. Be polite.

3. Take time to cool down.

4. Share your feelings.

5. Don't use putdowns.

6. Listen to the other person.

7. Pretend you are the other person.

8. Ask an adult to help.

9. Let others know when you are wrong.

10. Run away if someone threatens you or insists on fighting.

ALL ABOARD THE ANGER EXPRESS

Objective:

Students will tell healthful ways to express anger.

Life Skill:

I will express my anger in healthful ways. (PF6)

Materials:

All Aboard The Anger Express student master (page 198), a copy for each student

Motivation:

1 Begin the discussion by asking students how they would feel if someone pushed them. Explain that when another person does something we do not like, we do something in return. A person might be annoyed if someone pushed him/her. Possibly the person might have a stronger feeling than just being annoyed.

2 Introduce the term anger. **Anger** is the feeling of being annoyed, and/or furious. Ask students for examples of reasons that a person might become angry. Students might mention being left out of a game on the playground, wanting to play with a ball that another student would not share, and so on.

3 Explain that a person who is feeling angry may want to do something to the person who made him/her feel that way. Explain that anger is a feeling that everyone has at times. Explain that there are healthful ways of dealing with anger and there also are harmful ways of dealing with anger.

4 Ask students for examples of ways that people sometimes deal with angry feelings. They might mention name calling, biting, throwing objects, pushing, yelling, breaking things, refusing to cooperate, or not doing their work. Explain that these are harmful ways of dealing with anger. They are harmful because they can harm the person who is angry and also harm the other person.

5 Discuss healthful ways to deal with anger. Coming to an agreement is a healthful way to deal with anger. Following are some healthful ways to deal with anger.

- **Take time to think about it.** Sometimes it is difficult to realize how angry you are. Wait until you calm down before doing anything.
- **Talk to the person who made you angry.** It is possible that the person who made you angry does not realize how you feel.
- **Ask an adult for help.** You may not know what to do. A trusted adult will listen and help resolve the situation.
- **Draw a picture.** Sometimes it relieves angry feelings if you draw a picture of the person or situation that made you angry. Share the picture with the teacher or with the person who caused the anger.
- **Take a deep breath and relax.** If you take a few deep breaths and think about something you like to do, you will calm down.
- **Punch a pillow.** You can express angry feelings in this way without causing harm to yourself or to anyone else.
- **Do some physical activity.** Activities such as swimming, riding a bike, or jumping rope can help you release the extra energy you have when you are angry.

6 Play the Anger Express Game. Explain that you will be the conductor of a locomotive and that each student will become a part of the train as the train moves around the classroom. As students get on one by one, they will place their hands on the hips of the last person on the train. As each student "boards" the train, (s)he will tell one way to express feelings of anger in a healthful way.

Evaluation:

Distribute a copy of the *All Aboard The Anger Express* master to each student. Instruct each student to print his/her name on the blank space in the sentence at the top of the master. Students are to complete the master by drawing three pictures of situations that make them angry. Students should take their pictures home to share with their parents or other adults. Have them talk with this adult about healthful ways they can deal with their angry feelings.

All Aboard The Anger Express

I, —————, will express anger in a healthful way.

STRESS PULL

Objective:

Students will tell healthful ways to handle stress.

Life Skills:

I will choose healthful ways to handle stress. (PF7)

I will participate in physical activity. (PF8)

Materials:

A thick rubber band cut so that it is about four inches in length

Motivation:

1 Explain what the term stress means. **Stress** is the response of a person's body to the demands of daily living. Feelings of stress result from many different kinds of situations and experiences called stressors. A **stressor** is any demand that causes changes in the body. Taking a test in school or having a birthday party are examples of stressors.

2 Use the rubber band to illustrate the effects of a stressor. Grasp each end of the cut band and show students that you can stretch the rubber band to different lengths. Give examples of two different kinds of stressors such as a pet running away and a first day at school. Show that the rubber band might be stretched to the limit by the anxiety connected to the pet running away. However, the band might be stretched to a lesser degree by the anxiety connected to the first day at school. Ask students for other examples of stressors and, using the rubber band, discuss how severe the effects of each example might be. Add different kinds of exam-

ples, if necessary, such as having an argument with a friend; breaking a special toy; being afraid of an older boy in the neighborhood; worrying about getting a poor grade; and wanting to be chosen for a particular team on the playground.

3 Explain to students that if the feelings of stress are not relieved, the effects of the stress can "snap back" and cause additional pain just as the rubber band can snap back and cause pain. Explain that feelings of stress that are not relieved may cause a person to lose his/her temper, to break things, and to do things (s)he would not ordinarily do.

4 Discuss ways to relieve and reduce the feelings of stress. Use the following examples: talk to an adult and explain what is bothering you and ask for help; get sufficient sleep; eat foods that contain vitamins; spend time with friends; share feelings with a friend; and so on. Mention that crying also is a good way to relieve stress.

5 In addition to these ways of relieving stressful feelings, discuss the benefits of physical and recreational activities. Explain that physical activities use a person's muscles to get rid of extra energy. Activities such as swimming, biking, and skating are a good way to relieve stressful feelings. Explain that recreational activities are activities that are creative and fun, such as camping, going to a sporting event, or learning to play the guitar. Explain that watching certain kinds of television programs might be considered as recreation. However, watching too much television would not be beneficial.

Evaluation:

Explain that a self-contract helps a student set a goal and make a plan to reach that goal. Have students write on the top of a sheet of paper "My Self-Contract For Stress." They should list three of their stressors. After each stressor, they should list three ways they can relieve their stress.

WHO'S CALLING?

Objective:

Students will tell ways to stay safe from people who might harm them.

Life Skill:

I will follow rules to stay safe from persons who might harm me. (PF18)

Materials:

Telephone (not hooked up)

Motivation:

1 Explain to students that it is not possible to tell from looking at or listening to a person if that person might try to harm them. Explain that one way to protect themselves is to be especially careful around strangers. Students need to know that most strangers will not harm children. However, some strangers may try to harm children. These strangers may not look different from other people and they may seem to be very friendly. Explain that it is important for students to learn to protect themselves.

2 Explain that you are going to illustrate one particular way that a person might try to harm a child. Ask for a volunteer to help you with a demonstration. Pretend you are a stranger who is calling the student. Share the following script with the volunteer so that (s)he will answer your questions in the way that a typical student might answer the telephone. Pretend to have the telephone ring and then proceed with the following conversation.

Student: Hello.
Stranger: Hi! Who is this?

Student: This is Fran.
Stranger: Hi, Fran. This is Mrs. Smith. Is your mother at home?
Student: No.
Stranger: Do you know when she will be home?
Student: No.
Stranger: Is anyone else at home?
Student: No.
Stranger: Fran, I have a package your mom wanted me to deliver to your house and I lost your address. Would you give me your address and I'll stop by in a little while to deliver her package?
Student: Sure. I live at 1234 5th Street.
Stranger: Thanks. When I come over, just open the door and I'll give you the package.

3 Ask students to identify the different items of information that were given to you, the stranger. They should list the child's name; the fact that the mother was not home; that the child did not know when she would be home; that no one else was at home; and the address. Explain that if the stranger was a person who wanted to harm a child, the student would be in possible danger.

4 With a volunteer, demonstrate another telephone conversation with the student giving the following different answers.

Student: Hello.
Stranger: Hello. Who is this?
Student: With whom do you wish to speak?
Stranger: Is your mother at home?
Student: She's busy right now and can't come to the phone. Can I take a message?
Stranger: I need to deliver a package for her and I lost your address. Will you

please give me your address so that I can deliver the package for her?

Student: If you leave me your name and phone number, my mother will call you back shortly.

Stranger: Never mind. Goodbye.

5 Discuss with students the reason that the second conversation protects the safety of the student. At the end of the conversation, the stranger had no information about the student. If the stranger was a person who wanted to harm a child, this student would be safe.

Evaluation:

Ask students to identify the information that was not given to the stranger in this conversation. They should list the child's name; that the mother was not home; and the address.

DODGING DRUGS

Objective:

Students will explain that drugs may change the way a person acts.

Life Skills:

I will not try alcohol or other drugs. (PF14)
I will stay away from persons who use harmful drugs. (PF14)

Materials:

Soft, spongy ball

Motivation:

1 Introduce the term drugs. A **drug** is something other than food that changes the way the body and/or mind work. Explain that alcohol is a drug. Point out that alcohol affects a person's body in different ways. (S)he may become ill. (S)he may become confused. In addition, many automobile accidents are caused by people who have been drinking alcohol.

2 When people use drugs, their behavior is affected. They will not be able to think clearly. They will not act in ways that they ordinarily would. Their behavior can become out of control and often becomes violent. When this happens, the drug user and any people around him/her can be harmed. This is the reason that it is very important for students to make a decision not to try alcohol and other drugs. It is also the reason to stay away from any person who is using harmful drugs.

3 Mark off a circle and have the students stand around the outside of the circle. Ask for two volunteers who will be on the inside of the circle. Tape a card that reads "I use drugs" on each of the volunteers. Be sure that the students on the outside of the circle know what is printed on the cards.

4 Explain that the students on the outside of the circle are drug-free and they can stay that way by avoiding contact with the two students on the inside of the circle. The two volunteers on the inside of the circle will try to get the drug-free students to join them. Explain that the drug-free students may be harmed by any contact with those on the inside of the circle. Explain that in this strategy, the harmful contact will be the result of their being hit by the ball.

5 The students on the inside of the circle will use the soft, spongy ball to throw at the students who are on the outside of the circle. The ball represents a "drug ball." The students in the circle will use it to draw others into their lifestyle of using drugs. If a student on the outside of the circle is hit by the ball, (s)he moves to within the circle and associates with the drug people. Explain that as more and more students are drawn into the circle, the number of drug users increases and the risks of becoming involved in violent behavior increase.

6 Explain to students that it is important for them to choose to stay away from people who use drugs. Explain that it is not always easy to make that choice. Students must learn to say NO if anyone tries to get them to try any drugs, including alcohol.

Evaluation:

Have the entire class move within the circle. One at a time, the students are to identify a way to stay away from people who use drugs. As each way is identified, the students leave the circle and return to the drug-free environment.

YOUR TOUCH IS UNSAFE

Objective:

Students will explain the difference between a safe and an unsafe touch.

Life Skills:

I will expect family members to treat me in kind ways. (PF3)

I will tell someone if family members treat me in harmful ways. (PF3)

I will say NO if someone tries to touch me in an unsafe way. (PF18)

I will get help if I have been touched in an unsafe way. (PF19)

Materials:

Two bells, alarms, or buzzers, paper, crayons

Motivation:

1 To prepare for this strategy, draw two outlines on the chalkboard, one a boy and one a girl.

2 Discuss healthful families. In healthful families, members respect and trust each other. Children in healthful families feel safe because they are loved and protected. Explain that not all families are healthful families. In some families, children are not always loved and protected. Stress that it is important for children to expect family members to treat them in safe and kind ways. If a family member treats them in a harmful way, it is very important for them to tell a trusted adult and ask for help.

3 Introduce the terms safe touch and unsafe touch. A safe touch is a touch that feel right. When a mother hugs a child, that is an example of a safe touch. The mother's hug makes the child feel loved and protected. An unsafe touch is a touch that does not feel good; it feels wrong. When someone tickles a child and the child does not want to be tickled, that may be an example of an unsafe touch. Unsafe touches often involve private body parts. Explain that private body parts are the parts of the body that a bathing suit protects. The buttocks, a boy's penis or the part between his legs, and a girl's vagina or the part between her legs, and breasts are private body parts.

4 Explain to students that it is important for them to let someone know if they experience an unsafe touch and that they do not like unsafe touches. Suppose someone is tickling a person and (s)he does not like it. (S)he should say NO and tell the person to stop. If that person does not stop, (s)he should get away from that person and stay away. (S)he should get away from any touch that feels wrong or that hurts.

5 Explain to students that they should tell an adult they trust about any unsafe touch. Tell this trusted adult who touched them and where they were touched. Ask the adult for help. If the first adult doesn't help, the student should go to another trusted adult and ask for help. Have students identify the adults they trust and who might help them if they needed help.

6 Explain that you are going to make several statements that describe safe or unsafe touches. Go over the statements before reading them to the class. Note that certain items do not refer specifically to touches but they represent unsafe areas. As you read those particular statements, it may not be clear to the students whether or not to ring the bell. Explain that some situations may lead to unsafe touches.

7 Ask for two volunteers at a time. Give each volunteer a bell, alarm, or buzzer. Instruct the volunteers to ring their bells if the statement you make describes an unsafe touch. The volunteers will not ring their bells if your statement describes a safe touch. Ask for new volunteers after reading two or three statements, so that as many students as possible will have a chance to participate.

8 Read the following statements to the students one at a time.
- A relative tickles you in the area of a private body part and you do not like it. (ring)
- Your father hugs you after you show him your report card. (no ring)
- A person asks you to place your hand on his/her private body part. (ring)
- Someone rubs your neck and it makes you feel uncomfortable. (ring)
- A person speaks naughty words to you. (ring)

- A person shows you pictures of people with no clothes on. (ring)
- Someone hugs you when your pet dies. (no ring)
- (Point to a private body part on one of the outlines on the chalkboard.) You are touched here. (ring)
- A relative kisses you in a way you do not like and you are told to keep it a secret. (ring)
- Your mother kisses you goodnight. (no ring)
- A coach pats you on your back when you played a good game. (no ring)
- A babysitter kisses you goodnight in a way that does not seem right. (ring)
- An adult holds your hand because you are afraid. (no ring)

Evaluation:

Ask students to think of trusted adults they would go to for help if they needed it. Give students a sheet of paper, and have them draw a picture of one of those adults.

S-A-F-E

Objective:

Students will tell what to do when they are around weapons such as guns or knives.

Life Skills:

I will follow the SAFE rule: Stop, Avoid getting closer, Find an adult, Explain what I saw. (PF15)

Materials:

S-A-F-E student master (page 209), a copy for each student

Motivation:

1 Introduce the term weapon. A **weapon** is an object that can be used for fighting. A weapon is used to harm another person. Explain that there are many different kinds of weapons but that guns and knives are the weapons that are most commonly used. Stress that it is dangerous to be near weapons such as guns or knives. It is also dangerous to be near any person who has a gun or a knife or to be near any activity that involves guns or knives.

2 Explain that most states in the United States have laws about having and using guns. For example, it is against the law in most states for people under the age of 21 to buy a gun. These laws are made to protect people because guns can cause serious injuries and deaths. If students see a young person carrying a gun, they can know that person is breaking the law. Explain that if a person who is carrying a gun or a knife has an argument with someone, (s)he might use the gun to try to settle the argument.

3 Explain that many times innocent people are injured or even killed for no reason because they are nearby when someone is using a knife or firing a gun. This is the reason that students should stop and stay away from anyone who is carrying a gun. And they should hurry to find a trusted adult and tell the adult about the gun.

4 Explain that this strategy concerns keeping safe at home if gunshots are heard in the neighborhood. Stress that in such a event, the most dangerous response would be to look out a window to see what is happening. Explain that many people who use guns shoot randomly; that is, they shoot in any direction for no particular reason. This is the reason that looking out a window would be dangerous. Review the following suggestions for keeping safe at home if gunshots are heard in the neighborhood. These tips should be followed until the sound of gunshots is no longer heard.

- Inform an adult in the home.
- Keep away from windows.
- Keep away from outside walls, especially those that face the street.
- Get behind a solid piece of furniture, if possible.

5 Explain to students that they are going to cheer for safety. Divide the class into four groups. Write the following letters on the chalkboard: S-A-F-E. Assign each group one of the letters, explaining what each letter means as follows:

S — STOP
A — AVOID GOING NEAR THE SITUATION
F — FIND AN ADULT
E — EXPLAIN WHAT YOU SAW

207

As the students in each group call out their assigned letter, they are to give the meaning as if they were giving a cheer. Then the next group does the same thing, and so on. At the end of the fourth letter, the groups together say SAFE.

Evaluation:

Distribute a copy of the *S-A-F-E* master to each student. Students are to draw a picture of a way they will stay safe. Then they are to take the handout home. Explain that there is a letter for their parents on the handout. At home, students are to tell their parents what S-A-F-E means and explain the pictures they drew.

S-A-F-E

Dear Parent:

Your child has been learning about violence. (S)he has learned certain rules to follow if (s)he is around weapons such as guns and knives. (S)he has learned about using the word S-A-F-E. Each letter in this word has a special meaning.

S — STOP
A — AVOID GOING NEAR THE SITUATION
F — FIND AN ADULT
E — EXPLAIN WHAT YOU SAW

Please review the meaning of these letters with your child. Your child has drawn a picture of the way (s)he will stay safe. Have him/her explain the picture to you.

Thank you,

CALL FOR HELP

Objective:

Students will name persons who can help them stay safe.

Life Skills:

I will try to be in places where I can stay safe. (PF4)

I will listen to wise adults and follow rules and laws. (PF17)

I will act in ways to keep myself safe. (PF18)

Materials:

Poster paper, marker

Motivation:

1 To prepare for this strategy, use a marker to make a large poster of a push-button telephone with the numbers and corresponding letters as they are on a real telephone.

2 Introduce the term self-protection strategies. **Self-protection strategies** are strategies that can be practiced to protect oneself and decrease the risk of becoming a victim. Students should be aware of where they are and whom they are with. Explain that there may be times when they do not feel safe. Perhaps it is a person who makes them feel uncomfortable and threatened. Perhaps they are walking down the street and someone in a car wants them to get into the car. Stress that it is important for students to follow rules of safety that their parents have taught them. They can protect themselves by getting away from a person who makes them uncomfortable. They can run away from a person in a car who is calling out to them. They can find an adult such as a law enforcement officer to help them.

3 Explain that there may be times when students go home after school and no one is home. Stress the importance of their staying safe. If they have a key, they need to be careful to remember their parents' rules about being home alone. If they have no key, encourage them to go to a neighbor who will help. The important thing is that they are in a safe place.

4 Explain to students that they can make an emergency telephone call to the police or fire department if they ever feel threatened. Explain about the special emergency number 9-1-1. It is important the students do not refer to this number as "nine-eleven," but rather as nine-one-one, which is the correct way to dial this emergency number. Explain that if this 9-1-1 emergency number is not available in your community, the <u>number 0</u> (for operator) can be used. Emphasize that it is the number 0, <u>not</u> the letter O.

5 Discuss the importance of speaking clearly and calmly when making an emergency call. The person who answers the emergency call is prepared to help but (s)he must be able to understand what is being said and must have complete information. Explain the following steps that should be followed when making an emergency call.

• Tell what has happened that has made you feel threatened.
• Tell your name.
• Tell where you are.
• Listen for instructions from the person who is talking to you.
• Follow those instructions.
• Do not hang up the telephone until the person you are talking to hangs up.

6 Tell the students that they will each have an opportunity to make an emergency call using your poster to press the numbers 9-1-1 or 0. You may choose to provide students with examples of scenarios. They are to talk with the imaginary person whom they are asking for help. For example, you may say, "You are home alone and you hear someone trying to open the door. You hear the doorknob being turned." The student is to say what (s)he would say after dialing the emergency number.

Evaluation:

Have students tell you the steps in making an emergency telephone call. Discuss why each step is important.

HAVING A BALL PROTECTING YOURSELF

Objective:

Students will name kinds of violence and ways to protect against violence.

Life Skills:

I will recognize that violent behavior is wrong. (PF1)
I will practice suicide prevention strategies. (PF9)
I will avoid discrimination. (PF11)
I will practice self-protection strategies. (PF18)

Materials:

Protecting Yourself From Violence student master (page 214), a copy for each student, golf ball, soft spongelike ball

Motivation:

1 Explain that it is necessary to understand that a person can be harmed if (s)he is near people who are violent or if (s)he is in a situation that is either violent or in danger of becoming violent. Explain the meaning of the term violence. **Violence** is the threatened or actual use of physical force to injure, damage, or destroy yourself, others, or property. Explain that there are many types of violence including the following:

- **Bullying** is an attempt by a person to hurt or frighten those who are perceived to be smaller or weaker.
- **Fighting** is taking part in a physical struggle.
- **Homicide** is the killing of another person.
- **Suicide** is the intentional taking of one's own life.

- **Child abuse** is the harmful treatment of a person who is under the age of 18; it includes physical abuse, verbal abuse, emotional abuse, sexual abuse, and neglect.
- **Domestic violence** is violence that occurs within the family or within other relationships in which people live together.

2 Explain that it is important to recognize violent behavior. It is important to recognize that violent behavior is wrong because another person is either threatened with harm or is actually harmed. Explain that everyone has a right to be safe. A person who chooses a violent behavior against himself/herself or another person is choosing a wrong behavior. Encourage students to talk with a trusted adult if they are feeling angry or discouraged so that they will not behave in a way that might harm themselves or other people.

3 Introduce the term discriminatory behavior. **Discriminatory behavior** is treating someone differently because of how that person may act, feel, or look. When a person chooses discriminatory behavior, (s)he may treat some people with respect and others with disrespect. When people are treated with disrespect, they may become angry and violent. Explain that it is wrong to knowingly treat a person with disrespect.

4 Introduce the term self-protection strategies. **Self-protection strategies** are ways to protect oneself and decrease the chance of becoming a victim. Explain that a **victim** is a person who is harmed by violence. Use the *Protecting Yourself From Violence* student master as a checklist of self-protection strategies students might practice.

5 Ask students what they might do to protect themselves if they are near a violent person or in a violent situation. Emphasize that, if nothing else, they can avoid becoming violent themselves and they can get away from a violent situation.

6 Show students the golf ball and the larger, soft, spongelike ball. Ask students what would happen if both balls were thrown at them at a fast rate of speed and there wasn't enough time to protect themselves. They should understand that if the golf ball hit them, they could suffer a serious injury, especially if they were hit in the eye or mouth. Students also should understand that if they were hit by the spongelike ball, they probably would not be injured.

7 Point out what the two balls show — that you can't tell from the size of an object how much damage it might cause. A person might think that the larger ball could cause more harm than the smaller ball. Explain that a violent person can cause harm and that even a minor situation that becomes violent can result in serious harm to a person.

Evaluation:

Review the content of the student master by having students repeat the strategies that were listed without referring to the master. Ask students for additional self-protection strategies.

Protecting Yourself From Violence

( )   1. I will tell an adult where I will be at all times.

( )   2. I will leave a phone number of where I will be and how I am getting there and getting home.

( )   3. I will not leave school with an adult unless that adult is approved by an adult at home.

( )   4. I will follow a safe route home from school and from other places.

( )   5. I will stay away from places where gang members or others who might harm me are present.

( )   6. I will stay away from people who are using drugs or from places where there are drugs.

( )   7. I will follow safety rules set by my parents to protect me at home.

( )   8. I will choose friends who do not harm others.

( )   9. I will follow good behavior rules at school.

( )   10. I will avoid being around weapons.

USING RESISTANCE SKILLS

Objective:

Students will identify resistance skills that can be used when pressured to engage in violent behavior.

Life Skills:

I will develop positive self-esteem. (PF2)
I will make responsible decisions. (PF12)
I will practice resistance skills. (PF13)

Materials:

Using Resistance Skills student master (page 217), a copy for each student

Motivation:

1 Introduce the term resistance skills. **Resistance skills** are skills that are used when a person wants to say NO to an action and/or leave a situation. (S)he perhaps is being pressured to do something that (s)he does not want to do or something that (s)he knows would be harmful to his/her health. Explain that resistance skills are also called refusal skills.

2 Ask the students if they have ever been pressured to do something about which they had concerns. Perhaps they were pressured to break a family rule such as crossing a street at a crosswalk. Perhaps they were pressured to take part in an activity that might become violent and harm another person. Remind students that any time drugs or weapons are present, violence could result.

3 Explain that knowing how to make responsible and wise decisions helps a person keep from becoming involved in a risky situation. A person who thinks about the consequences or results of a particular decision will be able to resist pressures to do something that might be harmful to self and to others. Such a person is in control of his/her actions.

4 Introduce the term self-esteem. **Self-esteem** is what a person thinks or believes about himself/herself. People who have good feelings about themselves have positive self-esteem. They will want to protect themselves and be safe and they will not want to harm others. One way for people to develop positive self-esteem is to work to do their best in school. Another way is to choose friends who will support and encourage them. A third way to develop positive self-esteem is to have a neat and clean appearance. A neat and clean appearance improves a person's feelings about himself/herself.

5 Explain that you are going to discuss four resistance skills that can be used to resist pressure to engage in a behavior that might become violent. The skills are as follows:
- Look directly into the other person's eyes when you say NO.
- Say NO in a firm voice.
- Walk away from the person or from the situation.
- Tell an adult in your family about your experience.

6 Distribute a copy of the *Using Resistance Skills* student master to each student. Review each illustration. Using scenarios that involve pressuring a student to take part in an activity, call on students to respond to the pressure by using one of the four skills illustrated on the master. Be sure each of the four skills is used in the students' responses.

Evaluation:

Have students take their copy of the student master home to share with their parents. Students are to tell their parents what the four skills are and that they know how to use each of the skills.

Using Resistance Skills

RESOLVING CONFLICT

Objective:

Students will describe ways to resolve conflicts without fighting.

Life Skills:

I will develop social skills. (PF5)
I will practice conflict resolution and peer mediation skills. (PF10)

Materials:

Construction paper, markers, scissors

Motivation:

1 To prepare for this strategy, draw an outline of a flame on construction paper. Cut out eight flames from this outline. On each flame, print a situation that might cause a child to become frustrated and that might lead to violent behavior. Following are eight suggested situations. However, you may choose to use your own suggestions.

- A friend pushes me.
- A friend takes my toy.
- Someone gets ahead of me in line.
- Someone tells a lie about me.
- Someone calls me a name.
- Someone says something bad about a family member.
- Someone steals a homework paper.
- Someone calls me a "chicken" if I do not join others in an activity that could become violent.

2 To prepare further for the strategy, using construction paper, draw an outline of a water bucket. Cut out eight buckets from this outline. The water buckets will be used to

identify a positive way to handle each of the suggested situations.

3 Introduce the term conflict. A **conflict** is a disagreement between two or more persons over two or more choices. Explain that conflicts occur in everyone's life. They occur naturally in every area of life: in a family, at school, and in a neighborhood. It is not unusual for people to get very emotional about a conflict. They may get angry. They may feel frustrated. If the conflict is not resolved, their emotions may get out of hand and they may become violent. **Conflict resolution skills** are skills a person can use to resolve a disagreement in a healthful, safe, legal, respectful, and nonviolent way.

4 Introduce the term social skills. **Social skills** are skills that can be used to relate well with others. People who have social skills have good manners. They treat others with respect. They are able to see the other person's point of view. Point out that these skills are essential if students are to resolve conflicts in healthful and responsible ways.

5 Introduce the terms peer and peer mediation. A **peer** is a person who is similar in age or status. **Peer mediation** is a process used to resolve conflicts in which a person helps his/her peers resolve disagreements in healthful, safe, legal, respectful, and nonviolent ways. Explain that it is helpful sometimes to have a peer who is not involved in the conflict help resolve the conflict. Because the peer is not emotionally involved, (s)he often can be very helpful.

6 Select eight volunteers and attach a flame to each volunteer. As each student identifies a way to handle the situation that is printed on his/her flame in a positive way without fighting, tape a bucket to the flame to indicate that the situation is under control. Positive ways might include staying calm, asking an adult to help, sharing feelings with the other person, and removing yourself from the situation.

Evaluation:

Using the bucket outline, cut out a bucket for each student in the class. On one side of the bucket, have students write about a situation that can lead to a conflict. On the other side of the bucket, students are to write a positive way to handle the situation.

I'M MANAGING MY ANGER

Objective:

Students will identify ways to express anger and disappointment.

Life Skills:

I will respond to my environment in an empowering way. (PF4)
I will practice anger management skills. (PF6)

Materials:

Grocery bags, scissors, crayons, string, other miscellaneous items to use for making puppets

Motivation:

1 Before the lesson, develop several possible scenarios for puppet shows to illustrate situations that could cause a third grade student to be angry or disappointed. Examples might be: a student does not speak English well and other students tease him/her; a student is disappointed because (s)he was not chosen to be captain of the softball team. The puppet shows should portray one or more characters discussing his/her feelings of anger or ways to overcome disappointment.

2 Introduce the term nurturing environment. A **nurturing environment** is the surroundings in which a person lives that promotes good health. A nurturing environment provides the best opportunity for a person to be at his/her best. Living in a nurturing environment increases the likelihood that a person will not behave in violent ways because his/her parents care about the children in the family and teach them how to resolve problems without violence. Parents in a nurturing environment teach their children the difference between right and wrong and teach them to make responsible decisions.

3 Introduce the term hope. **Hope** is the feeling that what is desired is possible and that events in life may turn out for the best. Explain that a person who lives in a nurturing environment learns that (s)he will be able to cope with disappointment. Use the example of the student who did not get chosen to be team captain. If that student has hope, (s)he will be patient and know that (s)he will have another chance to be a captain. (S)he will set a goal and make a plan to be ready the next time a captain is chosen. A person who is filled with hope is optimistic about the future and does not feel trapped.

4 Explain that students may not be able to control their environment. They may not live in a nurturing environment but there are some steps they can take to control what they do. They can feel empowered. **Empowerment** is the belief that a person controls his/her own life in the future. Suggest the following: ask a trusted adult for help; attend school every day; play in safe areas; learn to set goals and make plans to reach them; and stay away from people who behave in violent ways.

5 Introduce the term anger. **Anger** is the feeling of being irritated, annoyed, and/or furious. Explain that being angry is a feeling that everyone experiences at times. Explain that it is important for students to recognize their anger triggers. **Anger triggers** are thoughts or events that cause a person to become angry. For example, if a friend calls you a mean name (the anger trigger), you would become angry.

6 Explain that the way a person deals with anger can be either healthful or harmful to that person. For example, a person who is angry may want to get back at the person who made him/her angry. This would be a harmful way to deal with anger. Ask students for other examples of harmful ways a person might deal with anger. Point out that harmful ways of dealing with anger often result in violent actions.

7 Explain that it is not always a person who can cause another person to become angry. Situations that are out of a person's control also can be the cause of angry feelings. No matter what causes angry feelings, stress that it is important to learn skills that will help handle angry feelings in a positive or healthful way. Skills are methods used to help reach a desired goal. In this strategy, the goal is to learn to deal with angry feelings in positive ways that will avoid the possibility of violent actions.

8 Discuss how students can express their anger in healthful ways. Suggest the following examples of skills to use:
• Talk with a trusted adult to get help with resolving the situation that caused your angry feelings.
• Draw pictures of the person or situation that made you angry.
• Take a deep breath and relax until you calm down.
• Ride your bike, jump rope, or play a game with your friend so that you can release the extra energy you have because you are angry.

9 Divide the class into small groups. Assign to each group one of the scenarios for puppet shows that you have developed. Work with students to make puppets for the characters in the scenarios. Have each group present their show to the class.

10 After each presentation, have students discuss what skills they might use to handle feelings of anger or disappointment aroused by the scenario presented in the puppet show.

Evaluation:

Have each student write a short paper describing what the anger trigger was in each of the puppet shows. Then, have students identify three anger management skills and discuss how each skill could be used to help the character who was angry.

STRESS BURST

Objective:

Students will outline ways to manage stress.

Life Skills:

I will practice stress management skills. (PF7)
I will participate in physical activity. (PF8)

Materials:

Balloons, small strips of paper (1" x 3"), pencils

Motivation:

1 To prepare for this strategy, use small strips of paper (1" x 3") and on each strip print an example of a stressor that could cause feelings of distress. Use the following examples and add some examples of your own: a pet dies; a family member becomes seriously ill; you get poor grades; you feel left out at school; a grandparent dies; family members can't get along with each other; a brother or sister is using drugs; a gang is operating in your neighborhood; older students are bullying you. Stuff one of the strips of paper into each balloon, inflate the balloons, and tie a knot to prevent air from escaping.

2 Introduce the term stress. **Stress** is the way the body changes when demands are made on it. Feelings of stress are an everyday experience and can be the result of many different kinds of experiences called stressors. A **stressor** is a demand that causes changes in the body. Examples of stressors are taking a test in school, getting ready for a relay race, or having a disagreement with a friend. Explain that everyone experiences stress.

3 Explain that feelings of stress that cause a person to feel upset can be called distress. **Distress** is a harmful response to a stressor that produces negative results. On the other hand, feelings of stress that cause a person to feel excited can be called eustress. **Eustress** is a healthful response to a stressor that produces positive results.

4 Explain that it is important for people to learn skills to manage their feelings of stress so that the effects of the stress do not harm them. Stress can affect a person's body in several different ways such as increasing heart and breathing rates, and difficulty in sleeping. If such effects are not relieved, a person's body becomes exhausted.

5 Introduce the term stress management skills. **Stress management skills** are methods that can be used to cope with the harmful effects produced by stress. Discuss the following skills to cope with and reduce the feelings of stress: asking an adult for help; getting sufficient sleep; eating healthful foods; spending time with friends; sharing feelings with a friend; helping others; or caring for a pet.

6 Explain to students that one of the best ways to manage stress is to be physically active. Activities such as swimming, riding a bike, or rollerblading help a person maintain physical fitness while relieving the effects of stress. Participating in recreational activities, such as camping, dancing, and taking painting lessons, will stimulate a person's mind and relieve the effects of stress.

7 Divide the class into two teams and form two single lines. Place two chairs with a balloon attached to each chair across the room. At the word "go," the first person in each line runs to a chair, picks up the balloon, sits on the balloon so that it bursts, and finds the strip of paper that was inside the balloon. The student will then read what is written on the strip of paper and suggest a healthful stress management skill that would relieve and reduce the stress that the situation would cause. The student then runs back to the line, and another student repeats the action.

8 Each time a stressor and a stress management skill are identified, the teacher should review each answer that was given and then place another balloon on the chair.

Evaluation:

Instruct the students to draw up a health-behavior contract. Explain that a health-behavior contract is a contract that a student makes with himself/herself. The contract should state a goal concerning healthful ways to handle feelings of stress that each student would like to reach. The contract should also include a plan to reach that goal.

TORN APART

Objective:

Students will differentiate between people and groups who choose responsible behavior and people/gangs who are violent.

Life Skill:

I will resist gang membership. (PF16)

Materials:

Poster board, double-sided and single-sided transparent tape, sheets of tissue paper, marker

Motivation:

1 To prepare for this strategy, draw a circle on poster board. Inside the circle, draw several stick figures. Attach a strip of double-sided tape to the figures inside the circle. On the outside of the circle, draw more stick figures. Attach a strip of single-sided tape to these stick figures.

2 Explain what youth gangs are. A **youth gang** is a group of young people who band together and participate in violent, unlawful, or criminal behavior. Belonging to a gang can be very risky because of the activities a member is required to take part in. Members of a gang associate only with each other and often commit crimes against other gangs and people.

3 Explain that certain activities are associated with gang membership. These include stealing, staying out of school, using alcohol and other drugs, getting in fights, selling drugs, and taking part in drive-by shootings. Drive-by shootings often are the result of fights be-

tween gangs, drug dealing, or random acts of anger.

4 Remind students that people who choose responsible behavior attend school regularly because they know how important it is to get an education. They do not use alcohol or other drugs; they do not settle differences with another person by fighting; they do not sell drugs; they do not take part in drive-by shootings.

5 Provide each student with a piece of tissue paper. Give each student an opportunity to approach the poster board and attach his/her piece of tissue paper to any one of the stick figures. Students will find that the tissue paper will adhere to the stick figures on the inside of the circle. The tissue paper will not adhere to the stick figures on the outside of the circle. Students are to try to pull their tissues away from the stick figures on the inside of the circle.

6 Ask students to describe what they observed. (The tissue stuck to the stick figures inside the circle and tore when students tried to separate the tissue from the stick figure.) Explain that the stick figures inside the circle represent gang members and that the stick figures outside the circle represent people who are not gang members.

7 Point out that when a person joins a gang, (s)he will find it difficult to leave the gang. (S)he may face threats of harm if (s)he tries to leave. Review again from step 3 the kinds of dangerous activities that are associated with gangs. Remind students that for their own protection, they should stay away from gangs and gang members.

Evaluation:

Make paper shields to place over the stick figures on the inside of the circle on the poster board. As you place a paper shield on a stick figure, call on students to give a reason for not becoming a member of a gang.

VIOLENT PILE-UP

Objective:

Students will explain why drug use increases the risk of violence.

Life Skill:

I will avoid alcohol and other drugs. (PF14)

Materials:

Alphabet blocks

Motivation:

1 Introduce the term drug. A **drug** is something other than food that changes the way the body and/or mind work. Explain that alcohol is a harmful drug. Alcohol has many effects on the body. A person who drinks alcohol may develop illnesses such as damage to the stomach, brain damage, and cancer. Explain that alcohol can cause people to lose control of the way they behave. Feelings that would normally be under a person's control may not be managed.

2 Explain that there are many other harmful drugs besides alcohol. When people use harmful drugs, their personalities and behavior are affected. Some of the effects are as follows: being annoyed easily, not thinking clearly, being angry toward others, being less patient, and being depressed. A drug user is less patient, experiences greater stress and more frustration, and is short tempered. Some drugs cause people to experience periods of violence while they are under the influence of the drugs.

3 Review the definition of violence. **Violence** is the threatened or actual use of force to harm yourself, others, or property. Explain that drug use is a major factor in cases of violent crime. When people are using drugs, they cannot think clearly and may engage in activities that they would not take part in if they were sober. Some people who use drugs commit crimes to get money to buy more drugs.

4 Stack the alphabet blocks and explain that each block represents a drug. Point out that as you add a block to the stack, the effects multiply. For example, if there is a drug user in a family, the effect of taking more and more of the drug can eventually pile up and cause serious problems in the family. Refer to step 2 and remind students of some of the ways drugs affect a person's personality and behavior.

5 Point out to students that it is important that they protect themselves from people who are using drugs because they could become the victims of violent actions. Explain that drug users may not intend to harm another person, but that they lose control of their thinking and their decisions. Point out that, for these reasons, it is essential that students avoid using alcohol and other drugs.

6 Discuss what students can do if they have a drug user in their family or if they know someone who uses drugs. For instance, they can get help at school from a teacher, a guidance counselor, or from a community agency such as a mental health agency.

Evaluation:

Using the blocks, make a stack by adding one block at a time. Explain that each block represents a drug. As you add a block, call on a student to name how the use of a drug might increase the risk that the drug user might become violent.

SCRAMBLED INSIDE

Objective:

Students will identify and describe types of abuse: emotional, sexual, physical, and neglect.

Life Skills:

I will strive for healthful family relationships. (PF3)
I will develop resiliency to "bounce back" if I was reared in a dysfunctional family. (PF3)
I will practice self-protection strategies. (PF18)
I will participate in recovery if a victim. (PF19)

Materials:

Two eggs, bowl

Motivation:

1 Explain that **child abuse** is the harmful treatment of a person under the age of 18 and includes physical abuse, verbal abuse, emotional abuse, sexual abuse, and neglect. Physical abuse is cruel treatment that harms the body. Signs of physical abuse include bruises, burns, cuts, missing teeth, broken bones, and internal injuries. Verbal abuse is using words to harm a person. Emotional abuse involves harm to a person's mind, self-esteem, and personality. Signs of emotional abuse are poor relationships with friends, distrust, a great deal of fear, and poor self-esteem. Sexual abuse involves inappropriate sexual behavior between an adult and a child. Neglect involves lack of proper care and guidance. Signs include malnourishment, poor health, and lack of appropriate clothes.

2 Show the first egg to the students. Explain that the yolk of the egg represents a person's brain and that the white represents protection for the brain. Tell students that this egg has been protected. Remind students how people protect their heads (brains) by wearing a helmet when riding a bike or when skating. Crack the egg and empty the contents into a bowl. Students will note that the yolk is whole. The white of the egg has protected it.

3 Shake the second egg vigorously. Explain that this egg represents a child who has been physically abused. Crack the egg and empty the contents into a bowl. Students will observe that the yolk and the white are scrambled — they are mixed together. The yolk (brain) was not protected. Point out that a child who has been physically abused cannot think clearly because his/her brain may have been harmed.

4 Explain that unfortunately some children grow up in homes where they are abused. Perhaps the parents do not mean to abuse their children. They may never have learned how to resolve conflicts without violence. Children who grow up in this kind of family can practice self-protection strategies. **Self-protection strategies** are strategies that can be used to protect oneself and decrease the chance of becoming a victim. If these children practice self-protection strategies, they will develop resiliency. Explain that **resiliency** is the ability to prevent or to recover, bounce back, and learn from misfortune, change, or pressure. These children can ask the person who is abusing them to stop. They can try to stay away from that person. They can tell a trusted adult about the situation and ask for help.

5 Explain that children who are victims of abuse need help and that there is help available. These children need to recover from the pain of their experience and be counseled about how to get on with their lives.

Evaluation:

Have students practice using the following skills by pretending they are being threatened by another person: 1) look the other person in the eye, 2) say NO in a firm voice, 3) leave the situation, 4) tell an adult what is happening.

WEAPON AWARENESS

Objective:

Students will describe procedures to follow for safety around weapons.

Life Skill:

I will practice responsible behavior around weapons. (PF15)

Materials:

Sheets of paper

Motivation:

1 To prepare for this strategy, you will need five sheets of paper on each of which is written a different scenario. The five scenarios are as follows:

1. Three students find a gun on the playground.
2. You notice a weapon on the table in your friend's home.
3. You notice a weapon in another student's book bag.
4. You notice a weapon in a trash basket in school.
5. You notice another student carrying a weapon on the way to school.

2 Discuss with students how dangerous it is to be near a person who is carrying a weapon. Explain that a **weapon** is something used for fighting. A weapon is used to injure another person. The most commonly used weapons are guns and knives. Stress that in many instances, innocent people are injured or even killed because they happened to be

near a situation where a weapon was involved.

3 Discuss the rules your school has established about weapons. Explain that such rules are designed for the safety of all students because weapons are so dangerous. This is the reason that it is so important for students to learn to be responsible around weapons.

4 Review with students the following suggestions for being responsible around weapons. The suggestions can be learned by remembering the acronym for the word safe.
· S — STOP
· A — AVOID GOING NEAR THE SITUATION
· F — FIND AN ADULT
· E — EXPLAIN WHAT YOU SAW

5 Ask for five volunteers and give each one of them a sheet of paper on which you wrote a scene. Explain that they are to act out the scene without using words. They each can choose other students to help them in the presentation. After each scene is acted out, the class must report what they observed. List the observations on the chalkboard.

6 Review each of the scenes. Discuss how the suggestions for keeping safe around weapons should be applied to each of the five scenes. Ask students what they would do if they had an experience similar to one of the scenarios.

7 Emphasize that each of the four steps represents a responsible behavior students should practice to be safe around weapons.

Evaluation:

Have students make posters about weapon safety. The posters may include a drawing and/or a jingle.

STAYING STRAIGHT

Objective:

Students will identify the advantages of cooperating with law enforcement officers and other people with authority.

Life Skills:

I will respect authority and abide by laws. (PF17)

I will change behavior if a juvenile offender. (PF20)

Materials:

Piece of yarn about 10 feet long, paper, scissors, tape

Motivation:

1 To prepare for this strategy, make one sign that reads "I have followed laws." Also make five paper badges. On each badge write one of the following statements.
- I will follow rules given by a police officer.
- I will not harm others.
- I will not sell drugs for another person.
- I will not have a weapon in my possession.
- I will not steal.

2 Discuss the concept of laws. A **law** is a rule of conduct or action that is regulated by people in authority. People who live in a community, city, or state are ruled by laws. These people understand that laws protect the safety and rights of everyone in the community, city, or state. Discuss school rules and explain that school rules protect students while they are in school.

3 Discuss authority. **Authority** is the power and right to make and carry out laws. Peo-

ple in authority make sure that everyone is protected and safe. If someone breaks a law, a person in authority has the power to apply the law and treat the individual according to what the law says. Ask students for other areas of life that involve following rules and authority. Perhaps they will mention games and sports. Explain that teams have rule books and that the rules must be followed to play that particular sport. There are rules that protect players, rules about time periods, and rules about penalties.

4 Discuss some of the laws in your town or city, such as driving laws. Explain what would happen if drivers of automobiles didn't pay any attention to laws concerning traffic lights, cross walks, or speed limits. Mention other areas of life where laws protect people, such as laws about stealing and/or destroying another person's property.

5 Introduce the term respect. To **respect** is to admire someone's positive characteristics. People who respect others treat others as they themselves would like to be treated. People who respect authority understand that the laws they follow are made to protect people and to prevent violence.

6 Introduce the term juvenile offender. A **juvenile offender** is a person under the age of 18 who breaks a criminal law. Juvenile offenders need help in learning respect for other people and for the laws of the community. There are programs in the community and agencies that help juvenile offenders learn right from wrong.

7 Select two students to hold the ends of a piece of yarn that is approximately ten feet in length. With tape, attach the five badges to the yarn at intervals. Read what is written on each badge. Select another student who will stand at one end of the yarn wearing a sign, "I have followed laws."

8 Blindfold a volunteer who will try to reach and tag the student who is wearing the sign. Place the volunteer's hand near the opposite end of the yarn from where the student with the sign is standing. The volunteer can reach and tag the student by holding the yarn and following the laws written on the five badges.

9 Pick a second volunteer and blindfold him/her. Have the two students who are holding the yarn with the badges step aside. The student with the sign will remain where (s)he was. Do not tell this volunteer that you are removing the yarn with the attached badges. This volunteer is to try to reach and tag the student who is wearing the sign "I have followed laws." This volunteer will have great difficulty because the guidelines (the yarn and badges) are not there to follow. Explain that if people do not follow laws, they have great difficulty keeping safe and protected.

Evaluation:

Attach a ten-foot piece of yarn from one part of the room to another. Have each student make a badge and write on it one law (or rule) they will follow. Students will then attach their badges to the yarn.

I'M PROTECTED

Objective:

Students will name kinds of violence and ways to protect against violence.

Life Skills:

I will recognize that violent behavior is wrong. (PF1)

I will practice suicide prevention strategies. (PF9)

I will avoid discrimination. (PF11)

I will practice self-protection strategies. (PF18)

Materials:

Construction paper, markers, scissors

Motivation:

1 To prepare for this strategy, cut five arrows from construction paper about two inches wide and twelve inches long.

2 Introduce the term violence. **Violence** is the threatened or actual use of physical force to injure, damage, or destroy yourself, others, or property. Explain that a person can be either a perpetrator or a victim of violence. A **perpetrator** is a person who commits a violent act. A **victim** is a person who is harmed by violence. Explain that many young people become engaged in violence because they are unable to cope with experiences in their lives that are overwhelming to them. No matter what the reason is, violent behavior is wrong because it results in harm to individuals.

3 Explain that young persons might become so discouraged with or depressed that they might consider harming themselves or com-

mitting suicide. Explain that it is important to have caring family members and good friends who will help a young person through tough times. Explain also that young people who are discriminated against often become angry enough to engage in violent behavior. Explain the term discriminatory behavior. **Discriminatory behavior** is making distinctions in treatment or showing behavior in favor of or prejudiced against an individual or group of people. Discrimination often means that a person is being treated disrespectfully and differently from others. When people show respect for others, they are encouraging them to be at their best.

4 Introduce the topic of self-protection strategies. **Self-protection strategies** are strategies that can be practiced to protect oneself and decrease the risk of becoming a victim. One important strategy is to always be alert. Pay close attention to the persons who are around you. If anyone is extremely angry, or has a weapon, or is threatening you or another person, get out of that situation as quickly as possible. Do not stay in an area where a person is engaging in violent behavior.

5 Review the following strategies that students can practice to protect themselves. Ask students for additional self-protection strategies they might practice.
- Never let a stranger into your home.
- Never give your name and address to a stranger over the phone.
- Never let anyone know that you are home alone.
- Never accept a ride from a stranger or from someone you do not trust.
- Stay away from areas that are considered gang territories.
- Do not talk to strangers who approach you.

- Stay away from people who are using drugs or from places where drugs are being sold.
- Get away from any person who is carrying or using a weapon, such as a gun or a knife.
- Get away from people who are angry and using threats.
- Tell a trusted adult if you see a weapon on the sidewalk or in school.

6 Have each student design a shield using construction paper. On the five arrows you prepared, print a type of violence, such as the following: fighting, stealing, using a gun, using a knife, hitting, pushing, threatening to harm a person, and threatening to break into a home.

7 Ask for a volunteer to come to the front of the classroom and hold his/her shield in front of him/her. Give five other students one of the five arrows. Have one of these students take his/her paper arrow, read what is printed on the arrow, and strike the volunteer's shield. The volunteer will respond "I am well protected because....(state a self-protection strategy that (s)he could use to avoid becoming a victim of violence.)" Repeat this activity using a different volunteer with a shield, and a student with a different arrow.

8 Repeat the activity with a volunteer who has no shield, so is not protected. When this volunteer is struck with an arrow, (s)he will respond "I have no protection so I may become a victim of violence." Use this activity to discuss the importance of practicing self-protection strategies to protect oneself and others against violence.

Evaluation:

Hold up arrows to the class with the same or additional acts of violence printed on them. As you show each arrow to the class, have students identify ways to protect themselves from those violent actions.

PULLED TOWARD VIOLENCE

Objective:

Students will identify resistance skills that can be used when pressured to engage in violent behavior.

Life Skills:

I will develop positive self-esteem. (PF2)
I will make responsible decisions. (PF12)
I will practice resistance skills. (PF13)

Materials:

Yarn (about a ten-foot piece)

Motivation:

1 Introduce the term resistance skills. **Resistance skills** are skills that are used when a person wants to say NO to an action and/or leave a situation. This person prefers to say YES to good health. Resistance skills are also called refusal skills. Explain that everyone has experienced situations in which they were pressured to do something they knew they should not do or something that might lead to violent behavior. Ask students if they have ever been pressured to engage in an activity that they considered questionable. Have students share examples of such experiences.

2 Explain that persons who have positive self-esteem want to protect themselves and keep themselves safe because they have good feelings about themselves. They are less likely to act in ways that might harm themselves or others. Explain that positive self-esteem contributes to a person's confidence level. Persons with positive self-esteem can deal with difficult situations and make responsible decisions. Persons who want to develop positive self-esteem can do so by working to do their

best in school; by getting involved in school activities; by choosing supportive friends; and by maintaining a neat and clean appearance.

3 Discuss decision-making skills. Decision-making skills are a series of steps to follow to make sure that a decision is wise and responsible. People who practice these skills know how to resist pressures to do something they do not want to do or something that might harm themselves or others. They know when to say NO.

4 Discuss various skills young persons can use to protect themselves from becoming involved in violence. Following is a list of suggested ways for effectively resisting pressure to engage in actions that threaten health; threaten safety; break laws; result in lack of respect for self and others; disobey guidelines set by responsible adults; and detract from character and moral values. Discuss each skill.

- Be honest. Express yourself without being anxious or threatening. Be in control of yourself and the situation.
- Say NO. Say it clearly and firmly. As you speak, look directly at the person who is pressuring you.
- Match your actions and your words. When you say NO, walk away from the person. Don't stay to discuss the matter any further.
- Avoid being in situations in which you know you might be pressured. If a situation seems dangerous to you, get away and stay away.
- Avoid being with persons who choose harmful actions. Choose to be with people who choose healthful actions.

5 Select two students to hold the ends of a piece of yarn that is approximately ten feet long. They should stand apart from each other with the yarn stretched to full length. Choose one of the students to act as a person who will try to pressure the other to do something that might turn violent. This student will make a statement such as "Let's steal some candy at the store" and at the same time give his/her end of the yarn a slight tug. For each statement, the student who is holding the other end of the yarn is to state a resistance skill that is relevant to the pressure. As this student states a resistance skill, (s)he is to give his/her end of the yarn a slight tug. Repeat with more examples of statements that pressure a student to do something that might turn violent.

6 Repeat the activity, but instruct the student who is being pressured not to state any resis-

tance skill. The student who is pressuring should try to be convincing and should give his/her end of the yarn a slight tug each time. This activity will demonstrate that the student who does not use resistance skills will get "pulled in" to whatever activity someone pressures him/her to do. Use this demonstration to stress the importance of practicing resistance skills in order to avoid violence.

Evaluation:

Divide the class into two groups. Have one group make statements that indicate a possible violent act to the other group. This latter group should respond by making statements concerning appropriate resistance skills.

PEACEFUL POETRY

Objective:

Students will describe ways to resolve conflicts without fighting.

Life Skills:

I will develop social skills. (PF5)
I will practice conflict resolution and peer mediation skills. (PF10)

Materials:

None

Motivation:

1 Explain that life without conflicts is impossible. A **conflict** is a disagreement between two or more persons or between two or more choices. Conflicts may be the result of differing opinions. For example, conflicts occur between friends, among family members, among students in school, and among residents in a neighborhood. Explain that people can disagree and still be friends. Skills can be practiced and learned so that people can come to a satisfactory agreement about conflicting opinions. Explain that if a conflict is not resolved, the people can become frustrated, and choose a behavior that might lead to violence.

2 Share some examples of conflicts that students might experience. A student might tell a lie about another student. A student might push ahead of other students in a line. A student might criticize another student. Ask students for other examples.

3 Discuss conflict resolution skills. **Conflict resolution skills** are skills a person can use

to resolve a disagreement in a healthful, safe, legal, respectful, and nonviolent way. Explain that people who learn these skills can think clearly about disagreements they may have with others. Discuss the following skills:

· <u>Stay calm.</u> Do not try to settle a disagreement while you are still feeling angry or frustrated. Count to 10.
· <u>Use social skills.</u> **Social skills** are skills that can be used to relate well with others. Treat others with respect. Be polite.
· <u>Describe the conflict.</u> Make sure you and the other person understand what you disagree about.
· <u>Share your feelings.</u> Use I-messages. I-messages are statements that refer to you, your feelings, and your needs. An example: "When you called me a name, I felt put down, and I was angry."
· <u>Listen to the other person.</u> Let the other person know that you really want to resolve the conflict.
· <u>List possible solutions.</u> Sit down with the other person and list possible ways to settle the disagreement.
· <u>Agree on a solution.</u>
· <u>Keep your word.</u> Do what you say you will do.
· <u>Ask an adult for help.</u>

4 Introduce the terms peer and peer mediation. A **peer** is a person who is similar in age or status. **Peer mediation** is a process used to resolve conflicts in which a person helps his/her peers resolve disagreements in healthful, safe, legal, respectful, and nonviolent ways. A person the same age as the two persons who are disagreeing can help them come to an agreement. If your school has set up a peer mediation program, give your students an opportunity to see how it works so that they can begin to gain more conflict resolution skills.

5 Divide the class into groups of three for a co-operative learning activity. Each group is to identify a conflict and write a poem about how that conflict could be resolved without fighting. One person in each group will read the group's poem to the class.

6 After each poem is read, review the conflict and the conflict resolution skill recom-mended in the poem. Ask students if they have other suggestions for resolving the conflict described in each poem.

Evaluation:

On the chalkboard, list the suggested skills to resolve conflicts. For each skill, have students identify other conflict situations in which the skill might be used to resolve the conflict.

WANTED: ANGER MANAGER

Objective:

Students will identify healthful ways to express anger and disappointment.

Life Skills:

I will respond to my environment in an empowering way. (PF4)
I will practice anger management skills. (PF6)

Materials:

Wanted: Anger Manager student master (page 242), a copy for each student

Motivation:

1 Introduce the term anger. **Anger** is the feeling of being irritated, annoyed, and/or furious. Explain that everyone experiences feelings of anger. Stress that it is OK to feel angry. However, it is important to learn how to handle anger in ways that will not harm oneself or others.

2 Explain to students that it is important to recognize anger triggers. **Anger triggers** are thoughts or events that cause a person to become angry. Have students identify situations that have caused them to feel angry. They may mention arguments with friends, name calling, being left out of events or activities with friends, and doing poorly on a test in school. They also may mention conditions such as poverty or illness. When a person realizes that (s)he is angry, it is a good idea to think about what the anger trigger was so that (s)he can begin to learn what sorts of situations arouse feelings of anger.

3 Discuss anger cues. **Anger cues** are changes in the body or signs that a person is

angry. Examples of anger cues are reddening of the face, increase in heart rate, sweaty palms, and rapid breathing. It is important for students to learn to recognize anger cues not only in themselves but also in others.

4 Ask students how they feel when they are angry. They may say that they feel like screaming, striking out at the person who has caused the anger, or kicking an object. Explain that these are examples of harmful ways to handle anger because they harm self or another person or destroy property. Explain that if people do not handle their anger in healthful ways, they may become violent.

5 Introduce the term hidden anger. **Hidden anger** is anger that is not dealt with in a healthful way and may result in inappropriate behavior and poor health. Hidden anger is often the underlying cause of violence because the feelings of anger begin to multiply. Eventually, this hidden anger cannot be contained and it overflows. The person may act out very inappropriately by having a temper tantrum, starting a fight, or hurting himself/herself or someone else. For this reason, it is important to do something about angry feelings in healthful ways rather than in harmful ways.

6 In order to express their feelings in a healthful way, students might consider the following ways:

• Keep an anger self-inventory. One way to become skilled in recognizing anger triggers and evaluating feelings of anger is to keep an inventory and answer questions such as "What am I feeling? What is causing me to feel this way? Is my anger justified? Am I still angry? How can I express my anger in a healthful way?"

- **Talk to an adult and ask for help.** Adults can help a student recognize what (s)he is feeling, and what are healthful ways to cope with those feelings.
- **Share their feelings with the person who caused the anger.** The other person may not realize that (s)he caused the anger.
- **Exercise to relieve the stress.** Vigorous physical activity can help relieve tension by providing an outlet for the energy that builds up when a person is angry.

7 Introduce the term nurturing environment. A **nurturing environment** is a set of conditions and surroundings in which a person lives that promotes optimal growth and development. Explain that nurturing means to train, to educate, and to support. In a nurturing environment, a person learns to have hope. **Hope** is the feeling that what is desired is possible and that events in life may turn out for the best. Having hope increases a person's ability to cope with disappointment. In a nurturing environment, people also are more likely to learn to act in nonviolent ways and to protect themselves from the violent actions of others. Parents or other adults in a nurturing environment teach their children how to resolve conflict without violence and how to manage anger.

8 Introduce the term adverse environment. An **adverse environment** is a set of conditions and surroundings in which a person lives that interferes with optimal growth and development. An adverse environment is the opposite of a nurturing environment. People who live in an adverse environment may not be able to control their environment, but they can become empowered.

Empowerment is the belief that you control your own destiny. These people can control what they do. They can determine to become protected in some possible ways as follows: They can ask a trusted adult, who will act as a role model, for help and advice; they can attend school every day and learn as much as possible; they can learn to set goals and make plans to reach those goals; they can find safe areas in which to play and to stay away from persons who act in violent ways.

9 Distribute a copy of the *Wanted: Anger Manager* master to each student. This master is a want ad, such as might appear in a local newspaper. Students are to fill in the blanks after each heading. For example, under "Job Description," the students will identify a kind of situation that an Anger Manager would have to control. Under "Qualifications," students will identify personal characteristics they would look for in a person who could be an Anger Manager. Under "Anger Management Skills," students will identify skills that an Anger Manager could use to control anger. Students will share their masters after the skills they have identified have been checked for appropriateness by the teacher.

Evaluation:

Make a list of the situations identified by students on their *Wanted: Anger Manager* masters. Divide the class into groups and assign some of the situations to each group to identify the skills they would use to handle the anger.

Wanted: Anger Manager

JOB DESCRIPTION:

QUALIFICATIONS:

ANGER MANAGEMENT SKILLS NECESSARY:

HEAVY BAGGAGE

Objective:

Students will outline ways to manage stress.

Life Skills:

I will practice stress management skills. (PF7)
I will participate in physical activity. (PF8)

Materials:

The Responsible Decision-Making Model transparency (page 609), transparency projector, book bag or backpack, books

Motivation:

1 Ask for a volunteer. This volunteer will hold an empty book bag or backpack at his/her side and stand at the front of the classroom. Have the class note that the student is holding the book bag or backpack easily. Start adding one book at a time and explain to the class that each book that is added represents a stressor.

2 Explain what a stressor is. A **stressor** is a demand that causes changes in the body. Examples of stressors are taking a test in school, getting ready for a relay race, or having an illness. Ask the class for examples of other stressors that might be represented by each book that is added to the book bag. Have them use examples of stressors that affect their lives.

3 Ask the volunteer who is holding the book bag how the addition of each added book affected him/her. (S)he will say that the book bag gets heavier and more difficult to hold with the addition of each book. The stressors (books) place strain on the arms and

makes the student feel tired. This effect is a change in the person's body and is called stress.

4 Define the term stress. **Stress** is the response of the body to the demands of daily living. Feelings of stress are an everyday experience. Explain that the effect of stress is like carrying heavy baggage. Stress interferes with a person's daily activity. For this reason, it is important to learn how to manage stress in order to relieve effects of stress such as headaches, sleeplessness, and nervousness. Young persons who experience prolonged stress may become depressed and even may become violent.

5 **Stress management skills** are techniques that can be used to cope with the harmful effects produced by stress. Examples of skills are asking an adult for help; getting sufficient sleep; eating foods that contain vitamins; spending time with friends; sharing feelings with a friend. Explain that there are two types of stress management skills. The first type focuses on doing something about the cause of stress. Using responsible decision-making skills can help solve a problem or situation that is causing stress. Use *The Responsible Decision-Making Model* transparency to discuss with students how to use the model to decide how to cope with a stressful situation. The second type of skill focuses on keeping the body healthy and relieving the anxiety caused by the stress. Explain that a very important example of this second type of skill is to participate in physical activity.

6 Discuss some of the benefits of physical activity that would keep a person healthy and also relieve the anxiety caused by stress as follows:

- Maintains physical fitness, increases your energy and improves your overall health status.
- Allows you to spend time in a positive manner without turning to activities that are harmful and/or illegal.
- Gives you an outlet for your anger and feelings of aggression and you will be less likely to express yourself in inappropriate or violent ways such as fighting and arguing.
- Eases feelings of loneliness and teaches you how to cooperate with others when you participate in team sports.
- Helps you get to know people who share your interests and talents.
- Requires you to follow established rules and guidelines and to "play fair." You learn to abide by the rules and to respect authority.

- Teaches you how to express feelings of disappointment and frustration when your team loses.

7 Refer to the stressors that students identified (step 2) and have them identify stress management skills they could use for each of the identified stressors. For example, a student might have said a test in school is a stressor. A stress management skill for this stressor might be to budget time on a regular basis to study for tests.

Evaluation:

Use the books that were packed into the book bag. Remove one book at a time and have students identify an additional stressor and an appropriate stress management skill to cope with that particular stressor.

TROUBLE BREWING

Objective:

Students will differentiate between people and groups who choose responsible behavior and people/gangs who are violent.

Life Skill:

I will resist gang membership. (PF16)

Materials:

Tea bag, two clear plastic cups, clear plastic wrap

Motivation:

1 Introduce the term youth gang. A **youth gang** is a group of young people who band together and participate in violent, unlawful, or criminal behavior. Members of a gang associate only with each other and often commit crimes against other youth gangs or against people in general. A gang usually has a name and operates in a certain area called their "turf." Gang members often use certain colors of clothes so that they are easily recognized.

2 Explain that young people join gangs for different reasons. Some are looking for excitement; some cave in to pressure by gang members; some join because they are bored with their lives; and some are alienated from their families and want a sense of belonging. In many cases, young people who want to join a gang do not realize the danger involved. Prospective gang members have to prove themselves to be worthy of joining the gang. They may be required to steal, to buy drugs illegally, or to commit a violent crime. They often are the victims of abuse from older gang members.

3 Place a tea bag in a clear plastic cup that contains water. Explain that the tea bag represents a gang. The longer the tea bag is in the water, the greater will be the amount of discoloration. Draw the analogy that the longer a person has contact with a gang, the more influence the gang has on the person. Also, the longer the contact, the more difficult it is for the person to break away from the gang and the risk of becoming involved in violent behavior increases.

4 Fill the second clear plastic cup with water. Cover the top of this cup with clear plastic wrap. Remind students that the tea bag represents a gang, as you place a tea bag on the clear plastic wrap. The class will notice that, in this case, the tea bag is not in contact with the water so the water will not become discolored by the tea bag.

5 Point out that the plastic wrap served as a protector that did not allow the "gang" to be an influence. Draw the analogy that there also are people who can help students resist gang membership. Have students identify these people. Some examples are their families, law enforcement authorities, teachers and other school personnel, schoolmates, friends, and so on.

Evaluation:

Have students set up an acrostic on a sheet of paper using the word RESIST. Using each letter of RESIST as the first letter of a sentence, write sentences that describe how to resist becoming a member of a gang.

WARNING: DRUG USE = VIOLENCE

Objective:

Students will explain why drug use increases the risk of violence.

Life Skill:

I will avoid alcohol and other drugs. (PF14)

Materials:

None

Motivation:

1 Introduce the term drug. A **drug** is a substance that changes the way the body and/or mind work. Alcohol is an example of a drug. Explain that the human body normally maintains an internal, chemical balance. Anything that upsets this internal balance affects a person's ability to function. Drugs change the chemical balance because they affect the nervous system, which is the body's control center. The nervous system is composed of the brain and spinal cord and nerves that branch from the brain and spinal cord. Drug use affects the function of the brain and leads people to behave in ways they might not when they are not using drugs. This might include violent behavior. Point out how important it is for students to avoid the use of any drug, including alcohol.

2 Explain that people who do not use drugs are in control of their behavior; can make responsible decisions; can relate well with others; express feelings in healthful ways; are more apt to have a positive self-concept; and abide by laws. People who use drugs are not in control of their behavior; cannot make responsible decisions; do not relate well with others; lose control of their feelings; are more apt to have a negative self-esteem; and are apt to resist laws.

3 The use of alcohol and other drugs is a risk factor that makes a person more vulnerable to violent behavior because of the effect on the person's nervous system. Review the following drugs with students.

- Alcohol. Alcohol is a drug that depresses the nervous system. Alcohol use may result in many different problems such as liver damage, damage to the stomach, abnormal heart functioning, cancer, and brain damage. Alcohol use seems to be related to feelings of anger and aggression, or unprovoked attacks. These feelings would normally be under control, but are less controlled when a person is under the influence of alcohol.
- Sedative-hypnotic drugs. These drugs also depress the nervous system. They are sometimes called "downers." They contribute to aggressive and assaultive behavior. Users tend to be argumentative and irritable.
- PCP. PCP use over a period of time affects a person's ability to see clearly. PCP causes most users to become angry, aggressive, and violent.
- Cocaine. Cocaine use is associated with feelings of irritability and paranoia (suspicion and distrust of others).
- Amphetamines. These drugs stimulate the nervous system. They are sometimes called "uppers."
- Heroin. Heroin is a form of narcotics, which depress the nervous system. Use of heroin causes feelings of anger and aggression.
- Anabolic steroids. Steroids represent a class of drugs that poses a serious threat of violent behavior because they produce feelings of aggression and paranoia.

- <u>Marijuana.</u> Marijuana use causes the heart to beat faster than usual and can cause lung damage. Marijuana users often experience mood swings and restlessness.

4 Explain that drug use not only has an effect on the drug user's behavior, but also increases the risks that others who are not drug users may become the victims of violence. Stress that drug users are not in control of their behavior and that they may injure another person without intending to do so. This is the reason that it is so important to stay away from persons who are using drugs.

5 Have students design warning labels similar to the warnings on a package of cigarettes.

The warnings should be concerned with how drugs increase the risk of violent behavior. Share all the labels and put them on the bulletin board.

Evaluation:

Divide the class into two groups. One group will identify a connection between drugs and violence. The other group will identify a way to deal with each connection. For example, a connection might be that a person who drinks alcohol gets loud and has a short temper. The response might be to walk away from such a person and associate with others who are not drinking.

NO USE FOR ABUSE

Objective:

Students will identify and describe types of abuse: emotional, sexual, physical, and neglect.

Life Skills:

I will strive for healthful family relationships. (PF3)
I will develop resiliency to "bounce back" if I was reared in a dysfunctional family. (PF3)
I will practice self-protection strategies. (PF18)
I will participate in recovery if a victim. (PF19)

Materials:

None

Motivation:

1 Explain that **child abuse** is the harmful treatment of a person under the age of 18 and includes physical abuse, verbal abuse, emotional abuse, sexual abuse, and neglect. Physical abuse is harm to the body. Signs of physical abuse include bruises, burns, cuts, missing teeth, broken bones, and internal injuries. Verbal abuse is the use of words to harm a person. Emotional abuse involves harm to a person's mind, self-esteem, and personality. Signs of emotional abuse are poor peer relationships, distrust, excessive fear, and negative self-esteem. Sexual abuse involves inappropriate sexual behavior between an adult and a child. Neglect involves lack of proper care and guidance. Signs include malnourishment, poor health, and lack of appropriate clothes. Child abuse is a type of violence.

2 Explain that being abused or neglected as a child increases a person's risk for violent behavior as an adult. Abused children often have difficulty in forming friendships and in doing schoolwork. They grow up in homes in which family members do not respect each other. Their parents may not know how to resolve conflict without fighting or some other type of violent behavior. Explain that many abusive and neglectful parents do not intend to harm their children and often are sorry about the abuse. Point out that the parents' problems may be so overwhelming that they do not know how to stop their harmful behavior.

3 Explain that children from this kind of home can practice self-protection strategies. **Self-protection strategies** are strategies that can be practiced to protect oneself and decrease the risk of becoming a victim. Remind students that a **victim** is a person who has been harmed by violence. Introduce the term resiliency. **Resiliency** is the ability to prevent or to recover, bounce back, and learn from misfortune, change, or pressure. Abused children can ask the person who is abusing them to stop. They can stay away from that person. They can say NO in a firm voice. And they can tell a trusted adult and ask for help.

4 Discuss the fact that abused children need help. Mention some possible sources of help in your community, such as mental health centers, public health clinics, and the school counselor. These sources will help a child recover from the violence. If necessary, they will find a safer home for the child.

5 Explain that you are going to read a Dear Helper letter to which the students will write a response. The responses should offer advice such as assuring the writer of the letter that no person should be abused and that people who abuse others need help. The responses should also include what help is available, such as community resources or professional help. Read the following letter.

Dear Helper,
I am very scared and confused. My father often beats me for no apparent reason. He gets moody and the slightest thing can set him off. Sometimes he punches me. At other times, he smacks me and calls me names like stupid. Most of the time, he tells me he is sorry and he will not do it again. Yet he does not keep his word. I love him and I am afraid that if I tell someone, he will be put in jail or he will become even more angry with me and become more violent.

Sincerely,
Hurt and confused

Evaluation:

Have students share their advice suggestions on ways to deal with a person who abuses another person. Consolidate the responses into a helpful list for students to follow. The list also can identify local community resources that can be of help.

SIGNS OF SAFETY

Objective:

Students will describe procedures to follow for safety around weapons.

Life Skill:

I will practice responsible behavior around weapons. (PF15)

Materials:

Safety Signs student master (page 253), a copy for each student

Motivation:

1 Ask students for examples of weapons. They may mention guns and knives. Define the term weapon. A **weapon** is an instrument or device used for fighting. Weapons are usually used to injure another person. Weapons of all sorts are used in violent crimes, and persons of all ages are victims of those violent crimes. According to recent statistics, young people are at a special risk.

2 Stress the fact that many innocent bystanders are the victims of random violence. Explain that random violence is accidental rather than planned and often involves persons who just happen to be nearby. This is the reason that it is so dangerous to be near a person who has a weapon.

3 Discuss school rules about weapons. Tell students they have a responsibility to themselves and to other students to report to a teacher if they see another student with a weapon, such as a gun or a knife. The student with the weapon may not intend to use it. (S)he may be just showing off. However,

if this student gets in an argument, (s)he may be tempted to use the weapon.

4 Explain that many families have guns in their homes. A gun in a home should not be loaded and should be kept in a securely-locked place. Parents in these families assume the responsibility of teaching their children safety rules about guns. Explain that although this strategy may be more concerned with weapons that students might see away from home, students should always be responsible about their behavior concerning weapons. They should apply safety procedures about weapons no matter where they see weapons.

5 There are procedures to follow to keep safe around weapons. The procedures can be remembered easily by remembering the word SAFE and an acronym formed with the letters in that word.
- S — STOP
- A — AVOID GOING NEAR THE SITUATION
- F — FIND AN ADULT
- E — EXPLAIN WHAT YOU SAW

6 Distribute a copy of the *Safety Signs* student master to each student. Point out the shapes of the different signs on the master. The STOP sign is an octagon — it has eight sides. The YIELD sign is a triangle. The CAUTION sign is diamond shaped.

7 Direct the students to draw a weapon on each sign. They are then to describe how that sign relates to a safety procedure concerning that particular weapon. For example, the safety procedure about a gun drawn on the STOP sign might be to stop short of going near a weapon. The safety procedure about a knife drawn on the YIELD sign might be to yield and tell an adult about the knife. Have students share their signs and their safety procedures.

Evaluation:

Have students work together to make a safety checklist based on student signs. The checklist should be a list of responsible behavior that students can practice around weapons. Suggest that students share the checklist with their parents or other adults.

Safety Signs

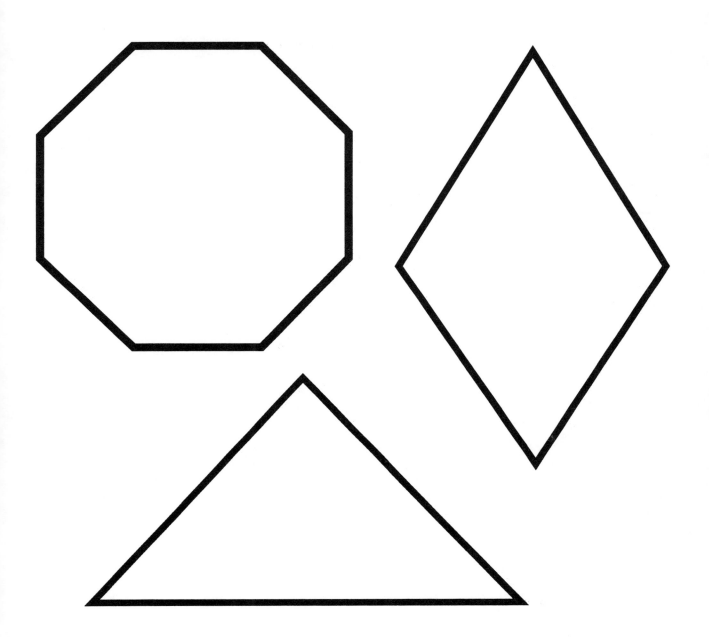

BEING RESPECTFUL

Objective:

Students will identify the advantages of cooperating with law enforcement officers and other persons with authority.

Life Skills:

I will respect authority and abide by laws. (PF17)
I will change behavior if a juvenile offender. (PF20)

Materials:

None

Motivation:

1 Discuss what the term respect means in regard to laws. To respect laws means to understand that laws and rules protect people. Discuss the different kinds of laws that exist in your community, such as driving laws, pedestrian laws, and drug laws. Explain that these laws protect people who live in the community.

2 Discuss law enforcement authorities. Law enforcement authorities protect and assist citizens of the community. They work to prevent accidents and criminal activity. However, law enforcement authorities cannot control criminal activity or protect citizens without the cooperation of citizens in the community. Most adults in a community understand the importance of respecting laws and law enforcement authorities.

3 Discuss authority. **Authority** is the power and right to govern and to apply laws. Ask students to identify people who have authority in the community in which they live. They will mention police officers, the mayor, or the governor. Mention others who have authority. Parents have authority over family rules. The school principal has authority over school rules. People who abide by laws and respect authority understand that the laws have been passed for the good of all people. They choose to protect their health and safety and the health and safety of others.

4 Explain what happens when a young person does not respect authority or abide by laws. A **juvenile offender** is a person under the age of 18 who has broken a criminal law. Explain that many first-time juvenile offenders decide to change their behavior and do not commit a crime again. Some juvenile offenders appreciate the help that is offered to them and respond favorably to rehabilitation. Rehabilitation is the process of restoring to a normal state of constructive activity through medical or professional treatment. Explain that juvenile offenders who do not change their behavior often go to prison.

5 Use this strategy as a cooperative learning experience. Have students work in groups to write three additional lines of verse to sing with the melody of the song "*RESPECT*." The first line will be R-E-S-P-E-C-T. For example, the four lines may be similar to the following:

R-E-S-P-E-C-T
My principal will protect me
When I am doing my work at school.
My principal will tell me I'm so cool.

One member from each group can share the group's verse with the class. Have the groups sing the verse.

Evaluation:

In an old magazine at school or at home, have students find a picture of a person who serves to protect people in a community. If possible, they are to cut the picture from the magazine and include it with a short report on how the person in the picture helps others abide by laws and why (s)he should be respected.

VPF 20 (VIOLENCE PROTECTION FACTOR)

Objective:

Students will name kinds of violence and ways to protect against violence.

Life Skills:

I will recognize that violent behavior is wrong. (PF1)
I will practice suicide prevention strategies. (PF9)
I will avoid discrimination. (PF11)
I will practice self-protection strategies. (PF18)

Materials:

Protective Factors To Prevent Violence transparency (page 588), transparency projector, bottle of sunscreen lotion with the SPF (sun protection factor) indicated, tissues, red water-base marker, two index cards, wide transparent tape, butcher paper

Motivation:

1 To prepare for this strategy, using the water-base marker, draw an outline of a person on each of the two index cards. Cover one of the index cards with wide transparent tape.

2 Introduce the term violence. **Violence** is the threatened or actual use of physical force to injure, damage, or destroy yourself, others, or property. Explain that it is dangerous not to know what actions are violent or what situations might eventually involve violence. Emphasize that it is wrong to harm yourself or others. Explain that there are many types of violence, such as the following:

- **Bullying** is an attempt by people to hurt or frighten those who are perceived to be smaller or weaker.
- **Fighting** is taking part in a physical struggle. A fistfight is an example of fighting.
- **Assault** is a physical attack or threat of attack. Many people require emergency medical care after an assault; many are fatally injured.
- **Homicide** is the accidental or purposeful killing of another person.
- **Suicide** is the intentional taking of one's own life.
- **Sexual harassment** is unwanted sexual behavior that ranges from making sexual comments to forcing another person into unwanted sex acts.
- **Child abuse** is the harmful treatment of a person under the age of 18 and includes physical abuse, verbal abuse, emotional abuse, sexual abuse, and neglect.
- **Domestic violence** is violence that occurs within the family or within other relationships in which people live together.

3 Explain further that it is possible for people to become so discouraged and hopeless that they decide to choose suicide rather than to go on living. Explain that there are ways people can protect themselves from thinking about or attempting suicide. They can build a network of caring people who will listen and offer advice. They can make a list of their strengths and the positive aspects of their lives. They can become involved in rewarding activities, such as learning a craft, or helping others.

4 Introduce the term discriminatory behavior. **Discriminatory behavior** is making distinctions in treatment or showing behavior in favor of or prejudiced against an individual or group of people. Explain also that when persons are discriminated against, they may become so frustrated and angry that they become involved in violent activities. It is behavior that treats some individuals or groups of individuals in a different manner from others, usually disrespectfully. Remind students that everyone should be treated with respect.

5 Show students the bottle of sunscreen lotion. Point out the SPF (sun protection factor) that is indicated on the label of the bottle. Explain that if people put this lotion on their bodies before going out in the sun, they will have some protection from the ultraviolet rays of the sun. Explain that the higher the SPF number is, the greater the protection that they will have. Explain about another type of protection. You are calling this VPF, or violence protection factors. Violence protection factors are self-protection strategies. **Self-protection strategies** are strategies that can be practiced to protect oneself and decrease the risk of becoming a victim.

6 Using the red water-base marker, draw an X over the body outline on each of the index cards. With a tissue, try to wipe off each of the X marks. The X on the card that has tape on it will wipe off. The X on the other card will not wipe off. Explain that the card with the tape represents a person who has put sunscreen lotion on his/her body before going out in the sun. For the purposes of this strategy, this card also represents a person who practices violence protective factors and has a "coating" of VPFs.

7 Use the *Protective Factors To Prevent Violence* transparency to discuss the 20 protective factors that are listed. Remind students that a **protective factor** is a way that a person might behave and characteristics of the environment in which (s)he lives that promote health, safety, and/or well-being. Protective factors are in contrast to risk factors. A **risk factor** is a way that a person might behave and characteristics of the environment in which (s)he lives that increase the likelihood of having something negative happen to his/her health, safety, and/or well-being. Use the *Protective Factors To Prevent Violence* transparency to discuss the 20 protective factors that are listed. As you discuss each protective factor, point out that the risk factor would be the opposite behavior or environmental factor. For example, risk factor 1 would be failure to recognize violent behavior.

Evaluation:

Make a full-size body outline by tracing the outline of a student's body on butcher paper. Give each student a strip of transparent tape. Each student is to name one of the 20 protective factors and then place his/her strip of tape somewhere on the body outline. The strips should represent all 20 protective factors so that the "body" has a VPF of 20.

INSTANT RESISTANT

Objective:

Students will identify resistance skills that can be used when pressured to engage in violent behavior.

Life Skills:

I will develop positive self-esteem. (PF2)
I will make responsible decisions. (PF12)
I will practice resistance skills. (PF13)

Materials:

Model For Using Resistance Skills transparency (page 610), transparency projector, ball

Motivation:

1 Introduce the term resistance skills. **Resistance skills** are skills that are used when a person wants to say NO to an action and/or leave a situation. Resistance skills are sometimes called refusal skills. People should use resistance skills when they are being pressured to do something they do not want to do or something they know would be harmful to their health.

2 Review the *Model For Using Resistance Skills* transparency. This transparency presents a list of suggestions for effectively resisting pressure to engage in actions that threaten health; threaten safety; break laws; result in lack of respect for self and others; disobey guidelines set by responsible adults; detract from character and moral values; and possibly become violent. As you review each skill, ask students if they have questions. Be sure they understand. For example, in step 3, you might use a relevant example such as refusing an invitation to a party at which alcohol and other drugs might

be used. Encourage students to say NO and to walk away from the person who is doing the pressuring rather than standing around to discuss it further or to be pressured further.

3 Divide the class into two groups. Group 1 will be the pressure group. Group 1 will brainstorm a list of as many statements as possible that could be used to pressure their peers to engage in a violent behavior or one that might become violent. Following are suggested statements that might be used:

- Since the garage is open, let's see what we can take.
- Hey, he left his locker open. Let's see if he has something we need.
- That rich kid left his jacket. He'll never miss it.
- Nobody's looking, let's check out the locker room.
- Let's leave school and steal food from the grocery store for lunch.
- I heard about a gang meeting over on Main Street, let's go see what's going on. Your mother doesn't need to know.

4 Group 2 will be the instant resistant group. To practice resistance skills, Group 2 will brainstorm as many reasons as possible why they would not engage in any behavior that is violent or that could become violent. Following are suggestions that might be used:

- I want to respect myself.
- I want to respect others.
- I don't want to get expelled from school.
- I don't want to do anything to jeopardize my education.
- I don't want to get into a fight.
- I have too many interesting things I like to do.
- I'm not willing to take that kind of risk.
- I'm not willing to do anything illegal.

5 Have the groups face each other across the room. Give a member of Group 1 a ball. This person looks at a person directly across from him/her and pressures that person using one of the items that Group 1 listed, such as "That rich kid left his jacket. He'll never miss it." Then the Group 1 person will toss the ball to the Group 2 person who must respond by using a resistance skill, such as "I want to respect others. The jacket is his." Then the Group 2 person will toss the ball back to the Group 1 person. Repeat this procedure several times. Summarize by saying that the members of Group 2 were INSTANT RESISTANT because they had several resistance skills ready to use effectively.

6 Explain that persons who have good decision making skills know when to resist and say NO. They take responsibility for their decisions. They think ahead to possible consequences and choose not to harm themselves or others. They are in control of their lives.

7 Introduce the term self-esteem. **Self-esteem** is what a person thinks or believes about himself/herself. When people believe they are worthwhile, they have positive self-esteem. They have good feelings about themselves and they are motivated to protect themselves and to be safe. They do not act in ways that would harm themselves or others. Persons who want to develop positive self-esteem do their best in school. They are involved in school activities; they have friends who encourage them to be at their best; they keep a neat appearance. A neat appearance influences how others perceive them, which in turn influences their self-image.

8 Encourage students to count on protective factors such as making responsible decisions and having positive self-esteem to help them practice and use resistance skills.

Evaluation:

Explain to students that they need to think quickly to be INSTANT RESISTANT. They are to list ten reasons they do not want to engage in violent behavior.

PUZZLED BY CONFLICT

Objective:

Students will describe ways to resolve conflicts without fighting.

Life Skills:

I will develop social skills. (PF5)
I will practice conflict resolution and peer mediation skills. (PF10)

Materials:

Five puzzles created from the *Puzzle Pattern* master (page 262), *Conflict Resolution Skills* transparency (page 606), transparency projector, five envelopes, paper, chalkboard, chalk

Motivation:

1 To prepare for this strategy, use the *Puzzle Pattern* master to cut out enough pieces to create five puzzles. Scramble the pieces and place an equal number of pieces in five envelopes. To prepare further, on the chalkboard write several examples of situations that might be the sources of conflict for fifth-grade students.

2 Ask for five volunteers and have them sit together at a table. Explain that you are going to give each volunteer an envelope. Without talking to each other, they are to use the puzzle pieces to form five identical puzzles. They can give each other pieces and take pieces from each other, but they cannot talk. The rest of the students should observe. (If you choose to have more than one group of volunteers, be sure to cut out enough pieces for each group to make five puzzles.)

3 After the five volunteers have completed the five identical puzzles, take time to discuss what happened. What did the volunteers experience? They most likely will mention frustration and perhaps impatience. Did anyone get angry?

4 Discuss ways that this task might have been easier to accomplish. Students might mention that if the volunteers could have talked with each other, it would have been easier. Discuss why talking might have helped. For example, they might have given one another tips or persuaded another volunteer to share a specific piece.

5 Repeat the same experiment using the suggestions that the students made for making the experiment easier to accomplish. After the puzzles are completed, note how the use of the suggestions helped. Explain that the task was easier after they had learned to work together and to communicate with each other. They were better able to resolve the problem of putting the five puzzles together.

6 Introduce the term conflict resolution skills. **Conflict resolution skills** are skills a person can use to resolve a disagreement in a healthful, safe, legal, respectful, and nonviolent way. Explain that conflicts occur naturally in every area of life. Learning how to come to an agreement about an issue over which there are conflicting opinions is an important skill to learn. Without learning conflict resolution skills, a person might easily become frustrated and angry and exhibit a behavior that could become violent.

7 Use the *Conflict Resolution Skills* transparency to discuss ways to responsibly settle disagreements. Explain that many of the conflict resolution skills are also social skills. **Social skills** are skills that can be used to relate well with others. A person who has developed social skills is said to be socially competent. Socially competent people are more likely to treat their peers fairly and with respect because they use good manners and they care about other people.

8 Introduce the terms peer and peer mediation. A **peer** is a person who is similar in age or status. **Peer mediation** is a process used to resolve conflicts in which a person helps his/her peers resolve disagreements in healthful, safe, legal, respectful, and nonviolent ways. Explain that a peer mediator has no authority over the people involved in the conflict. One of the roles of the peer mediator is to bring the people in conflict together

in a neutral setting. Perhaps your school has already established a peer mediation program. If so, give your students an opportunity to observe or take part in the process.

Evaluation:

Have students work in groups. Each group is to select one of the situations written on the chalkboard. Each group is to write a script for a role play using the chosen situation as a theme. The conflict is to be resolved without fighting and with the use of a least two conflict resolution/peer mediation skills. Have each group perform its script for the class. For each script, the class is to identify the source of the conflict and the two kinds of skills used in resolving the conflict.

Puzzle Pattern

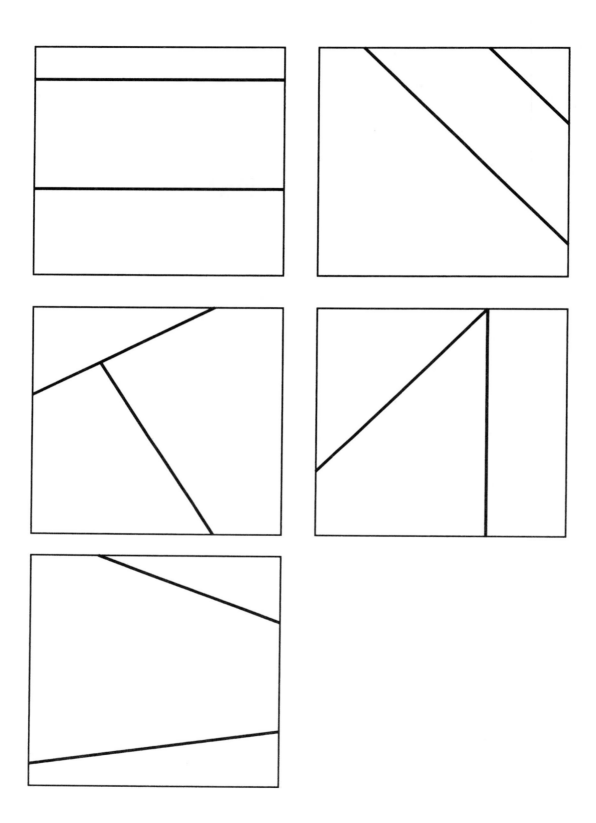

DILUTING ANGER

Objective:

Students will identify healthful ways to express anger and disappointment.

Life Skills:

I will respond to my environment in an empowering way. (PF4)

I will practice anger management skills. (PF6)

Materials:

Anger Management Skills transparency (page 600), transparency projector, pale yellow sponge, pitcher of water, red food coloring, large bowl, recipe or index cards (a card for each student)

Motivation:

1 Explain what anger is. **Anger** is the feeling of being irritated, annoyed, and/or furious. Everyone experiences feelings of anger at times. It is important that feelings of anger are managed in such a way that people do not harm themselves or others.

2 Introduce the term anger triggers. **Anger triggers** are thoughts or events that cause a person to become angry. Discuss examples of anger triggers such as being reprimanded in front of other students or failing a test in school. Ask students to think of other anger triggers they have experienced.

3 Introduce the term anger cues. **Anger cues** are changes in the body or signs that a person is angry. Anger cues include reddening of the face, rapid breathing, sweaty palms, and tense muscles. Show the yellow sponge to the students and the pitcher of water to which red food coloring has been added. Ex-

plain that the sponge represents their bodies and the red water will represent an anger trigger. Ask for volunteers to tell about an anger trigger they have experienced. Explain that as each student tells about an anger trigger, you are going to pour a little water on the sponge. Students will note that the addition of the red water to the sponge will change the color of the sponge. Relate the change in the color of the sponge to the effect of anger triggers on a person's body. A person's body changes when the person is aroused to anger just as the sponge changes. Anger cues result in body changes that make it difficult for angry people to control their actions. They may become violent.

4 Discuss hidden anger. **Hidden anger** is anger that is not dealt with in a healthful way and may result in inappropriate behavior and poor health. Symptoms of hidden anger include sleeplessness, depression, and tense muscles. Explain that when angry feelings are not expressed, they build up within the person. Eventually, the hidden anger cannot be contained and it overflows. The person may have a temper tantrum, start a fight, and/or say or do something that is inappropriate. The buildup of hidden anger can contribute to violent actions.

5 Squeeze the sponge to get all the red water out of it. Demonstrate that if there is just a small quantity of red water in it, a small squeeze might be sufficient. However, if there is a large quantity of red water in the sponge, it will take more effort to rid the sponge of all the red water. Relate this to the fact that a person must learn to get rid of angry feelings by using anger management skills.

6 Explain that when people use healthful ways to relieve angry feelings, they do not harm themselves or others. Use the *Anger Management Skills* transparency to discuss skills that help express anger in appropriate ways.

- Keeping an anger self-inventory can help you recognize what triggers arouse your anger. You can evaluate your angry feelings and determine how you might respond the next time you experience an anger trigger.
- Using self-statements to control your anger can help you respond to anger triggers and anger cues. Self-statements are reminders you can be use to calm down and wait before expressing angry feelings. Examples of self-statements are "I'm not going to let him/her get to me;" "It's not worth it to get so angry about this;" "Easy does it— I'm going to keep my sense of humor about this."
- Participating in physical activity helps defuse anger and relieves tension by providing a physical outlet for the energy that builds up with anger.
- Using physical expression to blow off steam will channel the extra energy that goes with angry feelings. Try punching a pillow, squeezing a tennis ball, or screaming into a pillow.
- Using I-messages and active listening are ways to express angry feelings in a healthful way. I-messages are statements that refer to you, the way you feel, and your needs. They are a way to communicate your feelings. An example is "I waited for you and missed the game and that made me angry." Feelings do not get bottled up inside you when you use I-messages and the other person can respond to you. On the other hand, active listening avoids shutting out the feelings that another person is expressing to you.
- Keeping a sense of humor when you become angry and laughing at yourself can help defuse angry feelings.

- Expressing yourself through creative activities helps lessen the effects of anger. Drawing a picture of what is happening or how you are feeling can help when it is difficult to put your feelings into words.
- Talking with parents and mentors can help you recognize what you are feeling, why you are feeling this way, and what are some healthful ways to cope with those feelings.
- Writing letters to express angry feelings, which may or may not be sent to another person, provides a means to express yourself and time to think through the situation.
- Planning ahead to deal with your anger allows you to test different approaches to expressing anger and different responses in different theoretical situations.

7 Explain that angry feelings that are not managed show up as hidden anger. Explain that it is important to do something about angry feelings as soon as they are felt. Illustrate this by repeating the sponge and red water experiment. Identify an anger-causing situation and pour a small amount of red water on the sponge. Then have a student mention an anger management skill that would relieve the situation and have the student squeeze the water out of the sponge.

8 Discuss how a person's environment can influence the way (s)he responds to feelings of disappointment and anger. When people live in a nurturing environment, they are more apt to learn how to cope with life situations. A **nurturing environment** is a set of conditions and surroundings in which a person lives that promotes optimal growth and development. However, if people live in an adverse environment, they will have to work on their own to develop coping skills. Explain that an **adverse environment** is a set of conditions and surroundings in which a person lives that interferes with optimal growth and development. People who live in an adverse environment often cannot cope with life situations well and are more apt to resort to violent behavior. It is important for these people to know that they can learn to "bounce back" and cope with life situations. Explain the term empowerment. **Empowerment** is the belief that a person controls his/her own destiny. Although people cannot control their environment, they can control what they do about it. For example, they can decide to stay in school to get an education. They can relate with people who do not engage in violent behavior.

Evaluation:

Give each student a recipe or index card. Have each student design a personal recipe for reducing anger or coping with disappointment. For example, the recipe ingredients might include a pinch of patience, a huge hug, a dash of calming music, and so on. Each recipe is to be a healthful skill and still meet the needs of the individual. Have students share their recipes with the class.

RESPONDING TO STRESS

Objective:

Students will outline ways to manage stress.

Life Skills:

I will practice stress management skills. (PF7)
I will participate in physical activity. (PF8)

Materials:

Stress Management Skills transparency (page 602), transparency projector, roll of white paper, index cards, one for each student, tape, marker

Motivation:

1 To prepare for this strategy, use the roll of white paper and the marker to draw a life-size outline of the body. Tape the outline to the chalkboard.

2 Introduce the term stressor. A **stressor** is a demand that causes changes in the body. Daily hassles, such as concern about physical appearance, struggles with peers, homework assignments and tests, trying out for a team, or being left out by peers, are stressors that account for much of the stress that students experience. Ask students for examples of stressors they have experienced.

3 Introduce the term stress. **Stress** is the response of the body to the demands of daily living. Discuss responses that a stressor might cause in a person's body, such as anxiety, headaches, sleeplessness, increased heart rate, rapid breathing, sweaty palms, and feelings of anger or impatience.

4 Interrupt your discussion at this point to give each student an index card. (S)he is to write

on one side of the card an example of a stressor that (s)he has experienced. The other side of the index card should remain blank. Collect the index cards and tape them (blank side up) to the outline of the body that was previously taped to the chalkboard. In this way, students will not be able to see what is written on any card.

5 Introduce the term stress management skills. **Stress management skills** are techniques that can be used to cope with the harmful effects produced by stress. Use the *Stress Management Skills* transparency to discuss skills that a persons can learn to manage stress. Discuss each item with the class.

- Using responsible decision-making skills. Refer to the Responsible Decision-Making Model (Figure 23) to review the steps involved. Point out that when you apply the steps in the model to a difficult situation, you will feel less anxious and have more confidence that you can handle the situation that is causing your stress.
- Using breathing techniques. Try breathing in deeply through your nose and then slowly blowing the air out through your mouth. This has a calming effect on your body.
- Eating a healthful diet. It is always wise to eat a well balanced diet, but it is especially important when you are stressed.
- Getting enough rest and sleep. When you are resting or sleeping, your muscles relax and your heart rate slows.
- Participating in physical activities. Physical activity provides an outlet for the energy that builds up in your body when you are stressed. Participating in physical activities has other benefits, such as maintaining fitness, improving appearance, and feeling better about yourself.

- Using a time management plan. Keep a daily calendar and write down the tasks you need to get done each day. Decide what you will do first and plan how much time you can spend on each task. Check off each task as you finish.
- Writing in a journal. Writing is a healthful way to express what you are feeling. The easiest way to start is to write about what is concerning you today.
- Having close friends. When you are with your friends, you can share your feelings without being judged. Just having someone listen can make you feel better.
- Talking with parents and other trusted adults. A parent or other adult can listen, be supportive, and often can help you solve the problem that is causing your stress.
- Helping others. When you help someone who needs help, you experience a "high" and you feel good about yourself. Helping persons less fortunate than you are can make your stress seem less important.
- Caring for pets. Caring for a pet can be a relaxing method of reducing stress.
- Changing your outlook. Try thinking about your situation and turning your problem into a challenge. In other words, be an optimist instead of a pessimist.
- Keeping a sense of humor. Laughing relieves pent up emotions and allows you to take a positive look at the situation.

6 Have students take turns going to the chalkboard and removing one of the index cards that were taped to the body outline. They are to read the example of a stressor that is printed on the card and tell the class a stress management skill that might be used to relieve the stress caused by that stressor.

Evaluation:

Have students identify several stressors in their lives. Have each student make and follow a personal plan for stress management. After the plans are complete, collect the plans and use them to evaluate the life skills.

WHAT'S THE ATTRACTION?

Objective:

Students will differentiate between people and groups who choose responsible behaviors and people/gangs who are violent.

Life Skill:

I will resist gang membership. (PF16)

Materials:

Two shoe boxes, 20 index cards, decorative paper

Motivation:

1 To prepare for this strategy, cover both shoe boxes with paper. Cover one with decorative paper; cover the other one with plain paper. Then prepare the index cards. On ten of the cards, write a description of a behavior that might relate to gang activity. Examples might be missing school, not graduating, having a criminal record, using harmful drugs, not participating in school activities, fighting, selling drugs, using firearms, stealing, and being alienated from family. Place these ten cards in the box that is covered with the decorative paper. On the other ten index cards, write a description of a behavior that might relate to students who are responsible and conscientious. Examples might be attending school, graduating from high school, earning good grades, respecting authority, lettering in a sport, participating in community events, being close to family, participating in school activities, helping friends, and respecting others. Put these ten cards in the shoe box covered with plain paper.

2 Ask students which shoe box they find to be the most attractive. They undoubtedly will choose the decorative box. Ask students for their reasons for choosing the box they did. Open the decorative box and ask ten students who chose the decorative box to come forward and select an index card from the box. Each one is to read what is written on the card (s)he has. When all ten cards have been read, explain that this shoe box represents a gang. Stress that the outside of the box was attractive, but the inside was not attractive. The inside represents trouble.

3 Introduce the term youth gang. A **youth gang** is a group of young people who band together and participate in violent, unlawful, or criminal activity. Gang members usually hang around together and often commit crimes against other gangs or against other people. Discuss the serious consequences of belonging to a gang. Being a member of a gang increases exposure to: illicit drugs; alcohol abuse; firearms and other weapons; fighting; dropping out of school; and arrest and imprisonment. Families of gang members may: fear for their safety; suffer damage to their property; and suffer personal injury.

4 Now open the plain shoe box. Have ten students come forward, select a card, and read what is written on it. When all ten cards have been read, explain that this shoe box represents responsible students. Explain that sometimes it may not seem as appealing or attractive to follow guidelines and to choose friends who are responsible. However, the benefits are many. Persons who choose responsible behavior: enhance their self-esteem; promote their health; are able to set goals and make plans to reach their goals; help prevent illness, injury, and premature death; and improve the quality of their environment.

Evaluation:

Students should keep a diary for one week, identifying the peers with whom they spend time and recording what they do with these peers. They are to record whether or not the activity they engaged in with a peer(s) was responsible. Follow up with a class discussion on the influence of peers on behavior.

DRUG PERMEATION

Objective:

Students will explain why drug use increases the risk of violence.

Life Skill:

I will avoid alcohol and other drugs. (PF14)

Materials:

Drug Permeation teaching master (page 272), nontransparent cup, red food coloring, pitcher of water, paper towels, old magazines, tape, strips of white paper, pen

Motivation:

1 Introduce the term drug. A **drug** is a substance that changes the way the body and/or mind work. Explain that alcohol is a drug. Alcohol use is linked to many accidental injuries and deaths. When people use alcohol or other drugs, their judgment is impaired. They cannot think clearly and may not be able to make responsible decisions. Aggressive feelings and behavior that normally would be under a person's control cannot be managed when a person is under the influence of alcohol or other drugs.

2 Review the definition of violence. **Violence** is the threatened or actual use of force to injure, damage, or destroy yourself, others, or property. Emphasize that drugs intensify feelings that may overflow and result in violent actions. These violent actions may affect not only the drug user but also other persons with whom the drug user is connected. If possible, discuss any event(s) that has happened in your community that would be examples of a drug user's behavior affect-

ing others such as his/her family, friends, and so on.

3 Put water in the nontransparent cup until it is about one-half full. Add sufficient red food coloring to make the water very red. Place a copy of the *Drug Permeation* teaching master on some paper towels or other absorbent material. Place the nontransparent cup in the center of the master. Explain that this cup represents a person, and that this person is closely connected to several other persons. These persons are represented by the faces on the master. Ask the students to pretend that they are the person represented by the cup. Have them tell who the other faces might represent, for example, a mother, brother, friends.

4 Now explain that the person represented by the cup is going to begin using alcohol or another harmful drug. As you begin to pour water very slowly from the pitcher of water into the cup, say such things as "This person drinks alcohol;" "This person snorts cocaine;" "This person smokes marijuana;" "This person has had an injection of an anabolic steroid," and so on. Eventually, the water in the cup will overflow and the red water will spill onto the master and stain the faces drawn on the master.

5 It is possible that some of the faces on the master do not become stained by the red water. Explain that some persons who have close connections to a drug user may not be harmed themselves, but they may be affected in other ways. For example, one of these persons might be the mother of a child who was harmed. Ask students for other possible examples.

6 Explain that drug use increases the likelihood of violence for at least two reasons. First, the use of drugs intensifies feelings. Drug users may become more angry than they would ordinarily be and would be unable to control this more intense anger. Second, the use of drugs dulls the part of the brain responsible for reasoning and judgment. These people could not think as clearly as they ordinarily would.

7 Point out the benefits of choosing to avoid alcohol and other drugs. When people choose a drug-free lifestyle, they are choosing to arm themselves with an important protective factor. These persons will be more likely to be in control of their behavior, to be able to make responsible decisions, to relate well with others, and to express their emotions in healthful ways.

Evaluation:

Have students find and cut out ads for alcoholic beverages in old magazines. Remind students that alcohol is a drug. Using the white strips of paper, students are to write warning labels explaining the relationship between drug use and violence. They are to tape the warning labels to the ads and make a bulletin board display from the ads and labels.

Drug Permeation

Grade 5
• Objective 8
• Protective Factors 3, 18, 19

SETTING THE RECORD STRAIGHT

Objective:

Students will identify and describe types of abuse: emotional, sexual, physical, and neglect.

Life Skills:

I will strive for healthful family relationships. (PF3)
I will develop resiliency to "bounce back" if I was reared in a dysfunctional family. (PF3)
I will practice self-protection strategies. (PF18)
I will participate in recovery if a victim. (PF19)

Materials:

Construction paper, markers

Motivation:

1 Introduce the topic of abuse. **Abuse** is the harmful treatment of a person. Explain that children who have been abused often get poor grades in school and have difficulty in forming friendships. They may behave in violent ways. Children who have been abused also may become involved with alcohol and other drug use.

2 Explain that emotional abuse might involve withholding love or constantly ignoring a child. Abuse of this kind may result in the child having negative self-esteem. A child who witnesses his/her parents abusing each other also is emotionally abused.

3 Sexual abuse includes fondling of a child's genitals, intercourse, rape, and other forms of sexual exploitation. Explain to students that sexual abuse is against the law.

4 Physical abuse includes inflicting injury by punching, beating, kicking, biting, burning, or otherwise physically harming a child. The injury may be the result of discipline or physical punishment that is inappropriate for the child's age. In some cases, the abuser did not intend to hurt the child. Signs of physical abuse include bruises, burns, cuts, missing teeth, broken bones, and head and internal injuries.

5 Neglect is failure to provide for a child's basic needs. Neglect can be physical, educational, or emotional. Physical neglect includes abandonment and refusal to seek health care for the child. Educational neglect includes failure to register a child for school, giving permission to let the child stay out of school unnecessarily, and inattention to the need for receiving special education.

6 Introduce the term dysfunctional family. A **dysfunctional family** is a family in which feelings are not expressed openly and honestly, coping skills are lacking, and members do not trust each other. Explain that young people who have been reared in a dysfunctional family can be resilient. **Resiliency** is the ability to prevent or to recover, bounce back, and learn from misfortune, change, or pressure. These young people can decide to make their environment as nurturing as possible. For example, they can stay in school to get an education. They can find adults who will serve as role models and mentor them. A **mentor** is a person who guides and helps young people.

7 Emphasize the importance of practicing self-protection strategies that protect and decrease the risk of becoming a victim. For example, an abused child must find a way to

Copyright © by Meeks Heit Publishing Company.

273

stay away from the abuser, if that is possible. The child must let a trusted adult know what is happening so that the child can be helped. Explain that victims of abuse and other forms of violence need help and that help is available. Victims of violence often need help to recover from physical injuries and from emotional pain. They also need help in stopping cycles of violence in their families.

8 Divide the class into four groups for SETTING THE RECORD STRAIGHT: emotional abuse group, sexual abuse group, physical abuse group, and neglect group. Explain that each group is going to make a CD recording. Give each group construction paper and a marker. They are to cut out a circle in the shape of a CD, give their group a name and write a title and an eight line verse that contains at least the mention of two self-protection strategies that an abused child could practice.

9 One of the members of each group should introduce the group giving the group name and the name of its hit tune. Then the group is to sing their hit song.

Evaluation:

Use a true-false quiz to evaluate student knowledge of emotional abuse, sexual abuse, physical abuse, and neglect. Following are some suggested questions:

1 A child who is not given a coat to wear in cold weather may be a neglected child. T

2 Sexual abuse includes being allowed to stay out of school. F

3 A child who is never hugged at home may be emotionally abused. T

4 Physical abuse includes slapping and hitting. T

5 A child who is constantly criticized at home is likely to have a positive self-esteem. F

6 Abused children are likely to get good grades in school. F

7 Every child should have an adult who is responsible for him/her. T

8 Sexual abuse is against the law. T

9 A baby sitter who fondles a child's genitals is sexually abusing the child. T

10 A child who is not given enough food to eat is physically abused. F

BULLET-TEN

Objective:

Students will describe procedures to follow for safety around weapons.

Life Skill:

I will practice responsible behavior around weapons. (PF15)

Materials:

Safety Around Weapons transparency (page 612), transparency projector, construction paper, markers, scissors, glue

Motivation:

1 Students should understand that guns are only one kind of weapon. A **weapon** is an instrument or device used for fighting. Explain that guns and knives are the most commonly used weapons. However, any object that is used to injure or destroy a person is a weapon. Explain that some instruments, such as knives, were originally designed for everyday types of activities. For example, a knife is a standard tool in kitchens for the preparation of food. However, when a knife is used in a fight, it becomes a weapon.

2 Explain that violent crimes involve many different kinds of weapons and that innocent bystanders often are the victims of crimes. Remind students that many acts of violence are not planned. They are random, or accidental, acts. This is why it is dangerous to be near a person who has a weapon or near any activity in which a weapon is involved.

3 Explain that many families own guns and that guns in a home should not be loaded

and should be stored in a securely locked place. Parents in these families assume the responsibility of teaching their children safety rules about guns. Stress that no matter where students see guns, they should always apply safety procedures.

4 Remind students of your school's rules about guns. Explain that these rules are designed to protect everyone in the school. Every student plays a vital role in keeping the school a safe place to be. Introduce the topic of practicing responsible behavior around weapons. Students should never underestimate the potential danger of seeing a weapon such as a gun being carried by another person or lying on the ground. Stress to students that each person has a responsibility to protect himself/herself from possible injury from a weapon.

5 Explain that an acronym is a word formed from the first letters of successive sentences. Usually the word formed is a word that can be remembered easily. The acronym in this case is SAFE. Explain that each of the sentences that form the acronym represents a responsible behavior to practice around weapons. Practicing responsible behavior is a way of protecting yourself. Review each sentence with the class.
- S — STOP.
- A — AVOID GOING NEAR THE SITUATION.
- F — FIND AN ADULT.
- E — EXPLAIN WHAT YOU SAW.

6 As you discuss the acronym, remind students that it is never safe to touch a weapon, such as a gun, that is found lying on the sidewalk or in the gutter or a gun that is seen being carried by another student. Emphasize the importance of protecting oneself.

7 Use the *Safety Around Weapons* transparency to review responsible procedures to follow to be safe around weapons.

8 Give each student a sheet of construction paper. Students are to draw and cut out a bullet, large enough upon which to print. (You may need to draw a bullet on the chalkboard as a pattern.) Each student is to write a responsible behavior tip for weapon safety on his/her bullet and decorate the bullet in any way (s)he chooses.

9 Select a place in the classroom to display the bullets. Have the class select ten bullets using the best safety tip, creativity, and attractiveness as criteria. Place these ten bullets on a BULLET-TEN board in the classroom.

Evaluation:

Have each student create a booklet that identifies ten responsible behavior tips for weapon safety. On the back page of the pamphlet, students are to design a pledge statement which states a promise that they will practice in regard to safety around weapons. The pledge should contain spaces for three additional names. Then each student is to share his/her pamphlet with three persons who are to signify that they agree to practice the ten responsible behavior tips by signing their names to the pledge.

SAFE AND DRUG-FREE ZONES

Objective:

Students will identify the advantages of cooperating with law enforcement officers and other people with authority.

Life Skills:

I will respect authority and abide by laws. (PF17)
I will change behavior if a juvenile delinquent. (PF20)

Materials:

Roll of paper, construction paper, tape, markers, scissors

Motivation:

1 To prepare for this strategy, unroll paper and tape it to a wall of the classroom in preparation for making a mural. Explain to the class that for the first few minutes of the class, they will use markers to make a representative drawing of their community. Several students can be drawing at the same time. Drawings may include their school, parks, playing fields, apartment buildings, and so on. Allow about 15 minutes to do the mural.

2 Discuss the community in which the students live. Remind students that in any community there are laws that the people living in that community must respect for the community to be safe. Mention different kinds of laws, such as driving laws, pedestrian laws, and drug laws, that protect the people in a community. In addition, the people in a community understand that there are persons with authority to govern and apply the laws. May-

ors, district attorneys, judges, and police officers are examples of persons with authority.

3 Explain that in school there are rules that are designed to protect everyone in the school and keep them safe. Remind students of your classroom rules. Explain that you have the responsibility and authority to apply the rules of your classroom. Explain that the school principal has the responsibility of making sure that everyone respects school rules.

4 Introduce the term authority. **Authority** is the power and right to govern and apply laws. People who hold positions of authority protect everyone who lives in the community, state, or nation. Explain what it means to respect authority. It means to have a high regard for the people who are in positions of authority. Students who show respect for school rules and for the principal, for example, understand that they also are showing respect for everyone else in the school. They are treating others the way they would like to be treated. Explain that young persons who develop respect for others have a good chance of being successful members of society and of staying out of trouble.

5 Introduce the term juvenile offender. A **juvenile offender** is a person under the age of 18 who breaks a criminal law. Some juvenile offenders realize the mistake they made and they never commit a crime again. They learned a lesson. Other juvenile offenders need help in becoming law-abiding citizens. There are many programs designed to help juveniles. They may be put on probation. **Probation** is a sentence in which an offender remains in the community under the supervision of a probation officer for a specific period of time. Under probation, a juvenile offender has certain restrictions, such as obeying their parents, attending school, and not associating with other offenders.

6 Explain that if juvenile offenders do not respond favorably to a program like probation, they may be assigned to a detention center. They are not allowed to go back to the community until they have served a sentence. Explain that young persons who change their behavior if they have been juvenile offenders recognize the dangers of being involved in criminal activity. They recognize that they could lose their freedom and cause other persons to suffer. The important thing is that help is available for juvenile offenders who want to change their behavior.

7 Introduce the topic of safe and drug-free zones. Safe and drug-free zones are areas of a community in which a person can feel safe. These zones are protected by laws and by law enforcement authorities. Explain that law enforcement authorities cannot protect citizens or control criminal activity without the cooperation of citizens in the community.

8 Ask students if they know of areas in their communities that are already safe and drug-free. Discuss what those areas are. Then ask for volunteers to go to the mural, one at a time, and identify a place in the community that they would like to be safe and drug-free. Ask each volunteer the reason(s) that (s)he would like that particular area to be safe and drug-free. Students might pick a playground where they play every day after school. They may choose the street where they live. They may choose the area they walk through to get to the public library.

Evaluation:

Give each student a sheet of construction paper. Each student is to design a Safe and Drug-Free Zone symbol. Students are to share their symbols with the class. Ask your principal for permission to post these symbols around the school building.

CRIME BAROMETER

Objective:

Students will identify types of crime and violence.

Life Skills:

I will recognize that violent behavior is wrong. (PF1)
I will avoid discrimination. (PF11)

Materials:

Types Of Violence transparency (page 589), *Ways To Avoid Discriminatory Behavior* transparency (page 608), transparency projector, ten sheets of paper, index cards

Motivation:

1 Introduce the terms crime and violence. A crime is an action that involves breaking the law. **Violence** is the threatened or actual use of force to injure, damage, or destroy yourself, others, or property. Explain that a person can be a perpetrator or a victim of violence. A **perpetrator** is a person who commits a violent act. A **victim** is a person who is harmed by violence.

2 Introduce the terms passive behavior, aggressive behavior, and assertive behavior and discuss how they relate to the risk of becoming a perpetrator or a victim of violence. **Passive behavior** is the holding back of ideas, opinions, and feelings. People who demonstrate passive behavior usually have difficulty expressing their concerns. They usually choose to say or do nothing rather than to express an opinion. These people do not know how to express angry feelings and anger can build until finally there is a violent reaction.

They become perpetrators. On the other hand, passive people often are victims of violence because they are perceived as people who will not tell someone else when they are harmed.

3 Aggressive behavior is the use of words and/or actions that show disrespect toward others. Aggressive behavior includes name calling, making loud and sarcastic remarks, interrupting others, and monopolizing conversations and situations. Aggressive people want to have their way and when they do not have it they often become perpetrators. Aggressive persons also are more likely to provoke others so they often become victims of violence.

4 Assertive behavior is the honest expression of thoughts and feelings without experiencing anxiety or threatening others. People who demonstrate assertive behavior are respectful of others and so are less likely to become either perpetrators or victims because they are less likely to provoke others.

5 Explain that it is important to understand that violent behavior harms not only oneself but others. This is the reason that students must be encouraged to take a firm stand that violence is wrong. Because knowledge of various types of violence helps make students aware of violent actions that need to be stopped, use the *Types Of Violence* transparency to discuss these various types. Use the information on the transparency as a basis of the discussion.

6 Remind students that even the threatened use of force or power is violent behavior. One kind of behavior that provokes violence is discriminatory behavior. **Dis-**

criminatory behavior is making distinctions in treatment or showing behavior in favor of or prejudiced against an individual or group of people. Persons who are discriminated against may become angry that they are treated unfairly and with disrespect. Discriminating words and actions often result in violent behavior. Using the *Ways To Avoid Discrimination* transparency, discuss how discriminating against others is a risk factor. Stress that it is important to show respect for all persons so that others can be at their best and contribute to the society in which they live.

7 For this strategy, write one of the following numbers on the ten sheets of paper: 10, 20, 30, 40, 50, 60, 70, 80, 90, 100. Line these sheets up on the floor in numerical order, either from 10 to 100 or from 100 to 10. Leave at least 12 inches between each sheet of paper.

8 On index cards write examples of violent actions such as those noted on the *Types Of Violence* transparency. Students may identify additional violent behavior to be written on index cards.

9 Distribute the index cards. One at a time, have a student identify the violent behavior that is written on his/her card. At this point, determine that *everyone* in the class understands what that violent behav-

ior involves. Everyone should understand before proceeding. The student with the card is then to decide which of the ten numbers on the sheets of paper that you placed on the floor represents his/her perceived seriousness of the violent behavior. The student will then line up behind the sheet with that number. For example, if a student thinks that fighting is one of the more serious crimes facing his/her peers, (s)he may line up behind the sheet on which 90 is written.

10 After lining up, the student will explain on what basis (s)he determined the seriousness of the violent behavior written on his/her card. Other students in the class may then ask questions, which can lead to a discussion of what students believe are the serious violent actions they face.

11 Continue with this procedure until all students who have the index cards have discussed the violent behavior identified on their cards.

Evaluation:

Have students search newspapers for reports of crimes or violent actions. Students should cut out the articles and in a class discussion have them compare the violent actions described in the newspaper with the types of violence that were discussed in class.

GUIDELINES FOR VIOLENCE PREVENTION

Objective:

Students will identify protective factors and risk factors for violence.

Life Skills:

I will develop positive self-esteem. (PF2)
I will strive for healthful family relationships. (PF3)
I will develop resiliency to "bounce back" if I was reared in a dysfunctional family. (PF4)
I will develop social skills. (PF5)

Materials:

Protective Factors That Prevent Violence transparency (page 588), *Risk Factors That Promote Violence* transparency (page 587), *Ways To Develop Positive Self-Esteem* transparency (page 592), transparency projector, poster board, rope, string, sheets of two colors of paper, blindfold

Motivation:

1 To prepare for this strategy, make a large target from the poster board. At the center of the target, print the words A PRODUCTIVE AND POSITIVE EXPERIENCE. Tape the target to the chalkboard or wall in the classroom in an area where there is room around the target.

2 Also in preparation, cut 20 strips from each color of paper. Referring to the *Protective Factors That Prevent Violence* transparency, write one protective factor on each of the 20 strips of the first color. Referring to the *Risk Factors That Promote Violence* transparency, write one risk factor on each of the 20 strips of the second color.

3 Review the definitions of risk factors and protective factors. **Risk factors** are ways that a person might behave and characteristics of the environment in which a person lives that increase the likelihood of having something negative happen to a person's health, safety, and/or well-being. **Protective factors** are ways that a person might behave and characteristics of the environment in which (s)he lives that promote health, safety, and/or well-being. Using the *Protective Factors That Prevent Violence* transparency, explain that Factors 2 and 5 are examples of factors that refer to behaviors while Factors 3 and 4 are examples of factors that refer to a person's environment.

4 Introduce the term self-esteem. **Self-esteem** is what a person thinks or believes about himself/herself. People who have good feelings about themselves have positive self-esteem and are motivated to protect themselves. They respect other people and are less likely to act in ways that harm others. Having positive self-esteem gives a person confidence. Use the *Ways To Develop Positive Self-Esteem* transparency to encourage students to do everything they can to develop and/or maintain a positive self-esteem.

5 Introduce the term social skills. **Social skills** are skills that can be used to relate well with others. Social skills are similar to other kinds of skills. They are learned. Many young people learn social skills in their families. Point out the following social skills that help relationships not only with peers but also with adults: using manners; asking for help when you are in a difficult situation; being able to express affection for someone; being able to express gratitude; responding to another person's need.

6 Use the *Risk Factors That Promote Violence* transparency to discuss two factors that refer to a person's environment. Introduce the terms discussed in Risk Factors 3 and 4. A **dysfunctional family** is a family in which feelings are not expressed openly and honestly, coping skills are lacking, and family members do not trust each other. An **adverse environment** is a set of conditions and surroundings in which a person lives that interferes with growth, development, and success. Point out that a dysfunctional family is an adverse environment. Explain that people who live in adverse environments can be resilient. **Resiliency** is the ability to prevent or to recover, "bounce back," and learn from misfortune, change, or pressure. These people can stay in school and get an education. They can avoid alcohol and other drugs. They can ask trusted adults at school for help. They can choose friends who will encourage them to do their best. By choosing behaviors like this, people will help change their environment from an adverse one to a nurturing one.

7 Ask for a volunteer. Distribute the 20 strips of paper on which are written risk factors. Explain that this student will strive to have a productive and positive experience by reaching the target. The volunteer will have no guidelines for attaining this goal. Blindfold the student and turn him/her around once or twice before facing him/her in the direction of the target. In the meantime, have the 20 students who have the strips of paper gather in the area between the volunteer and the target. Now have the volunteer try to reach the target. The volunteer will bump into many of the 20 students as (s)he tries to reach the target. When the volunteer bumps into a student, the student will say what risk factor (s)he represents. For example, the student might say, "You fail to recognize vio-

lence." Give the volunteer a time limit in his/her efforts to reach the target. Then remove the blindfold from the volunteer. If all 20 risk factors have not been identified at this point, have the remaining students tell about the risk factors they represent.

8 Distribute the 20 strips of paper on which are written protective factors. Ask for four volunteers. These volunteers will hold the ends of two 10-foot lengths of string extending from the target into the classroom area. The strings should be about three feet apart. Ask for another volunteer. Blindfold and turn him/her around once or twice before facing him/her toward the target and within the two lengths of string. Place the volunteer's hands on the strings. In the meantime, have the 20 students who have the strips of paper gather in the area along the outer sides of the two lengths of string. They are to hold on to the string. As the volunteer moves toward the goal and touches a student, the student will say what protective factor (s)he represents. For example, the student might say, "You manage anger effectively." By the time the volunteer reaches the target, (s)he will have identified all 20 protective factors.

9 Discuss the experiences of the two volunteers. Explain that the first volunteer had no guidelines to follow in order to experience a productive and positive experience. Risk factors increase the likelihood that (s)he will behave in violent ways and/or will be harmed by the violent actions of others. Stress the difference between the first volunteer and the second volunteer. The second volunteer was guided along a path toward a productive and positive experience because (s)he practiced protective factors to reduce the likelihood that (s)he will be a participant in or victim of violent actions.

282

Evaluation:

One at a time, have students identify a risk factor and for each risk factor that is identified, have students share how practicing a protective factor might eliminate the risk factor.

TAKING AD-VANTAGE

Objective:

Students will examine the importance of resiliency in dealing with life crises.

Life Skills:

I will respond to my environment in an empowering way. (PF4)

I will develop resiliency to "bounce back" if I live in an adverse environment. (PF4)

I will practice suicide prevention strategies. (PF9)

Materials:

Old magazines, scissors

Motivation:

1 Introduce the terms nurturing environment and adverse environment. A **nurturing environment** is a set of conditions and surroundings in which a person lives that promotes growth, development, and success. In this type of environment, a person is likely to remain safe from violence. An **adverse environment** is a set of conditions and surroundings in which a person lives that interferes with growth, development, and success. In this type of environment, a person is likely to be exposed to violence.

2 Explain that the environment in which people live can control the choices available to them. People who live in a nurturing environment have many advantages. They have adequate food, clothing, and shelter. They are encouraged to develop their talents, and to set goals. On the other hand, people who live in an adverse environment are at risk. They may not have adequate food, clothing, and shelter. They may become so discour-

aged that they drop out of school. They may have no hope for the future. They are more likely to be perpetrators or victims of violence.

3 Point out that young persons who grow up in an adverse environment may feel they have nothing to live for. They may consider suicide as a way of escape. It is important to remind students about suicide prevention strategies that can help prevent thoughts of suicide. Refer to Protective Factor 9.

4 Introduce the term resiliency. **Resiliency** is the ability to prevent or to recover, bounce back, and learn from misfortune, change, or pressure. Persons who are resilient choose positive ways to deal with life's misfortunes. Remind students that persons who are armed with protective factors (refer to Objective 2) are more likely to demonstrate resiliency. It is possible for young persons who live in adverse environments to become resilient. They may not be able to control their environment, but they can control how they respond to their environment. Explain that this is empowerment. **Empowerment** is the belief that a person controls his/her own destiny. They can make even small changes that will move their environment toward being a nurturing environment. Explain that everyone experiences misfortunes and life crises that are unavoidable. Remind students that all misfortunes and life crises require persons to make decisions about ways to handle them. It is important to choose positive ways to deal with them.

5 Discuss advertisements. Explain that ads in newspapers and magazines and on television are designed to influence people to buy products and services. An advertisement on television or radio is called a commercial. Many advertisements are designed to persuade people to improve the status of their health. Ads appear where they will be seen or heard by persons who are most likely to be concerned with the item or idea being advertised. For example, athletic shoes are advertised on TV during sporting events. Explain that advertisers use a variety of techniques in ads and commercials in order to make their messages appeal to you.

6 Explain to students that they are going to design ads that will help promote positive ways for students to deal with misfortunes and life crises. Their ads should encourage students to promote their health. Make up a sample ad. An example might be a picture from a magazine that shows a baseball player get-

ting ready to hit a pitched ball. Include a caption that shows a positive way to deal with a misfortune, such as "A person who faces life's curves doesn't have to strike out."

7 Display the ads created by the students and have them describe the messages and meanings of their ads.

Evaluation:

Have each student select an ad other than his/her own. Each student is to write a description of the ad and what the ad means to him/her personally. Others may share other meanings that they may find from the same ad.

WHAT THE WORLD NEEDS NOW

Objective:

Students will identify resistance skills that can be used when pressured to engage in violent behavior.

Life Skills:

I will make responsible decisions. (PF12)
I will practice resistance skills. (PF13)

Materials:

Paper, pencils

Motivation:

1 Introduce the terms peer and peer pressure. A **peer** is a person who is similar in age or status. **Peer pressure** is pressure that people of similar age or status exert on others to encourage them to make certain decisions or behave in certain ways. Explain that peer pressure is one of the most common reasons that young people decide to engage in actions that place them at risk. One reason that young people find it difficult to resist peer pressure is that they have a strong desire to "belong." Another reason is that they do not know how to say NO to a behavior that might be risky.

2 Explain that people who have responsible decision-making skills know <u>when</u> to say NO. These persons have learned to make decisions based on particular guidelines, such as their health, safety, and self-respect. In making a decision, they stop and think about the possible consequences. They are in control of their behavior. However, they may not know <u>how</u> to say NO.

3 Introduce the term resistance skills. **Resistance skills** are skills that are used when a person wants to say NO to an action and/or leave a situation. Resistance skills are also called refusal skills. Explain to students that they need to practice ways to resist pressures to engage in violent behavior.

4 Discuss the following ways to effectively resist pressure to engage in an activity that might become violent.
- <u>Be honest.</u> Express your thoughts and feelings without threatening the person who is pressuring you.
- <u>Say NO clearly and firmly.</u> Look directly at the person and make eye contact with the person who is pressuring you.
- <u>Match your words and your actions.</u> Leave the person who is pressuring you so that (s)he understands that your decision is final. Your actions should not leave the situation open for further discussion of the matter.
- <u>Think ahead.</u> Don't put yourself in situations in which you will experience the same pressure again.
- <u>Avoid being with persons who choose harmful actions.</u> Choose to be with persons who make responsible decisions about their behavior.

5 Divide the class into two groups. Group 1 will develop a list of statements that might be used to pressure students in Group 2 to engage in violent behaviors. You may choose to have the students in Group 1 work in subgroups so that everyone is involved in the activity. They may think of statements such as "Don't be chicken," "You won't get caught," "No one will know," "Don't you want to be like the rest of us?" Allow about ten minutes for the group to develop their statements.

6 Group 2 is to think about the kinds of statements that Group 1 will probably use to pressure them to engage in violent behaviors and they are to develop a list of counter statements that could be used to respond to those pressures. For example, a response to "You won't get caught" might be "If I don't do what you're asking me to do, I won't have to worry about getting caught." Allow about ten minutes for this group also.

7 While the two groups are working, select three students to be the singers. These three students should rehearse the first line of the song "What the World Needs Now Is Love, Sweet Love." The singers are to stand at the front of the classroom. After a student from Group 1 stands and makes a statement to Group 2 to pressure them to engage in violent behavior, the singers will sing the first line of the song. Then a student from Group 2 will respond with a counter statement applying the skills listed in step 4. For example, the Group 2 student would make eye contact, and speak clearly and firmly. Follow this procedure until you think enough pressure statements and responses have been made.

Evaluation:

Have each student identify and list additional pressure statements and counter responses (s)he can use to resist pressure to engage in violent behaviors.

DON'T BELIEVE WHAT YOU SEE

Objective:

Students will describe sources of hidden anger and healthful ways to express it.

Life Skills:

I will practice anger management skills. (PF6)
I will practice stress management skills. (PF7)
I will participate in physical activity. (PF8)

Materials:

Anger Management Skills transparency (page 600), *Stress Management Skills* transparency (page 602), transparency projector, two shoe boxes, decorated wrapping paper, pictures of people engaging in healthful and positive activities, pictures of negative events or activities

Motivation:

1 To prepare for this strategy, decorate the two shoe boxes so that they are attractive. In one of the shoe boxes, place the pictures of people engaged in healthful and positive activities, such as enjoying a sports event or walking or jogging. In the other shoe box, place the pictures of negative events or activities, such as a victim of violence, people fighting with each other, or people who look depressed.

2 Introduce the term anger. **Anger** is the feeling of being irritated, annoyed, and/or furious. Anger may be the result of experiences such as being disappointed, frustrated, or wronged. These kinds of experiences are called anger triggers. **Anger triggers** are thoughts or events that cause a person to become angry. Ask students to provide examples of anger triggers, such as being

criticized by a friend or being blamed for something you did not do. Anger needs to be recognized and dealt with in a manner that does not harm the angry person or others.

3 Discuss inappropriate ways to express anger, such as projection and displacement, that may lead to violent behavior. **Projection** is blaming others for actions or events for which they are not responsible. For example, a person who is angry about a poor grade may project his/her anger on the teacher who graded the test. **Displacement** is the releasing of anger on someone or something other than the cause of the anger. For example, a person who is angry about a family situation might release his/her angry feelings by destroying property or harming someone. Explain that the inability to express anger in healthful ways is a risk behavior.

4 Discuss hidden anger. **Hidden anger** is anger that is not dealt with in a healthful way and may result in inappropriate behavior and poor health. When angry feelings are not expressed in healthful ways, they become hidden. Hidden anger can multiply within a person and (s)he may experience harmful changes in his/her body. Explain that a person may not be aware that (s)he is hiding angry feelings. When anger is not expressed, a person may have headaches, be unable to sleep, or be depressed. Hidden anger is often the cause of violent behavior. Discuss the kinds of experiences that might cause a person to become angry, such as being insulted, being hit by another person, or having something stolen.

5 Show the two shoe boxes to the class without telling the students what is inside each box. Have them describe how each box looks. Explain that outward appearances can be deceiving and this is true of both shoe boxes and persons. The looks on the outside may not be indicative of how one feels on the inside. Show students some of the pictures from the shoe box that has positive pictures in it first. Then open the other box and show students some of the negative pictures. Explain that although both boxes look the same on the outside, what was on the inside was completely different. Draw the analogy with people. Explain that although some people may seem happy, below the surface they may be very angry and are hiding their angry feelings.

6 Show the *Anger Management Skills* transparency. Explain that feelings of anger can be coped with effectively without causing harm to self or to others. Discuss each item on the transparency.

- Keep an anger self-inventory. The Anger Self-Inventory (Figure 16) can help you evaluate your angry feelings and determine which anger management skills would be appropriate to use.
- Use self-statements for anger control. Self-statements are positive statements to use to stay in control when you are angry. Examples are "I'm not going to let him get to me," "Getting upset won't help," or "Time to take a deep breath."
- Participate in physical activities. Physical activity can help defuse anger and relieve tension. It provides an outlet for the extra energy that you feel when you are angry.
- Use physical expression to blow off steam. Punching a pillow or squeezing a tennis ball can channel your extra energy when you are angry.
- Use I-messages and active listening. I-messages are statements used to express feelings. When a person uses I-messages,

(s)he assumes responsibility for expressing his/her feelings. I-messages should include reference to the specific behavior that caused the anger, the effect of that behavior on the individual, and the feeling that resulted. An example of an I-message is "I waited for you to go to the game and we were late and I was angry." Active listening allows you to get more information about the situation that made you angry.

- Keep a sense of humor. Finding the humor in a situation and laughing at yourself can help defuse angry feelings.
- Express yourself through creative activities. Write a poem or draw a picture that would describe your situation. In addition to lessening the effects of anger, these types of activities give you a sense of accomplishment.
- Talk with parents and mentors. Adults can help you recognize what you are feeling, why you are feeling this way, and what are healthful ways to cope with those feelings.
- Write a letter to express your angry feelings. By writing a letter, you can express your angry feelings without confronting anyone. You may choose not to send the letter, however.
- Plan ahead to deal with your anger. Examine what kinds of anger triggers arouse your anger and practice what you might do when they occur again.

7 Introduce the term stress. **Stress** is the response of the body to the demands of daily living. Stressors are the source or cause of stress. A **stressor** is a demand that causes changes in the body. Have students think about the kinds of stressors that affect them. They may feel pressure to do well in school. They may have difficult family circumstances that concern them. They may have a serious illness in the family. Or they may be trying out for a team and they hope they make it. Life situations like these are stressors. If the demands on people are overwhelming, they may feel depressed, frustrated, or angry. Introduce the term stress management skills. **Stress management skills** are techniques that can be used to cope with and prevent the harmful effects produced by stress. Use the *Stress Management Skills* transparency to discuss ways to relieve stress.

8 Remind students of the benefits of physical activity and recreation as ways to help manage anger. People who maintain their physical fitness levels are more likely to feel better about themselves and their appearance and to be able to manage their feelings of anger. Explain that some young persons turn to vio-

lent behavior because they are bored. They do not know how to make constructive use of their time. On the other hand, young persons who are involved in a physical activity or recreation program on a regular basis learn self-discipline. They learn to set goals and make plans to reach those goals.

Evaluation:

Have students write a brief paper describing a situation that caused them to become angry. Then have them select one of the anger management skills and provide a specific example of how that particular skill could have helped them express their anger effectively.

CREATIVE SOLUTIONS

Objective:

Students will identify effective approaches to conflict resolution that exclude fighting.

Life Skills:

I will participate in physical activity. (PF8)
I will practice conflict resolution and peer mediation skills. (PF10)

Materials:

Conflict Resolution Skills transparency (page 606), transparency projector

Motivation:

1 Explain that life without conflict is impossible. A **conflict** is a disagreement between two or more persons or between two or more choices. Conflicts occur naturally in every area of life, including in a family. Conflicts also occur within an individual when that person has to make up his/her mind about which choice (s)he will make.

2 Explain that people respond to conflict in three distinct ways. They can try to avoid the conflict by denying that there is a conflict. In this way, someone else makes a decision on how the conflict will be resolved. The second way in which people respond to conflict is to be confrontational and try to settle the disagreement in a hostile, defiant, and aggressive way. This type of person wants to "win" at all costs. The third response is to use conflict resolution skills. **Conflict resolution skills** are skills a person can use to resolve a disagreement in a healthful, safe, legal, respectful, and nonviolent way. When conflicts are resolved using these skills, there is no "loser." Both sides are "winners."

3 Explain that people who do not learn to resolve conflicts in a responsible and healthful way may: experience problems with their physical health; not have meaningful relationships with others; and be more likely to become a victim or a perpetrator of violence. Explain that these experiences can result from a buildup of angry feelings and frustration from the unresolved conflict. This buildup of emotions can be overwhelming to people and they may begin to behave in harmful and even violent ways. At this point, remind students that if they do not participate in a physical activity program, they lack a very effective anger management skill. Explain that a person's body becomes more and more tense and has a surge of energy when (s)he experiences angry feelings. Participating in a physical activity helps defuse the anger by relieving the tension and providing an outlet for the extra energy.

4 Discuss the skills listed on the *Conflict Resolution Skills* transparency. Explain that these skills are positive and responsible ways to resolve a disagreement. Arguing over conflicting opinions is not an effective way to deal with a disagreement because the focus in on the opinions and not on the cause of the disagreement. Using conflict resolution skills allows the people involved in the disagreement to reach a solution that is acceptable to everyone involved.

5 Introduce the terms peer and peer mediation. A **peer** is a person who is similar in age or status. **Peer mediation** is a process used to resolve conflicts in which a person helps his/her peers resolve disagreements in healthful, safe, legal, respectful, and nonviolent ways. Successful peer mediation programs often reduce the need for adult involvement in school disciplinary matters.

If your school has a peer-mediation program already established, your students will already be familiar with it.

6 Have students share some of the common types of conflict they have experienced before providing them with the following scenario:

> It is the last quarter of a very close basketball game. On a fast break, Glenn takes a shot instead of passing the ball to a teammate who was open. Glenn misses the shot and the other team gets the rebound and goes on to win the game. Patrick is the teammate who was open and he is upset after the game. He calls Glenn a jerk and complains that Glenn should have passed the ball to him.

7 Using the *Conflict Resolution Skills* transparency, have students describe how conflict resolution skills could have been used by Glenn and Patrick.

Evaluation:

Divide students into groups of about five. Each group is to identify a common scenario that might result in a conflict. Each group is then to describe what skills could be used to help deal effectively with the conflict. Each group is to present its discussion to the class. Students in the class can develop additional ways to deal with conflict.

Grade 6
- Objective 7
- Protective Factors 18, 19

BLOCKING OUT RAPE

Objective:

Students will discuss rape, acquaintance rape, rape prevention, and guidelines to follow if raped.

Life Skills:

I will follow self-protection strategies. (PF18)
I will participate in recovery efforts if a victim. (PF19)

Materials:

Seven sheets of paper, markers

Motivation:

1 To prepare for this strategy, make seven signs using sheets of paper and markers. Each sign will consist of a self-protection strategy that helps protect a person from risk of rape. The seven self-protection strategies for the signs are as follows: 1) I date in groups. 2) I've established some degree of trust with the person I date. 3) I and the person I date do not use alcohol or other drugs. 4) I am not alone with my date at home. 5) My date acts in ways that show respect for me. 6) My date does not pressure me to engage in harmful behaviors. 7) My date is about the same age as I am.

2 Introduce the term rape. **Rape** is the threatened or actual use of physical force to get someone to have sex without giving consent. Explain that although females are the primary victims of rape, males also may be the victims of rape.

3 Explain that rape is not always committed by a stranger. **Acquaintance rape** is rape

that is committed by someone known to the victim. Explain that acquaintance rape often happens on a date when sexual feelings get out of hand. This is the reason that it is important for a person to let a date know about his/her decisions about limits before getting into a situation in which it would be difficult to resist and to say NO. Explain that most cases of acquaintance rape are not planned but the consequences can be serious and sometimes are violent.

4 Introduce the term self-protection strategies. **Self-protection strategies** are strategies that can be practiced to protect oneself and decrease the risk of becoming a victim. Following are some general self-protection strategies to use to avoid being raped:
- Do not tell others if you are going to be home alone.
- Do not give strangers your name, address, or telephone number on the telephone.
- Do not leave a party, shopping mall, or other place with a stranger.
- Carry a device for making a loud noise, such as a whistle, and use it at the first sign of danger.

5 Explain that there are other self-protection strategies that apply specifically to avoiding acquaintance rape as follows:
- Set clear limits for sexual behavior.
- Communicate these limits to persons whom you date.
- Avoid sending mixed messages in which you say NO while continuing to encourage sexual advances.
- When you experience unwanted sexual advances from someone, firmly tell the person to stop.

- If the person does not stop, respond by making loud noises and resisting.
- Avoid drinking alcohol and using other drugs that interfere with your judgment and ability to respond.
- Avoid being in places where there is no one who will hear your call for help should unwanted sexual advances occur.

6 Explain that both rape and acquaintance rape should be reported to the police and that the victim should get immediate medical attention before showering or changing clothes.

7 Explain that victims of rape and other violence experience many emotions such as anger, fear, shock, and confusion. It is important that these victims get help in recovering from the experience. The goal of recovery is to help the victim survive the pain, heal, and move ahead with self-confidence. If help is needed, services that offer help are listed in telephone directories and newspapers. The school counselor can be an excellent source of help.

8 Have seven students form a circle with their elbows locked. One other student is to stand in the center of the circle. Give each of the seven students who are forming the circle one of the prepared signs to hold (see step 1). Explain to the class that the student within the circle is protected by those who form the circle around him/her. Have each of the seven students read his/her sign on which is written a self-protection strategy. Explain that the person in the circle has a lowered risk of being raped when surroundedby these protective factors for preventing rape.

9 You may have another student approach the circle with a sign such as "I would like to invite you to my home since no one is at home." Explain that the as long as protective factors are present, the chances of the person inside the circle becoming a victim are substantially reduced. However, if the circle of protection breaks down and a risk factor is allowed to enter one's life, chances increase that a rape might occur.

Evaluation:

Have students develop additional self-protection strategies that would help protect them from becoming victims of rape. Print these factors on sheets of paper and demonstrate how the circle of protection can become larger by having additional students join the original circle representing additional self-protective factors.

REMEMBERING THE FACTS

Objective:

Students will discuss sexual harassment and guidelines to follow with regard to sexual harassment.

Life Skill:

I will practice self-protection strategies. (PF18)

Materials:

Seeing Is Believing transparency (page 297), transparency projector

Motivation:

1 Introduce the term sexual harassment. **Sexual harassment** is unwanted sexual behavior that ranges from making sexual comments to forcing another person into unwanted sex acts. Sexual harassment should never be tolerated by either males or females. Any inappropriate activity, such as obscene jokes, comments about a person's body, or unwanted hugging or kissing that threatens or bothers a person, is sexual harassment.

2 Explain that flirting is different than sexual harassment. The key words in the difference between the two behaviors are unwanted and unwelcome. Flirting is a normal behavior in which interest in persons of the other sex is expressed in appropriate ways that do not demean others.

3 Introduce the term self-protection strategies. **Self-protection strategies** are techniques that can be practiced to protect oneself and decrease the risk of becoming a victim. In order to maintain your self-respect and to show respect for others, you need to be aware of persons who do not respect you or your friends. Suggest that students use the following checklist to follow if they think they are being sexually harassed.

1. Ask the person who is harassing you to stop.
2. Write down exactly what occurred and when it occurred.
3. Get witnesses.
4. Discuss the situation with your parents.
5. Tell the appropriate person at school.

4 Stress that if a charge of sexual harassment is made against anyone, very specific details must be remembered and included with the charge.

5 Use the *Seeing Is Believing* transparency as follows: Instruct the students that you are going to show them a transparency and that they are to observe the picture closely. You will show the transparency for ten seconds only, after which you will ask the following questions. Have students write their answers so that they can check them later. You may choose to add questions of your own.
- What did the man say to the woman?
- Who may have also overheard the comment made by the man?
- What do you believe was the reaction of the woman who overheard the comment?
- What was the date the comment was made?
- At what time was the comment made?

6 Ask students if they think they were good observers. Explain that the purpose of this strategy is to make students aware that there are many situations in which they must be observant. Encourage students to practice being observant in everyday experiences.

Evaluation:

Show the *Seeing Is Believing* transparency again. Have each student check his/her answers from step 4 and note what answers were missed or were incorrect.

Seeing Is Believing

BRIGHT IDEAS

Objective:

Students will discuss ways to prevent assault and homicide.

Life Skill:

I will practice self protection strategies. (PF18)

Materials:

Color Me Safe student master (page 300), a copy for each student, crayons

Motivation:

1 Explain that sometimes people become so upset that they attack another person. Introduce the term assault. An **assault** is a physical attack or threat of attack. Such an attack attempts to inflict harm and puts the victim of the attack in danger. It is not unusual for an assault to become so violent that it ends in a case of homicide. **Homicide** is the accidental or purposeful killing of another person.

2 Discuss situations that might cause people to become so upset that they would attack another person. Examples might be a situation in which a person is constantly put down and criticized; frustration over a failure; seeing a loved one attacked by another person; jealousy; and despair.

3 Introduce the term stalking. **Stalking** is harassing someone with the intent to threaten or harm or form a relationship with that person. A stalking action sometimes begins when a relationship ends and the stalker wants to scare the victim into continuing the relationship. Stalking also may occur when a person wants to form a relationship with someone (s)he does not know. Stalking is a very serious form of harassment and often involves assaults.

4 Discuss ways that students might protect themselves from being possible victims of assault and homicide. Introduce the term self-protection strategies. **Self-protection strategies** are strategies that can be practiced to protect oneself and decrease the risk of becoming a victim. For example, if a student has a gut level feeling that a certain person is dangerous, (s)he should trust his/her instincts. The student should be on guard when that person is near him/her. The person should be avoided if possible.

5 Distribute a copy of the *Color Me Safe* student master to each student. Point out that the master shows a palette with spaces for five different colors. Students will use crayons to fill in the spaces. Each color they use will represent a symbol that correlates with a self protection strategy that will help prevent them from becoming victims of assault and homicide. For example, a circle colored red may indicate that red means stop, so the corresponding strategy may be "When I am upset with another person and I feel like fighting, I will STOP, think for a minute, and walk away." A circle colored yellow may indicate caution, so the corresponding strategy may be "I will use CAUTION if I observe someone following me when I am walking."

6 Instruct students to color the spaces and then to write their own self-protection strategies in the form of statements in the appropriate corresponding lines. The statements are to describe a self-protection strategy students can use to help prevent assault and homicide.

7 Have students share their strategies with the class. Discuss the importance of not engaging in acts of violence or of becoming victims of acts of violence.

Evaluation:

Have students choose a selection of strategies from the strategies developed by the class, and develop a handbook of self-protection strategies that can be duplicated and distributed to other students.

Color Me Safe

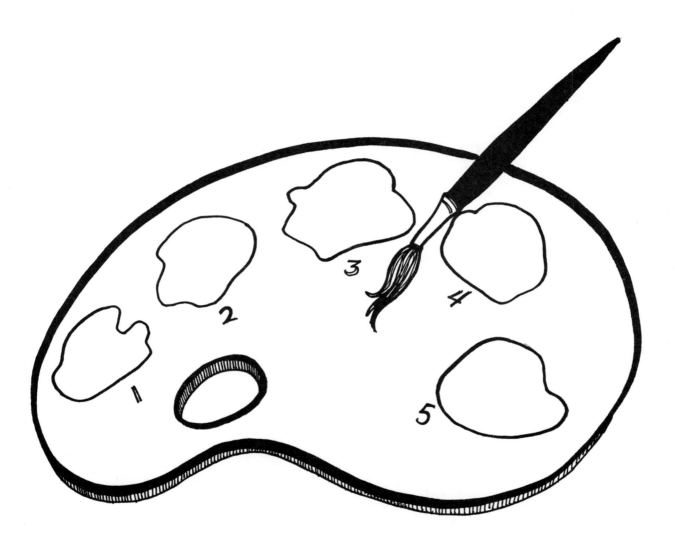

SUICIDE SIGNS

Objective:

Students will discuss ways to prevent suicide.

Life Skill:

I will practice suicide prevention strategies. (PF9)

Materials:

Slips of paper

Motivation:

1 To prepare for this strategy, prepare ten strips of paper. On each of these strips, write one of the following experiences that are common to adolescents.

- Breakup with boyfriend or girlfriend
- Conflict with brother or sister
- Change in parents' financial status
- Parental divorce
- Losing a close friend
- Trouble with a teacher
- Changing to a new school
- Personal injury or other physical injury
- Failing grades
- Ongoing arguments with parents

2 Explain that when persons feel as though they had nothing to live for, they may become extremely depressed. These persons may not feel that they are accomplishing anything. They may not feel connected to other persons. Explain that at some point, they may consider suicide as an option. Introduce the term suicide. **Suicide** is the intentional taking of one's own life. Explain that suicide is the third-ranked cause of death among persons ages 15 to 24.

3 Explain that there are many life experiences that can cause a young person to think of suicide. These include experiences such as difficulty at school, divorce or separation of parents, death of a family member, or a physical handicap. Experiences like these are called stressors. A **stressor** is any demand that causes changes in the body. The demands may be physical, such as preparing for a race. The demands may be mental, such as studying for a test. Going on an important date may be a stressor.

4 Introduce the term suicide prevention strategies. **Suicide prevention strategies** are techniques that can be used to help prevent a person from thinking about, attempting, or completing suicide. Remind students that suicide is a final choice; suicide cannot be undone. Discuss the following strategies that a person might use to prevent thinking about suicide:

- Know suicide hotline numbers. One 24-hour hotline number that is available to any youth in crisis is the National Youth Suicide Hotline. The number is 1-800-621-4000.
- Know what to do when you feel down. It is important to figure out the cause of your depression and do something about it. Make a list of things you can do to make yourself feel better.
- Build a network of support. A network may include friends, family members, teachers, or school counselors who will listen to you and help you through tough times.
- Get involved in rewarding activities. Playing a sport, learning a craft, or helping others through community services help a person to feel productive and motivated.
- Know what to do if someone shows warning signs. Some suggestions are: listen; let

the person know you care; ask a responsible adult for help; do not ignore any signs; do not leave the person alone.

5 Divide the class into groups. (The groups need to be large enough for a discussion to take place.) Give each group one of the slips of paper on which is written a common adolescent experience (Step 1). Each group is to discuss the particular experience and decide on healthful ways for a student to handle such a situation. After the groups have had about fifteen minutes for their discussions, they are to share their solutions with the class. After each group's presentation, allow other students in the class to suggest solutions other than suicide for that particular experience.

6 Explain that there are local resources that provide help and information about suicide prevention. Encourage any student who is facing a difficult life situation to talk about it with a parent or trusted adult. Remind students that the school counselor is trained to help at such times.

Evaluation:

Have students pretend that they have been given the job of the editor who writes an advice column for the local newspaper. Have each student write a fictitious letter to the column editor stating a problem. The editor is then to answer the letter, focusing on positive steps to prevent a possible suicide. Students can share their letters with the class.

A SAFE COMBINATION

Objective:

Students will outline procedures to follow to be safe around weapons.

Life Skill:

I will practice responsible behavior around weapons. (PF15)

Materials:

Shoe box, marker, scissors

Motivation:

1 To prepare for the strategy, using a marker, make the shoe box look like a safe. You can do this by drawing a circular combination lock at one end and a handle that can be used to open the safe. Use the scissors to cut a slit on the top of the box.

2 Introduce the term weapon. A **weapon** is an instrument or device used in fighting. Guns and knives are the most commonly used weapons. Because many young persons illegally carry a weapon, the number of cases of violence has increased. Carrying a weapon, particularly a gun, increases the risk that a person will injure or kill another person or will be injured or killed himself/herself. Explain that a person might carry a gun and have no plans to use it. (S)he might just intend to scare or threaten another person. However, in an emotional moment, this person might use the gun impulsively and the other person might be injured or killed.

3 Explain that many injuries and deaths are caused by the unintentional use of weapons, and that injuries and deaths caused by intentional or unintentional use of weapons can occur in schools, in homes, and in neighborhoods. Many of the victims of such cases are innocent persons who just happened to be near the person with the weapon. Therefore, it is essential for students to be responsible and to be aware of ways to protect themselves as well as others.

4 Explain that many schools have taken security measures to prevent students from bringing guns or other weapons to school. These measures have been taken to protect everyone in the school. If your school has a policy about weapons, review the policy with students. Remind students that they play a vital role in keeping the school safe. Discuss what they should do if they see a student carrying a weapon or if they see a weapon somewhere in the school building or anywhere else. They should get away from the student. They should not touch the weapon. They should tell a teacher or the counselor what they saw. These steps would be responsible actions to take to protect oneself.

5 Instruct students to consider guidelines they can practice to be responsible and to protect themselves. Each student is to write a safety tip (s)he can practice if (s)he sees a weapon. After they each write a tip on a sheet of paper, they are to fold the paper and slip it through the slit on the top of the safe (the shoe box).

6 After students have written their safety tips and placed them in the safe, explain that what is contained within the safe is the right combination of information that can be applied to the very serious job of being safe around weapons. Open the safe and have each student select one of the safety tips. Make sure that a student does not get the tip that (s)he wrote. One at a time, have students read the safety tips to the class. Discuss each tip. Remind them that no matter where they see a weapon, they need to behave responsibly.

Evaluation:

Have the class develop a list —The Top Ten Ways To Behave Responsibly Around Weapons. Students are to select the ten most practical tips that were placed in the safe. Discuss each of the ten tips. Discuss the reasons that the students picked those particular tips as being the most practical.

MAKE UP YOUR MIND

Objective:

Students will discuss ways to resist pressure to belong to gangs and to participate in group acts of violence.

Life Skill:

I will resist gang membership. (PF16)

Materials:

None

Motivation:

1 Select two students to leave the classroom for a few minutes. Do not tell these students why you are asking them to leave. After they have left, explain to the class that they are going to take part in an experiment. You are going to orally give the class some simple math problems complete with answers. They are to raise their hands every time you state a problem, even though the answer is incorrect. For example, you may say that 13 plus 15 equals 28. This is a correct answer and the students will raise their hands. Then give another problem, such as 12 plus 23 equals 34. This is an incorrect answer and again the students will raise their hands. Make sure that everyone in the class is clear about the instructions.

2 Send for the two students who have been waiting outside the classroom. Explain that you are conducting an experiment that involves your orally giving some simple math problems complete with answers. Instruct the two students that they are to raise their hands only when the answer to the problem is a correct answer. They are not to raise their hands if the answer is incorrect.

3 Begin the experiment with everyone participating. Very likely, when you give a problem with an incorrect answer, the students who were out of the classroom will be confused when the other students raise their hands. Most likely, they also will raise their hands because of the peer pressure. Continue the experiment giving mostly problems with correct answers and occasional problems with incorrect answers. Note the behavior of the two students who were out of the classroom at the beginning of class.

4 Discuss peer pressure. **Peer pressure** is pressure that persons of similar age or status exert on others to encourage them to make certain decisions or behave in certain ways. If the students who had left the room raised their hands even for incorrect answers, point out that they were influenced by the behavior of the other students. They experienced peer pressure. Ask the two students what their reaction was when they realized that although an answer was incorrect, their classmates raised their hands. Ask the two students why they raised their hands.

5 If the two students who had left the room did not raise their hands when the answer was incorrect, ask them why they did not become influenced by the actions of others. Ask them what their reaction was when they realized that although an answer was incorrect, their classmates raised their hands.

6 Use this classroom demonstration to discuss other pressures, such as the pressures some students experience when being urged to join a youth gang. A **youth gang** is a group of young people who band together and participate in violent, unlawful, or criminal behavior. Discuss how joining a gang might seem attractive at first because of peer pressure from a member of a gang. A young person who is being pressured might believe that the gang will offer him/her protection or that the gang would provide a sense of brotherhood and belonging. Stress that anyone who is experiencing such pressure to do something as potentially dangerous as joining a gang needs to examine the situation very carefully.

7 Explain that belonging to a gang can be very risky for a number of reasons. A gang member is exposed to illicit drug use and drug dealing; to the use of firearms and other weapons; to fighting and being injured or killed; and to being arrested and imprisoned. Gang members often acquire a criminal record that makes it difficult to find employment later on. Even the families of gang members may fear for their own safety.

8 Discuss the importance of staying in school to get an education, setting goals, and making plans to reach those goals. Encourage students to protect themselves from becoming either a perpetrator or a victim of violence by resisting pressure to join a gang.

Evaluation:

Develop some scenarios in which peers are pressuring a student to participate in certain behaviors that might develop into acts of violence. For example, you might say "You are pressured by a friend to be a friend to certain persons only." "You are pressured to take part in an activity that might physically harm another student." Have students describe what they might do in each case to resist the pressure. Using a variety of scenarios, develop common threads to handle peer pressure in a positive manner.

THE ROLE OF DRUGS

Objective:

Students will examine the role that drug use and drug trafficking play in increasing the risk of violence.

Life Skill:

I will avoid alcohol and other drugs. (PF14)

Materials:

Different Types Of Drugs transparency (page 611), transparency projector, roll of sturdy paper towels, markers

Motivation:

1 Introduce the term drug. A **drug** is a substance other than food that changes the way the body and/or mind work. Use the *Different Types Of Drugs* transparency to discuss the types of drugs and their effects on the body. Explain that in addition to harming the body, using drugs affects the way people think and behave. Their ability to make responsible decisions and to be in control of their feelings and emotions is seriously impaired. As a result, they are likely to become aggressive and violent.

2 Explain that there are two risk factors that increase a person's vulnerability to becoming either a perpetrator or a victim of violence. A **perpetrator** is a person who commits a violent act. A **victim** is a person who is harmed by violence. The two risk factors are using drugs and being involved in drug trafficking. Drug trafficking includes the purchase, sale, or distribution of drugs.

3 Drug users are likely to be perpetrators of violence because drugs affect their moods and behavior and cause episodes of violent behavior that become out of control. Drug users' victims may be their children, their spouses, or their friends. Another reason that drug users often become perpetrators is the high cost of drugs. Drug users sometimes have to commit violent crimes in order to get money to buy more drugs.

4 Explain that there also is a heightened risk of being a perpetrator or a victim of violence if a person participates in drug trafficking. Because drug sales and purchases are illegal, it is not unusual for deadly weapons to be involved in drug transactions. In many instances, innocent bystanders are the victims of violent acts associated with drug trafficking.

5 Use the roll of paper towels. Do not tear off the individual towels at the perforation marks. Explain to students that they will use a marker to write a statement on each towel that indicates how they can be responsible and avoid using drugs, including alcohol. They also might include statements that indicate how they might avoid situations in which there is illegal drug use and/or trafficking. Students may work individually or in groups to develop this "Roll Of Responsibility," which will serve as a guide to help keep them safe by reminding them about the dangers of being involved in any way with illegal drugs.

6 When the "Roll Of Responsibility" is complete, have some students carefully open the roll across the front of the classroom. Then have other students read the statements that are written on the towels. Emphasize the importance of each student taking responsibility for avoiding drug use and for avoiding situations in which there is illegal drug use and/or trafficking.

Evaluation:

Have students select one of the statements concerning how to avoid illegal drug use and/or trafficking and make an individual pledge card concerning that particular statement. The pledge card will remind the student that (s)he has made a responsible decision.

I Am Cooperative

Objective:

Students will identify ways to reduce violence by following laws and cooperating with law enforcement authorities.

Life Skills:

I will respect authority and abide by laws. (PF17)
I will change behavior if a juvenile offender. (PF20)

Materials:

Paper, markers, tape

Motivation:

1 Introduce the term moral development. **Moral development** is the process of gradually learning to base one's behavior on personal beliefs of right and wrong. Explain that this process takes place over many years as a child is growing. The last stage in moral development is one in which a person has a conscience and operates according to a set of principles. Explain that a **conscience** is an inner sense of right and wrong that prompts responsible behavior and causes feelings of guilt following wrong behavior. Persons who have a conscience live by a moral code that does not include behavior such as lying, stealing, or hurting others. These persons have determined that such behavior is wrong. They understand that certain actions violate the rights of others and they do not want to violate the rights of others.

2 Introduce the terms law and authority. A law is a rule of conduct or action recognized to be binding and enforced by a controlling authority. Laws represent what the majority of the people in a community, state, or nation believe. Laws are designed to protect rights. **Authority** is the power and right to govern and apply laws. For example, a school principal has the authority and responsibility to apply and enforce school rules. (S)he also would be responsible for applying city or state laws that apply to schools. A mayor and the police force in a town or city have the authority and responsibility to apply and enforce laws of the town or city.

3 Explain that some young persons are juvenile offenders. A **juvenile offender** is a person under the age of 18 who breaks a criminal law. Juvenile offenders have not developed a moral code of behavior and do not take responsibility for their actions. They challenge authority and do not abide by laws. Explain that help is available to assist juvenile offenders in changing their behavior. They can be helped to understand that they are at risk if they continue their delinquent behavior. They can be helped to understand they can lose their freedom and not regain it for a long period of time. Many juvenile offenders take advantage of programs that are designed to rehabilitate them. **Rehabilitation** is the process of helping juvenile offenders change negative behavior to positive behavior.

4 Explain that being a responsible citizen involves respecting and following both rules in school and laws in a community. Explain that being responsible means being reliable and dependable. Introduce the term commitment. A **commitment** is a pledge to do something. When persons in a school or in a community make a commitment to support their school and their community, they pledge to cooperate and work together for the common good. This includes supporting rules and laws that promote the health and safety of everyone in the school and community.

5 Write the following statement on the chalkboard: "I will be a cooperative and responsible citizen of my school and community by...." Distribute paper and markers. Students are to complete this statement by identifying a way they will help reduce violence by following school rules and/or community laws. You can provide examples such as by avoiding being friends with persons who destroy property, or by respecting and cooperating with law enforcement authorities in my neighborhood.

6 Explain that the class will form a "Cooperation Train." Give each student a strip of tape. One student will be chosen as the conductor and will lead the way. Each student will join the train one at a time. As each student joins the train, (s)he reads what (s)he wrote on the paper and then attaches his/her sheet of paper to the back of the last

person on the train. This person will then place his/her hands on the hips of the person in front of him/her and will follow the train around the classroom. This action is repeated by each student in the class until all statements have been read and all students have joined the train.

7 Using the statements that were written on the sheets, have the students form a master list of ways to help reduce violence by following school rules and community laws. They can do this by reviewing all the statements, eliminating the ones that repeat, and choosing the most relevant ones for the master list.

Evaluation:

Play a game similar to GHOST. To play this game, each student must make a statement about ways to cooperate with rules and laws without repeating what another student has said. The winner of the game will be the person who has not repeated a statement and who can be the last to contribute a new statement.

REACHING OUT

Objective:

Students will identify support systems available for persons who have been victims of violence.

Life Skill:

I will participate in recovery if a victim. (PF19)

Materials:

None

Motivation:

1 Be sure that students understand the meaning of the word victim. A **victim** is a person who is harmed by violence. Explain that some victims are seriously injured physically; some are injured mentally; and some die. Victims may be permanently disabled. They may suffer great fear. They may develop negative self-esteem because of the experience. Explain that no matter how a victim is harmed, all victims of violence need help.

2 Ask for a volunteer to come to the front of the room. You will ask this student to lie flat on his/her back on the floor. (If necessary, arrange for him/her to lie on newspapers or other protection from the floor's surface.) You are to stand next to the student. Instruct the student to try to stand up without using his/her arms or hands. The student may not be able to do this. If the student does manage to stand, have the class become aware of the fact that it would have been much easier if the student could have used his/her arms or hands. Explain that arms and hands would have served as a support system in this example.

3 Explain that the student on the floor represents a person who was a victim of violence. Victims of violence need support systems in order to get back on their feet. In the case of the student on the floor, if (s)he could not get up, (s)he needed help. Perhaps you finally helped him/her to get up. Perhaps (s)he asked you for help.

4 Explain that it is important for victims of violence to recover from their experience and return to their normal state of health. Explain that it is not always possible to recover without reaching out for help. Many times, victims do not ask for help because they are not aware that help is available. They do not know they can reach out and get help with their recovery. Explain that the goal of recovery programs is to help the victim survive the pain, heal, and move forward with his/her life. One way of reaching out for help is to have a strong network of family and friends with whom the victim can talk and share his/her feelings.

5 Explain that in many communities there are health care facilities that offer help in the form of counseling and medical care if it is necessary. There may be support groups, where victims of the same types of violence can meet together to support and help each other. In some communities, there are telephone hot lines available from which victims can get information and advice.

6 In order for students to become aware of the support systems for victims of violence that exist in their community, have them look through the yellow pages of the local telephone directory. Explain the format of the yellow pages and have them locate agencies or groups that offer help such as a battered women's center. Emphasize that help is available in almost *every* community.

Evaluation:

Check students' ability to access community resources for help for victims of violence by bringing in a telephone directory with yellow pages from a nearby city or community. Spot check that the students know how to find information for localities other than their own.

CRIME CALLIGRAPHY

Objective:

Students will identify types of crime and violence.

Life Skills:

I will recognize that violent behavior is wrong. (PF1)
I will avoid discrimination. (PF11)

Materials:

Ways To Avoid Discriminatory Behavior transparency (page 608), *Types Of Violence* transparency (page 589), transparency projector, *Alphabet Calligraphy* master (page 315), a copy for each student, art paper, ink, calligraphy pens or medium-tip black markers

Motivation:

1 Introduce the terms crime and violence. Crime is any action that involves breaking the law. Explain that there are many types of crimes. If the crime involves an intent to harm another person(s), it is called a violent crime. **Violence** is the threatened or actual use of physical force to injure, damage, or destroy yourself, others, or property. Violence harms all of society by causing deaths, personal injuries, loss of personal property, psychological trauma to individuals and families, destruction of public property, and in addition, causing people to fear for their lives.

2 Introduce the terms perpetrator and victim. A **perpetrator** is a person who commits a violent act. A **victim** is a person who is harmed by violence. Explain that it isn't always "the other fellow" who becomes a victim. This is a reason that it is important for

individuals to be aware of what is going on around them. Discuss random violence. Random violence is a type of violence in which the assailant does not intentionally choose a victim. Drive-by shootings are an example of random violence. Random violence usually involves innocent victims.

3 Point out that violent actions have become an everyday occurrence in our society. Television programs and movies are saturated with violence. Newspaper headlines daily remind us that people are more and more expressing themselves in violent ways. In addition, many children witness violence in their homes and communities. As a result of all this exposure to violence, it is not unusual for a person to become desensitized. **Desensitization** is the process of lessening a person's response to certain things by overexposing that person to these same things. In other words, when people become desensitized, they accept violent actions that once scared or shocked them. This is one reason that it is important for students to recognize violent behavior and to evaluate their own attitudes and behavior. By doing so, they will recognize that violent behavior is wrong.

4 Explain that one type of behavior that is apt to lead to violence is discriminatory behavior. **Discriminatory behavior** is making distinctions in treatment or showing behavior in favor of or prejudiced against an individual or group of people. **Prejudice** is suspicion, intolerance, or irrational hatred directed at an individual or group of people. When people are discriminated against they becomes angry about being treated unfairly and with disrespect. It is not unusual for these people to eventually become so angry and frustrated that they react in a violent manner. In addition, the person who practices discriminatory behavior can lose control and become violent. This person also can provoke someone to the point that (s)he will become a victim. Use the *Ways To Avoid Discriminatory Behavior* transparency to discuss ways individuals can stop discrimination. You will need the following definitions to share with students:

• **Stereotype** is a prejudiced attitude that assigns a specific quality or characteristic to all people who belong to a particular group.

• **Synergy** is a positive outcome that occurs when different people cooperate and respect one another and, as a result, more energy is created for all.

• **Empathy** is the ability to share in another's emotions or feelings.

5 To help students become more aware of violent behaviors, use the *Types Of Violence* transparency. Discuss each item using the descriptions provided. Make sure that students understand the terms. Stress that it is important for students to take a firm stand that violence harms people and therefore is wrong.

Evaluation:

Distribute copies of the *Calligraphy Alphabet* master. Give each student a sheet of art paper. If you have calligraphy pens and ink available, allow students to share these materials. If not, have students use medium-tip black markers. Have them write a paragraph using calligraphy and summarizing what they have learned about crime and violence. The paragraphs should contain a minimum of five facts.

Alphabet Calligraphy

Aa Bb Cc Dd Ee Ff Gg
Hh Ii Jj Kk Ll Mm Nn
Oo Pp Qq Rr Ss Tt Uu
Vv Ww Xx Yy Zz

LIFE SAVERS

Objective:

Students will identify protective factors and risk factors for violence.

Life Skills:

I will develop positive self-esteem. (PF2)
I will strive for healthful family relationships. (PF3)
I will develop resiliency to "bounce back" if I was reared in a dysfunctional family. (PF3)
I will develop social skills. (PF5)

Materials:

Protective Factors That Prevent Violence transparency (page 588), *Risk Factors That Promote Violence* transparency (page 587), *Ways To Develop A Positive Self-Esteem* transparency (page 592), transparency projector, poster board, one sheet for each group, dice, index cards, 40 cards for each group, markers, one for each group, "Life Saver" candies in assorted colors

Motivation:

1 Introduce the term protective factor. A **protective factor** is a way that a person might behave and characteristics of the environment in which (s)he lives that promote health, safety, and/or well-being. Contrary to these protective factors are risk factors. A **risk factor** is a way that a person might behave and characteristics of the environment in which a person lives that increases the likelihood of having something negative happen to a person's health, safety, and/or well-being. Use the two transparencies, *Protective Factors That Prevent Violence* and *Risk Factors That Promote Violence* as the basis of a discussion of both types of factors. Di-

rect students to think about which factors relate to a person's behavior and which relate to a person's environment.

2 Explain that growing up in a dysfunctional family is rated as the greatest risk factor for behaving in violent ways or becoming a victim of violence. Remind students that a **dysfunctional family** is a family in which feelings are not expressed openly and honestly, coping skills are lacking, and family members do not trust each other. Explain that perhaps two of the reasons that a person growing up in a dysfunctional family might become involved in violence are a lack of positive self-esteem and a lack of social skills.

3 Explain that **self-esteem** is what a person thinks or believes about himself/herself. People with negative self-esteem are self-centered. They have little regard for others. They are likely to have few social skills. **Social skills** are skills that can be used to relate well with others. Examples of social skills are using manners, feeling free to ask for help when it is needed, following instructions, expressing caring feelings for another person, and learning to deal with rejection. Explain that social skills are learned, usually at a young age within the family. However, social skills may not be taught in a dysfunctional family. Explain that having social skills is related to self-esteem. A person who has positive self-esteem has confidence in his/her ability to relate well with others. Use the *Ways To Develop Positive Self-Esteem* transparency to point out ways to develop and maintain a positive self-esteem.

4 Discuss resiliency. **Resiliency** is the ability to prevent or to recover, bounce back, and learn from misfortune, change, or pressure. Explain that many people who are reared in a dysfunctional family become resilient. They may not have control over their environment, but they learn to control their responses to their environment. They choose to be with peers who practice protective factors. They look for ways to improve their relationships within the family. They look for responsible adult role models who will serve as mentors. A **mentor** is a person who guides and helps younger people.

5 Divide the class into groups. Give each group poster board, markers, and index cards. Explain that each group is going to make a game board for a game called "Life Savers" (see illustration). Some of the spaces on the game board are to be designated as risk factors and others as protective factors. Explain that "Life Saver" candies will be used as markers for the game.

6 Using index cards, each group is to make 20 risk cards and 20 protective cards. On the face sides of 20 cards, they are to print RISK FACTOR. On the face sides of the other 20 cards, they are to print PROTECTIVE FACTOR. For the 20 protective cards, the group is to print a protective factor on the back sides of the cards. Because it is a protective factor, they assign spaces to move the marker forward. For example, a protective card might read "You spend time with a family member: move ahead one space." For the 20 risk cards, they are to print a risk factor on the back sides of the cards. Because it is a risk factor, they assign spaces to move the marker backwards.

7 When each group completes preparing their game board and cards, they are to shuffle the cards separately and put them in two piles, face up. Then each group member is to select a different color candy to use as his/her marker. Group members can roll the die to see who goes first. When the game begins, one die is rolled. The player moves his/her marker the number of spaces indicated by the roll of the die. When a player lands on a space, (s)he must draw a card from the pile of index cards indicated by the space (s)he landed on. If his/her marker landed on a risk factor space, (s)he must pick a card from the risk factor pile and do what the card indicates. Groups may exchange their game boards and cards.

Evaluation:

Have each student draw a poster in the shape of a "Life Saver." Where the term "Life Saver" is printed on the piece of candy, they are to print a protective factor. Then they are to include a statement as follows: The life saver I have selected is....

RISING TO THE OCCASION

Objective:

Students will examine the importance of resiliency in dealing with life crises.

Life Skills:

I will respond to my environment in an empowering way. (PF4)

I will develop resiliency to "bounce back" if I live in an adverse environment. (PF4)

I will practice suicide prevention strategies. (PF9)

Materials:

Donut

Motivation:

1 Explain that there are two basic types of environments in which young people grow up. A **nurturing environment** is a set of conditions and surroundings in which a person lives that promotes growth, development, and success. An **adverse environment** is a set of conditions and surroundings in which a person lives that interferes with growth, development, and success. The kind of environment in which a person lives can and does limit the choices available to him/her. For example, young people who live in adverse environments face many crises. They may have parents who do not have jobs. They may be exposed to violence in their neighborhoods. They may not have enough food to eat or appropriate clothes to wear.

2 Explain that life is not always fair and that very difficult times happen to everyone. It is important to "rise to the occasion" when difficult times occur. Show the donut to the students. Explain that the ingredient in the donut that makes it rise is yeast. The ingredient in humans that is like yeast is resiliency. **Resiliency** is the ability to prevent or to recover, bounce back, and learn from misfortune, change, and pressure. Young people from adverse environments need help to break out of and recover from the cycle of such conditions as poverty, drug use, drug trafficking, and unemployment.

3 Although people in adverse environments cannot control the conditions of their environment, they can be empowered. **Empowerment** is the belief that a person controls his/her own destiny. People who are empowered learn to control their responses to their environment and make it as nurturing as possible. They begin to do whatever is possible to promote their own growth and development. They stay in school. They begin to develop a network of peers and adults who will be supportive and encouraging. They are determined to be optimistic and to look for ways they can respond positively to the life crises they face. They choose not to harm themselves or others, but rather to focus not on what they have lost but what they have. They focus on ways to deal with what they do not have. This kind of attitude changes the bitter taste that their environment may have caused. This kind of attitude describes resiliency.

4 Explain that a psychiatrist named Murray Banks once used a donut to explain how people gain resiliency. Dr. Banks said, "As you ramble on through life, whatever be your goal, keep your eye upon the donut, not upon the hole." Ask students to explain what Dr. Banks might have meant by that saying. Have them give examples of life crises and tell how a person might keep his/her eyes on the donut instead of the hole.

5 Discuss suicide. **Suicide** is the intentional taking of one's own life. Explain that people who are not resilient may think about suicide. They have no hope in the future and nothing to live for. They become depressed. They need to practice suicide prevention strategies that can help them prevent even thinking about suicide. **Suicide prevention strategies** are techniques that can be used to help prevent a person from thinking about, attempting, or completing suicide.

One strategy is to develop a network of support so that they will have someone to talk with. They can determine what is causing them to be depressed and counter that with listing their strengths and the positive aspects of their lives. This will help them think clearly about what is bothering them so that they can think of positive responses to their situation.

Evaluation:

Have students create four-line jingles that describe and emphasize the importance of resiliency. Students can share their sayings with the class.

REPEAT AFTER ME

Objective:

Students will identify resistance skills that can be used when pressured to engage in violent behavior.

Life Skills:

I will make responsible decisions. (PF12)
I will practice resistance skills. (PF13)

Materials:

Model For Using Resistance Skills transparency (page 610), transparency projector, index cards

Motivation:

1 Review the meaning of the term violence. **Violence** is the threatened or actual use of physical force to injure, damage, or destroy yourself, others, or property. Explain that a particular activity may not seem violent in itself, but the potential of its becoming violent may be very evident. This is the reason that it is necessary to stop and consider the possible consequences of a decision that a person must make. Explain that a decision made in a moment may have consequences that last a lifetime.

2 Explain that knowing how to make wise and responsible decisions is a very important skill to learn and practice. Remind students that people who practice decision-making skills make decisions based on their own health and safety, on their self-respect and the respect of others, and on guidelines set by their parents or guardians. They are in control of their decisions.

3 Introduce the term peer pressure. **Peer pressure** is pressure that people of similar age or status exert on others to encourage them to make certain decisions or behave in certain ways. Peer pressure can be positive or negative. When people who practice decision-making skills encourage others to make wise choices, the peer pressure is positive. When people pressure others to make harmful or violent choices the peer pressure is negative.

4 Introduce the term resistance skills. **Resistance skills** (or refusal skills) are skills that are used when a person wants to say NO to an action and/or leave a situation. Explain that a person who practices decision-making skills knows <u>when</u> to say NO. A person who practices resistance skills knows <u>how</u> to say NO. Use the *Model For Using Resistance Skills* transparency to discuss ways for effectively resisting pressure to engage in actions that threaten health; threaten safety; break laws; result in lack of respect for self and others; disobey guidelines set by responsible adults; or detract from character and moral values. Discuss each step, making sure that students understand the importance of resisting negative peer pressure.

5 Give each student an index card. Each student is to describe a situation in which someone his/her age is being pressured to take part in a violent action or to engage in a risk factor that increases the likelihood that violence will occur. Collect the index cards and shuffle them.

6 Have students sit in a circle. Select one of the index cards and read it. Call on one student to respond by using the suggestions in the Model (step 4). For example, the card might say that someone is pressuring a student to paint obscene words on a wall in the school building. In this case, the student might respond by saying "NO, I do not want to destroy school property." Then the next student in the circle must respond by repeating what the first student said and add an additional reason for saying NO. For example, the second student would say "NO, I want to obey school rules and stay on the student council." Then the next student in the circle would repeat what the first two students said and add another reason to say NO. Continue around the class. A student who is not able to remember all the answers given before him/her is out of the game. When a person is out of the game, start again with a different index card with a different situation.

Evaluation:

Shuffle the index cards. Give each student one of the cards. Each student is to explain how (s)he would effectively use resistance skills to avoid negative peer pressure to participate in an activity that might be violent or become violent.

DISSOLVING ANGER

Objective:

Students will describe sources of hidden anger and healthful ways to express them.

Life Skills:

I will practice anger management skills. (PF6)
I will practice stress management skills. (PF7)
I will participate in physical activity. (PF8)

Materials:

Hidden Anger Word Search student master (page 325), a copy for each student, *Anger Management Skills* transparency (page 600), transparency projector, sugar cubes, water in a cup, bowl

Motivation:

1 Introduce the term anger. **Anger** is the feeling of being irritated, annoyed, and/or furious. Explain that everyone experiences feelings of anger. Anger is an emotional state experienced in response to being hurt or frustrated. **Anger triggers** are thoughts or events that cause a person to become angry. Examples of anger triggers are being criticized, getting a poor grade on a test, or being rejected by peers. Ask students for other examples of anger triggers. It is important for students to recognize when they are angry. Explain what anger cues are. **Anger cues** are changes in the body or signs that a person is angry. Anger cues may include increased heart rate, sweaty hands, reddening of the face, and a dry mouth. Explain that it is all right to feel angry, but angry feelings should not be expressed in ways that harm self and others. People who do not learn

how to express anger in healthful ways harm not only themselves but also others.

2 Introduce the term hidden anger. **Hidden anger** is anger that is not dealt with in a healthful way and may result in inappropriate behavior and poor health. There are many emotional and physical consequences of hiding anger such as headaches, fatigue, depression, and sleeplessness. Sometimes people do not even realize how angry they really are because they have suppressed their angry feelings. Hidden anger can contribute to many physical problems such as ulcers, headaches, or high blood pressure. Angry feelings that are suppressed over a period of time begin to multiply. Eventually, this hidden anger cannot be contained and it overflows and may result in violent actions.

3 Relate these emotional and physical consequences to stress. **Stress** is the response of the body to the demands of daily living. Stressors are the source of stress. A **stressor** is a demand that causes changes in the body. Point out that hidden anger is an example of a stressor. Other examples are taking an exam, running in a race, and using drugs. Explain that response to a stressor can be positive or negative. **Eustress** is a healthful response to a stressor. When a person trains diligently for a race while envisioning himself/herself as a winner and then wins the race, (s)he experiences eustress. **Distress** is a harmful response to a stressor that produces negative results. For example, the person training for a race might be overwhelmed at the number of other people who are training for the race. The person may begin to doubt his/her chances of winning and end up not winning. (S)he would experience distress as a result. Explain that it is important for students to learn to cope with the stressors in their lives and to strive to respond in positive ways.

4 Distribute copies of the *Hidden Anger Word Search* student master. Explain to students that they are to look for eight terms that are examples of the effects of hidden anger. In a word search, the words may be written across, up and down, diagonally, or backwards. The letters of two or more words may cross each other. The following terms are included in the word search:

- **ulcers** are body sores that occur on the skin or on mucous membranes
- **depression** is a state of feeling sad and an inability to concentrate
- **boredom** is a lack of interest
- **nightmares** are frightening dreams
- **sarcasm** is bitter language usually directed at an individual
- **sleeplessness** is inability to get to sleep
- **fatigue** is weariness
- **irritability** is the state of being angry, annoyed, or impatient

5 Discuss the term communication. **Communication** is the sharing of feelings, thoughts, and information with another person. Learning to communicate is important in all relationships, but it is especially important in learning to express angry feelings in a healthful way. Explain that a responsible and healthful way to communicate is to use I-messages. **I-messages** are statements that contain (1) a specific behavior, (2) the effect that the behavior or event has on the individual, and (3) the feeling that resulted. I-messages refer to the individual, the individual's feelings, and the individual's needs (Figure 11). When a person uses I-messages, (s)he assumes responsibility for sharing feelings. An I-message gives the opportunity for a response without the other person feeling attacked. An example of an I-message is as

follows: "When you called me a name, everyone laughed at me, and I was angry."

6 Explain that an alternative to an I-message is a you-message. A **you-message** is a statement that blames or shames another person instead of expressing feelings. An example might be "You spoiled the football game for me when you forgot to pick me up." A you-message does not give the opportunity for a response. It attacks the other person and may generate negative feelings and even provoke a fight.

7 Show the sugar cube to the students. Explain that the sugar cube represents the anger that is inside a person. Explain that the use of I-messages helps dissolve anger. Give several examples of situations that would make a person angry, such as calling a person names, promising to call and not calling, talking about a person behind the person's back, not inviting a person to a party that everyone else in the class is invited to, forgetting to tell a person that everyone else is going to meet at a certain time, and so on. To each situation, have a student respond with an I-message that would be a healthful way of expressing the angry feelings. As a student responds, pour a little water on the sugar cube to demonstrate the anger being dissolved because it is expressed.

8 Explain that the use of I-messages is an example of an anger management skill. Show the *Anger Management Skills* transparency to discuss other skills that a person can use to defuse angry feelings as follows:

- <u>Keep an anger self-inventory.</u> The *Anger Self-Inventory* (Figure 16) can help you evaluate your angry feelings and determine which anger management skills would be appropriate to use.

- Use self-statements for anger control. Self-statements are positive statements to use to stay in control when you are angry. Examples are "I'm not going to let him get to me," "Getting upset won't help," or "Time to take a deep breath."
- Participate in physical activities. Physical activity can help defuse anger and relieve tension. It provides an outlet for the extra energy you feel when you are angry.
- Use physical expression to blow off steam. Punching a pillow or squeezing a tennis ball can channel your extra energy when you are angry.
- Use I-messages. When people use I-messages, they assume responsibility for expressing their feelings.
- Keep a sense of humor. Finding the humor in a situation and laughing at yourself can help defuse angry feelings.
- Express yourself through creative activities. Drawing a picture of the person who caused your anger or of the situation that caused your anger is often easier than using words.
- Talk with a parent or a mentor. Sharing your feelings with an adult can help you recognize what you are feeling, why you are feeling this way, and what are healthful ways to cope with those feelings. A **mentor** is a person who guides and helps younger people.
- Write a letter to express your angry feelings. By writing a letter, you can express your angry feelings without confronting anyone. You may choose not to send the letter, however.
- Plan ahead to deal with your anger. By examining what kinds of anger triggers you experience, you can rehearse what you might do when they occur again.

9 Emphasize the benefits of the anger management skill of participating in physical and rec-

reational activities. Physical activities help maintain physical fitness, manage stress, and increase energy. Some benefits include keeping the mind intellectually healthy and giving opportunities to be creative and to be with people who share interests and goals. Participation in physical activity and recreation can protect a person from being a perpetrator or victim of violence.

Evaluation:

Have students keep an "Anger Journal" for one week. Each time they feel angry, they are to describe the situation that made them angry. Then they are to write an I-message to express their anger.

Hidden Anger Word Search

```
H  L  O  V  R  B  T  I  O  I  O  L
W  E  T  U  L  C  E  R  S  D  J  K
E  B  A  O  G  G  S  Y  I  E  P  S
T  B  N  D  R  U  T  I  E  P  M  A
H  O  I  B  A  E  X  R  N  R  R  R
B  R  T  R  I  C  A  P  F  E  E  C
A  E  U  L  C  M  H  S  A  S  B  A
W  D  R  D  T  I  S  E  E  S  B  S
G  O  N  H  P  C  L  E  S  I  I  M
R  M  G  U  D  W  B  U  K  O  Y  B
R  I  S  E  C  T  U  O  L  N  N  U
N  U  N  E  U  G  I  T  A  F  S  I
I  R  R  I  T  A  B  I  L  I  T  Y
```

WALKING-A-MILE IN MY SNEAKERS

Objective:

Students will identify effective approaches to conflict resolution that exclude fighting.

Life Skills:

I will participate in physical activity. (PF8)
I will practice conflict resolution and peer mediation skills. (PF10)

Materials:

Conflict Resolution Skills transparency (page 606), transparency projector, six pairs of old sneakers, paper, pencils, six index cards, old magazines, scissors, glue, markers

Motivation:

1 To prepare for this strategy, prepare three sets of index cards. Each set will contain two cards. Three situations follow that describe conflicts between two seventh-grade students. Write the same situation on the two index cards that make up one set. On each set, identify the names of two students who are in conflict. For example, if Juan and Ricardo are in conflict, write Juan's name on one card of the set, and Ricardo's name on the other card of the set. The following are suggested situations:

- Juan and Ricardo each like the same girl, Becky. Juan asked Becky to go to the game with him Friday night. He told Becky that Ricardo couldn't go to the game. When Ricardo asked Becky to go to the game, she told him what Juan had told her. Ricardo was really angry.

- Sue and Ellen are neighbors. Sue agreed to take care of Ellen's puppy while Ellen's family was going to be away over the weekend. When it was time for Ellen to leave with her family, no one was at home at Sue's house and Ellen could not believe that Sue forgot what she had promised to do.

- Maria and Tom live near each other. Maria had no way to get to the school concert and she asked Tom if his parents were going to take him to the concert, and if so, could she get a ride with him. Tom said OK. When it was time for Tom to pick Maria up, he didn't show up. When Maria saw Tom the next day, Tom said he tried to call her to tell her he couldn't pick her up but there was no answer. Maria knows that someone was home at her house and that if Tom called, someone was there to answer.

2 Introduce the term conflict resolution skills. **Conflict resolution skills** are skills a person can use to resolve a disagreement in a healthful and responsible way. Explain that life without conflict is impossible, so learning how to resolve conflicts satisfactorily becomes an important life skill.

3 Explain that unresolved conflicts are a threat to a person's health. For example, anger is a common reaction to a conflict and it is not unusual for two people involved in a conflict to get angry and start an argument. However, arguing does not resolve a conflict. Arguing only creates more angry feelings and allows them to build. Also explain that if a person is angry and avoids trying to resolve the conflict, the same buildup of angry feelings and frustration occurs.

4 At this point, remind students about what happens if they allow anger and frustration to build and not express it in a healthful way. As anger builds in a person, his/her body responds by tensing muscles and having a surge of energy. If this person does not have a physical outlet to "work off" the extra energy and relieve the tension, (s)he is more likely to express his/her anger in inappropriate ways that may be harmful to self and others. Explain that physical exercise provides many benefits besides relieving tension. For example, people who exercise regularly are physically fit. They use their time wisely and reduce their stress level.

5 Explain that allowing angry feelings to build is contrary to the skills that are effective in resolving conflict. Use the *Conflict Resolution Skills* transparency to discuss healthful and responsible ways to resolve a conflict.
- Remain calm. Take a time out. Count to 10.
- Set the tone. Let the other person know that you want to be fair.
- Define the conflict. The situation that caused the conflict is the focus, not the people involved.
- Take responsibility for personal actions. Apologize if any of your reactions were inappropriate.
- Use I-messages. I-messages allow you to be nonthreatening but assertive.
- Listen. Let the other person know that you are sincere about wanting to resolve the conflict.
- List possible solutions. Brainstorm and evaluate the possibilities.
- Agree on a solution.
- Keep your word.
- Ask for help if the conflict is still not resolved.

6 Explain that asking for help might involve a trusted adult. It could also involve a process called peer mediation. **Peer mediation** is a process used to resolve conflicts in which a person helps his/her peers resolve disagreements in healthful, safe, legal, respectful,

and nonviolent ways. In this process, a peer establishes ground rules to which the people in conflict must agree. During the process, the peer mediator remains neutral. If your school has such a program already established, have your students report on how effective it is.

7 Divide the class into six groups. Give each group an index card. Two groups will have situation #1, two groups will have situation #2, and two groups will have situation #3. However, although two groups have the same scenario, there will be a different name on the card so they will be representing a different person involved in the conflict. Each group is to think about how the person they represent is feeling or thinking about the situation and write these emotions and/or thoughts on strips of paper.

8 Now, the two groups who were given the same situation are to work together to resolve the conflict. Considering one situation at a time, have a representative from Group #1 take the strip(s) of paper from his/her group and put them in one pair of sneakers. A representative from Group #2 is to put the strip(s) of paper from his/her group in the other pair of sneakers. Read situation #1. Then the two representatives are to exchange pairs of sneakers before they talk. Have them pull out each strip of paper and read what is on it. Explain that this represents taking the time to listen or to "walk in the other person's sneakers" as you work to resolve conflict.

9 Proceed in the same manner with the groups that were given situation #2, and then with the groups that were given situation #3.

Evaluation:

Have students cut out pictures of shoes (tennis, track, dress, and so on) from old magazines and make collages. On the collages, they are to write a message about the importance of "walking a mile in someone else's sneakers" when resolving conflict. They are also to write a message about the importance of resolving conflict without becoming violent. Have students share their collages and messages with the class.

RAPPING ABOUT RAPE PREVENTION

Objective:

Students will discuss rape, acquaintance rape, rape prevention, and guidelines to follow if raped.

Life Skills:

I will practice self-protection strategies. (PF18)
I will participate in recovery efforts if a victim. (PF19)

Materials:

Tape recorder and blank tapes (optional)

Motivation:

1 Introduce the topic of rape. **Rape** is the threatened or actual use of physical force to get someone to have sex without giving consent. Both males and females can be victims of rape, although more females than males are victims. In many cases, the victim does not know the person who is committing the rape. However, rape is not always committed by a stranger. Acquaintances also commit rape. **Acquaintance rape** is rape that is committed by someone known to the victim.

2 Introduce the term self-protection strategies. **Self-protection strategies** are strategies that can be practiced to protect oneself and decrease the risk of becoming a victim. Explain that learning strategies to protect oneself applies to many situations such as being at home, caring for children, driving or riding in a car, or walking or jogging. Following are some specific self-protection strategies that apply to protecting oneself from the risk of being raped.

- Don't let others know when you are home alone.
- Do not hitchhike.
- Scream or yell if you think someone is following you, or carry a device for making a loud noise.
- Do not leave a party or a shopping mall with a stranger.
- Do not walk alone at night on unlit streets.
- Do not give your name, address, or phone numbers to strangers either in person or on the phone.
- Do not let a stranger into your home.
- Report continuous, obscene, or bothersome phone calls to the telephone company and police.
- Never accept a ride from a stranger.

3 Explain that acquaintance rape often happens on a date when sexual feelings get out of hand. It is important for a person to let a date know about his/her decisions about expressing sexual feelings before getting into a situation in which it would be difficult to say NO. Explain that most acquaintance rapes are not planned. They are impulsive actions and the consequences can be serious and even violent. Many cases of rape are associated with the use of alcohol. Explain that many cases of rape go unreported for different reasons. The victim may be afraid of retaliation, publicity, embarrassment, or fear of ruining a relationship.

4 Stress that if rape occurs, it is essential for the victim to report the rape and to get immediate medical help. Reporting a rape is a personal decision. However, by reporting the incident, a victim may prevent another person from becoming a victim. Most important, however, is the fact that a victim of rape needs medical attention. The following guidelines should be followed by a rape victim who reports a rape.

- The victim should not bathe, shower, or change clothes because semen, hair, and other materials under the fingernails or on the victim's clothing may help identify the rapist if the rapist is not known to the victim.
- The victim should report any information that can be remembered about the rapist. Details about the rapist's physical characteristics, clothes, or car may prove valuable in obtaining a conviction.

5 Explain that victims of rape and other crimes need to recover and get on with their lives. In addition to possible physical injury, a rape victim is often angry, confused, shocked, and depressed. The medical examination is essential to determine if there is any physical harm for which help is needed. In addition, there are counseling and support services that are available. The goal of recovery programs is to help the victim survive the pain, heal, and regain his/her self-confidence.

6 Divide the class into groups. Each group is to pretend that it is a popular rap group and give itself a name. Then the group is to write a ten-line rap that contains a message about self-protection strategies to help prevent rape and acquaintance rape and/or what to do if rape occurs. For example, a group might name itself "The Rape Rappers" and their hit rap might be "Protect Yourself." Allow the groups at least 20 minutes to write and rehearse their raps. Encourage student to have dance steps and hand motions to accompany their raps.

7 Announce that there will be a recording session and that someone from each group will introduce the group, telling the group name and the hit rap that will be performed. Record the introductions and raps from each group. After the recording session, ask students to review the messages that were presented in the rap songs. Play the tape recording for parents at the next parent-teacher meeting.

Evaluation:

Have students each develop a true-false test with ten items concerning rape and acquaintance rape. At least four of the items on the test must be false. For each false item, the student must provide the correct answer. For example, one test item might be "It is not considered rape if a boyfriend forces his girlfriend of two years to have sexual intercourse with him." Because this is a false statement, the student would have to explain why that situation would be considered rape.

CONTAINING HARASSMENT

Objective:

Students will discuss sexual harassment and guidelines to follow with regard to sexual harassment.

Life Skill:

I will practice self-protection strategies. (PF18)

Materials:

Hat or bowl, wastebasket, sheets of paper

Motivation:

1 To prepare for this strategy, write a different example of sexual harassment on several sheets of paper. The following examples are suggested: 1) Someone rubs his/her body against yours. 2) You baby-sit for a family. When the male adult takes you home, he offers you extra money for a kiss. 3) You receive obscene phone calls from a classmate. 4) A classmate keeps leaving sexually-explicit notes in your locker. 5) A classmate follows you and stares at you. 6) Someone threatens you if you will not date him/her. 7) Someone shows you sexually-explicit pictures. 8) The person who sits in back of you in class keeps pinching you after you have told him/her to stop. 9) A person in another class keeps making comments about your body. 10) A classmate insists on telling sexually-explicit jokes.

2 Introduce the term sexual harassment. **Sexual harassment** is unwanted sexual behavior that ranges from making sexual comments to forcing another person into unwanted sex acts. Sexual harassment is any activity that threatens or bothers a male or female, such as sexual remarks, obscene jokes, unwelcome phone calls, or letters. Sexual harassment should never be tolerated by either males or females. Incidents of sexual harassment can occur anywhere, even in school.

3 Explain that people are sometimes confused about the difference between sexual harassment and flirting. The main difference is that sexual harassment is unwanted, unwelcome, and degrading. Comments about a person's body or other inappropriate comments do not promote healthful relationships. On the other hand, flirting is normal behavior in which interest in people of the other sex is expressed in appropriate and nondegrading ways. Sexual harassment often occurs in a situation in which one person is in a position of authority and may want to control the other person.

4 Introduce the term self-protection strategies. **Self-protection strategies** are strategies that can be practiced to protect oneself and decrease the risk of becoming a victim. One key to self-protection involves a person trusting his/her gut feelings about another person or a situation. For example, a person may be uncomfortable when (s)he is around a certain individual. (S)he might not be able to say exactly what makes him/her feel uncomfortable. This person should trust his/her gut feelings and avoid that particular individual.

5 Explain what a person might do if (s)he feels (s)he is being sexually harassed. The following strategies are guidelines that can be followed:

- Tell the person to stop in very specific terms.

- Write down specifics about the situation, such as what was said or done, and when and where it happened.
- Determine if anyone witnessed what was said or done and get any witness to write down what (s)he saw or heard.
- Discuss the situation with a parent or other trusted adult.

6 Put the papers with the examples of harassment written on them in a hat or bowl. One at a time, have students select a slip and read the example to the class. Each student is to tell what (s)he could do to stop the type of harassment that is written on the paper, then throw the paper into the wastebasket. For example, the student might say "I am going to protect myself by telling my classmate to stop telling sexually-explicit jokes. If (s)he does not stop, I will write down exactly what was said and give a copy to the teacher, guidance counselor, or principal." Proceed in this manner until all the examples of sexual harassment have been read and responses given.

Evaluation:

Have students pretend that they are reporting on a sexual harassment case that occurred in school. They are to write a newspaper article using fictitious names. They are to describe what the harasser did, how the victim of the harassment handled the situation, and the action that they believe would be appropriate for the school to take.

ASSAULT AND BATTERY

Objective:

Students will discuss ways to prevent assault and homicide.

Life Skill:

I will practice self-protection strategies. (PF18)

Materials:

An old battery, pieces of colored yarn, tape

Motivation:

1 Introduce the terms assault and homicide. **Assault** is a physical attack or threat of attack. An assault involves an attempt to inflict harm and puts a person in danger. Introduce the term homicide. **Homicide** is the accidental or purposeful killing of another person.

2 Discuss reasons a person might harm another. Use the analogy of a fully charged battery. Explain that when a battery is charged, it is full of potential energy. Discuss how a person's "battery" might become overcharged and, as a result, the person might harm another person.

3 Students are to identify a list of situations or conditions that might cause a person's battery to become charged. As a cause is identified, a student is to tape a piece of yarn to the dead battery to show that it is being charged with more voltage. The following suggestions might be used to add to the students' list.
- A person loses a job and is desperate about his/her family.

- A person is under the influence of a drug.
- A person has been drinking alcohol.
- A person is experiencing poverty.
- A situation is viewed as racist.
- A person is constantly put down and criticized.
- A boyfriend is jealous of a girlfriend.
- A boy is frustrated over not being able to make a team.
- A girl lacks friends.
- A girl sees a loved one attacked by another person.

4 Explain that in some situations a person becomes overcharged and acts out by assaulting another person or persons. Sometimes the assaults are so violent, they become cases of homicide. Discuss self-protection strategies. **Self-protection strategies** are strategies that can be practiced to protect oneself and decrease the risk of becoming a victim. Discuss strategies a person might use to keep himself/herself away from people who might be overcharged. Use the following suggestions as a starter and have students identify other ways that a person might protect himself/herself. As each suggestion is given, a student is to remove a tape from the battery, indicating that it is possible to discharge a potentially violent situation.
- Do not spend time with anyone who is using drugs.
- Get away from anyone who is buying or selling drugs.
- Get away from anyone who has a gun, knife, or other weapon.
- Stay away from people who want to fight.
- Don't walk through a vacant field by yourself.
- Don't go over to a car to give a stranger directions.

- Don't tell anyone on the phone that you are home alone.
- Don't walk alone at night on an unlit street.
- Stay away from buildings that are known to be hangouts for drug users.
- Do not join a gang.
- Resist any peer pressure to take part in a questionable activity.
- Avoid situations where you might be alone with an adult whom you do not trust or whom you know is abusive.

- Do not leave a party or a mall with a stranger.
- Do not hitchhike.

Evaluation:

Have students create bumper stickers to educate others about self-protection strategies that would help prevent assaults. Ask a representative of your local law enforcement to select the best bumper sticker.

STAYING CONNECTED

Objective:

Students will discuss ways to prevent suicide.

Life Skill:

I will practice suicide prevention strategies. (PF9)

Materials:

Construction paper, tape, scissors

Motivation:

1 To prepare for this strategy, cut sheets of construction paper into four strips, each 11 inches long and 2 inches wide. You will need one strip for each student in the class.

2 Introduce the topic of suicide. **Suicide** is the intentional taking of one's own life. There are several reasons that preteens and teens sometimes think about or attempt suicide. They may view suicide as a way to gain attention; they may want to get even with someone who rejected them; they may see suicide as a way of escape from their pain. Their pain may have been caused by any number of situations, such as feeling alienated from their families and friends, experiencing the separation or divorce of their parents, experiencing the death of a parent, having poor peer relationships, or having physical defects that worry them.

3 Explain that many young people who attempt suicide experience severe depression. **Depression** is a feeling of hopelessness, sadness, or helplessness. Explain that everyone commonly experiences short periods of depression. Long periods of depression, however, are not normal. Explain that there

are many indications that a young person may be experiencing depression. These indications include a loss of interest in personal appearance, withdrawal from family and friends, loss of interest in schoolwork, and inability to concentrate.

4 Introduce the term suicide prevention strategies. **Suicide prevention strategies** are techniques that can be used to help prevent a person from thinking about, attempting, or completing suicide. Discuss the following recommendations that also can be used to help a person who seems to be considering suicide.

- Know suicide hotline numbers. The National Youth Suicide Hotline, 1-800-621-4000, is a 24-hour hotline that is staffed by trained volunteers. These volunteers will listen, offer support, and help with a plan of action.
- Know what to do when you feel depressed. Figuring out the cause of depression is vital. A person who is angry can use anger management skills (refer to Protective Factor 6) or stress management skills (refer to Protective Factor 7).
- Build a network of support. Stay connected with people who will listen, offer advice, and help through tough times.
- Immerse yourself in rewarding activities. When you are involved with activities you enjoy, you will feel better about yourself, and be better able to manage the cause of your depression.
- Know what to do if someone shows warning signs. Do not ignore warning signs of suicide in another person. Let the person know you care. Ask a responsible adult for help. Do not leave the person alone.

5 Explain that if the students suspect someone is thinking about suicide, that person should always be taken seriously. A responsible adult should be notified immediately. If emergency help is needed, call 9-1-1 and stay with the person until appropriate help arrives. When the crisis is over, continue to give this person support and encouragement. It is important for this person to stay connected to friends and adults who care for him/her and to stay connected.

6 Ask students to form a circle. Give each student a strip of construction paper. Have one student tape the ends of his/her strip together to form a ring. The student is then to mention one way (s)he can stay connected to others. (Remind students that staying connected to others is a suicide prevention strategy.) For example, the student might say "I will spend more time with my family." Then the next student in the circle will link his/her strip of construction paper through the ring made by the first student and close it to form a link by taping the ends together. In this way, the two students are linked together.

The second student will then mention one way (s)he can stay connected to others. The student might say "I sing in the choir." Continue this procedure with each student in the class linking his/her strip to the previous links and then telling a way (s)he can stay connected.

7 Eventually all students in the class will be part of the chain. They will all be connected. Summarize by saying that one of the most effective suicide prevention strategies is to stay connected to others by spending time with family and friends and to stay connected at school by participating in school activities.

Evaluation:

Have the students stay in the circle. Have one student break his/her link from the group. The student will then give a warning sign that indicates someone is considering suicide. Continue this procedure around the circle. Warning signs can be repeated.

FOUL SHOT

Objective:

Students will outline procedures to follow to be safe around weapons.

Life Skill:

I will practice responsible behavior around weapons. (PF15)

Materials:

Sheets of paper, wastebasket

Motivation:

1 To prepare for this strategy, write risk situations associated with weapons on separate sheets of paper. You will need a risk situation for each student. Following are suggestions for risk situations you might use:

- You discover a gun in a drawer at home.
- You hear gunshots outside your window.
- You find a gun in the trash outside your apartment.
- A classmate puts a knife in your locker.
- A schoolmate asks you to hide a gun for him.
- A classmate asks you to his/her house but you know his/her parent sell drugs and you know there probably are guns in the house.
- A classmate wants your older brother to buy a gun for him/her.
- You see a knife sticking out of a class-mate's book bag.
- You overhear comments about a break-in at a recent convenience store.
- You witness a heated argument between two students.
- You see a person under the influence of alcohol who is carrying a gun.

- Someone warns you not to tell the teacher about something you saw.
- You are asked to join a gang.
- You are a member of a gang and you are uncomfortable about some of the activities you are expected to be involved with.
- You accept a ride with a stranger.

2 Discuss weapons. Remind students that a **weapon** is an instrument or device used for fighting. Ask students for examples of weapons. They will likely mention guns and knives first. Guns and knives are the most common weapons used in violent acts. Explain that guns are readily available today and that they often are in the hands of people who possess them illegally. These people may not know how to use the guns and as a result there is a risk that the guns might be discharged accidentally. However, many owners of illegal guns intend to use the guns to injure other people.

3 Explain that sometimes a person carries a gun and has no intention of using it. Perhaps the person wants to look or feel "cool." Perhaps (s)he wants to impress someone. It is important to understand that even though there was no plan to use the gun, the situation is still risky. This gun carrier might get into a heated argument and, without intending to, might use the gun to try to settle the argument.

4 Stress that because weapons are so dangerous, it is extremely important to have a set of guidelines concerning responsible behavior in regard to weapons. Each student should think seriously about ways to protect himself/herself because the threat of weapons is so prevalent in our society.

5 Review information about the game of basketball. In this game, a player might be called for a foul. The foul may be intentional. At other times, it is not intentional. Explain that weapons can be viewed in a similar way to fouls. Weapons can harm others. In some cases, the harm is intentional. A person might pull a knife and deliberately stab another person. In other cases, the harm is unintentional. A person might be holding a gun and not know that it is loaded. (S)he might point it at someone and accidentally shoot the person.

6 Explain that you are going to play a basketball game. Divide the class into two teams. Place a wastebasket in the middle of the floor equally distant from the two teams. Decide which team will go first. Give a student on this team a sheet of paper on which is written a risk situation. The student should read the risk and then take a foul shot by crumpling the sheet of paper and tossing it into the wastebasket. If the crumpled sheet lands in the wastebasket, the team gets one point for the "basket." If the team member can give a positive way to reduce the likelihood of harm from the risk situation, the team gets a second point. Continue, alternating teams and keeping score.

Evaluation:

Have students design a checklist for safety around weapons. The items on the list should reflect responsible behavior that the students should practice to protect themselves from dangers associated with being around people who are carrying weapons or with finding weapons.

WHAT'S BREWING?

Objective:

Students will discuss ways to resist pressure to belong to gangs and to participate in group acts of violence.

Life Skill:

I will resist gang membership. (PF16)

Materials:

Boiling water (might use a thermos), coffee cup, small bowl, ice cubes

Motivation:

1 Introduce the topic of youth gangs. A **youth gang** is a group of young people who band together and participate in violent, unlawful, or criminal activity. Many gang activities involve violent activities against other gangs or against the general population. Gang members associate only with one another. Being a gang member often exposes a person to illegal drugs, alcohol abuse, and weapons.

2 Explain that young people join gangs for different reasons. They may be alienated from their families and want to "belong" somewhere. Some join because they are bored and are looking for something that looks exciting. The desire for acceptance is very strong in young people, and many who feel alienated from their peers are attracted to gangs to meet that need. Young people who have no job skills because they drop out of school also are at a risk for gang involvement. Stress that the hazards involved in gang membership are not always evident at first.

3 Explain that prospective gang members often have to prove themselves by performing harsh tests of their courage and loyalty. Some of these tests include violent and illegal actions, such as drug dealing, robbery, beating up another person, and even killing a member of a rival gang.

4 Explain that in contrast to young people who do not belong to gangs, gang members are more likely to carry a weapon, to engage in fighting, to use alcohol and other drugs, and to deal in drugs. Gang members often acquire a criminal record that affects their employment opportunities.

5 Prepare the following demonstration. Pour one-half cup of boiling water into the coffee cup. Explain that the boiling water represents a young person's angry feelings. Ask students if they would want to place their fingers into the water in the cup. They would not, of course, because it is hot and they might get burned. Place an ice cube in the water. The ice cube cools the water a bit. Ask students for suggestions for ways to cool off when they are angry, such as counting to ten, talking to a friend, writing in a journal, going for a walk, shooting baskets, riding a bike, and so on.

6 Now pour one-half cup of boiling water into the bowl. Explain that this represents the angry feelings of one of their peers. Pour another one-half cup of boiling water into the bowl. Explain that there are now the angry feelings of two peers. Continue in this way until the bowl is full. Explain that as you are adding boiling water, you are adding the angry feelings of an additional person each time. The full bowl of angry feelings represent what a gang is like.

7 Ask students if they think one ice cube would do much to cool boiling water. They will say no. Discuss gang violence. "What's brewing" in a gang often is more heated than it would be in an individual. It takes more to cool off a gang than it takes to cool off an individual. Discuss incidents of gang violence that have been reported in newspapers where individuals have been caught up in the heat of gang activity and "what's brewing" became hotter and hotter. Remind students that the risks of belonging to a gang are very serious. Have students identify resistance skills they might use if they are pressured to join a gang and/or pressured by a group of peers to engage in violent behaviors. (Refer to the strategy for Objective 4.)

Evaluation:

Have students bring in pictures of themselves, or take some Polaroid shots of them. Have each student attach his/her picture to a sheet of white paper. Each student is to write his/her name and a byline for himself/herself. For example, Laurie Smith—I am my own person. Then each student is to write a profile of himself/herself explaining ways (s)he can resist pressure to belong to a gang.

TRAFFICKING TICKET

Objective:

Students will examine the role that drug use and drug trafficking play in increasing the risk of violence.

Life Skill:

I will avoid alcohol and other drugs. (PF14)

Materials:

Different Types Of Drugs transparency (page 343), transparency projector, *Trafficking Ticket* student master (page 611), a copy for each student

Motivation:

1 Introduce the topic of drugs. A **drug** is a substance that changes the way the body and/or mind work. Explain that drug use can harm the body and lead to illness and disease. In addition to causing body changes, drugs affect the way a person thinks and behaves. Drug use causes mood changes resulting in a person's having episodes of behavior that can get out of control. Drug users have stolen money from their families or have robbed places of business in order to be able to buy drugs.

2 Use the *Different Types Of Drugs* transparency to discuss the effects of drugs as follows:
- Alcohol. The effects of alcohol use include physical illness and diseases, such as liver damage, abnormal heart functioning, cancer, and brain damage. Alcohol also affects a person's control over his/her emotions.
- Sedative-hypnotics. These drugs contribute to assaultive or hostile behavior.
- PCP. In addition to the problems in perception, PCP use is associated with mem-

ory and speech problems, seizures, and anxiety.
- Cocaine. Cocaine use is associated with personality changes, anxiety, depression, and hostility. Cocaine use may cause irregular heart rate.
- Amphetamines. The effects of amphetamine use include hostility, irritability, irrational mistrust of others, and impulsive behavior.
- Heroin. Use of heroin results in feelings of anger, aggressiveness, and physical dependence.
- Anabolic steroids. The effects of these drugs include high blood pressure, cancer, liver damage, and sexual problems.
- Marijuana. Marijuana use results in increased heart rate, impaired short-term memory, anxiety, and lung damage.

3 Discuss drug trafficking. Drug trafficking involves the purchasing, selling, or distribution of illegal drugs. Drug trafficking is illegal. Explain that it is not unusual for deadly weapons to be involved in drug sales and purchases. Drug users and drug traffickers are at risk for both committing violence and being a victim of violence. Their violent acts often extend beyond themselves to include family members, friends, and even innocent bystanders through injury and death

4 Distribute a copy of the *Trafficking Ticket* student master to each student. Students are to design and complete a traffic ticket stating a specific offense associated with drug use or drug trafficking and a penalty for the offense. For example, the trafficking ticket may cite a person for selling cocaine. The penalty might be a prison term, an assignment to a drug rehabilitation program, a fine, and several hours of community service. After students have completed their traffic tickets, have them share their citations and penalties with the class.

5 If possible, invite a law enforcement officer to class to discuss local laws regarding drugs and penalties for drug offenses. Have students prepare questions in advance and have them take notes so they will have a record of the visit from the law enforcement officer.

Evaluation:

Have students pretend that they are law enforcement officers and that they have arrested 10 people for drug trafficking. Students are to list 10 ways that a person involved with drugs might be guilty of breaking the law.

Trafficking Ticket

Offense:

Penalty:

PROFILES OF ENFORCEMENT

Objective:

Students will identify ways to reduce violence by following laws and cooperating with law enforcement authorities.

Life Skills:

I will respect authority and abide by laws. (PF17)
I will change behavior if a juvenile offender. (PF20)

Materials:

Profile Of Enforcement student master (page 346), a copy for each student, paper, markers, pens, computer (optional)

Motivation:

1 Explain to students that all societies are governed by a set of rules called laws and that these laws are regulated by people in authority. Laws usually represent what the majority of people in a community, state, or nation believe and they are designed to protect the rights of everyone living in the community, state, or nation. People who abide by laws recognize that laws benefit everyone. For example, ask students to imagine what it would be like in your community if there were no traffic laws. Stress that traffic laws benefit the people in the community by allowing them to drive and/or walk safely within the community.

2 Explain that people who abide by laws assume responsibility for their actions. They are reliable and dependable. Because they want their rights to be protected, they are willing to cooperate in respecting and protecting the rights of others. People who abide by laws and respect authority live by a moral code. A **moral code** is a set of rules that a person follows in controlling his/her own behavior.

3 Explain that, unfortunately, not everyone lives by a moral code. A **juvenile offender** is a person under the age of 18 who breaks a criminal law. Explain that juveniles are responsible for one-third of all burglaries, one in seven of all rapes, and one in seven of all homicides. Explain that many young people who have been juvenile offenders accept help in changing their behavior. They recognize that if they continue their delinquent behavior they will likely be placed in an institution, which means they will lose their freedom for many years. They recognize that if they associate with others who are involved in criminal activity they are at risk for becoming a victim of violence.

4 Explain that there are many people and agencies involved in helping juvenile offenders. Many first-time offenders change their behavior without help because they realize the seriousness of what they did. Other offenders may need to be taught the difference between right and wrong because they did not learn this at home. Others may change their behavior as a result of peer pressure. Others need help in stopping an alcohol or drug habit that was the reason for their breaking a law. For others, there are many programs available that teach skills that help an offender change his/her behavior. Making the decision to change his/her behavior and get help is a very important decision for an offender to make so that (s)he can experience success and be a productive citizen.

5 Explain that there is no doubt that drugs can directly contribute to violent behavior through their effects on a person's mind and body. For example, alcohol is the drug that is most commonly associated with violence, probably because it is so widely used in our society. Drug trafficking is another connection with violent behavior. Another reason that drugs are associated with violence is drug trafficking. Review the definition of drug trafficking. Drug trafficking involves the purchasing, selling, and distribution of illegal drugs. Crimes often are committed by drug users because of the high cost of some drugs and the need to support their continued drug use. The use of weapons in drug deals increases the risk of injury or death for both the seller and the buyer.

6 Tell students that they are to interview a law enforcement person who works in the field of drugs. Be sure to include both male and female law enforcement people. In the interview, students should ask questions about local cases of violence related to the use or trafficking of drugs. They should ask about local laws concerning drugs and how (s)he thinks violence could be reduced in your community.

Have students write a report about the interview.

7 Show students the *Profile Of Enforcement* student master. Explain that the master is a suggested format for the interview. They can develop their own Profile based on the law enforcement person they interviewed. They might get a picture of the individual or draw a sketch of him/her. They might use markers or pens for writing the information on the Profile. Some students may choose to use a computer and computer graphics to design their Profile. Have each student share his/her completed Profile with the class. Have each student comment on how (s)he can best cooperate with law enforcement authorities to protect the rights of everyone living in your community.

Evaluation:

After the sharing session, have students identify at least five people in their community with whom they might cooperate in abiding by laws and respecting authority as they protect themselves against violence.

Profile Of Enforcement

Age:

Gender:

Reason for entering this career:

Years of schooling completed:

Training necessary for the job:

Most rewarding aspect of the job:

Most difficult aspect of the job:

What would make the job easier:

What (s)he does to cope with stress of the job:

PUTTING THE PIECES BACK TOGETHER

Objective:

Students will identify support systems available for people who have been victims of violence.

Life Skill:

I will participate in recovery if a victim. (PF19)

Materials:

Large sheets of heavy cardboard, markers, scissors, masking tape

Motivation:

1 Review the definition of violence. **Violence** is the threatened or actual use of force to injure, damage, or destroy oneself, others, or property. People who are the victims of violence suffer a great deal. The world that they may have thought was safe and predictable is suddenly unsafe and unpredictable. Victims may be seriously or permanently injured; they may feel terrified; they may be unable to concentrate because of their fear; they may be afraid that they have been exposed to HIV, the virus that causes AIDS; they may be very angry; and they may suffer financial and property loss. People who witness violent crimes also can be victims. They may have difficulty forgetting what they saw or heard. They may have nightmares about the incident.

2 Explain that victims of crimes may be faced with secondary victimizations, which are injustices that occur to victims after the initial crime. Victims may have to testify in the court trials of their perpetrators. This will mean that the victims must relive the experi-ence as they remember details of the incident. They may have to miss school or work to get to court.

3 Introduce the term victim recovery. **Victim recovery** is a person's return to physical and emotional health after being harmed by violence. It is extremely important that a person who has been a victim of violence recover from his/her experience. Often the families and friends of a victim also need to recover because many lives can be affected by what has happened to the victim. Explain that recovery may take place over a period of time.

4 Explain that there are many recovery routes that victims of violence might take. Discuss some possible victim recovery efforts as follows:

- Talk about it. It is important to share feelings, thoughts, and other experiences with trusted friends and family members.
- Get a thorough medical examination. Medical help may be needed if the victim was physically harmed.
- Seek counseling. Health care facilities offer counseling help. Physicians and school counselors are good sources of information concerning counseling.
- Join a support group. A victim can be helped by a support group of people who have had a similar experience. For example, there are support groups for survivors of domestic abuse.
- Learn and practice self-protection strategies. Victims need to be aware of situations that put them at risk. They need to do everything they can to protect themselves from becoming a victim again.

5 Explain that victims of violence, such as domestic abuse or child abuse, who avoid recovery efforts are at risk of continuing the cycle of violence. Some victims do not seek help because they have developed negative self-esteem. They have been abused for so long they may begin to believe that they are inferior. Some victims may continue the behavior that caused them to be victims the first time. For example, if a person who was injured because (s)he was involved in a drug deal continues to deal drugs, (s)he is putting himself/herself at risk again.

6 Divide the class into groups. Give each group a large sheet of heavy cardboard. The group is to design a puzzle that has at least eight pieces. On each piece, they are to print a way that a person who has been a victim of violence might be helped to recover. They also might include ways for the

family of a homicide victim, for example, to recover. The groups are to cut out their puzzle pieces.

7 Have each group choose a representative who will share the puzzle pieces the group has designed. After (s)he reads what is printed on each piece, (s)he will tape the piece to the chalkboard and continue in this manner until all pieces of the puzzle are taped on the chalkboard. The other groups will follow the same procedure.

Evaluation:

Have students identify and list people or organizations in their community who would be resources to help a victim of violence recover from the experience.

CRIME CLOCK

Objective:

Students will identify types of crimes and violence.

Life Skills:

I will recognize that violent behavior is wrong. (PF1)

I will avoid discrimination. (PF11)

Materials:

Ways To Avoid Discriminatory Behavior transparency (page 608), *Types Of Violence* transparency (page 589), transparency projector, large clock with second hand, beeper or buzzer, calculators (optional), paper, pencils, copy of *F.B.I. Uniform Crime Reports For The United States*

Motivation:

1 Introduce the topic of crime and violence. Crime is any action that involves breaking the law. **Violence** is the use of force with the intent to harm oneself or another person. A person who demonstrates violent behavior can be a perpetrator or a victim. A **perpetrator** is a person who commits a violent act. A **victim** is a person who is harmed by violence.

2 Explain that it is important for students to recognize violent behavior. Our society has become immune to violence. Movies and television programs are saturated with violent actions such as murder, assault, torture, and rape. Newspaper headlines that report crimes and violence are an everyday occurrence. Actions that formerly shocked and scared people are now so common that people have become

desensitized. **Desensitization** is the process of lessening a person's response to certain things by overexposing that person to these same things. People who witness actual occurrences of violent behavior in their homes and communities also can become desensitized. The danger of becoming desensitized is that a person no longer recognizes dangerous and wrong types of behavior that are associated with the likelihood of violence.

3 Explain that one source of violence is the practice of discriminatory behavior. **Discriminatory behavior** is making distinctions in treatment or showing behavior in favor of or prejudiced against an individual or group of people. **Prejudice** is suspicion, intolerance, or irrational hatred directed at an individual or group of people. Behavior that discriminates against others is learned behavior. People are not born prejudiced. Children can and should be trained to treat and respect other people early in their lives. Use the *Ways To Avoid Discriminatory Behavior* transparency to help students understand that avoiding discriminatory behavior begins with each individual.

4 Explain that people who are prejudiced and who practice discriminatory behavior are at risk for being both perpetrators and victims of violence. These people are apt to behave aggressively; that is, they use words and/or actions that tend to communicate disrespect for others. This type of behavior often borders on or escalates to violent behavior. And people who are aggressive are apt to provoke those who are the objects of their attacks. Anger can build up in these people and eventually can erupt into violence. Thus, aggressive people also can become victims.

5 Use the *Types Of Violence* transparency to acquaint students with the various types of behavior that are classified as violent. Use the descriptions on the transparency to discuss each type. As you do this, point out that in each case, there is a victim(s) and a perpetrator(s). Also point out the all violent behavior is wrong because it causes injury and/or death to oneself or others.

6 The Federal Bureau of Investigation publishes *The Uniform Crime Reports For The United States*, which is a report that identifies the incidence of violent crimes in American cities and counties. This report is used to compile statistics regarding the incidence of violence and crime in the United States.

7 Explain that each year there are approximately 800 violent crimes reported for every 100,000 people who live in the United States. Based on this statistic, ask students what they think their chances are of becoming a victim of crime.

8 Using the *F.B.I. Uniform Crime Reports*, you are going to emphasize how often certain crimes occur in the United States. For example, according to the Report, there is a burglary committed approximately *every 10 seconds*. Without telling the students what crime is committed every 10 seconds, use a beeper or a buzzer every 10 seconds for two minutes. Then ask students if they can guess what type of crime is committed that often in the United States. If they do not guess it is burglary, tell them. Explain that burglary is a property crime. **Burglary** is an unlawful entry of a structure to commit a theft. Using this information, have students compute how many burglaries are committed in an hour, day, month, and year.

9 Use another crime statistic and repeat the process. (There is a motor vehicle theft *every 19 seconds*, a case of larceny-theft *every four seconds*, an aggravated assault *every 29 seconds*, a homicide *every 21 minutes*, a sexual assault *every 5 minutes*, and so on.) Use your beeper or buzzer for each one, and have the students guess which crime is committed that often. In each case, make sure students know the definition of the crime. Definitions are available in the F.B.I. Report. In each case, also have students calculate how many times that particular type of crime is committed every hour, day, and year.

10 Ask students to identify ways that crime and violence harm society in general. Students may mention some of the following ways: loss of personal property, personal injury, death, emotional harm, and fear.

Evaluation:

Have students prepare brief reports such as might be included in a 6 o'clock news report. The reports should inform listeners about F.B.I. crime statistics and how these crimes injure both individuals and society.

Inclusion:

Have students with special learning challenges use calculators to compute the statistics on a crime for an hour, day, month, or year.

PROTECTIVE SHELL

Objective:

Students will identify protective factors and risk factors for violence.

Life Skills:

I will develop positive self-esteem. (PF2)
I will strive for healthful family relationships. (PF3)
I will develop resiliency to "bounce back" if I was reared in a dysfunctional family. (PF4)
I will develop social skills. (PF5)

Materials:

Protective Factors For Violence transparency (page 588), *Risk Factors For Violence* transparency (page 587), *Ways To Develop Positive Self-Esteem* transparency (page 592), transparency projector, hard-boiled egg, bowl of water, bowl of white vinegar, empty cigarette package that shows a warning

Motivation:

1 Show students a hard-boiled egg. Explain that the shell is a protective factor for the part of the egg that is inside the shell. Introduce the term protective factor. A **protective factor** is a way that a person might behave and characteristics of the environment in which (s)he lives that promote health, safety, and/or well-being. Protective factors help keep a person safe from becoming involved in violence.

2 Place the egg in the bowl of water and have students note that nothing happens to the shell. The inside of the egg is still protected. Use the *Protective Factors For Violence* transparency. Discuss each factor with the students. Refer to the two parts of the definition of protective factors—behavior and environment—as you discuss the list. Have students identify which factors relate to a person's environment and which to a person's behavior.

3 Introduce the term risk factor. A **risk factor** is a way that a person might behave and characteristics of the environment in which a person lives that increases the likelihood of having something negative happen to a person's health, safety, and/or well-being. Consider again the hard-boiled egg and explain to students that just as harsh treatment might break the protective shell of the egg, so risk factors affect the protection a person has and increase the likelihood of damage to the person.

4 Move the hard-boiled egg from the bowl of water and put it in the bowl with vinegar. Use the *Risk Factors For Violence* transparency and discuss each factor. Explain that these are risk factors that might make them vulnerable to becoming victims or participants in violent actions. Discuss each risk factor. Point out that risk factors are in opposition to protective factors.

5 After discussing the list of risk factors, have students observe the hard-boiled egg that has been soaking in vinegar. They will notice that the shell has been affected, exposing the interior of the egg. Draw the analogy to the way in which risk factors affect people and make them more vulnerable to violence.

6 Discuss changing risk factors to protective factors. For example, how might a person change Risk Factor 2 (having negative self-esteem) to Protective Factor 2 (having positive self-esteem)? Use the *How To Develop Posi-*

tive Self-Esteem transparency to discuss ways that people who have negative self-esteem could work to improve their feelings about themselves.

7 Discuss Risk Factor 3 and Protective Factor 3. Introduce the terms dysfunctional family and healthful family. A **dysfunctional family** is a family in which feelings are not expressed openly and honestly, coping skills are lacking, and family members do not trust each other. A **healthful family** is a family in which feelings are expressed openly and honestly, coping skills are adequate, and family members trust each other. Explain that young people who grow up in dysfunctional families may not have a responsible adult role model. They do not learn ways of coping with life crises. They do not learn how to form responsible relationships with their peers. These young people can learn to be resilient. **Resiliency** is the ability to prevent or to recover, bounce back, and learn from misfortune, change, or pressure. Explain that to be resilient, young people must feel empowered—they must believe that they can control their own destiny. They may not be able to change their dysfunctional family background, but they can control how they respond to it.

8 Suggest ways that these young people might strive to improve their family relationships. They can learn and practice social skills. **Social skills** are skills that can be used to relate well with others. Examples of social skills are using manners, feeling free to ask for help in difficult situations, showing respect for other people, demonstrating an interest in other people, and expressing affection for others. Young people can respond to their situation by seeking a respon-sible adult role model who will act as a mentor. A **mentor** is a person who guides and helps a younger person.

Evaluation:

Show students the warning label on a cigarette package. Have each student write ten warning labels concerning violence. The warning labels should be based on the risk factors for violence. The transparency should not be available to students during this quiz. Share the following suggestions as examples:

WARNING: Having an available firearm increases the risk of violence.

WARNING: Belonging to a gang increases the risk of violence.

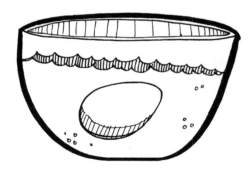

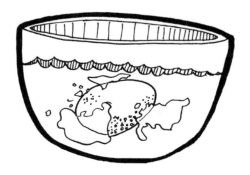

SOUR BALLS AND LOLLIPOPS

Objective:

Students will examine the importance of resiliency in dealing with life crises.

Life Skills:

I will strive to live in a nurturing environment. (PF4)

I will develop resiliency to "bounce back" if I live in an adverse environment. (PF4)

I will practice suicide prevention strategies. (PF9)

Materials:

Sour balls, lollipops

Motivation:

1 Remind students that their environment is *everything* around them in the places in which they live. Explain that a **nurturing environment** is a set of conditions and surroundings in which a person lives that promotes growth, development, and success. On the other hand, an **adverse environment** is a set of conditions and surroundings in which a person lives that interferes with growth, development, and success. Explain that people who live in a nurturing environment have hope. **Hope** is the feeling that what is desired is possible and that events in life may turn out for the best. People who live in adverse environments often experience hopelessness, anger, and frustration.

2 Explain to students that a book written by Rabbi Kushner is titled *When Bad Things Happen To Good People*. Ask students what they think the title means. Explain that life is not fair and that some-times life crises are "bad" things that do happen to people who are undeserving of bad treatment. Give examples: good workers lose jobs; loved ones die unexpectedly; someone in a family is chemically dependent; a family experiences poverty, or homelessness; people living in certain areas are affected by natural disasters such as earthquakes and floods; a person is permanently disabled after an accident, and so on.

3 Ask students to think about growing up in an adverse environment as a life crisis. Introduce the term resiliency. **Resiliency** is the ability to prevent or to recover, bounce back, and learn from misfortune, change, or pressure. People who are resilient accept a life crisis and learn to recover from it. They make decisions and take constructive steps to cope with the crisis. For example, people living in an adverse environment look at their situation and decide what part of their situation they might improve so that it becomes more of a nurturing environment. They decide to stay in school and get an education. They decide to reduce their risks of becoming a victim or a perpetrator of violence and choose to practice protective factors.

4 Explain that people who are not resilient may become so depressed that they consider suicide. These people need to practice suicide prevention strategies. They can develop a network of friends and trusted adults who will listen, offer advice, and help through tough times. They can examine what is causing their depression and take steps to overcome it. They can get information from the National Youth Suicide Hotline that is a 24-hour hotline staffed by trained volunteers.

5 To illustrate environments, give a lollipop (sugar-free or otherwise) to some students and sour balls to the rest. Ask students to describe what they taste. Obviously, some will say sweet; others will say sour. Explain that just as some students experienced a sour taste, some people seem to go through life with a sour taste. They do not master the experience of a life crisis.

6 Discuss what happens to a person who has a sour attitude toward life. Discuss ways this attitude might affect the person's relationships and outlook on life. Talk about ways that a person's sour attitude might increase the likelihood of violence by antagonizing other people or by holding grudges and perhaps seeking revenge.

Evaluation:

Working in groups, have students develop scenarios that illustrate a person or people dealing with a life crisis and exhibiting resiliency. Groups are to act out their scenarios for the class.

Inclusion:

Have students with special learning challenges discuss their acceptance of their crisis — having a learning difficulty. For example, a student with dyslexia might recount how (s)he felt when (s)he first learned about his/her dyslexia. How has (s)he coped with his/her challenge? Has (s)he been resilient?

PEERSUASION TWIZZLERS

Objective:

Students will identify resistance skills that can be used when pressured to engage in violent behaviors.

Life Skills:

I will make responsible decisions. (PF12)
I will practice resistance skills. (PF13)

Materials:

Using Resistance Skills student master (page 357), a copy for each student, transparency projector (optional), red licorice twizzlers, black licorice twizzlers

Motivation:

1 Remind students about the definition of the term violence. **Violence** is the threatened or actual use of physical force to injure, damage, or destroy yourself, others, or property. Explain that many young people get involved in violent actions because of peer pressure. **Peer pressure** is pressure that people of similar age or status exert on others to encourage them to make certain decisions or behave in certain ways. There are two main reasons that young people agree to actions that put them at risk. First of all, the need to identify with a person or to belong to a group is very strong in young people. The second reason is that many young people lack skills to resist pressure. They do not know how to say NO.

2 Introduce the term resistance skills. **Resistance skills** are skills that are used when a person wants to say NO to an action and/or leave a situation. People who have resistance skills can effectively resist pressure to

engage in actions that threaten health; threaten safety; break laws; result in lack of respect for self and others; disobey guidelines set by responsible adults; and detract from character and moral values.

3 Discuss how decision-making skills affect a person's ability to resist peer pressure. Explain that there are three styles of making decisions. An **inactive decision-making style** is a decision-making style in which people fail to make choices and the failure determines what will occur. People who are procrastinators use this inactive style. A **reactive decision-making style** is a decision-making style in which people allow others to make decisions for them. People who adopt this style are easily influenced by others and so are very vulnerable to peer pressure. A **proactive decision-making style** is a decision-making style in which people examine the decision to be made; identify and evaluate actions that can be taken; select an action and assume responsibility for the consequences. These people maintain control of their decisions.

4 Stress that people who choose a proactive decision-making style know <u>when</u> to say NO. People who practice resistance skills know <u>how</u> to say NO.

5 Divide the class into three groups. The students in the first group (Group 1) each get two red twizzlers; they have the reputation of engaging in violent behaviors. The students in the second group (Group 2) each get two black twizzlers; they have the reputation of behaving responsibly. The third group (Group 3) have the reputation of having difficulty making decisions and so are easily influenced by others.

6 Begin the strategy by having the students in Group 1 meet together and decide on a violent action they will do together. For example, they may decide to assault a student who is wearing a particular kind of jacket and to take the jacket. The students in Group 1 are then to try to convince the students in Group 3 to join them. Group 1 students are to be as convincing as possible, talking about the excitement and the daring aspect of their venture. Whenever a student in Group 3 agrees to join Group 1, (s)he is given a red twizzler by a member of Group 1. After a few minutes, end the experiment and have students discuss the kind of pressure they felt to join Group 1. What kind of pressure was the most difficult? Why? Have they experienced pressure like that in other situations?

7 Now have members of Group 2 meet together to decide on an exciting venture that they will do together. This venture will be a positive one such as being involved in a community project, helping to clean up after an earthquake, or volunteering to help with the school play. Then members of Group 2 will meet with members of Group 3 and try to convince them to join in the venture they have chosen. Whenever a student in Group 3 decides to join Group 2, (s)he is given a black twizzler by a member of Group 2. After a few minutes, end the experiment and have Group 3 students discuss the kind of encouragement they received to join Group 2. Was the appeal from Group 2 as convincing as the appeal from Group 1? Why or why not?

8 Have students look at the red and black twizzlers. Remind them that each color represents a different kind of behavior. The black is healthful and responsible; the red is violent. Remind them that PEERSUASION can lead to actions that are healthful or harmful and violent.

9 Distribute copies of *Using Resistance Skills* (or show it as a transparency with a transparency projector). Have students review ways that Group 1 pressured others to engage in harmful and violent behavior. Have students explain what resistance skills might have been appropriate. Students can demonstrate these resistance skills using role play.

Evaluation:

Have students complete four versions of the following sentence. I will not become involved in violent behaviors such as:

1. _____

_____

_____

2. _____

_____

_____

3. _____

_____

_____

4. _____

_____

_____

Using Resistance Skills

When I receive PEERSUASION to join my peers in violent behaviors, I will use the following resistance skills:

1. _____

2. _____

3. _____

4. _____

5. _____

OVERFLOWING ANGER

Objective:

Students will describe sources of hidden anger and healthful ways to express it.

Life Skills:

I will practice anger management skills. (PF6)
I will practice stress management skills. (PF7)
I will participate in physical activity. (PF8)

Materials:

Anger Self-Inventory transparency (page 601), transparency projector, water, white vinegar, baking soda, bowl, two glasses

Motivation:

1 Introduce the term anger. **Anger** is the feeling of being irritated, annoyed, and/or furious. Explain that everyone experiences feelings of anger and that it is all right to feel angry. However, angry feelings need to be expressed, but not in ways that harm self and others. Discuss harmful ways to let out feelings of anger: damaging property; hitting and physically hurting another person; hurting oneself by choosing to use alcohol or drugs. Ask students for other illustrations.

2 It is important for students to recognize their anger triggers and anger cues. **Anger triggers** are thoughts or events that cause a person to become angry. Ask students what kinds of anger triggers cause them to become angry. They may mention such events as not being chosen for a team, not being invited to a party, or getting a poor grade. Explain that there are cues that tell when a person is angry. **Anger cues** are changes in the body or signs that a person is angry. When people are angry, they can exhibit

changes such as a reddening of the face, clenched fists, sweaty palms, and increased heart rate. In order to relieve these physiological changes, people must learn to express their angry feelings in healthful ways.

3 Explain that anger that is not expressed is called hidden anger. **Hidden anger** is anger that is not handle in a healthful way and may result in inappropriate behavior and poor health. Explain that signs of hidden anger may appear in many ways and that people may not be aware that they are suppressing angry feelings. Unexpressed anger can contribute to high blood pressure, headaches, and other illnesses. If people allow hidden anger to remain suppressed they will find that they eventually cannot contain the anger. Their actions may eventually become violent.

4 The following experiment will help demonstrate what can happen when people do not express their anger. Pour one cup of white vinegar into a glass. Explain that white vinegar represents the angry feelings a person keeps hidden inside. Pour one cup of water into another glass. Ask students for an example of an anger trigger and add one tablespoon of baking soda to the glass of water to represent the anger trigger. As students suggest another trigger, add another tablespoonful of baking soda.

5 Next, add the water and baking soda mixture to the glass containing the white vinegar. Make sure you have a bowl or tray below the glass or do the experiment over a sink. When you add the water and baking soda to the vinegar, the ingredients will bubble up and overflow. Explain that this experiment illustrates what happens when people hide their anger. Eventually, the anger will overflow and they may act in a violent manner.

Ask students how overflowing anger might be expressed. They may suggest such ways as kicking, biting, destroying property, and so on.

6 Use the *Anger Self-Inventory* transparency to help students become skilled in recognizing anger triggers and in evaluating their feelings of anger. This inventory will help them examine the kinds of situations that cause their anger and how they might respond. The inventory can help them determine if a situation is worth a lot of their attention.

7 Introduce the terms stress and stressor. **Stress** is the response of the body to the demands of daily living. A **stressor** is a demand that causes changes in the body. Examples of stressors are inhaling the smoke of another person's cigarette, trying to solve a difficult math problem, and meeting a special person for the first time. Point out that anger triggers are a kind of stressor because they cause a person to respond by experiencing feelings of anger. Other kinds of stressors might cause a person to be frustrated, nervous, or worried. No matter what kind of stressor a person experiences, it is important to manage the stress.

8 Explain what stress management skills are. **Stress management skills** are techniques that can be used to cope with the harmful effects produced by stress. There are basically two types of these skills: one type focuses on doing something about the stressor; the other type focuses on keeping the body healthy and relieving anxiety.

9 Point out that one important skill that helps manage anger and other kinds of stress is participating in physical and recreational activities, such as jogging, biking, team sports, performing with a theater group, or attending a sporting event. Physical activities help a person maintain physical fitness and improve self-esteem. Recreational activities are both mentally and physically refreshing. They give a person an outlet for self-expression and an opportunity for developing new skills and talents.

Evaluation:

Have students write a brief description of a situation in which they were very angry at another person and did not express their anger in a healthful way. Then have students write an imaginary dialogue between themselves and the other person, describing how they would handle the situation if they had a second chance.

SHORT FUSE/LONG FUSE

Objective:

Students will identify effective approaches to conflict resolution that exclude fighting.

Life Skills:

I will participate in physical activity. (PF8)
I will practice conflict resolution and peer mediation skills. (PF10)

Materials:

Conflict Resolution Skills transparency (page 606), *The Process Of Peer Mediation* transparency (page 607), transparency projector, ball of red yarn, ball of yellow yarn, ball of green yarn, scissors

Motivation:

1 To prepare for this strategy, you will need to make a three-color ball of yarn. Cut three-foot strips of each color of yarn. Using the sequence of red, yellow, green, tie the ends together, and make a new three-color ball of yarn.

2 Explain that conflicts are a part of everyday life. They occur in every area of life, including the family, so it is necessary to learn how to respond to conflict in healthful and responsible ways. Introduce the term conflict response style. **Conflict response style** is a pattern of behavior a person demonstrates when conflict arises. There are three styles as follows:

1 **Conflict avoidance** is a conflict response style in which a person denies that there is a conflict and/or attempts to please others at his/her expense. People who choose this style allow others to resolve conflicts for them. Dis-

agreements are avoided and/or denied at any cost.

2 **Conflict confrontation** is a conflict response style in which a person attempts to settle a disagreement in a hostile, defiant, and aggressive way. A confronter wants to win or be right at all costs. Remind students at this point that when they feel angry or aggressive, participating in physical activities, such as swimming, jogging, and team sports, can help defuse anger and relieve tension.

3 **Conflict resolution** is a conflict response style in which a person uses conflict resolution skills to resolve a disagreement in a healthful and responsible way.

3 Use the *Conflict Resolution Skills* transparency to discuss effective steps that help solve conflicts in a responsible manner. You may need to remind students what I-messages are. An **I-message** is a statement that contains 1) a specific behavior or event, 2) the effect the behavior or event has on the individual, and 3) the feeling that resulted. I-messages are a nonthreatening way of expressing feelings. An example is, "When you called me a name, I felt put down, and I was angry."

4 Introduce the terms peer and peer mediation. A **peer** is a person who is similar in age or status. **Peer mediation** is a process used to resolve conflicts in which a person helps his/her peers resolve disagreements in healthful, safe, legal, respectful, and nonviolent ways. The peer mediator takes a neutral position, and establishes rules that the people in conflict must agree to follow. The peer then uses a process that includes conflict resolution skills to resolve the conflict. Use *The Process Of Peer Mediation* transparency to discuss the process. If your school has already established a peer mediation program, your students will no doubt be familiar with it. If your school has no such program, you may want to consider trying the process.

5 Show students a piece of red yarn. Explain that the red yarn represents a fuse—a short fuse. It also represents harmful ways of dealing with conflict. Show them a piece of yellow yarn as you tie it to the piece of red yarn. Explain that the yellow yarn represents ways to cool off. This gives you more time because the fuse is now longer and less likely to "blow." Next, show a piece of green yarn and tie it to the end of the yellow yarn. The green yarn has lengthened the fuse even more. The green yarn represents healthful ways to resolve conflict.

6 Have students sit in a circle. Using the three-color ball of yarn you prepared, give it to one student in the circle. Ask that student to wrap the end of the yarn around his/her finger and pass the ball to another student who wraps the yarn around his/her finger. This student checks to see what color of yarn is wrapped around his/her finger. Suppose it is yellow. Since yellow represents ways to cool off, the student mentions one way to cool off, such as going for a long walk. Suppose his/her finger was wrapped in red yarn. Since red represents a short fuse, (s)he will mention a way of resolving conflict that would be harmful. If his/her finger was wrapped in green yarn, the student would mention a healthful way of dealing with conflict since green represents healthful ways to resolve conflict. Students are to continue to pass the ball of yarn around until everyone in the class has had an opportunity to wrap yarn around his/her finger, check the color, and respond by mentioning a way to resolve

conflicts that is represented by the color of yarn.

7 After the web is complete, explain that students will experience many conflicts in their lifetime. They should notice that the people connected to them—friends, family, and so on—have different styles of resolving conflict. Stress that it is important to resolve conflicts in healthful ways and to stay away from people who have short fuses and choose to resolve conflicts in harmful ways.

Evaluation:

Have students think of conflicts they have experienced or are experiencing with a friend at school. Have them write a description of the conflict and how the conflict might be resolved in a healthful and helpful manner.

RAPE CRISIS HOT LINE

Objective:

Students will discuss rape, acquaintance rape, rape prevention, and guidelines to follow if raped.

Life Skills:

I will practice self-protection strategies. (PF18)
I will participate in recovery efforts if a victim. (PF19)

Materials:

Self-Protection When In Social Situations transparency (page 620), transparency projector, several index cards, three telephones (optional),

Motivation:

1 To prepare for this strategy, prepare several index cards by posing a question about rape on each card. You may think of additional questions in addition to the following suggestions to use on the cards.

1 My boyfriend forced me to have sex with him. Is that rape?

2 I've just been raped and I feel dirty. What should I do?

3 I've just been raped. Is it OK to take a shower before I call the police?

4 My uncle tried to have sex with me. Is that rape?

5 There have been two rapes in my neighborhood lately. What can I do to protect myself?

6 I am a male. I had a few beers with a man who hangs around by the school. Then he tried to touch my genitals. Was I at fault?

7 I am a female. I was just having fun with a bunch of guys. Then they started getting rough and pulled at my clothes. What can I do to get out of that kind of situation?

8 My friend was raped by a friend of her boyfriend. She did not report it because she doesn't want her boyfriend to know. But she's worried. What should she do? How can I help her?

9 If I agree to have sex with my boyfriend but he treats me real rough, is that rape?

10 I have been having sex with my boyfriend but I don't want to any more. He thinks I am kidding and he continues to force me to have sex with him. Is that rape?

2 Introduce the topic of rape. **Rape** is the threatened or actual use of physical force to get someone to have sex without giving consent. Explain that rape is not always committed by a stranger. **Acquaintance rape** is rape that is committed by someone known to the victim.

3 Explain that acquaintance rape can occur on a date if sexual feelings get out of hand. To some males, aggressive sexual behavior is considered a normal part of dating and they may not realize that everyone does not feel the same way. This is the reason that it is so important to communicate your feelings and decisions with a date before you get in a situation in which it would be difficult to say NO. Explain that most acquaintance rapes are not planned. They are impulsive actions. However, the consequences can be serious and the experience can become violent even though the victim knows the rapist. Explain that many acquaintance rapes unfortunately go unreported because the victim is embarrassed or does not want to ruin a relationship.

4 Explain that rape by a person who is not an acquaintance is usually a violent experience because the rapist is motivated by anger and a desire for power over another person. Alcohol is often associated with the occurrence of rape. Explain that although females are the primary victims of rape, males also may be victims.

5 Explain that in addition to the immediate medical attention that a rape victim needs, (s)he also needs help to recover from the emotional trauma of the experience. It is important for a victim of rape to develop a support network of trusted friends and family members with whom (s)he can talk and share feelings. There are counseling and support services available in most communities.

6 Discuss what to do if a rape occurs. There are now rape crisis centers in most urban communities where help is available. The following guidelines are recommended:
  • The rape should be reported to the police as quickly as possible so that the victim can get prompt medical help. The victim should not bathe, shower, or change clothes because semen, hair, and other substances under the fingernails or on the victim's clothing may help identify an unknown rapist.
  • The victim should report any information that can be remembered about the rapist. Details about the rapist's physical characteristics, clothes, or car may prove valuable in obtaining a conviction.

7 Introduce the term self-protection strategies. **Self-protection strategies** are strategies that can be practiced to protect oneself and

decrease the risk of becoming a victim. Use the *Self-Protection Strategies* transparency to discuss strategies that would decrease their risk of becoming a victim of rape.

8 Ask for three volunteers. They are to sit in front of the class and answer calls to the "Rape Crisis" hotline. (If you do not have phones, students can pretend they have phones.) They are to answer the calls using the notes they took during the class discussion. Distribute the index cards on which you have written questions. One at a time, have students ask the question written on the cards they have. The three volunteers are to take turns answering the questions.

Evaluation:

Explain to students that a rapist has been reported in their neighborhood. (A male is raping young males, and a male is raping young females.) They are to prepare a short script that might be used on radio or television to advise young people what self-protection strategies they might use to protect themselves and what to do if rape occurs.

GETTING THE PICTURE

Objective:

Students will discuss sexual harassment and guidelines to follow with regard to sexual harassment.

Life Skill:

I will practice self-protection strategies. (PF18)

Materials:

Self-Protection When Sexually Harassed transparency (page 621), transparency projector, poster paper, a sheet for each student, crayons or markers, old magazines

Motivation:

1 Introduce the term sexual harassment. **Sexual harassment** is unwanted sexual behavior that ranges from making sexual comments to forcing another person into unwanted sex acts. Sexual harassment can occur at any level of life to both males and females, but probably more often to females. Some people are confused about what actually constitutes sexual harassment and how it differs from a healthful flirtation. In verbal form, sexual harassment could include behaviors such as comments about an individual's body, sexually explicit or demeaning jokes, sexual proposals, and requests for sexual favors. Unwanted touching, hugging, and kissing are forms of physical sexual harassment. Sexual harassment is sexual behavior that is exploitive and unlawful and should never be tolerated by either males or females in any situation.

2 Incidents of sexual harassment occur in the workplace, in the military, and, unfortunately, in schools. Most people who have been sexually harassed feel embarrassed, demeaned, intimidated, and angry about the experience. If sexual harassment occurs in a school setting between a teacher or coach and a student, the student may feel anxious about going to school and his/her school performance may suffer.

3 Explain that there are at least three distinctions between sexual harassment and a healthful flirtation. First, sexual harassment is unwanted and unwelcome. When a male or female states that (s)he is not interested in developing a relationship, having a date, or having a sexual encounter, it should be clear that any further request or advance is unwanted and unwelcome. Second, sexual harassment is degrading. Comments about an individual's body, sexually explicit or demeaning jokes, leering, and sexual proposals that are inappropriate degrade another human being. They do not promote relationships that are respectful and caring. Third, sexual advances, favors, or comments that occur because one person is in a position of authority over another can be viewed as attempts to control the other person. This is especially true when refusal will be a risk for the person being sexually harassed. Behavior in which one person manipulates and controls another does not contribute to healthful and responsible relationships.

4 Explain that victims of sexual harassment are often in vulnerable situations. They may find it difficult to respond in spite of the fact that they are very angry. If victims let time elapse between the time of sexual harassment and the time they report it, there is often misunderstanding about the victim's motive. Sometimes victims do not want to admit that they endured harassment over the period of time they did. Victims sometimes believe that they were at fault. They may wonder what they did to invite such treatment and this may lead to self-doubt. Victims may wait until a later time to report an incident when they may have more self-confidence.

5 Introduce the term self-protection strategies. **Self-protection strategies** are strategies that can be practiced to protect oneself and decrease the risk of becoming a victim. For example, if a person is uncomfortable with a particular individual, (s)he should trust his/her instincts and avoid that individual. Show the *Self-Protection When Sexually Harassed* transparency. Explain that the first five steps refer to steps a student might take with his/her parents. Steps 6 and 7 would involve getting legal advice. Stress that there has to be very specific proof of any sexual harassment charge.

6 Distribute a sheet of poster paper to students, and have them make posters. At the top of the poster, they are to write "Sexual harassment is...." Then they are to cut a picture from a magazine and tape it in the center of the poster. At the bottom of the poster, they are to complete the sentence, based on the picture they chose. Examples might be "Sexual harassment is...(picture of a telephone ad)...making obscene phone calls to another person." or "Sexual harassment is...(picture of a muddy-looking child in a detergent ad)... dragging someone through the mud and using dirty language." or "Sexual harassment is...(picture of books)...sharing sexually-provocative material with another person."

7 Have students share their posters with the class. Begin by saying that it is important for everyone to "get the picture" about sexual harassment.

Evaluation:

Explain to the class that schools and places of business have policies regarding reports of sexual harassment. Students are to pretend they are on a committee to write the section of a student handbook that deals with sexual harassment. They are to define the term, give examples, and state policies and procedures for reporting incidents of sexual harassment.

HARM-A-SIDE

Objective:

Students will discuss ways to prevent assault and homicide.

Life Skill:

I will practice self-protection strategies. (PF18)

Materials:

Small strips of paper, a strip for each student, waste basket

Motivation:

1 Before starting the strategy, prepare a strip of paper for each student. On each strip, write an example of a risk behavior that might put a person in danger. Following are some suggestions:
- Going over to a car to give a stranger directions.
- Walking alone through a vacant field.
- Spending time with people involved in drug trafficking.
- Arguing with someone who is under the influence of alcohol or other drug.
- Telling a stranger over the phone that you are home alone.
- Leaving your doors unlocked when you are home alone.
- Walking home alone late at night.
- Riding in a car in which the driver has been using alcohol or another drug.
- Accepting a ride with a stranger.
- Giving a stranger a ride.
- Leaving your car unlocked when it is parked.
- Leaving your keys in your car when it is parked.
- Disregarding the feeling that someone is following you.

- Opening the door when you are home alone and you do not know who is ringing the doorbell or knocking on the door.
- Walking home alone at night through unlighted streets because it is the shorter route.

2 Begin the strategy by introducing the terms assault and homicide. An **assault** is a physical attack or threat of attack. Assaults attempt to inflict harm and put a person in danger. **Homicide** is the accidental or purposeful killing of another person. Review some of the suggested risk behaviors in step 1 that increase the likelihood of becoming a victim of assault or homicide.

3 Introduce the term self-protection strategies. **Self-protection strategies** are strategies that can be practiced to protect oneself and decrease the risk of becoming a victim. Students should always be aware of people who might try to harm them or of situations that might involve them in dangerous or illegal activity. They should do whatever they can to protect themselves.

4 Give each student one of the strips of paper that you prepared. Explain that written on each strip of paper is an example of a risk behavior. Place a waste basket in front of the room. One at a time, the students are to come to the front of the class and read what is on his/her strip of paper. Then (s)he is to place "harm-a-side" by telling an important self-protection strategy that might be practiced rather than engaging in the risk behavior. An example might be "I will place harm-a-side by not arguing with people under the influence of drugs." (The risk behavior written on this student's strip of paper was "Arguing with someone who is under the influence of alcohol or other drug.") The student will then throw his/her strip of paper into the waste basket. As students identify self-protection strategies they will practice, you may want to keep a record of them on the chalkboard or elsewhere.

Evaluation:

Have students design a Self-Protection Strategies Checklist in which they identify 10 strategies they can follow to protect them from danger. Have them use the following format.

(   ) 1. I will not jog alone at night.
(   ) 2. I will keep the door locked when I am home alone.

The checklist can be used as a quiz to measure whether or not students can identify 10 self-protection strategies. You may want to arrange for your class to share their checklists with another class at your school. The students in the other class would check the protection strategies they are already practicing. Then your class could tabulate the answers. They might compute percentages and make bar graphs to illustrate what they have learned.

SIGNS OF SUICIDE

Objective:

Students will discuss ways to prevent suicide.

Life Skill:

I will practice suicide prevention strategies. (PF9)

Materials:

Alphabet For Sign Language student master (page 370), a copy for each student, transparency projector (optional)

Motivation:

1 Introduce the topic of suicide. **Suicide** is the intentional taking of one's own life. It is the third leading cause of death among people ages 15 to 24. Discuss the following facts about suicide:

- Thoughts. A person who is in the midst of a trying experience might have the fleeting thought, "I would be better off dead." It is a fleeting thought. However, there are young people who dwell on the thought.
- Attempts. Each year, almost one-half million young people attempt suicide. Sometimes the nature of the attempt, such as cutting oneself with a knife, allows time for treatment, which keeps the attempt from being completed.
- Completions. Approximately 5,000 people, ages 15 to 24, commit suicide each year. The most frequently used methods used in completed suicides among young people are use of a firearm, hanging, and intentional poisoning.
- Parasuicide. **Parasuicide** is nonlethal suicidal behavior by a person who does not intend to die. Usually parasuicide is a " cry

for help." The person wants others to know that (s)he is in pain and needs help.

2 Explain that *severe depression* is a major cause of suicide thoughts and attempts. **Depression** is a feeling of hopelessness, sadness, or helplessness. Everyone experiences periods of depression, but normally the periods do not last. Short periods of depression are especially common during adolescence. However, long periods of depression should be taken seriously. Explain that people who are depressed tend to withdraw from others; they may be irritable and hostile; and they may lose interest in appearance, family, and friends. Discuss the following causes of depression in young people:

- Disappointment. A young person often has high expectations of other people or of events. If someone lets him/her down, or if something (s)he was counting on does not happen, (s)he may be so disappointed that (s)he gets depressed.
- A sense of hopelessness. Adolescents may feel uncertain about their future. They may feel that they have no control over what happens to them. They may feel trapped.
- Loss of self-esteem. Some young people are perfectionists. They set unrealistic goals for themselves. Some young people feel that their parents expect too much of them and the pressure they feel is overwhelming.
- Illness. Chronic or long-term illnesses can prevent young people from participating in activities with friends. These young people feel alienated and frustrated.
- Unfair comparisons. Some young people do not have a realistic view of themselves. When they compare themselves to people they see on TV or in the movies, they come up short. They think others are

smarter, more attractive, thinner, or more successful.

3 Discuss suicide prevention strategies. **Suicide prevention strategies** are techniques that can be used to help prevent a person from thinking about, attempting, or completing suicide. Explain that the National Youth Suicide Hotline provides a 24-hour hotline staffed by trained volunteers who listen, offer support, and help with a plan of action. Another strategy is for depressed people to figure out what is bothering them and list things they might do to make themselves feel better. Another strategy is to have a network of people who will listen, offer advice and help through tough times. Getting involved in rewarding activities, such as helping others or learning a craft, is another good strategy.

4 Give each student a copy of the *Alphabet For Sign Language* master or use it as a transparency. Students are to think of a sign that a young person might be severely depressed and considering suicide. Then they are to practice signing that sign using the alphabet for sign language. For example, a student might choose the

sign "loss of interest in appearance." Then the student would practice signing the five words. The student would then sign this for the class and the class would guess what the warning sign of severe depression is.

Evaluation:

Students are to make an acrostic for the term Suicide Prevention using the information learned in this lesson. An acrostic is formed when the first letters of the term are used as the first letter of a word to begin a sentence. For example, using the first three letters of the term:

Suicide is a final choice.
Unusually high expectations can cause disappointment.
Illness can alienate a young person from his/her friends.
C....

Continue with the remaining letters of the term Suicide Prevention. Have students share their acrostics.

Alphabet For Sign Language

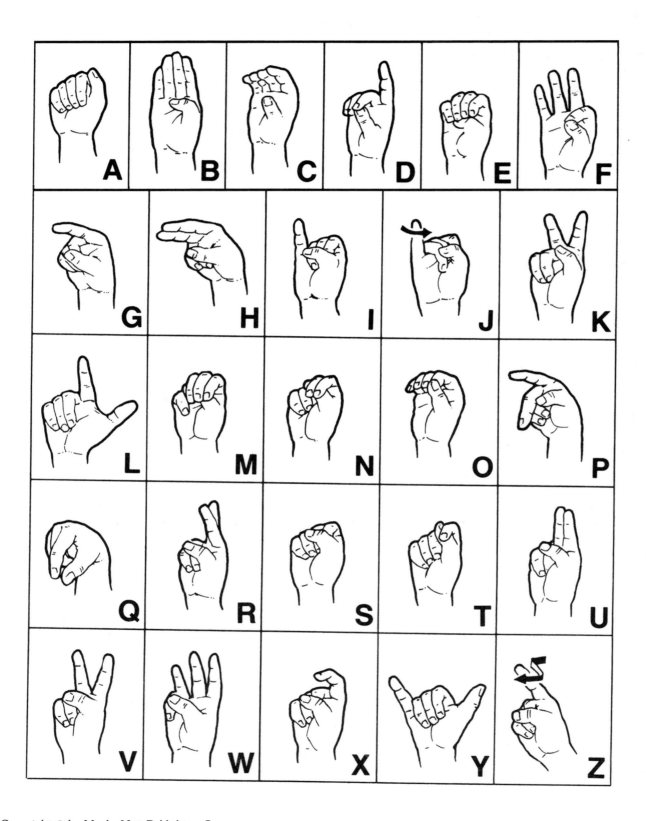

DYE-ING FROM GUNFIRE

Objective:

Students will outline procedures to follow to be safe around weapons.

Life Skill:

I will practice responsible behavior around weapons. (PF15)

Materials:

Safety Around Weapons transparency (page 612), transparency projector, large glass of water, betaine solution, vitamin C tablets dissolved in water, two droppers.

Motivation:

1 To prepare for this strategy, have the glass of water ready. Also be ready to add the betaine solution and the vitamin C with the droppers as you discuss risk factors and responsible safety tips.

2 Introduce the term risk factor. A **risk factor** is a way that a person might behave and characteristics of the environment in which a person lives that increase the likelihood of having something negative happen to a person's health, safety, and/or well-being. For example, taking a gun to school is a risk factor because that is a behavior that increases the likelihood that it might be used to harm another person. Drinking alcohol is a behavior that is a risk factor because drugs change the way a person thinks.

3 Have the class identify other risk factors such as being around drug traffickers or being by a window when there is the sound of gun shots outside. Each time a risk factor is identified, place a drop of betaine

solution in the glass that contains the water. Explain that this procedure represents the increased risk of someone "dye-ing from gunfire." Students should note that the addition of the betaine solution colors the water.

4 Discuss safety around weapons. Include safety tips that concern not only having a weapon, but also being around a person who has a weapon. Examples are: weapons should be kept in a safe place and out of the reach of children; a gun should not be pointed at another person, even in jest; and a person should leave a situation in which someone is carrying a gun. Each time a safety tip is identified, place a drop of the vitamin C solution in the water that has been colored by the betaine. Eventually, as you add drops of vitamin C solution, the color produced by the betaine solution will disappear.

5 Emphasize that by practicing responsible safety procedures around weapons, a person can help reduce the likelihood of having something negative happen.

6 Explain that the fact that many young people break the law and carry a weapon has increased the incidence of violence in the United States. These young people may carry a gun for a variety of reasons, but no matter what the reason, the risk is still present. They may have no intention of harming another person, but if they are carrying a loaded gun, it may go off accidentally. They may get into a heated argument and impulsively decide to use the weapon to settle the argument. Remind students that once the weapon is used, there is no way to cancel any injury that might have been inflicted.

7 Use the *Safety Aound Weapons* transparency to discuss safety guidelines as follows:

- <u>Do not purchase a weapon illegally.</u> Most states have laws forbidding the sale of guns to people under the age of 18.
- <u>Do not carry a concealed weapon.</u> Carrying a concealed weapon without a permit is against the law for people of any age.
- <u>Do not carry a weapon to school.</u> Protect your own safety and the safety of others by helping keep the school a safe place to be.
- <u>Encourage others to avoid buying, carrying, and/or concealing a weapon.</u> Have a positive influence on your peers.
- <u>Do not pretend you are going to use a weapon.</u> Joking about weapons may threaten others and provoke them into becoming violent.
- <u>Avoid being around people who buy, carry, conceal, or use weapons.</u> You can never be certain what will happen if another person has a weapon.
- <u>Do not argue with someone who has a weapon.</u> When you see someone who has a weapon, keep your distance. Stay calm.
- <u>Avoid being in situations in which there will be weapons.</u> Choose to be safe and stay away if you know that other students plan to carry weapons to a specific event.
- <u>If you find a weapon, leave it where you found it.</u> A weapon you find may have been used in a crime. If you pick it up, you may involve yourself needlessly.

- <u>Tell a responsible adult when you find a weapon.</u> A responsible adult will take the responsibility of removing the weapon and putting it in a safe place.

8 Review your school's policy concerning weapons with your students.

Evaluation:

Show students copies of news magazines such as *Time, U.S. News And World Reports,* or *Newsweek.* Have students write an article about weapons for a news magazine. The article should focus on a prevention program to be taught at the middle school level. Students should give the prevention program a clever name and describe the plan and some details of the program. The articles should each list at least three risk factors concerning weapons they have identified and five responsible safety tips concerning weapons. This would be an excellent opportunity for students to use computers and computer graphics.

Inclusion:

Students with special learning needs might be paired with other students to work together to peruse the magazines and plan the layout and design of the articles.

FEELING THE HEAT

Objective:

Students will discuss ways to resist pressure to belong to gangs and to participate in group acts of violence.

Life Skill:

I will resist gang membership. (PF16)

Materials:

The *Model For Using Resistance Skills* transparency (page 610), transparency projector (optional), chocolate candies that will melt when held in a hand

Motivation:

1 Introduce the term youth gang. A **youth gang** is a group of young people who band together and participate in violent, unlawful, or criminal behavior. Gangs usually have names and are territorial. They control a certain area of a city or a community. Members of a gang associate only with other members of their gang. They usually adopt certain colors of clothing so that they are easily recognized and identified as belonging to a certain gang.

2 Explain that **hard-core gang members** are the senior gang members with the most influence. **Regular gang members** are gang members who already belong to the gang and who back up the hard-core gang members. Their average age is 10 to 13. **Wanna-be's** are young persons who are not gang members, usually dress in gang colors, and engage in dangerous behavior to prove themselves to regular and hard-core gang members. Their average age is 10 to 13 and they engage in dangerous

behavior to prove themselves to the hard-core and regular members. **Could-be's** are young persons who are interested in belonging to the gang, perhaps because of a friend or family member. Initiation requirements may include drug dealing, illegal weapon activity, robbery, and beating up other people.

3 Explain that once a young person is in a gang, it is very difficult to dissociate from the gang. (S)he and his/her family may be threatened with harm or actually harmed.

4 Explain that young people join gangs for many different reasons. Some are bored and join for the excitement they think they will experience as members of a gang. Others cannot resist the pressure of peers to join a particular gang. Some young people are alienated from their families and peers and think that belonging to a gang will provide a sense of belonging. Regardless of the reason, many young people do not realize the hazards involved in being a member of a gang.

5 Ask for eight volunteers and have them come to the front of the classroom. Each volunteer is to hold out a hand. Place eight candies in each hand. Explain to the class that these eight volunteers belong to a gang and that the eight candies in each of their hands represent eight members of the gang. Have the volunteers walk around the room to show their classmates the candies in their hands. Now, ask these volunteers to make a fist in the hand that holds the candies. Tell them to keep the fists closed tightly.

6 Discuss the serious risks of belonging to a gang. Being a member of a gang often increases exposure to illicit drugs, alcohol abuse, firearms, and other weapons, fighting, dropping out of school, and arrests. A person who belongs to a gang can "feel the heat" or the pressure to conform to the rules and actions of the gang. Gang members have a record of dropping out of school and acquiring a criminal record. Gang members' families also often fear for their lives.

7 Now have the volunteers open their fists. Have students notice how the eight separate candies have changed as a result of "feeling the heat"—in this case, body heat. The candies have started to melt and stick together. Relate this to what happens to gang members and how gang psychology does not promote individual thinking.

8 Introduce the term resistance skills. **Resistance skills** are skills that are used when a person wants to say NO to an action and/or leave a situation. Resistance skills are sometimes called refusal skills. These skills can be used to effectively resist pressure to engage in actions that threaten health or safety; break laws; result in lack of respect for self and others; disobey guidelines set by responsible adults; and/or detract from character and moral values. Distribute copies of the *Model For Using Resistance Skills*, or use the transparency. Review the importance of learning skills that help a person resist peer pressure.

Evaluation:

Have students design posters with sayings that encourage peers to avoid gang membership. The posters can be displayed in your school or in the community.

DRIVING IN THE FAST LANE

Objective:

Students will examine the role that drug use and drug trafficking play in increasing the risk of violence.

Life Skill:

I will avoid alcohol and other drugs. (PF14)

Materials:

Different Types Of Drugs transparency (page 611), transparency projector, old magazines that might have pictures of race cars and other kinds of cars, scissors

Motivation:

1 To prepare for this strategy, cut out pictures of race cars and other cars from old magazines. Post the pictures around the room or circulate them. Begin a discussion of different kinds of cars. Ask students which kinds of cars are the fastest. Then discuss the kinds of people who drive cars. Which kind of drivers are more likely to be driving in the fast lane? What kinds of behaviors might you notice in people who drive in the fast lane? For example, they speed, they may take short cuts, they may break laws, they risk injury to themselves and to others. Explain that the faster these people drive and the more traffic they encounter, the greater is their risk.

2 Review the definition of drugs. **Drugs** are substances, excluding food, that alter the function of the body. Drugs not only cause damage to body organs, such as the liver, but also affect the way a person thinks and behaves. Under the influence of drugs, users can lose control of their emotions and get involved in inappropriate behaviors. Introduce the subject of drug trafficking.

Drug trafficking involves the purchasing, selling, or distribution of illegal drugs. Stress that drug trafficking is illegal. Death and bloodshed associated with drug distribution systems take a heavy toll on the participants themselves because drug trafficking usually involves the presence of deadly weapons. This violence often extends to innocent by-standers.

3 Use the *Different Types Of Drugs* transparency and the following additional information to remind students of some of the effects of using drugs.

- Alcohol. The effects of alcohol use include physical illness and diseases, such as liver damage, abnormal heart functioning, cancer, and brain damage. Alcohol also affects a person's control over his/her emotions.
- Sedative-hypnotics. These drugs contribute to assaultive or hostile behavior.
- PCP. In addition to the problems in perception, PCP use is associated with memory and speech problems, seizures, and anxiety.
- Cocaine. Cocaine use is associated with personality changes, anxiety, depression, and hostility. Cocaine use may cause irregular heart rate.
- Amphetamines. The effects of amphetamine use includes hostility, irritability, irrational mistrust of others, and impulsive behavior.
- Heroin. Use of heroin results in feelings of anger and aggressiveness, and physical dependence.
- Anabolic steroids. The effects of these drugs include high blood pressure, cancer, liver damage, and sexual problems.

- Marijuana. Marijuana use results in increased heart rate, impaired short-term memory, anxiety, and lung damage.

4 Return to the discussion of cars and drivers. Relate drivers who "drive in the fast lane" to people who get involved with drug use and/or drug trafficking. Ask students for ways that these groups of people are similar. For example, users and traffickers of drugs may take short cuts to get quick money for their drug habit, they break laws, and they risk injuring themselves and others.

5 Talk about what can happen when there is more than one driver in the fast lane. Ask students to think about the chances that two fast drivers who are fighting for position in the fast lane might collide with each other. Explain that collisions also occur in the fast lane of drug use and trafficking. People who are involved with drugs often have conflicts with other drug users and traffickers and the results can be violent.

6 Discuss the benefits of choosing to avoid alcohol and other drugs. A person who is drug-free is more likely to:
- Be in control of his/her behavior.
- Make responsible decisions.
- Desire to resolve conflicts in nonviolent ways.
- Relate well with others.
- Express emotions in healthful ways.
- Be skillful in managing stress.
- Have a positive self-image.
- Abide by laws.

Evaluation:

Have students design bumper stickers with slogans that discourage involvement in drug use and drug trafficking. Students might choose to use the pictures of cars cut from old magazines.

STAYING WITHIN THE LAWS

Objective:

Students will identify ways to reduce violence by following laws and cooperating with law enforcement authorities.

Life Skills:

I will respect authority and abide by laws. (PF17)
I will change behavior if a juvenile offender. (PF20)

Materials:

Two lengths of ropes, a blindfold, poster board, construction paper, tape, scissors, markers

Motivation:

1 Before beginning this strategy, explain that young people who do not respect authority or abide by laws often become juvenile offenders. A **juvenile offender** is a person under the age of 18 who breaks a criminal law. Many juvenile offenders recognize the risks of continuing to break laws and they get help in changing their behavior. This is an important step because if juvenile offenders do not get help, they are at risk for becoming a victim of violence. They also are at risk for losing their freedom.

2 Explain that people who respect authority and abide by laws live by a moral code. A **moral code** is a set of rules that a person follows in controlling his/her own behavior. A moral code serves as a guide that respects and protects a person's rights and respects and protects the rights of others.

3 Divide the class into six groups. Provide each group with construction paper, tape, scissors, and markers. The directions for the groups are as follows:
Group 1. One group member is to represent a person who has ill health as a result of using drugs. Other group members will "decorate" this person appropriately. For example, they might cut out black eyes to tape over this person's eyes.
Group 2. One group member is to represent a person who is involved in crime. Other members will "decorate" this person appropriately. For example, they might cut out a paper knife and tape it to the person.
Group 3. One group member is to represent a person who is in jail. Other members will "decorate" this person appropriately. For example, they might cut out bars to tape to the front of the person or make handcuffs out of tape.
Group 4. One group member is to represent a person who does not respect others. Other group members might "decorate" this person by cutting strips of paper, writing words that describe a person who does not respect the rights of others, and taping these strips of paper to the person. Appropriate words might include abusive and hostile.
Group 5. One group member is to represent a person who is not close to his/her family. Other group members will "decorate" this person appropriately. For example, the group might cut out a broken heart and tape it to the person.
Group 6. One group member is to represent a person who does not have good character and moral values. Other group members might cut out strips of paper, write words that describe a person who does not have good character and moral values, and tape these strips of paper to the person. For example, appropriate words might be liar and promiscuous.

4 While the groups are making their props, make a large target from poster board. At the center of the target, in large letters, print ABIDES BY LAWS, RESPECTS AUTHORITY. Tape the target to the chalkboard or wall at the front of the classroom.

5 When the groups have finished their props, ask the students who are representing their groups to come forward. They are to mingle in the area of the target. Ask for a volunteer and explain to this student that (s)he needs to make a decision about the use of drugs. Explain that the volunteer represents a person who does not abide by laws and does not respect authority. Blindfold the student and spin him/her around.

6 With the blindfold on, the student is to walk in the direction of the target. The representatives of the six groups will be in his/her way. When the volunteer bumps into one of the other students, the other student is to explain who (s)he is. For example, the Group 1 student might say, "I'm not healthy. I have used drugs." After the volunteer has bumped into other representatives, have

him/her take off the blindfold. Have the remaining students representing groups tell about themselves.

7 Ask for four more volunteers. They are to hold the two ropes to form a straight path toward the target. Have the students representing the six groups stand outside the two ropes. Put the blindfold on the volunteer student again, but have this student stand inside the ropes and place a hand on each of the two ropes. This llustrates that the student can use the ropes as "guide lines" to walk toward the target. Explain that the "guide lines" represent a moral code that helps a person get to the target without any serious consequences.

Evaluation:

Have students write letters to eighth grade students in another community in which they identify reasons for abiding by laws and respecting authority. The letters should include some risks of not abiding by laws and respecting authority.

GETTING BACK ON YOUR FEET

Objective:

Students will identify support systems available for people who have been victims of violence.

Life Skill:

I will participate in recovery if a victim. (PF19)

Materials:

Index cards, scissors, construction paper or cardboard paper, markers

Motivation:

1 To prepare for this strategy, write a way to recover from being a victim of violence on each of several index cards. Examples might be: meet with a support group; get help from a health clinic; get professional counseling; call a hotline for information or advice; share your feelings with a network of family members or friends; have a thorough medical examination; and learn self-protection strategies to protect yourself from becoming a victim again.

2 Introduce the term victim. A **victim** is a person who is harmed by violence. Victims suffer in many different ways. They may be permanently injured; they may suffer negative self-esteem; they may experience great fear; they may be afraid of having been exposed to HIV. Their lives are seriously affected. For example, statistics indicate that most children in inner cities have witnessed a murder and often they know the person who was murdered. These children also are victims. Discuss how such an experience might affect a child's outlook and future.

3 Introduce the topic of victim recovery. **Victim recovery** is a person's return to physical and emotional health after being harmed by violence. Explain that many people think that "time alone will heal their wounds." This is not always true. For example, victims of certain types of violence, such as domestic abuse, child abuse, and sexual abuse, who avoid recovery efforts are at risk of continuing the cycle of violence. Explain that violence is a learned pattern of behavior. If violence in a person's home or environment is an everyday experience while (s)he is growing up, violence becomes the pattern of his/her adult life also. The cycle must be broken so that the person can heal and go on to live his/her life with confidence. This is done best by seeking professional help.

4 Ask for a volunteer and have him/her come to the front of the class and stand on one foot. Explain that this person has been a victim of violence. (S)he may have been a victim himself/herself or may be a victim because a violent action involved his/her family or a friend. Have the volunteer continue to stand on one foot and explain that the volunteer has been "knocked off his/her feet" and needs support to get back on both feet.

5 Explain that the information that is written on each card is one possible road to recovery. One at a time, have a student come to the front of the class and read what is on his/her card. At the same time (s)he is to help the volunteer who is standing on his/her foot by providing a shoulder to lean on, or by providing support in some other way. As each student reads his/her card, discuss each recovery road as follows:

- <u>Meet with a support group.</u> There are many special support groups available in communities. For example, there are support groups for survivors of rape, domestic abuse, sexual abuse, and for family members of homicide victims. A victim of violence might ask the school counselor for help in finding a support group of people who have had a similar experience.
- <u>Get help from a health clinic.</u> Health clinics are available in most communities. They offer a variety of assistance, such as medical examinations and counseling.
- <u>Get professional counseling.</u> Professional counselors are trained in helping victims of violence recover. Recovery from the effects of violence may require considerable time and effort and may be costly. However, professional help may be the only road to recovery for some victims.
- <u>Call a hotline.</u> Hotlines have been set up in many communities. In some cases, a person can get information from the volunteer who answers the phone. In some cases, advice is available.
- <u>Share with a network of family members or friends.</u> It is important for victims to share feelings, thoughts, and experiences with other people. A network of family members and friends can help a victim through the recovery period.
- <u>Have a thorough medical examination.</u> Victims of violence need to care for themselves physically as well as mentally. A thorough medical examination will help determine if there has been physical harm for which treatment is necessary. It is possible that a victim might not know if (s)he has suffered a physical injury.
- <u>Learn self-protection strategies.</u> Remind students that self-protection strategies are techniques a person can practice to protect himself/herself and decrease the risk of becoming a victim. (You may wish to refer to Protective Factor 18.)

Evaluation:

Have students design bookmarks on which they identify and illustrate possible support systems for victims of violence.

NEWSWORTHY HEADLINES

Objective:

Students will identify types of violence.

Life Skill:

I will recognize that violent behavior is wrong. (PF1)

Materials:

Types Of Violence transparency (page 589), *Behavior And Violence* transparency (page 590), transparency projector, old newspapers, highlighter pens or pencils, construction paper, scissors, tape, markers, index cards, chalkboard, chalk

Motivation:

1 Introduce the topic of violence. **Violence** is the threatened or actual use of physical force to injure, damage, or destroy yourself, others, or property. A person can be a perpetrator of violence or a victim of violence. A **perpetrator** is a person who commits a violent act. A **victim** is a person who is harmed by violence.

2 Discuss the fact that violence in our society has become an everyday occurrence. Explain that constant exposure to violence in movies, on television and videotapes, and in newspaper reports can result in desensitization. **Desensitization** is the process of lessening a person's response to certain things by overexposing that person to these same things. A desensitized person sees violent acts that formerly frightened and scared him/her and does not get upset or angry or even afraid.

3 Use the *Types Of Violence* transparency to help students recognize violent behavior so that they can be encouraged to recognize that all violent behavior is wrong. Violence harms oneself and others. Remind students as you review the definitions on the transparency that violence can be the threatened or actual use of physical force.

4 Introduce the topic of behavior and explain that it is important for each student to be able to recognize types of behavior that are associated with the likelihood of violence. Use the *Behavior And Violence* transparency. Stress that people who behave passively may hold back feelings of anger. If these angry feelings build within these people, they may eventually explode with anger and become perpetrators of violence. People who behave passively also may become victims because they may not resist a perpetrator's abusive and harmful behavior.

5 Explain that on the other hand, people who behave aggressively are perpetrators; they are domineering and threaten and intimidate others. However, aggressive people may also become victims because when they threaten other people, those people may defend themselves. The result may be a fight and end up in violence.

6 Discuss the reasons that assertive behavior is a healthful choice. People who are assertive communicate clearly; they are confident; they relate well with others; and they are comfortable in expressing their thoughts without threatening others.

7 Divide the class into groups of five students. Give each group an old newspaper and highlighter pens or pencils. Ask each group to use the highlighter to mark articles in the newspapers that focus on different types of crime. Allow 10 to 15 minutes for the groups to examine their newspapers, highlight the articles that focus on crime, and read the articles they have highlighted. Use the *Types Of Violence* transparency and have students identify the types of crimes represented in the articles they highlighted. Have the class then discuss the prevalence of the types of violence that occur in your community.

8 Referring to the newspaper articles they have read, ask students to identify ways in which violence harms society. Students may mention some of the following ways:
• loss of personal property
• personal injury
• deaths of victims
• emotional harm to victims
• fear of injury or death

9 Ask students to return to their groups. Give each group construction paper, scissors, tape, and markers. The students are to replace the headlines on each of the articles they highlighted previously. Using construction paper, they are to write for each article a headline that indicates something positive about the community. They are to cut out the new headline and tape it over the previous headline.

10 After 10 to 15 minutes, have students share their revised headlines. Discuss the difference between a society in which the news is full of reports of crime and violence versus a society in which the news is full of reports of cooperation and positive actions.

Evaluation:

Devise a matching quiz using all the terms and definitions from the *Types Of Violence* transparency.

Inclusion:

Prior to giving the matching quiz using the terms and definitions from the *Types Of Violence* transparency, allow students with special learning needs an opportunity to play the match game. Print each of the terms on a separate index card and each of the definitions on a separate index card. Place all the cards face down in two stacks. Have students turn one card from each stack over at one time to try to get a match—a term and a matching definition. This will allow students the opportunity to review.

- Objective 2
- Protective 2, 3, 4, 5

VIOLENCE-PROOF VEST

Objective:

Students will identify protective factors and risk factors associated with violent behavior.

Life Skills:

I will develop positive self-esteem. (PF2)
I will strive for healthful family relationships. (PF3)
I will develop resiliency to "bounce back" if I was reared in a dysfunctional family. (PF4)
I will respond to my environment in an empowering way. (PF4)
I will develop resiliency to "bounce back" if I live in an adverse environment. (PF4)
I will develop social skills. (PF5)

Materials:

Protective Factors That Prevent Violence transparency (page 588), *Risk Factors That Promote Violence* transparency (page 587), *Ways To Develop Positive Self-Esteem* transparency (page 592), *The Nurturing Environment* transparency (page 594), *Social Skills* transparency (page 595), transparency projector, vests (any type that might be borrowed or brought from home), 12 index cards

Motivation:

1 Print one of the following types of violence on each of the 12 index cards: aggravated assault; sexual assault; emotional abuse; physical abuse; sexual abuse; kidnapping; carjacking; drive-by shooting; murder; suicide; rape; robbery.

2 If possible, have vests for about half of the students in the class. If that is not possible, the strategy can be done effectively with

vests for as few as three or four students. Ask for six volunteers. Give each volunteer two of the index cards on which you have printed a type of violence. Explain to the volunteers in confidence that the students who are wearing vests will be walking around the classroom. The volunteers also will be walking around the classroom, and they are to approach only students who are <u>not</u> wearing a vest and hand them one of the cards.

3 Explain to the class that the classroom is a community and that there is a gang in the community that engages in random violent activity. At this point, have the volunteers and the students wearing vests circulate around the classroom for three to five minutes. The volunteers will be following the directions you gave them in confidence.

4 Have students form a circle. Ask how many students were given a card. Explain that these students had contact with gang members and risked becoming victims or perpetrators of violence. Ask which students seemed to be protected. They should note that the students who were wearing vests were not given index cards.

5 Explain that the vests represented a protective factor. A **protective factor** is a way that a person might behave and characteristics of the environment in which (s)he lives that promote health, safety, and/or well-being. Use the *Protective Factors That Prevent Violence* transparency to discuss what factors might protect students from becoming victims or perpetrators of violence. Explain that students who did not wear vests were at risk.

6 Discuss risk factors. A **risk factor** is a way that a person might behave and characteristics of the environment in which a person lives that increases the likelihood of having something negative happen to a person's health, safety, and/or well-being. Use the *Risk Factors That Promote Violence* transparency to indicate what factors might make students vulnerable to becoming victims or perpetrators of violence. Explain that practicing protective factors and avoiding risk factors are responsible behaviors.

7 Call special attention to Protective Factors 2, 3, 4, and 5. Have students note that Risk Factors 2, 3, 4, and 5 are the opposite of the corresponding protective factors. Explain that it is possible for students to change risk factors to protective factors by becoming resilient. **Resiliency** is the ability to prevent or to recover, bounce back, and learn from misfortune, change, or pressure.

8 Discuss Protective Factor 2. Explain that **self-esteem** is what a person thinks or believes about himself/herself. If people who have negative self-esteem are resilient, they can work on developing positive self-esteem. Show the *Ways To Develop Positive Self-Esteem* transparency to suggest ways to do this.

9 Discuss Protective Factor 3. Explain the difference between a healthful family and a dysfunctional family. A **healthful family** is a family in which feelings are expressed openly and honestly, coping skills are adequate, and family members trust each other. A **dysfunctional family** is a family in which feelings are not expressed openly and honestly, coping skills are lacking, and family members do not trust each

other. If young people who were reared in a dysfunctional family are resilient, they might look for trusted adults who would be willing to be their mentors. A **mentor** is a person who guides and helps a younger person. In this way, the young people would have adult role models who would help them make up for the training and discipline they lacked at home. These young people can do their best in school and can choose friends who will encourage them to be at their best and develop positive self-esteem.

10 Discuss Protective Factor 4. Explain that a **nurturing environment** is a set of conditions and surroundings in which a person lives that promotes growth, development, and success. Remind students of the definition of a healthful family. Point out that a healthful family provides a nurturing environment. On the other hand, an **adverse environment** is a set of conditions and surroundings in which a person lives that interfere with growth, development, and success. Point out that a dysfunctional family provides an adverse environment. If young people who live in an adverse environment are resilient, they realize that although they cannot control their environment, they can control how they respond to their environment. They can be empowered. **Empowerment** is the belief that a person controls his/her own destiny. Use *The Nurturing Environment* transparency to challenge students to be empowered.

11 Discuss Protective Factor 5. Explain that **social skills** are skills that can be used to relate well with others. Young people who lack social skills often have difficulty relating with peers. Explain that social skills are usually learned at home at a young age and are practiced as a child grows. However, if young people who lack social skills are resilient, they can still learn social skills and how to use them effectively. Use the *Social Skills* transparency to discuss skills that are vital to relating well with others.

Evaluation:

Have students write pamphlets titled, "Are You At Risk?" in which they identify 10 risk factors that increase the likelihood of becoming a victim or perpetrator of violence.

LIFE-SAVING LYRICS

Objective:

Students will discuss the role of resiliency in dealing with hopelessness, poverty, discrimination, and other life crises.

Life Skills:

I will avoid discrimination. (PF11)
I will respect authority and abide by laws. (PF17)

Materials:

Ways To Avoid Discriminatory Behavior transparency (page 608), transparency projector, pencils, index cards, marker, tape

Motivation:

1 To prepare for this strategy, prepare the index cards. For step 7, students will each have an index card (with a word(s) printed on it) taped to his/her back. Each word(s) will indicate an example of a life crisis: loss of a job; death of a loved one; poverty; chemical dependency in the family; personal abuse; homelessness; learning difficulties; personal or family illness; natural disaster (such as earthquake or hurricane); disability due to an accident; and so on. Refer to step 7 for instructions on how the index cards will be used.

2 Explain resiliency. **Resiliency** is the ability to prevent or to recover, bounce back, and learn from misfortune, change, or pressure. People with resiliency are able to cope with misfortunes such as hopelessness, poverty, or discrimination. These people may feel angry and/or depressed about whatever life crisis they are experiencing. However, they choose not to harm themselves or others, but rather to focus on ways to go on with their lives despite the crisis. They do not focus on the problem. Their attitude is a life-saving attitude.

3 Introduce the term discriminatory behavior. **Discriminatory behavior** is making distinctions in treatment or showing behavior in favor of or prejudiced against an individual or group of people. **Prejudice** is suspicion, intolerance, or irrational hatred directed at an individual or group of people. Discriminatory behavior often results in violent behavior because those who are the target of discrimination are angry. They feel that they are treated unfairly and with disrespect. Explain that behavior that discriminates is a learned behavior. Children observe how the adults in their lives treat and respond to people who are different. They assume that the treatment they observe is acceptable and they follow suit.

4 Explain that anything that distinguishes one group from another can be divisive and can result in discriminatory behavior and prejudice. Discuss examples of groups that often are the object of discriminatory behavior, such as people with HIV/AIDS, racial groups, or people with disabilities. Students may suggest other groups.

5 Remind students that when they show respect to other people, they increase the likelihood that others will be at their best and contribute to the society in which they live. To help students to recognize behavior that discriminates against people, review the *Ways To Avoid Discriminatory Behavior* transparency. Discuss each behavior as follows:
- Challenge stereotypes. **Stereotype** is a prejudiced attitude that assigns a specific

quality or characteristic to all people who belong to a particular group. For example, a person might have an unfortunate experience with an individual who belongs to a particular ethnic group. This person then might think that everyone who belongs to that ethnic group would behave in the same manner. It is unfair to make generalizations based on stereotype. Fair treatment of others promotes nonviolence.

- Create synergy through diversity. **Synergy** is a positive outcome that occurs when different people cooperate and respect one another and, as a result, more energy is created for all. When people enjoy, appreciate, and respect all other people in their environment, they experience synergy. Synergy promotes nonviolence.
- Show empathy for all people. **Empathy** is the ability to share in another's emotions or feelings. Having empathy allows a person to understand what another individual is experiencing and to communicate to that individual by caring, helping, or encouraging.
- Avoid discriminatory comments. Words often cause emotional damage that is difficult to heal. It is better to think before speaking. Avoid making jokes at another person's expense. Avoid making snide remarks about another person. When people make a commitment to say kind and respectful comments about others, or say nothing at all, they are promoting nonviolence.
- Ask others to stop discriminatory behavior. When someone makes a discriminatory comment, it is best to express disapproval. People can make their feelings known without sounding self-righteous. In this way, others are helped to behave in ways that promote respect for others and nonviolence.
- Learn about people who are different. There are many ways to increase understanding about others: learn their language, read about other races and cultures, get to know a person as an individual.

6 Introduce the term moral code. A **moral code** is a set of rules that a person follows in controlling his/her own behavior. It is important to understand that everyone shares basic moral values, such as respect for authority and laws, that are essential for survival. Explain that people who have not developed a moral code do not understand the difference between right and wrong and do not appreciate the rights and feelings of others. Explain that these are qualities that will help people treat others fairly and with respect and also experience resiliency when they experience a crisis in their lives.

7 Divide student into groups to write songs. Decide ahead of time how many groups you want to have and how many students will be in each group. For example, if you have five groups, prepare five sets with five index cards in each set. On each set of cards, print a different crisis. The five cards in the first set might have homelessness written on them. The five cards of the second set might have poverty written on them. The five cards of the third set might have learning difficulties written on them, and so on.

8 Have students form a line and explain that you are going to tape an index card on each person's back. Explain that on each index card there is printed a type of crisis that a person might experience. After each student has an index card taped on his/her back, (s)he is to circulate and ask classmates questions in order to guess what crisis in printed on the index card that is taped to his/her back. However, there is one rule. Only questions that can be answered "yes" or no" can be asked. For example, a student might say, "Am I homeless?" If the answer is "yes," the student takes the index card from his/her back and places it on his/her front. Students continue to ask questions until everyone has guessed what his/her index card says.

9 Students will recognize that other students have the same crisis printed on their index cards. Explain that students with the same crisis are to be members of the same group for the next step.

10 Each of the groups should have paper and pencils and write "Life-Saving Lyrics" for a rap or for a song about ways to adjust to the crisis they have experienced. Their rap or song is to have a name and at least six lines. They are to think of a clever title for their rap or song and a clever title for their group. They might write an eight-line rap called "I'm no longer shakin'" and call their group "The Quakes." You may want to allow the groups 15 minutes to write their lyrics and to practice their raps or songs.

11 Have each group announce their group name and the title of their rap or song prior to performing for the class. Discuss the life-saving lyrics written by the different groups.

Evaluation:

Have students write short papers. Explain that the theme for their paper is "I cannot always control life crises, but I can control my response to them." If time permits, have students read each other's papers.

Inclusion:

Students with learning difficulties often experience anxiety, anger, and depression as they learn to cope and adjust to new styles of learning. They frequently ask "Why me?" or "Why do I have a learning disability when others my age learn so easily?" Explain that these feelings are normal, and expressing these feelings to caring adults and friends is healthful. It also is healthful to accept the challenge of learning. Provide these students with the option of writing their short paper on their response to having a learning disability.

ALIENATION

Objective:

Students will demonstrate resistance skills that are effective in resisting pressure to engage in violent behavior and/or belong to gangs.

Life Skills:

I will make responsible decisions. (PF12)
I will practice resistance skills. (PF13)
I will resist gang membership. (PF16)

Materials:

The Model For Using Resistance Skills transparency (page 610), transparency projector

Motivation:

1 To prepare for this strategy, choose a volunteer who will leave the classroom while you set up an experiment. When the volunteer has left the classroom, explain the experiment to the rest of the class.

2 Explain that you are going to ask the class several simple questions. They are to raise their hands when the answer to the question is no. If the answer is yes, they will not raise their hands. Explain that when the volunteer returns to the classroom, (s)he is also going to take part in the experiment. When the answer is no and students raise their hands, it is important that the class pretends that the answer was correct. Explain that the volunteer student will likely feel some pressure as the experiment proceeds.

3 Give students some examples of the kinds of questions you will ask. For example: does 9 x 11 = 101? They should raise their hands to indicate that the answer is *incorrect*. (The correct answer is 99.) Another example: Can

you get green paint by mixing blue and yellow paint together? The *correct* answer is yes, so they would not raise their hands.

4 Mix the questions you ask so that there is a mixture of questions to which the answers are correct and incorrect. Have the students observe the behavior of the volunteer as (s)he takes part in the experiment. Did (s)he seem confused? Did (s)he seem to want to raise his/her hand when the others did? How long did it take him/her to figure out what was going on? Ask the volunteer to share how (s)he felt while taking part in the experiment. Did (s)he like it when (s)he answered correctly and no one else was raising a hand? Would (s)he prefer to be doing whatever the rest of the class was doing?

5 You may choose to extend the experiment by using a simple signal to direct the class (other than the volunteer) to sometimes raise their hands for a correct answer. For example, you might raise your hand to your head when you want them to raise their hands for a correct answer. This would add to the pressure on the volunteer.

6 Review the definition of peer pressure. **Peer pressure** is the pressure that people of similar age or status exert on others to encourage them to make certain decisions or behave in certain ways. Explain that peer pressure is not always verbal. It does not always involve one person or persons trying to persuade another person to do something. Peer pressure can be nonverbal. It can involve a situation in which a person really wants to be like the others in a group and will go along with whatever is being done, without any persuasion. This classroom experiment is an example of nonverbal peer pressure.

7 Discuss decision-making skills and resistance skills. People who have decision-making skills know how to make decisions that protect health; protect safety; protect laws; follow guidelines set by responsible adults; and demonstrate good character and moral values. **Resistance skills** are skills that are used when a person wants to say NO to an action and/or leave a situation. Resistance skills are also referred to as refusal skills. Decision-making skills and resistance skills work together to help a person effectively resist decisions to engage in actions that threaten health; threaten safety; break laws; result in lack of respect for self and others; disobey guidelines set by responsible adults; and detract from character and moral values.

8 Use *The Model For Using Resistance Skills* transparency to discuss how a person can cope with peer pressure to engage in violent behavior. For example, a student may be pressured to join a youth gang. A **youth gang** is a group of young people who band together and participate in violent, unlawful, or criminal activity. Being a member of a gang increases a person's exposure to illegal drugs, alcohol abuse, firearms and other weapons, fighting, dropping out of school, and being arrested and imprisoned. Pretend that a student in the class is being pressured to join a gang. Use the steps in the Model to illustrate how (s)he should resist pressure to join a group that participates in violence.

Evaluation:

Have students respond to the following letter to Dear Helper, providing specific skills they would use to resist the pressure that the anonymous student is experiencing.

Dear Helper,
  My friend has joined a gang and now wants me to join also. He says he decided to join because the members of the gang will give him support dealing with other students who have been bothering him. I don't think my friend realizes what he will have to do as a gang member. I am concerned about my friend and do not want to do anything to lose his friendship. What can I do? I've never wanted to belong to a gang, but some of his arguments are very appealing. And after all, he is a friend.

Sincerely,
Concerned.

LETTING THE AIR OUT

Objective:

Students will examine ways in which unexpressed anger contributes to violence.

Life Skills:

I will practice anger management skills. (PF6)
I will participate in physical activity. (PF8)

Materials:

Hidden Anger transparency (page 599), *Anger Management Skills* transparency (page 600), *Benefits Of Physical Activity* transparency (page 603), transparency projector, rubber ball, sealant or patch, air pump

Motivation:

1 Show students the ball. Bounce the ball a few times. Explain that the bouncing ball represents life's ups and downs. Explain to students that the ball you are using always bounces back. Further, explain that people have ups and downs as they journey through life. People can be like the ball — they can bounce back when they experience difficulties and misfortunes if they know how to express their feelings in healthful ways.

2 Now puncture the ball with a hole small enough that it can easily be patched. The puncture represents a circumstance or event that causes hurt feelings and anger. Review the definition of anger. **Anger** is the feeling of being irritated, annoyed, and/or furious. Anger is a temporary state experienced in response to being hurt or frustrated. The hurt can be emotional, psychological, social, and/or physical. **Anger triggers** are thoughts or events that cause a person to become angry. Ask students to provide exam-

ples of anger triggers, such as being criticized by a friend, or being blamed for something that they did not do. Point out that as the air was leaving the ball, the ability of the ball to bounce back was seriously affected. Explain that the manner in which people deal with anger is extremely important to their total health – physical, mental, and social.

3 Explain that *everyone* experiences feelings of anger. What is important is how a person expresses the anger. First, it is important to recognize anger cues. **Anger cues** are changes in the body or signs that a person is angry. Anger cues may include acceleration of heart rate, dryness of the mouth, and facial signs such as knitted eyebrows, pursed lips, and flushing of the face. Ask students for other examples of anger cues they notice when they feel angry. Explain that it is all right to feel angry but that angry feelings should not be expressed in ways that harm self and others. Discuss harmful ways to let out feelings of anger: damaging property; hitting and physically hurting another person; and hurting oneself by choosing to use alcohol or drugs. Ask students for other illustrations.

4 Discuss hidden anger. **Hidden anger** is anger that is not dealt with in a healthful way and may result in inappropriate behavior and poor health. Explain that hidden anger may be exhibited in many ways and that people may not be aware that they are hiding angry feelings. Review the information on the *Hidden Anger* transparency. There are many emotional and physical consequences of hiding anger. People who do not learn how to express anger in healthful ways harm not only themselves but also others. Hidden anger often harms health status. Hidden anger may contribute to ulcers, high blood pressure, headaches, and to the development of psychosomatic illnesses. Most important, hidden anger also can contribute to violent actions. Hidden angry feelings begin to multiply and eventually this hidden anger cannot be contained. It overflows and may result in a violent situation.

5 Explain that anger that is expressed in healthful ways has the opposite effect. Illustrate this by patching the puncture with a sealant or with a patch and reinflating the ball. The sealant or patch illustrates that healing has taken place. Explain to students that a "scar" remains on the ball. However, the scar is no longer an open wound. Explain that everyone experiences difficulties and misfortunes. However, the response to these difficulties and misfortunes is what determines whether or not a person maintains positive health status. People who stay angry and who express their anger in destructive ways go through life with "open wounds." They remain vulnerable or open to more difficulties. People who express their anger in healthful ways are trying to work through a situation and move on in life. Eventually, they form a "scar" to indicate healing has taken place.

6 Show the students the part of the ball that has been patched. Explain that there is a term to explain the ability to express feelings and heal when life circumstances are difficult. **Resiliency** is the ability to prevent or to recover from, bounce back, and learn from misfortune, change, or pressure. Hidden anger interferes with resiliency. When people have angry feelings inside, they have a puncture that remains as an open wound.

7 Using the *Anger Management Skills* transparency, discuss the healthful ways to ex-

press anger. Discuss how each of these skills can be used to express anger in healthful ways:

- Keeping an anger self-inventory. The Anger Self-Inventory (Figure 16) can help students evaluate their angry feelings and determine which anger management skills would be appropriate.
- Using self-statements for anger control. Self-statements are positive statements students can use to help them stay in control when they become angry. Students should memorize and rehearse several self-statements such as "Take some deep breaths and relax" and "I'm not going to let him get to me."
- Participating in vigorous physical activities. Vigorous physical activity, such as dancing, jogging, and swimming, can work to defuse anger and relieve tension by providing a physical outlet for the energy that builds up with anger.
- Using physical expression to blow off steam. Physical expression, such as punching a pillow, squeezing a tennis ball, or screaming into a pillow, can channel the extra energy provided by the anger response.
- Using I-Messages and Active Listening. Using an I-message is a healthful way to express feelings because it focuses on what a person is feeling and does not place blame on the listener. The steps of an I-message are: I feel (emotion) when you (the other person's behavior) because (the effect it had on you). Active listening helps confirm that another person's feelings are understood and helps keep communication positive.
- Keeping a Sense of Humor. Finding the humor in a situation and laughing at self in a good-spirited manner can help defuse anger.

- Expressing yourself through creative activities. When it is difficult to put feelings of anger into words, drawing a picture depicting the person's feelings can help defuse anger.
- Talking with parents and mentors. When people feel anger triggers and cues, sharing their feelings with appropriate adults and mentors can help these people recognize what they are feeling, why they are feeling this way, and what are healthful ways to cope with those feelings. A **mentor** is a person who guides and helps younger people.
- Writing letters to express angry feelings. Writing a letter that may or may not be sent to another person helps defuse anger by providing a means of expression other than approaching another person. It provides the time needed to clearly communicate feelings.
- Planning ahead to deal with your anger. People can rehearse lifelike situations in advance and test different approaches to conflict and examine how they might express anger in a situation without losing control and doing something they might later regret.

8 Review the benefits of participating in physical activity using the *Benefits Of Physical Activity* transparency. As you discuss each benefit, stress the following:

- Maintaining physical fitness. An exercise program of just 25 minutes three days a week for seven weeks will make a difference in the way a person feels about himself/herself. (S)he will be less at risk to behave in violent ways.
- Making constructive use of your time. Participating in a regular routine of physical activities and/or recreation is a positive way to spend time.

- Defusing anger and aggression. Physical exercise is an outlet for the tension created by feelings of anger and a person is less likely to express the anger in inappropriate or violent ways.
- Managing stress. Participating in physical activities and/or recreation helps take a person's mind off the causes of his/her stress.
- Developing social skills. Participating in physical activity and recreation helps develop social skills, such as cooperating with others and easing feelings of loneliness.
- Feeling a sense of belonging. Participating in a physical activity or recreation program is a way to meet and to get to know people who share your interests and talents.
- Abiding by rules. Participants in physical activity and recreation programs learn to abide by rules and to respect authorities.
- Learning to accept defeat. Participants in physical activity and recreation programs learn the importance of sportsmanship because they learn ways to handle defeats.
- Improving self-image. Regular exercise improves a person's physical appearance and self-image as (s)he learns new skills.
- Practicing self-discipline. Physical activities require a person to set goals and identify ways to reach those goals by a training program.

Evaluation:

Have students write a short paper describing a recent anger trigger. Have them choose five of the anger management skills and discuss how each could have been used to help them express their anger in healthful ways.

Inclusion:

Discuss the questions: How do people "puncture" people who have special learning needs? Explain that these people may become frustrated and angry when they are teased by their peers or are labeled "slow" because they take longer to complete a task. Discuss the questions: When these situations happen, how do these people often express their anger? How can these people be helped to heal and to gain resiliency?

What's My Conflict Resolution Style?

Objective:

Students will describe effective means of conflict resolution and peer mediation to avoid fighting.

Life Skills:

I will practice stress management skills. (PF7)
I will practice conflict resolution and peer mediation skills. (PF10)

Materials:

Conflict Resolution Skills transparency (page 606), *The Process Of Peer Mediation* transparency (page 607), transparency projector, three index cards, chalkboard, chalk

Motivation:

1 Explain to students that life without conflict is not possible and that conflict is a stressor. Remind students that a **stressor** is a demand that causes a change in the body. Response to conflict or any other stressor can be either helpful or harmful. For example, arguing over differences is not an effective way to respond to conflict. Nothing gets settled. The focus is on emotions rather than on the conflict, and arguing generates angry and confrontational behavior. As anger builds, a person's behavior can become out of control. Remind students that stress management skills help a person respond, cope with, and prevent the harmful effects of a stressor.

2 Explain that in childhood most people learn ways of responding to conflict from their families. They may not even be aware of the fact that they have a conflict response style because responding to conflicts, no mat-

ter what the conflict is, becomes a habit. A **conflict response style** is a pattern of behavior a person demonstrates when conflict arises. Explain that it is never too late to change an old habit (style) and learn a new one. There are three basic conflict response styles.

- **Conflict avoidance** is a conflict response style in which a person denies that there is a conflict and/or attempts to accommodate others at his/her expense. (S)he will do anything to avoid a conflict. A person who chooses this style allows another person to resolve the conflict. (S)he may be choosing to avoid conflict rather than risk becoming the victim of more abusive or violent behavior.

- **Conflict confrontation** is a conflict response style in which a person attempts to settle a disagreement in a hostile, defiant, and aggressive way. A person who demonstrates this style wants to "win" or be right at any cost. This person has to be in control. (S)he resists being dominated by others and "losing" is not tolerated.

- **Conflict resolution** is a conflict response style in which a person uses conflict resolution skills to resolve a disagreement in a healthful and responsible way. A person who demonstrates this style views conflict as necessary and important. (S)he understands that conflict can be resolved without having a "winner" and a "loser" because everyone wins.

3 Introduce the terms conflict resolution skills and peer mediation. **Conflict resolution skills** are skills a person can use to resolve a disagreement in a healthful, safe, legal, respectful, and nonviolent way. If the two or more persons involved in a conflict cannot successfully resolve the conflict, they may use peer mediation. **Peer mediation** is a process used to resolve conflicts in which a person helps his/her peers resolve disagreements in healthful, safe, legal, respectful, and nonviolent ways. A **peer** is a person who is equal in age or status. In peer mediation, a peer maintains a neutral position as (s)he brings the persons in conflict together in an effort to resolve the disagreement. The skills used in peer mediation are very similar to conflict resolution skills.

4 Use the *Conflict Resolution Skills* transparency first. Discuss each skill. Stress that by using these skills, many conflicts can be resolved in mutually satisfactory ways. Then use *The Process Of Peer Mediation* transparency and discuss the steps of that process. If your school does not have a peer mediation program, you may decide to initiate one.

5 On each of the three index cards, write the name of a different conflict resolution style. Ask for three volunteers to play a game similar to "What's My Line?" The three students will each select a card and will not tell the class what is written on the cards they have. You will read one of the following scenarios to the class. Each volunteer will tell how (s)he would resolve the conflict using the style indicated on his/her card. After the three volunteers have responded, the class will guess which styles were demonstrated. The following are suggested scenarios. (You also may choose to use your own scenarios that would be more applicable to your situation.)

Buddy did not do a history assignment last night. He knew that David would get his assignment done, and besides, there was something else Buddy wanted to do last night. He figured David would give in again. The fact is that David is tired of letting Buddy copy his assignments. He told Buddy the last time this happened that he wouldn't let him copy another assignment. This morning, Buddy asked David for his assignment so that he could copy it.

Carol loaned a sweater to Molly to wear on a special date. Now, Molly keeps wearing the sweater to school and when Carol tells Molly to give it back, Molly keeps saying she will bring it to school tomorrow. But every time this happens, Molly says she forgot to bring the sweater. Carol and Molly are on the same track team, and Carol realizes how important it is for them not to have any disagreements during track season. However, she wants that sweater back and so far, no matter how hard she has tried, she hasn't been successful.

Jose and his brother Pedro have some responsibilities in the morning between the time their parents leave for work and the time Jose and Pedro leave for school. The family depends on their helping in the morning. Lately, Pedro has been leaving everything for Jose to do. Pedro says that he shouldn't have to help and that if Jose tells their parents, he will get even with him. Jose knows that his parents are depending on him and Pedro, and he knows that his parents are struggling to keep the family together. So lately, Jose has been doing not only his chores, but also Pedro's. He resents it that Pedro won't help, but he doesn't want to get Pedro in trouble with his parents. And he's tired of doing Pedro's share of the work.

6 Discuss the ways in which the three volunteers resolved the conflict described in the scenario. Ask the following questions. Which of the three styles (if any) would effectively resolve the conflict? Which style would best resolve the conflict if the other person was your best friend? What if the other person was someone you needed to maintain a good relationship with for some reason?

7 Collect the cards. Repeat the activity with three different volunteers and a different scenario. After each scenario, use the suggested questions in step 4, or use your own questions so that the class can examine the effects each conflict resolution style would have.

Evaluation:

Have students write a short description of their personal style of resolving conflicts. Have them decide which of the three represents their style. In their report, they should evaluate their style and determine what they need to change in order to respond to conflict in an effective way.

Inclusion:

Have students with special needs identify some of the kinds of conflicts they experience. Have them apply the three conflict response styles to each of the conflicts they identify.

WHEEL OF HARASSMENT

Objective:

Students will describe guidelines to follow when sexual harassment occurs.

Life Skill:

I will practice self-protection strategies. (PF18)

Materials:

Self-Protection When Sexually Harassed transparency (page 621), transparency projector, chalkboard, chalk

Motivation:

1 Introduce the term sexual harassment. **Sexual harassment** is unwanted and unwelcome sexual advances that range from sexual innuendos to coerced sexual behavior. This includes any activity that threatens or bothers a male or a female, such as sexual remarks, obscene jokes, physical touches, unwelcome phone calls, letters, or pressures for a date. Sexual harassment that gets out of control can become violent. Both males and females can be victims of sexual harassment.

2 Discuss the characteristics of sexual harassment. First, it is an activity that is not wanted by the victim. A person should make it clear that (s)he does not care for what is happening. Second, it is degrading. Comments about an individual's body, jokes that are inappropriate, or sexual proposals do not show respect and they affect a person's self-esteem. Third, harassing activities can be viewed as attempts to control another person. These characteristics are different from those that apply to responsible

relationships with members of the opposite sex. Males and females both like to flirt and tease. However, they maintain their self-respect and show respect for others.

3 Use the *Self-Protection When Sexually Harassed* transparency as a basis for a discussion. Discuss each item in the list as follows:
• <u>Ask the person who is harassing you to stop.</u> Be direct about what behavior is bothering you. Explain that it makes you uncomfortable.
• <u>Document the harassment.</u> Write down when the harassment occurred, exactly what happened, and your response to the harassment.
• <u>Get witnesses, if possible.</u> Document anything that anyone saw or heard.
• <u>Discuss the situation with your parents and/or other trusted adults.</u>
• <u>Follow the procedures in your school's policy on sexual harassment.</u> File a grievance with the appropriate person. This may be a boss on the job or a teacher or a school counselor.
• <u>If the harassment persists, think about legal</u> action. You may need to contact an attorney.

4 Introduce the term self-protection strategies. **Self-protection strategies** are techniques a person can practice to protect himself/herself and decrease the risk of becoming a victim. Explain that a person can protect himself/herself in three basic ways.
• First, always trust your instincts about people and about situations. If you have a gut feeling that a person or situation is dangerous, trust your instincts. Avoid the person and/or situation, if possible.
• Second, always be on the alert. Pay close attention to the people who are near you.
• Third, learn specific ways to stay safe. Do not take your safety for granted. You are

at risk when you think you could never be a victim.

5 Explain that many businesses have regulations and procedures that deal with sexual harassment that occurs in connection with a person's employment. You may want to suggest that students find news articles that deal with recent cases of sexual harassment. Post them on the bulletin board.

6 Explain to students that they are going to play a game similar to "Wheel of Fortune." Divide the class into two teams. You will choose a term that represents a form of harassment and on the chalkboard you will indicate blanks for each letter in the term you chose. The following terms are suggested for use in this game: acquaintance rape; suggestive remarks; sexual pictures; pinching; sexual jokes; sexual body motions; unwelcome kisses; sexual threats; touching; and sexual rumors.

7 Each member of a team has a turn to select a letter in an effort to discover what the term is. The first student picks a letter. If that let-

ter appears in the term, you (or a student) should fill in the appropriate blank(s). The student gets another turn if his/her first letter appeared in the term. After each successful turn, the student has the option of guessing what the term is or choosing another letter. If the student chooses a letter that does not appear in the term or if (s)he guesses incorrectly, a student from the other team takes a turn. Teams win points for each correctly identified term.

Evaluation:

Have students design a handout that includes information about sexual harassment and the guidelines for dealing with sexual harassment.

Inclusion:

Students with special needs are often the victims of sexual harassment. Ask for student volunteers to work with them to draw up their own set of guidelines for dealing with situations in which they feel threatened or harassed.

PROTECT YOURSELF

Objective:

Students will describe ways to prevent rape and guidelines to follow when rape occurs.

Life Skills:

I will practice self-protection strategies. (PF18)

I will participate in recovery if a victim. (PF19)

Materials:

Self-Protection When In Social Situations transparency (page 620), a copy for each student, transparency projector, a tape or disc of the song "R-e-s-p-e-c-t" sung by Aretha Franklin, tape player or CD player

Motivation:

1 Introduce the topic of rape. **Rape** is the threatened or actual use of physical force to get someone to have sex without giving consent. The rape may be oral, anal, or vaginal penetration that occurs without consent through force, intimidation, coercion, or deception. It is estimated that between 15 and 25 percent of females experience rape. Explain that rape is not always committed by a stranger. Acquaintances also commit rape. **Acquaintance rape** is rape that is committed by someone known to the victim.

2 Explain that many cases of rape go unreported for many different reasons. There may be fear of retaliation, publicity, or embarrassment, or fear of ruining a relationship. Rape is a behavior that usually is motivated by a combination of power, anger, and the desire for sexual gratification. When rape is committed by a person unknown to the victim, power and anger are likely to be the dominant motivating factors. This type of rape often is interpreted as an act of violence and domination that is expressed in a sexual manner rather than as an attempt to seek sexual gratification. The occurrence of rape often is associated with the consumption of alcohol.

3 Explain that acquaintance rape often occurs in a dating situation and is more likely to be impulsive rather than planned. Acquaintance rape is likely to be motivated by the desire for sexual gratification. Often the perpetrator and the victim view what happened quite differently. To some males, forceful sexual behavior is considered a normal part of courtship. Some males may misinterpret actions such as cuddling and kissing as indications of a desire to engage in intercourse. Honest communication skills are needed to avoid potentially harmful situations. Explain that although females are the primary victims of rape, males also may be raped.

4 Use the *Self-Protection When In Social Situations* transparency and discuss the 14 guidelines with the class.

5 Explain that these guidelines are self-protection strategies. **Self-protection strategies** are strategies that can be practiced to protect oneself and decrease the risk of becoming a victim. Give students a chance to comment or to ask questions.

6 Discuss what to do if a person becomes a victim of rape. The decision about whether or not to report a rape is a personal matter. However, it is important to remember that the information provided about a rape or attempted rape may prevent another person from becoming a victim. Even if rape is not reported, the victim should be tested for HIV infection. HIV is the virus that causes AIDS. The victim also should be tested for other sexually-transmitted diseases. There are two extremely important reasons to report a rape:

- Prompt medical attention is obtained. The rape survivor should not bathe or change clothes. Semen, hair, and materials under the victim's fingernails and on his/her clothing may help identify the perpetrator.
- Information about the perpetrator is documented. In particular, details about his/her physical characteristics, clothes, or car may prove valuable in obtaining a conviction.

7 Victims of rape and other violent acts often experience feelings of anger, fear, shock, confusion, and depression. In many instances, they blame themselves for what happened. Many people who have been raped choose to seek professional recovery help. The goal of victim recovery is to help the victim survive the pain, heal, and move forward with self-confidence. Some suggestions to help a victim recover are to develop a support network of family and friends; to seek counseling; and to join a support group of other victims of rape. There are now rape crisis centers in most urban communities.

8 Play the song "Respect." Discuss the words of the song with the students. After listening to the song, divide the students into groups and have each group write lyrics for a similar song entitled "Protect Yourself" using information learned from the class discussion and from the self-protection strategies. Students are to use the tune of "Respect." Have each group sing or recite their lyrics. Point out any different emphases that the different groups used in creating their lyrics.

Evaluation:

Have each student write a letter to a friend who has moved to a new area and is meeting new friends. The letter should give advice about new relationships and guidelines for self-protection strategies to avoid being raped.

SAFETY AROUND GUNS

Objective:

Students will describe guidelines to follow when there are weapons in the environment.

Life Skill:

I will practice responsible behavior around weapons. (PF15)

Materials:

Safety Around Weapons transparency (page 612), transparency projector, poster paper, a sheet for each student, markers, old newspapers

Motivation:

1 Introduce the topic of weapons. A **weapon** is an instrument or device used for fighting. A weapon is used to injure, defeat, or destroy. Guns and knives are the most commonly used weapons. Because guns are such deadly weapons, most states have laws about the possession and use of guns. In most states, it is illegal to sell a gun to anyone under the age of 18. However, laws forbid people of any age from carrying a concealed weapon without a permit. Most states also have laws that prohibit students from carrying guns to school.

2 Explain that many people possess guns illegally. Unfortunately, many of these people do not know how to use the guns and consequently are apt to have accidents with them. Many people possess guns for only one reason, to harm others. Carrying a weapon such as a gun increases a person's risk that (s)he will seriously injure or murder another person or be seriously injured and killed himself/herself.

3 Explain that even though a person does not intend to use his/her gun to physically harm another person, (s)he is taking a risk. The person may get into a heated argument and decide impulsively to use the gun to settle the argument. Or perhaps the person with the gun decides to intimidate or threaten another person. If the other person decides to resist the threat, the person with the gun may panic and start shooting. Emphasize that for whatever reason a person carries a weapon, the most responsible action to take is to get away from that person.

4 Discuss some of the legal reasons for owning a gun. For example, many sportsmen own registered guns for target shooting or for hunting; many civilians own registered guns to protect themselves or their families; law enforcement personnel and security guards carry guns; and people in some branches of the military are trained to use weapons.

5 Explain that because weapons are so dangerous, it is very important for students to be aware of protecting themselves against possible injury and death. Using the *Safety Around Weapons* transparency, discuss responsible ways of keeping safe as follows:
• <u>Do not purchase a weapon illegally.</u> People under the age of 18 cannot legally purchase a gun.
• <u>Do not carry a concealed weapon.</u> Laws are designed to protect you. Do not take risks that threaten not only your health and life, but also the health and life of others.
• <u>Do not carry a weapon to school.</u> You need your education. Do not risk the opportunities you have. School should be a safe place.
• <u>Encourage others to avoid buying, carrying, and/or concealing a weapon.</u> Have a positive influence on your peers. The fewer

weapons there are in a community, the less likelihood that there will be violence.

- <u>Do not pretend you are going to use a weapon.</u> Pretending may be misinterpreted. Don't joke about anything as potentially dangerous as weapons.
- <u>Avoid being around people who buy, carry, conceal, or use weapons.</u> There is no way to be certain about what can happen if another person has a weapon. People who deal with weapons may be involved in criminal activities.
- <u>Do not argue with someone who has a weapon.</u> Keep your distance. Do not provoke this person or get into an argument with him/her.
- <u>Avoid being in situations in which there will be weapons.</u> If you know that some people are going to carry weapons to a certain event, stay away.
- <u>If you find a weapon, leave it where you found it.</u> The weapon may be one that was used in a crime. Besides possibly injuring yourself, you may wipe out fingerprints that would be important to solving a crime. Don't touch it.
- <u>Tell a responsible adult when you find a weapon.</u> The weapon needs to be re-moved safely. Let a responsible person, such as a law enforcement officer, know where you saw the weapon so that (s)he can put it in a safe place.

6 Allow time for students to look through old newspapers and cut out items concerning incidents involving guns or other weapons. Point out that many accidental deaths occur from careless use or storage of guns. Using poster paper, have students create a message concerning weapons and responsible safety guidelines concerning weapons. They may direct their message to younger students, to parents, or to the community in general. They may choose to use drawings, such as cartoons, in addition to a printed message.

Evaluation:

Students are to write a checklist for responsible weapon safety. The checklist should contain at least 10 statements written as life skills. For example, a responsible life skill would be "I will never pick up another person's gun because it might be loaded." Review each student's checklist in class.

A-SALT

Objective:

Students will describe strategies to prevent assault and homicide.

Life Skill:

I will practice self-protection strategies. (PF18)

Materials:

Salt

Motivation:

1 Ask if there is a student in the class who has a cut on his/her hand. (If not, you can describe a cut and ask students to remember how it feels to have a cut.) Ask the student if (s)he will let you rub salt on the cut. The student will know that rubbing salt on a cut would sting and hurt. Explain that A-Salt (assault) is a crime that wounds another person and causes great harm. Define assault. An **assault** is a physical attack or threat of attack. An assault is intended to inflict harm on a person and puts the person in danger. An assault injury is any physical or body harm that occurs during the course of a rape, robbery, or any other type of attack on a person.

2 Discuss homicide. **Homicide** is the accidental or purposeful killing of another person. Most homicide victims know their assailants. In fact, one in six homicides occurs within families, primarily among young adults. Homicide is the leading cause of death for African-Americans ages 15 through 34. Homicide between inti-

mates is often preceded by a history of physical and emotional abuse.

3 Discuss who is likely to be a victim of an assault. For example, poor people are at great risk of becoming victims of a violent crime. This risk is increased for elderly people who live alone in high crime neighborhoods. Often the victim knows the perpetrator. Except for rape and petty larceny (purse snatching), males are more apt to be the victims of assaults.

4 Discuss where and when assaults are more apt to take place. For example, crime rates tend to be higher in cities than in suburbs and rural areas, although crime rates are increasing there also. Crime rates are high in older, low-income neighborhoods in large cities. Robberies of homes take place more often in the daytime while robberies of businesses take place mostly at night. Weekends are times of higher rates of many types of assaults such as homicide and rape. Weekend crimes are more apt to be associated with the use of alcohol and drugs. Violence may occur as a consequence of the pharmacological effects of drugs or of economically motivated crimes to support drug use, or interactions related to the manufacture, buying and/or selling of drugs. Other factors are the availability of guns and the effect of viewing violence on television.

5 Introduce the term self-protection strategies. **Self-protection strategies** are strategies that can be practiced to protect oneself and decrease the risk of becoming a victim. Although it is impossible to prevent all acts of violence, practicing self-protection strategies will greatly increase a person's chances of staying protected. There are many situations in which students should be aware of protecting themselves.

6 Discuss protection at home. Following are some recommended tips:
- Do not give your house key to anyone other than to a trusted friend.
- Do not hide extra keys outside your home.
- Never let a stranger into your home.
- Ask to see identification before allowing a repair person to enter your home.
- Be cautious about giving out information on where you live either in person or on the phone to a stranger.
- Report continuous obscene or bothersome telephone calls to the telephone company or police.
- Keep a list of emergency telephone numbers such as for police or fire.

7 Discuss protection when caring for children. Following are some recommended tips:
- Never open the door to strangers.
- Ask the children's parents (or other regular caretakers) what to do in emergency situations.
- Never tell anyone who calls on the telephone that you are alone with the children.
- Never leave a young child unattended outside the home for even a brief period of time.

8 Discuss protection while driving or riding in cars. Following are some recommended tips:
- Always park in a well-lighted area where there are other people and other cars.
- Never leave keys in the ignition and the engine running.

- Do not allow yourself to run out of gas.
- Try to drive in safe, well-lighted areas at night.
- Keep a flashlight and road flares in the trunk of your car.
- Be cautious of anyone approaching your car when it is stopped.

9 Discuss protection when in public places. Following are some recommended tips:
- Avoid walking alone at night or in high-risk areas.
- Never hitchhike.
- Never accept a ride from a stranger or someone you do not trust.
- Walk briskly with your head up and move in a confident manner.
- Do not talk to strangers who approach you.
- Carry a whistle or buzzer to attract attention if you need help.
- Only use pay telephones that are in populated, well-lighted areas.
- When you use a public telephone, do not have your back to a street or a lobby; have your back to the telephone.

10 Discuss protection when jogging. Following are some recommended tips:
- Avoid jogging alone, at night, and in isolated and secluded areas.
- Vary your jogging routes and routines.
- Run in the opposite direction and run to a populated area if you are harassed by someone in a car.
- Carry identification and change to make a telephone call.

11 Discuss protection while socializing. Following are some recommended tips:
- When dating someone for the first time, do so in a group situation or public place.
- Do not use alcohol or any other drug.

- Set limits for expressing affection, and communicate these limits to others.
- Avoid behavior that might be interpreted as sexually teasing or seductive.
- Be aware of the warning signs of a potential perpetrator: disrespectful attitude toward you; dominating attitude; obsessive jealousy; unnecessary physical roughness; and a history of violent and/or abusive behavior.

12 Discuss self-defense techniques. **Self-defense techniques** are techniques that can be used when someone is harming or threatening to harm a person. Suggest to students that they get information about self-defense courses that are offered by qualified instructors in your community. These courses allow a person to learn how to act in a crisis and to rehearse replacing fear with anger when threatened with an attack.

Evaluation:

Have students list in writing at least 10 protective strategies for protecting themselves from assaults. For example, I will carry a whistle or some other sort of noise maker to use if I am being followed.

SUPPORT NETWORK

Objective:

Students will describe suicide prevention strategies.

Life Skill:

I will practice suicide prevention strategies. (PF9)

Materials:

Suicide Prevention Strategies transparency (page 604), transparency projector, index cards, pens or pencils, ball of yarn

Motivation:

1 Introduce the topic of suicide. **Suicide** is the intentional taking of one's own life. It is a leading cause of death in children, pre-teens, and adolescents. Children and pre-teens who are vulnerable to suicide are those who are poorly treated at home, who desire to punish their parents, who are worried that they will be severely punished for their rebellious behavior, who are having difficulties in school, and/or who have worries about their physical appearance/health. Adolescents who are vulnerable to suicide are those who abuse alcohol and other drugs, have experienced the death of a parent or marital separation or divorce of their parents, have feelings of alienation from family and friends, fear independence, are the subject of ridicule or isolation from peers, and/or have difficulty in coping with body changes and sexuality.

2 Because many young people who attempt suicide are experiencing severe depression, discuss healthful ways of coping with depression. **Depression** is a feeling of hopeless-ness, sadness, or helplessness. Symptoms of depression include loss of interest in appearance, in family, friends, and/or school. Unfortunately, depression in young people often goes unnoticed and untreated. The five main causes of depression in young people are:

- Disappointment when expectations are not met
- A sense of hopelessness because of being uncertain about the future or feeling trapped
- A loss of self-esteem if expectations are high and are not met
- An illness that alienates them from peers
- Unfair comparisons with others, especially those seen on TV or in the movies

3 Following are suggestions that would benefit a person who is feeling depressed: share thoughts and feelings with at least one trusted adult; have a warm, affectionate relationship with family members; make a list of things to do each day and attempt to accomplish as many items on the list as possible; dress neatly and be well groomed; make a list of strengths and review them often; engage in vigorous aerobic exercise; plan social activities with friends; eat nutritious, balanced meals; get an appropriate amount of rest and sleep; and keep a journal.

4 Discuss the signs that a young person might be considering suicide. These signs include: a drastic change in personality; withdrawal from family and friends; loss of interest in personal appearance; loss of interest in schoolwork; difficulty getting along with peers and family members; use of chemicals such as alcohol and marijuana; change in sleeping and eating habits; giving away of personal possessions; and verbal or written statements about suicide or death. A person who displays any of these signs should always be taken seriously. Support and concern are needed. Respect for confidentiality should not be honored and a responsible adult should be immediately notified. If there is difficulty in contacting a specific responsible adult, call a suicide hot line, the local emergency number (9-1-1), or the police or fire department. Stay with the person until appropriate help arrives. After the crisis is over, recognize that this person will need continued support and encouragement.

5 **Suicide prevention strategies** are techniques that can be used to help prevent a person from thinking about, attempting, or completing suicide. Use the *Suicide Prevention Strategies* transparency and discuss each strategy as follows:

• Know suicide hotline numbers.
  The National Youth Suicide Hotline number (1-800-621-4000) is toll-free and phones are staffed by trained volunteers.

• Know what to do when you feel down.
  When you feel depressed, it is important to have a plan of action. Make a list of what you can do to make yourself feel better.

• Build a network of support.
  Identify people who will listen to you, offer you advice, and help you through tough times.

• Get involved in rewarding activities.
  Playing a sport, learning a craft, or helping others through community service are examples of rewarding activities.

• Know what to do if someone shows warning signs.
  Take the person seriously; make sure that (s)he knows you care; tell a responsible adult who will get help.

6 Because everyone goes through difficult times, emphasize the need and importance for everyone to have a network of family/friends/adults who will be supportive during those times. Distribute an index card to each student. Have students write the names of the people who are a part of their support network. They should include at least one family member, one adult other than a family member (e.g., coach, teacher, friend's parent), and one friend. If possible, have them include a phone number for each person they identify. Then give them the phone number for the suicide prevention hotline in your area. Suggest that students keep their index card in their purses or wallets.

7 Explain that they are going to take part in an activity called the Support Network. Have students sit in a circle. Ask for a volunteer to start the network. Give this student the ball of yarn. This student will wrap the end of the yarn around his/her index finger and will say the name of a person (s)he has listed as a member of his/her support network and toss the ball of yarn to another student in the circle. This student will repeat a name on his/her list and again toss the yarn to another student. Repeat this process until all students in the class are connected by the ball of yarn and have thus formed a network. Explain that each person in the network can now provide help and support to the others. The support network is especially important when suicidal indications are recognized.

Evaluation:

Students are to design a Suicide Prevention Fact Sheet. Their fact sheets should contain the following: reasons that adolescents attempt suicide; suggestions for coping with difficult times; indications or signs that a person might be thinking of suicide; and suicide prevention strategies to follow when suicidal signs or indications are recognized in another person.

GANGING UP

Objective:

Students will evaluate the consequences of belonging to a gang.

Life Skill:

I will resist gang membership. (PF16)

Materials:

Length of yarn, five index cards with "Pick a fight" printed on each card, one index card with "Talk it out" printed on it, *Model For Using Resistance Skills* transparency (page 610), a copy for each student, transparency projector

Motivation:

1 Introduce the subject of youth gangs. A **youth gang** is a group of young people who band together and participate in violent, unlawful, or criminal activity. Gangs usually have names and are territorial—they exist in definite areas of a community. Members of a gang associate together and often commit crimes against other youth gangs or against the general population. Most gang members adopt certain colors and/or dress styles that are easily recognized and identified with a particular gang. Although most gang members are males, there are some gangs composed of only females.

2 Explain that most gang members are between the ages of 10 and 21. Young people join gangs for many different reasons. Because the desire for acceptance is so strong during late childhood and adolescence, vulnerable youth often are attracted to gangs. Some are looking for excitement and think they will find it in gang membership. Others

are alienated from their families and are easily influenced by peers. Activities available through gang membership, such as crime and drug sales, can provide an avenue for the generation of income and status when options through legitimate channels are perceived as unavailable. However, many young people do not realize the hazards involved in joining a gang.

3 Explain that to become a member of a gang, a young person has to prove himself/herself by taking part in initiation rites that are often dangerous and illegal. Older gang members often take advantage of younger prospective gang members and expose them to serious penalties if they are caught. Because of the secrecy of gang initiations, prospective members have no way of knowing what they might be asked to do.

4 Emphasize that gang activity is associated with violence and drug use. Gang members often acquire a criminal record that makes it difficult to find employment later on. It is important for students to learn how to resist pressure to become involved with any activity that would jeopardize their futures. Using the *Model For Using Resistance Skills* transparency, discuss each skill.

1 Differentiate among aggressive behavior, passive behavior, and assertive behavior. Emphasize that when a person uses assertive behavior (s)he is in control of himself/herself and is not in danger of being pressured to do something that (s)he does not want to do.

2 Explain that saying NO is sufficient to resist any pressure to do something harmful or illegal.

3 Explain what nonverbal behavior is and discuss the example of the cigarette.

4   Students can practice the skill of walking away from a person who is encouraging them to do something harmful or illegal.

5   Encourage students to think ahead in order to avoid situations in which they would be pressured to do something they do not want to do.

6   Remind students that they can avoid association with people who choose harmful behaviors.

7   Remind students of their responsibility to themselves and to others to resist pressure to engage in any activity that is harmful or illegal.

5 Ask for two volunteers and have them come to the front of the room. Each is to hold an end of a piece of yarn. Explain to the class that these two persons are having a conflict. Identify one of them as a member of a gang. Give six other students the six index cards that you have prepared. These six students are to join the gang member, one at a time, to encourage him/her to behave in a certain way by reading what is on the card (s)he was given. The first student joins the gang member and reads what is on his/her card. When the second student joins, they both read together what is on their cards. Continue in this way until all six students have joined the gang member and all six have read together what is on their cards. At the end, five people will be saying "pick a fight" and one will be saying "talk it out." The five students were gaining momentum to "pick a fight." The one student who wanted to "talk it out" could not be heard as the momentum increased. Being a gang member can involve agreement to violent actions, even though as an individual (s)he might want to do something else. The pressure can be very strong to behave in a certain way.

Evaluation:

Distribute a copy of the *Model For Using Resistance Skills* to each student. Divide the class into groups to write the scripts for role plays in which a student is pressured to join a gang. Scripts are to include refusal skills that describe how the student might resist the particular pressure.

THIS WEEK'S TOP TEN LIST

Objective:

Students will evaluate the consequences of using drugs and being involved in drug sales and trafficking.

Life Skill:

I will avoid alcohol and other drugs. (PF14)

Materials:

Paper, markers

Motivation:

1 Introduce the topic of risk situations. **Risk situations** are circumstances that increase the likelihood that something negative will happen to a person's health, safety, and/or well-being. Explain that people who choose to use and/or traffic in drugs are putting themselves in a risk situation. In addition, these people run the risk of becoming a perpetrator or a victim of violence. They may become perpetrators because alcohol and other drugs impair the way a person thinks and behaves. Their behavior may become hostile and violent. Drug users and/or traffickers may become victims because their judgment becomes impaired and they are likely to drop their guard.

2 Review the definition of drugs. A **drug** is a substance that changes the way the body and/or mind works. Drugs not only can cause physical problems, such as liver disease, but also can cause people to lose control of their behavior. Review the definition of drug trafficking. Drug trafficking is buying, selling, or distributing illegal drugs.

3 Explain that in order to choose responsible behavior, people need to be in control of their decisions and actions. They need to be able to think clearly and to respond quickly to different situations. They need to be able to think about the consequences of their behavior. Explain that there is considerable evidence that connects drug use and violence. Discuss the following evidences:

• <u>Fighting and assaults.</u> People who use drugs are unable to manage their anger and identify peaceful solutions when they experience stressful situations. Instead, their emotions may explode and they begin to fight or assault someone.

• <u>School expulsion.</u> Using drugs places young people at risk for completing their education. Besides breaking school rules about fighting, drug users are often expelled from school on the basis of school policies about drug use.

• <u>Sexual assault and acquaintance rape.</u> Using drugs impairs a person's judgment and reduces his/her inhibitions. (S)he can unwittingly put himself/herself into a compromised position, a position that (s)he ordinarily would not choose. (S)he can become a victim of a sexual assault. On the other hand, under the influence of drugs, a person is less apt to be in touch with the responses of others and so does not respond appropriately. This person may not respect the other person's response, and may force unwanted sexual contact.

• <u>Theft.</u> When people who use drugs run out of money to buy more drugs, they may become desperate and steal from family and friends in order to satisfy the drug habit.

• <u>Domestic violence.</u> **Domestic violence** is violence that occurs within the family or within other relationships in which people live together. Drug users do not think rationally and may act in inappropriate ways to settle a disagreement.

- Suicide. Explain that when people who are already depressed use a drug, such as alcohol, which is a depressant, the drug intensifies the depression. Under these conditions, a person may believe that suicide is a solution to his/her problems.
- Homicide. **Homicide** is the accidental or purposeful killing of another person. Alcohol and other drug use is considered a factor in more than half of all homicides.

4 Divide students into groups. They are to brainstorm a list of reasons that it is dangerous to be involved in drug use and/or trafficking. Then each group is to rank these in order and, using markers, make "This Week's Top Ten List" of reasons not to be involved in drug trafficking. The groups are to tape their lists to the chalkboard. Have students circulate to read all the lists. Then discuss each group's list with the class.

Evaluation:

Students are to select three of the reasons identified in the lists for not being involved in drug trafficking. In a two-page paper, they are to support why those reasons are important to them.

AWFUL LAWFUL

Objective:

Students will describe the importance of respecting laws and law enforcement authorities.

Life Skills:

I will respect authority and abide by laws. (PF17)
I will change behavior if a juvenile offender. (PF20)

Materials:

Paper and pencils, computer and printer (optional), chalkboard, chalk

Motivation:

1 Explain that there are two factors that are the foundation for learning respect for authority and laws. The two factors are the development of a moral code and values. A **moral code** is a set of rules that a person follows in controlling his/her own behavior. **Values** are the beliefs, goals, and standards held by a person. Explain that a moral code involves values such as respect, responsibility, trustworthiness, and caring. Respect is a high regard for others. Responsibility is being reliable and dependable. Trustworthiness is acting in responsible and effective ways. Caring is being interested in and concerned for others. Explain that values such as these confirm the dignity of a human being and promote and protect a person's rights.

2 Explain that the development of a moral code takes place over a period of years during childhood and early adulthood. The emergence of a conscience in early childhood is one stage in this development. **Con-** science is an inner sense of right and wrong that prompts responsible behavior and causes feelings of guilt following bad behavior. As a conscience develops, a child begins to know the difference between a truth and a falsehood. Explain further that the next level of moral development involves making decisions based on answering the following question: "What will people think of me if I behave this way?" At this stage, young people understand what behavior is expected, what behavior is right, and what behavior is wrong. Finally, in the development of a moral code, people reach a level where they operate by a set of principles and understand that certain actions would violate the rights of others.

3 Explain that people who do not have a moral code do not respect authority or abide by laws. They resist authority and break laws. Introduce the term juvenile offender. A **juvenile offender** is a person under the age of 18 who breaks a criminal law. Explain that juveniles are responsible for one-third of all burglaries, one in seven rapes, and one in seven of all homicides. Help is available for juvenile offenders who want to change their behavior patterns. If a juvenile offender continues to resist authority and break laws, (s)he will be at a high risk of being a perpetrator or victim of violence. Explain that there are many programs available that help juvenile offenders learn the difference between right and wrong so that they can develop a moral code and follow it.

4 Students will need a sheet of paper and a pen or pencil. Explain that you are going to give them a term and they will have three minutes to write the words that come into their minds when they hear the term. Give them an example. If you said "holiday," they would start a list of the words or phrases that they thought of when they heard that word. They might list such words as no school, vacation, fun, summer, and so on. You are going to look for the longest list at the end of three minutes. Make sure each student is ready. Then give them the term "law enforcement authorities" and begin timing them.

5 After three minutes, the students should stop writing. Ask several students to share their lists with the class. Channel the discussion into talking about the importance of law enforcement authorities in protecting people in a community by enforcing community laws.

6 Divide students into groups. Each group is to develop a television program that highlights a law enforcement officer. The program should have a title and the plot of the program should be described. Then each group should design an ad for their program that will appear in a magazine called "A Guide For TV Viewing." They can type or hand letter their ads or use computer graphics.

Evaluation:

Students are to watch and report on a television program or a movie that involves law enforcement authorities dealing with some type of violence. Stress that students are to get their parents' permission before watching the television program or movie. Their report should include the type of crime, the victims, the role of the law enforcement authorities, and ways that others cooperated in solving the crime or otherwise helping the law enforcement authorities. Discuss the completed reports in class.

RECIPE FOR RECOVERY

Objective:

Students will describe ways that people who have been victims of violence may be helped toward recovery.

Life Skill:

I will participate in recovery if a victim. (PF19)

Materials:

Index cards, one for each student, pens or pencils, file box

Motivation:

1 Introduce the term victim. A **victim** is a person who is harmed by violence. People who are the victims of violence may suffer physical injury. They may be seriously or permanently injured. They may suffer from financial and property loss. They may suffer from emotional distress and psychological trauma. Explain that sometimes emotional trauma that follows an incidence of violence often is more devastating than physical wounds.

2 Discuss victim recovery. **Victim recovery** is a person's return to physical and emotional health after being harmed by violence. Victims often need treatment for physical injuries; treatment for emotional pain; support from family and friends; repayment for money or property losses; and skills to stop the cycle of violence. Recovery efforts include programs that help a victim survive pain, heal, and move forward with self-confidence again. Explain that victims of certain types of violence, such as domestic abuse, continue to be victims rather than engaging

in recovery efforts because they have developed negative self-esteem. People who have negative self-esteem may begin to believe that they deserve the abuse or do not deserve the respect of others. Explain that they are at risk of becoming a victim again if they continue the behavior that caused them to be victims the first time.

3 Discuss possible recovery paths for different types of violence. Victims of rape, for example, need to have an immediate physical exam to determine their condition and so that evidence can be collected. They may be examined by a sexual assault nurse examiner (SANE) who has specialized training in the treatment of rape victims. Rape crisis centers staffed with trained medical personnel and volunteers are available in many communities. Hospitals and women's centers offer counseling and support groups to victims of rape.

4 Discuss recovery from domestic abuse. The first step toward recovery from domestic abuse is for the victim to come to an awareness that (s)he deserves a life that is free from abuse and violence. The victim has to realize that (s)he is powerless to change the abusive behavior of the person who abuses him/her. Once the victim leaves the relationship, there is help available. (S)he may join a support group, get counseling, and take advantage of opportunities to learn new job skills.

5 Discuss recovery from child abuse. Children who have been abused often attempt to keep what is happening a secret. They are in a very difficult circumstance because in most cases they trusted the person who harmed them. These children must be helped to realize that no matter what they may have done, they did not deserve to be abused. First of all, these children have to talk with someone they trust, and get understanding and help. The National Child Abuse Hotline helps people locate professionals in their communities who are trained to deal with survivors of child abuse.

6 Discuss recovery for people who survive the homicide of a family member or friend. These people are in a state of shock and denial that may last for weeks or months. They need help in making funeral plans, possibly dealing with the criminal justice system, and changes in their family structures, or new family problems. They can be helped by joining in a support group and by counseling.

7 Explain that no matter what the act of violence was, a victim needs help in recovering. There are many sources of help. You may consider inviting the school counselor to speak to your class about the sources available in your community.

8 Give each student an index card. On one side of the card, the students are to write a description of a person who is a victim of a crime, or a description of a person/family who is a victim because someone they know has been harmed by violence. For example,

the person who is the victim might be a person who was raped. The family that has been a victim might be a family who has had a family member kidnapped and murdered. On the other side of the card, students are to write a recipe for recovery. Recipes must include information that supports the importance of and reasons for using the following five ingredients.

<u>Recipe for Recovery From Sexual Assault</u>

- A dash of help from clergy to relieve guilt
- Two tablespoons of calls to hotlines
- Four cups of visits to a health clinic
- One-third cup of self-esteem
- Three teaspoons of a support group
- Two pounds of support from family and friends

Evaluation:

Students are to use their recipes to identify five life skills that people who have been victims of violence can practice for recovery. For example, a life skill might be: I will call a hot line. I will speak with a member of the clergy. I will help others who have been victims of crime.

SECTION

4

Violence Prevention Literature

USING THE VIOLENCE PREVENTION LITERATURE

CHAPTER 4

In their textbook on children's literature, Huck, Hepler, and Hickman define literature as "the imaginative shaping of life and thought into the forms of structure" (Huck, Hepler, and Hickman, 1993). This definition is appropriate for the use of literature with violence prevention education. Because literature, whether in the form of short stories, poetry, scripts for plays, or reader's theatre, can be a powerful tool for extending knowledge and exploring emotions, its infusion into the violence prevention curriculum is valuable. The following discussion focuses on the benefits of using literature, the kinds of literature included in the violence prevention curriculum, and extensions of literature.

THE BENEFITS OF USING LITERATURE

Literature can provide safe avenues for students to have the "lived through" experience of situations and lives different from their own, experiences that can enable them to better understand and cope with the world around them (Rosenblatt, 1978). This may be the most valuable tool of literature in the violence prevention curriculum. As such a tool, literature should be examined in a new light.

Literature is both a window for other lives and a mirror for one's own life (Bishop, 1993). Literature can provide a window for a person of one culture and set of life experiences to view other people. As a reader, a student can move through time and space with a freedom and a clarity not equal in the "real" world, but these "lived through" experiences are no less than real. They can change and mold a reader, leaving understanding and impressions that last a lifetime.

That same literature can provide a mirror that can strengthen, encourage, and teach those students who have these "lived through" experiences. Within this violence prevention literature are mirrors for students who have experienced violence and abuse — mirrors

that are still much needed in the world of children's and young adult literature. Readers who know the pain of domestic violence, the despair of discrimination, and the struggle of victim recovery can see themselves and know that their experiences and struggles are not isolated ones and are not in vain. These mirrors can help readers to identify abuse in their own lives or better understand why certain types of behavior are risky. They also can provide safe avenues for readers to express their emotions, emotions that are often confusing or even overwhelming.

In addition to the rich benefits of the myriad of "lived through" experiences that literature can provide, using literature with the violence prevention curriculum allows opportunities for strengthening comprehension, using critical thinking, exploring creative writing, meeting the needs of individual students, and involving family members. Because the ability to read and comprehend is vital to students' growth and success, infusing literature into several curriculum areas is important. Literature has been infused into the violence prevention curriculum for this reason.

THE KINDS OF LITERATURE

Three kinds of literature are included in the Violence Prevention Literature section: short stories, poetry, and scripts for both puppet plays and reader's theatre.

<u>Short Stories</u>. Short stories are the most familiar type of literature available to students, but the extensions of those stories need not be limited to what teachers commonly refer to as "skill and drill." Educators should search for ways to extend the experience with literature and heighten the connections the students may make. Writing, art, and drama activities may be used to accomplish this.

<u>Poetry</u>. Poetry can provide an opportunity for students to explore their lyrical and creative side. Poetry is often

the most powerful and personal way for students to share their thoughts, feelings, and understanding of a text or an issue. Key to the successful use of poetry is creating a favorable and positive atmosphere. Educators should always affirm their students' efforts at creating poems.

Puppet Plays. Puppet plays are often the most interactive form of literature for young children. Even the most simple puppets made from paper bags can take on a life of their own. Children also can use puppets to talk about issues that normally make them feel uncomfortable. One example is child abuse; the script "A Visit With Dr. Sara" provides an opportunity for children to discuss their feelings about this issue.

Reader's Theatre. Reader's theatre provides an opportunity for students to add their voices and feelings to the issues studied. **Reader's theatre** is a process in which students use a script or create a script of their own to perform a story (Young, 1990). For example, having students create a reader's theatre script is suggested in the teaching strategy accompanying the grades 9–12 story, "One Step Removed." In this story, the mother and sister are silent. However, students who identify with them more than they do with the main character of Jason might create a reader's threatre script with their voices. Then their voices might be included and made central to the story.

The performance of reader's theatre is similar to that of a play. However, the lines of a play are memorized while the lines of reader's theatre are only well practiced. What is more important to reader's theatre is the vocal production of the lines. Participants work on expression and delivery, emphasizing their understanding and interpretation of the character. Blocking also is important. The entire tone of a reader's theatre performance can be changed by merely changing where the performers stand and how they move. Reader's theatre allows the student to take complete ownership of a piece of literature through the creation and performance of a reader's theatre script.

EXTENSIONS OF LITERATURE

The educator's role is to make use of the powerful tools of literature, including both the mirrors and the windows. Below are suggestions for using literature, many

of which focus on extending the lived through experiences students face. These literature extensions are grouped into four areas: generic extensions, artistic extensions, writing extensions, and process drama extensions.

General Extensions:
• Whenever possible, allow the students to read through the story, poetry, or script first on their own. Then they can reread the story together in groups or as a class.
• Watch, listen, and wait for opportunities to have students to make connections to their own lives.
• Encourage students to hear different voices in the text and to explore multiple perspectives on the same topic or issue.
• If an activity does not work, try it once more at a later time.
• Always write or work with the students, being willing to share your own responses or creative works. Have the students take ownership of the stories.

Artistic Extensions:
• Collages are a good way for students to explore abstract concepts or feelings. A **collage** is a collection of objects put together to form a piece of artwork representing a particular idea or theme. Any material can be used in collages, even trash. The objects are usually glued to a piece of drawing paper, cardboard, or posterboard.
• Mobiles offer advantages similar to those of collages, and again can be made from almost any material. A **mobile** is a collection of objects (often pictures or drawings) hanging by string at different different distances along a central piece. Dowel rods and coat hangers are often used as the central piece.
• Clay also can be used in interpreting the meaning of a text. The form or image can be changed as many times as necessary, but once it is finished, the image can be made permanent. Students can use potter's clay, which must be fired, or self-hardening clay.
• Masks can be made out of paper mâché, paper plates, or paper bags. These masks can be used in role playing the texts or used in reader's theatre.
• Illustrating a story or interpreting a poem through illustration provides an opportunity to make what they will of the text. You may choose to have students work in groups so that those who are not par-

ticularly skilled in drawing might benefit from the experience of those who are and not feel inferior when comparing the end product. Group drawings also allow for discussion of community and interdependence when students share how they arrived at their illustration.

- Murals are one way group interpretation of a text can be explored effectively. A **mural** is a large (often wall-sized) piece of artwork. The mural can be comprised of one scene or many scenes around a specific theme. White butcher paper is a good material to use for murals.
- Cartoons and comic strips are another way students can illustrate a text. Old film strips can be erased with alcohol and cotton and used for this activity.
- Setting poetry to music, either spontaneously-created music or known music, is an engaging way of exploring a poem. Television tunes, such as the introduction to Gilligan's Island often lend themselves well to adaptation.

Writing Extensions:

- Writing a journal entry or letter from one perspective in a text lends a personal note to the literature experience. The students can take on the voice and perspective of one or more characters. Different students' interpretations of the same perspective may be compared.
- Creating a newspaper chronicling events from the text allows students to employ critical thinking skills. Students must analyze what they know and have learned and then synthesize that information to create the new form of presentation.
- Writing telegrams or letters to communicate the events of the text allows students to weigh and sift the important facts surrounding events and topics.
- Writing reviews or advertisements for the text is one way students can show what they feel is worthy or important to the text.
- Writing a continuation of the text at a later period allows students an opportunity to predict how the circumstances might change, or how the characters involved might be affected or have changed.
- Comparing and contrasting the different characters from each text force students to make a closer examination of the text. Predict how a character in one text might respond to a character in another text.

- Create a character sketch of someone from the text. Describe that person not only through the reader's eyes, but the eyes of the other characters.
- Create a reader's theatre script for the text. Perform the script with class members. Students may form a casting company and explain why specific actors are chosen for each part.
- Writing poetry is one of the most powerful and personal ways for students to express their understanding, interpretation, or feelings about a text. The writing of poetry must be done in a positive atmosphere. Students need to be affirmed for their efforts.

Process Drama Extensions:

- Holding a panel discussion on the topic is one way to empower the students. It makes them the experts. Encourage them to explore different viewpoints during the discussion.
- Creating a tableau from one portion of the text is a powerful way to personalize the text, allowing students to give form to their thoughts and interpretations. A **tableau** is a living picture in which the students use their bodies to depict the scene chosen. Students are then asked questions about the scene. They can answer these questions in the context of their role in the tableau. For example, if students depict the scene from Goldilocks and the Three Bears when the bears find their porridge gone, the student depicting the mama bear might be asked what (s)he was thinking and feeling at the time.
- Role play, either as an extension of the text or an exploration of the topic, also can be useful. A role play calls for active critical thinking as the students continue to analyze what they know to balance what they say and do in role. Role play not only allows for a safe experience of thoughts and feelings about the topic but also requires students to use their critical thinking skills. The teacher creates a framework for the role play. For example, after reading "Please, Mr. Sandman," the class could role play a group of concerned parents brainstorming ways to prevent suicide. The teacher might play the role of chairperson of the meeting, or mediator.
- Mime can be used effectively in role playing different scenarios such as peer pressure, discrimination, anger management, and protective behaviors.

- Reader's theatre is a processing which students use a script or create one of their own to perform a story (Young, 1990). Different from a play, reader's theatre uses only blocking, voice, and facial expressions or body movements to portray the action and emotion of the story. Scripts are read, not memorized, and can be adapted to meet the students' needs. When creating a script from a poem or story, students should look for the different voices in the text, and can even join those voices for emphasis where possible for a chorus or echo effect. Reader's theatre scripts can be found in libraries and education stores, but allowing students to create their own script gives much-needed meaning and ownership to the activity.
- Interview students as a character from a text using a talk show format. Encourage the students to think, talk, and respond as they believe the character would.

THE RESPONSIBLE USE OF LITERATURE

There are guidelines for the responsible use of the violence prevention literature and accompanying teaching strategies in this section of the book:

- Always read the violence prevention literature <u>before</u> reproducing it for students to read in class or at home.
- When asking students to read the literature at home, consider sending an accompanying letter to adult family members. The letter might include the objective and life skills that are intended to be met. It might explain that students will process this information with your help. Adult family members might be encouraged to read and discuss the literature with the entire family.

REFERENCES

Bishop, R.S., & Dashiell, P. (1993) *Multicultural Literature in the Classroom: Developing Multiple Perspectives*. Columbus, OH: The Martha L. King Center of The Ohio State University.

Huck, C., Hepler, S., & Hickman, J. (1993) *Children's Literature in the Elementary School. Fifth ed*. New York: Harcourt Brace.

Rosenblatt, L. (1978) *The Reader, The Text, The Poem*. Carbondale, IL: Southern Illinois University Press.

Young, T. (1990) Reader's theatre. *Reading Horizons*.

A Boy, A Doll, And Some Cookies

Objective:

Students will tell ways to handle disagreements without fighting.

Life Skills:

I will use manners and treat others fairly. (PF5)

I will try to work out disagreements without fighting. (PF10)

Materials:

A Boy, A Doll, And Some Cookies (page 427), colored butcher paper, colored markers

Motivation:

1 Introduce the term conflict. A **conflict** is a disagreement between two or more people. Explain that everyone has disagreements with other people at some times. Explain that it is important to learn how to handle disagreements without getting into a fight.

2 Explain that there does not have to be a loser in *every* conflict. By learning to deal with a conflict in positive ways, both sides in the conflict can "win." Getting angry and getting into a fight are not healthful ways to resolve a conflict. It is better to find healthful ways to resolve, or work through, a conflict rather than to spend time and energy getting angry and getting into a fight. Explain that you are going to read a story about a fight.

3 Read the story *A Boy, A Doll, And Some Cookies* aloud to the students.

4 Discuss the following questions with students. Suggested answers are given after each question.

Why was Jane angry at Wendy?
> Jane thought Wendy had told a boy that she liked him.

What did Wendy do after Jane broke her doll?
> She jumped on her and started a fight.

5 Explain that there are ways to resolve a conflict so that nobody is harmed. Discuss with students the following suggestions for resolving conflicts in healthful ways.

- *Stay calm.* Speak softly. Do not get excited.
- *Be polite.* Show others that you want to treat them respectfully.
- *Take time to cool down.* If you are feeling angry, take time to get over the anger before you do anything.
- *Share your feelings.* Tell the other person why you feel the way you do about the disagreement.
- *Don't use putdowns.* A putdown is a remark that is critical or unkind about the other person.
- *Listen to the other person.* Listen and try to understand why the other person disagrees with you.
- *Pretend you are the other person.* Imagine that you are the other person. This often helps to understand that person's feelings.
- *Ask an adult to help.* Adults, such as a parent, a teacher, or a police officer, are available to help settle a disagreement.
- *Let others know when you are wrong.* If you take time to stay calm or to cool down, you may realize that you have made a mistake. When you admit that you are wrong, the disagreement will be ended.
- *Run away if someone threatens you or insists on fighting.* Realize that you might

be harmed if you continue the disagreement. Protect yourself.

6 Have students draw two pictures on separate sheets of paper. One picture is of a person who has settled a disagreement in a way that does not harm himself/herself or other people. This person should have a happy face. The other picture is of a person who has been in a fight. This person will be unhappy.

Evaluation:

Give students examples of conflicts that a person their age might face. Examples might include two people who want to use the same book in the library, two people who want to be captain of a team at recess, and two people who think they are first in line at the drinking fountain. For each situation, tell a result of the conflict. For some examples, tell a result where the two people resolve the conflict without harming themselves or others. For other examples, tell a result in which the two people harm themselves or others. Tell students that when you describe a situation in which the conflict is resolved in a harmful way, they should hold up their picture of an unhappy person. When you describe a situation in which the conflict is resolved in a healthful way, students should hold up their picture of a happy person.

A Boy, A Doll, And Some Cookies

By Patricia M. Dashiell

Wendy stared at the broken doll on the ground. She couldn't believe it. Jane had grabbed it out of her hands and threw it down, cracking the china head.

"Why did you do that?" Wendy asked, still surprised to see her birthday present on the ground.

"That's what you get for telling Christopher I like him."

"What do you mean?"

Jane glared at Wendy. "You told Christopher that I like him, and he came and kissed me!"

"He did?"

"Yeah, and it's all your fault."

"No, it isn't."

"Yes, it is!" insisted Jane. She took her boot and stomped on the doll's face, grinding it beneath her. "That'll teach you to tell lies about me, babyface!"

"Don't!" cried Wendy. But it was too late. Her doll could never be repaired now.

Wendy looked up at Jane and then threw herself at her. The two girls fell to the ground rolling over and over as they pulled at each other's hair and hit wherever they could. Suddenly Ms. Robbins came running across the playground and pulled Jane and Wendy apart.

"Stop it this instant!" the teacher cried, as she struggled to separate the girls.

Jane and Wendy had to go to the office where the principal made them apologize, shake hands, and write letters to their parents to take home and get signed. Wendy knew she was in trouble.

At home, her parents sent her to her room after dinner without dessert and said she would be grounded for a week—no playing after school and no television.

At school, though, Wendy was still mad at Jane, and Jane avoided Wendy at lunch and recess. Jane also told other classmates lies about Wendy. She said that Wendy wet the bed at night. So Wendy told her friends that Jane was afraid of the dark.

Jane started pinching Wendy whatever chance she got, and soon Wendy was doing the same thing.

"Wendy, you've got to stop," said Sheryl, her best friend. "You're gonna get in trouble again."

The two girls were swinging on the tire at recess.

"Why? She started it. I never told Christopher anything."

"Are you sure?"

"Yes! Don't you believe me?" asked Wendy.

"Yeah. But Jane doesn't."

"So?"

"So you've got to make her believe you."

"How?"

Sheryl stopped the tire with her feet and thought for a moment. "You tell her."

"She'll just start pinching me," Wendy said.

"You could ask Ms. Robbins to help you."

"No way! Then I'd really be in trouble with our teacher."

"No, you wouldn't. She'd be glad you're trying to do something."

"I don't want her help," insisted Wendy. She shoved off with both feet and set the tire to swinging wildly again.

"Hey!" cried Sheryl, trying to hold onto the rope. When she got both hands around the rope and had dragged her feet on the ground to slow them down, she continued. "How about asking the counselor?"

"Sheryl, I just don't want to have some adult help."

"Why not?"

Wendy shrugged her shoulders as she answered. "I want to see if I can handle this one."

"Well, that's all I can think of, Wendy."

"Aw, come on. You gotta help me. My arms are getting black and blue and boy, are they sore."

Wendy got up from the swing and walked over to the slide. She sat in the shade below it and propped her feet up on the bottom rung. Sheryl came and sat next to her. "You could write her a note?" she suggested to Wendy.

"Maybe she wouldn't read it when she saw it was from me."

"You could at least try."

"Yeah. You could tell her that you didn't say anything to Christopher. And —"

"And what?"

"And you could say you're sorry."

"Sorry! What am I supposed to be sorry for?" demanded Wendy. "You're supposed to be my friend."

"I am ," Sheryl sighed, "but I think you should say you're sorry 'cause you were wrong when you jumped on her."

Wendy stared at her friend for a few moments and then took her legs down off the step. Crossing them beneath her, she started tugging at the grass. "Okay. I'll do it. "

Sheryl sat with her friend for a while. She knew that admitting you are wrong is hard to do. Then she thought of another idea. "Hey, Wendy!"

"What."

"Maybe you could give her something to go along with the letter to let her know that you mean it."

"Like what?"

"I don't know. Why do I have to figure everything out, anyway?"

" 'Cause you're my friend, Sheryl."

Sheryl rolled her eyes and gave a big

sigh. She thought for a few moments before she came up with the perfect answer. "Okay. Why don't you give her your dessert, those cookies that your mom makes."

Wendy was quiet for a few minutes. Those cookies just might work, she thought. "That's a pretty good idea. But I think I'll wait 'til tomorrow when I have twice as many."

The next day, Wendy left the letter and a bag of cookies on Jane's desk just before recess. The two girls watched Jane from the other side of the room.

"At least she didn't crumple up the letter," whispered Sheryl.

Just then Ms. Robbins announced that it was time for recess. Grabbing the bag of cookies, Jane headed out the door. Wendy and Sheryl followed her and were surprised to see Jane walk right over to Christopher.

"What's she doing?" asked Wendy.

"She's giving him the cookies!" cried Sheryl.

"Why would she do that?"

"I don't know."

"Look, Sheryl, she's going over to the tire with him. And, wow, she's letting him push her."

"Why would she do that?"

"Maybe she does like him."

"Maybe."

"Sheryl?"

"Yeah?"

"Should I tell Christopher that they're my cookies?"

"No!"

Jane stopped pinching Wendy and asked to move her desk next to Christopher's. That ended up being better because the teacher said it was time to move everybody around.

Sheryl and Wendy finally got to sit next to each other for the first time that year. All because of a boy, a doll, and some cookies.

A PIECE OF TRASH

Objective:

Students will tell what to do when they are around weapons such as guns and knives.

Life Skill:

I will follow the SAFE rule: Stop, Avoid getting closer, Find an adult, Explain what I saw. (PF15)

Materials:

A Piece Of Trash (page 432), paper, crayons, stapler

Motivation:

1 Introduce the story by asking students for examples of items which might be found in the trash. Tell them that sometimes you can find unexpected things in the trash which can be dangerous. Explain that they are going to listen to a story about a piece of trash.

2 Read the story aloud to the students.

3 Discuss the following questions. Suggested answers are given after each question.

How do you think Theo and Sam felt about the gun?
They were excited to hold a real gun, curious about it, and scared of it.

What did they do with the gun that was not safe?
They held it, looked inside it, and tried to shoot it. If it had been loaded with bullets, either one or both of the boys could have been seriously injured.

4 Define **weapon**. A **weapon** is an instrument or device used for fighting. A weapon usually is used to injure a person. There are many different kinds of weapons. When people think about weapons, they usually think about guns and knives because these are the things often used to harm other people.

5 Stress that being around weapons can be very dangerous. Tell students if they see a gun or knife, or anyone carrying a gun or a knife, they need to stop and get away as soon as possible from the area or the person. Then they need to tell a trusted adult immediately about what they saw. Explain that there is no way to tell if a gun is loaded, and there is a possibility that a loaded gun could go off accidentally.

6 Explain that there are school rules concerning guns and knives and that these rules help to protect all the students in the school. If a student breaks the rules and carries a gun or knife to school, (s)he is endangering everyone.

7 Discuss several situations in which a student might come in contact with a weapon. One example might be finding a gun on a shelf in a closet at home. Another example might be finding a knife on the floor under a desk. Ask the students what they should do in order to practice safe behavior around weapons. Ask the students to identify trusted adults, such as a teacher or parent, whom they could tell if they find a weapon.

Evaluation:

Begin to read the story *A Piece Of Trash* aloud to the students again. Stop after Sam exclaims, "Man, that's a gun!" Ask students to discuss what Theo and Sam should do next to practice safe behavior around weapons.

A Piece Of Trash

By Patricia M. Dashiell

"What's that?"

"Something."

"What?"

"Something I'm not sure I want to show you."

"Aw, come on."

"Okay."

Theo sat on the ground and unwrapped the bundle he had been carrying. His friend Sam leaned over his shoulder to watch.

"Man, that's a gun!" exclaimed Sam.

"Yeah. I know."

"Where did you get it?"

Theo looked uncomfortable. "I...I found it."

"Where?"

"Somewhere."

"Theo, tell me, please," begged Sam.

Theo waited and then whispered, "I found it in the trash can in the alley behind our house."

"What were you doing digging in the trash can?" asked Sam as he sat next to his friend.

"Well, I sort of saw someone drop it in the trash can while I was playing hide and seek with Andre."

Sam shook his head. "You saw someone drop the gun in the trash?"

"Yeah. Well, he was pushing something way down to the bottom, and I wanted to see what it was," answered Theo. He finally turned to look at his friend. "What do you think we should do with it?"

"We?"

"Yeah, we're friends. We share."

"I don't know if I want a gun. Do you want to keep it?"

"I don't know," sighed Theo. He was beginning to think that he should have left the gun in the trash can.

"Does it have bullets in it?"

"I don't know. How can you tell?"

"You could shoot it," suggested Sam after a few moments. Theo picked it up and pointed it at different things around him. First he pointed it at the fence, then a car. The telephone pole looked too hard, and so did the dumpster across the street. Finally he handed the gun to his friend.

"You try first."

"Gosh, it's heavy."

"Yeah."

"You know, Theo, I don't want to shoot it." Sam handed the gun back.

"Do you know how to look inside?"

"Nope. Do you?"

"No."

"Why don't you try," said Sam.

"What if it goes off when I'm trying? I might get hurt or maybe even shoot you."

"Yeah."

Both boys sat thinking for a while. Neither one of them had ever seen a real gun before. Both of them thought it was neat and sort of scary at the same time. Each of them thought about what it would be like to keep it.

"I don't think my parents will let me keep it, Sam."

"I know my mom wouldn't. She would say I'm not old enough."

"When do you think you'd be old enough?" asked Theo.

Sam thought for a moment. "I don't really know. Maybe in high school or something."

"Do you think we could hide it until then?"

"It might break or someone else could find it by then, Theo. That's not for years and years."

"Yeah, second grade is a long way from high school."

"So what are you going to do?" asked Sam.

"Maybe I should give it to somebody," said Theo. Or at least tell somebody about it."

"Who?"

"I don't know."

"Maybe they'd think you stole it."

"But I didn't."

"But they might think you did."

"I don't want to get in trouble."

"You could put it back," suggested Sam.

"In the trash can?"

"Yeah."

"Someone else might find it." Theo started wrapping the gun back up in the cloth he found it in.

"So?"

"Well, it's mine."

"No, it isn't," said Sam.

"Yes, it is," insisted Theo.

"Then take it home."

"I can't."

"Then what are you going to do?" asked Sam.

"I guess I'll put it back where I found it."

"I'll help you."

"Okay."

The two boys walked slowly back to the alley behind Theo's house. Sam lifted up a bunch of trash so his friend could shove the gun down to the bottom of the trash can.

"Thanks. Are you gonna tell your dad?"

"Do you think I should?"

Sam just shrugged his shoulders.

"Yeah," said Theo, "I guess I will."

"I'll go with you."

"Okay."

Sam and Theo walked slowly back down the alley to Theo's house, hoping they did the right thing.

A SPECIAL SHOW AND TELL

Objective:

Students will name people who can help them stay safe.

Life Skills:

I will try to be in places where I can stay safe. (PF4)

I will listen to wise adults and follow rules and laws. (PF17)

I will act in ways to keep myself safe. (PF18)

Materials:

A Special Show And Tell (page 437), crayons

Motivation:

1 If possible, invite a police officer to visit your classroom. The police officer might read the story *A Special Show And Tell* to the students, and/or answer questions. Or, you can read *A Special Show And Tell* aloud to the students.

2 Explain that there are many people in a home, school, and community who try to protect children and can help them stay safe. Explain that a police officer is one of the people who can help them stay safe.

3 Discuss the following questions about the story with your students. Suggested answers are given after each question.

Who are some people who might help keep them safe?
Parents, police officers, teachers, and so on.

What did you learn about police officers from this story?
Police officers are just like other people in many ways. They have families, and they work hard at their jobs like other people do.

Why didn't Officer Dan let the children hold his gun?
It is never safe for a child to hold a gun. Guns are not toys.

How many of you have ever met a police officer? What was (s)he like?
Answers will vary.

4 Discuss how police officers help keep children safe. Police are always available to answer questions or to help a person who needs help; they are always watching for dangerous situations in which a person might be harmed; they help people who have accidents, and so on.

5 Explain that police officers make sure people obey rules. Explain that rules are made to help protect people. Discuss types of rules students can follow such as classroom rules, school rules, and rules that their parent(s) set at home. These rules are designed to help students and other people stay safe.

6 Point out that students can protect themselves. Students can try to stay in places where they are safe. If they are lost, they can find one of the people identified as helping them stay safe. They can choose to spend time with people who encourage them to do their best and to choose actions that are safe. They can stay away from people who try to harm them. They can tell a trusted adult if someone tries to harm them.

Evaluation:

Have students draw a picture of a person who can help them stay safe. Ask students to share their pictures with the class. They can take their pictures home to share with their parents. Ask students to talk with their parents about people who can help keep them safe.

A Special Show And Tell
By Patricia M. Dashiell

Steve stood nervously in front of the classroom, waiting for the laughter to die down. Even the teacher was laughing.

"Now, what did you say?" asked Ms. Robbins.

"My dad is my show and tell today," insisted Steve again.

"Really?" asked his teacher.

"Yes." Why doesn't she believe me, thought Steve. And where is my dad?

"Where is he?" Ms. Robbins glanced at the clock. "It's 8:45 already."

"I don't know," Steve replied in a small voice, "but he is coming," he added loudly.

"Well, we'll get on with our work. When he comes, we'll stop."

"All right," mumbled Steve, disappointed that his dad had not arrived yet.

Throughout the morning, Steve could not pay attention to his work. He even missed two words on his spelling test. He kept wondering where his father was.

Just before lunch, there was a knock on the door. Before Ms. Robbins could answer it, the door opened and in walked Steve's father, wearing his uniform.

Ms. Robbins looked worried when she saw the police officer in her room. "May I help you?"

Before he could answer, Steve jumped out of his seat, knocked his chair over, and threw himself at his father. "Daddy, I was worried."

"Why, Stevie? I told you I would come, didn't I?"

"Yes, but you're late."

"I'm sorry, son. I couldn't help it."

"Were you catching some more bad guys?"

"Yep." Steve's father rumpled his son's hair and then picked him up for a quick hug. He turned toward Ms. Robbins and asked, "Am I too late?"

"For show and tell? No, of course not." Ms. Robbins turned to the class.

"Children, stop working on whatever you are doing and meet me on the carpet. We are going to have a special show and tell."

Some of the students had been staring at Steve's father the whole time. Everyone quickly got up and scrambled to the carpet, fighting for spaces near the front.

"What should we call you?" asked Ms. Robbins as she led Steve's father to the carpet. Steve followed, happily swinging his hand in his father's.

"You may call me Officer Dan."

"Fine. Why don't you take the chair up front. Steve, do you want to introduce your dad?"

Steve nodded yes and went to stand next to his dad, who was sitting in the armchair reserved for special use.

"This is my dad. You may call him Officer Dan. He's a police officer and does a lot of hard work to keep us safe. He's here for my show and tell. I told him to let you ask questions."

Steve sat down and waited. The room was really quiet at first, and then, one by one, students started raising their hands.

Jonathan was called on first. "I didn't know police officers had kids."

"Yes, we do. We have families. Stevie here can tell you about the picnics he's gone on with other officers' families."

"Do you like being called a cop?" asked Cyndi.

"It doesn't bother me at all."

"How about Pig?" she continued.

"What's your name?"

"Uh, uh, Cyndi." Cyndi was scared that she had made him mad.

"Cyndi, where did you hear that word?"

"TV."

"Well, it's not a nice name for police officers. People who use it mean it to be rude. I don't like it when people are rude, but I'll still do my job and try to protect them."

Mike had been staring at the gun, so he asked next, "Have you ever shot anyone?"

"Yes."

"Did you ever kill anybody?"

"Yes, I did."

"Tell 'em how it made you feel, Daddy, like you told me," prompted Stevie, worried that his classmates would think his father was bad.

"It made me very sad, as I've told Steve. Last year I saw a man rob a corner store. He shot the clerk and ran down the street. He was running through the streets and I was chasing him. I warned him to stop, and he turned to shoot me. He missed, but I didn't. What he did was wrong, but I didn't want to kill him. I had to."

"You didn't want to?" asked Stacy. "The cops on TV are always killing people."

Steve's dad laughed. "Television is not the best place from which to learn things. Sometimes people are killed on television shows to make more people watch the show, but police officers do not just shoot people like that. We have very strict rules about when we should shoot our guns."

"Can I hold your gun?" asked Mike.

"That is not such a good idea. Police officers are responsible for their guns at all times, and I bet your mommy and daddy wouldn't like for you to touch this," Steve's father answered as he placed his hand on his gun.

"My daddy has a gun," offered Jessica.

"So does mine," echoed several of Steve's classmates.

His dad nodded his head a few times. "I know a lot of people have guns. Does your daddy let you play with his gun?" he asked Jessica.

"Nope."

"That's good. Guns are not toys. Does anyone else have any questions?"

"I do," said Susan.

"Okay."

"What's the best part about your job, Officer Dan?"

"That's easy," replied Steve's dad. "I like helping people best. I especially like helping children. Just a couple of weeks ago a girl your age was missing. We found her in less than a day and brought her back to her parents. That's the best part about my job."

Several children still had their hands raised, but Ms. Robbins walked toward the chair. "Thank you for coming, Officer Dan. We have enjoyed your visit. It's time for lunch now, children."

Several students groaned and complained that Steve's dad hadn't been there long enough.

"Come on now, get your lunches and line up at the door."

Steve sat in his dad's lap and hugged him. "You want to eat lunch with me?"

"What's for lunch?"

"Pizza!"

"Sure."

Steve smiled all the way through lunch and for the rest of the afternoon. He liked having his dad come to visit him at school. Everyone had wanted to sit next to them at lunch, and his classmates surrounded him at recess asking lots of questions.

This was the best Friday Steve had had all year.

FOREST FRIENDS

Objective:

Students will tell healthful ways to express anger.

Life Skill:

I will express my anger in healthful ways. (PF6)

Materials:

Forest Friends (page 443), five copies of the script; puppets to represent the characters: Robert Rabbit, Deenie Deer, Sally Squirrel, Randy Redbird, and Mother Rabbit; one paper bag for each student; crayons or colored markers

Motivation:

1 To prepare for this strategy, make puppets out of paper bags to represent each character in the script *Forest Friends*.

2 If there are students in the class able to read the script *Forest Friends* aloud, choose five of these students to perform the puppet show. Or, choose five students from a class in a higher grade to perform the puppet show for your class. Give these students copies of the script to read in advance, and assign the parts.

3 Introduce the term anger. **Anger** is the feeling of being irritated, annoyed, and/or furious. Tell the students they are going to watch a puppet show about what can happen when someone becomes angry. Have each puppet character introduce himself/herself. Have students perform the puppet show for the class.

4 Discuss the following questions regarding the puppet show. Suggested answers are give after each question.

> What happened to Robert Rabbit when he got angry?
> His face got red, he threw pebbles at the big frog, and he jumped on the slippery rocks and fell into the pond.

> Did Robert Rabbit express his angry feelings in healthful or harmful ways?
> Harmful, because throwing pebbles could have hurt the big frog, and he could have hurt himself jumping on the slippery rocks.

5 Explain that anger is a feeling that *everyone* experiences at times. Explain that there are healthful ways of dealing with anger and there are harmful ways of dealing with anger. Healthful ways result in a solution to the situation that caused the anger without anyone being harmed. Discuss healthful ways to deal with anger including:

- *Take time to think about it.* Sometimes it is difficult to realize how angry you are. Wait until you calm down before doing anything.
- *Talk to the person who made you angry.* It is possible that the person who made you angry does not realize how you feel.
- *Ask a grownup for help.* You may not know what to do. A trusted grownup will listen and help resolve the situation.
- *Draw a picture.* Sometimes it relieves angry feelings if you draw a picture of the person or situation that made you angry. Share the picture with the teacher or with the person who caused the anger.
- *Take a deep breath and relax.* If you take a few deep breaths, and think about an activity you like to do, you will calm down.

- *Punch a pillow.* You can express angry feelings in this way without causing harm to yourself or to anyone else.

6 Pass out one paper bag for each student, and crayons or colored markers. Have students make their own animal puppets.

Evaluation:

Have students sit in a circle on the floor with their puppets. Go around the circle, and ask students to share something that can make a person angry. They can finish the sentence, "My puppet gets angry when..." and describe a situation. After each student responds, have other students hold up their puppets and volunteer ways to resolve the situation in healthful ways. For example, if a student says that his/her puppet gets angry when a brother or sister teases it, then other students might suggest asking the brother or sister in a nice way to stop or asking a grownup for help.

Forest Friends

By Patricia M. Dashiell

Robert Rabbit comes home with his friends Deenie Deer, Sally Squirrel, and Randy Redbird.

Mother Rabbit:	What happened to you?
Robert Rabbit:	I fell in the pond today.
Mother Rabbit:	You fell in the pond?
Robert Rabbit:	Well, I sort of fell in the pond?
Mother Rabbit:	What do you mean, sort of?
Robert Rabbit:	I didn't fall in exactly.
Mother Rabbit:	What did you do then?
Deenie Deer:	Don't be mad. It wasn't his fault.
Mother Rabbit:	Did you see what happened?
Deenie Deer:	[all three together] We all did.
Sally Squirrel:	I did.
Randy Redbird:	Yes, we did.
Mother Rabbit:	Do you want to tell me what happened?
Robert Rabbit:	I think I should go to my room and dry off. [He hurries to leave so his mother won't stop him.]
Deenie Deer:	You see, Mother Rabbit, it happened like this. We were playing by the pond and just talking together.
Randy Redbird:	Yeah, we were just talking together.
Deenie Deer:	I'm telling the story.
Randy Redbird:	Okay.
Deenie Deer:	We were playing and decided to pretend to be frogs. And then it happened.
Mother Rabbit:	What happened?
Deenie Deer:	Robert fell in the pond.
Randy Redbird:	Well, not exactly.
Mother Rabbit:	Do you want to tell me what exactly happened?
Randy Redbird:	Well…[Sally Squirrel interrupts.]
Sally Squirrel:	We were by the pond pretending to be frogs, and this big frog started yelling at us and it happened.

Mother Rabbit:	Robert fell in?
Sally Squirrel:	Yes.
Robert Rabbit:	[Walking back in] Did they tell you what happened?
Mother Rabbit:	Well, I've heard from Deenie and Sally that you were playing by the pond, pretending to be a frog. Then this big frog started yelling for no reason at all, and you fell in. Does that sound right?
Robert Rabbit:	Doesn't it sound right to you?
Mother Rabbit:	Actually, no. It sounds like they are leaving something out.
Randy Redbird:	Well, they are.
Mother Rabbit:	What?
Sally Squirrel:	The part where Robert's face got all red.
Deenie Deer:	The part where Robert threw pebbles at the frog
Randy Redbird:	And the part where Robert was jumping on the rocks by the bank. The slippery rocks.
Mother Rabbit:	Why was he doing that?
Randy Redbird:	Because he got angry.
Mother Rabbit:	[A big sigh] I knew it must have to do with your temper. How many times have I told you that you should be careful of what you do when you are angry?
Robert Rabbit:	[In a very small voice] Lots of times.
Mother Rabbit:	Too many times. Now, tell me what happened.
Robert Rabbit:	Oh, we were playing by the pond and minding our own business like Deenie and Sally said. And there was a big frog. And he did yell at us. And I did jump on the rocks and fall in. But the reason the frog was yelling at us was because he saw us playing and tried to tell us how to jump like a frog. I said that I already knew how to jump like a frog and told him to leave us alone. He didn't like that and kept telling us how to play. He made fun of me and said I was the worst frog he had ever seen. Then, I got mad. I threw pebbles at him, but he

just kept jumping from rock to rock and laughing at me. Finally, I said I could show him what a good frog I was. I jumped over to the slippery rocks to show him that I was a good jumping frog.

Mother Rabbit:	Well?
Robert Rabbit:	Well, what?
Mother Rabbit:	What do you have to say now?
Robert Rabbit:	I guess I shouldn't have gotten so mad. When I get mad I sometimes do silly things. I shouldn't have thrown pebbles at him. I shouldn't have jumped on the slippery rocks.
Mother Rabbit:	And?
Robert Rabbit:	And, I'm sorry.
Mother Rabbit:	All right. Now you should tell the big frog you are sorry that you got so angry. And why don't all of you go with Robert when he tells the big frog he is sorry. And, why don't you ask the frog to play with you? [She waits for the friends to leave.] Oh, my, what a day. Now I have to get back to baking the carrot cake for dinner!

My Friend George

Objective:

Students will tell ways to say NO when other children want them to act in ways that would harm themselves or others.

Life Skills:

I will develop positive self-esteem. (PF2)
I will make wise choices. (PF12)
I will say NO when others want me to act in harmful ways. (PF13)
I will stay away from gangs. (PF16)

Materials:

My Friend George (page 448), a paper bag for the teacher and each student, colored markers or crayons

Motivation:

1 To prepare for this strategy, make a puppet out of a paper bag. The mouth of the puppet should be drawn on the flap so that the mouth can open and close. This puppet will represent the character George in the script *My Friend George.*

2 Use the puppet as a ventriloquist would use a dummy, and read *My Friend George* aloud to the students. Encourage the students to respond when they are asked questions.

3 Explain to students that if they are asked to do something that is not healthful or safe, they must say NO. Perhaps they were asked to tell a lie. Perhaps they were asked to take something that belonged to another student. Explain that these are examples of actions that would harm another person.

4 Ask students to think back to the puppet show, *My Friend George.* Point out that George's friend Joey wanted George to do things that George did not want to do. Explain that sometimes a friend like Joey might want them to do something that is not safe and might harm themselves or others. Remind students that even if a group of people want them to do something that might harm themselves or others, they must stand their ground and say NO.

5 Introduce the term decision. A **decision** is a choice. A wise decision is one that protects self and others. Explain that a person is more apt to make wise decisions if (s)he feels good about himself/herself. If (s)he feels good about himself/herself, (s)he is less likely to agree to any behavior that might harm himself/herself or others. Explain that students can do things to help them feel good about themselves. They can work to do their best in school, develop a special skill or talent, and choose friends who encourage them to do their best.

6 Have students make their own puppets out of paper bags and colored markers or crayons. Explain that they are going to use their puppets to help them practice saying NO.

Evaluation:

Explain that you are going to tell several situations in which a person is pressured to do something. If the situation would be harmful, students should pretend to make their puppets answer NO by opening their puppets' mouths. Students also should say NO in a strong, clear voice. The following are examples of situations to use. 1) A student wants you to fight him in the yard after school. 2) A friend wants you to steal something from another person. 3) Your friend wants you to hold the knife she found on the ground. 4) A friend wants you to throw a rock at someone's window.

My Friend George

By Patricia M. Dashiell

Teacher:	Today we are going to talk about saying NO. I have my friend George here. Say hi, George.
George:	Hi.
Teacher:	George needs to learn how to say NO, because he is always doing things that get him in trouble.
George:	But I don't mean to.
Teacher:	Or letting other people talk him into doing things he doesn't want to do.
George:	Like telling lies.
Teacher:	Like telling lies. George told me that one time he lied to his parents about where his little sister was because his friends were daring him to tell a lie.
George:	But what do you do if you want to keep your friends?
Teacher:	If your friends are asking you to lie, then they are not being good friends to you.
George:	What would you have said?
Teacher:	I would have said NO. [turns to class] Can you help George? Let's say NO together.
Class:	NO!
Teacher:	But saying NO is sometimes not enough. What if someone is asking you to lie? You can say friends don't make friends tell lies.
George:	NO! Friends don't make friends tell lies.
Teacher:	[to the class] Can you say that with him?
Class and George:	NO! Friends don't make friends tell lies.
George:	Okay, I got it. Ask me to lie now.
Teacher:	Hey, George. Why don't you come over to the park with me?
George:	You know I can't go there. My parents wouldn't let me.
Teacher:	Then don't tell them where we're going.
George:	NO! That's a lie. Friends don't make friends lie. Hey...I did it!

Teacher:	That's right, you did! What other things might you need to say NO to?
George:	Well, I took a pack of gum from the store once, but that's because Joey did it. He told me to take some too.
Teacher:	What could you have said to him?
George:	No?
Teacher:	How about, NO! Friends don't make friends steal.
George:	NO! Friends don't make friends steal. NO! Friends don't make friends steal.
Teacher:	[To the class] Can you help him again?
Class and George:	NO! Friends don't make friends steal.
George:	Will you test me now?
Teacher:	Pretend you're with me at the store. Hey, George, do you want some candy?
George:	Sure.
Teacher:	Well, I don't have any money, but I know how we can get some anyway.
George:	Really? How's that?
Teacher:	You stand in front of me, and I'll slip some candy into your pocket.
George:	Isn't that stealing?

Teacher:	It's only stealing if you get caught.
George:	NO! It's still stealing even if you don't get caught. Besides, friends don't make friends steal. Wow, that wasn't too hard.
Teacher:	You're right, George. It is just as easy to tell the truth as it is to lie, or not to steal as it is to steal.
George:	Hey, how did you get so smart anyway?
Teacher:	I went to school! How about trying one more thing to say NO to?
George:	Well, sometimes Joey makes fun of other kids and tells me to do it too.
Teacher:	Do you like to be made fun of?
George:	Uh, I guess not.
Teacher:	Hey, George!
George:	What?
Teacher:	Those ears of yours....
George:	What about them?
Teacher:	They stick up and look dumb.
George:	I was born this way. I can't help it. Why are you being so mean, anyway?
Teacher:	How did you feel when I made fun of you?
George:	I get your point. I felt awful.
Teacher:	Now what would you tell Joey?
George:	Definitely NO.
Teacher:	How about, NO. I don't like being teased, so why should I tease someone else?
George:	Okay, I got it.
Teacher:	Remember, George, friends don't make friends do things they don't want to do.
George:	Friends don't make friends do things they don't want to do. Friends don't make friends do things they don't want to do.
Teacher:	[to the class] Can you remember that? Say it with George.

Class and George:	Friends don't make friends do things they don't want to do.
Teacher:	Nice job. Just remember, you can always say NO, even if your friends are saying YES.
George:	Got it.
Teacher:	Good. Now, let's go get some ice cream.
George:	Just one more thing.
Teacher:	What is it?
George:	Do my ears really look dumb?
Teacher:	No, silly. I was just pretending.
George:	Whew! You had me worried for a while!

GRUMPY AND BUSY AND MEAN

Objective:

Students will explain that drugs may change the way a person acts.

Life Skills:

I will not try alcohol or other drugs. (PF14)
I will stay away from persons who use harmful drugs. (PF14)

Materials:

Grumpy And Busy And Mean (page 454), paper, colored markers or crayons

Motivation:

1 Read the poem *Grumpy And Busy And Mean* aloud to the students.

2 Discuss the following questions. Suggested answers are given after each question.

What is this poem about?
The poem describes how drugs affect people, how the narrator's brother takes pills, how the pills make his/her brother act mean.

How did the narrator feel about his/her brother?
(S)he may have been confused because (s)he loved his/her brother, but did not like the way he acted.

Is it always harmful to take pills?
No. Medicine that a doctor tells you to take and that is given to you by a responsible adult is not harmful. However, students should never take a drug that is not given to them by a responsible adult.

3 Introduce the term drug. A **drug** is a substance that changes the way the body/or mind works. Explain that alcohol is a drug. Explain that when people drink alcohol or take drugs that have not been prescribed to them by a doctor, they may not be able to think clearly or may not be able to control their feelings. Their behavior may be affected. They may not act in ways that they ordinarily would. Their behavior can become out of control and may become violent. When this happens, the person who uses drugs and any people around him/her can be harmed. This is one reason that it is very important for students to make a decision not to try alcohol and other drugs. It is also the reason to stay away from any person who is using harmful drugs.

4 Pass out the paper and colored markers or crayons. Have students draw a picture of a bottle of pills. Explain that these pictures represent drugs that have not been prescribed by a doctor. Collect the papers. In an empty section of the room, drop each paper on the floor so that the papers are scattered. Have students line up and put their hands on each others' shoulders. The person in front is the leader. Explain that (s)he will guide the rest of the students through a drug-free path. Students should avoid stepping on the pictures of drugs that have not been prescribed by a doctor or given by an adult, just as they should avoid using drugs in real life. The leader, with the train of students following, should try to walk around the room without stepping on any of the papers.

Evaluation:

Tell students you are going to give examples of situations in which a person is using drugs. If the example is a situation that is harmful to the person, the students should call out NO. If the situation is not harmful, the students should call out YES. Examples of situations that are harmful might include one in which a student finds a bottle with pills on the ground, a person uses a drug someone sold to them on the street, and a student takes a pill that (s)he has found in the medicine cabinet. Examples of situations that are not harmful might include one in which a doctor gives a student medicine for a sore throat, and a parent gives a child a pill that the doctor has prescribed.

Grumpy and Busy and Mean

By Patricia M. Dashiell

I have a brother, a father, a mother;
I have a family I love.
I have a brother, a father, a mother,
I sometimes don't understand.

Daddy gets grumpy and needs his newspaper.
Momma gets busy and needs her helper.
 (That's me!)
But my brother gets mean and needs the pills he hides
 from Daddy and Momma and me.
 (I wish he didn't.)

Papers I like.
Helping is fine.

But pills...
Maybe I'm small. Maybe I'm young.
Maybe I'm not 'cause I know the pills are wrong.

Grumpy is okay. I get grumpy.
Busy is alright. I get busy.
Mean is...
        ...mean!

SOME ARE AND OTHERS AREN'T

Objective:

Students will name persons who can help them stay safe.

Life Skills:

I will try to be in places where I can stay safe. (PF4)

I will listen to wise adults and follow rules and laws. (PF17)

I will act in ways to keep myself safe. (PF18)

Materials:

Some Are And Others Aren't (page 457), colored paper, colored markers or crayons

Motivation:

1 Read the poem *Some Are And Others Aren't* aloud to the students. Read it a second time aloud slowly.

2 Discuss the following questions. Suggested answers are given after the question.

What do we learn from the poem?
There are some people who are strangers and other people who are not. It is important to be careful around strangers.

Who are some of the strangers in the poem?
A man on the street, a woman in the car, someone at the store, someone at the park, anyone you don't know.

Who are some of the people in the poem who are not strangers?
A father, a mother, an aunt, an uncle, family, friends.

3 Encourage students who do not live in a nurturing environment to stay around people with whom they feel safe as much as possible. Encourage them to make friends at school with people who will help them do their best. At the same time, encourage students who do live in a nurturing environment to choose to be in safe places and with people with whom they feel safe.

4 Discuss the importance of letting someone know when they do not feel safe. Discuss people they can trust to help keep them safe. For example, remind them that:
- A school principal makes sure that only certain people are allowed in the school building.
- A teacher keeps his/her students safe by taking care of them during the school day.
- A school nurse cleans scrapes and cuts when students fall on the playground.
- A police officer patrols a neighborhood to make sure that people who live there are safe.
- A neighbor may have a "SAFE HOME" sign in the window to let children know they can come there for help if they do not feel safe.

5 Explain how important it is to cooperate with adults who help children stay safe. Even if children do not understand why these grownups have certain rules, they need to obey those rules if they are to be safe. Obeying rules is an important way for students to keep themselves safe.

6 Ask students to raise their thumbs up in the air. Explain that you are going to describe situations in which there are adults. Students should place their thumbs up or down to identify adults they can trust or adults who are strangers.

Students should give a "thumbs-up" sign when you identify an adult they can trust. Students should give a "thumbs-down" sign when you identify an adult who is a stranger. Examples of adults whom students can trust might include a parent, a school nurse, a teacher, a doctor, and a school principal. Examples of adults who are strangers might include a person in a car asking for directions, a person sitting on a bus, and a person shopping in a mall.

Evaluation:

Show students how to fold a sheet of paper into four equal parts. Students are to draw pictures of two people whom they trust and two people whom they would consider strangers. Have students share their pictures with the class and discuss why someone in the picture may be considered a trusted adult or considered a stranger. Students should take the papers home and share them with their parents.

Some Are And Others Aren't

By Patricia M. Dashiell

A man on the street
is a stranger,
a father is not.

A woman in a car
is a stranger,
a mother is not.

Someone at the store
is a stranger,
an aunt is not.

Someone at the park
is a stranger,
an uncle is not.

Anyone you don't know
is a stranger,
family and friends are not.

Play with your friends,
visit your relatives,
hug your family,
but
be careful of
a stranger.

A THIEF IN THE NIGHT

Objective:

Students will identify and describe types of abuse: emotional, sexual, physical, and neglect.

Life Skills:

I will strive for healthful family relationships. (PF3)

I will develop resiliency to "bounce back" if I was reared in a dysfunctional family. (PF3)

I will practice self-protection strategies. (PF18)

I will participate in recovery if a victim. (PF19)

Materials:

A Thief In The Night (page 460), one copy for each student, paper, colored markers or pencils, a phone directory

Motivation:

1 Introduce the story by asking students if they have ever scraped their knees or elbows. Ask them what a person does when (s)he has a small scrape. Students will answer that they might put medicine and a bandage on the scrape. Explain that the bandage helps the scrape heal. Ask students what a person does when (s)he breaks an arm or leg. Discuss how putting a bandage on the broken arm or leg is not enough to help the arm or leg heal. This person needs to see a doctor for extra help to fix the arm or leg and help it heal.

2 Explain that sometimes people are hurt and try to heal themselves, when they really need help from other people to help them to heal. Tell them that the story they are going to

read is about a kind of hurt that is different from a scrape or broken leg.

3 Give a copy of A Thief In The Night to each student. Have the students read the story to themselves.

4 When students have finished reading, discuss the following questions. Suggested answers are listed below the question.

> What happened to Mary's and David's house?
>> Their house was robbed.

> How did Mary and David feel after the robbery?
>> They felt scared that they might be robbed again. They were upset that their belongings had been taken. They did not feel safe.

> Why do you think Mary and David were afraid to admit they were scared?
>> They did not want to admit they were scared because they wanted to act grownup and because their parents did not seem scared.

> What could Mary and David do to feel safe besides sneak into each other's rooms?
>> They could have talked to their parents or another trusted adult. It is important to share feelings after being a victim of violence.

> Why do you think their parents had not noticed how scared they were?
>> Their parents may have been hiding their own feelings too, in order to be brave for Mary and David. They may have had many things on their minds

such as reporting the crime, dealing with the police, and buying an alarm for their house to warn them if a stranger enters their house. Sometimes it is hard for parents or other people to know what others are thinking. This is one reason it is important to share feelings and thoughts.

5 Discuss the importance of recovery if a victim of violence. A **victim** is a person who is harmed by violence. Explain that a person may be harmed in many ways. A person may be a victim of child abuse. **Child abuse** is the harmful treatment of a person who is under the age of 18. It includes physical abuse, which harms the body. It includes emotional abuse, which may be in the form of using cruel words to put down, threaten, or frighten another person. Sexual abuse involves sexual behavior between an adult and a child, and is wrong. Neglect involves lack of proper care, such as not feeding or clothing a child or leaving a child alone without proper supervision.

6 Remind students that in the story, Mary and David were still feeling scared even though the robbery had happened two weeks earlier. Discuss how victims of violence may take a long time to recover. In the time period soon after being harmed, victims may feel depressed, sad, angry, afraid, and may have difficulty sleeping and nightmares. Remind students that it is important to talk to a parent about their feelings if they or someone they know has been a victim of violence. If they are unable to talk to a parent, or do not feel comfortable talking to a parent, it is important to share feelings with a trusted adult such as a teacher, counselor, doctor, or relative.

7 Have students close their eyes and think about a belonging they really like. It may be a bicycle, a pair of sneakers, or a pet. Then ask them to think about how they would feel if this item were taken away. Have students share how they would feel with the class. Explain that these feelings are common after a person is a victim of a robbery.

Evaluation:

Have the students create a Victim Recovery Booklet of their own. In the booklet, students should identify people they might talk to if they were victims of violence. They might look up organizations, names of doctors, or medical facilities and other sources of help in the community and write these in the booklet.

A Thief In The Night

By Patricia M. Dashiell

Mary lay awake in bed wondering what time it was. She thought it must be hours and hours past her bedtime, but she could still hear her parents in the den. Mary knew she couldn't move until they went to their bedroom. She heard her brother on the other side of the wall, so she tapped softly on the wall to let him know she was awake. He, too, was waiting.

When he heard his sister, David put his hand flat against the wall, wanting to hold her hand. Only three nights ago he had asked to move his bed to the other side of his room. He had told their parents that he just wanted to change his room around. David didn't want them to know how scared he was. He was glad Mary understood. She, too, was scared.

Two weeks before the whole family had gotten up in the morning and found their house had been robbed while they were sleeping. No one had heard the thief or anything at all. The thief took their stereo, television, and the knife collection David had hanging on his bedroom wall. Grandpa had collected knives since he was a little boy and gave the collection to David on his eighth birthday, this past summer. David shuddered every time he thought of a thief coming into his room while he was sleeping.

He finally heard his sister come into his room. "David, are you still awake?"

"Yeah. Are you gonna stay?"

"Of course. Did you set the watch?"

"It's right here." He pointed to his father's sports watch wrapped around the headboard. "I set it for 6:30."

Mary crawled into bed and turned her back to her brother. Since she was two years older than her brother, she felt responsible. Neither one of them wanted their parents to know how much the robbery still bothered them. Their parents had installed an alarm in the house, but neither of the children trusted it.

"Mary?"

"Yeah?"

"Are you asleep yet?"

"No." Mary pressed her back against David's and reached out to squeeze his hand. "Are you having trouble sleeping?"

"Yeah. I'm afraid of—you know."

"Of what?"

"Of bad dreams. I keep dreaming that person comes back and takes me with him."

"David, he's not coming back. And even if he did, Mom and Dad wouldn't let that happen."

"How would they know someone was here? They didn't hear him the first time."

"If he tried to take you, you would wake up, and you could scream and scream until they came."

"What if I were too scared to scream?"

"I would scream for you. That's why I'm here."

Mary heard her brother sigh. Both children wondered when they would stop feeling so scared, when they would be as brave as their parents.

The next morning, neither one of them heard the watch alarm ring. Their mother walked in David's room to wake him up and found Mary sleeping with her arms wrapped protectively around her brother.

"Mary! David! It's time to wake up." She shook both her children gently on the shoulder.

"Huh?" Mary sat up rubbing her eyes. She stopped when she saw her mother looking at them and leaned over to poke her brother. "David, get up."

"What? Oh." David sat up and looked at his mother and his sister. Ashamed for his mother to find Mary in his room, he dropped his head and pulled at the blanket in front of him.

"Mary, why are you in here?"

"I, umm, had trouble sleeping."

"Why?" Her mother noticed the watch and reached over to pull it off the headboard. "And what is Daddy's watch doing in here?"

Mary shrugged her shoulders and looked at her brother. She didn't know how to explain. She didn't know how to say that she and David were terrified of a person they had never seen or heard, a faceless figure who had grown into a terrible monster in their dreams.

"Frank? Frank, come in here." Her mother called over her shoulder as she sat on the bed and pulled her children to either side of her. "Now somebody tell me what's going on. You two haven't slept in the same room in years."

She waited, but David and Mary remained silent. Looking up, she saw her husband coming into the room. "Good, maybe you can get them to talk. I found Mary sleeping in David's room and your watch on the headboard, and nobody wants to tell me anything."

Taking one look at his son huddled on the bed, David's father scooped David up in his arms and sat him down on his lap.

"How about it, champ. Is something wrong?" His father asked.

David nodded his head. Mary decided to explain.

"I've been sleeping in here because of the bad dreams that David's — well, we've been having."

"What bad dreams?" Her father prompted.

"Dreams about that person."

462

"What person?"

"The one who robbed us. David's scared he's gonna come and take him away, and I am afraid, too, I guess."

Her parents looked at each other in surprise.

"Honey, we had no idea you were this scared. Why didn't you tell one of us?"

Mary was glad her parents didn't seem mad.

"Daddy, you and Mommy aren't scared at all, and you got the alarm, and told us everything was all right. How could we tell you it wasn't?"

"Mary, your father and I always want to know how you feel. We...we thought that you felt safe and were not worried since you didn't say anything."

"We don't, though. We don't feel safe at all, and nighttime scares us most. Right, David?"

David nodded his head again and wrapped his arms around his father's neck. "I'm sorry," he whispered.

"For what?"

"For not being brave like you asked us to be."

His father looked at his mother and hugged David close. "I think we need to spend some time talking about the things that man took from us."

David looked up at his father. "You mean the TV and stuff?"

"No," his father whispered softly as he looked around at his family huddled together on the bed.

STEWART'S BIRTHDAY

Objective:

Students will name kinds of violence and ways to protect against violence.

Life Skills:

I will recognize that violent behavior is wrong. (PF1)
I will practice suicide prevention strategies. (PF9)
I will avoid discrimination. (PF11)
I will practice self-protection strategies. (PF18)

Materials:

Stewart's Birthday (page 466), *Protecting Yourself From Violence* (page 469), one copy for each student

Motivation:

1 Read *Stewart's Birthday* aloud to the students. Ask students how the story made them feel. Students may answer they felt sad, surprised, or angry.

2 Explain that it is important to recognize that a person can be harmed if (s)he is near people who are violent or (s)he is in a situation that is violent or may become violent. **Violence** is the threat of or use of force to harm a person or property. Explain that there are may types of violence including:

- **Fighting** is taking part in a physical struggle.
- **Homicide** is the killing of another person. It may be on purpose or it may be an accident.
- **Suicide** is the taking of one's own life on purpose.

- **Child abuse** is the harmful treatment of a person under the age of 18.
- **Domestic violence** is violence that occurs within the family or within other relationships in which people live together.

3 Explain that it is important to recognize violent behavior. It is important to recognize that violent behavior is wrong because a person or people may be harmed. Explain that everyone has a right to be safe. A person who chooses violent behavior is choosing a wrong behavior.

4 Introduce the term discriminatory behavior. **Discriminatory behavior** is acting differently toward or showing behavior that is in favor of or prejudiced against a person or group of people. When a person chooses discriminatory behavior, (s)he treats some people with respect and others with disrespect. When people are treated with disrespect, they may become angry or violent. Explain that it is wrong to treat a person with disrespect, and disrespect may lead to violence.

5 Introduce the term self-protection strategies. **Self-protection strategies** are strategies that can be practiced to protect oneself and to lessen the risk of being a victim. A **victim** is a person who is harmed by violence. Give a copy of *Protecting Yourself From Violence* to each student. Students can use this master as a checklist to review self-protection strategies they might practice.

6 Ask students to remember how they felt when you were reading the story and they discovered that Larnell was killed. Ask students what types of plans and goals Larnell might have had for the future. Students may say that Larnell wanted to play basketball, that he may have wanted to get married, or go to college. Remind students that because of violence, Larnell would never have the chance to do any of those things. Have students identify a person to whom they look up. Students may choose a parent, an older brother or sister, or a neighbor. Ask students to close their eyes and think about how they would feel if this person was harmed by violence. Have students share their feelings.

Evaluation:

Have students take a piece of drawing paper, fold it in half, and draw a line down the middle of the page. Have the students draw a picture to illustrate a type of violence on the left side of the page. On the right side of the page they should draw a picture of how to avoid the type of violence they have drawn. Use the drawings to create a Violence Prevention display.

Stewart's Birthday

By Patricia M. Dashiell

Stewart was so excited he couldn't keep his feet on the ground, almost. He wished he could hold Larnell's hand, but he knew his brother would think that was uncool. After all, Stewart wasn't a baby anymore. Today was his tenth birthday — double digits, Larnell told him. And Larnell knew about everything. He was fifteen and in junior high.

Stewart hopped up on the curb and back down, repeatedly, to let out some of his excitement. He and Larnell were on their way down to the Sam's-On-The-Corner where the older kids hung out and ate burgers and watched the girls. Stewart didn't care anything about the girls, but he liked being included in his brother's plans. Larnell had promised that later, they were going to see a movie. Just the two of them. They were going to get hotdogs and popcorn and drinks and candy, the whole movie thing.

Walking down the street, Stewart sneaked a look at his brother. He was envious of the strip of blue cloth his brother wore around his baseball cap. Larnell had friends, cool friends, who were his brothers. They hung out together and played together. Only Stewart knew that teenagers didn't play together, they just were together doing the same thing.

Larnell was tall for his age and a great basketball player. The neighborhood kids played ball together all the time, and everyone wanted Larnell on their team. Stewart knew Larnell dreamed of being in the NBA, but Larnell never said anything about it to anybody so Stewart kept quiet too. Stewart hoped his brother made it, though, just like he hoped he would grow tall himself. At ten, Stewart was the shortest kid in the fourth grade.

Stewart had dreams of his own, although he too did not share them. He wanted to go to college and study medicine. Nobody in his family had ever gone to college, but he wanted to. He knew he had to go in order to become a doctor. He'd seen those shows on TV where the kids were in college, and it didn't look too hard. In fact, school wasn't hard for him, but he kept that a secret, too. Getting A's all the time didn't look too good to his family and friends. If he brought home a good grade on his paper and showed it to anyone, they'd say he was being a showoff.

But none of that mattered. Here he was, walking down the street with his brother. It was seven o'clock and starting to get dark already. His stomach rumbled.

"When we gonna eat?" he asked, reaching over to pull on Larnell's jacket sleeve to get his attention.

Larnell shrugged him off. "Soon enough. I gotta talk with Devon 'bout something first." He looked at his brother for a moment. The kid was grinning from ear to ear just standing next to him. "When we get to Sam's, you stick close to me. Got it?"

"Yeah. But how long's it gonna take?"

"You don't mind about that. We'll get to the movie all right; just stick close to me."

Stewart nodded his head. Some of the kids at Sam's kind of scared him, but he would never admit that to anyone. Guns and knives were a way of life for them, but Stewart wanted no part of that. He wouldn't mind the friends, but he knew he could never hurt another person. He was weak that way.

Standing outside of Sam's, Stewart wondered how much longer it was going to take. Larnell and his friends looked mad about something, but Stewart was more interested in getting to the movie. He stood at the curb, scraping the mud from the bottom of his tennis shoes and trying to be patient. Patient like a double digit person ought to be. And then it started.

At first he thought that someone had set off firecrackers. He wondered why there would be firecrackers when it wasn't the Fourth of July. But the screech of tires and the screams broke through his thoughts. For a moment time stood still. The street noises faded into nothingness as the last of the gunfire echoed through the evening air. Stewart looked for Larnell when the gunfire stopped, wondering somewhere deep inside why he wasn't scared yet.

But Larnell wasn't standing with his friends anymore. He was lying on the ground in a growing pool of blood.

Funny that he couldn't hear the sirens racing toward him. The shouts of the Larnell's friends seemed so far away. Only when someone reached to pull the strip of blue off of Larnell's cap did the screaming fill Stewart's ears. The screams were his own.

"No! Don't you touch that! Larnell's gonna be mad at you!" Stewart ran over to his brother's body and grabbed for the piece of cloth.

"Let go, little man. You don't understand what's going down."

Someone was shaking him and pulling at the cloth clutched tightly between his fists. Stewart couldn't see who it was. There was something wrong with his eyes.

"No!" he screamed again. "He's my brother! We're going to the movies for my birthday. He won't go without his blue on his cap."

Why didn't they understand?" Stewart wondered. Although a part of him realized that Larnell had been shot, all he wanted to do was get to the movie. Everything would be all right once they got there.

Stewart wiped his sleeve across his eyes. Those were tears getting in his way. He was furious with himself. Big boys didn't cry. What would Larnell think? He tightened his fingers around the strip of cloth in his hand. But even as he did, he felt other fingers prying his loose. Amid the confusion he heard their voices.

"We gotta clear outta here."

"Man, the cops are on the way."

"Get that outta his hands, now!"

And then a new voice above the others. "My baby! Oh, no! Not my baby!"

Stewart felt his grip loosening. How could he fail Larnell now? Just as he started to scream once again, he felt himself being lifted by a woman. His mother! She was here. She would make everything right again. He flung his arms around her neck and let the tears come fast and furiously. He didn't care who saw him anymore. All he wanted was for everything to stop.

But for Stewart and his mother it was just beginning. The beginning of endless questions. Questions by the police and by Larnell's friends. Who saw what? Each side wanted to know the same answers, but for different reasons.

Will the killing ever stop?

Protecting Yourself From Violence

(   )   1. I will tell an adult where I will be at all times.

(   )   2. I will leave a phone number of where I will be and how I am getting there and getting home.

(   )   3. I will not leave school with an adult unless that adult is approved by an adult at home.

(   )   4. I will follow a safe route home from school and from other places.

(   )   5. I will stay away from places where gang members or others who might harm me are present.

(   )   6. I will stay away from people who are using drugs or from places where there are drugs.

(   )   7. I will follow safety rules set by my parents to protect me at home.

(   )   8. I will choose friends who do not harm others.

(   )   9. I will follow good behavior rules at school.

(   ) 10. I will avoid being around weapons.

ROSALIND

Objective:

Students will identify resistance skills that can be used when pressured to engage in violent behavior.

Life Skills:

I will develop positive self-esteem. (PF2)
I will make responsible decisions. (PF12)
I will practice resistance skills. (PF13)

Materials:

Rosalind (page 472), a copy for each student, a piece of construction paper, a black marker

Motivation:

1 Give each student a copy of the story *Rosalind* and have them read it to themselves. When they are finished, discuss the following questions. Suggested answers are given after each question.

What kinds of things did the girl write about in her diary?
She wrote about the things that happened in her day, and about her feelings.

What did Rosalind want the girl writing in her diary to do?
She wanted her to do her homework for her.

Is this cheating?
Yes. A student must always do his/her own work.

How did the girl who wrote in her diary feel about helping Rosalind do her work?

She did not want to cheat, but neither did she want to lose her opportunity to be Rosalind's friend. She was afraid of being left out.

Why do you think the girl felt guilty even though she did not cheat?
She might have felt guilty because she had been prepared and willing to cheat.

2 Introduce the terms peer and peer pressure. A **peer** is a person who is like you in age or interests. **Peer pressure** is pressure that this person puts on you to try to get you to make a certain decision or behave in a certain way. Rosalind was using peer pressure to encourage her classmates to do her homework. Point out that Rosalind was not a true friend. A true friend would not try make you do something wrong or harmful, or do anything you do not want to do.

3 Ask the students if they have ever been pressured to do something they didn't want to do that may have been harmful to themselves or others. Perhaps they were pressured by a friend to break a rule such as not crossing a street at a crosswalk. Perhaps they were pressured to throw stones at a house. Remind students that anytime drugs or weapons are involved, violence could result.

4 Introduce the term resistance skills. **Resistance skills** are skills that are used when a person wants to say NO to an action and/or leave a situation. (S)he perhaps is being pressured to do something that (s)he does not want to do or something that (s)he knows would be harmful to his/her health. Explain that resistance skills also are called refusal skills.

5 Explain that knowing how to make responsible and wise decisions helps a person resist becoming involved in a risky situation. A person who makes a responsible decision should feel good about himself/herself because (s)he is doing the right thing.

6 Introduce the term self-esteem. **Self-esteem** is what a person thinks or believes about himself/herself. People who have good feelings about themselves have positive self-esteem. They will be motivated to protect themselves and be safe, and they will not want to do anything to harm themselves or others. One way for people to develop and build positive self-esteem is to work to do their best in school. Another way is to choose friends who will support and encourage them. A third way to develop positive self-esteem is to have a neat and clean appearance. A neat and clean appearance bolsters a person's feelings about himself/herself.

7 Explain that you are going to discuss four resistance skills that can be used to resist pressure to engage in a behavior that might become violent. The skills are as follows:
• Look directly into the other person's eyes when you say NO.
• Say NO in a firm voice.
• Walk away from the person or from the situation.
• Tell an adult in your family about your experience.

8 Tape a piece of construction paper on the chalkboard. Ask students for examples of ways peers might try to convince them to do something that might harm themselves or others. Write several of these statements on the construction paper. Take the construction paper off the chalkboard and crumple it into a ball. Show the crumpled paper ball to the students. Tell them the paper represents something that is very dangerous and might harm them.

9 Toss the paper ball to a student. When you toss the paper ball to a student, give statements that a person might make to pressure another person. For example, you might say, "You have nothing to lose if you take this" and toss the ball. Other statements might be "Everyone else is doing it," "You don't want to be left out, do you?" and "I know you'll like it if you try it." When the student catches the ball, (s)he must respond by looking directly at you, saying NO in a firm voice, and answering your statement. For example, the student might say, "NO, it doesn't matter if everyone else is doing it," or "NO, I won't like it," or "NO, if you were my friend you wouldn't try to make me do this." After the student responds, (s)he can toss the ball back to you. Continue this process with other students.

Evaluation:

Tell the students to think back to the story *Rosalind*. Tell them that you are going to pretend to be Rosalind and ask students to do your homework for you. You might say to a student, "If you do this for me I will invite you to my party," or "If you don't do this you won't be my friend." Using the resistance skills that they have learned, students are to respond.

Rosalind

By Patricia M. Dashiell

Dear Diary,

January 6

There's a new girl in school now. Her name is Rosalind, and she's pretty. Everyone crowded around her at recess because she had a computer game with her with a whole purse full of cartridges. I want to be her friend too.

January 8

Rosalind sat with me at lunch! I was so happy she chose me. Who could believe she just came here two days ago? She's the most popular girl at school. Her dad's in the Air Force so she moves around a lot. At recess she talks about all the countries she's lived in. Maybe I should let my hair grow long like hers.

January 9

Rosalind's having a birthday party next weekend. A sleepover. She said she might invite me. There are twelve girls in our class. Only eight girls get to come. I hope I'm one of them.

January 10

I talked with Rosalind on the phone for twenty minutes. Mom made me get off, and I was mad. Anyway, I think I'm gonna get an invitation....

January 12

Tomorrow's Monday, and Rosalind is going to hand out her invitations. I'm gonna wear my jeans with the cool vest Mom bought me for Christmas. I want to look good.

January 13

I didn't get invited. Rosalind said I was ninth. I asked her why, and she said that I hadn't helped her enough yet. Maybe someone will get sick.

January 14

I figured out what Rosalind meant. Kids help her with her homework so they can play with her computer games. I don't want to be like that.

January 17

This week has been so miserable that I didn't want to write. Susan, Jennifer, Carol, Amy, Virginia, Jackie, Christy, and Melanie have been acting stuck up. They huddled around Rosalind at lunch and recess and gym, talking and whispering and giggling. I felt like nothing. Like I wasn't even there. And Christy is supposed to be my best friend. I told her that if she wanted to be friends with Rosalind, then she couldn't be my friend anymore. She just walked off, and I felt so stupid. I wish I hadn't said that.

January 18

Christy called to tell me about the party. I didn't say anything, but I didn't hang up either. They went skating and had pizza, and they rented movies with popcorn and chips and brownies and did makeovers and everything. I lied and said my mother was calling me before Christy finished telling me the rest. I didn't want to hear it.

January 20

I told Rosalind that if she needed help in math, I would help her. I'm not sure why. Maybe it was because she said she was going to have another sleepover.

January 21

I'm confused. Rosalind doesn't want me to help her with her math. She wants me to do it for her! I think that's wrong—cheating or something. But, everyone is doing it. I told her no. She just walked away and gave her homework to Christy. I'm better in math than Christy!

January 23

I don't think Rosalind does any of her work. I don't have any friends anymore.

January 25

I'm not invited to the party again. I don't have anything to do this weekend.

January 26

I tried to talk to Granny about all this without really saying what was going on. I couldn't be a snitch. She just said I should be a friend to make a friend. I wonder if that means I should be a friend to Rosalind by doing her homework for her. I'm not sure Granny would say that's what she meant, but what else can I do?

January 28

I told Rosalind I'd do it. We didn't have any math homework today, though. I hate waiting.

January 29

Rosalind wasn't in school today. Another day of waiting.

January 30

Rosalind was gone again today. Susan, Jennifer, Carol, Amy, Virginia, Jackie, Christy, and Melanie were called down to the office during science and never came back. I wonder what's going on.

January 31

Rosalind was caught. She's been suspended for two weeks. Her friends were suspended for three days. The principal came in to talk with us, and I kept my face down the whole time. Why do I feel so guilty?

A Visit From Doctor Sara

Objective:

Students will identify and describe types of abuse: emotional, sexual, physical, and neglect.

Life Skills:

I will strive for healthful family relationships. (PF3)
I will develop resiliency to "bounce back" if I was reared in a dysfunctional family. (PF3)
I will practice self-protection strategies. (PF18)
I will participate in recovery if a victim. (PF19)

Materials:

A Visit From Doctor Sara (page 477), one copy for each student, *I Could Talk To...* (page 481), one copy for each student, a heavy book

Motivation:

1 Give students a copy of *A Visit From Doctor Sara*. Have them read it to themselves. Assign students to read the parts of the teacher and students in *A Visit From Doctor Sara*. You will read the part of Doctor Sara. Have the students read their assigned parts aloud to the class.

2 Explain that everyone has the right to be loved and to be safe. However, some people may harm other people, even children and members of their own family. Introduce the term child abuse. Child abuse is the harmful treatment of a person who is under the age of 18. It includes physical abuse, which harms the body. It includes emotional abuse, which may be in the form of using cruel words to put down, threaten, or frighten another person. Sexual abuse involves sexual behavior between an adult and a child, and is wrong. Neglect involves lack of proper care, such as not feeding or clothing a child or leaving a child alone without proper supervision.

3 Explain that a person may hurt another person by touching a private body part. As Doctor Sara explained in the story, private body parts are the body parts covered by a bathing suit or underwear. Stress that if a person touches you in a way you don't like, you have the right to say, "Stop touching me." Tell students if a person touches their private body parts, and if this touch makes them feel uncomfortable, or feels wrong, they must tell a grownup they trust, such as a parent, teacher, or school nurse. If the grownup doesn't believe them, they must tell another grownup. Stress that if a person touches them in a way that makes them uncomfortable, it is not the student's fault.

4 Ask a student to stand up in front of the class and hold his/her arm straight out to the side. Place a heavy book in his/her hand and watch the student become uncomfortable. Ask the student if (s)he feels comfortable or uncomfortable. When (s)he answers that (s)he is uncomfortable, take the book from the student. Explain that when a person is abused, (s)he feels uncomfortable too, even though this is a different way. A person may feel physically tired, angry, anxious, and want help. These are some feelings that are common in people who have been abused.

5 Explain that unfortunately some children grow up in homes where they are abused. Children who grow up in this kind of family can practice self-protection strategies. **Self-protection strategies** are strategies that can be practiced to protect oneself. Tell students that self-protection strategies include talking to a trusted grownup, avoiding places that are unsafe, not being alone after dark, and knowing how to dial 9-1-1 for help. Children practicing self-protection strategies will develop resiliency. Explain that **resiliency** is the ability to prevent or to recover or bounce back when something bad happens to them. These children can ask the person who is abusing them to stop. They can try to stay away from that person.

And, they can tell a trusted adult about the situation and ask for help. Explain that children who are victims of abuse need help and that a variety of help is available, including support groups and hotline numbers.

Evaluation:

Give a copy of *I Could Talk To...* to each student. Have them fill in the blank spaces. Tell them they can bring this paper home to keep.

A Visit With Doctor Sara

By Patricia M. Dashiell

Teacher:	Today we have a visitor who will talk to us about touch. Can anyone tell me what touch is?
Student 1:	It's one of our senses.
Teacher:	Good answer. What else?
Student 2:	It's something we can do with our fingers.
Teacher:	That's right. Well, class, there are times that touch is unsafe. We are going to talk about that today with my friend Doctor Sara. She's a doctor who works with kids and knows all about them.
Student 3:	Yeah.
Teacher:	So, here's Doctor Sara. You may ask her any questions you may have. I'm going to be working at my desk so you'll feel free to talk.
Doctor Sara:	I thought I would begin by telling you that I am a doctor who works mainly with children. Does anyone know what another name is for doctors like me?
Student 4:	A pedi...a pedi... I can't say it.
Student 2:	I know. Pediatrician. I know 'cause I have one.
Doctor Sara:	Good. How many of you have a pediatrician you see regularly?
All Students:	I do, I do!
Doctor Sara:	I'm glad to see you are all working to stay healthy. I also have three children of my own, so I am a doctor and a mother too.
Student 5:	Doctors have children?
Student 6:	Of course they do. What a dumb question.
Student 5:	I was just asking, and besides, remember rule number three.
Student 6:	Okay. I'm sorry.
Doctor Sara:	What's rule number three?
All Students:	Never tease or make fun of other students. If you hurt someone's feelings, apologize right away.

Doctor Sara:	That's a good rule. I am going to talk with you about rules in a way, too. As your teacher said, we can all touch things. We can touch objects and animals and plants and people. Can anyone tell me some objects you can touch?
Student 2:	Do you mean, like, toys?
Doctor Sara:	Yes.
Student 2:	You can play with them.
Doctor Sara:	What else can you touch?
Student 1:	What about plants?
Student 7:	You can pull off leaves.
Student 6:	And you can pick flowers.
Student 1:	I have plants in my yard that, if you touch them, the leaves curl up.
Doctor Sara:	Really? It sounds as if those plants didn't like to be touched.
Student 1:	I guess so. I don't really know.
Doctor Sara:	What are some ways you can touch people?
Student 3:	You can hit 'em.
Student 4:	Or hug them or kiss them.
Doctor Sara:	That's exactly right. You can hug them or kiss them. You can snuggle with them or hold hands.
Student 7:	Or sit on their laps.
Doctor Sara:	Are all those kinds of touch safe touches?
Student 2:	All but hitting people.

Doctor Sara:	What are some other unsafe touches?
Student 3:	Slaps.
Student 5:	Pinches.
Doctor Sara:	I think you all know that the kinds of touches that are unsafe shouldn't happen. If someone is hurting you with unsafe touches, then you need to tell someone you consider safe, like a teacher or a doctor or a nurse or a parent.
Student 3:	What if...what if it is a parent who is doing the unsafe touches?
Doctor Sara:	Then you need to tell someone else. Let's go back to hugs, kisses, and snuggles. Are those always safe touches?
Student 1:	Yes.
Student 4:	I think so too.
Student 3:	Sometimes kisses and hugs can make you...uncomfortable.
Doctor Sara:	You are right. Sometimes people can hug, kiss, or cuddle you in places and ways that may make you feel uncomfortable. If that happens, you can tell the person to stop, and why you want him or her to stop. If that person doesn't stop, then you should tell someone you consider safe. The places that might make you feel uncomfortable with kisses or hugs or cuddling are places that are covered up when you are wearing underwear or a bathing suit. But, any time you don't like someone to touch you, in either safe and unsafe ways, you don't have to let him or her touch you — no matter who it is. Well, sometimes doctors have to make you uncomfortable when you are hurt or sick, but then you know they are doing what they can to help you. And, a nurse or parent is always there to look out for you.
Student 3:	Did anyone ever make you feel uncomfortable?

Student 1:	(in a loud whisper) You're not supposed to ask things like that.
Doctor Sara:	It's okay. That's why I am here. Yes, when I was a little girl, I had someone in my family who made me uncomfortable.
Student 7:	Is that why you decided to become a doctor?
Doctor Sara:	That's part of the reason. I like helping people, especially children, and that is what my job is every day. I think my time is up. But I will be eating lunch with you, and be with you at recess too. So if any of you want to talk to me by yourself, I will be here.
Student 3:	I'm glad you came.
All Students:	Me too. So am I.
Doctor Sara:	I'm glad I could come.

I Could Talk To...

Trusted adults with whom I could talk if I am a victim include:

1.

2.

3.

Other confidential sources of help for victims include:

National Domestic Violence Hotline
1-800-333-SAFE

National Child Abuse Hotline
1-800-422-4453

Alcohol and Drug 24-Hour Help
1-800-562-1240

Sexual Abuse Crisis Hotline
1-800-433-7273

Runaway Hotline
1-800-231-6946

A FIRST PURCHASE

Objective:

Students will describe procedures to follow for safety around weapons.

Life Skill:

I will practice responsible behavior around weapons. (PF15)

Materials:

A First Purchase (page 484), one copy for each student, paper, colored markers or pencils

Motivation:

1 Give each student a copy of A First Purchase and have them read it to themselves. When they have finished, assign students to read the parts of John, Sadale, Devon, and Michael. Have these students read the story aloud to the class.

2 Discuss the following questions. Suggested answers are given after the question.

When John showed the gun to his friends, what did the friends do that might have been harmful?
They handled the gun, and one of them looked down the barrel of the gun and pulled the trigger.

Should John have brought his gun to school?
Students should answer NO. However, if a student(s) answers that he should bring it for protection, explain that carrying a weapon to school is not only a crime but also it is extremely dangerous.

What do you think you should do if you find a gun?
After students provide their answers, lead into the following discussion on safety around weapons.

3 Discuss with students how dangerous it is to be near a person who is carrying a weapon. Explain that a **weapon** is an object used for fighting. A weapon is used to injure another person. The most commonly used weapons are guns and knives. Stress that in many instances, innocent people are injured or even killed because they happened to be near a situation where a weapon was involved.

4 Discuss the rules your school has established about weapons. Explain that such rules are designed for the safety of all students because weapons are very dangerous. This is the reason that it is so important for students to learn to be responsible around weapons.

5 Review with students the following suggestions for being responsible around weapons. The suggestions can be learned by remembering the acronym for the word safe.

- S — STOP
- A — AVOID GOING NEAR THE SITUATION
- F — FIND AN ADULT
- E — EXPLAIN WHAT YOU SAW

6 Have students write one of the letters S, A, F, or E in black markers on their paper. The letters should be large so they can be seen from far away. Review the S-A-F-E rule again. Ask all the students who wrote an S on the paper to jump up and hold their papers over their heads. Ask them to call out what the S stands for, (STOP), and sit down. Continue this process with students who wrote an A, an F, and an E on their papers.

7 Give examples of situations in which a person may be around a weapon. Examples may include finding a gun in the trash can, a friend offering to sell you a gun, seeing the outline of a gun in another student's bookbag, or a friend telling you about a gun (s)he is hiding in his/her house. After each example is given, have the students who wrote an

S on their paper jump up and call out STOP, followed by the students who wrote an A on their paper who will call out AVOID GOING NEAR THE SITUATION, and so on.

Evaluation:

Have students draw pictures around the letters they have written on their paper. The pictures should illustrate people practicing responsible behavior around weapons. Use these pictures to make a "Weapon Safety" bulletin board.

A First Purchase

By Patricia M. Dashiell

[Three boys are sitting together on the playground just talking. A fourth boy walks up to join them.]

John:	Hey, guys, what's up?
Sadale:	Nothing much.
Michael:	That's for sure. I can't believe that school's been out for only a month. I'm already thinking about going back so I can have something to do.
Devon:	You don't like school, do you?
Michael:	Of course not. That's stupid.
Devon:	It's not stupid. Saying you want school to start is stupid.
Michael:	I didn't say I wanted school to start.
Devon:	Yes you did.
John:	Hey, guys, cut it out.
Sadale:	[to John] Where've you been? I haven't seen you in a while.
John:	Out.
Sadale:	Doing what?
John:	None of your business.
Michael:	What do you mean, none of your business?
John:	I don't have to tell you everything.
Devon:	Hey, friends are supposed to talk to each other — not be all mysterious.
John:	I'm not being mysterious. If you must know, I was shopping.
Michael:	With your mother?
John:	No.
Devon:	What'd you get?
John:	Something.
Sadale:	Where'd you get the money?

John:	Saved up my allowance.
Devon:	So what'd you buy?
John:	I bought some protection. You know, a piece.
Michael:	Of what?
John:	A piece.
Michael:	Are you deaf? A piece of what?
John:	Gosh, you are stupid. I bought a gun.
Sadale:	No way? \
Michael:	Are you kidding? | [all together]
Devon:	You lie! /
John:	Okay, don't believe me. But I did.
Devon:	Show us!
John:	[pulls small gun out of his pocket] It's right here. See for yourself.
Michael:	You gotta be crazy! What does a fifth-grader need with a gun? You aren't using your brain, boy. You're gonna get in trouble.
Sadale:	Yep! You're gonna fry.
John:	Am not. All my brothers have guns, and I need protection as much as they do.
Devon:	How much was it?
John:	Twenty bucks.
Michael:	That's it? Can I hold it?
John:	Sure. [He hands it over.] I could've gotten a better one, but I'm tired of never having any money to spend.

Sadale:	Hear you on that one. Still, to blow all that money on a gun. Man, I wouldn't do that. I'd get something else.
Devon:	Pass it here. [He turns it over in his hands and looks down the barrel.] I never saw one like this for real before. It's heavier than I thought. [He points it at the slide and pulls the trigger.] Hey, it's empty. Did you buy any bullets?
John:	Not yet, but I'm gonna. I gotta get 'em from someone else.
Michael:	How did you know how to buy one? And why did the guy in the store let you have it?
John:	I didn't go to any store.
Sadale:	You didn't?
John:	Nope. I heard my brothers talking about it a couple times. There's this guy up at the high school who has a whole trunkful of them. And he'll sell to anyone as long as you got the money.
Michael:	Are you gonna use it?
John:	Sure. Wouldn't you?
Michael:	I dunno.
Sadale:	I would. Better someone else gets shot than me. Are you gonna take it to school?
John:	Sure. Why not?
Devon:	Death for you if you get caught.
John:	Don't worry. I won't.
Michael:	Do your parents know you did this?
John:	Of course not. They wouldn't understand.
Sadale:	Your brothers?
John:	Nah. But they wouldn't care if I did. I bet they had guns in the fifth grade and just didn't tell nobody.
Sadale:	Well, maybe. I just don't know if you need one.
Michael:	I think it's cool. Hey, John, if I get the money, would you tell me where to go?
John:	Yeah. But you don't get an allowance. Where are you gonna get the money?

Michael:	Dad leaves money lying around all the time. I take a bit sometimes. I can save up just like you.
Devon:	You think I should get one?
John and Michael:	Yes! \
Sadale:	No! / [at the same time]
John:	[to Sadale] What's wrong with you?
Sadale:	Nothing.
John:	Why are you so chicken?
Sadale:	I'm not chicken.
John:	Give him the gun, Devon.
Sadale:	I don't want it.
John:	What a baby!
Sadale:	[Stands up] I'm not a baby, John. We're supposed to be friends, and you're being stupid. Leave me alone. [Walks away]
Michael:	What's his problem?
John:	[Shrugs his shoulders] I don't know, and I don't care. Let him be. How about getting something to eat?
Devon and Michael:	Sure thing. Maybe on the way you could show us where you bought it?
John:	Yeah, I could do that. Let's go.

A DEED NOT DONE

Objective:

Students will identify healthful ways to express anger and disappointment.

Life Skills:

I will respond to my environment in an empowering way. (PF4)
I will practice anger management skills. (PF6)

Materials:

A Deed Not Done (page 490), a copy for each student

Motivation:

1 Give a copy of *A Deed Not Done* to each student. Read the poem aloud to the students. Read the poem a second time. Have students act out the poem as you read it. For example, if you say "I'm so angry I could shout," have the students shout.

2 Discuss the following questions with the students. Suggested answers are given after each question.

> How did the person in this poem feel about the broken necklace?
> (S)he felt angry and frustrated that (s)he was blamed for something (s)he did not do.

> How did the person usually express anger?
> By kicking, shouting, screaming, and hitting.

> What did (s)he decide to do about his/her anger?
> Wait it out.

3 Introduce the term anger. **Anger** is the feeling of being irritated, annoyed, and/or furious. Explain that being angry is a feeling that everyone experiences at times. Explain that it is important for students to recognize their anger triggers. **Anger triggers** are thoughts or events that cause a person to become angry. For example, if a friend calls you a mean name (the anger trigger), you would become angry.

4 Explain that the way a person deals with anger can be either healthful or harmful to that person. For example, a person who is angry may want to get back at the person who made him/her angry. This would be a harmful way to deal with anger. Ask students for other examples of harmful ways a person might deal with anger. Point out that harmful ways of dealing with anger often result in violent actions.

5 Explain that it is not always a person who can cause another person to become angry. Situations that are out of a person's control also can be the cause of angry feelings. No matter what causes angry feelings, stress that it is important to learn skills that will help a person manage angry feelings in a positive or healthful way. Skills are methods that can be learned in order to reach a desired goal. In this strategy, the goal is to learn to deal with angry feelings in positive ways that will avoid the possibility of violent actions.

6 Discuss how students can express their anger in healthful ways. Suggest the following examples of skills to use:

• Talk with a trusted adult to get help with resolving the situation that caused your angry feelings.

- Draw pictures of the person or situation that made you angry.
- Take a deep breath and relax until you calm down.
- Ride your bike, jump rope, or play a game with your friend so that you can release the extra energy you have because you are angry.

7 Introduce the term nurturing environment. A **nurturing environment** is a set of conditions and surroundings in which a person lives that promotes growth, development, and success. A nurturing environment provides the best opportunity for a person to be at his/her best. Living in a nurturing environment increases the likelihood that a person will not behave in violent ways because his/her parents care about the children in the family and teach them how to resolve problems without violence. Parents in a nurturing environment teach their children the difference between right and wrong and teach them to make responsible decisions.

8 Introduce the term hope. **Hope** is the feeling that what is desired is possible and that events in life may turn out for the best. Explain that a person who lives in a nurturing environment learns that (s)he will be able to cope with disappointment. A person who is filled with hope is optimistic about the future and does not feel trapped.

9 Explain that students may not be able to control their environment. They may not live in a nurturing environment but there are some steps they can use to control what they do so they can feel empowered. **Empowerment** is the belief that a person controls his/her own destiny. Some of these steps are: ask a trusted adult for help; attend school every day; play in safe areas; learn to set goals and make plans to reach them; and stay away from people who behave in violent ways.

Evaluation:

Have each student draw a picture of something that makes him/her angry. Students can share their pictures with the class. When they share their picture, they should list a healthful way they might express their anger.

A Deed Not Done
By Patricia M. Dashiell

I'm so angry I could shout,
tug my hair and pull it out.
I could punch, and I could kick,
stomp my feet and throw a brick.

I tried to talk, I tried to plead,
I didn't break the string of beads.

My father and my mother,
my sister and my brother,
didn't listen, refused to see,
that it couldn't possibly be me.

I'm so angry I could shout,
tug her hair and pull it out.
I could punch, and I could kick,
stomp my feet and throw a brick.

I tried to explain, to make them understand;
I said I saw the necklace in my cousin's hand.

They shook their heads and rolled their eyes;
They think I'm telling all out lies.
They asked me why I thought she would,
I had no answer that sounded good.

I could kick, and I could punch,
and make my cousin lose her lunch.
I could scream, and I could shout,
but I won't; I'll wait it out.

MORE THAN I AM

Objective:

Students will outline ways to manage stress.

Life Skills:

I will practice stress management skills. (PF7)
I will participate in physical activity. (PF8)

Materials:

More Than I Am (page 492), one copy for each student

Motivation:

1 Announce to the class that they are going to have a surprise quiz that will be graded. Start passing out copies of *More Than I Am* face down so that students can not read them. As you are passing out the paper, students should feel stressed and/or nervous.

2 Ask students how they are feeling at the moment. Students may answer that they are nervous, sweating, or that their heart rate is faster. Tell the students that there really is no surprise quiz and that they will read a poem about stress.

3 Have students read *More Than I Am* to themselves.

4 Introduce the term stress. **Stress** is the response of the body to the demands of daily living. Feelings of stress are an everyday experience and can be the result of many different kinds of experiences called stressors. A **stressor** is a demand that causes changes in the body. Examples of stressors mentioned in the poem are getting good grades, doing well in sports, and having too much to do. Explain that *everyone* experiences stress.

5 Explain that people can do many things to help relieve stress. Ways to manage stress include talking about your feelings with a trusted adult, spending time with friends, writing in a journal, getting enough sleep, and caring for pets.

6 Explain to students that one of the best ways to manage stress is to participate in physical activities. Activities such as swimming, riding a bike, or exercising help a person maintain physical fitness while relieving the effects of stress. Participating in recreational activities, such as camping, dancing, and painting also can help relieve stress.

Evaluation:

Have students write their own poem that identifies ways they can manage stress.

More Than I Am
By Patricia M. Dashiell

Sometimes I feel
like I'm torn
between
school and home,
homework and practice.

"Watch your grades."
"Hit the ball."
"Eat your dinner."
"Finish your chores."
"Stay here."
"Go there."
"It's time to leave."
"It's time for bed."
"I'm counting on you."
"We're counting on you"

So much
that I don't
know who
or what
or where
I am.

❖❖❖❖❖❖❖❖❖❖❖❖❖❖❖❖❖❖

YES AND NO

Objective:

Students will examine the role that drug use and drug trafficking play in increasing the risk of violence.

Life Skill:

I will avoid alcohol and other drugs. (PF14)

Materials:

Yes And No (page 494), a copy for each student, six shoe boxes with a hole cut in one end big enough to fit a hand, a brush, a piece of egg carton, a piece of steel wool, a sock, a handful of grass, and a piece of cheese

Motivation:

1 Prepare the six shoe boxes by placing one of the items in one of the boxes at the end opposite the hole. Have the students take turns putting their hands in the boxes and feeling the object. Students should write down what they think the item is on a piece of paper.

2 Tell the students what the objects were. Explain that they have just tried to discover what they were by the use of touch only. Explain that alcohol and other drugs impair a person's senses so that trying to function while using alcohol and other drugs is like trying to figure out what an object is without using the sense of sight.

3 Define drugs. A **drug** is a substance that changes the way the body and/or mind work. Explain that drug use can harm the body, can affect the way a person acts, and can cause illness, disease, and even death. Drug use changes a person's behavior so that (s)he is more likely to lose control and may become violent.

4 Give a copy of the story to each student. After the students read the story discuss the following questions. Suggested answers are listed after each question.

What was Sean doing?
Sean was pretending to use drugs by making fake drugs.

Why was he doing that?
He did not want to use drugs. However, he thought pretending to use drugs was his only way to avoid using them in his school and neighborhood.

Evaluation:

Have the students give examples of ways to say NO to using alcohol and other drugs. Examples would include, "NO, I don't use drugs," and "NO, I don't want to harm myself." Students can pair off and practice saying NO to alcohol and other drugs. One student can pretend to offer alcohol or other drugs, and the other student can refuse. Then they can reverse roles.

Yes And No

By Patricia M. Dashiell

Sean pulled the bottle out of his jacket and poured the pills out onto the counter. He checked his watch to make sure he had enough time before his mother got home from work. An hour was enough.

After retrieving the mirror, the razor blade, and the powder from his stash of supplies in his room, Sean proceeded to fix his "dope" for the week. Searching for the right capsules in the drug store had taken much longer this time. Plus, he was worried that he might draw attention to himself. Sean did not want to get caught—not by either side.

Carefully he pulled apart each of the capsules lying on the counter and dumped the medicine down the sink. Before returning each capsule to the counter, he cautiously blew into each end, trying to empty each one out as best as he could. He sprinkled some of the white powder from the bag on to the mirror and separated into the right amount it with the razor blade. With the tiny funnel he had found in the back of his mother's makeup cabinet, he began to fill each capsule. The whole process worked better if he sifted the powdered sugar first, but unsifted sugar would have to do for now.

Filling the capsules took careful precision. Sometimes he wondered why he bothered, but the memory of being caught by his friends with pills that had been squashed flat still scared him.

"Man, Sean, you sure bought it on that load. Who did that to you?" asked Jose, looking at the worthless pills in his bag.

Sean's heart was hammering so loudly in his chest that he was sure they would discover his secret, but Jose and the others just started griping about how hard it was to find good stuff anymore. They just went on and on about the guys who tried to rip you off just because you weren't old enough to beat them up. In any case, Sean was glad for the excuse given to him by his friend.

He worked at filling each of the capsules as full as possible while keeping an eye on the clock. He still needed to roll his joints if he wanted to have everything ready for school tomorrow. With just ten minutes to go, Sean quickly wiped down the counter, turned on the water, and returned his supplies to his room.

494

At his desk, he feverishly sharpened his pencil until he thought he had enough shavings. Pulling out the cigarette papers he had "borrowed" from his grandfather, Sean dropped a pinch of shavings into the center of the paper, creased it to spread the shavings out, and rolled and twisted it expertly between his fingers. How many had he made before, dozens, hundreds, thousands? And for what?

Six o'clock. His mother should be coming through the door any minute now. Returning to the kitchen, he turned off the water and grabbed two plastic baggies from the kitchen drawer. Putting the pills in one and the joints in another, Sean stuffed both into the outside pocket of his backpack. He picked up his jacket and returned to his room to start his homework. As he spread his books and papers out on his desk, he knew he had made it once more. His mother would think he had been hard at work since returning home from practice, and he was ready for school again. This time his drug supply had gotten dangerously low. He was not about to take from any of his friends. This was the only way to protect himself.

The next morning he stood before the mirror and checked his clothes. Jeans with a hole in one knee, denim shirt, jacket with the bags in the inside pocket, hightops, and a cap worn backward. He pulled the cap off and smoothed his hair back once more. His mother hated how long it was now, but slicked straight back you couldn't really tell—at least not till later on in the day when it fell in front of his eyes.

"You've really changed, Sean," he told himself. None of his friends from his old neighborhood would recognize him now. None of them would even understand why he must be who he is now. None of them. How could they understand if even he didn't? Sean no longer even looked at himself in the mirror. He had no answers for the questions he knew lay behind his eyes. If he was already this confused in junior high, what would happen next year at the high school?

He had grown up on "just say NO." At least it seemed that he had been hearing that all his life. But no one ever told him what to do when NO was not an option. Period. Final.

Here he was pretending to be what he wasn't, hiding from what he was, and leaving his dreams buried in the back of the closet, behind the gym bag, inside a funnel coated with powdered sugar. His whole life was a lie. In fact, he was a lie.

Shouldering his backpack, he turned to leave the room. Bounding down the stairs he called goodbye toward the kitchen hoping to escape. No such luck.

"Sean, wait!" His mother crossed the hall and stood in front of him. "Let me get a good look at you, baby."

She held his face in her hands and stared straight at him. Sean tried to gently pull away, but her hands held firm. To jerk his face would be disrespecting her, so he waited. With her right thumb, she wiped a smudge of peanut butter toast crumbs from the corner of his mouth.

"You remember. You remember your ma today."

"Yes'm," he mumbled between clenched teeth as he reached up to move his mother's hands. "I'm gonna be late."

"Go, then. Go."

Sean wasted no time getting out the door, but paused to lean against the hallway after shutting the door. He listened to the sliding click of the deadbolt. His mother would be leaving for work in less than a half hour, but still she took no chances.

That word—Remember. That one word could hold a thousand. One word to tell him that she loved him, that he was to be a good boy, that he was to make his father's memory proud, that she was counting on him. Remember. All those messages wrapped up in that one word—in a word Sean

496

could not forget. But even his mother, who kept him safely locked away from the world while he was at home, did not understand that he could not remember that special word with its many messages in a school where guns were best friends, and drugs and alcohol were food and drink.

No, he would forget. For only in forgetting was he able to say NO the only way he could.

LANGUAGE ARTS

A KIND OF WELCOME

Objective:

Students will identify types of crime and violence.

Life Skills:

I will recognize that violent behavior is wrong. (PF1)
I will avoid discrimination. (PF11)

Materials:

A Kind Of Welcome (page 499), a copy for each student, two balloons, an 18" dowel rod, two pieces of string approximately two feet in length, a piece of wool fabric

Motivation:

1 Take a dowel rod and tie an inflated balloon to each end. Show students how the balloons hang naturally. Rub each balloon vigorously with the wool fabric. When you let go of the second balloon and hold the dowel rod level, the balloons will repel each other. Tell the students that people sometimes stick together" with other people who are similar to them, or avoid people who are different. However, in science, this is the opposite, because opposites attract and similar things repel.

2 Give a copy of *A Kind Of Welcome* to each student. Tell students this is a story about discriminatory behavior. **Discriminatory behavior** is acting differently toward or showing behavior that is in favor of or prejudiced against a person or group of people. When a person chooses discriminatory behavior, (s)he treats some people with respect and others with disrespect. When people are treated with disrespect, they may become angry or violent. Explain that it is

wrong to treat a person with disrespect, and disrespect may lead to violence.

3 Have the students read *A Kind Of Welcome* to themselves.

4 Discuss the following questions with the students. Suggested answers are given after each question.

> How do you think Rachael felt the first day of school?
> She may have felt scared, lonely, tired, and angry at her mother for sending her to this school.

> What are some forms of discriminatory behavior?
> Answers may include discriminatory behavior against people of different races, religions, sexual orientation, and gender.

5 Explain that discriminatory behavior, such as ethnic jokes, negative remarks, and rejecting a person, is wrong and that students should not only avoid these types of behavior but ask others to stop discriminatory behavior. Other ways to avoid discriminatory behavior are to learn about people who are different from you, respect people who are different from you, and get to know people who are different from you.

Evaluation:

Have students rewrite the locker room scene of *A Kind Of Welcome*. In this version, have the students insert a character into the story who stands up for Rachael, and teaches the other students how to avoid discriminatory behavior. Ask student volunteers to tell how their new character avoids discriminatory behavior.

A Kind Of Welcome

By Patricia M. Dashiell

Of all the things I would face at this new school, I knew physical education class would be the worst. I knew that without a teacher present, the locker room was where the whispers I had been hearing all day long would become open taunts. And, I shuddered at the thought of having to change in the locker room. Why did Momma make me come here?

I thought about the last argument we had before she closed her mind and her mouth.

"Momma, my old school is just fine. I don't want to go to that old H.P. Weatherford Academy. The name is stupid enough," I had fought to keep the whining out of my voice, but my voice rose with each word anyway.

"Why do we have to go through all of this again, Rachael? Do you think I've been breaking my back all those years just to let you go to some lousy school?"

"No, but..."

"I'm tired of your but's, Rachael. As long as you've been in school, we've been talking about the eighth grade. You know how much it means to me for you to go to college. You're the only one of my babies who's got what it takes. I'm not going to let you mess it up like your brothers."

"Momma, I'll go to college. I want to. You know that. But why do I have to transfer to H.P. Weatherford?"

Momma shook her head at me.

"I have told you that I looked at all the high schools, and none of them is as good as this one."

"But, Momma, I don't belong there. I'm different from all of them."

"That doesn't matter, Rachael. You are going there to get a good education. That's what matters."

"But Momma..." I stopped when I saw her eyes. Those eyes told me not to say another word.

We stared at each other before I ran to my room. But it didn't matter how much I sulked in my room and moped around the house over the summer. I still found myself climbing all those steps into H.P. Weatherford this morning.

The whispering began almost immediately. Walking down the hall to my first class I heard the whispers. None of the whispers were clear, but I knew that all the girls were whispering about me. They were staring at me. I had known I would be different from all the other girls. Even the school uniform somehow looked different on me. I saw that too.

The morning was so long, and I had to go to a new class every forty-five minutes. Lunch was miserable, eating by myself at one of those long cafeteria tables. Then it was time to head toward the locker room where they would all get a good look at me and stare even more. I sighed as I pushed open the door.

The locker room was long and narrow with rows and rows of benches. At the end of each bench were lockers, and most of the girls were already seated on the benches and had started to change. The room quieted down as they noticed me. I felt frozen by the silence.

After what seemed like a lifetime, I forced myself to move and sat on the nearest bench. The two girls who were already seated there jumped up and moved, grabbing their clothes and clutching them.

"What did they think, that I was going to steal them? This is even worse than I imagined it would be," I thought. I hoped the gym teacher would show up soon.

"Look at her! "

I whipped my head around and stared, but I could not tell who had spoken. The silence was unbearable. I turned back around and continued changing while everyone else in the room watched me.

"What's *she* doing here?"

Another whisper. I couldn't stand it anymore. After I finished tying my shoes, I marched over to the nearest girl and shoved my face inches from hers. It made me feel funny to see her flinch, but I stared straight into her eyes.

"Do you have something you want to say to me or ask me?" I pulled back some, but continued to stare.

"No...I...I don't know what you mean." She tried to take a step away but the wall was just behind her.

"I may be a little different from you, but I have ears and I can hear. Should we play Twenty Questions so you can find out everything you want to know about me? Or should I just stand here and let you conduct your little inspection?" My voice was rising, and I fought to keep it even. "We might as well get this over with so you can all get on with your lives."

The girl in front of me looked close to tears. I suppose that my voice had been rather loud. But honestly, I felt like some sort of explorer in a new land who was being greeted as a freak.

Looking around the room, I began to despair of ever fitting in here. A girl sitting three benches over cleared her throat and spoke up. "Why are you here? We've never had your kind here."

"Your kind. I'm a kind," I thought. Suddenly I saw all these girls as little girls playing with each other and spending the night with each other. They had probably been going to old H.P. Weatherford all their lives. Who was I to come here now?

"I bet she's some kind of quota or something," said the girl next to the one who had spoken.

"I am not," I said hotly. I made it here on my own, and I deserve to be here. My mother is paying for every day of my education and I plan to make her proud of me." I stood up and began walking toward the gym. The girls moved away from me in silence. I paused at the door and turned back for a moment, "I am here to stay." I lifted my chin just a little bit higher and emphasized each word carefully, "I am here to stay."

As I stepped into the gym, I heard the gym teacher yelling at the rest of the class to hurry up because they were late. She asked why nobody was ready. Their answer was silence.

FOR BETTER OR WORSE

Objective:

Students will examine the importance of resiliency in dealing with life crises.

Life Skills:

I will respond to my environment in an empowering way. (PF4)
I will develop resiliency to "bounce back" if I live in an adverse environment. (PF4)
I will practice suicide prevention strategies. (PF9)

Materials:

For Better Or Worse (page 504), a copy for each student, a piece of string, a rubber band

Motivation:

1 Give a copy of *For Better Or Worse* to each student and have them read it to themselves. Have students read *For Better Or Worse* to themselves.

2 After students have read the story, explain that Aaron's mother was a victim of domestic violence. **Domestic violence** is violence that occurs within the family or within other relationships in which people live together. Explain that women are more likely to be killed by a former or current partner than by all other groups of people combined. This is one reason domestic violence is a very serious problem in this country.

3 Explain to students that Aaron was living in an adverse environment. An **adverse environment** is a set of conditions and surroundings in which a person lives that interferes with growth, development, and success.

Aaron lived in an environment where he and his mother were exposed to dangerous situations. He witnessed violence in his home. The amount of violence is high in adverse environments. People who live in adverse environments sometimes feel hopelessness about life options. These people are at risk for suicide. **Suicide** is the intentional taking of one's own life. Other people living in adverse environments feel angry about poverty, and fearful of the risk of violence.

4 Tie the two ends of the string together so the string and rubber band are the same size. Show students the rubber band and the string. Place the rubber band at the top of your index finger and shoot the rubber band toward a wall, away from the students. Then do the same thing with a string. The string will fall. Point out that the rubber band has spring and responds when it is pulled or stressed, but the string doesn't. The string merely fell.

5 Explain that the rubber band has resiliency, while the string does not. **Resiliency** is the ability to prevent or to recover, bounce back, and learn from misfortune, change, or pressure. Many people who are reared in adverse environments are like the rubber band and develop resiliency. Others are like the string and do not develop resiliency, and fall.

6 Explain that young people such as Aaron who live in adverse environments should feel empowered. **Empowerment** is the belief that you control your own destiny. Although people cannot always control the environment in which they live, they can control what they do. They must do everything they can to avoid violent behavior and develop resiliency.

Evaluation:

Ask students to identify people and resources in their school and community to
whom they could go for help. Write their answers on the chalkboard. Then write the following hotline numbers on the chalkboard.
Leave the list on the chalkboard for the day
in case a student wished to copy any information for themselves.

National Domestic Violence Hotline
1-800-333-SAFE

National Child Abuse Hotline
1-800-422-4453

Alcohol and Drug 24-Hour Help
1-800-562-1240

Sexual Abuse Crisis Hotline
1-800-433-7273

Runaway Hotline
1-800-231-6946

For Better Or Worse

By Patricia M. Dashiell

"One...two...three..." Aaron tried not to count, but he couldn't help himself. "Four...five...six..." He steeled himself against the blows as if to try to ward them off. He winced and prayed for it to end. How much more could he stand? He wondered about that more and more these days.

When had it started? The first day of fourth grade came to mind. He had been late coming back from Caleb's house. His stepfather, Tom, started yelling about chores not being done. Tom had yelled before, but not this way. It was that night that the beatings started, the night Aaron realized how helpless he really was.

Suddenly the beating stopped. Aaron hesitated until he heard the front door slam. With all the courage he could muster, Aaron wiped the tears from his face and went to his mother's room.

Gingerly, he pushed the door open and tiptoed inside. Even after the past four years, he was not prepared for the sight in front of him. Clothes had been pulled out of drawers and strewn about the room. Every picture on the dresser had been destroyed, the glass broken, and the photographs torn. The bedside lamp lay on the floor; the cord was missing from the base.

Aaron cautiously walked around the bed to the bathroom where his mother was washing the blood from her face. He noticed her hands shaking as she carefully wiped below her eyes with the washcloth.

"Aaron, you shouldn't be in here."

"It's okay. I heard him leave."

"Oh, Aaron, I'm sorry."

"For what?" he cried as he knelt on the carpet before his mother.

She waved her arms around at the bathroom and toward the bedroom. "For this."

"It's not your fault, Mom."

"I got us into this." She dropped her hands to her lap and wrung the washcloth between her hands. "I didn't know, I didn't know."

"What did he say this time?" Aaron gently took the cloth from his mother's hands and rinsed it in the sink. Gingerly, he began to clean her face. At times like this he felt so awkward and clumsy.

504

"He said that I left the garage door unlocked last night."

"Did you?"

"I don't think so."

"What would it matter if you did, Mom? What's the harm?" Aaron's throat tightened as he forced himself to lower his voice. "Whatever it is, you don't deserve this."

His mother took the washcloth back and stood up without saying a word. Walking into the bedroom, she began piling clothes on the bed. Aaron went to help her, and they began folding them.

"Aaron, you don't deserve this. You don't deserve a mother who cannot keep you safe."

"Mom, I am safe. You're the one who isn't. I hate this." His voice broke. "I hate him," he whispered fiercely.

"Don't. It's not him."

"Then what is it? How can you say Tom isn't to blame for all of this. Did you look at your face?"

His mother reached up to touch the welts that had formed across her check. "No, I couldn't. It doesn't matter."

"How can you say that?"

"As long as he leaves you alone nothing else matters."

"If he ever came near me I'd..."

"You'd run outside and over to Caleb's house."

"That's not what I was going to say."

"I know, honey, but you're no match for him. He'd probably...he'd...just promise me, Aaron."

"Promise you what?"

His mother sat on the bed and pulled Aaron down beside her. "Promise me that you'll never anger Tom. I just couldn't bear it if he hit you."

"How can you bear it now, Mom?" Aaron dared to ask.

"Promise me?"

"Mom..."

"Promise me, Aaron."

His heart ached at the desperation he heard in her voice and the tear he saw slide down her cheek. She never cried. No matter how bad it got, Aaron never saw his mother cry. "I promise."

"Thank you, honey."

Wrapping her arms around Aaron, she pulled him close. The two of them sat like that for what seemed like hours.

"The two of them," Aaron thought. "Just the two of them would be better." Never before had he dared to ask.

"Mom?"

"Yes?"

"Why don't you leave him?"

She pulled away and stared at him. "Where did that come from?"

"I was just thinking how nice it was when it was just us. It could be just us all the time. You could do it."

"Tom would never let me."

"He'd have to."

"I wouldn't know what to do. I can't."

"Can't or won't, Mom?"

"Aaron!"

"Four years is enough. He's not going to change."

"I've...I've never had a job. You don't remember how hard it was when your father left. We were just barely making it until Tom came along."

"I could help. I'll quit school and get a job. We don't need him, Mom." He was pleading shamelessly now. Maybe she would listen this time.

"You can't quit."

"You can't go on like this."

"This is my problem, Aaron, not yours."

"It's our problem, Mom, and I'm not gonna let him hurt you again. If you won't do something I will."

"You will?" his mother asked softly. She reached up and smoothed his

hair away from his eyes. "You've really grown up, Aaron." She searched his face with her eyes.

"It would be very hard," she finally said.

"I know."

"I'd have to find a job somewhere."

"I know," he repeated with rising hope.

"I wouldn't make much money. No new tennis shoes and clothes for you."

"Anything, Mom. Anything to never see you like this again."

"Then I'll try. For you, Aaron, I'll try. And not only for you, Aaron. For myself."

MORE THAN A LIPSTICK

Objective:

Students will identify resistance skills that can be used when pressured to engage in violent behavior.

Life Skills:

I will make responsible decisions. (PF12)
I will practice resistance skills. (PF13)

Materials:

More Than A Lipstick (page 510), a copy for each student, a thin sheet of tissue, a handkerchief, marbles, *The Model For Using Resistance Skills* transparency (page 610)

Motivation:

1 Give each student a copy of *More Than A Lipstick* and have them read it to themselves.

2 After students have read the story, discuss the following questions. Suggested answers are given after each question.

> Why do you think Cherra wanted to steal the lipstick?
> Students may answer that she wanted to fit in, her friend wanted her to, or that she wanted it and didn't have the money.

> Why do you think Cherra asked Janice to steal?
> She may not have wanted to do it alone, she may have been testing Janice's friendship.

3 Introduce the terms peer and peer pressure. A **peer** is a person who is like you in age or status. **Peer pressure** is pressure that this person puts on you to try to get you to make a certain decision or behave in a certain way. Cherra was using peer pressure to encourage Janice to steal. A true friend would not try to make you do something wrong or harmful, or do anything you do not want to do.

4 Ask the students if they have ever been pressured to do something they didn't want to do that may have been harmful to themselves or others. Perhaps they were pressured by a friend to break a law, such as shoplifting. Perhaps they were pressured to throw stones at a house. Remind students that any time drugs or weapons are involved, violence could result.

5 Introduce the term resistance skills. **Resistance skills** are skills that are used when a person wants to say NO to an action and/or leave a situation. (S)he perhaps is being pressured to do something that (s)he does not want to do or something that (s)he knows would be harmful to his/her health. Explain that resistance skills also are called refusal skills. Review *The Model For Using Resistance Skills*.

6 Explain that knowing how to make responsible and wise decisions helps a person resist becoming involved in a risky situation. A person who makes a responsible decision should feel good about himself/herself because (s)he is doing the right thing.

7 Take a thin sheet of tissue and hold it end-to-end so that it is stretched. Do the same thing with a handkerchief. Select two students, each to hold one of the items. Distribute marbles to the students in the class. Each marble represents a pressure that a peer places on them. Select two students at a time. Each student places a marble on the tissue and the handkerchief. As the marbles are placed, the students will identify a pressure that students face. Explain that the handkerchief and tissue represent people who handle stress. Continue to have students place marbles on the tissue and the handkerchief until the tissue breaks. Explain that the tissue, or person, did not have the ability to resist the peer pressure and broke apart. Explain that some people have the ability to handle peer pressure easier because they have resistance skills.

Evaluation:

Have students write on a piece of paper a situation in which a person might feel peer pressure. Put all of the sheets of paper in a pile. Distribute the papers to the students randomly. Have students read the situation aloud to the class and suggest a way that the person described might say NO.

More Than A Lipstick

By Patricia M. Dashiell

Janice stared out the window, waiting for Cherra to finish picking through the lipsticks in the basket. Although the cool air conditioning was a welcome relief to the sweltering heat outside, Janice was tired of hanging out in a drug store. Besides, all their friends were probably down at Burger World eating ice cream or something.

"You finished yet?"

"Nope."

Janice walked over to examine the smears of lipstick coloring Cherra's wrist. "I like the darker ones," she offered pointing to the nearest colors.

"Really? I was sort of thinking pink rather than mauve."

"With your skin?"

"What's wrong with my skin?"

"Dark colors go with dark coloring. With that tan and your hair, you need something mauve or even brown."

"Brown? You gotta be crazy, girl!"

"Fine. Insult your best friend. I was only trying to help." Janice turned back to the window in a huff. She knew she was overreacting but she was tired of the whole situation.

"Jan...Jan, I didn't mean anything." Cherra walked around in front of her friend to face her.

"Yeah, right."

"No, honestly, you don't wear the stuff so I just...well, kind of question what you know."

"Just because my parents are from the dark ages and won't let me wear makeup," Janice said hotly while staring right at Cherra, "doesn't mean that I don't read."

"Huh?"

"I read this great article on coloring the other day. You're a winter and, with your skin and all, you should wear browns and stuff. Not everyone can wear browns, you know?"

"Really?"

"Yeah."

510

Cherra pulled on Janice's arm. "Come back here and pick a brown for me."

Janice resisted for a moment, before allowing herself to be pulled back to the basket of lipsticks. Being sweaty and sticky always made her grumpy, but that was no reason to pick on Cherra. She grabbed Cherra's wrist and carefully studied the array of colors once more.

"How about that one?"

"You think?"

"Definitely. You'll look hot. "

Cherra began applying the lipstick to her lips, leaning forward to inspect her face in the mirror.

"What are you doing?"

"Making sure I start looking hot right now."

Janice glanced back at the man standing behind the counter at the front of the store. "You just can't put that stuff on. It's not...hygen...hygen...whatever. Are you gonna buy that? "

"Maybe. What do you think?" Cherra turned around and pursed her lips dramatically. "If you were a guy, would you want to kiss me?"

Pulling the tube of lipstick out of Cherra's hand, Janice checked the price. "Not for $5.97 plus tax. Let's get out of here. You haven't even gotten your allowance yet."

"So."

"So you can't afford this. "

"I can with creative financing. "

"Creative what?"

Cherra took the lipstick back and dropped it into her open purse hanging at her side.

"What are you doing?"

"Hush! "

Janice dropped her voice to a whisper. "What in the world do you think you're doing?"

"I can't afford it, but Super Drug can. They build loss into their finances anyway."

"Put it back!" Janice demanded, eyeing the clerk once more.

"No."

"Put it back now, Cherra."

"I don't want to. And you know what?"

"What?"

"I think," said Cherra, reaching into the basket of lipsticks once more, "that you want one too."

Before Janice could stop her, Cherra dropped the second lipstick into Janice's purse and quickly closed the zipper.

"Cherra!"

"Lower your voice, Jan," Cherra said calmly. "Everybody does it."

"Everybody who?"

"Lisa, Jodi, Tamika...everybody."

"Well, I'm not everybody." Janice fumbled with the zipper of her purse. "I'm not gonna 'creatively finance' this."

"Yes. You are." Cherra caught Janice's hands in her own. "We're friends, and you said that you wanted to fit in better. Now's your time to fit. We can go down to Burger World and brag. Think what they'll say about your coup."

"I don't wanna do it, Cherra."

"We're in junior high. Junior high kids do this stuff all the time. Grow up, Jan, or you'll get left behind."

Janice stood biting her lip and glancing back at the clerk. She measured with her eyes the distance to the door. Staring at Cherra she wondered how everything could have changed so quickly. If anyone had ever asked her if Cherra stole, Janice would have defended her friend. But now she knew differently.

Seeing her friend waver, Cherra squeezed Janice's hands quickly before letting go. "It's easy. Let's get outta here."

Fitting in. Everybody does it. Whoever thought junior high would be this complicated. Sighing, Janice nervously turned toward the door. She wondered if her feet would make it all the way down the aisle and out the door. If only she had never suggested they come inside to cool off. If only...

Janice and Cherra walked toward the door, Cherra as if nothing was wrong and Janice in fear. They almost made it.

"Girls, would you like to explain to me where you are going?" The store manager stood in front of them.

THE PHONE CALL

Objective:

Students will discuss ways to prevent suicide.

Life Skill:

I will practice suicide prevention strategies. (PF9)

Materials:

The Phone Call (page 516), a copy for each student, *Suicide Prevention Strategies* transparency (page 604), transparency projector

Motivation:

1 Introduce the term suicide. **Suicide** is the intentional taking of one's own life.

2 Give a copy of *The Phone Call* to each student. Have students pair off and read *The Phone Call* to each other. One student will read the part of the Volunteer, the other person will read the part of the Teenager. The students should fill in the blanks with their own names where appropriate.

3 After students have finished reading, discuss the following questions. Suggested answers are given after each question.

How did the teenager feel?
(S)he felt sad, scared, and lonely.

How was the teenager handling those feelings?
(S)he was considering suicide. Calling the hotline was a cry for help.

How might other people suspect that the teenager was considering suicide?
(S)he might be sad, lonely, or depressed for a long period of time, might withdraw from others, might not show an interest in school or other activities, might make statements about suicide, and may give away possessions.

4 Explain that there seem to be many reasons that children and preteens attempt suicide. They may be abused, have difficulty at school, lack love from their families, experience the separation or divorce of their parents, experience the death of a person or other loved adult, have poor peer relationships, or have physical defects that worry them. Teenagers who are vulnerable to suicide are those who abuse alcohol or other drugs, have feelings of alienation from their families, fear independence, are the subject of ridicule or isolation from peers, and/or have difficulty in coping with body changes and sexuality.

5 Discuss suicide prevention strategies. **Suicide prevention strategies** are techniques that can be used to help prevent a person from thinking about attempting and completing suicide. Review the information on the *Suicide Prevention Strategies* transparency. These include knowing suicide hotline numbers, knowing what do when a person feels depressed, talking to trusted adults, and being involved in rewarding activities. A person who shows warning signs should always be taken seriously. A responsible adult should be notified immediately. If emergency help is needed, call 9-1-1 and stay with the person until appropriate help arrives. When the crisis is over, continue to give this person support and encouragement. It is important for this person to stay connected to friends and adults who care for him/her.

6 Have students write letters to a Suicide Prevention Helper from an imaginary person who is at risk for suicide. Read aloud the following example of a letter:

Dear Helper,
My girlfriend just broke up with me and I am depressed. I don't know what to do. I don't feel like seeing anyone or going to school and want to hibernate in my room.

Sincerely,
Unhappy

7 Students should pass their letters to another student and write a response to the new letter they have received. Read the following example of an answer to Unhappy's letter aloud.

Evaluation:

Have students create a handbook for suicide prevention to share with other classes or to put in the library. Divide students into groups, and assign each group a topic from the following list: facts about young people and suicide, warning signs of suicide, ways to prevent suicide, and resources for suicide prevention.

Dear Unhappy,
Breaking up with a girlfriend or boyfriend can be painful. Your feelings are not unusual. But there are positive ways to deal with your feelings. You might speak to a parent or counselor. You are a worthwhile person with many positive traits. Talking to a trusted adult can help you to begin to gain positive feelings back.

Sincerely,
Dr. Helpyou Feelgood

The Phone Call

By Patricia M. Dashiell

Volunteer:	Crisis Hotline. Hello.
Teenager:	[silence] Um…
Volunteer:	Hello?
Teenager:	[someone clearing a throat]
Volunteer:	Can I help you?
Teenager:	Um, yeah. I mean no. Well, I don't know…[voice trails off]
Volunteer:	Why don't we try? My name is_____. What's yours?
Teenager:	I didn't know you had to give your name.
Volunteer:	[quickly interrupting] You don't have to tell me your name unless you want to. What would you like me to call you?
Teenager:	Uh…_____.
Volunteer:	Okay, _____, why don't you tell me why you're calling?
Teenager:	Isn't this, I mean, didn't I call a help line?
Volunteer:	Oh, yes, but I'm wondering why you called.
Teenager:	I saw your commercial on TV, and I didn't have anything better to do.
Volunteer:	Why is that?
Teenager:	Why don't I have anything better to do?
Volunteer:	Yes.
Teenager:	I just don't.
Volunteer:	What grade are you in?
Teenager:	Eighth.
Volunteer:	How's school?
Teenager:	It's okay.
Volunteer:	Why don't you tell me about it.
Teenager:	There's not much to tell.
Volunteer:	Do you have friends at school?
Teenager:	Not at this one.

Volunteer:	What do you mean?
Teenager:	I just moved to this school, and all my friends are at my old school.
Volunteer:	How long have you been in the new school?
Teenager:	Six months.
Volunteer:	That's not very long.
Teenager:	It's too long.
Volunteer:	Too long for what?
Teenager:	Never mind.
Volunteer:	Too long for what, _____?
Teenager:	For caring.
Volunteer:	About school?
Teenager:	No.
Volunteer:	Then what?
Teenager:	About Chris.
Volunteer:	Who's _____.
Teenager:	Someone who was my friend.
Volunteer:	Was? (S)he's not your friend any more?
Teenager:	No.
Volunteer:	Did you have a fight?
Teenager:	No.
Volunteer:	Did (s)he move away?
Teenager:	No.
Volunteer:	Then what?
Teenager:	[silence]
Volunteer:	Do you want to tell me about it?
Teenager:	[sigh] You already know.
Volunteer:	I don't understand, _____.
Teenager:	My friend was Chris Smith.
Volunteer:	Oh...
Teenager:	Even you heard.

Volunteer:	I read about it in the newspaper. Were you the friend who found him/her?
Teenager:	Yes.
Volunteer:	How did that make you feel?
Teenager:	I don't know.
Volunteer:	_____, why are you calling?
Teenager:	Maybe Chris did that because (s)he had to.
Volunteer:	Had to what?
Teenager:	Maybe (s)he had to get away from it all.
Volunteer:	Get away from what?
Teenager:	Everything.
Volunteer:	So why are you calling?
Teenager:	I didn't just find him/her.
Volunteer:	[silence]
Teenager:	I was there. I was going to do it too.
Volunteer:	Why didn't you?
Teenager:	I wasn't sure if I wanted to.
Volunteer:	Do you want to now?
Teenager:	Want to what?
Volunteer:	Do you want to kill yourself?
Teenager:	I still have the package of pills.
Volunteer:	That's not what I asked, _____.
Teenager:	We made them up together from the medicine cabinets in our houses.
Volunteer:	Do you want to kill yourself?
Teenager:	[whisper] No.
Volunteer:	I'm not sure I heard you.
Teenager:	[louder] No.
Volunteer:	Good. What do you want?
Teenager:	The same thing Chris did.
Volunteer:	What is that?
Teenager:	[all in a rush now] I want my parents to understand me. I want to fit in at school. I want to matter. I want to know what I'm supposed to be doing. I want to know that if I died it would be a bad thing not a good thing. I

	want somebody to want to get to know me, the real me. I want the hurting to stop. It hurts so much. I want...I want...I want Chris back.
Volunteer:	I know it's hard. But we can handle this together, if you're willing to go step by step.
Teenager:	Are you sure?
Volunteer:	Absolutely, if you're willing to try.
Teenager:	I think I am.
Volunteer:	I have the name and phone number of someone in your area that you might want to talk to.
Teenager:	[pause] All right. But, can I talk with you for a little while first?
Volunteer:	Of course, _____. I'm here for you.
Teenager:	I think I'm counting on that.
Volunteer:	Then, that's the first step.

WHEN I WAS MAD

Objective:

Students will identify effective approaches to conflict resolution that exclude fighting.

Life Skills:

I will participate in physical activity. (PF8)
I will practice conflict resolution and peer mediation skills. (PF10)

Materials:

When I Was Mad (page 522), a copy for each student, transparency of *Conflict Resolution Skills* (page 606), transparency projector

Motivation:

1 Explain that life without conflict is impossible. A **conflict** is a disagreement between two or more people or between two or more choices. Conflicts occur naturally in every area of life, including in a family. Conflicts also occur within an individual when that person has to make up his/her mind which choice (s)he will make.

2 Tell students they are going to read a poem about conflict resolution. Give a copy of *When I Was Mad* to each student and have students read it to themselves.

3 Explain that there are different ways to resolve conflicts, just as they read in the poem. Tell that the narrator in the poem feels that neither the way some people settled conflicts when his father was growing up nor the way some people settle conflicts today are right.

4 Explain that people who do not learn to resolve conflicts in a responsible and healthful way may: experience problems with their physical health; not have meaningful relationships with others; and be more likely to become a victim or a perpetrator of violence. Explain that these experiences can result from a buildup of angry feelings and frustration from the unresolved conflict. This buildup of emotions can be overwhelming to people and they may begin to behave in harmful and even violent ways. At this point, remind students that if they do not participate in a physical activity program, they lack a very effective anger management skill. Explain that a person's body becomes more and more tense and has a surge of energy when (s)he experiences angry feelings. Participating in a physical activity helps defuse the anger by relieving the tension and providing an outlet for the extra energy.

5 Discuss the skills listed on the *Conflict Resolution Skills* transparency. Explain that these skills are positive and responsible ways to resolve a disagreement. Arguing over conflicting opinions is not an effective way to deal with a disagreement because the focus is on the opinions and not on the cause of the disagreement. Using conflict resolution skills allows the people involved in the disagreement to reach a solution that is acceptable to everyone involved.

6 Introduce the terms peer and peer mediation. A **peer** is a person who is similar in age or status. **Peer mediation** is a process used to resolve conflicts in which a person helps his/her peers resolve disagreements in healthful, safe, legal, respectful, and nonviolent ways. Successful peer mediation programs often reduce the need for adult involvement in school disciplinary matters. If your school has a peer-mediation program already established, your students will already be familiar with it.

7 Have students share some situations in which there might be conflict. Write these situations on the chalkboard. Divide students into groups of four. They can choose one of the situations listed on the chalkboard and, using the steps on the *Conflict Resolution Skills* transparency, discuss how the people involved could resolve the conflict healthfully.

Evaluation:

The groups of students should prepare a brief skit about their situation. The skits should include the situation that lead up to the conflict, and then the steps the people involved take to resolve the conflict healthfully. The groups should perform the skits for the class.

When I Was Mad

By Patricia M. Dashiell

"When I was mad," my dad would say,
"I'd meet the kid outside to settle it. On
the playground, at the park,
or anywhere was fine. Our friends
would form the ring. Our hands
would raise. Our feet would dance.
And between the blows,
it would all be worked out.
What's a few bruises?" he would ask.

"Now," I say, "We still have playgrounds,
parks, and other places.
We even have friends.
But we don't raise our fists or
make our feet dance. We raise our guns and
knives and make our feet run.
We work it all out."

He is silent. Life has changed.
But still, I think I'd trade a gun
for a fist, a knife for an insult.
Yet even then, I wonder
  if both dad's way and
my way is not right.
I wonder if there's a
  new way. I
wonder, because I
  wonder
if I'll be a dad to say,
"When I was mad..."

FRIENDS WHO ARE REALLY NOT

Objective:

Discuss ways to resist pressure to belong to gangs and to participate in group acts of violence.

Life Skill:

I will resist gang membership. (PF16)

Materials:

A copy of *Friends Who Are Really Not* (page 525), a copy for each student, colored butcher paper for a bulletin board

Motivation:

1 Introduce the term youth gangs. A **youth gang** is a group of young people who band together and participate in violent, unlawful, or criminal behavior. Explain that gangs usually have names and an area they believe to belong to them. They often use graffiti to mark their territory. Gang members hang out only with each other. They often commit crimes against other youth gangs or against the general population. Gang members often wear certain colors and dress in ways to be easily recognized. Youth gangs are usually made up of members from the same backgrounds. Gang members often refer to the groups to which they belong as "crews" or "posses."

2 Give students a copy of *Friends Who Are Really Not* and read it to themselves. Ask students how this poem relates to youth gangs. Explain that to join a youth gang, a person often has to do things that might harm himself/herself and others. Stress that people who are true friends would never

pressure a friend to do something that might harm him/her or other people.

3 Discuss with students why young people join gangs. Young people join gangs for different reasons. Some join because they want to feel like they belong. Others join because they live in an unsafe place. They want the protection of other gang members. Young people who are experiencing difficulties seem to be attracted to gangs. They may live in poor areas, struggle in school, and have few job skills. Still other young people join gangs for money and status. They see no other way to get these without getting involved in crime and drug trafficking. Young people from families that have money also join gangs. They may join because they are bored or lonely. They may want to rebel against their family. They may want a sense of excitement. Other reasons young people join gangs are the excitement of gang activity, peer pressure, and family tradition. Many young people who join gangs have no idea how dangerous this will be.

4 Explain that belonging to a gang can be very risky for a number of reasons. Gang members are more likely to be around illegal drugs and weapons. They get into fights more often. They are more likely to get arrested and spend time in jail. Family members of active gang members are at risk as well. They may be harmed. Their property may be stolen or damaged. Gang activities are very risky. The two most common crimes gang members commit are robbery and assault. Belonging to a gang also often means being with young people who have enemies. Rivalry exists among gangs. Gang rivalry and hatred results in fighting and other acts of violence.

5 Stress that it is important for students to resist gang membership by taking the following steps. Students should:

1. Avoid being around gang members;
2. Avoid being in locations that are gang turf or where gang activity takes place;
3. Avoid wearing any color or clothing that is gang-related;
4. Avoid taking part in graffiti writing or being around graffiti-marked walls;
5. Avoid alcohol and other drugs;
6. Avoid having tattoos with gang symbols;
7. Avoid staying out late at night;
8. Attend school and school activities regularly;
9. Be involved in family activities;
10. Set goals and make plans to reach them.

6 Divide the class into groups of four or five. Explain that each group is a rock or rap group that is developing an album with the theme of how to resist belonging to a gang. The group is to come up with titles of five songs they would have in their album. Examples of titles would be "You Can't Make Me A Part Of Your Gang," and "Gang Busters." Students should create a name for their album. Groups can create a short song to sing to the class that provides ways to resist gang membership.

Evaluation:

Have students draw album covers showing positive ways to handle life's demands. The cover can show how life can be great without belonging to a gang.

Friends Who Are Really Not

By Patricia M. Dashiell

Friends who are really not:

They test you, and push you,
and finding you worthy
embrace you,
but not for long.

So you try to gain respect,
but you really lose respect.
You work to save face,
and find that you've actually lost face.

What to do . . . but do what you must:

So you lie, or cheat, or steal,
or beat another up to maintain
that precarious standing
in a group of friends
who are really not,

friends who take you into danger.
and laugh when you get scared,
friends who lead you to dark places,
and leave you to fight your way out alone.

You work to keep those friends:

And in the end you find that what you have
are friends who are really not.

TERMINATING MARVIN

Objective:

Students will evaluate the consequences of belonging to a gang.

Life Skill:

I will resist gang membership. (PF16)

Materials:

Terminating Marvin (page 527), a copy for each student, two packs of sugar, two transparent cups, sheets of paper

Motivation:

1 Have the students draw a line down the center of a piece of paper. On one side of the paper, have them make a list, "Things I know about gang membership."

2 Give each student a copy of *Terminating Marvin* and have students read it to themselves.

3 Introduce the term youth gang. A **youth gang** is a group of young people who band together and participate in violent, unlawful, or criminal behavior. Being a gang member often exposes a person to illicit drugs, alcohol abuse, firearms, and other weapons. Young people join gangs for different reasons. They may be alienated from their families and are seeking to belong somewhere. Some join because they are bored and are looking for something that looks exciting. Many young people join gangs to feel a sense of belonging. The hazards involved in gang membership are not always evident at first.

4 Show the class two packets of sugar and two transparent cups. One of the cups should be filled with water. Explain that the packs of sugar represents two people who want to be independent, make their own choices about life, and be individuals. Open one packet of sugar and pour it into the empty cup. Ask students to observe what happened. Point out that the sugar has not changed in its new environment. Open the other packet of sugar and pour it into the cup of water. Ask students what happened. Point out that the sugar dissolved in the water and is not able to be seen. The sugar has changed dramatically in its new environment and is part of the water. Explain that the water represented a gang that accepted another person. And like many gangs, the gang members have a great influence on its members. A person who joins a gang can lose his/her identity, change behavior, and not be able to make his/her own choices.

5 Discuss with students ways to resist gang membership. These include:

- Avoid being around gang members.
- Avoid being in locations where gang activity takes place.
- Avoid writing graffiti.
- Avoid alcohol and other drugs.
- Avoid staying out late at night.
- Attend school and school activities regularly.
- Set goals and make plans to reach them.

Evaluation:

Have students complete the following statement on the other side of the paper they started prior to reading the story. "After reading the story, I learned the following five things about gangs..." Have students share their answers. Write the most common answers on the chalkboard and have students tell ways to resist pressure to join a gang.

Terminating Marvin

By James Heath

"Go down, chump. Go down."

Marvin didn't know who was saying that, but he didn't like it.

Marvin turned toward the voice to tell it to shut up, but before he could breathe, something collided with his hip, eating him up. A switch on the side of his head snapped on. A light flashed blindingly behind his eyes, then everything faded black.

Even with his eyes closed, Marvin knew he wasn't in his own room. He did not try to open his eyes. Somehow he knew that wasn't a good idea, not yet. The room was full of sounds. The main sound was a beep beep beep. It was constant, patient, unmistakable. Marvin could hear voices too, but not so clearly. Then he got very tired again and went back to sleep.

Marvin woke up next time out of a dream. He'd been running down the street. He was running away, but didn't know from what. He kept looking backwards, trying to see what was chasing him, but he couldn't recognize it. A voice warned, "Here it come, Marvin, here it come." The voice! He knew that voice. Then he felt pain. He woke up and one eye snapped open.

Marvin saw a bright light, lighting up a white room. He was right, the room definitely wasn't his. Marvin forgot everything about the dream, forgot everything except how much he was hurting. There was so much pain, he couldn't cry out. He could barely breathe. Marvin looked across the room. The bed he was in was metal with sides that stuck up like a pen around him. Marvin saw his right arm. It was in a cast from the tips of his fingers up almost to his shoulder. He had a tube stuck in his wrist that was attached to a plastic bag full of fluid that dripped through the tube into his arm. Marvin closed his eyes and tried to breathe, but the best he could do was short, shallow gasps. Marvin discovered another vivid area of pain—his jaw. It hurt. He fell back asleep.

When Marvin woke up again, two men in jackets and ties were waiting, standing at the foot of his bed, staring at him. The bigger one took a few steps forward. Deliberately he looked over Marvin's injuries.

"I'm Sergeant Wright," he said. 'That's Detective Solomon. Are you up for a little chat, Marvin?"

"Okay," Marvin said.

"Can you tell us how you got beat up?"

"I got beat up?" Marvin asked. "So that's what happened."

Sergeant Wright grinned at him. "Your right arm's broken. They sewed up your head—48 stitches. Three ribs on your right side are cracked. You almost lost an eye. Plus, your right hip was shattered. And you've been snoozing about four days. You think all that might have happened when you slipped in the shower?"

"Guess not."

"You know not," the other one said stepping forward. "C'mon, Marvin, how about we help each other out here. You're a Snake, right? So who got you? Knights? Razors? Who?"

At the sound of the word Snake, Marvin's stomach got so tight he thought he had to go to the bathroom. "I don't know, man. I ain't sure."

"Okay, Marvin. Tell you what." That was the bigger one speaking again. "I'm going to leave my card right on the bedside table. If you remember anything, you give me a call. Detective Wright. Okay?"

"Yeah, no problem."

"Good enough," Detective Wright said. "Get some rest, Marvin. You need it. See you, Miss."

Until then, Marvin didn't realize anybody else was there, but right away he knew it was Keisha. He realized he'd been smelling her perfume all the time the cops were talking at him. Marvin smiled, even though it hurt his jaw to do it. "Whatcha doin', girl?"

"Hey, Marvin," she said. She stood up from the chair and leaned over him. Keisha brushed her lips on Marvin's forehead, careful not to touch his swollen eye.

"They're going to send you home in a couple days, Marvin." Keisha sounded worried. She didn't look too happy.

"That's good," Marvin said.

Keisha shook her head. "No, it's not, Marvin."

"How come?"

"What do you think's going to happen when Goathead and Slick and the rest find out you're home?" Keisha asked.

Marvin's stomach felt the same as when the detective mentioned the

Snakes. The name Goathead brought back his dream, the voice, telling him, "Here it comes, Marvin." Marvin got flashes, impressions of his brothers looking mad and mean. Pain punctured his memory. He felt his arm breaking, he saw fists smashing into his ribs.

Keisha had been out of school for most of three years, working for an insurance company. She had been Marvin's girl for four years. Last Christmas, Marvin gave her a diamond ring. He didn't graduate from high school but, as Slick put it, Marvin had major bucks. His Snake family saw to that.

"Oh, Marvin," Keisha exclaimed. Marvin was pleased. Obviously she never expected anything like it. "It's so beautiful." Then she got quiet and looked at Marvin. "Does this mean what I think it does?"

Marvin didn't know. He just had gone into the store and asked the man what kind of rings girls liked most.

"Diamonds, my friend, the bigger the better," the man said. The ring cost five thousand dollars. A lot of cash, but it didn't clean him out.

"What do you think it means?"

That's when they started talking about marriage. At first, Marvin said, "No way, chick. What do we need that for? What's wrong with the way we're living now?"

A couple of weeks after that fight, they made up. A few days after, Keisha started talking about what their life could be if they moved, had their own apartment, and didn't have to worry about anybody but themselves. Marvin could forget about returning to school and instead take the GED. Keisha would help him prepare. Then, Marvin could work at the insurance company. Keisha's boss said married people are steady; they could find a job for Marvin.

Keisha expected Marvin's reaction. "What do I need a chump job for? I get more money in a week than you and all those guys see together in six months."

Keisha was ready, "You think I'm a chump, Marvin?"

Three weeks later she told him she was pregnant.

"That's cool," Marvin said. "I'm gonna be a daddy."

"No, Marvin," Keisha said. "That's not cool. This baby isn't gonna

have a daddy in prison or lying dead on the street. This baby isn't gonna have a gang chump for a daddy."

That week, Marvin met Slick in the yard. Marvin didn't know how to tell Slick what he and Keisha had decided Marvin had to do.

"Keisha's having a kid," he managed.

"Yeah," Slick said. Everybody knew that already. Snakes knew everything about each other. That's the way it was in a family, no secrets.

"We're gonna get married. We're gonna get our own place."

"That's cool," Slick said. Some Snakes were married, mostly older guys. Lots of brothers lived with their women. It wasn't a problem.

"Out of town," Marvin continued.

Slick sat up straight. "You can't do that. You're a Snake."

Marvin didn't move. From here on, no mistakes. "Way it's gotta be, Slick. 'Bout to get married. Having a kid. He isn't ending up out on the street. Got to give him a chance."

Slick was suddenly standing inches from Marvin. Marvin was taller, bigger than Slick but he didn't feel that way, looking down into Slick's eyes.

"You know what you talking about, Marvin. Only one way out, brother. Termination."

"I know," Marvin said.

"Well, I gotta talk to Goathead. Set it up. If you're sure."

It only took a week to set up. The playground across from the middle school was neutral ground. When gang leaders needed to talk about business, they went there. Other gang activities took place there too. Things like Termination.

On the appointed day, some of the junior Snakes threw rocks, one at a time, taking out the street lights around the playground. Now at midnight, shift change time for the cops, the playground was pitch black. Around the corner Marvin waited, his heart beating faster than the seconds counting off on his watch. At just after midnight he walked through the gate. He could barely make out the dark shapes under the hoop at the end of the the playground. Five guys. Goathead, the Snake leader, would be there. He knew Slick would be there since Slick got Marvin into the gang in the first place. With each step he took, Marvin's feet got heavier. As he moved closer, he saw Jake, E-Man, and Quinn. He stood looking into the darkness at their faces.

"Marvin. You sure about this, man?" Goathead asked.

"Gotta do it, yo," Marvin said.

Goathead nodded. "And you know what you're getting yourself into." He wasn't asking a question.

Everybody knew Termination. You stand, hands at your side, and your brothers beat on you. Not with weapons, just taped-up hands. If you try to strike back or even get out of the way, you're dead. Somebody right there kills you, gun or knife, right there, right then. The longer you stand on your feet, the better your chances. Go down too soon, you get stomped. Stay up, they just might walk away from you. When you wake up— if you wake up— you got to leave the neighborhood and never come back. Come back, you're dead.

Goathead nodded and the brothers moved around Marvin, a savage circle. Marvin wanted to see where Slick ended up. He thought Slick might take it a little easy. But he couldn't take his eyes off Goathead. He knew Goathead would start. Suddenly all the air exploded out of his stomach and Marvin was paralyzed. He needed to bend over, but he knew that would get him shot. Almost simultaneously two fists slammed into his arms. The blows started to come so fast he couldn't tell one from another.

Marvin wasn't getting any air, and panic spread through him. Marvin feared he'd faint.

"Go down, chump," Marvin heard someone say. "Go down, chump, go down."

Marvin didn't know who was saying that, but he didn't like it. He turned toward the voice. As he tried to open his mouth to tell whoever it was to shut up, he felt something collide with his hip. A light flashed blindingly behind his eyes, then clanged away into a deep, dull black. The last thing Marvin heard was "Chump going down. Here it comes, Marvin, here it comes."

The door to his hospital room opened slowly and Slick entered. He crossed the room to Marvin's bed. "I heard you were alive. Couldn't believe it.

Came by to see so myself." Slick's hands were stuffed inside the pouch of the hooded sweatshirt he was wearing.

Marvin looked at Slick but didn't say anything back. Keisha didn't say a word either.

"What's your plan, Marvin?" Slick wanted to know.

"Go on home when they let me out," Marvin said.

"You never get there Marvin, you know that. Don't you remember? You been terminated, man. You aren't ever going home. You better find a new home and fast."

Terminated. Finally it sank in.

Slick moved closer to Marvin's bed. Marvin watched Slick's hands inside the pouch. They moved and the pouch bulged with the movement. Slick pulled a closed fist slowly out of the pouch.

Keisha sucked in her breath with fear. Marvin shut his eyes. Was this what he survived the Termination for, to be shot or stabbed anyway?

"Hey, man, take this." Slick opened his palm and showed a car key. He tossed the key to Keisha. "When you leave, you pick him up, Keisha. Car's on High Street. Old, beat up Honda. Drive out of the city and don't even look around."

Slick leaned closer. "E-man hit you with a pipe. Wasn't right."

Marvin held out his arm, ignoring the pain, and grabbed Slick's hand.

"Be cool, Marvin. Take care of that kid." And then Slick was gone.

A NIGHT TO FORGET

Objective:

Students will describe ways to prevent rape and guidelines to follow when rape occurs.

Life Skills:

I will practice self-protection strategies. (PF18)
I will participate in recovery if a victim. (PF19)

Materials:

A Night To Forget (page 535), a copy for each student, strips of paper one foot in length and three to four inches wide, one for each student, sheets of blank paper, *Self-Protection When In Social Situations* (page 620), a copy for each student

Motivation:

1 Introduce the term acquaintance rape. You are in many social situations. Sometimes you meet new people. At other times, you socialize with friends and other people you already know. When you socialize, you do not expect to be harmed, especially when you socialize with people you know. Unfortunately, a perpetrator might be an acquaintance, such as someone you know from school, or a neighbor. A perpetrator might be someone with whom you have had a few dates. One type of violence that occurs far too often is acquaintance rape. **Acquaintance rape** is rape that is committed by someone known to the victim. Give students a copy of *Self-Protection When In Social Situations*. Review the material with students.

1. Stay away from places where you will be alone, when you are with a person you do not know well, or whom you do not trust.
2. Do not go anywhere with a stranger, even if you are supposed to meet other people.
3. Trust your gut feelings about other people.
4. Choose to be with other people when you socialize with someone the first few times.
5. Do not use alcohol or other drugs.
6. Set limits for expressing affection and communicate these limits to others.
7. Do not pressure another person to drink alcohol or to express affection beyond limits.
8. Avoid behavior that might be interpreted as sexual teasing or seductive.
9. Respect the limits other people have set for expressing affection. Never pressure someone beyond limits.
10. Ask the other person to tell you clear limits when you are confused or feel you are getting mixed messages.
11. Do not assume you and another person want to express affection in the same ways or have the same limits.
12. Use physical force if someone continues sexual behavior after you have set limits.
13. Attend workshops, seminars, or classes to be clear on issues regarding acquaintance rape.
14. Pay attention to warning signs that indicate a person might harm you: disrespectful attitude toward you, dominating attitude, extreme jealousy, unnecessary physical roughness, and/or a history of violent and/or abusive behavior.

2 Give students a copy of *A Night To Forget* and have them read it to themselves.

3 Divide the students into six groups. Provide students in the class with strips of paper, each about one foot in length and three to four inches wide. Have each student write a statement that is a rape prevention technique on the strip of paper. Some examples may be: have your keys ready beforehand as you are getting inside your car, keep lights around homes at night, lock all doors at home, and do not jog alone at night. Have each person sit in the front of the room side-by-side. Explain that students have formed a barrier to rape, and that if someone wanted to break through this wall, that person would

have a difficult time because of the protection. However, you can pull one person out of the line to simulate not practicing a rape prevention behavior. Then an opening has developed and a person can be vulnerable to rape.

Evaluation:

Have students draw a line down the middle of a page to divide it into two columns. In the left column, have the students write down 10 ways that they put themselves at risk, such as jogging alone at night. In the right column, have them write down self-protection strategies they might use for each of these ten ways; for example, jogging with a friend or a large dog.

A Night To Forget

By Patrica M. Dashiell

Somehow I found myself beating on Tess' door, torn between shame and fear. Over and over I beat my fist against the solid wooden door, scarcely feeling the pain of the gravel being ground deeper into the flesh of my palm as I curled my fingers more tightly. Suddenly, the door opened, and I half fell into Tess' arms. One look at my face and I knew she would know. Keeping my eyes on the floor, I dared not look up. I tried to concentrate on breathing. One. Two. Three.

"Gosh, Angie, did you plan on breaking the door down? I was up in my room doing—what in the world happened to you?" She stopped to stare at the edges of my tattered shirt I had tied back together rather clumsily.

"Can I come in?"

"Of course. Angie, what happened?"

I brushed past her and walked toward the kitchen. "I need something to drink," I mumbled as I walked past. "I was out running, and I fell down."

She followed me out to the kitchen. "You were running at 10:30 at night? Don't you know how stupid that is?"

"Yeah, I do. So you don't have to remind me."

I stuck my head in the refrigerator, welcoming the cold air on my face.

"Just help yourself to whatever. Mom went to the store today. Angie, what did you say you were doing?"

"Running, why?" I tried to keep my voice even. How can I explain? How can I explain how stupid I am?

"You're not dressed for running, at least I never knew anyone who ran in a blouse and a skirt. And your legs are all scratched up. Why is that?"

"I changed in the car."

"Really?"

She sounded suspicious. I stepped away from the refrigerator and moved toward the cabinets that held the glasses, keeping my back to her the whole time.

"Angie?"

"Yeah?"

"What really happened? You look more as if you fell out of a moving car. And if you changed, why is your blouse all torn?"

"Can we go up to your room?" I swallowed hard, fighting to hold the tears in. I wanted to tell her. I wanted her to stop it all from happening.

"Sure."

I led the way upstairs, my long hair hiding my face. I wanted desperately to take a bath, but couldn't see how I could ask. Flicking off the lights, I crossed to the window, staring out into the black night, trying to figure out what to say.

"What in the world are you doing, Angie? Are you crazy?" Tess turned the lights back on and came over to where I stood, leaning against the window frame. Reaching out, she turned my face toward her with one hand and gasped. "What happened to your face?"

"I fell."

"Yeah, right, and I'm the queen of England. Come on, Angie, you've never lied to me before. Did you get in a fight with Kevin?"

Kevin! I had forgotten. How could I forget Kevin? He was never going to understand. Who would want a girlfriend who had been—used?

"No, I fell," I insisted as I sank to the floor, not daring to look at my friend.

She stood for a moment looking at me and then left the room. Returning with a wash cloth in hand, she knelt before me and carefully began wiping the dirt and gravel from my face. Her gentle touch broke the grip I was holding on the flood building within me, and the tears came pouring forth. Dropping the cloth, she leaned forward as sobs wracked my entire body.

"Why, Tess? Why couldn't I stop him? Why was I so stupid?"

"Shhh, Angie. Take a deep breath."

I tried, but couldn't. The pain welled up from deep within and washed over me. It no longer mattered who I was. I no longer mattered. I gave in to the horror of what had happened and screamed the fear that was tearing at my heart, the screams I should have let out earlier. Maybe if I had screamed. I thought I heard my name, but the pain made it seem far away.

Suddenly someone was shaking my shoulders. I tried to pull away, but two strong hands held me tightly. Hands! His hands. "No!" I screamed and fought to pull away.

"Angie. Angie, it's me. Tess' mother."

Tess. Tess was my friend. But who was holding me?

"Angie, you've got to let us help you. What happened?"

"Angie? It's me, Tess, tell us what happened? Who did this to you?"

And then the wave was gone, leaving me utterly empty. Darkness filled the void, as the hurt subsided to an incredible ache in my heart.

"Angie?" Tess' mother had both arms wrapped around me. The pressure was oddly reassuring, and I fought to get my breath.

"Angie, can you hear me?"

I nodded my head.

"Keep taking deep breaths, honey, just relax." Gently releasing me, she stroked my hair with one hand and supported my back with the other. "You need to tell us what happened."

Where do I begin?

"Tess, go call her mother. I'll stay right here with her."

My mother. What would she think? She said my skirt was too short to be wearing to work. It was all my fault.

"What was all your fault, Angie?"

I was startled to realize I had spoken aloud. I suppose there is no getting around this. In a voice I didn't recognize as my own, I heard myself say, "I was raped." The words fell flat on the floor, creating a barrier between me and Tess' mother.

"Oh, no. Please not that," she whispered. In a louder voice she asked, "Who did this to you?"

"The manager."

"At work?"

"Yes."

"What did he do? I mean, can you tell me exactly what happened?" What was keeping Tess so long? How could I begin to explain? I sighed. "I stayed late to help him close the store. I've kind of gotten in the habit of doing that. I want to, I mean I wanted to get a raise."

"And?"

"And he offered to walk me to the car, and we stood outside the back door talking for a while. He talked the whole time about how I was doing well and how he would put in a good word for me to the branch office..." My voice trailed off as I struggled to continue.

"It's okay, honey, I'm listening."

"He said he thought I would make a good manager, and I got so excited that I hugged him, and he...."

"Go on. It's all right."

All right? Nothing was all right anymore. "He held on when I started to pull away. I was so confused when he started kissing me. I tried to get away, but I couldn't. I couldn't even scream. When it was over, he just kicked me in the side as I lay on the gravel and said tramps never made managers." I started to cry again. "He said...He said...."

She just waited for me to finish.

"He said I was fired and never to come back to work."

I heard her swear under her breath. I waited for her to tell me it was all my fault. To tell me that I had ruined everything.

"Angie?" She had me by both shoulders again, shaking me hard. "Angie, look me in the eyes."

Reluctantly, I raised my head.

"Angie, this is not your fault." She spoke very slowly and clearly. "Do you hear me? This is not your fault at all."

I wondered why she couldn't see. I wondered how she could say that when I had hugged him. I started it. But did it matter? I was nothing. Felt nothing. It was as if ice flooded my veins and chilled my heart.

She shook me again. "None of this is your fault, Angie. As soon as your mother gets here, we're going to take you to the hospital."

At those words everything came back in focus. "No," I said sharply, managing to free myself from her grasp. I pulled my knees up and wrapped my arms around them. "I don't need a doctor; I need a bath."

"We need to get you checked out, to see if you need any medical attention."

"No!"

"Angie, honey, they'll have to examine you."

"No."

"We need to see if you're all right."

"No." It was no more than a whimper now.

"I know you don't want to do this, but we need to take care of you. Your mother and I will be there. Tess, too, if you want. Just relax."

538

No. No. No. I had said no. I had pleaded. He didn't listen. He didn't stop. He didn't.

I buried my head in my chest and started crying again. Tess' mother hugged me and kept telling me that it was all over, that everything was going to be all right. But she was wrong. I knew it wasn't over. It was just beginning.

PLEASE, MR. SANDMAN

Objective:

Students will describe suicide prevention strategies.

Life Skill:

I will practice suicide prevention strategies. (PF9)

Materials:

Please, Mr. Sandman, (page 542), a copy for each student, *Suicide Prevention Strategies* transparency (page 604), transparency projector

Motivation:

1 Give each student a copy of *Please, Mr. Sandman* and have students read it to themselves.

2 Introduce the term suicide. **Suicide** is the intentional taking of one's own life. Discuss the following questions with students. Suggested answers are given after each question.

> Why do you think Lyla wants to end her life?
> She tells about losing her best friend, her job, and the interest of her boyfriend. She is feeling alone and helpless.

> Did Lyla plan for this day? How?
> Her father and mother were out. She had given away her watch. She watched how characters on television committed suicide. She had the pills ready.

3 Explain that suicide is not a solution. Suicide does not solve any problems.

There are many reasons that children and adolescents sometimes attempt suicide. They may be abused, have difficulty at school, lack love from their families, experience the separation or divorce of their parents, experience the death of a person or other loved adult, have poor peer relationships, or have physical defects that worry them. Teenagers who are vulnerable to suicide are those who abuse alcohol or other drugs, have feelings of alienation from their families, fear independence, are the subject of ridicule or isolation from peers, and/or have difficulty in coping with body changes and sexuality.

4 Discuss suicide prevention strategies. **Suicide prevention strategies** are techniques that can be used to help prevent a person from thinking about attempting and completing suicide. Explain that suicide prevention strategies include knowing suicide hotline numbers, knowing what do when a person feels depressed, talking to trusted adults, and being involved in rewarding activities.

5 Write a suicide prevention hotline number, such as the National Youth Suicide Prevention Hotline number: 1-800-621-4000, on the chalkboard. Tell students to write this number down in case they ever know someone who is at risk for suicide. A person who shows warning signs should always be taken seriously. A responsible adult should be notified immediately. If emergency help is needed, call 9-1-1 and stay with the person until appropriate help arrives. When the crisis is over, continue to give this person support and encouragement. It is important for this person to stay connected to friends and adults who care for him/her.

6 Explain to students that suicide is a leading cause of death in young people. Suicide is a serious health problem that is preventable. Have students develop a headline for a newspaper printed in the year 2050. The headline should indicate why suicide has declined. For example, students may write, "Decline In Suicide Attributed To More Students Sharing Feelings With Trusted Adults," or "Teens Choose Aerobics Over Suicide To Handle Daily Stressors." Hang these all over the bulletin board.

Evaluation:

Have each student write a letter to Lyla, pretending it is several days before the story takes place. Each student should pretend (s)he is a classmate of Lyla's who has noticed her warning signs and is concerned. In the letter, students should discuss at least three suicide prevention strategies.

Please, Mr. Sandman

By James Heath and Patricia M. Dashiell

Lyla Hart sat in the middle of her bed, the sheets and blanket pushed down against the foot in a roll. She wore the same clothes as yesterday—a T-shirt taken from her sister's closet, her father's heavy wool socks, and her oldest pair of jeans with the holes in the knees.

Lyla looked straight at the window across from the foot of her bed. She had been able to see the sun through the crack where the curtains did not meet before it rose out of sight. Earlier, she had stared directly into the sun. She'd heard you could burn your eyeball that way. She'd done it anyway. Now the sun was too high to see and she had pulled the curtains together to block the light. Here, inside, it was like a bleak, rainy day. That didn't matter; there wasn't anything much she wanted to look at anymore. She'd taken the pills. Her door was locked. She was just waiting.

She wondered what time it was. Automatically she lifted her right arm to look at her wrist. Then she remembered, she'd given her watch to her boyfriend. If you could even call him her boyfriend. Recently, he certainly hadn't been acting as if he cared very much about her. Like, just last Wednesday when she found him at his locker and she asked what they were going to do Friday night. She remembered the conversation.

"What's Friday night?" Todd asked.

"Friday night," Lyla answered. "We usually go out Friday night, right?"

"Oh yeah," he said. "I kind of told Brownie and Taylor I'd hang out with them. Probably go to the mall or something."

Lila didn't say anything, she just looked at him. Todd leaned against his locker and took a breath but didn't say anything. He just stared at Lyla. Then he said, "You want to meet us there?" He didn't look as if he hoped she'd say yes.

"No, you guys go. Have a good time. Call me Saturday or something."

Todd grabbed Lyla's hand. "Look, is there something wrong? I mean, did I do something?"

She pulled her hand back and said, "No, I'm fine."

So on Friday, Lyla gave him her watch. She just walked up to him at his locker and gave it to him.

He was surprised, just like she thought he would be. "What's this for?"

"You like it, don't you?" She knew he did. The watch had been a birthday present to her from her father. It was an Army-style watch with an olive band. When she had first showed it to Todd he'd said, "Dude, if you ever get bored of that watch, I could take it off your hands for you." What he liked was the way the web band went with his old Army jacket.

"Well, yeah," Todd said, taking it out of her hand but not completely ready to accept it. She hadn't spoken to him at all since they'd first talked about going out Friday night. He had been asking Nikki and her other friends if she was ticked off at him.

"Look," Lyla said, "you can have it. I mean, I want you to have it."

She knew Todd wanted it from the way he kept looking at it.

"But, hey, look," he said. "I mean, your dad gave it to you and everything. And besides, you like it, right?"

"He really, really wants it," she thought. "In fact, he likes the watch more than he likes me. He wants me to say I don't like it so he can have it and not feel guilty."

"My father's a jerk," was all she said.

Todd caressed the watch. "Yeah, well, I mean, if you really don't want it, sure." He turned to Brownie who came up while he and Lyla were talking. Lyla started walking away.

"Hey," Todd called. "Thanks a lot."

Lyla just lifted her hand and gave a backwards wave. She didn't turn around. "Just remember where it came from when you find out about me," she muttered under her breath.

Lyla's head began to throb and she gritted her teeth against the pain. What was taking so long? Shouldn't she be getting sleepy? Funny, in all the time she had thought about this moment, she had not stopped to wonder what it would actually feel like. On TV all you ever saw was someone sprawled across the bed, clutching an empty bottle of pills.

Lyla wasn't going to end up like all of those people. The bottle was in the trash outside. Her glass was in the dishwasher. Her room was clean—probably for the first time in years. And she was ready.

Turning her eyes toward the door, she checked to see if her door was still locked. "Duh! Good one, Lyla," she thought. "Nobody's even here." Her father was still at work, her sister was living who knew where, and her mother was out wherever, being the world's oldest teenager.

"Oh, man," her mother would say to Lyla whenever they saw each other—which was about twice a year, "Those earrings are sooo cool. Where'd you get them?"

Lyla started to feel sick to her stomach. And that made her want to call up Nikki. Now how stupid was that? And what made her think of Nikki?

"Oh," she thought, "because last time my stomach felt like this was when we drank those bottles of wine."

That night had started out so cool. Nikki's parents were away. The pizza was delivered late so they got it for free. But then, right in the middle of Nikki's imitation of their science teacher, the room had seemed to spin around and around. Next thing Lyla knew she was on the floor and didn't know how she got there. Suddenly she'd thrown up, and then Nikki was on her case about throwing up on the new rug, and knocking the wine bottle over on the floor. What a nightmare.

Lyla closed her eyes. That helped her stomach a little. Two months ago she would have been on the phone with Nikki in a flash, but Lyla hadn't seen Nikki in weeks. When she and Nikki had been best friends, the best parts of the day were meeting Nikki in the morning, having lunch together,

and last period when they'd sneak out of study hall and hang out. But somewhere, sometime, they'd stopped doing that.

Lyla tried to forget how strange she was feeling; instead she thought about Nikki. They'd been best friends all last year and were together all the time except for work. Lyla had worked at the Valley Animal Hospital until she'd been fired, which was totally unfair, because she hadn't been late nearly as much as they had said. About the time that Lyla got fired, that was about the same time she and Nikki had stopped being best friends anymore. If that was the way Nikki wanted it, fine. Lyla just wished she could see Nikki's face when she got the news.

The pain behind her eyes was growing worse. "I need to stop thinking," she thought.

Who would have thought all those pills would make her feel so wretched. What happened to peaceful sleep? Why didn't the Sandman just come along and put her to sleep? She tried to stop thinking about what she would do next and wondered why the pills were taking so long to do their job. Too bad she'd given away her watch.

Lyla concentrated on watching the specks of dust fly through the filtered sunlight streaming between the curtain folds. Then slowly she realized that her head felt fuzzy, that she no longer felt a part of her last great plan. The afternoon, the waiting, was actually happening to someone else. Lyla was the casual observer pausing to stare at the latest sad ending to a young life.

She was surprised to find tears slipping down her cheeks and she reached up to wipe them away.

This wasn't the way it was supposed to be. She felt terrible all over. And she couldn't control her thoughts. She had begun to think about things that she cared about and looked forward to.

"Oh no," she thought as she struggled against the descending cloud. But it was too late. Mr. Sandman had made his last visit to Lyla Hart.

LANGUAGE ARTS

ONE STEP REMOVED

Objective:

Students will evaluate the consequences of using drugs and being involved in drug sales and trafficking.

Life Skill:

I will avoid alcohol and other drugs. (PF14)

Materials:

One Step Removed, (page 547) a copy for each student, *Different Types Of Drugs* transparency (page 611), transparency projector

Motivation:

1 Introduce the term drug. A **drug** is a substance that changes the way the body and/or mind work. Explain that drug use can harm the body, drugs can affect the way a person acts, and can cause illness, disease, and even death. Drug use changes a person's behavior so that (s)he is more likely to lose control and become violent. People who use alcohol and/or other drugs are at increased risk for being involved in fighting, sexual assaults, domestic violence, and suicide. Use the *Different Types Of Drugs* transparency to discuss the terms.

2 Introduce the subject of drug trafficking. **Drug trafficking** involves the purchasing and/or selling of illegal drugs. Explain that drug trafficking is associated with violence for several reasons. Since drug trafficking is illegal, the drug trade is not enforced by law authorities. Therefore, it is run by people who do not obey any laws and who make up their own rules. People involved in drug trafficking often carry weapons to protect them-

selves and to protect their drugs. Carrying a weapon puts them at higher risk of being involved in violence.

3 Ask students for examples from the media of people who have died of drug overdoses. Have the students list all the people that had some responsibility for the death of the person who overdosed. Examples might include the people who grew the drugs, the people who processed the drug, the people who transported the drug, the people who sold the drug, and the people who were with the person while (s)he was taking the drug.

4 Give each student a copy of *One Step Removed* and have the students read it to themselves. After they have read the story, have students rewrite a version of the story from another character's point of view. Point out that they may choose from any character in the story including one of the detectives, Jason's father, Jason's sister, and the girl who gave the party.

Evaluation:

Prepare a sign-up sheet with the names of different types of drugs. Have students go to the library and research the effects a specific type of drug can have on a person's body. Have students prepare a brief oral report and a visual aid to display in the class. Visual aids might include a poster, a diorama, photographs, or transparencies.

One Step Removed

By James Heath

On Thursday evening, the first week of June, the Dunstans were just finishing their dinners when the doorbell began to buzz. None of them could remember the last time someone had come by right at dinner time. Something about the doorbell set Jason on edge. Whoever was out there was patient. He or she just kept pushing the button as regular as an alarm clock.

Mr. Dunstan got up to answer the door. A moment later, Jason went through the living room to look out the window. The car in the street was not a police cruiser, but it was the same make the Afton Police drove. He had seen them often enough to know. Jason could hear murmuring at the door, then he heard his father say, "Of course." More murmurs, then, "Just a minute."

Jason darted into the kitchen so he was seated again at the table when his father reentered. Jason's mother and sisters looked at him expectantly, but he remained silent.

Mr. Dunstan stopped in the middle of the kitchen, looking puzzled. "Do you know what they want?" he asked, staring straight at Jason.

"Who?" Jason asked nonchalantly, trying to act as if he did not know that they were police officers.

"Two police officers. Detectives, I think. They want to talk to you."

"Me?" He pretended surprise. "What about?"

Mr. Dunstan shook his head and stared at his son for a moment. "I thought you might know," he answered quietly.

"No, Dad." Jason fought to keep his face carefully blank.

"They're waiting out in the front hall. We had better go speak with them." Jason merely looked at him, making no effort to get up out of his chair. "Come on, Jason. They're waiting."

Mrs. Dunstan started to protest, but her husband shook his head at her.

Jason rose and crossed in front of his father. Mr. Dunstan followed him.

Two men stood in the foyer between the living room and the dining room. One was much bigger and a little older than the other; he wore a jacket and tie. The other wore a tie, too, and a navy blue windbreaker.

Jason could easily see the gun on his hip. It made his stomach shrink.

Jason looked them both in the eyes, almost defiantly as if to say, "You have no business here!" But his stomach did not feel any better. Here were two strange men in his house, unexpected and unwelcome visitors. While they looked as if you might meet them in a supermarket or sit next to them at a ball game, he knew they had not come to pay a friendly visit.

"Why are they here?" he wondered, as he tried not to drop his gaze.

The bigger man stepped toward Jason and held out his hand. "I'm Sergeant Booth, Jason. This is Detective Dylan. Sorry to bother you like this. I guess you know what this is about."

"Not really," Jason said, shaking hands first with Sergeant Booth and then Detective Dylan.

"No?" the sergeant said. He stopped short and stared back at Jason.

"It's pretty obvious he doesn't believe me," Jason thought.

"Mr. Dunstan, is it okay if we go sit in the living room here?" Booth asked, indicating the darkened room to their left, but not taking his eyes off Jason's face.

"Certainly."

No one moved at first. Tension filled the foyer quickly. Finally Sergeant Booth took a step into the living room. "Is there a light switch close by?"

With the silence broken, Mr. Dunstan shook himself and pointed at the switch. He turned toward Detective Dylan. "Do you want to speak with Jason alone?"

"You're seventeen, right?" Dylan asked Jason, still looking straight into his face.

Jason nodded. Slowly turning back toward face Jason's father, he phrased his answer carefully, "The law does not require that you be present, Mr. Dunstan." He paused. "But, if Jason would like you to stay…"

"That's okay, Dad. You can go," Jason said rather quickly. Something might come up he'd rather his parents not know about.

Mr. Dunstan hesitated.

"Really, Dad, it's no big deal."

Jason deliberately turned away from his father and entered the living room. Family photographs in elegant frames sat on the four end tables that bracketed two large leather sofas which faced each other. The coffee table held still more photographs, some of Jason and his sisters. On the mahogany mantel above the fireplace stood Jason's school trophies from football and track.

The police officers moved slowly into the room, taking in its details. The plush carpet, the rich paneling, the oriental rug, and the photographs all told the story of how this family lived. After looking around the entire room, stopping once to pick up a picture of Jason with his family, Booth settled himself on the larger sofa. Dylan sat on the other. This left Jason to choose which detective he wanted to sit beside. He chose Booth.

Detective Dylan took out a small notebook, but it was Sergeant Booth who started the interview.

"So, Jason," he began, "you really have no idea why we want to talk to you?"

Jason definitely had some ideas but he was not exactly sure which ideas might be the interest of these two cops. In any case, he did not want them to know any of his business. "I don't know? Maybe that fight between Ronnie Atkins and Brion Moore?" he offered. "I heard Brion is still in the hospital."

"Basically." Booth rested his elbows on his knees. "Is there any more you can tell us about that?"

"You mean more than I already told the guys who were asking questions that night?"

"Oh, that's right. You were there that night. I thought I read your name in the report." The sergeant leaned back, making himself more comfortable. "Sure. Is there anything else you can tell us about that?"

"I don't really think so. I didn't see it happen. I was in another part of Amy's house."

Booth looked over at Dylan who flipped back in his notebook a few pages. Dylan nodded at Booth before asking, "That would be Amy Lee, the girl who had the party?"

"Right." The notebook was beginning to make Jason nervous. "Look, is Ronnie in trouble about what happened to Brion?" He paused, but the two police officers remained silent. He went on, "I heard it wasn't Ronnie's fault. I mean, is that why you're going around asking more questions?"

Booth looked at Dylan. Dylan wrote something down. Jason pulled the pillow from the corner of the couch and placed it in his lap, trying to settle his stomach.

"Why don't you tell us about what happened, Jason," suggested Booth. "Just start at the beginning, and maybe you'll remember something you forgot to tell us."

"Well, like I said I wasn't there. But I heard that Ronnie was just trying to get by Brion and Kerry to get to the bathroom and..."

"That would be Kerry Meyers?" Dylan offered after checking his notes again.

"Yeah." These guys were beginning to make Jason's knees weak.

"They've done a lot of homework," he thought. "Anyway, the hall is like really narrow, you know? And Ronnie bumped Brion, and then Brion basically freaked out and started choking Ronnie. Ronnie shoved him up against the wall, and that was it. Brion went down and, I guess, passed out. A bunch of kids tried to help him with that stuff that smells like ammonia, you know, and doing the CPR thing."

"Were you one of those?" Dylan asked.

"What are they saying?" Jason wondered. "I already told them I wasn't there."

550

"No," Jason answered, trying to keep his voice still. Turning his shoulders slightly away from Dylan, he chose to look at Booth and added, "By the time I got back to the hall it was pretty crowded. And somebody had already called 9-1-1."

"Where had you been?" Dylan persisted.

"Where had I been? You mean, when they were having the fight?"

"Yeah, then too. But also before, while the party was going on."

"Jason felt his chest begin to constrict. His whole head felt like it was emptying out, like the blood was draining down into his stomach. His throat was dry, really dry. "I don't know." He swallowed hard. "I guess mostly downstairs in the family room. That's where the music and most of the kids were."

"Most of the kids?" Dylan was pushing toward something Jason did not understand yet, but knew he did not want to understand, either.

Jason tried to lighten the interview. "Well, you know. I mean, Amy's parents were out to dinner or something. So some of the kids were in different parts of the house. You know, making out and stuff."

"Were you in different parts of the house, Jason?"

Jason tried to stop himself from seeing the extra bathroom upstairs where he had spent most of the party before Brion ruined everything. He tried not to think, either, of the money he had made or how much more he could have made had it not been for Brion. But the more he sent his thoughts in different directions, the more they went back where he didn't want them. He felt as if these cops were taping what was running through his head.

Jason was not used to being on the defensive. He was used to being the one in control. And he was good at it, at being in control. As he felt the control over this interview leaving him, his anger flared. "I thought you wanted to know what I could tell you about the fight. Look, I told you, and that's all I know."

Ignoring the outburst, Dylan leaned casually back into the sofa and crossed his legs. "We do need to know that, Jason. It's just we've already talked to quite a few of your friends. We've been investigating this incident for the last two weeks."

The strength Jason felt from his outburst suddenly vanished. Dylan let the information sink in before adding, "Some other questions have come up."

"Like what?" Jason tried to sound tough but his cracking voice betrayed him.

"Jason, were you aware of any drug use at this party?" challenged Booth.

"Booth twisted to face Jason directly, and the cushions shifted under his weight. Jason had the sensation of being bounced up into the air, sending him more into a panic than he already was. His heart began to pound so much that he could feel the beating pulse in his wrists, neck, temple, and even in his armpits.

"Not really," he managed.

Dylan interjected, "Does that mean 'No, there were no drugs,' or 'Yes, there may have been drugs?'"

Jason dug in. Despite fear that he was on the verge of sheer panic, he managed to sound angry. "Look, Sergeant Booth, it was a party, okay? Party? You've heard of it? When has there ever been a party where there weren't some kids who got high or had a couple of beers?"

Dylan wrote in his notebook. He looked up across the coffee table at Jason. "That means yes, there were drugs at this party. Can you confirm that?"

"Yes," Jason said. "I'm almost positive there were drugs, but I couldn't swear to it."

"No kidding," Dylan said. He leafed back through his notebook. "That's not exactly consistent with our information so far."

Jason wanted to say something hard and clever and resourceful, something to put these cops back a step or two. He wanted to show them they were not getting to him at all. But he couldn't do so because they were getting to him. All he could do was to stare belligerently at Detective Dylan. So when Sergeant Booth asked quietly if he had heard that Brion was dead, he did not immediately realize what was being said. Jason asked him to repeat it.

"Brion Moore died yesterday. He never really regained consciousness."

Jason was dumbfounded. Although he did not understand how or why, almost everything about this interview suddenly shifted. Every single word that had been said became utterly important. He tried to remember exactly how the conversation had been going, but the throbbing in his temple was growing worse. Jason found it difficult to concentrate.

"So you didn't know that, Jason?" Booth offered.

"No, I didn't." Jason found himself on a dangerously careening roller coaster. His voice turned shrill. "What happened? I mean, how come he died?"

"It's okay," Booth said, softly, patting Jason's knee. "Don't get worked up. That's why we're here asking questions." Jason tried to calm down as he took a deep breath. Then, in the same tone of voice Booth dropped his bombshell. "Jason, do you know where Brion got his cocaine?"

Jason knew what he had heard. He understood the question but he could not make himself move or answer or respond. For a moment he felt paralyzed. He felt like he couldn't breathe. He shut his eyes and took a deep breath.

He heard Detective Dylan say, "Hello, Mr. Dunstan, why don't you stay."

Jason eyes flew open. His father stood patiently, like a butler awaiting instruction.

"Are you all right now?" Booth asked. Jason nodded. "That's a boy. Tough question for you now, Jason. Do you use cocaine, too?"

Jason had no strength, no will, no feelings. He shook his head.

"Any illicit drugs at all?"

"Some weed. Not all that often."

The police officers looked at each other and then over at Mr. Dunstan. His face disclosed nothing but misery as he caught himself against the arm of the couch.

"Hang on there, sir," Dylan thought. "You haven't heard anything yet."

"So let me ask you, Jason. Did you sell Brion the cocaine he was using that night?"

Jason barely nodded.

"Is that a yes?"

Jason nodded again. "That's a yes," he echoed the detective.

Booth sighed. He and Dylan stood. Jason hardly noticed until he felt Booth's hand on his arm compelling him to stand as well. "Why don't you step right out there," Booth pointed to the space in front of the coffee table. Jason, not sure what was happening or why, did as Booth told him.

"Excuse me, sir," Dylan said as he rose from the couch, indicating that Mr. Dunstan should step back. Then he stopped behind Jason. Booth said, "Jason, you don't have a knife on you, do you? Or any other kind of weapon?"

"No," Jason said, finally surprised at what was happening. "Dad?"

Taking Jason's left wrist and pulling it, Dylan said, "Please put your wrists together."

"Dad?" Jason repeated. Dylan handcuffed his wrists together.

Mr. Dunstan found his voice. "What's happening? Are you arresting Jason?"

"Jason," Sergeant Booth said, "I am placing you under arrest for the death of Brion Moore."

Jason twisted toward Booth. Dylan let him turn just enough so he could see Booth reading a card. "You have the right to remain silent. You have the right to an attorney and to have one present during questioning."

Neither Jason nor his father said anything until Booth was finished and had put the card away. Then Jason found his voice. "Look, I told you, I wasn't there. Nobody said I was anywhere even close. I hardly knew him."

Jason stood very still. He saw again, in perfect detail the extra bathroom upstairs where he had set up shop during the party before Brion had ruined everything.

"Blood samples were drawn when Brion Moore was admitted to the Medical Center," Booth went on. "The reports were forwarded to us this afternoon. Brion's blood showed heavy cocaine intoxication. That was the proximate cause of death. In this state—since you sold him the cocaine—that makes you responsible for his death."

NEW KID IN TOWN

Objective:

Students will identify ways to reduce violence by following laws and cooperating with law enforcement authorities.

Life Skills:

I will respect authority and abide by laws. (PF17)
I will change behavior if a juvenile offender. (PF20)

Materials:

New Kid In Town (page 557), a copy for each student, *Ways To Change Behavior If A Juvenile Offender* transparency (page 624), transparency projector

Motivation:

1 Introduce the term juvenile offender. A **juvenile offender** is a person below the age of 18 who breaks a criminal law. Explain that juvenile crime has been on the rise in the past two decades. Point out that juveniles are responsible for one-third of all burglaries, one in seven of all rapes, and one in seven of all homicides. Juvenile offenders also commit less serious offenses, called status offenses. **Status offenses** are types of behavior for which an adult would not be arrested, such as skipping school, alcohol use, running away, defying parents, and staying out late.

2 Introduce the term rehabilitation. **Rehabilitation** is the process of helping juvenile delinquents change negative behavior to positive behavior. In most cases, juvenile court systems attempt to rehabilitate juvenile offenders.

3 Give each student a copy of *New Kid In Town* and have students read it to themselves. When they have finished reading, divide them into groups of four. Have each group create a one-paragraph character sketch of Jake through the eyes of another character mentioned in the story. Examples of characters they might use include the security guard, Jake's mother, Jake's aunt, and Jake's classmates. When the groups are finished, have a person from each group read their character sketch aloud.

4 Discuss that most young people who commit a crime do not continue their criminal behavior. However, for some juvenile offenders, changing their behavior is more difficult. They may not have learned right from wrong while they were growing up. They may be encouraged by peer pressure, or may abuse alcohol and other drugs. Explain that there are steps juvenile offenders can take to work toward changing behavior. Review the information on the transparency *Ways To Change Behavior If A Juvenile Offender* with students. Discuss the following information.

Improve Family Relationships. In most cases, juvenile offenders have difficult family relationships. When young people are juvenile offenders, usually the entire family benefits from getting help.

Spend Time With Other Trusted Adults. Youth leaders, teachers, coaches, and clergy are trusted adults who may be helpful. They can teach juvenile offenders what is responsible. Offenders can learn by watching how these adults behave.

Ask Trusted Adults For Feedback. **Feedback** is information that helps someone know how well they are doing. When trying to change, it is always helpful to have feedback.

Work To Improve Self-Esteem. **Self-esteem** is what you think or believe about yourself. As self-esteem improves, there is less chance of behaving in harmful ways.

Choose Friends Who Obey Laws. When juvenile offenders want to change behavior, they may need to change friends. They need friends who support responsible behavior. These friends should obey laws. They need to stay away from young people who do not obey laws. This helps prevent the temptation to do things that get them in trouble again.

Make Repayment For Wrong Actions. Repayment is a way to make up for what has been taken, damaged, or hurt. Repayment might involve paying back money that was stolen. Returning stolen property to the rightful owner is another kind of repayment. Damage to property might be repaired. Replacing property is another kind of repayment.

Become Involved In School Activities. As part of recovery, juvenile delinquents can become involved in school activities. Then they will be with other young people with whom they share an interest. They will spend time with peers in positive ways.

Develop Job-Related Skills. It is important for young people to prepare themselves for the future by developing job-related skills. This increases the chance of obtaining and keeping a good job after finishing school.

Volunteer In The Community. Volunteering in the community may include helping to clean up a neighborhood or helping at a homeless shelter. By helping others, juvenile offenders can be of value to others. This is a new way of behaving.

Join A Support Group. Many correctional facilities, hospitals, and social service agencies offer support groups for juvenile offenders. These support groups offer the opportunity to discuss how difficult it will be to change behavior. Members can discuss ways to help each other maintain a violence-free lifestyle.

Evaluation:

Have the students write a sequel to the story on their own. The sequel is to be in the format of a letter written by Jake ten years later. Jake is to tell what happened to him, and how he continued to change his behavior after spending time in juvenile hall and moving to his new school.

New Kid In Town

By James Heath

Jake's the new kid in town. In the city, you wouldn't be able to tell Jake from nobody else. Out here in the suburbs, it's like a different country and you couldn't miss him unless you were blind.

Forget he combs his hair slicked back, which makes him totally different from any other kid in this school. All you would have to do is just watch him walking. The way he walks is saying something. His walk says, "This is me here, and nobody else. And if you don't like that, tough." Everybody knows right away, this is one tough guy. I knew right away I wasn't gonna mess with him and he knew it. We're pretty tight now.

Don't get the impression that Jake's this kind of kid that's going around looking for trouble, 'cause that's not true. I mean, he's been in trouble, and he isn't afraid of trouble, but he's not looking for trouble—not anymore anyway. He's just out here living with his aunt, going to school for the main reason that if he didn't leave the city he was living in, his whole life would be trouble. I know because he told me the whole story.

Basically, how he got to live in this town was he didn't want to join the Knights, which is the gang in his old neighborhood.   You might have heard of them. On a scale of good to bad, they're off the bad end of the scale. Whatever you can think of, they've done that already and probably worse besides.

When Jake was little, about nine years old, he and his friends would hide in the bushes at the edge of the park and throw rocks at cars. Once in a while, a driver would slam on the brakes, just leave the car right there in the middle of the road, and go chasing after them. That was what they liked, the feeling they would get of being all juiced up. Jake and the kids he hung out with, they didn't do drugs. But when they were chased, there was this feeling, like adrenaline; it got them all juiced up and excited. It was a rush.

After a while, though, the rush wore off and throwing rocks wasn't so exciting anymore, so they graduated to other stuff like fighting and stealing. He would steal just small things at first, like a pack of gum or baseball cards. It was more exciting. But, also, in his neighborhood if you didn't do bad stuff, you wouldn't have respect. Street life, it's all about respect—you got it or you don't.

Where Jake comes from, everything is respect or no respect. What you're doing all day long is all about that. And respect is not this thing that once you got it, that's it. Respect is day to day, every day, like food. You don't just eat supper on Monday and not have to eat anymore again for the rest of the week. You gotta eat every day. Same with respect. You got to get it every day. If you don't get respect in that neighborhood, people are gonna mess with you. Only out here in the suburbs, nobody but a couple of kids even understand that.

Jake came here straight from NCC, which stands for Northwest Correctional Center. It's a reform school. Here's how Jake got there. He and his boys had sort of graduated from boosting baseball cards and gum to bikes. Last time he stole a bike, somebody must have told on him, 'cause next thing he knows, this cop calls him up at home. He asks Jake where he was that afternoon.

And Jake, he answered, "Home," which he wasn't.

The cop goes, "Don't lie to me, boy. I know you were up in the Elmwood area. I know what you look like. I'm coming down to your house to have a look at you."

Jake figured the cop really did know him so he said, "All right, I did it."

Right away the cop came down and arrested him and took him to juvenile hall. Jake didn't much like spending the weekend in juvie, so he was cool for almost the whole time of his probation. Then one day he was at the mall.

He was checking out those hats you wear sideways or backwards. And in walks a bunch of Knights. So, Jake ducks behind one of those racks and waits until he can leave the place without the Knights seeing him. Then, he runs outta there and in the opposite direction of the Knights. Man, he got outta there all right but he forgot he had been trying on those hats. Suddenly he hears this security guard yelling at him.

Well, when Jake hears the guard he just takes off running, not knowing what's up. Then he remembers the hat and stops. The guard grabs him and asks, "Why did you steal that hat?"

Jake goes, "I didn't steal it. I was just trying it on and forgot."

558

And the guard says, "Yeah, right. And you were running just because you felt like it. You're coming with me, boy."

The guard started dragging Jake with him, but Jake jerked his arm away and ran off. He hid out for an hour in the trash shed at the end of the mall thinking that would be enough. But when he comes out, they're still looking for him.

Jake ducked outside and took off across the parking lot which was pretty full. He kept hiding in bushes and under cars, but the security guards kept asking people if they had seen him. So finally there's this bunch of people looking for him. A lot of police cars came skidding into the parking lot and right across the grass toward the playground, so Jake just put his hands up in the air.

He spent that weekend in the juvie system too, but this time he was pretty angry— he hadn't meant to do anything wrong. He had meant to pay for the hat.

This was when Jake got into his most serious trouble. Just after his mom bailed him out, he decided to steal a car and take a joyride—to get even, to get his respect back. He got caught right away when he ran a red light. Next thing, Jake is surrounded by cops again. That time he ended up in reform school for six months to two years.

Jake says reform school is a bad place. Every move you make is watched. You have to get permission to do everything, even to go to the bathroom. They put you in categories there. In Category 1, you can do anything you want pretty much—have more free time, go home weekends, and buy soda from the staff soda machine. But practically the only way anybody could be in Category 1 was to be the kind of kid who wouldn't be in reform school in the first place.

When Jake got there, he was automatically put in the lowest category since the file of all his incidents was so thick. The staff guy says to him, "So, I guess you're a pretty bad guy, is that right?"

Jake didn't say anything. The staff guy said, "Insubordination. Extension of category status, indefinite."

Jake said, "What are you talking about?"

After he was sentenced but before he got taken to NCC, Jake's social worker told him that if he was good he'd get out soon. So for three months, he didn't do anything bad. Then one time when the social worker came to visit him, Jake asks her, "I've been good for all this time, I don't see me getting out any sooner. When do I get out of here?"

And she says back, "Six months to two years. You have at least three more months. But you have too much of a record. You're probably staying the whole time." So Jake stopped trying to be good and just was himself. He had lost a lot of respect being good all that time, but it didn't take him very long to get his respect back.

He got his respect back by mouthing off to the staff now and then. If you had respect, the other kids would lay off you most times.

In the school part, Jake did good, almost all A's. Before he was going to get out, he was supposed to finish the grade as valedictorian of his class. Only two days before school ended for the session, they told him that his time was up and he was leaving.

"What?" he said. "You know I want to finish as valedictorian. Get something good out of this place."

But they said his time was up.

When Jake got out, school was about to start so he went right from NCC into high school in the city. First week of classes, he was in trouble again. The reason was, he needed to get respect. He had to prove to the guys that he should get respect even though he was away in reform school all that time. Next thing he knows, he was suspended from school for disrespecting his teachers. That was a funny thing, Jake said. One way of getting respect was giving out disrespect.

The pressure from the Knights started again. In the city, you're either in a gang or you get messed with by a gang. It's either-or, no other choices. Jake kept putting the gang guys off. He said he was thinking about it. They kept saying he didn't have a long time to think.

A couple weeks later, he was at football practice. Most of the players on the team were Knights. Jake was running with the ball, when he got tackled— by about five guys. His shoulder got dislocated. One of the guys, a Knight, said, "You still thinking, Jake? We're waiting."

His mother said that was the final straw. She had to get him out of the city. Lucky for Jake, his aunt lives out here in the suburbs. Even though his aunt says all the time she don't want any more kids. "I finally got mine out of the house," she complains all the time. "Why am I being punished with a troublemaker like Jake?"

Jake is doing okay here. His grades are better and the teachers like him okay. He's got some friends like me, that don't get into trouble. Except maybe for goofing off once in a while in class. He is even gonna try out for the football team. Sometimes new kids come to our school that dress different, sound different, and have a hard time feeling like they fit in. But, if they try hard they can usually get along okay. Like Jake.

THE PLAGUE, THE THORN, THE ALBATROSS

Objective:

Students will identify types of violence.

Life Skill:

I will recognize that violent behavior is wrong. (PF1)

Materials:

The Plague, The Thorn, The Albatross (page 563), a copy for each student, *Types of Violence* transparency (page 589), transparency projector

Motivation:

1 Have students bring five articles that describe types of violence to class. The articles should be from different magazines, newspapers, and journals and should be a mix of local, national, and international stories. For each article, have students write the answers to the following questions: What type of violence occurred, where did it take place, who was the perpetrator(s), and who was the victim(s).

2 Give students a copy of the poem *The Plague, The Thorn, The Albatross* and have them read it to themselves. Break them up into four groups and ask each group to give a reading of the poem. The reading should be creative and might be in the form of a role play, musical, rap, or any interpretation the group chooses. Allow groups time to practice. Have each group perform their reading for the class.

3 Discuss different types of violence, using the *Types Of Violence* transparency.

Bullying is an attempt by a person to hurt or frighten people who are perceived to be smaller or weaker

Fighting is taking part in a physical struggle

Assault is a physical attack or threat of attack

Homicide is the accidental or purposeful killing of another person

Suicide is the intentional taking of one's own life

Sexual Harassment is unwanted sexual behavior that ranges from making unwanted sexual comments to forcing another person into unwanted sex acts

Rape is the threatened or actual use of physical force to get someone to have sex without giving consent

Child Abuse is the harmful treatment of a person under 18 and includes physical abuse, emotional abuse, sexual abuse, and neglect

Domestic Violence is violence that occurs within the family or within other relationships in which people live together

Evaluation:

Have students watch an evening's worth of television. Have them record the number of acts of violence and the types of violence shown on the television shows. Put the results on the chalkboard. Calculate the number of acts of violence in each program. Calculate which types of violence occurred most frequently.

The Plague, The Thorn, The Albatross

By Patricia M. Dashiell

Crime is the plague of our youth.
   a death knoll echoing through
   our homes, our neighborhoods
   our schools, our malls
   claiming its victims from one to twenty-one
   but not without cure

Crime is the thorn of our nation.
   a wound in our side
   placed there by loved ones and strangers alike
   festering
   with no healing in sight
   but there for the plucking

Crime is the albatross of our future.
   hanging around the necks of young and old
   the overwhelming burden
   the hindering weight
   that pulls us back from our journey
   but a destiny not set in stone

LANGUAGE ARTS

MORE THAN WORDS

Objective:

Students will name kinds of violence and ways to protect against violence.

Life Skills:

I will recognize that violent behavior is wrong. (PF1)

I will practice suicide prevention strategies. (PF9)

I will avoid discrimination. (PF11)

I will practice self-protection strategies. (PF18)

Materials:

More Than Words (page 566), one copy for each student, a bowl of water, salt, pepper (black and cayenne), toothpick, liquid dish detergent, magazines, poster board, glue, scissors, colored butcher paper

Motivation:

1 Dip the toothpick into the dish detergent and place it aside.

2 Have the students gather around you and the bowl of water. Discuss how the world is made up of different kinds of people, who have different backgrounds and skin colors. As you talk, sprinkle the salt and two kinds of pepper liberally into the bowl. Explain that different kinds of people can get along if they try, but sometimes all it takes is just one person showing discriminatory behavior to change that. Dip the toothpick into the water and watch as the salt and pepper pulls to the edge of the bowl. Tell the students that the one person often begins with words.

3 Give each student a copy of *More Than Words* and have the students read it to themselves. Discuss the following questions with students. Suggested answers are given after each question.

How do you think the person in the poem feels?
Students might suggest that the person feels sad, hurt, frustrated, lonely.

What do you think might have happened to make the person feel that way?
(S)he might have been left out, teased, hurt, rejected.

What are some reasons people make fun of others?
Examples might include: for their appearance, for their race, or for lack of abilities.

4 Introduce the phrase, "Different is different, not better or worse." Have the students tell you what they think you mean by that. Also discuss how it is often easier to make fun of people who are different than it is to try to understand them. In seeking to understand each other, we can eliminate discrimination and prejudice. Explain that people who are faced with discriminatory behavior may feel hurt, sad, and lonely. People who have these feelings may be at risk for harming themselves.

5 Explain that when people are faced with discriminatory behavior they may become angry and violent. Explain that it is necessary to understand that a person can be harmed if (s)he is near people who are violent or if (s)he is in a situation that is either violent or in danger of becoming violent. Explain the meaning of the term violence. **Violence** is the threatened or actual use of physical force to injure, damage, or destroy yourself, others, or property.

6 Explain that it is important to recognize violent behavior. It is important to recognize that violent behavior is wrong. Explain that everyone has a right to be safe. A person who chooses a violent behavior against himself/herself or another person is choosing a wrong behavior. Encourage students to talk with a trusted adult if they are feeling angry or discouraged so that they will not behave in a way that might harm themselves or other people.

7 Remind students that discriminatory behavior can lead to violence. Tell students they can make a commitment to avoid discriminatory behavior by doing the following. Tell students they should avoid discriminatory comments. For this reason, they should always think before they speak. If they make

a commitment to say kind and respectful comments about others or nothing at all, they promote nonviolence. Students should ask others to stop discriminatory behavior When someone makes a snide remark or tells a joke about an individual belonging to a specific group, they should show disapproval. They should not laugh or go along with the behavior. Students also can learn about people who are different. As they learn more about others, they appreciate the talents they have to offer.

Evaluation:

Have students find articles in newspapers and magazines describing events in which there has been discriminatory behavior. Students should draw a picture, or write a poem, or illustrate in a creative way of their choosing how they can help stop discriminatory behavior. These student works and the newspaper articles can be posted on the bulletin board to make a collage.

More Than Words

By Patricia M. Dashiell

Words spoken,
either softly or harshly,
casually or purposefully,
hurt me more
than anything else.
I cringe to hear
my skin, my eyes, my hair
the subject of your conversation,
your taunts.
I ache to prove to you that we are
brother and sister,
mother and father,
grandparent and grandchild
from now to eternity,
from the past to the present;
that we are bound
by earth and sea and sky,
by life and death, joy and despair;
that beneath the words spoken
lies a sword which may pierce my heart,
but will wound you as well.

❖❖❖❖❖❖❖❖❖❖❖❖❖❖❖❖❖❖❖❖❖❖

CLOUDED VISION

Objective:

Students will identify protective factors and risk factors associated with violent behavior.

Life Skills:

I will develop positive self-esteem. (PF2)
I will strive for healthful family relationships. (PF3)
I will develop resiliency to "bounce back" if I was reared in a dysfunctional family. (PF3)
I will respond to my environment in an empowering way. (PF4)
I will develop resiliency to "bounce back" if I live in an adverse environment. (PF4)
I will develop social skills. (PF5)

Materials:

Clouded Vision (page 570), a copy for each student, boxes of varying sizes, gift wrap, a checkbook with a sticker saying WEALTH, fake prison ID card, a blank booklet with the title "Fulfilling Your Dreams," an obituary column from the newspaper with the word DEATH written across it, white poster board, *Risk Factors That Promote Violence* transparency (page 587), *Protective Factors That Prevent Violence* transparency (page 588), transparency projector

Motivation:

1 Prepare the following materials before class. Wrap two of the boxes with gift wrap so they look attractive. In one of the boxes place the prison ID card, and in the other put the blank booklet. Decorate two other boxes so they look unattractive. One could be dirty, and one could be wrapped in an old newspaper. Place the obituary in one box and the checkbook in the other.

2 In class, have the students look at the boxes and choose which they would like to receive as a gift. Divide the class into four groups and give each group a box. Have them open the box and share the contents with the class. Point out that the outside of something is not an accurate indicator of what is on the inside. Appearance does not tell character, content, or capability.

3 Give the students a copy of *Clouded Vision* and have them read it to themselves. Discuss with students what the poem says about poverty. Point out that the author seems to say that poverty can be ignored, avoided, or set aside. Society often views the poor as "nobodies." But, we can choose to see poverty as something that we do not accept, and as something that can challenge us to better our lives and the lives of others.

4 Explain that poverty is a symptom of an adverse environment. An **adverse environment** is a set of conditions and surroundings in which a person lives that interferes with growth, development, and success. Explain that to some extent the saying, "Life is not fair," is true when we examine the environment in which people live. The environment in which you live can and does limit the choices available to you. Living in an adverse environment is a risk factor for violence. The amount of violence in adverse environments is very high. Homicide and other forms of violence are closely related to poverty and high rates of unemployment. Young people who are poor are the most likely to be victims and perpetrators of violence. Young people who live in inner-city areas are far more likely to be perpetrators or victims of violence than are people who live in rural areas.

5 Discuss protective factors. A **protective factor** is a way that a person might behave and characteristics of the environment in which (s)he lives that promote health, safety, and/or well-being. Use the *Protective Factors That Prevent Violence* transparency to discuss what factors might protect students from becoming victims or perpetrators of violence.

6 Discuss risk factors. A **risk factor** is a way that a person might behave and characteristics of the environment in which a person lives that increases the likelihood of having something negative happen to a person's health, safety, and/or well-being. Use the *Risk Factors That Promote Violence* transparency to indicate what factors might make students vulnerable to becoming victims or perpetrators of violence. Explain that practicing protective factors and avoiding risk factors are responsible behaviors.

7 Call special attention to Protective Factors 2, 3, 4, and 5. Have students note that Risk Factors 2, 3, 4, and 5 are the opposite of the corresponding protective factors. Explain that it is possible for students to change risk factors to protective factors by becoming resilient. **Resiliency** is the ability to prevent or to recover, bounce back, and learn from misfortune, change, or pressure.

8 Discuss Protective Factor 2. Explain that **self-esteem** is what a person thinks or believes about himself/herself. If people who have negative self-esteem are resilient, they can work on developing positive self-esteem.

9 Discuss Protective Factor 3. Explain the difference between a healthful family and a dysfunctional family. A **healthful family** is a family in which feelings are expressed openly and honestly, coping skills are adequate, and family members trust each other. A **dysfunctional family** is a family in which feelings are not expressed openly and honestly, coping skills are lacking, and family members do not trust each other. If young people who were reared in a dysfunctional family are resilient, they might look for trusted adults who would be willing to be their mentors. A **mentor** is a person who guides and helps a younger person. In this way, the young people would have adult role models who would help them make up for the training and discipline they lacked at home. These young people can do their best in school and can choose friends who will encourage them to be at their best and develop positive self-esteem.

10 Discuss Protective Factor 4. Explain that a **nurturing environment** is a set of conditions and surroundings in which a person lives that promotes growth, development, and success. Remind students of the definition of a healthful family. Point out that a healthful family provides a nurturing environment. On the other hand, an **adverse environment** is a set of conditions and surroundings in which a person lives that interferes with growth, development, and success. Point out that a dysfunctional family provides an adverse environment. If young people who live in an adverse environment are resilient, they realize that although they cannot control their environment, they can control how they respond to their environment. They can be empowered. **Empowerment** is the belief that a person controls his/her own destiny.

11 Discuss Protective Factor 5. Explain that **social skills** are skills that can be used to relate well with others. Young people who lack social skills often have difficulty relating with peers. Explain that social skills are usually learned at home at a young age and are practiced as a child grows. However, if young people who lack social skills are resilient, they can still learn social skills and how to use them effectively.

Evaluation:

Have students bring in items from their trash for several days. The items should be clean and dry. Have the students form groups of three or four. Have the groups create a collage of the items. Show each collage to the rest of the students and comment on the characteristics of the "work of art" such as attractiveness, originality, and creativity. Remind students it is not the packaging or the environment that matters, but what you do with that packaging and environment. Although everyone would like to live in a nurturing environment, we do not always have that opportunity. Explain that just as you can create a work of art from trash, you can still succeed in any area or reach goals even though you may come from an adverse environment.

CLOUDED VISION
By Patricia M. Dashiell

Beneath the dirt and grime
lies the treasure of a beating heart.
Beneath the torn and tattered clothes
lies the wealth of a life not yet done.
Beneath the hunger, the outstretched hand,
lie the riches of possibility.

Do I chose to see the grime, the clothing, the hunger?
Dare I see the treasure, the wealth, and the riches?

Over the treasure of a beating heart
lie dirt and grime.
Over the wealth of a life not yet done
lies torn and tattered clothing.
Over the riches of possibility
lies hunger, an outstretched hand.

Dare I see the treasure, the wealth, and the riches?
Do I chose to see the grime, the clothing, the hunger?

A Touch

Objective:

Students will describe guidelines to follow when sexual harassment occurs.

Life Skill:

I will practice self-protection strategies (PF18)

Materials:

A Touch (page 573), a copy for each student, *Self-Protection When Sexually Harassed* transparency (page 621), transparency projector

Motivation:

1 Give students a copy of *A Touch* and have them read it to themselves. Ask students what sexual harassment is. Allow them to provide answers, then define the term for them. **Sexual harassment** is unwanted sexual behavior that ranges from making sexual comments to forcing another person into unwanted sex acts.

2 Explain that the workplace and the school are the most common settings for sexual harassment. Sexual harassment may occur when someone with whom you work says sexual things to you that are not appropriate. It may occur if someone tries to force you to kiss him/her. A person might touch you in ways you do not want to be touched. Discuss how sexual harassment also might occur at school. The most common types of sexual harassment reported in schools are sexual comments and sexual jokes; inappropriate gestures; staring up and down; and touching, grabbing, and pinching in sexual ways.

3 Discuss the effects sexual harassment may have on the victim. It may cause the victim to feel embarrassed, ashamed, or threatened. Students who have been sexually harassed often do not want to attend school. They find it difficult to attend classes. They stay home or cut classes to avoid further harassment. People who are sexually harassed at work often are afraid to report the harassment because they feel it may threaten their job.

4 Explain that there are steps that should be taken when a person is sexually harassed. Review the material on the *Self-Protection When Sexually Harassed* transparency.

1. Ask the person who is harassing you to stop. Be direct about what behavior is bothering you. Describe the situation and the behavior that made you uncomfortable.

2. Keep a record of what happened. Write down the date and time, describe the situation and behavior, and explain how you handled the situation. Save any notes, letters, or pictures.

3. Check to see if there are guidelines to follow for the specific situation. For example, if the harassment was at school, check school guidelines; if at work, check work guidelines.

4. Report the harassment to the appropriate person in charge. This may be a boss, teacher, or school counselor.

5. Determine if you want to take legal action.

5 Divide the class into groups of four. Have each group pretend they are a department in a company that has the responsibility to establish policies to prevent sexual harass-

ment in the workplace. Each group should
make a company handbook regarding sexual
harassment. The handbook should include
the definition of sexual harassment, ways to
prevent it, reporting procedures, and disciplinary actions. Each group should present its
handbook to the class. Have students compare and contrast their policies and discuss
some of the differences.

Evaluation:

Obtain a sample sexual harassment policy
from a local business or government agency.
Share the policy with the class. Compare
the policies in the handbooks the students
made. Discuss how many of the policies are
applicable to students in school.

A Touch
By Patricia M. Dashiell

a
touch
a
whisper
a
stare
can mean
love
or...

lust

❖❖❖❖❖❖❖❖❖❖❖❖❖❖

Family, Teacher, and Student Masters

USING THE FAMILY, TEACHER, AND STUDENT MASTERS

In designing *Violence Prevention: Totally Awesome™ Teaching Strategies for Safe and Drug-Free Schools*, the authors wanted to provide educators with a ready-to-use and practical program that includes a curriculum guide, factual information in the form of a student book, *Totally Awesome™* Teaching Strategies, as well as violence prevention literature. Also included in this program are family letters and family, teacher, and student masters. The masters included in this section can be reproduced as transparencies and used with a transparency projector, or they can be reproduced as handouts. The following discussion examines ways to use the family letters and ways to use the family, teacher, and student masters.

WAYS TO USE THE FAMILY LETTERS

To be effective, violence prevention education must involve parents and other significant adult family members concerned with the health and safety of their children. For this reason, family letters are included for grades K–2, grades 3–5, grades 6–8, and grades 9–12. These letters summarize what students will learn in the violence prevention curriculum. They can be duplicated and given to parents and other adult family members.

WAYS TO USE THE FAMILY, TEACHER, AND STUDENT MASTERS

Masters are located in two places in this book: within the *Totally Awesome™* Teaching Strategies and in this section of the book. Some masters are designed for use with only one *Totally Awesome™* Teaching Strategy. When this is the case, the master appears on the page following the specific *Totally Awesome™* Teaching

Strategy. Other masters can be used with different teaching strategies because these masters focus on the protective factors. In this section of the book, the 38 figures that appear in the student book, *Violence Prevention: How To Be Hip, Cool, And Violence-Free*, are included as full-page masters. The information contained in each master pertains to one or more of the protective factors that are included in the violence prevention curriculum and can be used with several different *Totally Awesome™* Teaching Strategies. These masters can be used to make transparencies. Also, they can be duplicated and used to:
- educate parents and other adult family members about protective factors;
- accompany the *Totally Awesome™* Teaching Strategies.

To Educate Parents And Other Adult Family Members. The family letters summarize what students will be learning in the violence prevention curriculum. The 38 masters that are duplicates of the figures in the student book provide information about protective factors to prevent violence. Educators might want to duplicate some of these for parents and other adult family members. Then they too will know ways to prevent young people from being perpetrators or victims of violence. This information may also help them to reduce the likelihood they will be perpetrators or victims of violence.

To Accompany *Totally Awesome™* Teaching Strategies. The masters in this section also are designed to be used with the *Totally Awesome™* Teaching Strategies in Section 3. They may be used to introduce topics, to reinforce concepts, and to summarize ideas. They also may be used for evaluation purposes. Tests can be designed around these masters. Students may be asked to demonstrate their comprehension of concepts by using the masters as the basis for a summary presentation to the class.

Some general guidelines should be considered in using these masters in presentation situations. Students and other members of the audience should be seated in such a way that they are able to view the projected materials. If the group is especially large, the master should be reproduced in such a way that the type or other visual material is large enough to be read and distinguished by everyone. When the masters are reproduced as transparencies or handouts, the copyright information must be included on the page. Educators using these masters in any form in presentations with other educators should credit the source of the material. Reproduction of this part of the book in another book or as part of a curriculum is prohibited without the written consent of the publisher.

Grades K–2
Family Letter

Dear Family Adults:

I am beginning to teach violence prevention skills. I am using *The Meeks Heit Violence Prevention Curriculum,* which focuses on helping students develop life skills. The students will learn how to resist behaving in harmful and violent ways. They will learn ways to protect themselves from the violent actions of others. They also will learn the importance of resiliency. Resiliency is the ability to prevent or to recover, bounce back, and learn from misfortune, change, or pressure. Today, much is known about violence. For example, we know if young people behave in certain ways, they greatly reduce their risk of being harmed or harming others. They can choose to behave in these ways. I want to motivate my students to behave in certain ways. I want them to agree to the following violence-free pledge:

❖❖❖ Violence-Free Pledge ❖❖❖

- I will not act in ways that harm others.
- I will not say hurtful words or act in harmful ways toward people who are different.
- I will change the way I act if I treat others in harmful ways.
- I will behave in ways to develop positive self-esteem.
- I will make wise choices.
- I will say NO when others want me to act in harmful ways.
- I will stay away from gangs.
- I will use manners and treat others fairly.
- I will try to work out disagreements without fighting.
- I will express my anger in healthful ways.
- I will choose healthful ways to handle stress.
- I will participate in physical activity.
- I will follow rules to stay safe from persons who might harm me.
- I will not try alcohol or other drugs.
- I will stay away from people who use harmful drugs.
- I will expect family members to treat me in kind ways.
- I will tell someone if a family member tries to harm me.
- I will say NO if someone tries to touch me in an unsafe way.
- I will get help if I have been touched in an unsafe way.
- I will follow the SAFE rule around weapons: stop, avoid getting closer, find an adult, and explain what I saw.
- I will try to be in places where I can stay safe.
- I will listen to wise adults and follow rules and laws.
- I will act in ways to keep myself safe.

I hope that you will discuss violence prevention at home and encourage your child to make the violence-free pledge.

Sincerely,

Grades 3–5
Family Letter

Dear Family Adults:

I am beginning to teach violence prevention skills. I am using The Meeks Heit Violence Prevention Curriculum, which focuses on helping students develop life skills. The students will learn how to resist behaving in harmful and violent ways. They will learn ways to protect themselves from the violent actions of others. They also will learn the importance of resiliency. Resiliency is the ability to prevent or to recover, bounce back, and learn from misfortune, change, or pressure. Today, much is known about violence. For example, we know if young people behave in certain ways, they greatly reduce their risk of being harmed or harming others. They can choose to behave in these ways. I want to motivate my students to behave in certain ways. I want them to agree to the following violence-free pledge.

❖❖❖ Violence-Free Pledge ❖❖❖

- I will recognize that violent behavior is wrong.
- I will practice suicide prevention strategies.
- I will avoid discrimination.
- I will practice self-protection strategies.
- I will behave in ways to develop positive self-esteem.
- I will make responsible decisions.
- I will practice resistance skills when asked to do something violent.
- I will use social skills.
- I will practice conflict resolution and peer mediation skills to handle disagreements without fighting.
- I will respond to my environment in an empowering way and overcome difficulties such as living in poverty or crowded conditions.
- I will express anger in ways that will not harm myself or others.
- I will learn to cope with stress.
- I will participate in regular physical activity.
- I will resist belonging to a gang.
- I will stay away from gang members.
- I will avoid using alcohol and other harmful drugs.
- I will stay away from people who use drugs or who are involved in drug trafficking.
- I will strive for healthful family relationships.
- I will develop resiliency and "bounce back" if I have experienced difficulties in my family such as a broken home.

- I will protect myself by following rules to stay safe from violence.
- I will participate in a recovery program if I have been a victim of a crime.
- I will practice responsible behavior if someone has a weapon.
- I will not carry weapons.
- I will respect authority and abide by laws.
- I will change my behavior if I have been a juvenile offender.

I hope that you will discuss violence prevention at home and encourage your child to make the violence-free pledge.

Sincerely,

Grades 6–8
Family Letter

Dear Family Adults:

I am using *The Meeks Heit Violence Prevention Curriculum* to motivate my students to learn and use life skills to prevent violence. They will learn how they can resist behaving in violent ways, protect themselves from the violent actions of others, and develop resiliency. Resiliency is the ability to prevent or to recover, bounce back, and learn from misfortune, change, or pressure.

Today, much is known about protective factors to prevent violence. Protective factors are ways that people might behave and characteristics of the environment in which they live that promote their health, safety, and/or well-being. I plan to teach the students about the following protective factors that prevent violence:

1. recognizing violent behavior;
2. having positive self-esteem;
3. being reared in a healthful family;
4. living in a nurturing environment;
5. using social skills;
6. practicing anger management skills;
7. practicing stress management skills;
8. participating in physical and recreational activities;
9. practicing suicide prevention strategies;
10. practicing conflict resolution and peer mediation skills;
11. avoiding discriminatory behavior;
12. making responsible decisions;
13. practicing resistance skills;
14. avoiding alcohol and other drugs;
15. practicing responsible behavior around weapons;
16. resisting gang membership;
17. respecting authority and abiding by laws;
18. practicing self-protection strategies;
19. participating in recovery if a victim;
20. changing behavior if a juvenile offender.

Of course, learning about protective factors is not enough. Young people have to practice certain behaviors in order to be violence-free. I will ask my students to honor the following violence-free pledge.

❖❖❖ Violence-Free Pledge ❖❖❖

- I will recognize that violent behavior is wrong.
- I will avoid discrimination.
- I will behave in ways to develop positive self-esteem.
- I will strive for healthful family relationships.
- I will develop resiliency to "bounce back" if my family life is difficult or if I have a broken home.
- I will treat family members with respect.
- I will expect family members to treat me with respect.
- I will use social skills.
- I will respond to my environment in an empowering way and overcome difficulties such as poverty and/or crowded living conditions.
- I will develop resiliency and "bounce back" if I live in an adverse environment.
- I will practice suicide prevention strategies and do something positive if I feel depressed.
- I will make responsible decisions.
- I will use resistance skills when I am pressured to behave in a violent way or use harmful drugs.
- I will express my anger in ways that will not be harmful to myself or others.
- I will cope with stressful situations in positive ways.
- I will participate in regular physical activity.
- I will use conflict resolution skills and peer mediation instead of fighting.
- I will practice self-protection strategies to keep from becoming a victim of violence.
- I will participate in a recovery program if I am a victim of violence.
- I will stay away from people who carry weapons.
- I will not carry weapons.
- I will stay away from gang members and gang turf.
- I will resist belonging to a gang.
- I will not use alcohol or other harmful drugs.
- I will stay away from people who use harmful drugs or who are involved in drug trafficking.
- I will respect authority and abide by laws.
- I will change my behavior if I have been a juvenile offender.

I hope that you will discuss violence prevention at home and encourage all family members to make the violence-free pledge.

Sincerely,

Dear Family Adults:

I am using *The Meeks Heit Violence Prevention Curriculum* to help students in my class learn life skills they can use to resist behaving in violent ways, protect themselves from the violent actions of others, and develop resiliency. Resiliency is the ability to prevent or to recover, bounce back, and learn from misfortune, change, or pressure.

This curriculum is based on what is known about risk factors and protective factors for violence. Risk factors are ways that people might behave and characteristics of the environment in which they live that increase the likelihood that something negative will happen to their health, safety, and/or well-being. Some risk factors for violence are:

1. failing to recognize violent behavior;
2. having negative self-esteem;
3. being reared in a dysfunctional family;
4. living in an adverse environment;
5. lacking social skills;
6. being unable to manage anger;
7. being unable to manage stress;
8. not participating in physical and recreational activities;
9. having suicidal tendencies;
10. resolving conflict in harmful ways;
11. practicing discriminatory behavior;
12. lacking responsible decision-making skills;
13. being unable to resist negative peer pressure;
14. using alcohol and other drugs;
15. carrying a weapon;
16. belonging to a gang;
17. challenging authority and breaking laws;
18. being involved in risk situations;
19. avoiding recovery if a victim;
20. repeating violence if a juvenile offender.

Risk factors refer only to the statistical probability that something negative will happen. When young people have risk factors in their lives, it does not mean that they will actually behave in violent ways or be harmed by others. Young people have varying degrees of control over the different risk factors. For example, young people can control whether they use drugs or belong to gangs. However, they do not have control over the family in which they were reared and whether their families are rich or poor.

584

Protective factors are ways that people might behave and characteristics of the environment in which they live that promote their health, safety, and/or well-being. Some protective factors to prevent violence are:

1. recognizing violent behavior;
2. having positive self-esteem;
3. being reared in a healthful family;
4. living in a nurturing environment;
5. using social skills;
6. practicing anger management skills;
7. practicing stress management skills;
8. participating in physical and recreational activities;
9. practicing suicide prevention strategies;
10. practicing conflict resolution and peer mediation skills;
11. avoiding discriminatory behavior;
12. making responsible decisions;
13. practicing resistance skills;
14. avoiding alcohol and other drugs;
15. practicing responsible behavior around weapons;
16. resisting gang membership;
17. respecting authority and abiding by laws;
18. practicing self-protection strategies;
19. participating in recovery if a victim;
20. changing behavior if a juvenile offender.

During class, we will examine these risk factors and protective factors. In addition, I will discuss the importance of behaving in certain ways. I want to motivate students to practice the behaviors that are listed in the following violence-free pledge.

❖❖❖ Violence-Free Pledge ❖❖❖

- I will recognize that violent behavior is wrong.
- I will behave in ways to develop positive self-esteem.
- I will strive for healthful family relationships.
- I will develop resiliency to "bounce back" if I have experienced family difficulties such as a broken home.
- I will respond to my environment in an empowering way recognizing that I control my own destiny.
- I will develop resiliency to "bounce back" if I live in an adverse environment (poverty, overcrowded conditions).
- I will use social skills.
- I will avoid discrimination.
- I will respect authority and abide by laws.

- I will make responsible decisions.
- I will use resistance skills when pressured by peers to behave in illegal or violent ways or to use drugs.
- I will not join a gang.
- I will stay away from gang members and gang turf.
- I will express my anger in ways that do not harm myself or others.
- I will participate in regular physical activity.
- I will cope with stress in positive ways.
- I will use conflict resolution skills and peer mediation to solve disagreements rather than fighting.
- I will protect myself from violence by following guidelines to stay safe.
- I will acquaint myself with guidelines to follow to prevent acquaintance rape.
- I will participate in a recovery program if I am a victim of violence.
- I will practice responsible behavior if I am in a situation in which there is a weapon.
- I will not carry weapons.
- I will follow guidelines to prevent assault and homicide.
- I will practice suicide prevention strategies and speak with someone if I am depressed.
- I will recognize signs of suicide in other people and get them help.
- I will not use alcohol or other drugs.
- I will stay away from people who use harmful drugs or who are involved in drug trafficking.
- I will respect authority and abide by laws.
- I will change my behavior if I have been a juvenile offender.

I hope that you will discuss violence prevention at home. As a family, you can agree to the violence-prevention pledge.

Sincerely,

Figure 1
Risk Factors
That Promote Violence

Risk Factors are ways that you might behave and characteristics of the environment in which you live that increase the likelihood of having something negative happen to your health, safety, and/or well-being.

1. Failing to recognize violent behavior.
2. Having negative self-esteem.
3. Being reared in a dysfunctional family.
4. Living in an adverse environment.
5. Lacking social skills.
6. Being unable to manage anger.
7. Being unable to manage stress.
8. Not participating in physical and recreational activities.
9. Having suicidal tendencies.
10. Resolving conflict in harmful ways.
11. Practicing discriminatory behavior.
12. Lacking responsible decision-making skills.
13. Being unable to resist negative peer pressure.
14. Using alcohol and other drugs.
15. Carrying a weapon.
16. Belonging to a gang.
17. Challenging authority and breaking laws.
18. Being in risk situations.
19. Avoiding recovery if a victim.
20. Repeating violence if a juvenile offender.

Figure 2
Protective Factors
That Prevent Violence

Protective Factors are ways that you might behave and characteristics of the environment in which you live that promote your health, safety, and/or well-being.

1. Recognizing violent behavior.
2. Having positive self-esteem.
3. Being reared in a healthful family.
4. Living in a nurturing environment.
5. Using social skills.
6. Practicing anger management skills.
7. Practicing stress management skills.
8. Participating in physical and recreational activities.
9. Practicing suicide prevention strategies.
10. Practicing conflict resolution and peer mediation skills.
11. Avoiding discriminatory behavior.
12. Making responsible decisions.
13. Practicing resistance skills.
14. Avoiding alcohol and other drugs.
15. Practicing responsible behavior around weapons.
16. Resisting gang membership.
17. Respecting authority and abiding by laws.
18. Practicing self-protection strategies.
19. Participating in recovery if a victim.
20. Changing behavior if a juvenile offender.

Figure 3
Types of Violence

Bullying   An attempt by a person to hurt or frighten people who are perceived to be smaller or weaker

Fighting   Taking part in a physical struggle

Assault   A physical attack or threat of attack

Homicide   The accidental or purposeful killing of another person

Suicide   The intentional taking of one's own life

Sexual Harassment   Unwanted sexual behavior that ranges from making unwanted sexual comments to forcing another person into unwanted sex acts

Rape   The threatened or actual use of physical force to get someone to have sex without giving consent

Child Abuse   Harmful treatment of a person under 18 and includes physical abuse, emotional abuse, sexual abuse, and neglect

Domestic Violence   Violence that occurs within the family or within other relationships in which people live together

Figure 4
How Behavior Influences the Likelihood of Being a Perpetrator or Victim of Violence

People with Passive Behavior:
- Hold back ideas, opinions, and feelings;
- Have difficulty expressing concerns;
- Rarely start arguments with others.

They may be **perpetrators** because they hold back feelings for so long that they may become angry and act out in unexpected ways.

They may be **victims** because they have difficulty resisting abusive and harmful actions of others, which invites further harm.

People with Aggressive Behavior:
- Use words and actions that show disrespect for others.

They may be **perpetrators** because they often bully, threaten, and fight others.

They may be **victims** because they may provoke others, causing them to retaliate.

People with Assertive Behavior:
- Express thoughts and feelings honestly without experiencing anxiety or threatening others.

They are less likely to be **perpetrators** because they resolve conflict by sharing thoughts and feelings and listening to others.

They are less likely to be **victims** because they resist abuse from others.

Figure 5
Patterns of Behavior Self-Test

Directions: Read each of the following scenarios. Determine how you might respond. Think about your response. Are you behaving in ways that might provoke others? Are you behaving in ways that might invite others to abuse you? Are you behaving in ways in which anger and resentment is building inside you? Do you have any patterns of behavior that may lead to violence? If so, how might these behavior patterns be changed?

1. You are playing softball on the playground after school. It is your turn to bat. One of the other players grabs the bat out of your hand and runs up to the plate. You respond by:
   a. pushing him/her off the plate and calling him/her names
   b. not saying anything, after all, your turn will come
   c. calling to him/her and asking if he realized that it was your turn to bat

2. You have taken your friend to a restaurant for his/her birthday. You made reservations but the host tells you that you must wait for a table. After waiting for a long time, you notice that customers who arrived later than you are being seated. You respond by:
   a. complaining loudly so that all the customers can hear about your situation
   b. remaining quiet to avoid spoiling the birthday celebration
   c. asking the host about your order in line and explaining that you are having a special celebration

3. You are working on a paper in class and are trying to concentrate. The student behind you keeps kicking your chair. It is driving you crazy. You respond by:
   a. turning around and kicking his/her desk so that his/her books fly off the desk
   b. ignoring it as best as you can
   c. telling him/her that (s)he might not realize that (s)he is kicking your desk, but it is making it hard for you to concentrate, and to please stop

4. You have invited your friend to sleep at your home. Your friend begins to snore so loudly you can't fall asleep. You respond by:
   a. knocking your friend off the bed and saying if you can't sleep, neither can (s)he
   b. putting your pillow over your head and trying to ignore it
   c. nudging your friend carefully until (s)he changes positions and quiets down

5. A new teammate on your basketball team is not playing very well. (S)he keeps missing the basket, never looks where (s)he is going, and keeps bumping into you. You respond by:
   a. bumping him/her back and yelling that (s)he stinks at the game
   b. ignoring him/her, hoping that it won't happen again
   c. taking him/her aside and asking if (s)he wants to stay later to practice with you so that you two can figure how to play together best.

If most of your responses are a:
You are choosing **aggressive** responses to situations. If you demonstrate aggressive behavior, you are at risk of being a perpetrator or victim of violence. When you demonstrate aggressive behavior, you use words and/or actions that tend to communicate disrespect toward others. People who demonstrate aggressive behavior are likely to be violent. Because aggressive behavior tends to provoke others, people who demonstrate aggressive behavior also are at risk for being victims of violent actions of others.

If most of your responses are b:
You are choosing **passive** responses to situations. If you demonstrate passive behavior, you are at risk for being a victim or a perpetrator of violence. When you demonstrate passive behavior you tend to hold back ideas, opinions, and feelings. People who demonstrate passive behavior often hold angry feelings inside and may become perpetrators. When angry feelings that are held back begin to build up inside, the result may be an explosion of violence. People who demonstrate passive behavior also are more often selected to be victims of violence because they are less likely to resist and less likely to tell someone else when they are harmed.

If most of your responses are c:
You are choosing **assertive** responses to situations. Assertive behavior is healthier than passive or aggressive behavior. People who demonstrate assertive behavior clearly communicate with others. Assertive behavior promotes high-quality relationships. People who demonstrate assertive behavior are least likely to be perpetrators and/or victims of violence.

Figure 6
Ways to Develop Positive Self-Esteem

1. Set goals and make plans to reach them.
2. Develop a special skill or talent.
3. Make a list of things you do well.
4. Work to do your best in school.
5. Be involved in school clubs and community activities.
6. Develop a trusting relationship with at least one adult.
7. Choose friends who encourage you to do your best.
8. Spend time with friends and adults who give you support.
9. Volunteer to help another person.
10. Keep a neat appearance.

Figure 7
The Family Continuum

The Family Continuum depicts the degree to which a family promotes skills needed for loving and responsible relationships.

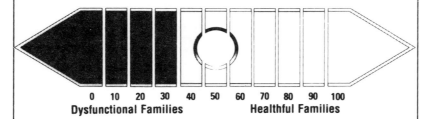

0 10 20 30 40 50 60 70 80 90 100
Dysfunctional Families   **Healthful Families**

Dysfunctional Families
1. do not show respect for each other;
2. do not trust each other;
3. are confused about guidelines for responsible behavior;
4. are not punished or are punished severely for wrong behavior;
5. do not spend time with each other;
6. do not share feelings or do not share feelings in healthful ways;
7. do not have effective coping skills
8. resolve conflicts with violence;
9. abuse alcohol and other drugs;
10. abuse each other with words and actions.

Healthful Families
1. show respect for each other;
2. trust each other;
3. follow guidelines for responsible behavior;
4. experience consequences when they do not follow guidelines;
5. spend time with each other;
6. share feelings in healthful ways;
7. practice effective coping skills;
8. resolve conflict in nonviolent ways;
9. avoid alcohol and other drugs;
10. use kind words and actions.

Figure 8
The Nurturing Environment

I have only just a minute.
Only sixty seconds in it,
Forced upon me—
Can't refuse it
Didn't seek it,
Didn't choose it,
But, it's up to me to use it.
I must suffer if I lose it,
Give account if I abuse it.
Just a tiny little minute—
But eternity is in it.

Benjamin Eligah Mays
Former President of Morehouse College

Figure 9
Social Skills

Social Skills are skills that can be used to relate well with others. When you are **socially competent,** you are skilled in:

1. Using manners;
2. Asking for help;
3. Giving and following instructions;
4. Expressing affection;
5. Expressing and responding to a complaint;
6. Dealing with rejection;
7. Dealing with a stressful conversation or event;
8. Dealing with shyness;
9. Responding to the feelings of others;
10. Dealing with excessive fear.

Figure 10
I-Messages

The three parts of an I-message are:

1.	2.	3.
The specific behavior or event…	The effect of the behavior or event…	The feeling that resulted…
▼	▼	▼
(When you…)	(It affected me because…)	(and I felt…)

Figure 11
Active Listening

Active listening is a type of listening in which you let others know you heard and understood what was said. Active listening includes the following types of responses:

Type of Response	The Listener...
Clarifying Response.......	Asks for more information.
Restating Response	Repeats what the speaker said in his/her own words.
Summarizing Response ..	Summarizes the main idea or ideas.
Confirming Response	Acknowledges and shows appreciation for the speaker's feelings.

Figure 12
Coping with Life Crises

Anger is one of the five stages that occur in life crises. When a person experiences a life crisis, (s)he may go through five stages. Using the example of parents getting a divorce, this is how the person might respond:

1. **Denial** .... (My parents won't really get a divorce.)

2. **Anger** .... (I hate my father for wanting a divorce.)

3. **Bargaining** ...... (If I promise to behave better, they won't get a divorce.)

4. **Depression** ...... (I can't stop crying when I think about my parents' divorce.)

5. **Acceptance** ..... (At least I will still see my father every weekend after the divorce.)

Adapted from Elisabeth Kübler-Ross (1975)

Figure 13
Hidden Anger

Hidden anger is anger that is not recognized or is expressed in a harmful way and may result in inappropriate behavior or poor health. The following types of behavior may be signs of hidden anger:

- Being negative
- Making cruel remarks to others
- Being flippant
- Procrastinating
- Blowing up easily
- Having very little interest in anything
- Being bored
- Sighing frequently
- Being depressed

Figure 14
Anger Management Skills

1. Keeping An Anger Self-Inventory
2. Using Self-Statements To Control Your Anger
3. Participating In Physical Activities
4. Using Physical Expression To Blow Off Steam
5. Using I-Messages And Active Listening
6. Keeping A Sense Of Humor
7. Expressing Yourself Through Creative Activities
8. Talking With Parents And Mentors
9. Writing Letters To Express Your Angry Feelings
10. Planning Ahead To Deal With Your Anger

Figure 15
Anger Self-Inventory

What am I feeling?

What is causing me to feel this way?

Is my anger justified?

Am I still angry? (If yes, continue.)

What are healthful ways I can express my anger?

Figure 16
Stress Management Skills

1. Using Responsible Decision-Making Skills
2. Using Breathing Techniques
3. Eating A Healthful Diet
4. Getting Enough Rest And Sleep
5. Participating In Physical Activities
6. Using A Time Management Plan
7. Writing In A Journal
8. Having Close Friends
9. Talking With Parents And Other Trusted Adults
10. Helping Others
11. Expressing Affection In Appropriate Ways
12. Caring For Pets
13. Changing Your Outlook
14. Keeping A Sense Of Humor

Figure 17
Benefits Of Physical And Recreational Activities

1. You Develop Physical Fitness.
2. You Use Your Time Wisely.
3. You Have A Physical Outlet To Work Off Anger.
4. You Reduce Your Stress Level.
5. You Practice Social Skills Such As Cooperation.
6. You Feel A Sense Of Belonging.
7. You Learn To Follow Rules And Respect Authority.
8. You Learn How To Accept Defeat.
9. You Improve Self-Esteem.
10. You Develop Self-Discipline.

Figure 18
Suicide Prevention Strategies

1. Know Suicide Hotline Numbers
2. Know What To Do When You Feel Down
3. Build A Network Of Support
4. Get Involved In Rewarding Activities
5. Know What To Do If Someone Shows Warning Signs

Figure 19
Conflict Response Styles

Conflict Avoidance

A person denies that there is a conflict and/or attempts to please others at his/her expense.

Conflict Confrontation

A person attempts to settle a disagreement in a hostile, defiant, and aggressive way.

Conflict Resolution

A person uses conflict resolution skills to resolve a disagreement in a healthful, safe, legal, respectful, and nonviolent way.

Figure 20
Conflict Resolution Skills

Conflict resolution skills are skills a person can use to resolve a disagreement in a healthful, safe, legal, respectful, and nonviolent way.

1. Remain Calm.
2. Set The Tone.
   - Avoid blaming.
   - Avoid interrupting.
   - Affirm others.
   - Be sincere.
   - Avoid putdowns.
   - Reserve judgment.
   - Avoid threats.
   - Separate the person from the problem.
   - Help others save face.
   - Use positive nonverbal messages.
3. Define The Conflict.
4. Take Responsibility For Personal Actions.
5. Use I-Messages To Express Needs And Feelings.
6. Listen To The Needs And Feelings Of Others.
7. List And Discuss Possible Solutions.
   - Will the solution result in actions that are healthful?
   - Will the solution result in actions that are safe?
   - Will the solution result in actions that are legal?
   - Will the solutions result in actions that are respectful of all involved people?
   - Will the solution result in actions that are nonviolent?
8. Agree On A Solution.
9. Keep Your Word And Follow The Agreement.
10. Ask For The Assistance Of A Trusted Adult Or Obtain Peer Mediation If The Conflict Cannot Be Resolved.

Figure 21
The Process of Peer Mediation

Peer mediation is a process used to resolve conflicts, in which a person helps peers resolve disagreements in healthful, safe, legal, respectful, and nonviolent ways. A peer mediator assists the people having a conflict in reaching a resolution.

1. The peer mediator introduces himself/herself and explains that (s)he will maintain a neutral position.
2. The peer mediator establishes ground rules and the peers in conflict agree to follow them.
   - Tell the truth.
   - Commit to resolving the conflict.
   - Avoid blaming.
   - Avoid putdowns.
   - Avoid threats.
   - Avoid sneering, pushing, and hitting.
   - Reserve judgment.
   - Listen without interrupting.
3. Each of the people in disagreement clearly defines the conflict.
4. Each of the people in conflict expresses his/her needs and feelings about the conflict.
5. Each of the people in conflict identifies possible ways to resolve the conflict.
6. The peer mediator offers additional ways to resolve the conflict.
7. Each of the suggested solutions is evaluated.
   - Will the solution result in actions that are healthful?
   - Will the solution result in actions that are safe?
   - Will the solution result in actions that are legal?
   - Will the solution result in actions that are respectful of all people involved?
   - Will the solution result in actions that are nonviolent?
8. The people in conflict attempt to resolve the conflict by agreeing to a solution. If this is not possible, the peer mediator negotiates an agreement.
9. An agreement is written and signed by all people.
10. A follow-up meeting is set to discuss the results of following the agreement.

Figure 22
Ways To Avoid Discriminatory Behavior

In his famous speech, Martin Luther King said, "I have a dream...my four little children will one day live in a nation where they will not be judged by the color of their skin but by the content of their character." Unfortunately, our society is still not living this dream. Change begins with the individual. Your efforts are very important in stopping discriminatory behavior. You can:

1. Challenge Stereotypes
2. Create Synergy Through Diversity
3. Show Empathy For All People
4. Avoid Discriminatory Comments
5. Ask Others To Stop Discriminatory Behavior
6. Learn About People Who Are Different

Figure 23

The Responsible Decision-Making Model

1. **Clearly describe the situation you face.**
   If no immediate decision is necessary, describe the situation in writing. If an immediate decision must be made, describe the situation out loud or to yourself in a few short sentences. Being able to describe a situation in your own words is the first step in clarifying the question.

2. **List possible actions that can be taken.**
   Again, if no immediate decision is necessary, make a list of possible actions. If an immediate decision must be made, state possible actions out loud or to yourself.

3. **Share your list of possible actions with a responsible adult such as someone who protects community laws and demonstrates character.**
   When no immediate action is necessary, sharing possible actions with a responsible adult is helpful. This person can examine your list to see if it is inclusive. Responsible adults have a wide range of experiences that can allow them to see situations maturely. They may add possibilities to the list of actions. In some situations, it is possible to delay decision making until there is an opportunity to seek counsel with a responsible adult. If an immediate decision must be made, explore possibilities. Perhaps a telephone call can be made. Whenever possible, avoid skipping this step.

4. **Carefully evaluate each possible action using six criteria.**
   Ask each of the six questions to learn which decision is best.
   a. Will this decision result in an action that will protect my health and the health of others?
   b. Will this decision result in an action that will protect my safety and the safety of others?
   c. Will this decision result in an action that will protect the laws of the community?
   d. Will this decision result in an action that shows respect for myself and others?
   e. Will this decision result in an action that follows guidelines set by responsible adults such as my parents or guardian?
   f. Will this decision result in an action that will demonstrate that I have good character and moral values?

5. **Decide which action is responsible and most appropriate.**
   After applying the six criteria, compare the results. Which decision best meets the six criteria?

6. **Act in a responsible way and evaluate the results.**
   Follow through with this decision with confidence. The confidence comes from paying attention to the six criteria.

Figure 24
Model for Using Resistance Skills

1. **Use assertive behavior.**
   There is a saying, "You get treated the way you 'train' others to treat you." Assertive behavior is the honest expression of thoughts and feelings without experiencing anxiety or threatening others. When you use assertive behavior, you show that you are in control of yourself and the situation. You say NO clearly and firmly. As you speak, you look directly at the person(s) pressuring you. Aggressive behavior is the use of words and/or actions that tend to communicate disrespect. This behavior only antagonizes others. Passive behavior is the holding back of ideas, opinions, and feelings. Holding back may result in harm to you, others, or the environment.

2. **Avoid saying, "NO, thank you."**
   There is never a need to thank a person who pressures you into doing something that might be harmful, unsafe, illegal, or disrespectful or which may result in disobeying parents or moral values. Your verbal NO should not be confused by misleading actions. For example,

if you say NO to cigarette smoking, do not pretend to take a puff of a cigarette in order to resist pressure.

3. **Use nonverbal behavior that matches verbal behavior.**
   Nonverbal behavior is the use of body language or actions rather than words to express feelings, ideas, and opinions. Your verbal NO should not be confused by misleading actions. For example,

4. **Influence others to choose responsible behavior.**
   When a situation poses immediate danger, remove yourself. If no immediate danger is present, try to turn the situation into a positive one. Suggest alternative, responsible ways to behave. Being a positive role model helps you feel good about yourself and helps gain the respect of others.

5. **Avoid being in situations in which there will be pressure to make harmful decisions.**
   There is no reason to put yourself into situations in which you will be pressured or tempted to make unwise decisions. Think ahead.

6. **Avoid being with persons who choose harmful actions.**
   Your reputation is the impression that others have of you, your decisions, and your actions. Associate with persons known for their good qualities and character in order to avoid being misjudged.

7. **Resist pressure to engage in illegal behavior.**
   You have a responsibility to protect others and to protect the laws of your community. Demonstrate good character and moral values.

Figure 25
Different Types Of Drugs

Alcohol. A drug that depresses the nervous system and often changes behavior.

Sedative-Hypnotics. Drugs that depress the central nervous system and are "downers."

PCP. A drug that changes the way people see things.

Cocaine. A drug that stimulates the central nervous system and frequently results in dependence.

Crack. A drug that is pure cocaine, which produces rapid ups and downs.

Amphetamines. Drugs that "speed up" the central nervous system.

Heroin. A drug that slows body functions such as heart rate and breathing and produces drowsiness and mood swings.

Anabolic Steroids. Drugs made from male hormones, that produce muscle growth and can change health and behavior.

Marijuana. A drug containing THC that impairs short term memory and changes mood.

Figure 26
Safety Around Weapons

1. Do not purchase a weapon illegally.

2. Do not carry a concealed weapon.

3. Do not carry a weapon to school.

4. Encourage others to avoid buying, carrying, and/or concealing a weapon.

5. Do not pretend you are going to use a weapon.

6. Avoid being around people who buy, carry, conceal, or use weapons.

7. Do not argue with someone who has a weapon.

8. Avoid being in situations in which there will be weapons.

9. If you find a weapon, leave it where you found it.

10. Tell a responsible adult when you find a weapon.

Figure 27
Typical Gang Member

Characteristics Of A Typical Gang Member Include:

Wardrobes
- wearing mostly one-color outfits such as all dark clothes;
- having a scarf or one particular color with every outfit;
- wearing a dark jacket or sweater with every outfit;
- regularly wearing oversized pants;
- wearing colored shoelaces in tennis shoes.

Tattoos
- having a tattoo of a rose, tear drops, or graffiti-like markings around the hand area, neck, forearm, shoulder, or leg.

Makeup
- heavy eye makeup;
- heavy rouge;
- dark lipstick.

Hair
- wearing hair cut in the "feathered look" at the top, and left loose in the back or pulled to the back with a pencil or Afro comb;
- wearing hair nets;
- two-tone hair coloring;
- wearing rollers and braids in hair.

Figure 29
Self-Protection When At Home

1. Keep windows and doors locked at all times, even when you are home.
2. Make sure your home has extra-security deadbolts on all entry doors.
3. Be aware that chain locks are easily ripped off a door.
4. Consider having a home security alarm system installed.
5. Consider getting a dog and placing "Beware of Dog" signs on your property.
6. Do not give out your house key to anyone other than a trusted friend.
7. Do not hide your extra keys outside your home.
8. Consider having a one-way viewer or peephole in your door.
9. At night, leave one or more lights on.
10. Have your mail, newspaper delivery, and other services discontinued when you leave for an extended period of time.
11. Ask a trusted neighbor to check your home and vary the position of the drapes.
12. Always have your keys ready before going to your door.
13. If there are signs that someone has entered your home, do not go inside. Go to a safe place and call the police.
14. Never let a stranger into your home unless you are sure it is safe to do so.
15. When speaking on the phone or answering the door, always give the impression someone else is in the home with you.
16. Ask to see identification before allowing a repair person to enter your home.
17. Do not open the door when someone asks to come in and make an emergency phone call. You can always make the call yourself if you want to do so.
18. Report any stranger who does not have identification to the police.
19. Be cautious about giving out information on where you live to people in person, on the phone, or by mail.
20. If you receive a crank phone call, do not talk to the person. Hang up immediately.
21. Report continuous, obscene, or bothersome phone calls to the telephone company and police.
22. Keep a list of emergency phone numbers such as the number for the police and fire departments by the phone.

Figure 30
Self-Protection When Caring for Children

1. Ask the child's caretakers to show you around the home before they leave. Be aware of exits and entryways.
2. Ask the caretakers what to do if an emergency occurs.
3. Keep outside doors and windows locked.
4. Keep lights on in various rooms so it looks like others are at home.
5. Never open the door to strangers.
6. Do not allow anyone to enter the house unless the caretakers have told you in advance to expect someone. Ask the caretaker what the person looks like.
7. Never tell anyone who calls on the phone that you are alone with the children.
8. If you hear a suspicious noise or think that someone is trying to break in, call the police.
9. If the caretakers come home drunk, do not allow them to drive you home. Call your parents.
10. If the caretakers do anything that makes you feel uncomfortable, call your parents.
11. If the caretakers do not return home when they are supposed to, call your parents and tell them you will be late.
12. Do not let other people know you will be alone.
13. Never leave a young child unattended outside the home for even a brief period of time.

Figure 31
Self-Protection While Driving and Riding In Cars

1. Always park in a safe and well-lighted area where there are other people and other cars.

2 Take special note of exactly where you are parked in a large parking lot.

3. Lock your car at all times and keep your keys with you.

4 Have someone walk with you to your car whenever possible.

5. Check the front and back seats to make sure that no one is hiding inside before getting in your car.

6. Never leave infants or small children in an unattended car even if you are leaving only for a brief time.

7. Never leave the keys in the ignition or the engine running.

8. Always take your keys with you when leaving your car.

9. Keep wallets, purses, unattached stereos, and other valuables out of sight.

10. Do not allow yourself to run out of gas.

11. Plan ahead and fuel your car only during daylight hours.

12. Keep your car in good condition to prevent breakdowns.

13. Try to drive in safe, well-lighted areas, especially at night.

14. Install a car phone to use in case of emergency.

15. Keep a sign in your car that says "Send Help" to display if your car breaks down.

16. Keep a flashlight and road flares in your trunk.

17. Stay in your car, keep your doors locked and windows rolled up, keep a lookout for passing police cars, and honk your horn if you see a police car when your car breaks down.

18. Do not get out of the car if someone other than a police officer stops and offers help. Roll the window down only a crack and ask the person to call the police.

19. Drive to a nearby phone and call 911 if you see someone in need of help.

20. Never pick up a hitchhiker.

21. Do not drive home if you think you are being followed. Go to a store, police station, or well-lighted area where there are other people. Call the police and report that you were being followed.

22. Be cautious of anyone approaching your car when it is stopped.

23. Keep your car doors locked and windows rolled up at all times to prevent carjacking. If you need ventilation, roll the windows down only a crack. Keep your sunroof closed. Avoid driving in a convertible with the top down.

24. Keep your car in gear when at a stoplight or stop sign. Allow enough distance between your car and the car ahead to drive away.

25. If a person armed with a weapon demands your car or your keys, do not resist.

26. Do not give out your keys to other people.

27. Consider getting an inside latch for your trunk. If you are ever forced into the trunk, you could escape.

28. Do not rent cars that are marked as rental cars.

29. Be a courteous driver on the street. If another driver makes you angry, ignore this person. Never begin a fight.

Figure 32
Self-Protection When In Public Places

1. Avoid walking alone at night or in high-risk areas.
2. Stay on well-lighted streets and avoid deserted areas, alleys, and staircases when walking alone.
3. Keep your distance if someone in a car stops to ask you for directions. Ignore the person or call out the directions to them.
4. Never accept a ride from a stranger or someone you do not trust.
5. Never hitchhike.
6. Wear comfortable shoes that allow you to run from trouble.
7. Do not talk to strangers who approach you.
8. Seek help in a nearby store or building with other people. Walk briskly with your head up, and move in a confident manner if you think you are being followed.
9. Carry a loud siren, whistle, or buzzer to get attention if you need it.
10. Avoid using bank money machines whenever possible. If you use a money machine, do so during the day.
11. Stay away from areas where there are gangs.
12. Carry a chemical spray such as tear gas to use in case you are attacked.
13. Carry a flashlight at night and use it to light up potentially dangerous areas. It also can be used as a weapon in an emergency.
14. Carry your purse tucked under your elbow and hold it firmly with one hand. (Instead of carrying a purse, consider wearing a waist pack and carrying only what you need.)
15. Avoid using alcohol or other drugs so that you think clearly and make wise decisions about what you should do.
16. Wait only in safe and well-lighted areas for public transportation. After boarding, stay with a group of people or sit near the driver if possible.
17. Do not go into places that are deserted.
18. Yell, scream, or shout loudly for help if someone is bothering you in a public place.
19. Be sure to vary your walking route if you routinely walk to and from school or work.
20. Speed up, cross the street, turn around, run, or do whatever you feel is necessary if you feel a person may be following you.
21. Do not turn your back toward a street or a lobby when you are using a public telephone; turn your back toward the telephone.
22. Use pay telephones only when they are in well-lighted places where there are many other people.

Figure 33
Self-Protection When Exercising Outdoors

1. Avoid exercising alone, at night, and at places where there are few other people.
2. Pay attention to your feelings and avoid areas that do not seem safe.
3. Vary routes and routines (change route, time of day, etc.) because people may stalk their victims and plan their attacks.
4. Avoid paths where a person could be hiding in bushes or trees and quickly grab you.
5. Run or walk quickly in the opposite direction and run to a place where there are other people if you are harassed by someone in a car.
6. Carry a personal siren, personal protection alarm, or whistle.
7. Consider taking a large dog with you when you exercise.
8. Do not use personal stereos with headphones because you will be less likely to hear someone approach you.
9. Keep your distance from strangers.
10. Carry identification and change to make a telephone call.
11. Always let someone you trust know the exact route that you will follow. Tell this person what time you expect to return.

Figure 34

Self-Protection When In Social Situations

1. Stay away from places where you will be alone when you are with a person you do not know well or whom you do not trust.

2. Do not go anywhere with a stranger even if you are supposed to meet other people.

3. Trust your gut feelings about other people.

4. Choose to be with other people when you socialize with someone the first few times.

5. Do not use alcohol or other drugs.

6. Set limits for expressing affection and communicate these limits to others.

7. Do not pressure another person to drink alcohol or to express affection beyond limits. Know that a person who has been drinking is accountable for sexual behavior.

8. Avoid behavior that might be interpreted as sexually teasing or seductive.

9. Respect the limits other people have set for expressing affection. Never pressure someone beyond limits.

10. Ask the other person to tell you clear limits when you are confused or feel you are getting mixed messages.

11. Do not assume you and another person want to express affection in the same ways or have the same limits.

12. Use physical force if someone continues sexual behavior after you have set limits.

13. Attend workshops, seminars, or classes to be clear on issues regarding acquaintance rape.

14. Pay attention to warning signs that indicate a person might harm you: disrespectful attitude toward you, dominating attitude, extreme jealousy, unnecessary physical roughness, and/or a history of violent and/or abusive behavior.

Figure 35
Self-Protection
When Sexually Harassed

1. Ask the person who is harassing you to stop. Be direct about what behavior is bothering you. Describe the situation and behavior that made you uncomfortable.

2. Keep a record of what happened. Write down the date and time, describe the situation and behavior, and explain how you handled the situation. Save any notes, letters, or pictures.

3. Check to see if there are guidelines to follow for the specific situation. For example, if the harassment was at school, check school guidelines; if at work, check work guidelines.

4. Report the harassment to the appropriate person in charge. This may be a boss, teacher, or school counselor.

5. Determine if you want to take legal action.

Figure 36
Self-Protection
When Being Stalked

1. Check the laws of your state regarding stalking. Thirty-seven states currently have antistalking laws. Know your rights and the best way to protect your rights. Know the limits of your protection as well.

2. Contact the police department to report the stalking. Consider pressing charges against the person who is stalking you. This may be enough to frighten and stop the person.

3. Keep a record of each case of stalking. Write down the date, time, what was said, and what happened. Save any evidence, including notes and letters that may have been written to you and answering machine tapes with messages left on them.

4. Try to obtain a restraining order. A restraining order is an order by a court that forbids a person from doing a particular act.

5. Tell your parents and school officials what is happening. They should be told everything so they can do what they can to help protect you.

6. Seek appropriate counseling or join a support group for victims of stalking.

Figure 37
Victim Recovery

1. Talk About What Happened
2. Get A Complete Medical Examination
3. Seek Counseling
4. Join A Support Group
5. Learn And Practice Self-Protection
   Strategies

Figure 38
Ways To Change Behavior if a Juvenile Offender

1. Improve Family Relationships
2. Spend Time With Other Trusted Adults
3. Ask Trusted Adults For Feedback
4. Work To Improve Self-Esteem
5. Choose Friends Who Obey Laws
6. Make Repayment For Wrong Actions
7. Become Involved in School Activities
8. Develop Job-Related Skills
9. Volunteer In The Community
10. Join A Support Group

SECTION
6

Violence Prevention Resources

USING THE VIOLENCE PREVENTION RESOURCES

CHAPTER 6

Educators may want to have other violence prevention resources to augment the use of *Violence Prevention: Totally Awesome™ Teaching Strategies for Safe and Drug-Free Schools*. In this section of the book, the authors have included a violence prevention annotated bibliography and a violence prevention resource guide. The following discussion focuses on ways each of these might be used.

WAYS TO USE THE VIOLENCE PREVENTION ANNOTATED BIBLIOGRAPHY

The Violence Prevention Annotated Bibliography includes a listing and description for violence prevention literature for a variety of reading levels on the following topics:
1. alcohol and other drugs,
2. conflict resolution,
3. crime,
4. discrimination,
5. environment,
6. gangs,
7. peer pressure,
8. physical, sexual, and emotional abuse,
9. self-protection,
10. suicide,
11. victim recovery.

This literature can be used in a variety of ways. Remember, always review materials before making a reading list for students. Determine whether the material is appropriate for students. Check readability. After making the reading list, discuss it with students. Provide suggestions. Students might make selections from this list and prepare book reports or oral reports. They may read and discuss one or more of these books with family members or with a school counselor. Educators in the primary grades may want to read one of these books to the students.

WAYS TO USE THE VIOLENCE PREVENTION RESOURCE GUIDE

The Violence Prevention Resource Guide contains a listing of the names and telephone numbers (and in many cases the address) of places that help with violence prevention, intervention, and/or treatment. This listing is divided into the following headings:
1. abuse,
2. alcohol and other drugs,
3. conflict resolution,
4. discrimination,
5. family/mentor programs,
6. juvenile crime,
7. physical and recreational activity,
8. rape,
9. self-protection,
10. suicide,
11. victim recovery,
12. weapon safety.

Many of the places that are listed provide free and/or inexpensive materials for educators. They also may provide services. For example, some of the telephone numbers listed are hotline numbers. These numbers can be dialed for immediate help. Educators may want to share the hotlines numbers with students. They also may want to have students contact specific places for information when they are writing reports or when they share a concern about a problem.

THE VIOLENCE PREVENTION ANNOTATED BIBLIOGRAPHY

ALCOHOL AND OTHER DRUGS

Berger, Gilda. (1992) *Joey's Story. Meg's Story. Patty's Story*. Brookfield, CT: Millbrook Press. 62 pages each.

These three books contain first person accounts of young people in alcohol and other drug rehabilitation programs. Each account explains why it is not easy to quit using alcohol and other drugs. Written for the intermediate reader.

Cormier, R. (1991) *We All Fall Down*. New York: Delacorte Press. 193 pages.

Buddy and his friends destruct property in Jane's house and hurt her sister. He is not sure why he did it because the alcohol clouded his mind. Later, he falls in love with Jane. How will he hide his problem with alcohol and his secret about the vandalism from her. Read on to discover the end-

ing to this tale of alcohol and physical abuse. Written for the young adult reader.

Monroe, Judy. (1994) *Alcohol*. Hillside, NJ: Enslow Publishers.

This book explores the physical, emotional, historical, and societal effects of alcohol. Suggestions for ways to avoid alcohol, and resources are included.

Taylor, C. (1991) *The House That Crack Built*. San Francisco: Chronicle Books. 32 pages.

A take off on *The House That Jack Built*, this picture book describes a crack house and the domino effects it has on the community, from the distractions to the death it holds. Eye-catching illustrations grab the reader's attention and make this book truly one for all ages.

CONFLICT RESOLUTION

Berenstain, Stan, and Berenstain, Jan. (1982) *The Berenstain Bears Get in a Fight*.

The popular Berenstain Bears family gets into fights like everyone else. Learn how they resolve their conflicts. Written for primary readers.

Greenfield, E. (1992) *Koya Delaney and the Good Girl Blues*. New York: Scholastic Inc. 126 pages.

Koya would rather smile than frown, laugh than cry. There is nothing unusual in that. But Koya

avoids conflict at all costs until she realizes that avoiding it only makes the conflict worse. Instead of hiding behind laughter, Koya learns to face her feelings within the bounds of a loving family and good friends. Written for the intermediate reader.

Havill, Juanita. (1989) *Jamaica Tag-A-Long*.

This book explores lessons in how brothers and sisters can resolve their conflicts. Written for primary readers.

Crime

Brown, Gene. (1993) *Violence in America's Streets.* Brookfield, CT: The Millbrook Press. 62 pages.

This book discusses crime, gun control, police brutality, and other aspects of crime and violence in America. Written for the middle-grade reader.

Cohn, J. (1994) *Why Did It Happen? Helping Children Cope in a Violent World.* New York: William Morrow. 30 pages.

Daniel learns that his favorite neighborhood storekeeper has been robbed. He is upset and frightened by the news. Daniel's parents and teacher encourage him to share his questions and fears.

Taylor, L.B. (1979) *Shoplifting.* New York: Franklin Watts. 117 pages.

Are all shoplifters poor? Do shoplifters take only expensive items? Taylor provides relevant information for identifying and avoiding shoplifting, including the consequences of stealing. Reference tools include an index and a bibliography. Written for the intermediate reader.

Wormser, R. (1991) *Lifers: Learn the Truth at the Expense of Our Sorrow.* New York: Julian Messner. 206 pages.

Young persons are landing in jail at an alarming rate. Here is a book about a group of prisoners sentenced to life imprisonment, who are attempting to prevent juveniles from experiencing the pain and hardship they have faced. Beginning and ending with the reminder that young people have the choice to obey or break the law, lifers share their choices and the consequences of the wrong behaviors in which they engaged. Personal vignettes, accompanied by black-and-white photos, help drive the reality of poor choices and their ensuing consequences home for the reader— a reality to help young persons become scared straight.

Discrimination

Hoffman, M. (1991) *Amazing Grace.* New York: Dial Books for Young Readers. 32 pages.

Grace loves to tell stories and to play stories. When her class decides to put on a play, Grace wants to be Peter Pan. But she is told she cannot because she is a girl and because she is African-American. Grace does not accept this as an answer. Vivid watercolors accompany this text for primary readers.

Mohr, N. (1979) *Felita.* New York: The Dial Press. 110 pages.

Leaving the barrio is difficult, but moving to an all white neighborhood when you are Hispanic seems impossible to Felita. Felita faces discrimination and hate crimes and her family must decide if the move is worth the racism they encounter. Written for the intermediate reader.

Naidoo, B. (1986) *Journey to Jo'burg: A South African Story.* New York: HarperCollins. 80 pages.

Thirteen-year-old Nalodi and her younger brother travel to Johannesburg, three hundred kilometers away, to find their mother. Facing hunger, thirst, and imprisonment for venturing into the white province, the two siblings work together to survive. Written for the intermediate reader.

Osborn, K. (1994) *Everything You Need to Know About Bias Incidents.* New York: The Rosen Publishing Group, Inc. 64 pages.

Written for the intermediate reader, this book focuses on the issues of racism and prejudice and bias crimes in our society. Getting at the heart of the issue, Osborn challenges the reader to recognize and avoid bias in their own lives and in their communities. Included are color and black-and-white photographs, an index, a glossary, a list of further reading, and list of resources.

Siegel, B. (1992) *The Year They Walked*. New York: Four Winds Press. 103 pages.

The Montgomery bus boycott was sparked by the defiant action of Rosa Parks, but it was fueled by decades of abuse and defeat. The boycott was flamed by the courage and desire for a better life by the thousand of African-Americans living in Montgomery. The faces and lives of the countless unknown who made this boycott possible and successful are portrayed with a sensitivity which will attract the intermediate reader.

Yep, L. (1979) *Sea Glass*. New York: Harper & Row. 215 pages.

Craig Chin doesn't fit in anywhere. His father doesn't think he is athletic enough, and his uncle doesn't think he is Chinese enough. Craig wants to have friends, doesn't want to argue with his father, and wants to learn Chinese. Before he can do those things, he must come to terms with who he is in his own eyes. Written for the young adult reader.

Environment

Myers, W. D. (1975) *Fast Sam, Cool Clyde and Stuff*. New York: The Viking Press. 190 pages.

Friends stick together. Friends help each other. Friends keep each other safe. This unique picture of life in Harlem will enlighten and encourage the intermediate reader.

Rosen, Michael, (Ed.). (1992) *Home*. New York: HarperCollins.

An anthology of stories, poems, and illustrations about different kinds of homes. Written by 30 authors and illustrators for primary grades. Proceeds from this book benefit the homeless.

Wolff, V.E. (1993) *Make Lemonade*. New York: Henry Holt and Company. 200 pages.

LaVaughn steps in as a babysitter to help seventeen-year-old Jolly and her two children. She eventually helps Jolly away from a life of poverty. Life as a poor young mother can be difficult. But LaVaughn's mother teaches her "If life gives you lemons, make lemonade." Written for the young adult reader.

Gangs

Goldentyer, D. (1994) *Gangs*. Austin: Raintree Steck-Vaughn Publishers. 80 pages.

Written for intermediate and young adult readers, Goldentyer uses the format of a teen hotline to examine and answer questions surrounding gangs. Topics covered include peer pressure, racial hatred, relationships, and pressures of gangs. Ways to resist pressures to join a gang and avoid gangs are also discussed. Sources for help, an index, a listing of books and videos, and black-and-white photographs are included.

Stark, E. (1992) *Everything You Need to Know About Street Gangs*. New York: Rosen Publishing Group, Inc. 64 pages.

What is a street gang and why do people join them? Readers will take a hard look at gangs through the life of Johnny Boston as his choices and his experiences are shared. In clearly written prose, Stark examines the issues and concerns surrounding gangs and discusses ways the reader can avoid them. Intermediate

and young adult readers will also benefit from the index, glossary, and listing of further reading.

Peer Pressure

Bauer, Marion Dane. (1986) *On My Honor.* New York: Clarion Books. 90 pages.

Joel has been warned about the danger of going near the river, but when his friend Tony pressures him, Joel goes to the river. He doesn't want Tony to think he's scared. Then, Tony drowns in the river. Joel must come to terms with the aftermath.

Crutcher, C. (1993) *Staying Fat for Sarah Byrnes.* New York: Greenwillow. 216 pages.

Having a girl for a friend is tough enough for a teenage boy, but having Sarah Byrnes for a friend is even harder. Sarah became a misfit when, as a small child, she was burned in a fire. Being fat earned Eric the same ranking. The two become friends despite the walls Sarah maintains to protect herself from being hurt again. This book explores how these two friends manage to stay friends in the midst of peer pressure and teasing from all those who are not willing to see past the outward appearance. Written for the young adult reader.

Physical, Sexual, Emotional Abuse

Bahr, A. C. (1986) *Sometimes It's Okay to Tell Secrets.* New York: Grosset and Dunlap. 28 pages.

Secrets are fine, but not all secrets should be kept. Bahr gives primary readers reasons to keep secrets such as presents, surprises, and imaginary friends. But secrets that make you feel unsafe should not be kept. These lessons are accompanied by soft watercolors.

Byers, B. (1985) *Cracker Jackson.* New York: Viking Kestral. 147 pages.

What can an eleven-year-old boy do to help his babysitter? Cracker Jackson rightly suspect that his babysitter is being abused by her husband, but he is forced to realize that abuse is never easily stopped. Cracker Jackson learns how he can help his friend.

Caines, J. (1986) *Chilly Stomach.* New York: Harper & Row. 32 pages.

When Sandy's uncle comes to visit, he kisses and touches her in ways that give her a chilly stomach. The simple text and soft colored drawings give the primary reader and opportunity to talk about the important issue of sexual abuse.

Lowery, L. (1994) *Laurie Tells.* Minneapolis: Carol-Rhoda Books. 40 pages.

Written in beautifully lyrical prose, this picture book for older readers explores how one young girl tells of the sexual abuse in her life. Readers learn the importance of finding a safe person to tell, and that it is all right to admit to feelings of shame and confusion. Muted watercolors accompany the text.

Polese, C. (1985) *Promise Not to Tell.* New York: Human Sciences Press, Inc. 66 pages.

Meagan is happy that her riding teacher Walt picks her out for special attention. But that attention soon turns into an uncomfortable time when

Walt pressures her to do things that make her feel uncomfortable. Walt lets her go with a promise not to tell, but Meagan learns there are promises that shouldn't be kept. Written for the intermediate reader, this book provides an avenue for discussing the issue of sexual abuse.

Self-Protection

Mufson, S., and Kranz, R. (1983) *Straight Talk About Date Rape*. New York: Facts on File, Inc. 123 pages.

Acquaintance rape is a form of rape. A friend, a coworker, or a date can be the perpetrator of acquaintance rape. The authors of this book make facts about this for mof rape available for the young adult reader and provides answers to common question concerning acquaintance rape. How to stay safe is a primary focus. Included are an index and a listing of resources.

Petty, K., and Kopper, L. (1988) *Being Careful with Strangers*. New York: Gloucester Russ. 21 pages.

Through colored pencil drawings and the accompanying text, readers learn how even cuddly things like puppies can be used as tools that strangers may use to harm children. This picture book lends itself to discussion. Written for the intermediate reader.

Quiri, P.R., and Powell, S. (1985) *Stranger Danger*. New York: Julian Messner. 41 pages.

Through scenarios, this book explains the dangers of strangers for the intermediate reader. It includes information on ways children can protect themselves from strangers who wish to harm them. Readers are instructed on how to identify strangers and how to keep themselves safe. Black-and-white line drawings and a list of further resources are included.

Swisher, K.L. (Ed.). (1992) *Sexual Harassment*. San Diego: Greenhaven Press, Inc. 208 pages.

Created for the young adult reader, this collection of essays helps to define and educate readers about sexual harassment in today's society. The essays focus around the questions that arise from this issue including what causes sexual harassment, and how sexual harassment can be reduced? Included are a bibliography, an index and a listing of resources.

Taylor, M. (1987) *The Friendship*. New York: Dial Books for Young Readers. 53 Pages.

Cassie Logan and her brothers are sent for medicine. Despite warnings to do otherwise, they venture to the Wallace store and find prejudice rather than help. They must come up with ways to obtain the medicine they need. Black-and-white line pencil sketches accompany this story for intermediate readers.

White, R. (1992) *Weeping Willow*. New York: Farrar Straus Giroux. 246 pages.

Tiny Lambert is a victim of rape. But her stepfather is the perpetrator, so what can she do? Determined not to be defeated by the abuse in her life, she turns her strength inward and chases her dreams. Written for the young adult reader.

Suicide

Crutcher, C. (1989) *Chinese Handcuffs*. New York: Greenwillow Books. 202 pages.

Dillon Hemmingway is forced to watch his brother commit suicide. Dillon battles that experience as he struggles to put his life back together. Dillon faces the pressures of adolescence as well as those of death and abuse. Written for the young adult reader.

Garland, S. (1994) *I Never Knew Your Name*. New York: Dial Books for Young Readers. 32 pages.

A young boy sorrowfully recounts the life of a lonely teenager in an attempt to understand why he would commit suicide. He gives a silent offer of friendship to a life already gone. Rich paintings clearly portray the feelings of loneliness, fear, and sadness for readers of all ages.

Kolehmainin, J., and Handwork, S. (1986) *Teen Suicide: A Book for Friends, Family, and Classmates*. New York: Learner Publications. 70 pages.

Suicide is not just about death. Suicide affects persons other than the victim, from family and friends to the entire community. In straightforward prose, this book explores reasons why teens often choose suicide and what options friends and family have in trying to help a hurting teen. Each chapter begins with a scenario and ends with possible solutions to avoid feeling that suicide is the only answer. A listing of books, videos, and films is included.

Kunz, R. B. (1986) *Feeling Down: The Way Back Up*. Minneapolis: Dillon Press, Inc. 46 pages.

The different facets of suicide are explored through the eyes of Kirk and his teenage sister, who attempts to kill herself. Talking with the family therapist, the family members learn how to communicate their true feelings and focus on the stress of keeping feelings bottled up inside. Readers see how important it is not to believe suicide is the only way to find relief from pain and confusion. A glossary is included in this book for primary readers.

Pevsner, S. (1989) *How Could You Do It, Diane?* New York: Clarion Books. 182 pages.

Bethany discovers her stepsister lying on a couch in their basement. But when Bethany attempts to wake Diane, she discovers that Diane has killed herself. Bethany and her family are left with unanswered questions. When they press for answers they all learn the signs were there all along. Can Bethany accept the answers she finds? Will the family members learn how to pull together again? Written for the young adult reader.

Victim Recovery

Greenberg, J. (1979) *A Season In-Between*. New York: Farrar Straus Giroux. 150 pages.

Carrie's world is turned upside down when her father is diagnosed with cancer. Tests, separation, and hospital visits become her concerns instead of school, play, and friends. Explore how she deals with the stress of family illness and grief for a loved one. Written for the intermediate reader.

Rylant, Cynthia. (1992) *Missing May*. New York: Orchard Books.

When May dies, her niece and husband help each other through their grief and the recovery process. Written for the intermediate reader.

THE VIOLENCE PREVENTION RESOURCE GUIDE

Abuse

Child Abuse Prevention
1-800-257-3223

Child Welfare League of America
440 First Street NW
Washington, DC 20001
1-202-638-2952

Clearinghouse on Child Abuse and Neglect
  Information
P.O. Box 1182
Washington, DC 20013

Family Service America. Inc.
1-800-221-2681

National Child Abuse Hotline
1-800-422-4453

National Clearinghouse on Battered
  Women's Self-Defense
524 McKnight Street
Reading, PA 19601
1-215-373-5697

National Committee for the Prevention of
  Child Abuse
332 S. Michigan Avenue
Suite 1600
Chicago, IL 60604
1-312-663-3520

National Domestic Violence Hotline
1-800-333-SAFE

National Youth Crisis Hotline
1-800-448-4663

Alcohol And Other Drugs

Al-Anon Family Group Headquarters
1372 Broadway
New York, NY 10018
1-800-344-2466

Alcohol and Drug 24-Hour Help
1-800-562-1240

Alcoholics Anonymous
307 7th Avenue, Room 201
New York, NY 10011
1-212-647-1680

Children of Alcoholics Foundation
P.O. Box 4185
Grand Central Station
New York, NY 10163
1-800-359-2623

MADD
18935 I 45th Street
Spring, TX 77388
1-713-589-6233

National Cocaine Hotline
P.O. Box 100
Summit, NJ 07901
1-800-COCAINE

National Council on Alcoholism
12 West 21st Street, Suite 700
New York, NY 10010
1-800-NCA-CALL

National Drug Information and Referral Line
5600 Fishers Lane
Rockville, MD 20857
1-800-662-HELP

National Federation of Parents for Drug Free
  Youth
1-800-554-KIDS

National Institute on Drug Abuse Hotline
1-800-662-4357

Conflict Resolution

Children's Creative Response to Conflict
Box 271
Nyack, NY 10960
1-914-358-4601

Committee for Children
172 20th Avenue
Seattle, WA 98122
1-800-634-4449

Resolving Conflict Creatively Program
163 Third Avenue #239
New York City, NY 10003
1-212-260-6290

Safe Kids/Safe Neighborhoods
New York City Dept. of Health
Box 46
New York, NY 10013
1-212-566-6121

Discrimination

Anti-Defamation League
823 United Nations Plaza
New York, NY 10017
1-212-490-2525

National Institute Against Prejudice and
  Violence
31 S. Greene Street
Baltimore, MD 21201
1-301-328-5170

Family/Mentor Programs

American Association of Marriage and
  Family Therapy
1717 K Street NW
Washington, DC 20006
1-202-429-1825

Big Brothers/Big Sisters of America
230 N. 13th Street
Philadelphia, PA 19107
1-215-567-7000

Boys and Girls Clubs of America
771 First Avenue
New York, NY 10017
1-212-351-5900

Family Service America, Inc.
1-800-221-2681
Toughlove
P.O. Box 1069
Doylestown, PA 18901
1-215-348-7090

Juvenile Crime

Center for the Study of Youth Policy
University of Michigan School of Social Work
1015 E. Huron St.
Ann Arbor, MI 48104
1-313-747-2556

Mothers Against Gangs
110 W. Madison Street
Chicago, IL 60602
1-312-853-2336

National Council on Crime and Delinquency
685 Market Street, Suite 620
San Francisco, CA 94105
1-415-896-6223

National Crime Prevention Council
1700 K Street, NW 2nd Floor
Washington, DC 20006
1-202-466-6272

U.S. Office of Juvenile Justice and
  Delinquency Prevention
633 Indiana Avenue NW
Washington, DC 20531
1-202-638-2144

Physical And Recreational Activity

Midnight Hoops Program
Columbia, SC 29250
1-803-777-5724

Outward Bound USA
384 Field Point Road
Greenwich, CT 06830

Rape

National Clearinghouse on Marital and Date
  Rape
1-415-524-1582

National Coalition Against Sexual Assault
P.O. Box 21378
Washington, DC 20009
1-202-483-7165

Rape Crisis Center
1-800-637-7273

Rape Crisis Hotline
1-800-433-7273

Washington DC Rape Crisis Center
P.O. Box 21005
Washington, DC 20009

Self-Protection

Missing Children Safety Council Child Watch
1-800-222-1464

National Child Safety Council
1-800-327-5107

National School Safety Center
4165 Thousand Oaks Blvd. Suite 290
Westlake Village, CA 91362
1-805-373-9977

Vanished Children's Alliance
1-800-826-4743

Suicide

Coping With A Loved One's Suicide
  Support Group
Center for Life Management
44 Birch Street
Derry, NH 03038
1-603-434-1500 ext. 133

National Adolescent Suicide Hotline
1-800-621-4000

Youth Suicide Prevention Center
P.O. Box 844
Bothell, WA 98011
1-206-481-0560

Victim Recovery

Good Grief Program
295 Longwood Avenue
Boston, MA 02115

National Association for Crime Victims'
  Rights
P.O. Box 16161
Portland, OR 97216

National Victim Center
309 W. 7th Street, Suite 705
Fort Worth, TX
1-817-877-3355

Parents of Murdered Children
100 East 8th Street
Cincinnati, OH 45202
1-513-721-5683

Runaway Hotline
1-800-231-6946

Save Our Sons and Daughters
435 Martin Luther King Blvd.
Detroit. MI 48201
1-303-833-3030

Victims Anonymous
9514-9 Reseda Blvd. No. 607
Northridge, CA 91324

Weapon Safety

Center to Prevent Handgun Violence
1225 I Street NW, Suite 1100
Washington, DC 20005
1-202-289-7319

Kids + Guns = A Deadly Equation
1450 Northeast 2nd Avenue, Room 904
Miami, FL 33132
1-305-995-1986

Glossary

GLOSSARY

A

Abuse: the harmful treatment of a person.

Acquaintance rape: rape that is committed by someone known to the victim.

Active listening: a type of listening in which you let others know you heard and understood what was said.

Adrenaline: a hormone that helps the body get ready for an emergency.

Adverse environment: a set of conditions and surroundings in which a person lives that interferes with growth, development, and success.

Aftercare: the support and supervised services that juvenile offenders receive when they are released and must live and interact in the community.

Ageism: behavior that discriminates against people in a specific age group.

Aggressive behavior: the use of words and/or actions that show disrespect toward others.

Alarm stage: the first stage of the GAS in which the body gets ready for action.

Alcohol: a psychoactive drug that depresses the nervous system.

Alienation: the feeling that one is apart from others.

Amphetamines: drugs that "speed up" the central nervous system.

Anabolic steroids: drugs made from male hormones, that produce muscle growth and can change health and behavior.

Angel dust: *see* PCP.

Anger: the feeling of being irritated, annoyed, and/or furious.

Anger cues: changes in the body or signs that a person is angry.

Anger triggers: thoughts or events that cause a person to become angry.

Anorexia nervosa: an emotional disorder in which there is excessive preoccupation with food, starvation, or exercising to lose weight.

Assault: a physical attack or threat of attack.

Assertive behavior: the honest expression of thoughts and feelings without experiencing anxiety or threatening others.

Authority: the power and right to govern and apply laws.

Autogenic training: a relaxation technique that involves a series of exercises to increase muscle relaxation.

B

Battered spouse: a person in a committed relationship that is physically, emotionally, or sexually abused by a partner.

Being empowered: a feeling of being inspired because you believe you control your own destiny.

Beta-endorphins: substances produced in the brain that help reduce pain and create a feeling of well-being.

Biofeedback: a technique for getting information about involuntary processes in the body at a particular time so that an involuntary physical function can be controlled.

Boot camp: camp which uses rigorous military-style drills, hard physical training, and structure in an effort to instill discipline and shock in juvenile offenders.

Bulimia: an emotional disorder in which an intense fear of being overweight and a lack of self-esteem result in secret binge eating, followed by self-induced vomiting.

Bully: a person who hurts or frightens people who are perceived to be smaller or weaker.

Bullying: an attempt by people to hurt or frighten those who are perceived to be smaller or weaker.

Burglary: an unlawful entry of a structure to commit a theft.

C

Caffeine: a stimulant drug that increases the rate of bodily activities.

Caring: being interested and concerned.

Carjacking: car theft that occurs by force or threat of force while the driver and/or passengers are in or near the vehicle.

Cherokee Nation Youth Fitness Camp: a program in Oklahoma for young people who belong to the Cherokee Nation.

Child abuse: the harmful treatment of a person under the age of 18 and includes physical abuse, verbal abuse, emotional abuse, sexual abuse, and neglect.

Child neglect: maltreatment that involves failure to provide proper care and guidance.

Clarifying response: a response in which a person asks for more information.

Cocaine: a drug that stimulates the central nervous system and frequently results in dependence.

Codependence: a mental disorder in which a person loses personal identity, has frozen feelings, and copes ineffectively.

Coercion: use of force to influence another person.

Collage: a collection of objects put together to form a piece of artwork representing a particular idea or theme.

Commitment: a pledge to do something.

Communication: the sharing of feelings, thoughts, and information with another person.

Concealed weapon: a weapon that is hidden partially or fully from view.

Confirming response: a response to acknowledge the feelings that the speaker expressed and to show appreciation for expressing the feelings.

Conflict: a disagreement between two or more persons or between two or more choices.

Conflict avoidance: a conflict response style in which a person denies that there is a conflict and/or attempts to please others at his/her expense.

Conflict confrontation: a conflict response style in which a person attempts to settle a disagreement in a hostile, defiant, and aggressive way.

Conflict resolution: a conflict response style in which a person uses conflict resolution skills to resolve a disagreement in a healthful and responsible way.

Conflict resolution skills: skills a person can use to resolve a disagreement in a healthful, safe, legal, respectful and nonviolent way.

Conflict response style: a pattern of behavior a person demonstrates when conflict arises.

Conscience: an inner sense of right and wrong that prompts good behavior and causes feelings of guilt following bad behavior.

Contract for life: a written agreement in which a suicidal person promises not to hurt himself/herself for a certain period of time and/or until (s)he receives professional help.

Could-be's: young persons who are interested in belonging to the gang, perhaps because of a friend or family member.

Crack: a drug that is pure cocaine that produces rapid ups and downs.

D

Daily hassles: the day-to-day stressors of normal living.

Decision: a choice.

Delayed gratification: allowing oneself to sacrifice in the present so that a benefit will be achieved in the future.

Delinquent behavior: is an illegal action committed by a juvenile.

Denial: a condition in which a person refuses to recognize what (s)he is feeling because it is extremely painful.

Dependence: when a person has to have a drug or they experience withdrawal.

Depression: a feeling of hopelessness, sadness, or helplessness.

Desensitization: the process of lessening a person's response to certain things by overexposing that person to these same things.

Detention centers: secure custody facilities that detain juveniles on a temporary basis.

Disability: a condition in the body that may require a person to do things in a different way.

Discriminatory behavior: making distinctions in treatment or showing behavior in favor of or prejudiced against an individual or group of people.

Dispiriting relationships: relationships that are characterized by a state of low spirits.

Displacement: the releasing of anger on someone or something other than the cause of the anger.

Distress: a harmful response to a stressor that produces negative results.

Diversion: an approach to dealing with juvenile offenders that offers services that are designed to provide alternatives to juvenile correctional facilities.

Diversity: the quality of being different or varied.

Domestic violence: violence that occurs within the family or within other relationships in which people live together.

Drug: a substance that changes the way the body and/or mind work.

Drug abuse: the use of drugs that lessens the user's ability to function normally or that is harmful to the user or others.

Drug-free lifestyle: a lifestyle in which people do not use harmful and illegal drugs.

Drug-free zone: a defined area around a school for the purpose of sheltering young persons from the sale of drugs.

Drug use: the legal or illegal way in which people use drugs.

Dysfunctional family: a family in which feelings are not expressed openly and honestly, coping skills are lacking, and members do not trust each other.

E

Elder abuse: maltreatment involving the elderly.

El Puente: a community-based youth center in Brooklyn, New York that offers a wide range of services and activities for young people.

Emotional abuse: maltreatment that involves assault in a nonphysical way.

Empathy: the ability to share in another's emotions or feelings.

Empowerment: the belief that a person controls his/her own destiny.

Environment: everything that is around a person in the place in which (s)he lives.

EQUIP: a unique rehabilitation program for juvenile offenders which combines several different approaches: social skills training, anger management, moral education, and support sessions with peers.

Eustress: a healthful response to a stressor that produces positive results.

Exhaustion stage: the third stage of the GAS in which there is wear and tear on the body, lowered resistance, and an increased likelihood of disease or death.

Extended family members: family members in addition to parents and siblings.

F

Family continuum: a scale marked in units ranging from zero to 100 to show the quality of relationships within family members.

Family relationships: the connections that you have with family members, including extended family members.

Fighting: taking part in a physical struggle.

Flooding: the sudden, rather than gradual, exposure of a person to what causes the fear.

G

Gang: *see* youth gang

Gang Alternative and Prevention Program: a program in Los Angeles, California that refers at-risk young people in elementary and middle school to a variety of recreational activities.

Gay-bashing: a physical assault on people who are homosexual, that is motivated by prejudice.

General adaptation syndrome (GAS): a series of changes that occur in the body when stress occurs.

H

Hallucinogenic drugs: substances that have the major effect of producing distortions in perception.

Handgun: a small hand-held weapon that discharges one bullet for each pull of the trigger.

Hard-core gang members: the senior gang members with the most influence.

Hate crimes: crimes motivated by religious, racial, ethnic, sexual orientation, or other bias.

Health status: the sum total of the positive and negative influences of behavior, situations, relationships, decisions, use of resistance skills, and self-esteem on a person's health and wellness.

Healthful family: a family in which feelings are expressed openly and honestly, coping skills are adequate, and family members trust each other.

Hedonistic gang: group of young people whose band together to get high on drugs.

Helper-T cell: a type of white blood cell that fights pathogens and destroys cancerous cells.

Heroin: a drug that slows body functions such as heart rate and breathing, and produces drowsiness and mood swings.

Heterosexism: behavior that discriminates against people who are gay, lesbian, and/or bisexual.

Hidden anger: anger that is not dealt with in a healthful way and may result in inappropriate behavior and poor health.

HIV: *see* human immunodeficiency virus.

Homeless youth: young people who along with their families, lack shelter; leave home without parental consent; or are thrown out of their homes.

Homicide: the accidental or purposeful killing of another person.

Homicide survivor: a person who suffers because a friend, family member, or partner has been murdered.

Hope: the feeling that what is desired is possible and that events in life may turn out for the best.

Hostility: a feeling of ill will and antagonism.

Hostility syndrome: the body changes that result from stronger responses of the sympathetic nervous system and weaker responses of the parasympathetic nervous system and immune system.

Human immunodeficiency virus (HIV): the pathogen that causes AIDS.

I

I-message: statement that contains 1) a specific behavior or event, 2) the effect the behavior or event has on the individual, and 3) the feeling that resulted.

Immune system: the body system that fights disease.

Inactive decision-making style: a decision-making style in which a person fails to make choices, and this failure determines what will occur.

Inspiriting relationship: a relationship that lifts the spirit and contribute to a sense of well-being.

Instrumental gang: groups of young people who band together and commit property crimes to get money.

Intergroup conflict: conflict that occurs between two or more groups of persons.

Interpersonal conflict: conflict that occurs between two or more persons.

Intragroup conflict: conflict that occurs between persons that identify themselves as belonging to the same group.

Intrapersonal conflict: conflict that occurs within a person.

Ism: beliefs, attitudes, assumptions, and actions that subject individuals or persons in a particular group to discriminatory behavior.

J

Jumping-in: a test for toughness in which a young person fights with two gang members at once for an established period of time.

Juvenile delinquent: a young person who has antisocial behavior or refuses to follow the law.

Juvenile detention: the temporary care of juveniles in physically restricting facilities while their legal case is pending.

Juvenile offender: a person below the age of 18 who breaks a criminal law.

L

Life skill: an action that keeps people healthy and safe and that are learned and practiced for a lifetime.

Life skill for violence prevention: an action that helps young people resist behaving in violent ways, protects themselves from the violent actions of others, and develops resiliency.

Loneliness: an anxious, unpleasant, and painful feeling that results from having few friends or from being alienated.

M

Marijuana: a drug containing THC that impairs short term memory and changes mood.

Mediate: to bring persons who conflict together.

Mental rehearsal: a technique that involves imagining oneself in a stressful conversation or situation, pretending to say and do specific things, and imagining how the other person will respond.

Mentor: a person who guides and helps younger people.

Midnight Basketball: a basketball program that is held late at night to keep young people from being on the streets.

Mobile: a collection of objects (often pictures or drawings) hanging by string at different distances along a central piece.

Moral code: set of rules that a person follows in controlling his/her own behavior.

Moral development: the process of gradually learning to base one's behavior or personal beliefs of right and wrong.

Mural: a large (often wall-sized) piece of artwork.

Murder: a homicide that is purposeful.

N

Negative self-esteem: the belief that a person is unworthy and unlovable.

Nonviolence: the avoidance of the threatened or actual of physical force to injure, damage, or destroy yourself, others, or property.

Nurturing environment: a set of conditions and surroundings in which a person lives that promotes growth, development, and success.

O

Outward Bound USA: an outdoor adventure program in which young people are challenged physically and mentally in a wilderness setting.

P

Parasuicide: a suicide attempt in which a person does not intend to die.

Parasympathetic nervous system: part of the nervous system that maintains the body's normal state and restores balance after an emergency.

Parent abuse: physical and emotional assault of parents by their children.

Parole: a conditional release from a sentence in a correctional institution.

Parricide: the murder of one's parents.

Partner abuse: a range of abusive actions including verbal, sexual, and physical abuse by an adult intimate partner.

Passive aggressive: appears cooperative and pleasant while inside feels very angry and hostile.

Passive behavior: the holding back of ideas, opinions, and feelings.

PCP: a drug that changes the way a person sees things.

Peer: a person who is similar in age or status.

Peer mediation: a process used to resolve conflicts, in which a person helps his/her peers resolve disagreements in healthful, safe, legal, respectful, and nonviolent ways.

Peer mediator: a person who assists the people who have a conflict in reaching a solution.

Peer pressure: pressure that people of similar age or status exert on others to encourage them to make certain decisions or behave in certain ways.

Peer programs: programs in which young people serve as role models, facilitators, helpers, and leaders.

Perpetrator: a person who commits a violent act.

Physical abuse: maltreatment that harms the body.

Physical activity: activity that requires a person to use energy and to move his/her muscles.

Positive self-esteem: the belief that a person is worthwhile and lovable.

Post traumatic stress disorder (PTSD): a condition in which a person relives a stressful experience again and again.

Predatory gang: groups of young people who band together to commit crimes and violence.

Pre-delinquent behavior: behavior that often lends to breaking the law and includes disobedience, lack of respect for authority, stealing, lying, excessive aggression, inattention at school, truancy, and fighting.

Prejudice: suspicion, intolerance, or irrational hatred directed at an individual or group of people.

Premoral level: a level of moral development whereby a child determines which behavior is right and which is wrong based on which behavior is likely to be punished and which behavior is rewarded.

Principle-centered: having guidelines that direct decisions.

Principled level: a level of moral development in which a person has a conscience, operates with a set of principles, and understands that certain actions would violate the rights of others.

Prison: a building, usually with cells, where convicted criminals stay.

Proactive decision-making style: a decision-making style in which people examine the decision to be made, identify and evaluate actions that can be taken, select an action, and assume responsibility for the consequences.

Probation: a sentence in which an offender remains in the community under the supervision of a probation officer for a specific period of time.

Procrastination: putting off doing something until a future time.

Progressive relaxation: a relaxation technique that involves relaxing the mind by first relaxing the body.

Projection: blaming others for actions or events for which they are not responsible.

Protective factor: a way that a person might behave and characteristics of the environment in which (s)he lives that promote health, safety, and/or well-being.

Psychological needs: things that are needed to feel important and secure and may include friendship, belonging, accomplishments, and status.

R

Racism: behavior that discriminates against people who are members of a certain racial or ethnic groups.

Rape: the threatened or actual use of physical force to get someone to have sex without giving consent.

Rape trauma syndrome: a condition in which a person who has been raped experiences emotional responses and physical symptoms over a period of time.

Reactive decision-making style: a decision-making style in which a person allows others to make decisions for them.

Reader's theatre: a process in which students use a script or create a script of their own to perform a story.

Recovery efforts: programs a victim may undergo, support a victim may receive, and skills a victim may gain in order to manage the emotional effects of being a victim of violence.

Recreational activities: activities that involve play, amusement, and relaxation.

Reframing: changing a person's outlook in order to see a situation in a more positive way.

Regular gang members: gang members who already belong to the gang and who back up the hard-core gang members.

Rehabilitation: the process of restoring to a normal state of constructive activity through medical or professional treatment.

Relationships: the connections that a person has with other people.

Resiliency: the ability to prevent or to recover, bounce back, and learn from misfortune, change, or pressure.

Resistance skills: skills that are used when a person wants to say NO to an action and/or leave a situation.

Resistance stage: the second stage of the GAS in which the body attempts to regain balance and return to normal.

Resources: available assets and may include time, money, and material possessions.

Respect: having esteem for someone's admirable characteristics and responsible and caring actions.

Responsibility: reliability and dependability.

Responsible Decision-Making Model: a series of steps to follow to assure that the decisions a person makes lead to actions that protect health, protect safety, protect laws, follow guidelines set by responsible adults such as parents and guardians, and demonstrate good character and moral values.

Restating response: response in which a person repeats what the speaker has said in his/her own words.

Restitution: a means of compensating the victim.

Risk factor: a way that a person might behave and characteristics of the environment in which a person lives that increases the likelihood of having something negative happen to a person's health, safety, and/or well-being.

Risk situations: circumstances that increase the likelihood that something negative will happen to a person's health, safety, and/or well-being.

Role conformity: a level of moral development whereby moral decisions are determined by answering, "What will people think of me?"

S

SANE: a nurse who has training in the examination and treatment of rape victims.

Scared Straight: a program in which adults who are serving prison time tell juveniles about the dangers of prison life.

Secondary victimizations: unfair treatments experienced by victims after they experience violence.

Sedative-hypnotic drugs: drugs that depress the central nervous system and are "downers."

Self-centered behavior: behavior in which a person acts in ways that fulfill his/her needs and wishes with little regard for the needs and wishes of others.

Self-defense techniques: techniques that can be used when someone is harming or threatening to harm a person.

_destructive behavior: behavior in which a harms himself/herself.

'ine: the effort or energy with which a ws a plan to do something.

vhat a person thinks or believes /herself.

Self-loving behavior: healthful and responsible behavior that indicates a person believes (s)he is worthwhile.

Self-preservation: the inner desire to keep oneself and others safe from harm and may include preserving physical, mental, and social health.

Self-protection strategies: strategies that can be practiced to protect oneself and decrease the risk of becoming a victim.

Serotonin: a naturally occurring chemical found in the brain, blood, and other parts of the body, that helps regulate primitive drives and emotions.

Sexism: behavior that discriminates against people of the opposite sex.

Sexual abuse: maltreatment that involves inappropriate sexual behavior between an adult and a child.

Sexual harassment: unwanted sexual behavior that ranges from making sexual comments to forcing another person into unwanted sex acts.

Sexually transmitted diseases (STDs): diseases that are transmitted from an infected person to an uninfected person during intimate sexual contact.

Sibling abuse: physical and emotional assaults directed toward a sibling.

Socially competent: uses social skills effectively.

Social reciprocity: the act of people treating others as they themselves wish to be treated.

Social skills: skills that can be used to relate well with others.

Sportsmanship: losing without acting out or winning without bragging, and treating other players in fair and courteous ways.

Stalking: harassing someone with the intent to threaten or harm that person.

Status offense: type of behavior for which an adult would not be arrested, such as truancy, alcohol use, running away, defying parents, and staying out too late.

Stereotype: a prejudiced attitude that assigns a specific quality or characteristic to all people who belong to a particular group.

Stress: the response of the body to the demands of daily living.

'leit Publishing Company.

Stress management skills: techniques that can be used to cope with the harmful effects produced by stress.

Stressor: a demand that causes changes in the body.

Suicide: the intentional taking of one's own life.

Suicide prevention strategies: techniques that can be used to help prevent a person from thinking about attempting, and completing suicide.

Summarizing response: a response to review the major idea or ideas expressed.

Sympathetic nervous system: part of the nervous system that prepares the body for emergencies.

Synergy: a positive outcome that occurs when different people cooperate and respect one another and as a result, more energy is created for all.

Systematic desensitization: a process in which a person is gradually exposed to something that arouses fear and learns to respond less to it.

T

Tableau: a living picture in which the students use their bodies to depict the scene chosen.

Trustworthiness: acting in a right, responsible, and effective way.

V

Values: the beliefs, goals, and standards held by a person.

Victim: a person who is harmed by violence.

Victim recovery: a person's return to physical and emotional health after being harmed by violence.

Violence: the threatened or actual use of physical force to injure, damage, or destroy yourself, others, or property.

Violence prevention curriculum: an organized plan for the effective implementation and evaluation of violence education.

W

Wanna-be's: young persons who are not gang members, usually dress in gang colors, and engage in dangerous behavior to prove themselves to regular and hard-core gang members.

Weapon: an instrument or device used for fighting.

Wellness: the quality of life that includes physical, mental-emotional, family-social, and environmental health.

Wellness Scale: a scale that depicts the ranges constituting the quality of life—from optimal well-being to high level wellness, average wellness, minor illness or injury, and premature death.

Y

You-message: a statement that blames or shames another person instead of expressing feelings.

Youth gang: group of young people who band together and participate in violent, unlawful, or criminal behavior.